63607

D1595133

Transport and Public Policy Planning

Transport and Public Policy Planning

edited by

DAVID BANISTER and PETER HALL

MANSELL, London, 1981

207762

380.5
T 7722

ISBN 0 7201 1580 9

Mansell Publishing Ltd, 3 Bloomsbury Place, London WC1A 2QA

First published 1981

© Mansell Publishing Ltd and the Contributors 1981

Distributed in the United States and Canada by The H. W. Wilson Company, 950 University Avenue, Bronx, New York 10452

This book was commissioned, edited and designed by Alexandrine Press, Oxford.

All rights reserved. No part of this publication may be reproduced or transmitted in any form or by any means, electronic or mechanical, including photocopy, recording, or any information storage and retrieval system, without permission in writing from the Publishers.

British Library Cataloguing in Publication Data

Transport and public policy planning.
  1. Transportation and state
  I. Banister, David II. Hall, Peter *b. 1932*
  380.5'09181'2   HE193

  ISBN 0-7201-1580-9

Printed in Great Britain by Henry Ling Ltd, Dorchester, and bound by Mansell (Bookbinders) Ltd, Witham, Essex.

Contents

PART TWO. METHODS OF SURVEY AND ANALYSIS IN TRANSPORT

The Contributors

MICHAEL BAKER, The Open University, Milton Keynes
DAVID BANISTER, University College London
MICHAEL BATTY, University of Wales Institute of Science and Technology, Cardiff
MARY BENWELL, Cranfield Institute of Technology
SUSAN CARPENTER, University of Oxford
DAVID CLARK, Lanchester Polytechnic, Coventry
ANDREW DALY, Cambridge Systems Inc., Den Haag
MARTIN DIX, University of Oxford
PETER ENNOR, Formerly Oxfordshire County Council
PETER HALL, University of Reading
DAVID HARTGEN, New York State Department of Transportation
BARRY HEDGES, Social and Community Planning Research, London
IAN HEGGIE, University of Oxford
MAYER HILLMAN, Policy Studies Institute, London
DAVID HOLLINGS, Steer, Davies and Gleave, Transportation Planning Consultants, London
JEFFREY JOHNSON, University of Cambridge
GERALD LEACH, International Institute for Environment and Development, London
BO LENNTORP, University of Lund
MARVIN MANHEIM, Massachusetts Institute of Technology, Cambridge
KIT MITCHELL, Transport and Road Research Laboratory, Crowthorne
MALCOLM MOSELEY, University of East Anglia, Norwich
POUL-OVE PEDERSEN, University Centre of South Jutland
PAUL PRESTWOOD-SMITH, Greater London Council
FRANK D. SANDO, Departments of the Environment and Transport, London
DAVID STARKIE, University of Adelaide
PETER STOPHER, Schimpeler-Corradino Associates, Miami
PETER STRINGER, The Catholic University, Nijmegen
KERRY THOMAS, The Open University, Milton Keynes
STEPHEN W. TOWN, Transport and Road Research Laboratory, Crowthorne

DEREK WAGON, London Transport Executive
PETER WARMAN, University College London
MELVIN WEBBER, University of California, Berkeley
ANNE WHALLEY, Policy Studies Institute, London
DAVID WIGGINS, Bedford College, London
HUW WILLIAMS, University of Leeds
IAN YOUNG, Communications Studies and Planning Ltd., London

Preface

This book is based on the papers presented at a series of seminars on the theme of Transport and Public Policy Planning, financed by the Social Science Research Council through a grant to David Banister and Peter Hall at the University of Reading. Each seminar comprised a 'core' group of participants who remained the same, as far as possible, throughout the series; this group was supplemented by specially invited experts on each particular theme. The group consisted of both academics and practitioners, with a predominance of the former; these academic members came from a multidisciplinary background, and most of them are currently carrying out fundamental research into the social aspects of transport. Additionally, the possible gulf between researchers and policy-makers was bridged by a number of key individuals from the Department of Transport in the British government and from the Department's Transport and Road Research Laboratory, and from the Greater London Council and local authorities.

Throughout, the purpose of the series was to examine the problems of transport from the perspective of the social sciences. But there was particular emphasis on how decisions are made, the problems of the distributional effects of transport decisions, and on the spatial and social variations in the supply of transport services. The aim was to find ways of conceptualizing the process behind these distributional problems, and thus to establish a methodology that linked policy and analysis.

Each contributor to the series has been given the opportunity to modify or revise his or her paper in the light of the seminar discussion and of subsequent thoughts; the seminar series, itself, was organized with this specific end product in mind.

ACKNOWLEDGEMENTS

All the papers in the book were specially commissioned for the seminar series with the exception of Gerald Leach's contribution. This paper is also published as chapter six in *A Low Energy Strategy for the United Kingdom*, written by Gerald Leach, Christopher Lewis, Ariane Van Buren, Frederic Romig and Gerald Foley, and published by the International Institute for Environment and Development Science Reviews (1979). Derek Wagon's paper has also been presented to the Metropolitan section of the Chartered Institute of Transport on 17th October 1978. David Starkie's contribution is an edited version of his seminar presentation, which itself was prepared at very short notice in lieu of the programmed speaker. In all the papers, the views expressed are the personal ones of the respective authors, and they do not necessarily reflect those of the organizations for which they work.

Many individuals have contributed to both the organization of the seminars themselves, and to the production of this volume, and we are grateful for their considerable assistance. In particular, the efforts of Mary Esslemont and Anne Bowsher are acknowledged—they had the herculean task of deciphering and typing the manuscript, and this book is a tribute to their perseverance. Other members of the secretarial staff in the Geography Department at Reading University all chipped in over the two-year period, and our thanks go to Chris, Jacqui, Rosa and Pam.

Finally we acknowledge the generosity and understanding with which the Social Science Research Council have allowed us to proceed, both during the seminar series, and in the production of this volume.

Introduction

DAVID BANISTER and PETER HALL

1. INTRODUCTION

As Rudyard Kipling once stated 'transportation is civilization'; this
prophetic comment is increasingly becoming true. We have now come to
accept a level of personal accessibility which was quite unknown even
a generation ago. Instead of living within walking distance of one's
workplace, people commute long distances to work by both public and
private transport. The corner shop is a thing of the past, and
leisure activities are now consuming an increasing proportion of our
time. Transport influences many aspects of our lives; directly
through the available means of travel; indirectly through the benefits
of cheaper goods or through the disbenefits of environmental pollution; and through the contribution it can make to industrial growth
and rising living standards. Although the influence of transport may
appear to be simple, the reality is complex.

This book attempts to unravel some of these complexities, and in
particular it examines the contribution that social scientists can
make to the analysis of transport. The contributions have been
invited from a wide range of researchers, both in the United Kingdom
and elsewhere in Europe and the United States. Although the papers
have an academic bias, nearly a third have been written by non-
academics – these include consultants, government researchers,
representatives from local authorities and transport operators, and
private or publicly funded research organizations. This diversity
illustrates the interest which transport has generated over the last
few years. In the introduction, the policy perspective in Britain is
sketched, both as the context within which the majority of the papers
are placed, and because many of the policy changes which have occurred
in Britain are mirrored elsewhere. The final section outlines the
structure and purpose of the book in greater detail, commenting on
each of the main themes in turn.

2. POLICY PERSPECTIVES

Over the last twenty years, increasing personal mobility has perhaps
produced the most fundamental change in people's lifestyles. In
Great Britain, as with other advanced Western countries, between 15-
20 per cent of Gross Domestic Product is spent on transport, and this

consists mainly of private and not public expenditure. Although
transport only provides the means to reach a particular activity, the
organization of transport systems has effects which spread through all
sectors of the economy. Obviously, with such a significant expenditure sector, there are important social externalities which have
consequences for the whole population as a result of decisions taken
at all levels. It is here that transport research has a new challenge
to face; to understand these problems and their causes, and to
identify both the possible solutions and the means to achieve them.
This emphasis has been reinforced by a change in direction in transport policy objectives in Britain and in other advanced industrial
countries. Thus, in the previous (Labour) British government's White
Paper on Transport Policy, one of the three main objectives, reflecting thought in government circles, was

> '... to meet social needs by securing a reasonable level of
> personal mobility, in particular by maintaining public trans-
> port for the many people who do not have the effective choice
> of travelling by car.'

(Department of Transport, 1977, para. 9).

To some extent, it may be argued that this emphasis reflected
political ideology, but it would be a mistake to pursue that too far.
It also, more importantly, reflected a general shift in perception
among transport researchers and policy-makers, as to the essential
nature of the transport problem. The approach used in the 1960s and
1970s had two main and closely related aspects. Firstly, it was
engineering-dominated in seeing the main problems as concerned with
efficiency of overall movement of people and goods; the central
problem was to reduce or remove the impedences to the free flow of
traffic, and with respect to public investment in transport, there
were two main agents. One was the engineer who was responsible for
road construction and maintenance, and the management of the road
system; the other was the operator who controlled public planning and
management.

Secondly, it was dominated by *economic considerations of allocative efficiency* as scarce resources must be utilized to the greatest
effect in order to reduce the real costs of transporting people and
goods. Both aspects logically led to a concentration on the average
benefits for study areas considered as a whole, not upon the detailed
analysis of which individuals or groups gained or lost. Improvements
in traffic flow and speed, translated into time savings that dominated
aggregate cost-benefit analysis, were the criteria that characterized
this approach. So the emphasis was on the consideration of the transport system as a business, rather than that of the effectiveness with
which it served the needs of the community as a whole.

The change in approach, captured in the quotation from the White
Paper (Department of Transport, 1977), contrasts with that mentioned
in several ways. Firstly, it acknowledges that the objectives of
transport policy cannot be summed up in one or two performance
criteria, but rather that there are different and even competing
objectives: allocative efficiency, social equity and environmental
impact, to name but three of the most important. Secondly, it
reflects a government concern over the rapid rise in levels of public
expenditure in transport. This growth, reaching peak levels in 1975-
76 (£3913m at 1979 survey prices), has now come to an end, and the
expected levels for 1980-81 will be £2914m (at 1979 survey prices –

HMSO 1979). So there has been a change from the large-scale investment projects, typified by the engineering approaches, to one of
making better use of the existing transport infrastructure, together
with small-scale incremental investment. These priorities are likely
to continue with the present (Conservative) government which is
committed to reducing public expenditure: very few large-scale transport investment decisions are likely to be made in the next five
years, unless they are considered to be a national priority (for
example, the completion of the M25), or the capital can be raised
elsewhere (for example, grants from the EEC for the construction of
the Channel Tunnel).

     Not only have the objectives of policy and the levels of resource
availability changed, but so has the involvement of different interest
groups. It is now assumed that the approach to policy formulation and
implementation will be socio-economic, and not dominated by a single
methodology. Different social sciences will contribute a variety of
insights and techniques, working in multidisciplinary interaction
with engineers, physicists, mathematicians and other 'hard scientists'. This change has meant that the focus and style of the debate
has moved towards a concern with the decision-making process and the
implications of decisions on equity. Coupled with this trend has been
the greater involvement of the public in decisions which are likely
to affect them, directly or indirectly, principally through the consultation and participation processes.

     Finally, transport problems should no longer be separated from
their wider environment. Attempts to solve a particular problem by a
transport solution might result in disbenefits elsewhere, either in
another field of transport, or in some other areas such as land use.
The focus is now one that specifically includes the inter-relationships between transport and non-transport problems. This points to
the necessity for a suitable methodological basis that explicitly
links policy to social impacts. Two particular examples illustrate
the importance of these inter-relationships. As transport is one of
the principal users of oil (34 per cent of the total inland consumption of oil in the United Kingdom, 1978; Department of Energy 1977),
it is essential to understand the social and technical implications
of the likelihood of increasing prices in real terms and the possibility of supply shortages. In this way the most effective management of
resources could be ensured, given the government's objective of energy
conservation. Secondly, there is the relationship between transport
and land use, and the effects that each has on the other. The importance of these interactions are acknowledged by the present planning
system in Britain through the Structure Plans and Local Plans, but the
nature of the interactions is less well understood.

     So in these four areas, the focus of transport policy has changed
over the last few years, and this change is mirrored in other Western
countries. The concern is with the use of multiple criteria for evaluation, including efficiency, distributional and environmental
effects; with the best use of limited public resources available for
investment; with understanding the decision-making process and the
involvement of a wide range of interested parties in analysis; and
with transport within a wide range of contexts so that the social
impacts of particular policies can be assessed. These changes in the
policy form the backcloth against which this book is placed.

3. THE PURPOSE AND STRUCTURE OF THE BOOK

As there have been fundamental changes in the direction of transport
policy and planning, the primary purpose of this book is to review the
current state of the art from a broad social science perspective. In
particular, the aim is to give an up-to-date summary of the research
which has been and is being carried out into transport and public
policy planning; papers are included on the nature of the transport
problem, the allocation of resources (in particular energy), the
growing importance of information and communications systems, the
distributional effects of decisions, and the theory and practice of
transport analysis. In each case, the papers outline the current
position, describe how this has developed, and then proceed to a
statement of where likely future directions will lead. As such, most
papers include extensive references for the interested reader to
follow up, and perhaps, most important, the language used is non-
mathematical so that the concepts and issues will be accessible to all
readers.

The book is divided into two main parts. The first focuses on a
statement of the present situation in transport. This review starts
with a series of personal perspectives from key individuals; in each
case, the author has outlined the contribution of his own discipline
to the analysis of transport, highlighting particular research issues
that should be addressed. From this review, the complexity and the
wide range of social effects can be assessed; its purpose is to
familiarize the reader with current research. This broad-based review
serves as an input to two contrasting scenarios, and forms the
structure within which the remaining three sections of the first part
of the book are placed.

Resources form the theme of the second section. Within the context of increasing energy resource constraint, the relationships
between energy and transport are outlined together with the implications of a low-energy scenario for transport. The effects of
increased energy costs for the public transport operator are covered,
and an often overlooked resource - walking is included. This section
ends with a paper that examines one 'high technology' investment
which has failed to live up to expectations.

Alternative technologies are then covered with papers on information and telecommunications systems. Here, the debate is over
whether the impact of the 'new' technology will actually result in
travel substitution or stimulation of new activities.

The final section of the first part of the book examines the
distributional effects of decisions. There is a careful analysis of
the changes which have taken place in household expenditure patterns.
These economic aspects are then placed within particular spatial
situations with an examination of the changing transport markets in
London and the problems of accessibility in rural areas; this latter
issue is illustrated with examples from Britain and Denmark. The
first part of the book ends with a consideration of the nature of
'needs' and their relevance to transport demand - here the fundamental
role of such indicators as accessibility is outlined, with particular
reference to the determination of social welfare. In the conclusion,
the contribution of the social sciences to the analysis of transport
problems is assessed, together with directions as to which issues are
the most crucial.

In the second part of the book, there is a major survey of the methods which have been used in transport analysis. Throughout this review, certain issues are emphasized, namely the development of the methodologies, the variety of techniques which are available, and the link between theory and practice.

In the first section, the use of survey methods as an investigative tool in transport research is introduced. The whole range of survey techniques is examined, ranging from the large-scale highly structured survey through semi-structured to unstructured attitudinal and in-depth survey methods. This developmental process is also related to the evolution of the transport planning process to illustrate how survey methodology has responded to the demands of policy-makers.

Secondly, there is a major review of the theoretical developments in aggregate travel demand forecasting methods, together with the more recent moves towards the application of behavioural travel models. These reviews are complemented by a new methodology which attempts to place a structural framework around the relationship between transport and land use. The advantages of behavioural models, together with the use of attitudinal models, psychometric methods and time-geographic approaches to the analysis of transport and public policy planning are then outlined. In each case the theoretical issues are contrasted with the problems of application, both within a research environment and in planning practice.

In the final section, the differences between the modelling predictions and the actual changes which have taken place in urban policy are highlighted with the case study of London; here, the policy modelling interface is outlined, together with an assessment of how the conflicts can be resolved. Some of the longer-term questions are asked about what travel-demand analysis is trying to achieve, and the contribution which the 'new' technology might make to this. This section concludes with an overview on the purpose of systems analysis in problem-solving and suggests that the perspective of evaluation should be broadened to include some of the practical issues which have been raised in the preceding papers. The conclusions to the book cover some of the main findings and research priorities identified, and attempt to place transport research within the framework of policy-making processes.

4. CONCLUSION

As stated at the outset, transport is a matter of 'passionate public concern' (foreword to Department of the Environment 1976), and this book attempts to give a comprehensive overview of the current state of transport research. Throughout, the emphasis is placed on the contributions which social scientists might make to the study of transport. The aim is to match the theoretical perspectives on the subject to the problems of implementation with which policy-makers have to concern themselves. So the focus is not one of mere description of policies and policy differences, but an attempt to explain them in terms of the shifting balance of the forces that produce them. As such, the contents of this book explicitly examine the links between policy and analysis, and investigate the processes of policy formulation and implementation, as well as the resulting pattern of outputs. The recommendation for the intending reader is to follow the advice given

by Samuel Johnson, when he suggested that 'a man ought to read just
as inclination leads him; for what he reads as a task will do him
little good' (Boswell 1819).

REFERENCES

Boswell, J. (1819) *The Life of Dr. Johnson*, Vol. 1, 9th July 1763,
    London, p. 292.
Department of Energy (1979) Advisory Council on Energy Conservation.
    Energy Paper No. 40, London: HMSO.
Department of the Environment (1976) *Transport Policy: A Consultative
    Document*, 2 vols. London: HMSO.
Department of Transport (1977) *Transport Policy*, Cmnd 6836. London:
    HMSO.
HMSO (1979) The Government's Expenditure Plans 1980-81, Cmnd 7746.
    London: HMSO.

PART ONE

Resources, Technologies and Choices for Transport

Perspectives on Transport

This group of papers focuses on a series of individual views of the nature of the transport problem, given by a political economist, a geographer/planner, an economist, a sociologist and a psychologist; these perspectives are then linked together through two contrasting scenarios. The aim is to establish a common background state-of-the-art review, which could serve as the basis for a wide-ranging investigation of how transport problems have been resolved both analytically and in practice.

Peter Levin's paper analyses policy-making processes under four principal headings. Output-based analyses trace outputs in terms of processes and explain them in terms of structures and environment. Process-based studies need to be made at the actual point of policy-making. Input-output studies relate policies to the governmental structure or environment. Structure-based studies ask whether changes in structure have any impact on decisions. All these studies need to be complemented by analyses of policy implementation.

Peter Hall's paper, on the geographer-planner's perspective, outlines the nature of contemporary social and economic change in advanced industrial economies, and the effect of that change on the use of geographical space. The British space economy is now following the same path as the American one, with massive shifts of people and jobs out of the older, larger urban areas: the conurbation cities are the chief losers, while smaller and medium sized towns - especially in the more rural regions of southern and midland England - are the main beneficiaries. Growth has been especially rapid in the ring around London, but is now spreading quite widely across the southern half of England. To some extent, as people had decentralized in advance of employment, that might have led to longer journeys to work; but this process might now be correcting itself.

David Starkie's paper concentrates on the economist's distinction between the efficiency objectives of planning, and the non-efficiency objectives. He argues that in Britain there has never been a systematic examination from an efficiency standpoint of the overall balance and amount of transport spending - as between road and rail,

capital and current spending or the treatment of externalities. Non-
efficiency questions concern the right role of subsidy, the objective
of protecting the environment and the conservation of energy. On all
of these topics there seems to have been much muddled thinking and
distorted analysis. Overall, Starkie comes to a depressing conclusion: that transport research has moved away from the really
important questions of resource allocation, to the pursuit of
relatively unimportant details.

Stephen Town's paper on the sociologist's perspective stresses
that there is little work on transport in Britain today that could
properly be described as sociological; transport planning is pragmatic
rather than theoretical, and the sociologists do not seem to be
interested. But there are times when the sociologist can help show
how choices and constraints affect behaviour - as in job choice, or
the distribution of inequities in resources and their cumulative
interaction. There could also be useful research from a sociological
perspective on the nature of the transport planning process and the
character of the transport industry. Finally, the sociologist may be
able to help in defining what alternative futures might imply, and in
demonstrating the origins and consequences of differences in opportunity.

Peter Stringer's paper contributes the perspective of a social
psychologist. Apart from the study of ergonomics, he cannot identify
much central psychological research in transport *per se*. But there
are points of contingent interest; the relationship between attitudes
and behaviour; the phenomenology of travel, or what transport 'means'
to people; the use of trade-off techniques to study preferences; the
role of the locus of control (inside the person, or imposed from
without) in choices such as that between the private car and public
transport; the study of two-way communication, or co-orientation, in
transport policy-making; the role of risk and uncertainty in decision-
taking; and the way people adjust to changed circumstances. Beyond
these, there might be a more fundamental study: that of the satisfactions people get from spatial movement. But no one seems to have
researched this area.

Due to the diversity of views expressed on the nature of the
transport problem, the final paper outlines two contrasting scenarios.
The purpose of the scenarios is to sketch the alternative backcloths
against which decisions are likely to be taken, given assumptions of
a low and a high economic growth rate. In this way, the adequacy of
present research methods can be assessed, alternative approaches can
be investigated, and research priorities determined: thus the focus
is problem specific rather than one based on disciplinary boundaries.

Policy-making processes

Peter Levin

1. INTRODUCTION

Why should the processes of making transport policies be worthy of
study? There are, I suggest, two main reasons. In the first place,
in recent years there have occurred many instances in which - in the
judgement of a significant body of opinion - something has gone
wrong. Deficiencies have been noted in (1) the outputs of the
processes (i.e. in policies themselves) - transport subsidies have
failed to benefit people without cars in proportion to their numbers,
rail and bus services have failed to be coordinated, some newly-
built roads have proved to be significantly under-used; (2) the
processes themselves - traffic forecasting methods have been severely
criticized in the Leitch report, highway inquiry procedures have
given rise to a great deal of complaint; (3) the organizational and
political structure within which the processes have operated - many
have argued that we have lacked a proper framework for the coordination of transport policy at both national and local level{1}. These
perceived deficiencies have given rise to concern about our ability
to identify and resolve the issues that beset transport policy at
the present time or will do so in the future: to improve our ability
in this respect will require that we examine and draw lessons from
past experience. Secondly, these processes are of interest in their
own right, as mechanisms through which government interacts with
society at large - for example, in responding to social, economic and
political change - and as case studies in organizational and political
behaviour. This is not to say, however, that studying them for their
intrinsic interest may not lead to the production of 'better'
policies.

Policy-making processes are exceedingly complex. Moreover at the
present time there is little in the way of established methodologies
for tackling them. While it is certainly possible to set out - as I
do below - a number of approaches to their study, they are little
more than that: in other words, they involve fastening on to some
more or less visible feature of the process - its output, inputs to
it, or some aspect of the process itself or the structure within which
it takes place - and exploring what lies behind it. We do, however,
have the advantage that there are a number of possible starting
points, so that it is possible to examine a particular process or

11

group of processes by employing several approaches simultaneously and
correlating their respective findings.

CONCEPTS

Before discussing approaches to 'process studies', one needs to have
and to describe some concept or model of the process and its relationship to the context within which it takes place. I have presented
such a model elsewhere (Levin 1976), but it may be helpful to define
here some of the concepts employed, since I shall make use of them in
the following sections of this paper. I think of a policy-making
process as comprising activities, both of a 'technical' kind, to do
with the generating and treating of information, and overtly 'political', such as bargaining, negotiation, enlisting support. A process
has an *output*, which takes the form of a policy: this is essentially
a specification for action of some kind, or a statement (for example,
a financial constraint) that has implications for whatever course of
action may later be specified and adopted. It is important to note
that a policy is not only a direct or indirect specification for
action: it also carries a degree of commitment to its implementation
on the part of those whose policy it is. (Indeed, a policy-making
process is one that generates commitment as well as a specification
for action.) A process also has *inputs*: these take the form of
information and the claims of certain interests, whether of individuals, organized groups, or people who stand to be similarly affected
by the output of a process. (The distinction between information and
interest parallels the distinction between the technical and overtly
political elements of a process.) Processes by which public policy
is made take place within a governmental *structure:* such a structure
may be roughly resolved into organizational elements (for example,
departments, sections, committees, professional groups, together with
the lines of authority and communication that link them); political
elements (for example, the loci of certain powers and institutional
interests and the network of obligations by which they are linked);
and procedural requirements, which set out the steps that must be
followed before a policy can be manifested in an Act of Parliament or
financial allocation, say (although these requirements are defined in
relation to processes, because they themselves are relatively unchanging over long periods of time it is helpful to think of them as
structural elements). A governmental structure exists within an
environment, namely the world outside and the patterns of life and
work that go to make up that world: this environment continuously
impinges upon government, through the medium of pressures, demands
and supports, and is in turn impinged upon, through the medium of
policies and their implementation. It may be noted that of the inputs
to a policy-making process, some will be drawn from that environment,
albeit mediated through the perceptions of individuals who are part
of the governmental structure; others will be generated within the
governmental structure itself, such as the claims of professional and
other institutional interests and information about other policies
that are already in operation. It is important to note that at every
stage of the process *human factors* may play some part - pre-
dispositions, abilities, ambitions, self-confidence and other human
qualities or frailties are more difficult to study than the more
visible or regular structural and environmental factors, but their

influence may be very considerable.

3. OUTPUT-BASED APPROACHES

Output-based approaches are essentially retrospective. They
involve taking a particular policy, tracing the process by which it
was formulated and adopted, and asking (a) to what extent the
substance of the policy can be explained by reference to the form and
nature of the process, and (b) to what extent the form and nature of
the process can be explained by reference to the characteristics of
the governmental structure and environment at the time. A study of
this kind is particularly appropriate to a policy that can be
characterized in relation to its 'predecessors' or to other policies,
for example as an innovation or incremental development or rationalization of some kind. That attribute, as well as the substance of
the policy, then provides a focus and a perspective for gathering and
juxtaposing data. Such studies do open up the possibility of evaluating the governmental structure, as when inter-departmental boundaries,
say, prove insuperable obstacles to the coordination of related areas
of policy. And even if it proves that human factors rather than
structural ones have had the major influence on policy - whether for
good or ill - it might be possible to propose a modification to the
structure that would militate against their playing a harmful part in
future.

Studies of this kind do however run up against some methodological
difficulties. It may be found that although a certain amount of
material in documentary form is available, the recollections of the
individuals concerned - on whom one would depend for further material -
are selective and liable to reflect a degree of defensiveness or
self-justification. Furthermore, explanation, which necessitates
identifying relevant attributes of the structure and environment and
establishing causal relationships between them and the process, is
not easy given the present state of the art and the complications
introduced by human factors. And it is not easy to generalize from
the one-off studies that have been carried out up to now, nor will it
be easy to generalize from future ones until a respectable 'bank' has
been built up. However, generalization will be aided by employing
this type of approach in conjunction with others.

A variation of this approach would be to make retrospective
studies of how policies that are now recognized as deficient had come
to be adopted. One would need here to be fairly explicit about the
criteria being used to identify deficiency. The two fundamental
grounds would be those of rationality and democracy, both of which
lend themselves to being applied to both outputs and processes.
Irrationality may be manifested in the simultaneous implementation of
policies that are mutually inconsistent (for example increasing
access needs in rural areas by shutting local schools and simultaneously reducing access provision by closing local rail lines;
imposing financial cuts on the National Health Service while failing
to make the wearing of seat belts compulsory and thereby reduce the
£44 million per annum which road accidents cost the NHS; building the
M25 through London's green belt, stimulating new development and
decentralization, while trying to attract new development to Dock-
lands), or in the implementation of projects which experience then
demonstrates to have been based on unsound predictions (Concorde, some

motorway schemes), or in the adoption of indiscriminately uniform
policies to meet needs that in fact vary widely from one locality and
situation to another. A failure of democracy may be manifested in a
widening of the inequities between different groups in the population
(urban road schemes have inflicted upheaval on the have-nots in order
to benefit the haves; public policies have contributed to the enhancing of the mobility opportunities of those who have the use of a car
at the expense of the opportunities of those who have not; the
distributional consequences of policies have not been worked out when
decisions have been taken). Why, it may be asked, has this come
about?

While studies of this particular kind would be likely to encounter
even more defensiveness than other retrospective studies, they are
nonetheless worth pursuing. They may uncover processes of non-
decision making (which may well be as significant as processes of
conscious, purposive decision making) (Bachrach 1969), and are likely
to highlight differences in values and attitudes that may usefully be
explored. Moreover, 'post-mortem' studies would seem more likely to
yield profitable lessons for the future. The inquiry carried out by
the Leitch committee, although an obviously special case, is an
illustration of this.

4. PROCESS-BASED STUDIES

Whereas output-based studies of the kind described above give access
to processes indirectly and retrospectively, it is sometimes possible
to make studies of processes at the very time that they are taking
place. Unfortunately such proximity may make it difficult to focus
clearly on events: unless there is a single, well-defined issue or a
particular scheme at stake - or sometimes even when there is - it is
difficult to distinguish events that will have a significant effect
on the output from those that will not. (Of course, the participants
in the process are likely to have the same difficulty.) The most
fruitful approach is perhaps to fasten on to the imperative that
triggers off a review of policy - for example a political imperative
such as exists when a 'new broom' government or minister takes office,
or a well-supported public campaign takes off, or an economic
imperative such as the bankruptcy of a motor manufacturer - and trace
the ensuing events. Contemporary studies are inherently difficult to
encompass in a tidy research project, and the unpredictability of the
subject and problems of securing access (likely to worsen as things
become more interesting, although there is usually someone who is
prepared to talk) will not help matters. Moreover the closer that
researchers get to the process that they are studying, the greater
the danger that there will be an 'observer effect' - that the process
will be affected by the very fact of being studied. Despite these
drawbacks, there is nothing that can compare with a contemporary,
close-quarters study of decision making for gaining an appreciation
of the dynamics of the process, especially the subtleties of the
interplay of personalities and the build-up of commitment, or for
learning the 'restricted code' of British policy making (in which,
for example, the statement "This is a very good paper but it needs
clarification" may have the meaning "Over my dead body....").

Although policy-making in Britain today is still a very secretive
process, there are elements of it that by their nature are exposed to

the public view, namely Parliamentary debates and committee proceedings, consultation stages and public inquiries. The latter in particular afford opportunities for observing the official mind at work and the way in which it responds to challenges (for example Levin 1979).

5. INPUT-OUTPUT STUDIES

Input-output studies involve, as the name implies, examining the extent to which policies reflect particular inputs, whether they originate within the governmental structure or in its environment. In the former category of input one might include the interests etc. of individuals and groups within the structure and the human factors associated with them; in the latter category one would place information about changes in the social and economic environment and pressures from certain groups. If a selective responsiveness of policies to certain inputs or types of input is apparent one would aim to relate this to the process and to the structure itself. Have the causes of the 'road lobby' or the 'amenity movement' or Transport 2000 made a mark on transport policies? If so, is this due to the 'merits' of their case, or to structural factors: have they had preferential access to the formative stages of policy making, have their interests coincided with the interests of certain groups within central government, or have they been in a position to exert an obligation on policy-makers to heed their views, for example by achieving 'client' status or by being – as one official remarked of Transport 2000 – a 'bloody nuisance'? If one were to take a particular pressure group and explore its impact over the whole range of transport policies, one might well find variations, the exploration of which could generate some valuable insights. Likewise it would be interesting to trace the impact of research findings upon policy and to explore the reasons for any differences that emerged: why are some findings taken up and acted on while others are ignored?

It is also possible to apply the input-output approach over a much longer time scale. If one were to trace changes in the pattern of life and work over the past sixty years and attempt to correlate them with changes in transport policy (and indeed with changes in the governmental structure), there might be interesting lessons to be learned about the responsiveness – or lack of it – of policy to changes in its environment, and also about how the environment has changed in response to the implementation of new policies. Has government monitored the requisite characteristics of its environment? (Has it ever been taken by surprise?) How many of its prophesies have been self-fulfilling ones? If research is closely coupled to policy, who keeps an eye on the independent variables? How did we come in 1976 to be in a situation where Anthony Crosland, the then Secretary of State for the Environment, could say "By common consent, we still lack a coherent national transport policy"? (Department of the Environment 1976). At the present time, when government finds itself operating in a more complex and rapidly changing environment than ever before, and at closer quarters than ever before, research into responsiveness and its mechanisms might yield some immediate and practical benefits.

6. STRUCTURE-BASED APPROACHES

During the 1970s a number of changes - some subsequently reversed -
were made in the structure of those parts of central government
concerned with transport and in the pattern of powers and duties
among the central department and local authorities. Is there anything
to be learned from these? Did we have better or worse transport
policies when transport was the responsibility of the Department of
the Environment? Is the effect of abolishing the post of Director
General Highways being monitored? (Would we have had different
policies if there had been a Railways Directorate as well as a
Highways one within the DOE?){2}. What is the effect of segregating
or de-segregating the different professional groups? If structure
actually affects policy - not to mention responsiveness to the world
outside - are there not useful lessons to be learned from researching
into the effects of the structural changes of the past decade? If,
on the other hand, structure has scarcely any impact on policy,
surely we ought to establish this too: it would save an enormous
amount of time and effort and public money on future reorganizations
if they could be shown to be irrelevant, and researchers could turn
their attention to human factors instead.

   An important component of the governmental structure within which
transport policy is made is the TPP (Transport Policies and
Programmes) system, whereby county councils submit annual bids for
shares of the block Transport Supplementary Grant. These arrangements involve not only the Department of Transport and the county
councils themselves, but also the regional offices of the Department
of the Environment. The original aim of the system was to reduce
central intervention in the detail of local transport policies, but
there have been vigorous complaints at local level that the system
has proved no less interventionist than that which it superseded
(although there have been instances where national policy regarding
revenue support of transport services has conspicuously not been
implemented). (Central Policy Review Staff 1977). There is evidently
scope for studies of how the TPP system works - these could be
carried out on a comparative basis - and one could go on from there
to make an evaluation of it. A difficulty arises, of course, in
deciding what criteria would be appropriate for such an evaluation.
One can apply criteria of rationality and democracy in a limited
sense - for example interpreting rationality as internal consistency
and drawing attention to failure to coordinate TPPs and structure
plans (say), or interpreting democracy as the dominance of consumer
interests over administrative convenience - but it would be difficult
to secure agreement over whether conformity to national policy would
be a more appropriate criterion than responsiveness to local
pressures.

7. POLICY IMPLMENTATION

In the above discussion of policy making, no reference has been made
to the existence of some point at which policy making ends and policy
implementation begins. This is because such points are essentially
in the eye of the beholder: one person might argue, on the evidence
of changes that are made to policy while it is being implemented,
that policy making can be said to be complete only when implementa-

tion too is complete (i.e. even if one can distinguish between the two processes, the latter overlaps with the former), whereas someone else might draw attention to the formal steps that both mark and of themselves generate commitments to policy (for example White Papers, formal approvals of spending plans) and find it convenient to regard such steps as denoting a break between policy making and implementation. Probably the more helpful approach is to take commitment-carrying statements of policy and examine the process of implementing them and the extent to which the policy actually gets implemented in the form specified. One central question here is whether the faithful implementation of a policy requires that its making and its implementation should be in the charge of a single body, or if not, requires that the implementing agency should be able to participate in policy making. Another major question, particularly important in view of the long time that some transport policies necessarily take to get implemented, is that of how best to allow for changes of circumstances (not to mention the appearance of new information) during implementation; to avoid implementing out-of-date policies a degree of robustness and flexibility is called for, but this is easier to call for than to secure {3}. At all events, there is undoubtedly much to be learned from seeing whether policies actually get implemented as specified, from understanding why (or not), and from an evaluation of the appropriateness of whatever action is ultimately taken.

NOTES

{1} For catalogues of these deficiences see Hillman, M. (1975) Social goals for transport policy, in *Transport for Society*. London: Institution of Civil Engineers; and Department of Environment (1976) *Transport Policy: A Consultation Document*. London: HMSO. Traffic forecasting is dealt with in the Leitch report (Department of Transport (1978) *Report of the Advisory Committee on Trunk Road Assessment*. London: HMSO).

{2} For the Department of the Environment organization charts in November 1970 and March 1972 see Draper, P. (1977) *Creation of the D.O.E.* London: HMSO.

{3} On the concept of robustness see Gupta, S.K. and Rosenhead, J. (1968) Robustness in sequential investment decisions. *Management Science*, 15 (2), pp. 18-29.

REFERENCES

Bachrach, P. (1969) *The Theory of Democratic Elitism*. London: University of London Press.

Department of the Environment (1976) Foreword to *Transport Policy: A Consultation Document*. London: HMSO.

Central Policy Review Staff (1977) *Relations between Central Government and Local Authorities*. London: HMSO.

Levin, P.H. (1976) *Government and the Planning Process*. London: Allen and Unwin.

Levin, P.H. (1979) Highway inquiries: a study in governmental responsiveness. *Public Administration*. Spring, pp. 21-49.

The geographer's and planner's perspective

PETER HALL

Geographers and planners have different – albeit closely-related – approaches to public policy questions like transport. Both are centrally concerned with the spatial analysis of patterns of activities (often represented by land uses) and how these affect behaviour. The difference is that geographers analyse them positively, while planners introduce a normative element: they ask how activities can be rearranged, so as better to meet certain set objectives, however these are derived.

We can therefore most usefully represent the geographers'-planners' perspective by asking three related questions:

1. What have geographers discovered empirically about the patterns of activities and how they are changing over time?
2. How far have geographers and planners developed new conceptual insights in looking at these patterns and changes?
3. To what extent have planning objectives evolved and changed?

It should immediately be clear that these questions cannot neatly be separated. Empirical investigation under (1) will naturally affect concept formation under (2), and will in turn be influenced by it. Similarly, concepts developed for positive analysis (2) will affect planning objectives (3), but will in turn evolve in response to those objectives.

1. EMPIRICAL OBSERVATIONS

In recent years, fairly exhaustive investigations have been made by geographers of changing patterns of work, residence, shopping and other service provision, and leisure in advanced Western industrial society. This work is particularly rich for Britain (Hall *et al.* 1973; DoE 1976) and for the United States (Berry 1973; Berry 1976; Berry and Gillard 1977; Sternlieb and Hughes 1975); it is now being extended systematically to Europe (Hall and Hay 1980; Kawashima 1980), to Japan (Glickman 1977), and to Canada and Australia (Bourne 1975;

Berry 1976). From this mass of analytic material, certain common
themes, but also certain contrasts emerge.

    First, in advanced industrial (or post-industrial) societies, the
normal trend is one of decentralization of people and of jobs. This
trend sets in earlier for residential location than for job location,
which follows with a lag. Thus in many British areas in the 1950s
there was relative decentralization of people (faster growth in
suburbs than in central cores) and relative centralization of jobs.
By the 1960s, many areas were experiencing relative decentralization
of both people and jobs; while larger urban areas might be showing
absolute decentralization of both (losses in core cities). In the
United States, these trends were earlier and more drastic; there,
many core cities are experiencing decline, and it appears that since
1970 larger metropolitan areas (central cities plus suburbs),
especially in the East and older Mid-West, are reaching a static
condition with a threat of future decline. In Europe, the trends are
less clear and even contradictory, with different countries exhibiting
divergent trends. At one extreme Britain and the Netherlands by the
1970s were following American pattern of decentralization, and at the
other Eastern Europe was still exhibiting strong centralization (loss
from rural periphery to central city) tendencies, while in Scandinavia
and in Southern and Central Europe a trend to centralization has been
replaced during the 1970s by one of decentralization on the Anglo-
American model. In Japan, centralization appears to have been the
norm.

    Much of this analysis tends to have been at a rather coarse level
of central city/suburban ring aggregates. Only Berry's work in the
United States, with its close analysis of commuting gradients, goes
further (Berry and Gillard 1977). We rather badly need a closer look
at some of these trends. For instance, it appears that employment
may decentralize at one scale (central city to suburban ring of
metropolitan areas) but centralize or re-centralize at another (into
smaller cities or employment concentrations within the suburban ring).
Some analysis at the metropolitan area already captures this (the
movement from London and New York to their surrounding rings of
smaller cities like Reading or Guildford, Stamford or New Haven, from
Los Angeles to Anaheim or San Bernadino, and from San Francisco to
San Jose); but finer-grained analysis would be more revealing. In
Britain the coarseness of workplace census coding (prior to the
supplementary grid reference analysis of 1971) so far precludes this.

    The implications of such decentralization patterns for transport
are well-known. As Michael Thomson has convincingly shown, different
spatial arrangements in cities are almost inevitably associated with
different patterns of dependence on the private car (Thomson 1977).
Even large urban aggregates can work well with higher car dependence,
so long as both residence and work are highly decentralized on the
Los Angeles model. Conversely, very centralized cities tend to
support a very dense public transport net - the more so if they are
very large: Paris, New York and Tokyo are the archetypes. The
problems arise in mixed forms - and these are characteristic of cities
like London, with a large central employment mass but also many
smaller employment centres, and a medium density of residential
populations. For large American urban areas, research has shown that
modal split on the commuter journey can be satisfactorily 'explained'
by these variations in spatial patterns; for similar areas in Britain,

the explanation is less good (Sammons and Hall 1977).

2. NEW CONCEPTUAL INSIGHTS

The new insights may usefully be summed up in one word: *disaggreg-ation*. Ten years ago, classical analysis of journey patterns tended
to deal with aggregates, distinguishing merely between car-owning and
non-car-owning households. Now we know that this is too simplistic.
The work of Hillman and his colleagues has shown that even in car-owning households, individual levels of mobility vary greatly
(Hillman, Henderson and Whalley 1973, 1976). Children by definition
have no access to private cars except by courtesy of their parents.
Women tend less often to hold licences than men; and even when they
do, they tend to have less access to cars. Therefore, for long
periods of the day, so-called car-owning households may have no car
access. The consequences of this may be more or less severe, depending on the patterns of activities and land uses, and on the associated
possibilities of walking (or bicycling) or using public transport.
In dispersed communities - such as characterize many new areas of
'village suburbanization' in Southern England - the difficulties may
be acute: here, access to jobs and shopping and even schools may
depend critically on the availability of the car. Work at Reading
University and elsewhere on the problems of access in these kinds of
community, which are increasingly characteristic as settlement
patterns in the more prosperous parts of Britain, has shown the extent
of these problems (Banister 1980).
    This point must be related to the changing patterns of lifecycle
mobility. Already, in advanced industrial societies like Britain, a
majority of married women are in employment. Like their husbands,
they have increasingly specialized skills. The labour markets they
need in order to satisfy these skills will be increasingly wide.
Though it may be possible by careful planning to bring a wider range
of jobs (and services) closer to the home, there will be an obvious
limit to this solution. The work of Hägerstrand and his colleagues
in Sweden, using time-space diaries of individual members of households, shows just how complex these patterns now tend to be (Hall
1977; Carlstein, Parkes and Thrift 1978). In these circumstances, a
second job in the family may virtually demand a second car - or
alternatively, a quite novel approach in terms of transport policy.
And this is especially true in the widespread areas of dispersed
settlement that, rightly or wrongly, have been produced in the last
twenty years through the interaction of private development pressures
and public planning controls. This Pandora's box is open: people
have dispersed and have found new lifestyles. It will not easily be
closed again - unless and until energy shortages bite much more
deeply. And that may not be until after the year 2000 (Hall 1977).

3. POLICY RESPONSES

Planning objectives have changed in parallel. It is no longer realistic, as it seemed in the mid-1960s, to base transport planning on
some coming age of universal car ownership; universal car *access* is
a very long way off. Emphasis has markedly shifted, in the past
decade, from road building to investment support - and latterly to
revenue support - for public transport. But in all this, there has

been too little attention to the subtle connections between patterns of movement.

To some extent, there has been a rough-and-ready *ad hoc* policy response of a political character. The structure plans of the shire Counties of South-East England, now appearing, tend in many cases to accept the current trend as inevitable. They thus support extensive road-building plans; they call for a limit on revenue support for conventional public transport, and for maximal concentration on unconventional forms of public transport (such as those being tested in the current DTp rural experiments) so as to broaden access for carless individuals. And in this they may be right – though at present, there is all too little detailed evidence.

4. SOME RESULTING QUESTIONS FOR RESEARCH

The major resulting questions will be fairly obvious.

First: can we square the circle by more sensitive land-use planning – so as to maximize car-based choice for those enjoying car access, while guaranteeing minimal defined levels of walking (or bicycling) access to jobs and services for others, and also some minimal skeletal network of public transport? What criteria would be needed for such a planning exercise? What trade-offs would be involved?

Secondly: failing that, or as a complement to it, how far can we adapt public transport to the new patterns of living and working – especially through unconventional forms such as jitney, dial-a-bus, shared taxi and car pooling schemes? What are the economics of such schemes (Kirby *et al.* 1974), and how far are they psychologically acceptable in a car-based society?

Thirdly: how far in the future will these policies be affected by fundamental changes in ownership and use of cars? Is the Transport and Road Research Laboratory right in its current trend methods of forecasting – or are the critics right in assuming that there will be a fundamental disjuncture (Adams 1977)? The report of the Leitch Committee (Advisory Committee on Trunk Road Assessment 1978) has thrown some light on this question – and has already led to a change in official forecasting methods, leading to a downward revision of future projections of car numbers. But further work is needed – and in 1980, the Leitch Committee's standing successor committee is just starting this.

REFERENCES

Adams, J. (1977) How many car owners? *New Society*, 42, p. 521.
Advisory Committee on Trunk Road Assessment (1978) *Report*. London: HMSO.
Banister, D. (1980) *Transport Mobility and Deprivation in Inter-Urban Areas*. Farnborough: Saxon House.
Berry, B.J.L. (1973) *Growth Centers in the American Urban System*. Cambridge, Mass: Ballinger.
Berry, B.J.L. (ed.) (1976) *Urbanization and Counter-Urbanization*. Urban Affairs Annual Reviews, Vol. 11. Beverly Hills: Sage.
Berry, B.J.L. and Gillard, Q. (1977) *The Changing Shape of Metropolitan America*. Cambridge, Mass: Ballinger.

Bourne, L. (1975) *Urban Systems. Strategies for Regulation - A Comparison of Policies in Britain, Sweden, Australia and Canada*. Oxford: Clarendon.

Carlstein, T., Parkes, D. and Thrift, N. (1978) *Human Activities and Time Geography*. London: Edward Arnold.

Department of the Environment (1976) *British Cities: Urban Population and Employment Trends 1951-71*, DoE Research Report 10. London: HMSO.

Glickman, N.J. (1977) *Growth and Management of the Japanese Urban System*. New York: Academic Press.

Hall, P. *et al*. (1973) *The Containment of Urban England*. London: George Allen and Unwin.

Hall, P. (1977) *Europe 2000*. London: Duckworth.

Hall, P., Hansen, N. and Swain, H. (1975) Urban Systems: A Comparative Analysis of Structure, Change and Public Policy. Laxenburg: International Institute for Applied Systems Analysis, mimeo.

Hall, P. and Hay, D. (1980) *Growth Centres in the European Urban System*. London: Heinemann.

Hillman, M., Henderson, I. and Whalley, A. (1973) *Personal Mobility and Transport Policy*. Broadsheet No. 542, London: PEP.

Hillman, M., Henderson, I. and Whalley, A. (1976) *Transport Realities and Planning Policy: studies of friction and freedom in daily travel*. Broadsheet No. 567, London: PEP.

Kawashima, T. (1980) *Urbanization Processes: Experiences of Eastern and Western Countries*. Oxford: Pergamon.

Kirby, R.F., Buatt, K.U., Kemp, M.A., McGillivray, R.G. and Wohl, M. (1974) *Paratransit - Neglected Options for Urban Mobility*. Washington DC: The Urban Institute.

Sammons, R. and Hall, P. (1977) Urban structure and modal split in the journey to work. *Urban Studies,* 14, pp. 1-9.

Sternleib, G. and Hughes, J. (1975) *Post-Industrial America: Metropolitan Decline and Inter-Regional Job Shifts*. Brunswick, NJ: Centre for Urban Policy Research, Rutgers University.

Thomson, M. (1977) *Great Cities and Their Traffic*. London: Gollancz.

The economist's perspective on transport policy

DAVID STARKIE

1.   INTRODUCTION

The most recent attempt to undertake an overall review of transport policy in the United Kingdom can be found in the Government Consultation Document of 1976 and the ensuing White Paper of 1977 (Department of Transport 1976, 1977). I want to use these two publications as a focus in examining the question: what are the economic research frontiers in relation to transport policy? I realize that in doing so I will be forced to ignore the broader issues not covered by the documents and possible research which might question the very basis of the policies emanating from this policy review.

For example, I do see a case for economists examining the role of transport in relation to macro-economic policy from either a Keynesian or monetarist viewpoint. In the Keynesian context there are, as Bayliss (1978) has shown, a number of unanswered questions regarding transport's role as an instrument of counter-cyclical policy. And, on the other hand, in the monetarist context there is the question of whether and in what way the transport sector contributes to the public sector borrowing requirement. But for immediate purposes I want to by-pass such considerations and concentrate on the 1976-77 policy review itself.

According to the Consultation Document, 'The prime objective of transport policy is an efficient system which provides good transport facilities at the lowest cost in terms of the resources used' (Department of Transport 1976, para. 3.1). But where this government document differs from previous government documents and White Papers is in the emphasis laid on other objectives: a reasonable degree of mobility for everyone, the maintenance of a good environment and the conservation of non-renewable resources. The conclusion is that 'the transport market must therefore be strictly managed in the interests of these three non-transport objectives' (Department of Transport 1976, para. 3.2). So taxation and subsidy may legitimately be used to modify the pattern resulting from market forces, though these forces must still be permitted to operate.

2.   TRANSPORT OBJECTIVES

The prime objective of an economically efficient transport system
poses the fundamental question: what are the effects on economic
efficiency of major changes in the balance of public expenditure in
the context of transport as outlined in the 1977 White Paper? It is
important because in the last few years considerable shifts have taken
place in the pattern of public expenditure in transport. Expenditure
at the beginning of the 1970s was approximately £2 billion (at 1976
survey prices) and according to the Department of Transport (1977,
para 15), it was expected to remain at about that figure till 'the
end of the decade' (i.e. 1980). But within that fairly fixed total,
radical switches of expenditure have taken place. For example, there
has been a complete change in the balance between capital and current
account, that is to say between investment and revenue subsidies.
Within the total, comparing 1971-72 with 1978-79, revenue subsidies
would have increased by about £300 millions and investment would have
decreased by £230 millions. Moreover, even within the investment
total, the composition was also changing radically; public transport
over this period was expected to increase by £170 million, road
investment to decrease by £400 millions. As a consequence, road
expenditure, roughly 50 per cent of public expenditure on transport
in 1971-72 would by 1978-79 constitute barely one third.

These changes, of course, constitute very substantial shifts of
resources between transport sectors. Looked at one way, shifts of
this magnitude, planned over such a limited space of time, could be
seen as encouraging, for they suggest that to a surprising degree,
government initiatives are able to adjust quickly and to enforce new
policy initiatives. But in fact such large transfers of expenditure
are a cause for concern when they take place in ignorance of their
underlying implications for the efficient allocation of resources, or
even in spite of them. And in this instance, the indications are
that there is very little knowledge of the efficiency consequences of
the very large, non-marginal changes that have been taking place; if
anything, links between expenditure and efficiency have weakened.
Beesley and Gwilliam (1977) noted, for example, that the White Paper
showed the 'sacrifices' in road investment, but did not give any
explanation of the transfer of resources.

This is a disturbing situation when we consider that most of these
'sacrifices' were taking place in a trunk roads sector which is
supposedly at the forefront of efficiency analysis. The English
motorway and trunk road programme contracted from about £400 million
in 1971-72 to about £270 million by 1977. Cost benefit analysis,
expressed in the COBA procedures, has been an established tool for
trunk road appraisal since 1972, yet nowhere in the Government documents of 1976 and 1977, nor indeed in the Report of the Advisory
Committee on Trunk Road Assessment, chaired by Sir George Leitch
(1978), has any indication been given of the optimum size of trunk
road expenditure, as inferred from the COBA analyses. Nor, as the
Leitch Committee did show, are we able to draw conclusions from
existing appraisals regarding the *relative* disposition of resources
between modes in specific sectors such as inter-city transport.

In response to these significant changes in resource allocation
within the transport sector, three main tasks emerge. First, a broad
economic framework should be established that will allow for some

comment on appropriate levels of expenditure in functional sectors
such as local transport and inter-urban transport. Naturally, it
could be argued that this is an impossible task, and that, given the
division of resources between major spending programmes, the issue is
best left to collective Ministerial judgement. Alternatively, it
could be argued that broad-brush indicative analyses are possible and
worthwhile. In the urban sector, for example, Glaister and Lewis
(1977) have suggested an efficient level of resource commitment to
public transport in London in the absence of road congestion pricing.
In the inter-urban sector, the author (Starkie 1979) has outlined an
approach for deciding upon the correct level and disposition of
resources between inter-city rail and road from an efficiency viewpoint. Both papers stress the importance of feedback from prices
charged to investment decisions, a feedback which Beesley and Gwilliam
(1977) also noted as being absent from previous commitments with
regard to both road and rail investment.

The second task, on the theme of efficiency in the use of
resources, is the question of the right balance between current and
capital expenditure as reflected in asset renewal and replacement
policies. A large proportion of expenditure in rail goes on renewing
and repairing existing assets,for example, British Rail argues (though
not entirely convincingly) that 95 per cent of its investment is asset
renewal expenditure (Department of Transport, 1978, table 25.2). Road
maintenance spending runs to several hundred million pounds a year,
and yet the pattern and level of expenditure is determined solely on
engineering criteria. The comment of the Marshall Committee in 1970,
that virtually nothing was then known about the optimum overall level
of maintenance from the point of view of the community, still rings
very true. In the railway field, some very useful work was done by
Joy and Foster (1967) in the 1960s on the renewal of railway assets
in the United Kingdom, and Nash (1974) has also carried out a fair
amount of work on road vehicle replacement. But, overall, this is an
area in which there is a need for substantial research, bearing in
mind the importance in public expenditure terms of simply renewing
existing assets.

The third area is the requirement to develop the efficiency
criteria in a second best context. Financial analysis and cost
benefit analysis have theoretical underpinnings in welfare theory.
Unfortunately, that theory has not been adapted or stretched far
enough in order to come to terms with the important constraints of
the real world. For example, the existence of capital rationing and
the more recent development of cash limits have to be taken account
of. In addition, there are the labour and managerial constraints.
The requirement is, therefore, to adapt and give theoretical respecta-
bility to efficiency criteria to take account of these considerations.
London Transport (1975) have made a start in this context, by suggesting an efficiency criterion for public passenger transport operating
in a controlled deficit environment, of maximizing passenger miles
per pound spent. This, it argued, was an operational surrogate for
maximizing net present values within a budgetary constraint.

The other really important facet of this question of second best
criteria is the observed size and therefore relevance of transport
related externalities. It has become fashionable to draw attention
to externalities in the context of public sector investment, and
transport is often singled out for particular scrutiny with the

implication that externalities are more persistent or prevalent in
this sector of the economy. However, one or two commentators have
recently questioned the validity of such a point of view. Mohring
(1976), for example, considers that 'external economies which have
been held to require special investment criteria for transportation
... have their exact counterparts in every other form of economic
activity'. Certain developments, such as the 1973 Land Compensation
Act which was formulated specifically to internalize negative
external effects from new public works including road and airports,
suggest that the residual externalities associated in the future with
new transport investments may in certain instances be quite unexcept-
ional. Even in urban transport where externalities might be expected
to dominate issues, there are signs that they might not be quite so
imposing as was once thought. This radical change of view was
expressed in the supporting papers to the Consultation Document
(Volume 2, Paper 3). Early estimates of congestion loss in cities
appear to have been gross over-estimates, and the fact that the
potential gains from traffic restraint are at best, moderate, appears
to have gone without comment, so far. It seems therefore that there
is an urgent case for research on the merits of this and related
views.

3. NON-TRANSPORT OBJECTIVES

The first of the so-called non-transport objectives outlined in the
1976/77 policy documents was to ensure 'a reasonable degree of
mobility for all'. It is to suggest that transport should be
treated to an extent as a merit good and this invokes the issue of
subsidy and economic efficiency, a comparatively unexplored research
area in the United Kingdom. The main exception to this conclusion is
the excellent essay by Pryke (1977) on the subject. Subsidies, as
Pryke points out, are a source of economic inefficiency as their very
existence usually results in the level of output in transport industries being higher than it would otherwise be and, as a consequence,
resources are diverted from other sectors. Indeed, they may be a
source of substantial inefficiency; Pryke's estimate for 1975 was
that expenditure by public passenger transport undertakings in the
United Kingdom, including the railways, exceeded commercial revenue
by about 55 per cent. Of course, there are social benefits to offset
the resource loss, but there are also social losses. Possibly,
depending on your point of view, these may be in the form of longer
commuting journeys or in the form of greater urban sprawl. Thus, a
number of questions are raised such as: where does the balance of
gain and loss lie, particularly in the context of the Consultation
Document's suggestion that rail subsidies benefited the rich? What
ways are there of giving subsidies without prejudicing operating
efficiency? What are the best ways of allocating subsidies from the
recipients point of view?
     The second non-transport objective was the protection of the
environment. Here, the role of the economist may be limited, not
because economic analysis cannot be applied to environmental issues,
but because there is a credibility problem. The clearest example of
this dilemma has been the difficulty of getting the man-in-the-street
to accept the idea of putting monetary values on aircraft or road
vehicle noise, exhaust pollution or accidents. Perhaps the role of

the economist should be to encourage the lay person to adopt a wider
perspective. For example, making people aware of the extent to which
they enjoy cheaper air flights or get cheaper consumer goods as a
result of there being transport related pollution. Also there is a
case here for challenging conventional wisdom - as for example the
questioning by Sharp and Jennings (1976) of the established view that
railways are environmentally pure.

The final objective highlighted in the Transport Policy White
Paper (Department of Transport 1977, para. 27) was the conservation
of energy. In the transport sector, energy consumption is primarily
considered in terms of the current account, with the result that
other important factors are ignored. One example here is the fact
that investment prompted by considerations of energy conservation
will itself involve the consumption of energy. This problem is
illustrated by the current review of the case for further main line
electrification in the context of the general prospects for energy
supplies (Department of Transport/British Railways 1979). The investment involved in the various options being examined is large (£230m
to £750m at 1978 cost levels), and there is a great deal of popular
pressure to value the savings in energy at a shadow price in excess
of the price prescribed by market forces. But at the same time
there is some evidence of myopia on the part of the enthusiasts who
fail to recognize that the very fact of putting in overhead gantries,
refining the copper wire, manufacturing the steel and building the
structure, is itself going to consume energy. It is by no means
clear that the energy balance alone comes out in favour of electrification. This is an area which requires further economic analysis.

4. CONCLUSION

Looking back to the last major transport policy review which culmina-
ted in the 1968 Transport Act, it seemed then as if we could see where
we were going in efficiency terms. The 1968 Transport Act had a well
thought out economic base to it. There was a certain direction to
policy which was comprehensible from an economist's point of view.
At that time it was thought there was a substantial commercial core to
the railways, and that the pieces not requiring subsidy could be
subject to cost benefit analysis along the lines of the Cambrian
Coast Line Study (Ministry of Transport 1969). In the road sector,
cost benefit analysis was really coming to the fore while the
Ministry's Road Track Cost Study (1968) had suggested a basis for
introducing economically efficient road vehicle taxation. Overall,
subsidies were rather small as there was very little bus subsidy and
rail subsidies were at last considered to be under control.

Ten years later, however, the picture has altered completely.
Public transport subsidies are now a major item of public expenditure.
Moreover, because the objective framework for transport policy has
broadened out and we are now faced with the problem of multi-purpose
objectives, these subsidies are no longer related to cost benefit
returns. Indeed the very role of cost benefit analysis is questioned,
and, in the wake of the Leitch inquiry, relegated to a less important
role in trunk road appraisals. In addition, the handing-over in the
context of Transport Policies and Programmes of block grants unrelated
to performance criteria has again eroded the economic framework which
was the setting for the 1968 Transport Act.

In the 1950s and early 1960s British transport economists seemed to expend more of their time and effort on the broader policy issues such as suggesting a framework for competition between road and rail (for example, Sargent 1958; Foster 1963) or establishing appropriate criteria for transport investments (Coburn *et al.* 1960; Beesley and Foster 1963). In the last ten to fifteen years, the emphasis appears to have swung towards research into isolated components of the whole; a supreme example is research into values of travel time where a recent review by Bruzelius (1979) lists over thirty British papers. Bearing in mind that research resources themselves are scarce, it seems that the time has come when, as transport economists, we can afford rather less fine tuning of much-played research themes. The problem we are faced with now is not essentially one of accurately meeting objectives, but really of defining appropriate objectives and the right balance to strike between them.

REFERENCES

Bayliss, B.T. (1978) The role of transport in counter-cyclical policy. ECMT Round Table 41, Paris.

Beesley, M.E. and Foster, C.D. (1963) Estimating the social benefit of constructing an underground railway in London. *Journal of the Royal Statistical Association*, 126, pp. 46-58.

Beesley, M.E. and Gwilliam, K.M. (1977) Transport policy in the UK. *Journal of Transport Economics and Policy*, 11 (3), pp. 209-23.

Bruzelius, N. (1979) *The Value of Travel Time*. London: Croom Helm.

Coburn, T.M., Beesley, M.E. and Reynolds, D.J. (1960) The London-Birmingham Motorway Study. Road Research Laboratory, Technical Paper 46.

Department of Transport (1976) *Transport Policy: A Consultation Document*, 2 vols. London: HMSO.

Department of Transport (1977) *Transport Policy*, Cmnd 6836. London: HMSO.

Department of Transport (1978) *Report of the Advisory Committee on Trunk Road Assessment* (Chairman Sir George Leitch). London: HMSO.

Department of Transport (1979) *Review of Mainline Electrification: Interim Report*. London: HMSO.

Foster, C.D. (1963) *The Transport Problem.* London: Blackie.

Glaister, S. and Lewis, D. (1977) An integrated fares policy for transport in Greater London: second best estimates computed from recent empirical findings. Proceedings of the Urban Economic Conference, Keele, July.

Joy, S. and Foster, C.D. (1967) Railway track costs in Britain. Symposium on Development in Railway Traffic Engineering, Institution of Civil Engineers, London.

London Transport (1975) London Transport's Corporate Aim Explained. London Transport Executive, mimeo.

Ministry of Transport (1968) *Road Track Costs*. London: HMSO.

Ministry of Transport (1969) *The Cambrian Coast Line*. London: HMSO.

Mohring, H. (1976) *Transport Economics*. Boston: Ballinger.

Nash, C.A. (1974) The treatment of capital costs of vehicles in evaluating road schemes. *Transportation*, 3 (3), pp. 225-42.

Pryke, R. (1977) The case against subsidies, in Foster, C.D. (ed.) *A Policy for Transport?* London: Nuffield Foundation, pp. 47-65.

Sargent, J.R. (1958) *British Transport Policy*.   Oxford: Oxford
    University Press.
Sharp, C. and Jennings, A. (1976) *Transport and the Environment*.
    Leicester: Leicester University Press.
Starkie, D.N.M. (1979) Allocation of investments to inter-urban road
    and rail. *Regional Studies*, 13 (3), pp. 323-36.

The sociologist's perspective on transport

STEPHEN W. TOWN

1. TRANSPORT AND SOCIOLOGY

When applied to a problem oriented subject such as transport research, there is considerable overlap between the different social sciences. However, the perspectives of a sociologist, psychologist and geographer will differ, even in respect of the same topic. Rather than dispute these disciplinary boundaries, the purpose here is to review those topics to which the sociologist can make a distinctive contribution.

There are two reasons for the growth of interest in a sociological perspective on transport. Paradoxically, both reflect issues peripheral to travel behaviour itself. The first is a concern about the distributional effects of the transport system at a time when growing car ownership and an associated decline in public transport have increased the opportunity for mobility by some people, but have decreased it for others. Secondly, there is a growing concern about the adequacy of conventional demand models for predicting behaviour, particularly where the future is unclear.

Little of the research presently being carried out in Britain could properly be described as sociological. Most of the work being done at the Transport and Road Research Laboratory and, with certain exceptions (for example, the Transport Studies Unit at Oxford), nearly all other research in this field could more properly be described as descriptive social research. Similarly, there seems to be little of distinctly sociological interest going on in America, although in Europe there are a few more interesting developments, chiefly in French urban sociology and Swedish time-geography.

There are two reasons for a lack of interest in social factors in the transport field. Firstly, transport planning is very pragmatic in approach. This stems from its origin in highway construction and the engineering profession; such a background is almost essential for many local authority transport jobs. This pragmatic engineering background can be contrasted with that of the land-use planner. In the history of that profession there is a streak of idealism, going back to William Morris, Ebenezer Howard, the Garden City movement and so on; this has resulted in a wider professional outlook which regards social

goals as an integral part of its objectives and at times has produced
a professional identity crisis.

The second reason is a lack of interest in transport on the part
of sociologists. Sociology is about how people organize their everyday lives within a given social structure, and generally transport
does not appear to be a primary focus of interest. Unlike most of the
institutional areas which concern sociologists - the sociology of
industry, of education, of religion - where the institutional boundaries provide a context which governs the form and content of
interaction, transport provides no such context. People travel in
order to carry out activities, not for the sake of travel; nor are
their values heavily shaped by the transport system as such. Even in
urban sociology - which appears to be the study of urban institutions
- the tendency is to take the spatial context as set and look at the
interactions within it. It is difficult to think of any general
sociological study which has contained a systematic analysis of personal mobility, either as a mediating influence in patterns of
interaction or even in terms of the distribution of power and opportunity.

2.   THE CONTRIBUTION OF SOCIOLOGY

Transport and travel, as such, are not of central interest to the
sociologist. However, there are subjects in which the sociologist
has a direct interest and where this discipline may help explain the
observed pattern of travel behaviour. These would be areas where the
sociologist looks at a broader facet of social structure in which
access or mobility plays a part. Their chief application to transport
studies would be to show what choices and constraints help determine
observed behaviour. A number of examples can be given.

Take the case of employment. Work trips are of interest to the
sociologist only because they connect two significant places at which
activities are carried out. The job a person holds is a function of
the individual's position in the labour market, and that market recognizes the importance of many factors: age, sex, skills and
experience, wage levels, job satisfaction. Depending on the supply of
jobs, accessibility may or may not also be important. If it is, it
may be used to mediate between the other interests of those involved
and the range of jobs available. In a South Wales mining area which
was studied by the author (Town 1978), there was a norm of short
journeys to work; you lived in the village surrounding your pit. With
pit closure, there was a rise in unemployment and a drift of workers
to factories outside the valley and up to twenty miles away on the
coast. However, these factories preferred to take younger men, and
given the high level of unemployment, could do this. Over the last
ten years, Regional Policies have attempted to redress unemployment in
the valley by bringing in jobs for the older workers who could not get
jobs on the coast. Jobs brought into the valley paid less than those
on the coast. However, because no travelling was involved, the
younger men from the valley who worked on the coast were prepared to
accept a lower wage rate and thus filled these local jobs instead.
This was often at the expense of the older men for whom they were
intended. Obviously it was to the advantage of employers to take on
these younger, more highly skilled men. In the resulting pattern of
job holding, travel to work played an important part since younger

men made a pay-off between lower wages and less travelling. However, the role of travel to work was to mediate between other facets of the labour market and could only be understood in those terms.

The pattern of social trips that an area generates should also be understood in terms of the meaning that this activity has for people. The level and distribution of social and recreational trips depends upon style of life - whether it is home based, localized or centred on a more diffuse community of interest (such as participation in a particular sport, pastime or pursuit). Although, at one extreme there are highly mobile life-styles, and at the other there are life-styles which make little use of mobility, mobility is only one component of a wider set of attributes and values. Car ownership and use may follow from a particular life-style rather than facilitate or cause it. Various studies of reductions in transport services indicate the extent to which people faced with changes in mobility can adjust their travel patterns without necessarily changing their basic life-style.

The question of the distribution of resources, and hence of opportunities, is another distinct area in which sociologists might have an interest. The inequities of travel opportunities that result from car availability or its absence are becoming reasonably well documented. However, transport is only one institutional area in which there are inequities. The same is true for housing, education, employment and so on. Very often these inequities build up one upon another, and the extent to which people can escape from any given one is limited. People who rely on buses also tend to live in poorer housing, have less well-paid jobs and have lower levels of educational attainment. It is well established that the middle classes get better value from many public and social services, such as health or education. It would be interesting to see how far this is also true for transport.

The question of need and deprivation may seem to follow from a discussion of the distribution of opportunities. However, it seems impossible to identify empirically what constitutes need. It appears that although some people have better transport provision than others (and make greater use of it), in general everyone copes. A discussion of need requires a value judgement about proper standards; this is outside the scope of scientific research. It might be more illuminating to focus attention on the way in which people with low levels of mobility adapt to their situation - through car sharing, community buses or other means - and thereby to understand the basis of their requirements of transport.

In a catalogue of possible sociological interests in transport, brief mention should also be made of a number of contextual topics. One is the study of social movements described by Peter Stringer in the following paper. The willingness of people to accept or protest about a transport innovation says a great deal both about how they see transport and its uses, and what sort of power they have.

The whole transport planning process, and the transport planner himself, richly deserve study. The engineering bias of this profession, which may be reflected in past emphasis on roads at the expense of other forms of transport, has already been referred to. Equally, one might question why, at the present time, public transport should receive so much attention when it accounts for only 12 per cent of all journeys, while walking (which accounts for 35 per cent) receives so little.

Finally, research on the transport industry itself may prove

fruitful and enlightening. There may be scope for improving the
efficiency of public transport. However, since labour costs form a
relatively high proportion of total costs, progress in this field
would involve a serious study of industrial relations which takes into
account the syndicalist tendencies of the transport workers.

3. CONCLUSIONS

In conclusion, it seems that there are two main topics to which
sociology can provide a context in the study of transport – prediction
and equity. It is clear that sociology cannot replace conventional
techniques of demand forecasting. These are necessary exercises,
although they have their limits. However, one should recall the
remark made by Humphrey Lyttleton when he was asked where he thought
Jazz would be in ten years' time; he replied 'if I knew that, I'd be
there now, man'. There is an uncertainty about the future which must
be recognized, and which cannot be overcome by the use of predictive
techniques. The role of sociology here is to clarify what the alternative futures might imply, what the consequence of these alternatives
would be for peoples' requirements, and then to leave the policy-maker
to make a conscious choice between alternatives on the basis of this
knowledge.

In the case of equity, there is the possibility of documenting how
differences in opportunity occur, and what their consequences are.
However, there is a great deal of uncertainty about what the term
means. Does a concern about equity stem from a decline in public
transport, a growth of car ownership, a dispersal of population, a
shift of activity centres, or a change in people's expectations? By
focusing on transport related issues alone, one tends to forget that
the people who today may be 'transport deprived' (if there is such a
thing) might forty years ago have been able to go where they wished
(given the higher population densities and better bus services of that
time). However, forty years ago these people would probably have been
too poor to benefit from that better public transport system.
Inequalities which in the past were manifest through wealth or other
basic institutional features (for example health, education), may now
be manifest through transport. The sociologist's job is to assess the
extent and consequences of this, not just as a matter of transport
policy, but as a matter of social policy.

REFERENCE

Town, S.W. (1978) *After the Mines: Changing Employment Prospects in
    a South Wales Valley*. Cardiff: University of Wales Press.

© Crown Copyright 1981. This paper expresses the personal views of the
    author, which are not necessarily those of the Department of the
    Environment or of the Department of Transport. The paper is published
    by permission of the Director, Transport and Road Research Laboratory.

The social psychologist's perspective

PETER STRINGER

1. INTRODUCTION

My own concern with the 'transport problem' has been as a researcher: looking variously at transportation in structure planning, from the viewpoint of public participation (Stringer and Ewens 1974; Stringer and Plumridge 1974; Stringer 1977, 1978); at consultation in trunk road planning (Thornton and Stringer 1979); and at psychological factors in travel mode choice (Stringer in press). However, the most interesting issues to arise from these research projects are methodological and appear to be more properly the subject matter of several later papers in this volume. Accordingly, I shall attempt here to make some preliminary suggestions about the kind of contribution which psychology, and more particularly applied social psychology, might make to transportation policy (for another account cf. Michon 1976).

It should be self-evident that psychology has a potential contribution to make in any area of human behaviour and experience. That it often does not make that contribution may be because it is edited out of another discipline's agenda. A prime example can be found in the work on modal choice models. In the foreword to his recent book on the subject, Ian Heggie (1976) drew attention to a number of psychological assumptions which had been made by modellers. They are amazing not only for their naivety, but because their proponents ignored the relative ease with which they might be tested empirically. They sat until recently as naive and untested assumptions precisely because psychology had been edited out of travel behaviour modelling.

This example suggests that a general role for psychology in transportation research might be to uncover those of its implicit assumptions which have a behavioural or phenomenological content, and to do so in a manner which shows how the assumptions could be tested. The analysis and formulation of problems for research on such a basis might be a more useful, as well as fundamental, contribution to the field of transportation than the attempt to produce substantive results for policy-makers to plug into their decisions. In the context of policy research psychology's valuable analytic role has been obscured by the expectation that it will operate only at an empirical and technological level - as, for example, in much of the ergonomic work which involves psychologists (e.g. Forbes 1972).

Allied to this distinction between possible contributions which psychology might make to another discipline are questions about the different levels of interest which that discipline's problems might have for psychology. It is conceivable that only a very few aspects of transportation may be interesting, fundamentally and in themselves, to psychology. In rather more instances one may find that transportation problems, as currently represented, are interesting only in so far as they reflect issues of contemporary concern in psychology. Other problems may be simply susceptible to routine technological intervention by psychologists, but otherwise carry no particular significance for the science of psychology. And yet others will be necessarily or contingently posed in a form which puts them entirely outside the scope of psychology in its present state.

In an academic context, of course, these different levels of interest carry strong evaluative connotations. From the viewpoint of those who wish to promote research which helps the formulation of policy, academic values (as distinct from academic criteria) can frequently cause irritation. But in the pragmatic business of drawing up a statement on feasible research priorities, these values must be taken into account. All manner of research can be delineated, encouraged and commissioned. But that is not the same as getting it done. To take full advantage of a contributing discipline, one must pay attention to its level of development and to the concerns of its more able exponents. Research problems need to be more carefully defined in the middle ground between the wishes of policy-makers and the capacities and interests of those who will do the research.

A doubt intrudes. The *possibility* that transportation might sometimes be not all that interesting a topic for psychologists raises the question as to whether transportation is very interesting at all. In its own right, that is. Any interest it does have may lie in anterior considerations. It may be more profitable or easier to do research on those anterior considerations rather than on the epiphenomenon. In the field of transportation we have an example of the contemporary emergence of extensive research domains which are defined almost exclusively by transient everyday events. A concern for those events is quite proper. But to make the research questions isomorphic with them may detract our attention from studying the more crucial underlying issues.

The area of psychology which has probably been most closely concerned with transportation is ergonomics. The management of vehicles by their drivers (cf. a forthcoming issue of the *International Review of Applied Psychology* on driving behaviour) and the behaviour of others inside and outside the vehicle have raised a large number of interesting and pertinent ergonomic questions. Ergonomics has received a significant part of its definition from transportation, and will continue to do so.

But apart from ergonomics it is difficult to identify much psychological interest in transport *per se*. What might be of interest – though I know of no attention given to it – would be a study of the kinds of gratifications and satisfactions to be derived from spatial movement. This would be distinct from studying the more mundane uses to which people put transport. It is possible that travelling satisfies the need for curiosity, which we know to be a basic source

of human motivation. The satisfactions could be very varied, from
visual and kinaesthetic sensations to social contact and interaction.
A research strategy of this kind can be found in the area of mass
communications research (cf. Blumler and Katz 1974).

     If there are few reasons why psychology should show a fundamental
interest in transportation, there are many more points of contingent
interest. A number of these are relevant to more than one area of
social policy, and for that reason it may be particularly worthwhile
investing research resources in them. I shall briefly refer to seven
areas of interest. They are not an exhaustive set. The choice is
somewhat personal. They are restricted to areas of *social* psychology;
not just because that is my particular concern, but because previous
psychological contributions to transportation have emphasized the
individual over the social. What follows is intended to represent
potential offerings of social psychology to transportation research.
Crucially it builds on some contemporary concerns of social
psychology, and it should be recognized in that connection that
processes rather than topics are involved.

2. THE ATTITUDE-BEHAVIOUR RELATIONSHIP

This question has preoccupied social psychologists for more than four
decades (cf. Thomas 1971). It is particularly difficult to resolve.
Underlying much social research is an assumption that a survey of
people's attitudes will enable one to predict their behaviour or
their level of satisfaction with proposed developments or innovations.
Psychological studies, however, have shown that one can rarely make
firm predictions of this kind. At best, we need more information;
for example, about people's behavioural intentions or the salience
for them of the particular object of attitudes being studied.
Attitudinal statements are misunderstood and taken as promissory
notes, when they are probably only ever intended as rather rough
indicative statements. Attitudes are uttered in a social context,
from one person to another. Their predictive content may depend on
the context. An attitudinal statement to a close friend may be
expected to guarantee more than one given to a social survey
interviewer. The behaviour which one attempts to predict will also
occur in a social context which may be quite different from that in
which the attitude is elicited. There is not space here to expand
the argument, but my conclusion would be that quite radical changes
are needed in the ways in which we use information about people's
values, opinions and beliefs so as to inform policy decisions.
Kerry Thomas and colleagues at Cranfield have attempted to improve
prediction of travel behaviour with the Fishbein model of attitudes
(cf. Tuck 1976). But my own feeling is that the model, though
sophisticated, still tinkers with the problem rather than offering
the basic reappraisal which is needed.

     One outline which does begin to fit the bill can be found in
Harré and Secord (1972, chapter 14). They point out that psychology,
unlike philosophy, has been unduly simplistic in its preparatory
analyses of the concept of 'attitude'. The study of attitudes is
complicated by the fact that each person usually displays a
different attitude system in cool, verbal situations from that
which occurs in action. Harré and Secord claim that the way to
penetrate the complex structure of attitudes and behaviour is by

analysis of the accounts which people produce in a justificatory
context. Such justificatory accounts are at the root of the authors'
explanations of social behaviour.

3. PHENOMENOLOGY OF TRAVEL

I suspect that we know very little of what travel 'means' to people
at large. Most of the information sought by transportation researchers is governed by their own interests. These may not coincide with
the public's experience. The concentration on time and cost as
predominant factors in mode choice models is an example. Qualitative
accounts in laypersons' own terms are lacking (though cf. Stringer in
press). But qualitative information often gives one a better 'feel'
for a problem area than precisely quantified data. Policy-makers
are certainly experienced at using both types of information. And
politicians would be lost without qualitative interpretations. An
example of social scientific research in this vein is the Rapoports'
work, e.g. *Leisure and the Family Life Cycle* (1975).

As a complement to possible sample surveys, they use a bio-
graphical method to engage in a systematic qualitative study of
selected individuals in specific family and community contexts. Two
basic problems for them, which make the work essentially 'social' in
emphasis, are the link between the individual and society and between
intimate small groups and large-scale organizations, and the dynamics
of life-cycle development in the family. They take opportunities for
leisure and the assumptions underlying leisure provision as their
starting-point, and examine the way in which individuals articulate
their interests in relation to them. The people-oriented approach
is used to suggest where and how in people's lives planners and
providers of leisure facilities could most validly direct their
efforts. The approach could readily be adapted to the study of
transport.

Another concept which is proving useful in guiding social
psychological research of a qualitative nature is the 'social
representation' (cf. Herzlich 1974). The distinctive characteristics
of the study of 'social representations', as opposed for example to
'attitudes' or 'images', are that it gives due attention to those
forms of individual understanding which are a specific expression
of *social* thought; and which are taken to be a mental construction
or remodelling of objects and events, often at a metaphorical level.
What is expressed in a representation is not based on perception,
taken as the direct evidence of the senses, but on a complex
elaboration overlaid with presuppositions from many varied sources.

4. TRADE-OFF TECHNIQUES

Multi-disciplinary approaches are required to many transportation
problems. The social science with which psychology has probably
collaborated least in the past is economics - though this is slowly
being rectified (there have now been four annual European colloquia
on economic psychology). Economic questions in transportation, as
in other fields, are dealt with by assuming a 'rational' or non-
psychological model of man. Trade-off techniques for analysing
preference patterns, such as Hoinville's (1977) 'priority evaluator',
were a natural development for policy areas in which benefits and

disbenefits balance and interact with one another. They have the
useful feature of a response format, in quasi-monetary terms, which
parallels one important aspect of decision-making - resource
allocation. Trade-off, one would imagine, is a familiar aspect of
everyday, private and domestic decision-making. Trade-off techniques
should have greater 'ecological validity' than most survey instruments.
But, in fact, we know rather little about processes such as those
underlying everyday decisions. What people are doing in a trade-off
operation - whether, for example, they proceed hierarchically or
lexicographically - needs to be more clearly understood if policy
decisions are to be based on the output of trade-off surveys.
Transportation would be a mutually productive field in which psychologists might study such questions.

5. LOCUS OF CONTROL; ATTRIBUTIONAL ANALYSIS

Conflicts between public and private service provision are at the
root of many transportation problems. Two sets of concepts which
social psychologists have made much use of recently could throw light
on the conflicts. 'Locus of control' is a concept which is used to
analyse people's perceptions of events in terms of the perceived
extent of 'external' or 'internal' control over them (Phares 1976).
People seem to vary systematically as to whether or not they feel
that they are themselves in control of events, or wish to be. These
variations have good explanatory power for a wide range of pieces of
behaviour. Thus, the presence or absence of personal control of
various kinds in a travel mode may bring into play rather deep-
seated aspects of a person's psychological make-up.
     The psychology of attributional processes (Shaver 1975) attempts
to explain how we interpret and understand other people's actions in
terms of the dispositions, desires and capabilities which we
attribute to them. Attribution is affected both by situational
factors and by personal motives. Attributional analysis might be
useful for looking at certain aspects of benefit and disbenefit in
transportation modes. For example, what are people's perceptions of
pollution and polluting agents? To whom do they attribute the
responsibility? What follows if they do not attribute to themselves
as car-owners or users the disbenefits of the car? How do they
square, if at all, a personal desire for cheap fuel and energy with
the risks attached to giant oil-tankers or nuclear reactors? Whom do
they blame for a disaster? Information on questions such as these,
and ways to make the electorate more sophisticated about its implicit
role in the related policy decisions, are urgently needed.

6. CO-ORIENTATION

Research on mass media and social communication has gone through an
instructive evolution in recent decades. Communication was first
thought of as a one-way process: the communicator does something to
the audience, his activities guarantee effective communication. The
model then evolved, partly under the influence of survey methodology,
into its 'market research' phase. Communication processes could be
understood, it was thought, in terms of audience characteristics and
audience expectations. The more recent 'co-orientational' approach
(Kline and Tichenor 1972; Clarke 1973) treats communications as a

fully two-way process, treating both parties as communicator *and* audience in an integrated system. It distinguishes agreement between the two parties from, for example, accurate perception or understanding of one another's viewpoint.

The relevance of this to transportation and other areas of social policy should be obvious. Effectively aligned policy decisions are dependent upon viewing the policy-maker and the public as reciprocating elements of an integrated system, rather than as isolated parties with distinct 'objectives/criteria' and 'needs', vainly trying to signal across an unbridgeable gap. The former viewpoint entails a value-laden assumption about social process. But so does the polarization between experts and consumers. Such assumptions are inevitable in social research whose results are explicitly to inform policy.

Co-orientation research is not far advanced. One of its most promising applications would seem to be in relation to public participation and consultation (cf. Stringer 1978; Uzzell 1980).

7. RISK AND UNCERTAINTY

Any area of planning involves a guess at the future with consequent uncertainties. The introduction of high technology tends also to introduce varying degrees of risk — that is, an uncertainty associated with undesirable consequences, often of a critical nature. Safety-oriented technology can lead to greater confidence and greater subsequent catastrophe, whether actual or perceived, when safety limits are overstepped. What makes a risk acceptable, even palatable, is an interesting psychological question. How, for example, do people evaluate low-risk/high-loss situations against high-risk/low-loss? Why does crossing the road on one's first trip to Paris seem less risky than the jet to get there? What are the pay-offs for ending different classes of risk?

Until very recently most of the behavioural studies of risk dealt with natural hazards. An example can be found in the discussion by Slovic *et al.* (1974) of decision-making under risk. They conclude that much new policy related to natural hazards will depend upon action by individuals within public constraints. It needs to be informed by knowledge of how people make choices in the face of uncertainty and how they might respond within different constraints. Choice cannot be simply described as an effort to maximize net marginal returns, nor in terms of culture and personality, nor of organizational and environmental conditions. It is a complex, multi-determined phenomenon. Many of the same conclusions are likely to emerge from the study of man-made hazards, with the added complication that a range of positive and negative attributions can be made to a possibly indeterminate set of agents contributing to the hazard. For more recent psychological approaches to risk cf. Otway and Fishbein (1977) and Slovic *et al.* (1976).

8. ACCEPTING ALTERNATIVES

A part of the uncertain future can be envisaged in the form of the alternatives which it will throw up. In the sphere of transporation there are alternative modes, goals and activities. The problem of moving forward toward a future which will include inexperienced novelties; of enabling people to appreciate their potential, give them

a reasonable evaluation and, if necessary reject them without undue
loss or disadvantage - is one which colours many areas of contemporary
living. It may seem outrageous or irrelevant to suggest that
psychotherapy is dealing with the same problem, usually at an
individual rather than a societal level. We need to understand how
people develop their attitudes towards novel situations and what
reasons they use for accepting or rejecting them - not so that they
can be engineered toward an inevitable acceptance of certain planning
solutions, but in order that they may control their own reactions in
a more critical and aware spirit.

Rather few psychological theories have a forward-looking
orientation. An exception is Kelly's (1955) personal construct
theory (cf. also Bannister and Fransella 1971). Its fundamental
postulate is that 'a person's processes are psychologically channel-
ized by the ways in which he anticipates events'. This implies,
among other things, that man is not so much reactive to the past as
reaching forward to the future. Many of the assumptions underlying
the theory are encapsulated in the term 'constructive alternativism':
'whatever nature may be, or howsoever the quest for truth will turn
out in the end, the events we face today are subject to as great a
variety of constructions as our wits will enable us to contrive'.
The unending possibility of alternative constructions, and in Kelly's
philosophy their desirability, inevitably lead one forward into the
future. It directs our attention not just to change and to novel
situations, but equally to the change which can result from novel
constructions of familiar situations. Many transport problems might
benefit more from personally managed cognitive adjustment than from
expert technological intervention.

9. CONCLUSION

I shall finish with three even more general pointers which social
psychology might offer to transportation studies.

Methodology
Psychology has, to its cost, come to appreciate only too well the
highly multivariate and systemic nature of its subject-matter, and
the dangers of trying to reduce it into univariate paradigms. It
might offer this preliminary 'mapping sentence' (Levy 1976) as one
guide for transportation studies:

'To what extent do (general/particular) (aspects) of
(transport systems) facilitate (users) to achieve (goals)
as revealed by (data sources) at (points in time)?'.

Each of the seven components indicated here is a multivariate focus
of inquiry; but each interacts with the others.

Theory
Most psychological theories tend today to be more encompassing than
those of a few years ago. For example, one would probably not wish
to dissociate cognition, value and behaviour, either theoretically or
in empirical studies. Thus, the evaluation of a transport system by
a psychologist might now ask simultaneously whether it gives greater/
fewer opportunities (cognition) at greater/less cost (value) with
more/less annoyance/dissatisfaction (value) and more/less behavioural
realization (behaviour). And it would be possible to give this

question a theoretical framework.

Metatheory

Hidden assumptions, particularly those of a value-laden kind, in psychological theories, methodologies, and constructs have received increasing attention in recent years. Applying the same consideration to transportation, one might, for example, point to the positivistic orientation of demand models. The orientation tends to be less useful in the human than the physical sciences; man's reactivity tends to negate positivism. The terminology of demand models suggests that something is 'demanded'. But what is *demanded*? And in what sense is it demanded? Again methods of modelling tend to reflect unthinkingly and overwhelmingly the wider concerns and ultimate goals of the modellers, and do not strive to any degree of isomorphism with the psychological processes of those whom they study.

REFERENCES

Bannister, D. and Fransella, F. (1971) *Inquiring Man*. Harmondsworth: Penguin Books.

Blumler, J.G. and Katz, E. (eds.) (1974) *The Uses of Mass Communications: Current Perspectives on Gratification Research*. London: Sage.

Clarke, P. (ed.) (1973) *New Models for Mass Communication Research*. London: Sage.

Forbes, T.W. (1972) *Human Factors in Highway Safety Research*. New York: Wiley.

Harré R. and Secord, P.F. (1972) *The Explanation of Social Behaviour*. Oxford: Blackwell.

Heggie, I. (ed.) (1976) *Modal Choice and the Value of Travel Time*. Oxford: Clarendon Press.

Herzlich, C. (1974) *Health and Illness: A Social Psychological Analysis*. London: Academic Press.

Hoinville, G. (1977) *Priority Evaluator Method*. Methodological Working Paper 3. London: Social and Community Planning and Research.

Kelly, G.A. (1955) *The Psychology of Personal Constructs*, Vols. I and II. New York: Norton.

Kline, F.G. and Tichenor, P.J. (eds.) (1972) *Current Perspectives in Mass Communication Research*. London: Sage.

Levy, S. (1976) Use of the mapping sentence for coordinating theory and research: a cross-cultural example. *Quality and Quantity*, 10, pp. 117-25.

Michon, J.A. (1976) The mutual impacts of transportation and human behaviour, in Stringer, P. and Wenzel, H. (eds.) *Transportation Planning for a Better Environment*. New York: Plenum, pp. 221-36.

Otway, H.J. and Fishbein, M. (1977) Public attitudes and decision making. RM - 77 - 054. Laxenburg, Austria: International Institute for Applied Systems Analysis.

Phares, E.J. (1976) *Locus of Control in Personality*. Morristown, NJ: General Learning Press.

Rapoport, R. and Rapoport, R.N. (1975) *Leisure and the Family Life Cycle*. London: Routledge, Kegan and Paul.

Shaver, K.G. (1975) *An Introduction to Attribution Processes*. Cambridge, Mass: Winthrop.

Slovic, P., Fishcoff, B. and Lichtenstein, S. (1976) Cognitive processes and societal risk taking, in Carroll, J.S. and Payne, J.W. (eds.) *Cognition and Social Behaviour*. Hillsdale, N.J.: Erlbaum.

Slovic, P., Kunreuther, H. and White, G.F. (1974) Decision processes, rationality, and adjustment to natural hazards, in White, G.F. (ed.) *Natural Hazards*. Oxford: Oxford University Press, pp. 187-216.

Stringer, P. (1977) The Press and Publicity for Public Participation. Interim Research Paper 12, Linked Research Project into Public Participation in Structure Planning. London: Department of the Environment.

Stringer, P. (1978) Tuning in to the Public: Survey before Participation. Interim Research Paper 14, Linked Research Project into Public Participation in Structure Planning. London: Department of the Environment.

Stringer, P. (in press) Time, cost and other factors in inter-urban travel mode choice, in Hartmann, H.A. and Molt, W. (eds.) *Advances in Economic Psychology*. Bern: Huber.

Stringer, P. and Ewens, S. (1974) Participation through Public Meetings: The Case in North East Lancashire. Interim Research Paper 2, Linked Research Project into Public Participation in Structure Planning. London: Department of the Environment.

Stringer, P. and Plumridge, G. (1974) Consultation with Organizations on the North East Lancashire Advisory Plan. Interim Research Paper 3, Linked Research Project into Public Participation in Structure Planning. London: Department of the Environment.

Thomas, K. (ed.) (1971) *Attitudes and Behaviour: Selected Readings*. Harmondsworth: Penguin Books.

Thornton, P. and Stringer, P. (1979) The role of local groups in trunk-road consulation: a case-study. *Journal of Voluntary Action Research*, 8, pp. 84-93.

Tuck, M. (1976) *How do we Choose? A Study in Consumer Behaviour*. London: Methuen.

Uzzell, D. (1980) A coorientational approach to participatory politics in an inner city ward. Unpublished PhD thesis, University of Surrey, Guildford.

Contrasting scenarios
for the future

DAVID BANISTER

1. INTRODUCTION

To help focus on the key issues and to ensure some longitudinal structure within the book, two contrasting scenarios are outlined. It
should be remembered that the purpose of these scenarios is not to
predict a particular future, but to provide a framework within which
to identify how presently available methods could be used to analyse
the issues raised by the scenarios. The second reason for introducing
the scenarios is to isolate those research areas in which present
methodology failed or proved to be inadequate; alternative approaches
can then be examined (part 2 of this book), and priority areas for
further research can be determined (the conclusions).

The scenarios have been divided into two parts: the first covers
the common background that outlines the 'non-transport' elements of
the situation in the year 2000. The second states the framework for
the scenarios, and this is followed by the factual background of the
'low' and 'high' growth alternatives. Finally, the actual scenarios
are stated under the headings of the White Paper (Department of
Transport 1977) with the different growth rates and the different
levels of government intervention.

2. COMMON BACKGROUND TO ALL SCENARIOS TO 2000

1. There will be a stable political situation

2. Population estimates for Great Britain – Office of Population
    Censuses and Surveys (1977).

    1975 54.5 million
    1980 54.4 million
    1985 54.8 million
    1990 55.6 million
    1995 56.3 million

An increasingly large proportion of the population will be in the
elderly age group.

3. Residential and industrial location: distribution will first be towards decentralization from the major centres, but there may be a secondary trend to recentralization on intermediate sized towns ($\approx$ 100,000) and some movement back into the inner city areas.

4. Employment: a continued decline in basic and manufacturing industries with some structural unemployment; and an increase in service sector employment and in technical services.

5. The working week will be reduced to 35 hours and there will be an increase in the time available for leisure activities; paid holidays will be increased to 6 weeks per annum. There will also be an increase in part time employment, particularly for females, and people at or near retirement age; the structurally unemployed may also take part time jobs.

6. No significant changes will occur in ownership, either in the transport or other sectors of the economy.

7. The centralization of facilities and activities over the next ten years will be complemented by subsequent decentralization to the community level with smaller units and less specialization in, for example, health facilities, shops, schools, and entertainment and recreational facilities. This may include auxiliary transport facilities (for example, mobile services) and the use of telecommunications. There may eventually be some stabilization with a balance between large and small units.

There will also be a certain amount of uncertainty within the system.

1. The use of North Sea oil revenue;
    changes in the fiscal system;
    investment abroad;
    repayment of loans;
    reinvestment in industry.

2. A change in the structure of the economy with more specialization in certain products; for example, high technology.

3. The density of population: whether this develops on a pattern that relates to decentralization or centralization.

4. The role of the family unit, and changes in size and structure.

5. The amount of discretion that is permissable at the local level in transport decision making.

6. Changes in the road licensing laws: alternatives here will remain open.

7. The role of technology: changes in the efficiency in the use of resources and the control of operations.

8. Changes in public attitudes and aspirations.

3. THE FRAMEWORK OF THE SCENARIOS

Two broad scenarios are outlined that include facets of alternative political, economic, spatial and social elements. Naturally, a wider range of scenarios could be presented, but the purpose of the scenarios is to focus on the issues in the first section of the book. So the two alternatives suggested here are restrictive and it must be realized that there is considerable interaction and feedback between the elements stated above.

Each economic situation must be seen within the political framework of minimal intervention or significant state intervention.

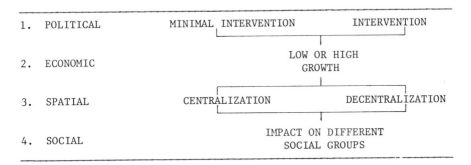

1. POLITICAL	MINIMAL INTERVENTION	INTERVENTION
2. ECONOMIC	LOW OR HIGH GROWTH	
3. SPATIAL	CENTRALIZATION	DECENTRALIZATION
4. SOCIAL	IMPACT ON DIFFERENT SOCIAL GROUPS	

However, social groups also influence the political framework through the electoral process and through pressure groups – so there is considerable vertical interaction. There is also lateral impact and feedback within the system – for instance a policy of high growth and decentralization may lead to a lower growth rate and subsequent centralization, and conversely the reverse may occur. We have taken a high and low economic growth rate as given and outlined the scenarios in terms of minimal and substantial state intervention (i.e. levels 1 and 2 in the diagram). The objective has been to concentrate on the distribution of the economic, spatial and social effects, and the methodologies that can be used to analyse them (i.e. levels 2, 3 and 4 in the diagram).

FACTUAL BACKGROUND TO THE YEAR 2000

	Low	Base level 1978* – White Paper	High
Car ownership	0.35 cars/head	0.25 cars/head	0.44 cars/head
Cars	21.5 million	14 million	25 million[2]
Motorcycles		1.3 million	
Car usage	+17%[1] (Leitch +31%)	Base level	+100%[2] (DoE + 80%)
Public transport patronage			
Bus	Rate of decline to reduce to about 1% p.a.	-2% p.a. pass-km -3.6 p.a. passengers	decline to continue at same rate (2% p.a.)
Rail	Slight increase (0.3% p.a.)	stable	substantial further decline
Energy consumption		29 million tons	
Cost of motoring	200[3]	100[3]	100[3]
Freight transport			
– road	remain stable	1492m tons by road[4]	to increase by 2% p.a.
– rail	increase by 2% p.a.	173m tons by rail[4]	remain stable
Motorways	1400 miles	1323 miles[4]	2000 miles
Other trunk roads	8600 miles	8381 miles[4]	10000 miles
Rail network	same	11,300 miles	contraction to 8000 miles
Capital expenditure on transport (not personal expenditure on purchase of cars)	reallocation within headings with more for subsidy and less for capital expenditure	£1802m – roads £619m – vehicle £982m, – other £201m	to increase on all fronts
Gross Domestic Product	Nominal increase (≈0.8% p.a.)		2.5-3% p.a. increase
Real disposable income	+10-20%		+60-80%

*The base situation states the actual present levels under each
heading or the recent trends.
1. British Railways forecast   3. Index for 1976
2. DoE/TRRL Forecasts.   4. British Road Federation (1978)
                                    Basic Road Statistics.

4. SCENARIO DIFFERENCES

Both follow the headings in the White Paper (Department of Transport 1977)

	LOW	
Energy	Nominal 0.8% p.a. growth. Conservation of resources the key - preservation of fossil fuels - fuel prices to at least double in real terms - possibility of rationing	
Political	**Minimal Intervention**	**Intervention**
Role of government	Very limited support for public transport	Continued support for public transport especially where no alternative service would be supplied
Investment	A cut in expenditure on road construction	A cut in expenditure on road construction, whilst there will be a corresponding increase in public transport expenditure
Local planning	Limited support for local rail services - some closures Limited or no concessionary fares	Local rail services to be maintained, but alternatives may be investigated Concessionary fares for elderly and children
Transport in towns	Limited control of cars at peak hours Some priority for public transport Congestion as a traffic regulator Charge the commuter the 'economic' rate for travel	Restraint on the use of the car - control of parking Priority for Public transport Traffic management Commuter rail services to continue to be supported
Rural areas	Very limited support - let the market mechanism operate	Continued support for public transport Encouragement of alternative modes of transport
Inter-urban passenger transport	Minimal investment - only replacement of existing assets Limited subsidy	Investment in railways with the HST - some government support

LOW

Political	Minimal Intervention	Intervention
Freight	Allocation of all costs to the user	Tighter control over operators Routeing policies to restrict the lorry Sidings to be built
Roads	Limited construction – charging for the use of road space	Limited construction – some bypasses – minimum maintenance – reduce quality of roads
Public consultation	Some form of consultation will take place before decisions are made	For any scheme with a major impact – an independent panel to consider all objections
Airports	Absorption of growth in existing airports	Some limited extension of terminal buildings
Pedestrians	No special provision for other road users and pedestrians	Limited provision for other road users and pedestrians
Other points	Decrease dependence on transport Increased use of telecommunications – substitute for movement	

HIGH

Energy	2.5-3% p.a. growth rate No possibility of shortage – Middle East situation resolved – North Sea resources greater than expected – fuel prices will not increase in real terms	
Political	Minimal Intervention	Intervention
Role of government	Gradual reduction in subsidies both for railways and the bus industry	Continued support for public transport – on an increasing level
Investment	Increase in road expenditure	Increase in road expenditure at the levels of the 1960s

	HIGH	
Political	Minimal Intervention	Intervention
Local Planning	Withdrawal of local rail services if not 'economically viable' Lower level concessionary fares – for elderly and children	Continued support for local rail services Concessionary fares – for elderly and children; also perhaps for the unemployed
Transport in towns	No restraint on traffic Very limited priority – share road space with private vehicles Some traffic management as at present Increase fares for commuters	Very limited restraint, except on environmental grounds Some priority for public transport Limited traffic management Increase subsidy for commuter rail services
Rural areas	Market solution based on minimum viable network Free entry and increased competiton	Increase in subsidies for rural transport Incentives for alternative modes
Inter-urban Passenger Transport	Competition encouraged through road/rail/air services No subsidies	Expansion in research and development in railways – extension of HST and APT network
Freight	Freedom to enter the market Larger lorries permitted to conform with other EEC countries	Freedom to enter market provided that certain legal requirements are met Some limited routeing policy Sidings to be built Restoration of canals
Roads	Increase motorway network to 2000 miles plus a further increase in trunk roads	Increase motorway network to 2000 miles plus a further increase in trunk roads – although the lobbyists may delay the increase
Public consultation	Some form of consultation will take place before decisions are made	For any scheme with a major impact – an independent panel to consider all objections – resources available to aid serious objections

	HIGH	
Political	Minimal Intervention	Intervention
Airports	Extensions of existing airports - new terminals and runways	Extension of existing airports plus major expansion at Stansted
Pedestrians	Some limited provision for other road users and pedestrians	Special provision for pedestrians and cyclists
Other points	Increased dependence on transport Increased use of telecommunications - complement to movement	

CONCLUSION

We have taken as given the political constraints and will be investigating how relevant methodologies can be used to analyse the questions
raised by the scenarios. The next section examines the economic
issues in terms of the availability and use of resources. The importance of information and communications system are then introduced;
in the final section of the first part of the book, the distributional
effects of decisions are outlined, within an economic, a spatial and a
social context.

ACKNOWLEDGEMENT

These scenarios were written in 1978. Thanks are due to Graham
Chapman and Peter Hall for useful ideas and discussion during their
preparation.

REFERENCES

Department of Transport (1977) *Transport Policy*, Cmnd 6836. London:
    HMSO.
Office of Population Censuses and Surveys (1977) Population
    Projections 1975-2015. Series PP2, No. 7. London: HMSO.

Resources: Availability, Allocation and Modal Choice

This section brings together related papers on energy resources and modal choice. It starts from the scenarios which concluded the preceding section. First, there are two alternative forecasts of likely energy resources and their influence on the development of new technologies. They are followed by a paper looking at the energy-efficiency of public transport, which reaches some surprising conclusions. Another contribution concludes that walking, an energy-frugal mode, has been ignored in much transport planning. Finally, an American analysis suggests that capital-intensive new public transport systems may fail to provide an adequate alternative to the private car.

In his paper on energy and transport, Michael Baker summarizes the patterns of oil consumption in the transport sector, and comments on the effects of changes in the availability and price of fuel. The possible alternatives considered include other liquid fuels and the potential for the battery car, given its limited range. Finally, there is a brief survey of other energy sources together with a series of questions on possible alternative futures.

Gerald Leach's paper usefully develops some of these themes by looking in greater detail at the patterns of movement of people and goods in the recent past, and then by critically considering forecasts of future change in car ownership, car traffic and freight traffic. It examines the scope for fuel saving, and concludes that over the next decade considerable economies will be possible for car travel. Economies are also possible in other modes, such as rail and air; but for air, these are likely to be greatly outweighed by the growth of traffic.

Peter Ennor's paper, on energy considerations in public transport, compares different modes. At the margin, the car is far more fuel-efficient than the nearly-empty bus. And, as the number of bus passengers falls, the bus becomes steadily less efficient in terms of energy consumption. The policy response, Ennor suggests, should be to try to make bus services more energy-efficient, by increasing average occupancy and cutting out little-used services; by resisting

the temptation to meet peak demand by extra buses; and by using buses
in the peak more efficiently, and through cutting out restrictions
on their use in the off-peak. Lastly, Ennor agrees with Hillman and
Whalley that the aim of land-use planning should be to reduce all
dependence on motorized transport, by making more places accessible on
foot or by bicycle.

Mayer Hillman and Anne Whalley give a summary of their recent
research on the role of walking as part of the total transport scene
in Britain. For short journeys walking is a dominant mode, and for
all journeys it accounts for one trip in three. But people lacking
car access, as well as those near to their destinations, are likely
to walk far more. Yet transport surveys still tend to ignore walking,
and transport policy-makers seem unaware of its importance. Because
of this, transport policy tends to have too little regard to the needs
of those who walk most and are at greatest risk - especially children.
And long-term planned changes in urban patterns have made life harder
for thosewho have to rely on walking. Yet, in terms of overall
economies in public spending - and also energy saving - there is a
strong case for a transport policy based on the encouragement of trips
on foot.

This conclusion contrasts with that of Melvin Webber who takes the
Bay Area Rapid Transit scheme in San Francisco as his example. The
case put forward is that the decision to go ahead with the BART
investment was based on fundamental flaws in the understanding of the
nature of travel behaviour. It is suggested that the means by which
public transport could be made attractive to the car driver would be
a system which tried to replicate as many features of the car as
possible, and this is what BART attempted to achieve. However, the
most important advantage of the car is its ability to allow almost
random access, and this cannot be provided by a rail system; hence
the predicted patronage figures are gross over-estimates. The only
alternative means of transportation which is likely to challenge the
supremacy of the car is a sytem offering the same many-to-many access
as the telephone or the car itself.

The conclusions reached in this section accept that the technology for change is available, but there is some dispute over
whether there is sufficient political goodwill for implementation.

The energy scenarios concentrate on the technological options and
do not cover the broader issues which relate to fundamental changes
that may occur in location patterns and life-styles. Questions are
posed about the implications of these changes for accessibility, for
land-use patterns, for trip patterns and for social interaction in
general. Some of these issues are returned to in the conclusions
to this book. The main point to emerge is that with careful use of
energy resources over the next twenty years, there should be no real
energy problems for the transport sector.

Within the context of energy, the role of public transport seems
to be bleak. There is particular concern over off-peak services and
the more lightly-used rural services. Unless cross-subsidization
from urban services could continue, rural buses might become
restricted to a set of skeletal services between towns, with some
small scale infilling. Perhaps public transport can be replaced by
a more effective car sharing scheme; although this would involve
major legal problems, legislation in Britain is easing the way for the
introduction of such schemes.

In estimating the role of walking, methods of data collection are critical. Respondents often forget short walk movements when recalling only trip information, but within an activity framework all time has to be accounted for, thus giving a more accurate estimate. Conversely, if just the numbers of trips are quoted, this may result in over-representation of the walk mode, as trip lengths are ignored. Some balance should be sought. On the other hand, it could be argued that walking is not travel as no resources are consumed except time. But time is a resource which is under the control of the planner, and there are also critical distances beyond which people are not prepared to walk. So distance and time are critical factors in mode choice. Walking, the forgotten mode, should merit a far greater priority in transport analysis.

This conclusion contrasts with that reached on the 'failure' of the Bay Area Rapid Transit system where detailed analyses failed to estimate accurately the demand for mass rapid transit. Walking permits random access on a local scale, and the only alternative to the car on the city-wide scale is likely to be some form of para-transit (for example, the jitney or the shared taxi). The impact of BART on accessibility in the whole of San Fransicso is marginal, as the dense network of roads gives an almost uniform accessibility surface.

Energy and transport

MICHAEL BAKER

1. INTRODUCTION
In a Western, or specifically United Kingdom context 'energy and
transport' is currently synonymous with 'petroleum and transport'.
(In 1978 over 99 per cent of energy use by transport in the United
Kingdom was from petroleum, see table 1.) However, within an
historical context petroleum is an aberration, there being approximately an order of magnitude difference between reserves of oil and
of coal. For example see figure 1 which shows King Hubbert's
projections of world coal and oil production.

This paper examines the petroleum use in transport and the
possible time scales over which changes within the transport sector
may take place. Within transport, road transport accounts for 78
per cent of energy use, and within road transport, cars are the major
user so that cars use half of all transport energy (tables 1 and 2).

Table 1. Energy use (10^6 therms) by transport 1978.

	Coal, etc.	Electricity	Petroleum	Total	%
Rail	19	102	384	505	3.7
Road			10697	10697	77.9
Water	2		516	518	3.8
Air			2005	2005	14.6
Total	21	102	13602	13725	100.0
Percentage	0.2	0.7	99.1	100.0	

Source: Department of Energy (1979b).

Table 2. Energy use (10^6 therms) by road transport 1978.

	Motor spirit	DERV	Total	%	%
Cars and m/c	6882		6882	64.3	50.1
PSV and Taxi	34	375	409	3.8	3.0
Goods vehicles	1157	2138	3295	30.8	24.0
Services and other					
Government	70		70	0.7	0.5
Miscellaneous	22	19	41	0.4	0.3
Total	8165	2532	10697	100.0	77.9

Source: Department of Energy (1979b).

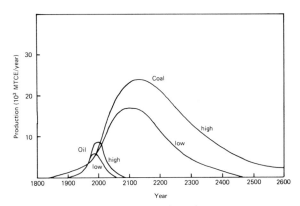

Figure 1. World coal and oil production (source: Hubbert 1973).

2. CHANGES IN PETROLEUM MARKETS

Between 1973 and 1974 there was a 100 per cent increase in price in
non-transport petroleum markets in real terms but only a minor
increase in the road transport market (see figures 2 and 3). This
has resulted in an absolute decrease in non-transport use of petroleum but only a temporary and minor decline in transport use of
petroleum (see figure 4).

    It is interesting to note that the price of crude oil only plays
a small part in the price of petrol. For example the breakdown of
the cost of petrol in 1975 and 1979 is as shown in table 3. Consequently a doubling of the price of crude would, in the first
instance, only cause about a 20 per cent increase in the price of
petrol.

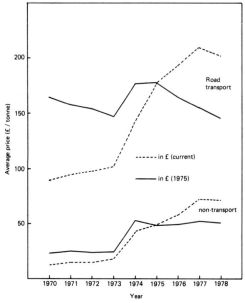

Figure 2. Average prices of petroleum (prices deflated by Retail Price Index) (source: Department of Energy 1979b).

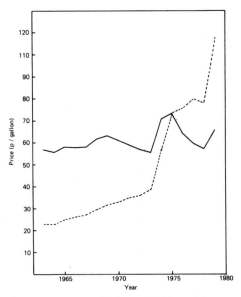

Figure 3. The price of petrol (prices deflated by Retail Price Index) (sources: Department of Transport 1978; Andrews 1979).

Table 3. Breakdown of petrol costs in 1975 and 1979.

| | 1975 | | 1979 | | |
	p/gallon	%	p/gallon	P_{1975}/gallon	%
Crude	16	22	23	(13)	20
Refining and distribution	20	27	43	(24)	36
Duty	22	30	37	(21)	31
VAT	15	21	15	(8)	13
Total	73	100	118	(66)	100

Note: Figures in brackets are prices deflated to 1975 values.
Sources: Department of Transport (1978), Department of Energy (1979b),
Andrews (1979).

3. PETROLEUM RESERVES

UK consumption and UK production of crude oil are shown in figure 5.
Also shown are projections of production (Department of Energy
1979a), and of consumption under various assumptions. These show UK
self-sufficiency in crude lasting from about 1980 or 1981 until some
point between 1990 and 2010 with a possible 'best estimate' of 2000.
    Within this 10 to 30 year period it would be possible to prevent
the current 'shortage' of oil. However, whether this is either
desirable or, within the European and global contexts, politically
feasible is another matter. Even if the shortages are not prevented
it would seem reasonable to assume that transport will continue to
take a greater share of the petroleum market due to differential
price rises, as has happened over the last five or so years (figures
2 to 4).

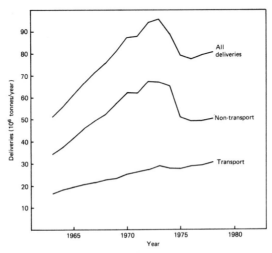

Figure 4. Deliveries of petroleum (source: Department of Energy 1979b)

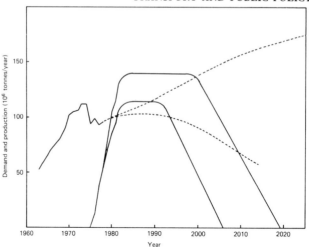

Figure 5. UK oil demand and production (sources: Department of Energy 1979a, 1979b).

4.   CARS

Within the transport sector the major use of energy is by cars (50 per cent, table 2). The next section deals mainly with car use. The major determinant of fuel use per mile for cars is engine size, so that the simplest way to reduce energy use by cars would be to reduce the average engine size of new cars. However, more than 70 per cent of new cars are bought by businesses and it seems likely that energy efficiency is, and will remain, low on their list of priorities.

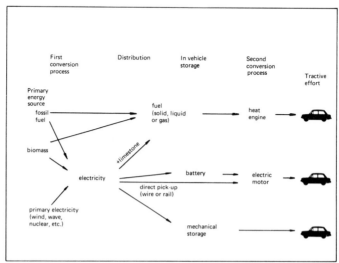

Figure 6.   Flow diagram showing possible routes to tractive effort (source: Charlesworth and Baker 1978).

Alternatives to liquid fuels for transport
As identified in 'Future Transport Fuels' (Chapman 1976) the main
alternatives to natural petroleum appear to be either liquids derived
from coal, or electricity stored in batteries. Some other alternatives are also shown in figure 6. The two more plausible routes
for converting primary energy to tractive effort are shown in figure
7 and the relative efficiences of these processes is shown in
figure 8.

However, this is not the complete picture since we are not
dealing with like vehicles. This is due to the differences in energy
storage between liquid fuels (47,000 MJ/tonne for petrol) and
batteries (180 MJ/tonne for lead-acid and a possible 430 MJ/tonne for
sodium-sulphur). The effect which increasing the energy storage
within a car, and so its range, has upon energy use is illustrated in
figure 9.

The comparison between the two vehicle types should not stop here,
since there will be widespread effects, of the choice between the
alternatives, on other energy markets. For example, if there is a
limit on the availability of coal, a liquid-fuelled vehicle fleet
could use it all leaving none for conversion to synthetic natural gas
for the heating market.

Daily ranges of cars
As mentioned above, battery and liquid-fuelled vehicles are not
directly comparable. One of the major problems when studying this
area is to try and determine the range requirements of a projected
battery car.

On the assumption that a battery car could be fully recharged
overnight, the range of interest is the maximum distance travelled in
any one day, so that we can see if the car can be used without
battery exchange. If battery exchange were possible, it is necessary
to know how many vehicles will exceed the range of one battery re-

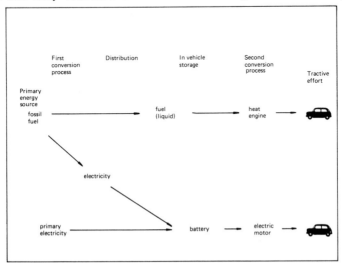

Figure 7. Flow diagram showing most likely routes to tractive
effort (source: Charlesworth and Baker 1978).

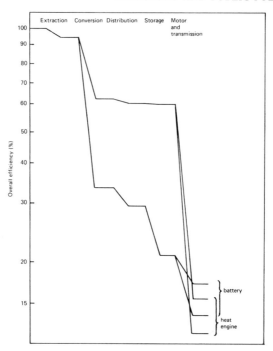

Figure 8. Overall conversion efficiencies for different routes to
tractive effort (source: Charlesworth and Baker 1978).

charge on any day so that the number of battery exchanges required
may be estimated for that day.
      In figure 10, the variation in annual mileage and weekly mileage
of cars from the National Travel Survey (NTS) has been plotted. To
estimate the daily variation in ranges (for battery exchange studies)
it is necessary to make a number of brave assumptions (as was done
for figure 11). So far, only one possible source of data has been
found to construct a variation in daily range table for individual
vehicles over a year (longitudinal), as opposed to variations in
range for many vehicles on one day (cross sectional). It is the
survey of Manchester residents made by British Railways in 1974
(Beadle and Paulley 1979). There are also some data in the NTS, but
not easily accessible and only for one week as opposed to one year
periods.

5. CONCLUSIONS

Work done at the Open University Energy Research Group has on future
transport fuels only been of a preliminary nature. It has identified
more questions than answers. Many of the areas identified in which
further research is required (Baker and Charlesworth 1977, Chapman *et
al*. 1976) are the concern of social research. For example it is
possible to design a short-range electric vehicle for mass production,
but very little is known about its market prospects, or whether there
will be consumer resistance to electric cars (with or without the

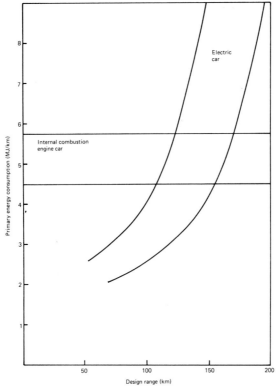

Figure 9.   Variation in energy consumption with designed range.

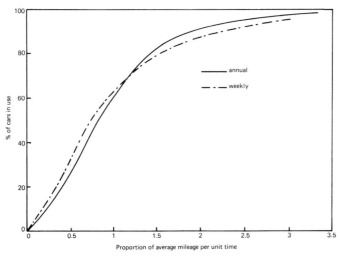

Figure 10.   Cumulative distribution of yearly and weekly car ranges
(sources: Department of the Environment 1975; Gray 1969).

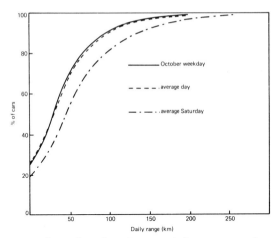

Figure 11. Cumulative distribution of daily ranges for cars.

possibility of battery exchange). On the supply side, the willingness
and ability of the motor vehicle industry to adopt a new vehicle
technology has not been examined. There are also several ways in
which the introduction of electric vehicles could lead to significant
changes in patterns of behaviour. These can be posed as yet
unanswered questions. Would the introduction of electric cars lead to
changes in patterns of transport demand such as an increase in rail
travel for long journeys? Would it lead to changes in patterns of
car ownership or increases in the car hire market? Would it lead to
changes in land-use patterns to accommodate shorter range vehicles?
Would it lead to the use of presently marginal land by the reduction
in traffic noise? Until answers are found to such questions it will
not be possible to make comprehensive comparisons between futures in
which road transport is fueled by electricity in batteries or liquids
derived from coal.

REFERENCES

Andrews, J. (1979) Some petrol prices may fall. *Guardian*, 21
    September, p.1.
Baker, T.M. and Charlesworth, G. (1977) Mobility without oil. *Built
    Environment*, December, pp. 276-79.
Beadle, A. and Paulley, N.J. (1979) A Survey of Long-distance Journeys
    made by Manchester Residents in 1974. Transport and Road Research
    Laboratory, SR487.
Chapman, P. *et al*. (1976) Future Transport Fuels. Transport and
    Road Research Laboratory, SR251.
Charlesworth, G. and Baker, T.M. (1978) Transport fuels for the post-
    oil era. *Energy Policy*, March, pp. 21-35.
Department of Energy (1979a) *Development of the Oil and Gas Resources
    of the United Kingdom 1979*. London: HMSO.
Department of Energy (1979b) *Digest of United Kingdom Energy
    Statistics* 1979. London: HMSO.
Department of the Environment (1975) *National Travel Survey 1972-3:
    Cross sectional analysis of passenger travel in Great Britain*.

London: HMSO.

Department of Transport (1978) *Transport Statistics Great Britain 1967-1977*.   London: HMSO.

Gray, P.G. (1969) *Private Motoring in England and Wales*.   Government Social Survey SS329.   London: HMSO.

Hubbert, M. King (1973) Survey of world energy resources. *Canadian Mining and Metallurgical Bulletin*, July.

The implications of a low-energy strategy for transport

GERALD LEACH

1. PAST TRENDS

Energy growth in the transport sector has been uniquely rapid. Since 1958 it has accounted for half the *total* increase in UK final energy consumption. For road vehicles alone, mainly cars, the growth was as much as 70 per cent of this total, all of it in oil-based fuels. The relevant figures are shown in table 1.

Table 1.   Growth of transport and total energy, UK 1958-76.

	Delivered energy (PJ)			
	1958	1976	Increase	(%)
Total inland energy use	5132	6053	921	100
Total inland transport	888	1339	451	49
Road transport	400	1047	647	70

Source: Department of Energy, *Digest of United Kingdom Energy Statistics* (various years).   London: HMSO.

This energy growth has mainly been due to a rising tide of cars. Figure 1 shows the long-run trend for Great Britain.   Over the period 1953-76 passenger movement per capita doubled (from 4200 to 8300 km/year) but movement by car leaped six-fold, with the car population increasing from 2.8 million to just over 14 million in roughly two decades.   From a four-mode system of bus, car, rail and bicycle (in that order), Britain has moved to a 'one and two halves' system of car, bus and rail, with the two halves in gradual and heavily-subsidized decline.

In freight the growth in tonne-kilometres has been much slower, as shown in figure 2.   Over the period 1956-76 it rose by 61 per cent, slightly faster than Total Industrial Production, which increased by 53 per cent in the same period (Central Statistical Office, various years).

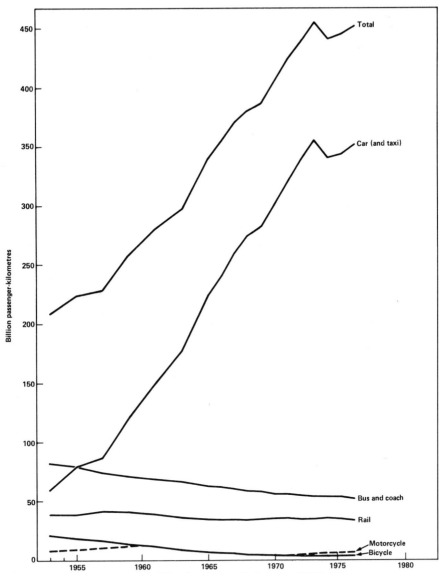

Figure 1. Passenger traffic in Great Britain, 1953–76.
(Source: Central Statistical Office, *Annual Abstract of Statistics*,
various years. London: HMSO.)

    The tonnage of freight moved has not followed this trend. It has
been roughly constant over a decade and has recently declined: 1.95
billion tonnes in 1966; 2.01 billion in the peak year of 1968; 1.78
billion tonnes in 1976.
    The United Kingdom now has a pattern of transport energy use
almost entirely based on oil and dominated by the car, the lorry and
the van, with the fuelling of international air and ship traffic

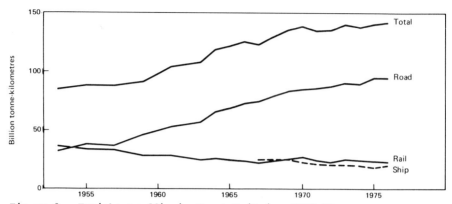

Figure 2.   Freight traffic in Great Britain, 1953-76.
(Source: Central Statistical Office, *Annual Abstract of Statistics*,
various years.   London: HMSO.)

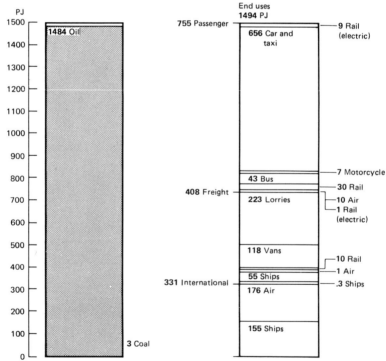

Figure 3.   Energy use in UK transport, 1976.
(a) Domestic flights, estimated from tonne-km flown.   (b) Lorries:
over 1.5 tonne unladen weight.   Vans: under 1.5 tonnes unladen
weight.   (c) Includes 16.2 PJ for fishing vessels as in UK Energy
Statistics.   (d) Excludes 1.9 PJ for rail self-generation of electricity.   Rail electricity includes this quantity plus purchases from
public supply (8.9 PJ) less sales to other sectors (0.5 PJ).

('bunkers') coming a close third. Figure 3 gives the 1976 breakdown
of transport fuel consumption to roughly the level of disaggregation
used in this study.

Table 2 gives a summary of activity levels, energy intensities and
energy use of the main UK transport modes in 1976. Once again, the
dominant roles of the car and road freight in the transport energy
problem stand out clearly. Aircraft cannot be included because the
statistics are inadequate. However, average energy intensities for
aircraft in the United States in 1972 - probably differing little
from UK performances - were 5.9 and 3.2 MJ/passenger-km for domestic
and international flights respectively (Basile *et al.* 1976) - greater
than any other comparable class of traffic. Furthermore, air traffic
is growing much faster in the United Kingdom than any other transport
mode: over the period 1968-76 the combined passenger and freight,
scheduled and non-scheduled tonne-mileage flown by UK airlines grew by
2.6 times.

Table 2. Traffic, energy intensity and energy use in UK transport,
          1976.

Passenger	Per capita activity level	Delivered energy intensity	Delivered energy per capita
	Passenger-km	MJ/passenger-km	GJ
Car	6480	1.81	11.7
Bus and coach	974	0.79	0.77
Motorcycle	123	0.98	0.12
Bicycle	72	–	–
Rail	615	(1.7)	1.0*
Total	8264	1.66	13.59
Freight	Tonne-km	MJ/tonne-km	GJ
All road	1756	3.5	6.1
(Lorries)	(1700)	(2.35)	(4.0)
(Vans)	(56)	(37.5)	(2.1)
Rail	424	(0.5)	0.21*
Ship	368	1.9	0.70
Total	2548	2.75	7.01

Sources: traffic levels as figure 1; energy, figure 3.
*Energy data are approximate: final electricity use is multiplied by
a notional factor of 3 (and added to petroleum) to allow for energy
losses in electricity supply.

These trends and patterns obviously cannot continue into a future
of rising oil scarcity and cost. Unless transport can achieve large
improvements in fuel economy and in the long run find alternatives to
oil, such as electricity, syncrudes from coal, or liquids from organic
wastes and crops, traffic growth will be depressed and eventually
decline.

The thrust of this paper is that technical measures for escaping

this predicament abound. The technical world is intensely aware of
the problem and foresees large potentials for oil-saving without
materially affecting performance in other respects, especially in the
vehicles where they most matter - the car, the van and the aircraft.
Once developed, these technical fixes could work swiftly because of
the generally rapid turnover of vehicle stocks. Furthermore, their
potential impact is much greater than any feasible savings from the
modal shifts often advocated as solutions to the 'energy crisis'. If
in 1976 bicycle and motorcycle traffic had trebled and bus and rail
passenger traffic doubled (all at the expense of the car) energy use
for UK passenger traffic would have been only 11 per cent lower than
it was. Such large shifts do not seem likely.

2. PRESENT PATTERNS

Passenger traffic
Many surveys confirm that higher incomes generate greater travel, car
travel and car ownership. Table 3 shows for 1976 how expenditure on
all transport rose faster than total expenditure as one moves from the
poorest to the wealthiest households, with most of the increase due to
private transport, or cars. Since many cars are bought and run on
business expenses which are not fully reported in household surveys,
the real trend is probably much steeper.

Table 3. Household expenditure on transport, 1976.

£ weekly household expenditure	Lowest income*	Middle income**	Highest income
Total	23.4	59.8	152.2
All transport	1.4	8.2	23.8
(percent of total)	(6)	(14)	(16)
Private transport	0.7	6.7	19.9
(percent of all transport)	(50)	(82)	(84)
Percent of households	16.5	8.4	3.2

Source: Department of Employment (1977)
*weighted average of four lowest income bands.
**close to average for all households.

The 1976 trend for car ownership by households is shown in
figure 4. While there is a strong saturation effect among wealthier
households, the curve for poorer households below the average 55 per
cent car ownership level rises steeply. Over a half of all households
fall in this group.
As GDP grows, in the absence of severe transport policies that
restrain cars one must thus expect travel generally and car travel in
particular to rise quite rapidly. An important effect reinforcing
this pressure involves retired people, who now make up over one-fifth
of all households. Car ownership in this large group is now low,
especially among single women, most of whom do not hold driving
licences. As a new generation of women accustomed to driving cars
reaches retirement they will almost certainly wish to continue doing
so.
However, several limiting effects on car ownership and traffic

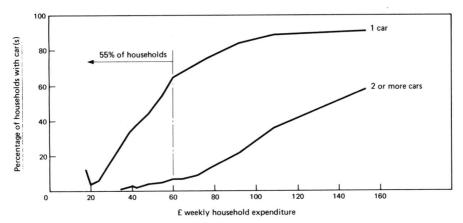

Figure 4. Household car-ownership levels, 1976.
Source: Department of Employment (1977) *Family Expenditure Survey
1976*. London: HMSO.

are likely to counterbalance these pressures. The great bulk of
households which in future acquire cars for the first time, especially
retired people, will not want large cars, nor want to drive them far.
Many will live in urban areas, where car ownership levels and annual
car mileages are lower than in rural areas (DTp 1977). Consequently,
average mileages per car-owning household (and per car) are likely to
fall. Ownership of second and third cars will also be held down by
substantial increase in the proportion of one-adult and single-parent
households assumed by official projections of household structure.

Apart from income, the types of journey that people make strongly
influence the choice of vehicle and traffic levels generally. The
1972-73 National Travel Survey found that only a fifth of journeys
were for commuting (Rigby 1977) where fixed routes and the cost of
parking cars may favour public transport. A further 10 per cent were
trips to and from school, where bus and walking dominate. Nearly all
the remaining journeys were for 'personal' reasons, where the freedom
to go anywhere at any time with any amount of goods and possessions
gives the car a strong advantage over public transport. The dispersal
of the urban population to suburban and rural areas will add to this
advantage in future, while in a more leisured and affluent society
such personal trips are likely to increase in importance. The 1972-73
breakdown of journeys by type and transport mode is shown in table 4.

Time-saving is another important consideration favouring the car
which is now included as a major component in economically based
traffic forecasts. Most passenger journeys are very short. As shown
in figure 5, when all walking trips are included two-thirds of
journeys are less than 4.8 km and only 2.8 per cent are longer than
40 km. Cars become progressively more important with greater journey
length, the significance of the bus declining at the 5-15 km range and
the train at above 30-40 km. For all journeys, on average, car users
spend only two-thirds the amount of time travelling that bus users
spend, but travel 50 per cent further (Rigby 1977). For long journeys
rail is often quicker but fares are a severe deterrent, especially

Table 4.   Journeys by type and transport mode, United Kingdom 1972/73.

				Modal split:	(%)		
Trip purpose	Rail	Bus	Car	Motor-cycle	Bicycle	Walk	Proportion of *all* trip purposes (%)
Work	4.5	20.4	45.3	2.5	5.4	22.0	20.8
In course of work	1.8	4.5	79.6	0.4	0.8	12.8	3.8
Education	1.1	18.0	10.2	0.2	3.1	67.4	9.9
Shopping	0.5	13.7	27.4	0.3	2.2	55.8	20.2
Personal business	0.8	10.9	44.3	0.4	2.0	41.4	7.8
Eat/drink	0.7	7.1	41.5	0.7	0.4	49.7	4.1
Entertainment	1.1	16.7	46.0	0.9	1.6	33.6	4 6
Personal social	0.9	11.5	51.8	0.9	2.6	32.3	14.2
Day trip/play	1.0	3.5	28.1	0.3	2.7	64.5	5.9
Escort	0.4	3.2	66.2	0.3	0.4	29.6	5.9
Other	2.0	9.9	52.6	0.5	3.9	31.1	2.8
Overall modal split (%)	1.6	13.2	40.6	0.9	2.8	40.8	100

Source: Rigby (1977)

when a family is travelling and the motorist counts only the marginal (or petrol) cost of a car trip.

We thus find from all these considerations strong pressures towards greater car ownership and travel, though with some saturation effects. The extent to which these will simply add to total travel – leaving residual bus and rail services at their present or even increasing levels – or will push bus and rail into further decline is most uncertain. Much depends on the final major factors in traffic projections, which are the absolute and relative costs of motoring and public transport.

At first sight the cost of petrol seems to be a major determinant in car travel. The steady upward surge of car traffic shown in figure 1, with its sudden decline in 1973-74 and more recent climb, is mirrored almost exactly by the cost of petrol at the pump (in real terms). Measuring this by the minutes an average male manual worker must toil to earn enough to buy one gallon of petrol, Blackmore and Thomas (1977) have shown that the time fell steadily from 74 minutes in 1953 to 25 minutes in 1973, and then rose sharply to 29 minutes in 1974 and just over 30 minutes in 1975 (all data for October). By October 1977 the figure had fallen to 28 minutes and has continued to drop since.

However, petrol forms only 30-40 per cent of average motoring costs over the year while its future pump price is virtually

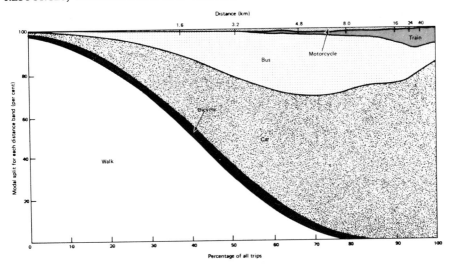

Figure 5.   Transport modal plot by distance travelled, United Kingdom
            1972-73.

Source: Rigby (1977)

impossible to predict, even if one could foretell crude oil prices,
owing to the large tax element in petrol, now close to half the price
at the pump. Expense account motoring provides a further cushion
against higher prices. What we can conclude is that given the two-
to three-fold increase in GDP and doubling of car fuel economy
assumed in this study over the next fifty years, the pump price of
petrol would have to rise roughly four- to six-fold in real terms to
deter the average motorist more than it does now.
     Meanwhile, despite the rising price of petrol since 1973 this
increase has not been much greater than that of all goods and services
and has recently halted, almost closing the relative gap. At the same
time, as shown in table 5, the total cost of motoring has risen much
less than bus and rail fares despite great productivity improvements
in bus and rail services and steeply rising subsidies and grants. In
1975 these were £502 million, or 45 per cent of operating costs, for
rail passenger services; and £260 million or about 27 per cent of
operating costs for bus services (Webster 1977). A recent
detailed analysis of the problem concluded that to halt the decline of
bus traffic, fares would have to be halved in real terms, involving
subsidies rising to £500-800m a year (£1975) by 1985, and that with
today's subsidy levels and expected growths in car ownership bus
traffic would fall over 1975-85 by some 30-40 per cent (Webster 1977).
In summary, most transport forecasters consider that declining bus

Table 5. Relative costs of transport and other items, 1965-77

	Consumer cost indices (1970=100)					
	1965	1970	1974	1975	1976	1977
All items	80	100	145	180	207	258
All car costs	79	100	152	197	216	
Vehicle purchase	85	100	138	176	204	
Petrol and oil	78	100	166	219	231	241
Rail fares	78	100	154	206	270	
Bus and coach fares	71	100	145	193	240	

Source: Central Statistical Office (various years) *National Income and Expenditure*. London: HMSO.

usage is almost inevitable (with subsidies) but that rail services could remain roughly constant (with subsidies), particularly because of business inter-city traffic and cheap fare schemes in off-peak periods.

Freight traffic

The three main freight modes (road, rail and shipping) serve entirely different markets. Shipping is slow and has few docking points: consequently, of UK domestic trade in 1975, 85 per cent was bulk cargoes of coal and oil. Rail is more flexible and rapid, but with limited track and loading facilities is also confined largely to bulk commodities. Road vehicles can reach anywhere, quickly, and have won out on cost, reliability and ease of handling for all but the heaviest bulk goods. These advantages and constraints are reflected in table 6, which shows how land-based freight traffic in Great Britain in 1976 (122 billion tonne-km) was shared by type of goods and traffic mode.

A fully disaggregated traffic projection would be based on a breakdown of this kind. But looking to 2000, let alone 2025, uncertainties are too great to warrant such detail. Many other uncertainties, such as the distribution of producers, routes, and

Table 6. Freight traffic by type and mode, Great Britain 1976.

	Percentage of total freight traffic			
	All	Road	Rail	Pipeline
Food, drink, tobacco	19.4	18.9	0.5	—
Building materials	19.5	17.0	2.5	—
Coal and coke	9.4	2.2	7.2	—
Petroleum products	8.3	3.4	2.2	2.7
Chemicals, fertilizers	6.3	5.4	0.9	—
Iron and steel	8.5	5.6	2.9	—
Other	28.6	25.9	2.7	—
All goods	100.0	78.4	18.9	2.7

Source: as table 5.

consumers and the produce mix within industrial and service sectors
also need to be considered and blur such fine distinctions. In our
projections we have allowed only for broad trends and relationships.

The dominant one is the link between freight traffic and Total
Industrial Production. A close approximation to the UK trends over
1966-76 is shown in table 7. The ratio of traffic volume (tonne-km)
and TIP shown in the third column was fairly steady until 1970 but then
began to drop quite sharply until the 1975-76 recession, probably due
to greater concentration of production and wholesale outlets and
changes in the mix of goods carried. In 1976 the ratio in absolute
terms was close to 3.2 tonne-km per £ of TIP (1.3 tonne-km per £ of
GDP). In the long term, a substantial reduction in this average
traffic-to-value ratio of goods seems likely. The point is simply
illustrated by comparing the retail value of a tonne-load of coal and
advanced hand calculators in 1976: £20-25 as against about £500,000.

Table 7. Growth of freight traffic and industrial production
1966-76.

	Indices (1970=100)		
	All freight traffic tonne-kilometres (Great Britain)	Total Industrial Production (United Kingdom)	Freight x 100 / TIP
1966	90.3	90.6	99.7
1967	89.5	91.7	97.6
1968	94.3	97.2	97.0
1969	98.3	99.8	98.5
1970	100.0	100.0	100.0
1971	97.8	100.3	97.5
1972	98.1	102.5	95.7
1973	101.4	110.0	92.2
1974	99.8	107.0	93.3
1975	101.8	101.7	100.1
1976	102.9	102.2	100.7

Sources: Traffic, as figure 1; TIP, as table 5.

These factors define total traffic volumes and are more important
than shifts between modes - especially from road to rail. The scope
for such transfers is rather limited, at least in the medium term,
since the distribution of industry, the many commercial factors that
influence choice of mode, and the great reduction in railway lines
and sidings, have produced two more or less complementary rather than
competitive markets. Since road now accounts for 80 per cent of
inland freight traffic only a major reinvestment programme for rail
(as in France) could effect any appreciable shifts.

Furthermore, any conceivable shifts will *not* make much difference
to total freight energy consumption. This crucial point is underlined
by the range of rail and road freight energy intensities shown in
table 8. At its best, with fully laden merry-go-round trains and
whole trainloads, rail can be highly efficient at about 0.35-0.45
MJ/tonne-km of freight carried, though average performance is worse.
These two modes account for 60 per cent of rail freight but it is only

the trainloads that compete with road. With other rail freight,
where traffic could be won from road, typical energy intensities are
0.5-1.5 MJ/tonne-km without allowing for shunting and empty running,

Table 8. Energy intensities of rail and road freight, United Kingdom.

	Payload (tonnes)	mpg	Energy intensity (MJ-tonne-km)
Rail (average)			
Merry-go-round: bulk freight			0.6
Whole trainloads: large single consignments			0.65
Freightliner: trunk hauls between specialized depots			0.91
Wagonloads: mixed traffic			0.96
Road (typical range)			
Large tractor + trailer 35 tonne gvw	30-35	6	0.62-1.1
Long distance containers 32 tonne gvw	10-20	7	0.79-2.1
Long distance aggregates, minerals, etc. 32 tonne gvw	18-21	7	1.2 -2.1
Oil delivery 5000 gallon tanker	14-17	8	1.3 -2.4
Finished goods to warehouses, export/import traffic 24 tonne gvw	10-16	8	0.97-2.6
Parcel trunk routes 10 tonne gvw	3-5	10	2.1 -4.4
Parcel collection/delivery 3 tonne flat truck or van	1-3	17	3-24
Deliveries to shops, etc. 3 tonne van	0.5-2	18	6-50
Shop deliveries to customers: services to offices, houses etc., 0.75 tonne van	<0.5	25	>9

gvw: gross vehicle weight. Diesel fuel at 174 MJ/gallon; petrol at
159 MJ/gallon.
Adapted from Advisory Council on Energy Conservation/Department of
Energy (1977).

road shipments at both ends of the rail journey, or the extra distance
of the rail route compared to direct door-to-door lorry service
(Advisory Council on Energy Conservation/Department of Energy 1977).
Since the competing road traffic has an energy intensity of 0.6-2.0
MJ/tonne-km, there is little difference between the two.
  However, over the longer term several factors suggest that rail
freight will and should increase in volume. As well as its environmental advantages, rail is less sensitive than road freight to rising
energy prices and through electrification can rely on other fuels than
oil. In 1977 fuel accounted for only 7 per cent of total rail
operating costs, while electrification is expected to cut these costs
by 30 per cent compared to diesel traction (British Railways Board
1978). In road freight, in December 1976, fuel accounted for 4-19
per cent of the operating costs of smaller lorries of 2-4 tonnes

unladen weight and as much as 13-29 per cent for the large 10-12 tonne
lorry traffic that could be transferred to rail (Freight Transport
Association 1977).

3. FUTURE GROWTH

The basic model and main 'factors of influence' used in our traffic
projections are shown in table 9. Traffic is broken into eleven types
(five for passenger, six for freight) and treated with varying detail
depending on the importance of each mode in total energy use.

Table 9. Traffic projection model.

Sub-sector	Activity level	Factors influencing projections
Passenger		
Car	vehicle-km	GDP; household number and structure; fuel prices; TRRL/ DTp 1978 forecasts to 2005; long-term saturation/congestion
Motorcycle	vehicle-km	Held constant (small)
Bus and coach	vehicle-km	Declining trend; subsidy costs; growth of car; TRRL/DTp fore- casts to 2005
Rail-intercity	train-km	Slowly declining trend; subsidy costs; growth of car
Rail- other	train-km	British Rail forecasts
Freight		
Vans	vehicle-km	Output of services sector; TRRL/ DTp 1978 forecasts to 2005
Lorries	tonne-km	Output of non-services sector (Total Industrial Production); traffic/value ratio of TIP; share of total freight
Rail	train-km (and tonne-km)	As lorries; British Rail forecasts
Ships (Inland and coastal)	tonne-km	As lorries; declining trends with petroleum products switched to pipeline
Ships (Bunkers)	growth index	Proportional to total UK freight traffic
Air (all services)	growth index	1978 'Airports Policy' White Paper forecasts; long-term saturation and congestion

Cars
Forecasts by the Transport and Road Research Laboratory (TRRL) of the
numbers of cars and car traffic have been dropping steadily over the
years, partly because of downward revisions of population and economic
growth, but also in reaction to actual trends. In 1978 the Leitch
Committee criticized the TRRL forecasting methods, based on ultimate
saturation levels, and set about producing its own 'causally based'
forecasts. These were not available for this study and so reliance

has been placed instead on the post-Leitch interim forecasts prepared by the TRRL for the Department of Transport (DTp 1978). These run to 2005 for all road traffic but also include 'possible ranges' for some key factors to 2025.

Table 10 gives the basic population, household and economic projections used in the TRRL/DTp forecasts and in this study. Apart from petrol prices, the assumptions for the two Low projections are very similar, except that we assume a slightly higher number of households, the basic unit of car ownership. For the High projections, the TRRL/DTp assumes substantially greater economic growth.

Table 10. Comparison of basic indicators in IIED and Department of Transport traffic projections.

			DTp	IIED
GDP per capita	1990	Low	138	140
(index: 1976 = 100)		High	157	150
	2000	Low	166	168
		High	208	187
Home population	1990		101.1	101.1
(index: 1976 = 100)	2000		102.5	102.7
Households	1990	Low	21.4	21.6
(millions)		High		21.6
	2000	Low	21.7	22.2
		High		23.1
Petrol price	1990	Low	115	–
(index: 1976 = 100)		High	177	–
	2000	Low	154	{ 200 (approx)
		High	300	

Figure 6 shows the assumed percentage of households owning at least one car. Our Low projection is exactly as the TRRL/DTp Low to 2025, while the High is slightly below the TRRL/DTp maximum possible range.

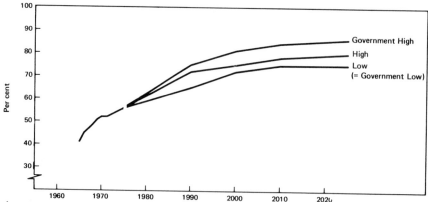

Figure 6. Percentage of households owning car(s), 1965-2025.

The assumption that ownership will rise to 75-80 per cent in 2025 means that much of the future demand will be for small cars with relatively low annual mileages, while the increasing proportion of one-adult households owning cars will hold down the number of second (and third) cars. Consequently, the figure of cars per car-owning household comes close to saturation in both scenarios in the year 2000. Table 11 records in detail the assumptions made about population, households, car numbers and other ownership variables.

Table 11. Car ownership and traffic, 1976-2025.

		1976	1990	2000	2010	2025
Population	Low	56.0	56.6	57.5	57.7	58.0
(millions)	High	56.0	56.6	57.5	58.3	59.0
Households	Low	19.9	21.6	22.2	22.4	22.8
(millions)	High	19.9	21.6	23.1	24.5	25.2
Households with car(s)	Low	58.5	65	72	75	75
(percent)	High	58.5	72	75	78	80
Households with car(s)	Low	11.6	14.0	16.0	16.8	17.1
(millions)	High	11.6	15.5	17.3	19.1	20.2
Cars/owning household	Low	1.24	1.28	1.31	1.33	1.33
	High	1.24	1.33	1.35	1.35	1.35
Cars/person	Low	0.26	0.32	0.36	0.39	0.39
	High	0.26	0.37	0.41	0.44	0.46
Cars	Low	14.4	18.3	20.9	22.3	22.7
(millions)	High	14.4	20.7	23.4	25.8	27.3
of which 2nd or more	Low	2.8	4.3	4.9	5.5	5.6
(millions)	High	2.8	5.1	6.1	6.7	7.1
Average km/car	Low	14.2	14.0	13.2	12.8	12.8
(thousands)	High	14.2	14.4	14.2	13.7	13.4
Average km/household with	Low	17.6	18.3	17.2	17.0	17.0
car (thousands)	High	17.6	19.2	19.2	18.6	18.1
Average car-km/person	Low	3.66	4.5	4.8	4.9	5.0
(thousands)	High	3.66	5.3	5.8	6.1	6.2
Total vehicle-km	Low	205	256	275	285	290
(billions)	High	205	298	332	355	365
(as index)	Low	100	125	134	139	141
	High	100	145	162	173	178

The projections for the total number of cars, together with past trends, some of the projections made by the TRRL since the middle 1960s, and the 1978 TRRL/DTp forecasts are illustrated in figure 7.

Table 11 also gives projections for car traffic. Here the basic assumptions are declines in average mileage per car and, after peaking in 1990-2000, per car-owning household. Some of the reasons for this

have already been mentioned: another is the assumed increase in
second cars which typically have lower mileages than the main family
car. The reductions are not large, as shown in figure 8, and are
within the range assumed by the TRRL/DTp forecasts. Nevertheless, car
traffic per person rises substantially, with a marked tendency to
saturate after 2000, reaching by 2025 a level that is 37 per cent to
69 per cent above today's.

The final projections of car traffic, on which the energy
projections are based, are shown in figure 9. In the Low case traffic
grows exactly as in the TRRL/DTp Low projection to 2005; and in both
cases there is virtually zero growth by 2025 at levels 41 per cent and
78 per cent above that of 1976.

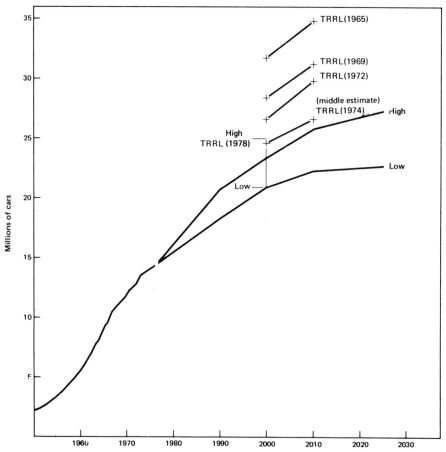

Figure 7. Number of cars, 1950-2025.
Sources: Historical data, as table 5. TRRL forecasts for Great
Britain multiplied by ratio of UK/GB car fleet in 1975 (1.023).
TRRL/DTp 1978 gives no car population projection: range given is
implied by other assumptions.

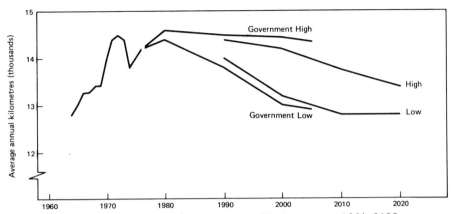

Figure 8. Average annual distance travelled per car 1964-2025.
Sources: Historical as figure 1 and DTp (1977) (total vehicle-km for
cars and taxis divided by number of cars).

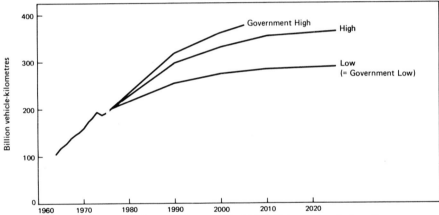

Figure 9. Car and taxi traffic, 1964-2025 (historical for Great
Britain; projections for United Kingdom).

Other passenger traffic

Because they are less critical for energy consumption than the car,
for other passenger vehicles the same traffic projections are used in
both the High and Low cases, as in the TRRL/DTp forecasts for bus and
coach travel.

The assumptions for the three main non-car modes (bus, rail and
motorcycle) are given in table 14. The declining trends for bus and
rail follow from the relatively high car projections. Nevertheless,
the rate of decline is so small so that by 2025 there are still quite
high levels of service from bus, coach and rail to serve the markets
not provided by the private car.

Projections for rail follow closely the 1978 forecasts produced
by the British Railways Board in its discussion document on rail
electrification (British Railways Board 1978). With bus and rail it

should be realized that a constant or rising level of *passenger*
traffic is consistent with the declines in vehicle traffic through
increased load factors.

Freight
Freight projections are based on the growth of (non-energy) industrial
output and the assumption that the traffic-to-value ratio of goods
will decline as the mix of production increasingly shifts from
primary, heavy goods to secondary, assembled manufactures, and energy
costs force 'tighter' distribution networks. The extent of this
decline is perhaps the greatest uncertainty in the model. Even
allowing for a 'base load' of coal, oil, iron and steel, which
accounted for 35 per cent of all freight tonne-km in 1975, the assumed
fall of 12 per cent to 19 per cent is possibly conservative. The
basic assumptions are consistent with those of the industry sector and
are given in table 12.

Table 12. Total freight traffic, 1976-2025.

		1976	1990	2000	2010	2025
Non-energy TIP	Low	40.72	47.8	56.3	59.6	62.0
(£ billion)	High	40.72	51.2	62.8	73.2	89.7
(as index)	Low	100	121	143	151	157
	High	100	130	159	185	227
Tonne-km/£ Non-energy TIP	Low	3.58	3.47	3.2	3.19	3.15
	High	3.58	3.47	3.2	3.1	2.9
(as index)	Low	100	97	89	87	81
	High	100	97	89	89	88
Traffic	Low	145.8	165	180	190	195
(billion tonne-km)	High	145.8	178	201	227	260
(as index)	Low	100	113	123	130	134
	High	100	122	138	156	178

The second step in the model is to allocate freight by modes. In
both cases, inland and coastal shipping continues its absolute and
percentage decline as oil and some coal traffic is transferred to
pipelines, which increase by about 60 per cent over the forecast
period, though from a very small base. (Because pipeline traffic and
energy use are both small they are ignored in later calculations.)
Some coal and oil traffic is also assumed to move from ship to rail.
Rail traffic increases steadily, largely due to the growth of bulk
shipments but also in the longer term because of transfers of some
heavy, long-distance traffic from road. The balance of freight tonne-
km is allocated to road. The resulting assumptions are given in
table 13 and figure 10.
    The third step in the model is to convert rail freight to *train*-
kilometres and to divide road freight into lorry and light van
traffic.
    The step is necessary for rail because energy use depends on all-
up weight and is dominated by the weight of the train, not the load
itself. In making the conversion the critical factor is the average
freight load per train, which has increased very rapidly in the past
decade, going from 225 tonnes in 1966 to 338 tonnes in 1976. Further
increases, though at a slowing rate, are assumed: namely, 380 tonnes

Table 13. Freight traffic by mode, 1976–2025.

		1976	1990	2000	2010	2025
Traffic by mode *(Billion tonne-km)*						
Road	Low	98.2	113	125	132	136
	High	98.2	124	144	165	193
Rail	Low	23.7	30	34	38	39
	High	23.7	31	36	41	47
Water	Low	20.6	19	17	16	15
	High	20.6	19	17	16	15
Other: pipelines, etc.	Low	3.2	3	4	4	5
	High	3.2	3.5	4	5	5
Traffic by mode *(Percent {rounded})*						
Road	Low	67.4	68.5	69.5	69.5	70
	High	67.4	70	71.5	73	74
Rail	Low	16.3	18	19	20	20
	High	16.3	17.5	18	18	18
Water	Low	14.1	11.5	9.5	8.5	7.5
	High	14.1	10.5	8.5	7	6
Other: pipelines, etc.	Low	2.2	2	2	2	2.5
	High	2.2	2	2	2	2

in 1990, 400 in 2000, 410 in 2010 and 420 tonnes in 2025, for both
High and Low cases. With these assumptions one reaches the required
projections for loaded train-km shown in figure 11 along with past
trends and the 1978 forecast by the British Railways Board. Since
energy use by rail freight is small the final results are not
sensitive to these assumptions.

    The breakdown into lorry and light van traffic is necessary
because of the extreme difference in energy performance – and in
potential fuel economies – between the two types of vehicle. In 1976
light vans of under 0.75 tonnes unladen weight carried about 3 per
cent of road freight tonne-km but accounted for over half the vehicle
mileage and one-third of fuel consumption by road freight (see table 2
and figure 3). Since their energy consumption is dominated by vehicle
weight and not by their typically small payloads, it is sensible to
project van traffic by vehicle-km, as in the TRRL/DTp projections.
The growth assumptions, shown in figure 12, are the same as the TRRL/
DTp forecasts in the Low case but fall below them in the High variant
and in both projections show a marked long-term saturation effect.

    Estimates of the small freight volume of vans then gives the
tonne-km of traffic by lorries, from which energy use is derived. The
traffic projections for lorries are very close to the total road
freight forecasts shown in figure 10.

Air and ship bunkers
Although important energy users, these last two transport sub-sectors
can be projected only in the crudest way because their future growths
are extremely uncertain. With air, the fuelling of international
traffic originating in or passing through the United Kingdom
completely dominates domestic traffic, while air freight is negligible

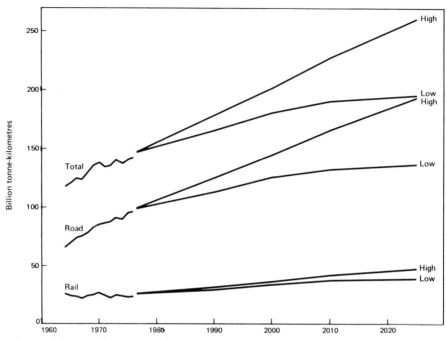

Figure 10. Freight traffic by mode, 1964–2025 (historical for Great Britain; projections for United Kingdom).

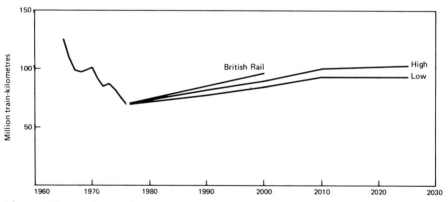

Figure 11. Rail freight: loaded train-km, 1965–2025 (historical for Great Britain; projections for United Kingdom).

compared with passenger traffic. Thus, as with international shipping, future growth depends mostly on global economic and other factors which cannot be forecast by a national model.

In outline, air traffic is assumed to grow at slower than historic rates, with a marked tendency to saturation after 1990–2000 owing to

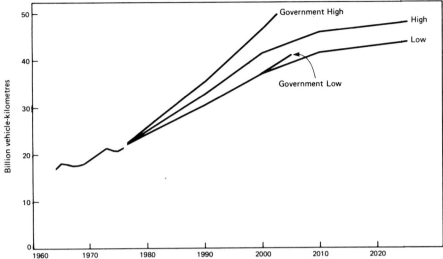

Figure 12. Light van traffic, 1964-2025 (historical for Great Britain; projections for United Kingdom).

airport congestion, environmental pressures against new airports, reductions in business travel due to better telecommunications, and fuel cost constraints. Nevertheless, aircraft movements increase over 1976-2000 by a factor of 2.15 to 2.65 in the Low and High cases, and by 2.4 to 3 times over the 1976-2025 period. International shipping is assumed to grow in line with UK freight and thus increases by 34 per cent to 73 per cent over the entire period.

TRAFFIC PROJECTIONS: SUMMARY

For convenience table 14 brings together all the traffic projections used in the transport sector.

4. FUEL SAVINGS: CARS

There is a growing consensus among engineers that the fuel consump-tion* of the average European car could be reduced by 40-50 per cent in the medium to long term, and even more by some advanced engine and transmission designs. Similar savings can be made in aircraft. With other vehicles potential savings range from 30-40 per cent for vans and 20-30 per cent for lorries and rail.

No single trick will produce these savings. They must come from many individual contributions, some of them relatively simple with low or negligible costs, others calling for protracted development along lines already under intensive investigation, all backed by the right incentives.

In this section we review briefly the most important of these

---

*Throughout this section fuel consumption refers to energy per unit distance (e.g. gallons/mile) and not to 'fuel economy' or miles/ gallon. Source data have been converted where necessary. Gallons are imperial units (= 1.2 US gallons, 4.55 litres).

Table 14. Summary of traffic projections, 1976–2025.

		1976	1990	2000	2010	2025
Million vehicle-km						
Car	Low	205	256	275	285	290
	High	205	298	332	335	365
Motorcycle	Low	6	6	6	6	6
	High	6	6	6	6	6
Bus and coach	Low	3.63	3.2	2.9	2.6	2.5
	High	3.63	3.2	2.9	2.6	2.5
Light vans	Low	21.9	30.7	37.2	41.6	43.8
	High	21.9	32.9	41.6	46	48
Million vehicle-km						
Rail: Inter-city	Low	109	104	100	95	90
	High	109	104	100	95	90
Other	Low	226	213	204	195	180
	High	226	213	204	195	180
Freight	Low	70	78	85	93	93
	High	70	82	90	100	112
Million vehicle-km						
Lorries	Low	95.2	109	120	126	130
	High	95.2	120	138	159	186
Ships: Coastal	Low	20.6	19	17	16	15
	High	20.6	19	17	16	15
As index						
Ships: Bunkers	Low	100	113	123	130	134
	High	100	122	138	156	178
Air	Low	100	175	215	230	240
	High	100	215	265	285	300

savings using the car as the basic example. In the next section,
short reviews are given for other vehicles along with our assumptions
on the timing and extent of fuel savings for all transport modes.

Cars
A useful starting point is to see where the energy of fuel is used
(and lost) in a typical car. Figure 13 shows an 'energy flow map' for
a car during a standard US Environmental Protection Agency
test driving cycle (Grey *et al*. 1978). While the numbers should be
treated as only rough approximations, since real cars and driving
cycles vary enormously, it is clear that targets for improving fuel
economy do not lie only in improved engine design but all the way
along the chain from the engine to the wheels.

Streamlining
At 50–65 km/h about half of the engine power of a car goes into
overcoming air resistance, the fraction rising steeply to around 75
per cent at 110 km/h. For medium to large cars this air drag can be
reduced at the design stage with no cost penalty by as much as 25 per

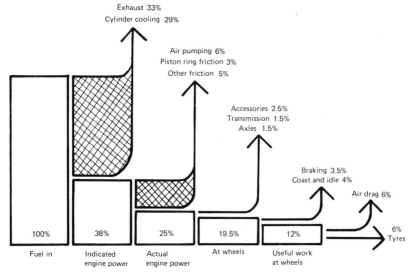

Figure 13.   Energy flow in a 'typical' car.

cent without sacrificing passenger and luggage space.   Small cars are
more difficult to streamline but drag reductions up to 30 per cent by
better design have been recorded (Advisory Council on Energy Conservation 1977).   Fuel savings by this approach would vary from negligible
for small cars used only in cities to 20 per cent or more for an
average car on a high speed motorway journey.

Allowing for the breakdown of car traffic by vehicle size and road
type shown in table 15, if we assume no drag savings for the smallest
cars or urban traffic, and for other cars fuel savings of 10 per cent
for rural roads and 20 per cent for motorways, potential fuel savings
for the UK fleet would be around 5-6 per cent.   This is in line with
a recent estimate of 8 per cent fuel savings from a 33 per cent drag
reduction for the US car fleet (British Railways Board 1978).

Given the relatively small motorway mileage indicated by table 15,
speed limits would not save much fuel (possibly around 1 per cent
overall) even though a reduction from the present UK limit of 110 km/h
to the US limit of 90 km/h typically reduces consumption by 17-18 per
cent (DTp 1978).

Tyre drag
Tyre rolling resistance accounts for about half of the work output of
cars but greatly exceeds air drag at low speeds.   This tyre drag can
be cut by about 25 per cent by switching from cross-ply to steel-cased
radial-ply tyres (Advisory Council on Energy Conservation 1977),
giving a 6-8 per cent fuel saving.   Since about one-quarter of UK tyre
production is still cross-ply, a complete switch to steel radials
would produce fleet fuel savings of 1.5-2.0 per cent as well as giving
safer driving.   Proper tyre inflation can decrease fuel consumption by
as much as 1 mpg or 3 per cent for the average vehicle (DTp 1977).
Possibly a further fuel saving of around 0.5 per cent could be
achieved here if all tyres were properly inflated.

Table 15.   Car traffic and fuel consumption by engine size and road
type UK, 1975.

Car engine size (litres)	Motorways km (fuel) %	Urban roads km (fuel) %	Rural roads km (fuel) %	All roads km (fuel) %
Under 1	1.3 (0.9)	8.0 (6.6)	6.9 (4.6)	16.2 (12.1)
1-1.5	3.6 (3.3)	22.3 (23.0)	19.2 (16.1)	45.1 (42.4)
1.5-2.0	2.4 (2.6)	15.0 (17.7)	12.9 (12.5)	30.3 (32.8)
2.0-3.0	0.4 (0.6)	2.8 (4.2)	2.4 (2.9)	5.6 (7.7)
Over 3	0.2 (0.4)	1.4 (2.7)	1.2 (1.9)	2.8 (5.0)
All cars	7.9 (7.8)	49.5 (54.2)	42.6 (38.0)	100.0 (100.0)

Estimated for 1975 from Department of Transport (1977), tables 26, 33;
Society of Motor Manufacturers and Traders data on annual mileages by
engine size; fuel consumption data for 172 different cars from *What
Car*, July 1977, and *Motor* 9 July 1977; and Department of Energy,
Digest of United Kingdom Energy Statistics (various years).   London:
HMSO.

Idle-off and coasting
In American cities cars in traffic are typically stationary for 13 per
cent of the time and decelerating for another 26 per cent (Burt 1977).
If UK levels are not very different it means that for around 40 per
cent of urban driving times engines are running to no purpose.
Devices that turn off the engine and restart it at a touch of the
accelerator and others that automatically shut off the fuel supply
during coasting are under development.   Estimates for fuel savings
from these devices have been put at 10 per cent (Cohn 1975) and 12 per
cent (Grey *et al.* 1978) for US cars in urban driving cycles.   If one
assumes 8-10 per cent for the British car, fuel savings would be at
least 4-5 per cent (see table 15).

Vehicle weight
Lighter vehicles are a direct route to saving fuel, so long as engine
power is reduced in proportion.   The reason is simply that energy
inputs for acceleration and losses from rolling friction and braking
are all directly proportional to weight.   The scale of possible
savings for the UK is indicated by figure 14, which shows fuel
consumption in urban conditions and vehicle curb weight for 52 new
1978 model cars ranging from the Fiat 126 to the 2.8 litre Granada
saloon.   Fuel consumption and weight are clearly closely related, the
average line following the formulae:

$$\text{fuel consumption (gallons/100 miles)} = 0.5 + 3.4T$$
$$\text{fuel consumption (MJ/km)} = 0.94(0.5 + 3.4T)$$

where T is curb weight in tonnes and one gallon contains 159 MJ.   From
this it follows that (for urban conditions and over this weight range)
a 10 per cent reduction in vehicle weight (either by purchasing
patterns or car design) would produce fuel savings close to 9 per
cent.

Lubricants and pumping
In the 'typical' car of figure 13 as much as half the indicated engine power goes into pumping and overcoming friction in the engine, transmission and axles. If these losses could be eliminated, fuel consumption would be halved at a stroke.

In the long term, advanced research may achieve about half this theoretical target. Grey has estimated that for the average American car proper valve sizing could reduce pumping losses by 60 per cent, giving a 13 per cent reduction in fuel consumption, and that low-friction Xylan coatings on moving parts could reduce engine and other friction by a half, giving a further 15 per cent saving in fuel (Grey *et al.* 1978). A more immediate prospect for average European cars is a 6 per cent fuel-saving from better engine and transmission lubricants with a further 5-10 per cent from better petrol formulae, giving a combined fuel reduction of 10-14 per cent as a feasible target for new cars within a decade (Blackmore and Thomas 1977).

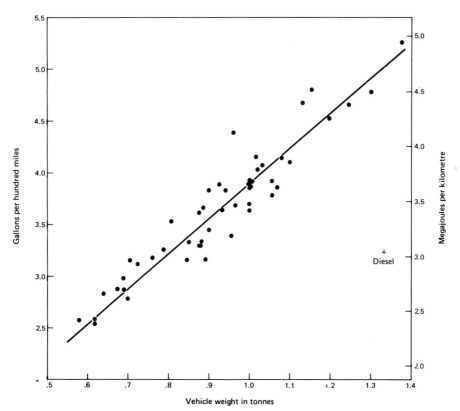

Figure 14. Car fuel consumption by vehicle weight, 1978 models. Sources: fuel consumption, Department of Energy (1978); vehicle curb weight from 1978 manufacturers' catalogues (Ford, British Leyland, Fiat).

Driving techniques
Jerky driving and 'flooring' the accelerator are well known ways of
wasting fuel and can increase consumption by up to 2 mpg in city
traffic (DTp 1977). Short of a determined driver education campaign,
a simple technical fix is to fit some form of two-pressure control on
the accelerator. The first, light pressure range may give a steady
90-100 km/h on open roads and adequate acceleration in urban driving.
If the driver wants greater power he must press harder – and receive a
warning of what he is doing. Twin choke carburettors which are now
commonly fitted to new cars give a similar warning. Careful economy
driving can go much further and reduce consumption in a mixed motorway
and urban driving cycle by up to 25-30 per cent with little sacrifice
in average speed (Anon. 1977a). A potential saving from these
measures is hard to quantify but could be around 3-5 per cent.

Maintenance and electronic controls
Many surveys show that most cars are badly tuned for most of the time.
Tests on 4450 cars chosen randomly in the United Kingdom found the
following frequency of faults (Advisory Council on Energy Conservation
1977).

Contact breaker requiring attention	58.4%
Mixture over-rich at idle	58.1%
Mixture over-rich at cruise	57.0%
Sparking plugs needing adjustment, cleaning, etc.	27.2%
Ignition timing over-advanced 6° or more	25.5%
Ignition timing over-retarded 6° or more	12.1%

Similar or higher frequencies were found in thirteen other
European countries in a 1973-74 survey, also by the Champion Sparking
Plug Company (Atkinson and Postle 1977). Other tests have shown
improvements in fuel consumption after tuning of 5-7 per cent
(Advisory Council on Energy Conservation 1977) and up to 19 per cent
for new cars on a standard EEC driving cycle (Atkinson and Postle
1977).

Devices which improve and maintain performance of ignition systems
and carburettors are now standard on US cars because of air emission
regulations. In Europe electronic ignition systems will shortly
become standard equipment on many vehicles and to meet EEC anti-pollu-
tion requirements carburettors will have their adjustments locked to
prevent incorrect resetting. Tests have shown that devices of this
kind can maintain correct tune for 50,000 miles with only minor
servicing and prevent deterioration in emissions and fuel performance
(Advisory Council on Energy Conservation 1977). Fuel savings from
electronic ignition alone are estimated at 3 per cent (Advisory
Council on Energy Conservation 1977), 5 per cent (Atkinson and Postle
1977) and 10 per cent (Anon 1976). With a mass production cost well
below the present £20-30, payback times from fuel savings should be
under one to two years (Advisory Council on Energy Conservation 1977).

Cold starting
When a vehicle engine and transmission are cold, fuel consumption is
much higher than when fully warmed up. Tests show that in city
conditions for a one mile trip consumption averages twice that when
fully warmed even at a summery 21^oC and about three times at -12^oC
(Blackmore 1977). After 24 km it is still 10-25 per cent above the
minimum warmed-up figure. Since 40 per cent of all car trips in the
UK are less than 4.8 km and 80 per cent are less than 16 km the

potential for fuel saving here is clearly large. Probably some 10 per cent of total car fuel usage is the excess due to warm-up (Advisory Council on Energy Conservation 1977).

A variety of technical solutions exist for cutting this waste. Thermostatically controlled fans to avoid cooling the engine when warming up could save about 3 per cent of fuel in urban driving (Advisory Council on Energy Conservation 1977), or say 1.5 per cent for the UK car fleet. Faster warming or insulated engines, fuel pre-heat and precise choke control could also help greatly. Another route is through better engine and transmission lubricants and fuels: savings of 1-5 per cent for cold weather trips up to 13 km and up to 3 per cent thereafter are considered feasible (Padmore 1977).

Variable transmission

Car engines suffer from the problem common to many prime movers and heating systems: they must be powerful enough to meet peak demands (when accelerating or cruising at high speeds) but most of the time they run at low loads, and are over-sized and inefficient. Gear boxes and automatic transmissions are attempts to put this right but fall short of the ideal, which is a properly sized (small) engine running continuously at full throttle through infinitely variable gearing or an energy storage device such as a flywheel, or both combined.

As far back as 1953 it was estimated that an *ideal* continuously variable transmission (CVT) would give fuel savings of 40-50 per cent over the speed range 50-110 km/h (Blackmore 1977). A more practical target today is a saving estimated at anything from 20 per cent (Grey *et al.* 1978) to 25-30 per cent (Advisory Council on Energy Conservation 1977) from CVT systems which, though they exist on the engineer's bench, have not yet proved to be sufficiently cheap, durable, reliable or efficient. Since no other single development in road vehicle design can give such a large fuel saving, CVT is naturally under intensive development.

Further off is the idea of coupling the engine through a CVT to a flywheel which can also pick up energy from the wheels through 'regenerative braking' as the car slows down. A micro-processor would continuously adjust the settings of the throttle, CVT, engine and flywheel clutches to give optimum performance with minimum fuel consumption. Fuel savings have been estimated at 28 per cent by the designers of one such system (Beale *et al.* 1976) at 50 per cent for urban driving (Advisory Council on Energy Conservation 1977) and for American cars an overall 35 per cent (Grey *et al.* 1978). However, on present knowledge these systems appear too expensive, heavy, possibly dangerous in collisions if the flywheel comes loose, and demand complex controls.

Improved engines

Much development effort is being made across the industrial world to improve the fuel performance of car engines while meeting tighter air pollution limits. The topic is extremely complex, but in the broadest outline centres on two strategies. One, for the medium term, is to run engines on a weaker petrol-air mix, either by adapting the internal combustion engine (ICE) or developing satisfactory diesel engines for cars. The second, longer term strategy is to develop inherently more efficient, low pollution 'open combustion' engines, especially the Stirling engine and the gas turbine. A third approach, the electric battery vehicle, will be discussed separately.

Table 16 outlines the problems, opportunities and trade-offs involved.
The first two columns give the engine efficiencies attainable with
present technology and what may be achieved in advanced engines ten
years from now, under full-load and the more taxing and common part-
load condition.

The advantage of the diesel at part-load (though not at full-load)
is clear but there is a trade-off in higher emissions (though without
lead) and higher cost. The Stirling engine offers very high

Table 16. Present and future engine characteristics.

	Engine efficiency (per cent)		Emissions and noise	Manu-facturing cost
	Full load	10% Load		
Conventional ICE	26 - 30	15 - 24	acceptable with controls; likely to degenerate noise: moderate	very low
Diesel	26 - 36	18 - 32	high in nitrogen oxides, smoke noise: high	moderate
Stirling (steam or organic vapour)	30 - 42	28 - 38	very good; not likely to degenerate noise: low	high
Rankine (steam or organic vapour)	20 - 30	15 - 22	very good; not likely to degenerate noise: low	high
Gas turbine	25 - 44	8 - 25	very good; not likely to degenerate noise: low	moderate; potentially low (ceramics)

Source: Adapted from Wilson (1978)

efficiencies and fuel savings, low pollution and noise, but could cost
more than a conventional engine because of formidable engineering and
control problems; nevertheless, it is being developed vigorously,
notably by Ford (United States), Philips (Holland) and United Sterling
(Sweden). The Rankine engine offers little, if anything, in fuel
savings and has severe problems of reliability, complicated controls
and poor start-up characteristics, so that interest in it has
declined. The gas turbine, which is being developed mainly in the
United States, is a very attractive long-shot but success strongly
depends on developing high temperature ceramic materials.

A broad consensus exists that lean-burn conventional engines will
be the major approach for European cars unless emission standards are
severely tightened, and that fuel savings of around 20 per cent could
be achieved in new cars by the late 1980s (Blackmore and Thomas 1977,
Advisory Council on Energy Conservation 1977). Diesel engines will be
the main competitor, offering savings of roughly 20-30 per cent within

a decade (Advisory Council on Energy Conservation 1977), but with
higher costs and problems of designing suitable medium-to-small
engines, may be limited to the large car or high annual mileage
market.

Combined savings for the car
How do these potential fuel savings add up? In a book published in
1977 which exhaustively reviews these issues (Blackmore and Thomas
1977), Blackmore offers a 'personal speculation of what is practically
realizable over the next decade' for European petrol-powered cars.
He concludes that a 33 per cent fuel saving is possible and 'a very
good target for the industry to aim at'. Individual savings as
improvements in fuel economy (mpg) are: engine design, 20 per cent;
gasoline design, 5-10 per cent; engine lubricants, about 3 per cent;
transmission lubricants, about 3 per cent; transmission design, 5-10
per cent; weight, air drag, tyres, accessories, about 10 per cent;
engine size and model mix changes, about 10 per cent; vehicle
maintenance, about 5 per cent; giving a combined total of 61-71 per
cent. As the effects are not entirely independent, Blackmore's (1978)
'conservative' final estimate is a 50 per cent improvement, equal to
a reduction in fuel consumption of 33 per cent.

   Substantially larger savings can be envisaged over a slightly
longer period if one includes other opinions and a fuller range of
options, including CVT. Using the estimated savings in the previous
sections, table 17 gives a total fuel reduction by 46-57 per cent, and
even this excludes some advanced concepts such as Xylan surface
coatings and valve resizing, or advanced engines such as the Stirling
cycle. Nor does it allow as large a shift to smaller, lighter
vehicles as we judge to be likely in the long term from the assumptions about household structure and car acquisition discussed earlier.
Grey *et al.* (1978) have envisaged even larger savings, running up to
67 per cent, for American cars without any allowance for weight

Table 17. Potential fuel savings for cars.

		Fuel savings %
(1)	Air drag	5-6
(2)	Tyre drag and inflation	2-2.5
(3)	Idle-off and coasting	4-5
(4)	10 per cent shift in average weight	9
(5)	Engine lubricants	3
(6)	Transmission lubricants	3
(7)	Petrol changes	5-10
(8)	Electronic controls	3-7
	Sub-total	30-38
(9)	Engine design	20
	Sub-total	44-50
(10)	Continuously variable transmission	10-20
	Total (excluding 3 and 6)	46-57

reduction. Furthermore, many industry experts canvassed for this
study, including Blackmore and Porter of TRRL and senior engineers and
long-term planners from Ford (UK), British Leyland and Shell
International, agree that a 50 per cent average fuel reduction may
well be possible by 2025 given sufficient industry incentives.

Allowing fifteen years for tooling up new production lines and
changing over the car stock, we have therefore assumed the following
average fuel reductions for the UK car fleet compared to 1976:   1990,
9 per cent; 2000, 34 per cent; 2010, 44 per cent; 2025, 50 per cent
(see also table 18). These assumptions are less optimistic than those
in the Department of Energy's 1978 'reference' forecast, where savings
of 22 per cent by 1985 and 40 per cent by 2000 are assumed for cars
and also for motor cycles and light vans (Department of Energy 1978b).

The additional costs for these fuel savings are most uncertain
but, over the long term, may not be at all high. Engine and vehicle
development is a continuous, evolutionary process of improvement for
which large research and development teams are carried as an overhead.
At any time the next leap ahead usually looks expensive; but as time
passes technical progress, cost reductions through mass production and
competition ensure that the leaps are gradually incorporated into new
vehicles without drastic price increases. This appears to have
happened over the last twelve years of car development, when engineering standards have greatly improved but vehicle costs have risen
more slowly than the average baskets of goods and services (see
table 5).

5. FUEL SAVINGS: OTHER VEHICLES

Table 18 presents a summary of assumed fuel savings for all types of
vehicle in the transport sector.

Table 18. Specific fuel consumption of average vehicles. (Index:
1976 = 1.)

	1990	2000	2010	2025	
Passenger					
Car	0.91	0.66	0.56	0.5	*
Bus and coach	0.95	0.85	0.85	0.85	*
Motorcycle	0.73	0.64	0.55	0.55	*
Rail (diesel and electric)	0.9	0.75	0.7	0.7	**
Freight					
Light vans	0.91	0.74	0.65	0.59	*
Lorries	0.95	0.9	0.81	0.73	
Rail (diesel and electric)	0.96	0.93	0.9	0.85	
Ships (coastal and international)	1.0	0.96	0.93	0.93	*
Air (all types)	0.9	0.8	0.7	0.5	

* Substantial battery electrification after 2000.
** Coal burning fluidized bed systems introduced after 2000.

Bus and coach
Savings are due to driver education and better maintenance (about 3
per cent) improved diesel engines (5 per cent from spark ignition)
(Advisory Council on Energy Conservation 1977) and closer matching of

engine size to load and improvements in transmission, rolling resistance, lubricants, etc. (7-10 per cent). Savings are fairly slow to
take hold because of long vehicle life.

Motorcycles
Rapid improvements comparable to that of the car are considered
possible. The large and early reductions are due to increasing
proportions of small machines, mopeds, etc. This sub-sector is not an
important fuel user.

Rail (passenger)
Through lightweight construction and a 40 per cent reduction in aerodynamic drag, the 240 km/h Advanced Passenger Train should have a fuel
consumption 20-30 per cent lower than conventional inter-city trains
(Anon 1978a). Lightweight bodies can save 7-15 per cent; regenerative
braking together with thyristor controls can cut consumption in urban
electric trains by 25-30 per cent; better driving, particularly in
freight trains, can save 10-15 per cent; and improved suspension and
track can save up to 33 per cent (Wickens 1977). Savings of 30 per
cent by 2010 for all types of traffic do not seem unreasonable even
with the comparatively long lifetime of engines and rolling stock.
    Substitution of diesel by electric traction starting in the mid-
1980s is assumed, following 'Plan B' of the Railway Electrification
discussion document published in May 1978 (British Railways Board
1978). Fuel savings (on a primary energy basis) are substantial; as
are operating costs, largely because of much lower maintenance needs
for electric locomotives. After 2000 the remaining diesel stock is
replaced by fluidized-bed, coal-burning turbogenerators or steam
turbines which are already under development; for example, by the
Energy Equipment Company and Babcock and Wilcox (Anon 1977b). Coal
reaches 10 per cent of total fuel consumption by 2025.

Light vans
Potential savings approach those of the car since these vehicles are
very similar in size, weight and loading. Substitution of petrol by
higher efficiency diesel engines is also more probable; but since
there is not the same incentive for operators to save fuel as for the
private motorists, and volume production of vehicles is less, fuel
savings after 1990 increase more slowly to reach 41 per cent rather
than 50 per cent.

Lorries
The linear decline in average fuel consumption assumed here may be
considered fairly conservative. Design options are similar to those
for buses with the addition of anti-drag devices on large vehicles
which can cut fuel consumption by about 7 per cent on a typical
journey (Anon 1978b). Further savings are assumed from a fairly
modest shift towards larger vehicles, with their much lower fuel use
per tonne-km (see table 8); and from higher average load factors,
where a 10 per cent improvement would reduce fleet consumption by
7-8 per cent. Porter of the TRRL has suggested that a 20 per cent
average fuel saving by 2000 (compared to our 10 per cent) could easily
be achieved, though further gains are much less certain (Porter 1978).

Rail (freight)
Savings are smaller than with passenger trains since good aerodynamic
design, regenerative braking and improved suspension are less

applicable. Lighter wagons, better driving and a range of minor
technical improvements are assumed to give an average saving of 15
per cent by 2025. Coal is introduced to the same extent as in
passenger trains. This is a minor energy using sub-sector.

Ships
Small savings due to improved engine and hull design are assumed. The
most important trend, beginning in 1990-2000, is the fairly rapid
replacement of oil-fired engines by coal-burning turbogenerators or
steam turbines, as in rail. However, substitution by coal is more
rapid and reaches a fairly high level (40 per cent of total fuel by
2025) since there is no competition from electricity and fuel costs
are a much higher proportion of operating costs, thus strongly
encouraging the shift from oil.

Air
The dominance of fuel costs in air transport has launched since 1973
much development of energy-thrifty designs. With engines, the next
generation of high-bypass turbofan designs for service in the 1990s
should use 12 per cent less fuel than the present family introduced
around 1970 (Hewish 1978). Including other conservation measures
such as lighter construction and low-drag supercritical wings or
'winglets', several next-generation aircraft offer fuel savings over
their contemporary equivalents ranging from about 17 per cent for the
Lockheed Reduced Energy Commercial Air Transport and the Boeing 757-
100 to about 33 per cent for the DC-9-80 and European Jet 2 and 44
per cent for the McDonnell Douglas Advanced Technology Medium Range
airliner (Anon 1978c). These prototype designs are thus well on the
way to fulfilling the 50 per cent reduction in average fuel consumption assumed here by 2025 and foreseen by the US National Aeronautics
and Space Administration (NASA) Task Force Report on 'Aircraft Fuel
Conservation Technology' (Allen 1977).

Electric vehicles
In the long term the main choice for transport fuels is between
liquids derived from coal (and organic wastes and plants) and electricity, with battery storage for road vehicles. Other substitutes
for natural petroleum, such as the synthesis of methanol or hydrogen
using electricity, can be ruled out because of the two- to six-fold
increase in total generating capacity that would be needed even with
present traffic levels (Advisory Council on Energy Conservation 1978).
     Electric vehicles offer well-known advantages so long as batteries
with sufficiently high energy densities or storage capacity can be
developed. Quiet, with no pollution (except at the power station),
and with low maintenance costs, they could be run from off-peak electricity and provide substantial load-smoothing storage in the supply
system - enhancing the economies of wind and wave electricity generation. Given that the intensive development of high capacity devices
such as the sodium-sulphur battery is successful, the economics of
battery vehicles also look good even against the energy-thrifty petrol
and diesel vehicles assumed here.
     For these reasons we have assumed that from about 2000 there is a
fairly rapid introduction of electric-battery cars, vans and buses,
but not of other vehicles because of range and weight limitations.
The assumptions are given in table 19. In the High case, owing to
greater pressures on oil resources, market penetration is slightly

higher for cars and energy intensities are slightly lower owing to
more rapid development of advanced batteries. Figures for 2000 are
based on lead acid batteries and for 2025 on sodium-sulphur or
equivalent technologies.

Table 19.   Traffic levels and energy consumption of electric vehicles.

		1990	2000	2010	2025
Percentage of traffic powered by electricity					
Car	Low case	small	5	20	30
	High case	small	10	25	35
Van	Both cases	small	10	20	40
Bus	Both cases	small	10	25	40
Energy intensity (MJ/vehicle-km)					
Car	Low case	−	0.58	0.46	0.39
	High case	−	0.55	0.44	0.38
Van	Low case	−	1.5	0.9	0.8
	High case	−	1.3	0.9	0.8
Bus	Both cases	−	5.0	4.3	4.0

   The largest uncertainty is over the percentage of traffic that is
electrified: our estimates are based on a canvassing of expert
opinion, which gave a wide range of guesses. If systems such as the
zinc-air battery (which allow rapid recharging during journeys) are
developed, traffic levels could be much higher than we have assumed.
   These assumptions are based on a fairly elaborate expression for
the performance of electric vehicles which links vehicle range, energy
intensity, battery weight and energy density, minimum acceleration
performance, unladen weight, maximum and average payload, electric
drive efficiency (including regeneration from braking) and the
maximum draw-down on the charged battery during any journey, using
data culled from recent technical sources (Energy Vehicle Development
Group 1977; Porter and Fitchie 1977; Weeks 1978; Chapman *et al.* 1976).
The model and basic data employed are described in Leach *et al.* (1979)
while some key results and assumptions for vans and small-medium
electric cars in urban traffic conditions are given in table 20.
   In all cases vehicle range without refuelling *en route* exceeds
90 km for the lead acid battery and 150 km with sodium-sulphur. This
would be more than adequate for the vast majority of car trips (see
figure 5): in fact most second cars and many first cars could have
a more limited range and better energy performance by using smaller
batteries. For urban buses and most vans on regular delivery trips
a 100 km range is more than adequate (Bayliss 1977). It will also
be seen that the energy intensities actually assumed (table 19) are
considerably higher than those given in table 20, even for the most
unfavourable conditions. This was deliberate in order to make the
assumptions conservative in the face of many large technical uncertainties.
   As for costs, these must be highly speculative. With vans and
buses, even with today's battery technologies and oil costs the
economics of electric vehicles appear attractive. For example, Lucas
Industries estimate that their latest generation of electrified

Table 20. Performance characteristics of electric vehicles.

Battery Type	Car		Van	
	Advanced Lead Acid	Sodium– Sulphur	Advanced Lead Acid	Sodium– Sulphur
Energy density (MJ/tonne)	150	500	150	500
Maximum draw-down (%)	75	75	75	75
Battery weight (kg*)	450	150	800	300
Vehicle unladen weight (kg)	600	600	1000	1000
Maximum payload (kg)	225	225	500	500
Range (km)	110	160	90	150
Energy intensity (MJ/km)	0.46	0.36	0.98	0.77
Typical payload (kg)	100	100	200	200
Range (km)	120	180	105	175
Energy intensity (MJ/km)	0.42	0.31	0.85	0.64

* In all cases power output compared to gross vehicle weight gives
good acceleration characteristics.

Bedford vans will cost 50 per cent more than a conventional vehicle
but that this penalty will be paid back in about five years running
at 11,000 km a year, and more rapidly with higher mileages. Looking
to the long term, the cost comparison given in Leach *et al.* (1979)
suggests that a small sodium-sulphur electric car will be considerably
cheaper to run than an 'advanced' (62mpg) petrol car if petrol costs
rise two to three-fold even if annual travel is only 10,000 km. The
comparison also shows that primary energy use is much lower for the
electric car than for one running on natural or coal-derived liquids.
However, we emphasize that any such comparison is most tentative since
it depends critically on battery costs and service life, vehicle and
maintenance costs, and relative fuel costs.

6. FUEL PROJECTIONS

To complete this sector it only remains to combine the traffic projections and the energy intensities for each transport mode to derive the
figures for oil, electricity and coal consumption. These calculations
are given in Leach *et al.* (1979) and the totals are shown in table 21
and 22 and figures 15 and 16.
     Despite the considerable traffic increases for most types of
vehicle, total energy use falls after the peak in 1990 in both cases
as conservation measures begin to bite. The reduction in oil is more
rapid, falling over the 1976-2025 period by 31 per cent in the Low
case and 16 per cent in the High case. But, as one might expect, in
the long term transport takes an increasing slice of total oil
consumption and is thus a major contributor to the North Sea oil
supply-demand 'gap' in the total scenario. Whereas in 1976 transport,
including ships' bunkers, took 44 per cent of total delivered
petroleum fuels (including feedstocks and non-energy uses), by 2000
and 2025 in both cases its share becomes close to 50 per cent.
     Of equal importance are the large changes in the share of

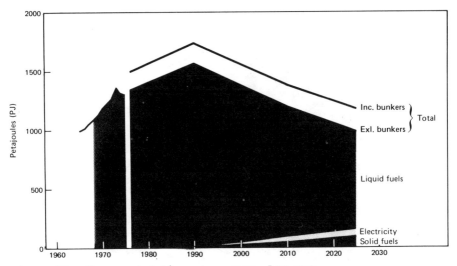

Figure 15.   Transport delivered energy: Low case

Table 21.   Transport delivered energy (PJ):   Low case.

	1976	1990	2000		2010		2025	
Liquids	1484	1722	1512		1285		1019	
Solids	small*	2	24		48		97	
Electricity (stored)	10	15	28	(12)	50	(33)	65	(49)
Total: incl. bunkers	1494	1739	1564		1383		1181	
Total: excl. bunkers	1339	1564	1381		1195		988	

* Ships, 0.3: 1.9 for rail electricity generation included under electricity.

Table 22.   Transport delivered energy (PJ):   High case

	1976	1990	2000		2010		2025	
Liquids	1484	1962	1739		1535		1272	
Solids	small	2	24		55		122	
Electricity (stored)	10	15	38	(22)	64	(47)	83	(66)
Total: incl. bunkers	1494	1979	1801		1654		1477	
Total: excl. bunkers	1339	1790	1597		1429		1222	

transport energy use that occur within the sector. As shown for the
High growth case in table 23, the share for cars drops from just under
44 per cent to 29 per cent, but for lorries, international shipping
and air, the proportions increase very considerably, the combined
total rising from 38 per cent to 58 per cent. For the first two modes
this is mostly due to high traffic growth, itself dependent on
industrial growth, since fuel savings are small; and in the case of
air, to high traffic growth.

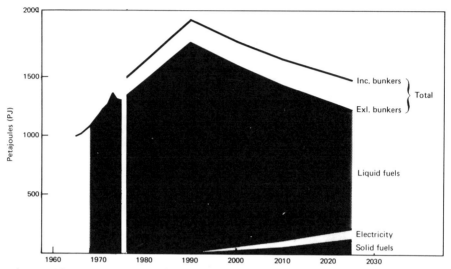

Figure 16.   Transport delivered: High case.

Table 23.   Percentage share of transport energy by main modes: High case.

	1976	1990	2000	2010	2025
Car	43.9	43.7	35.8	31.4	29.0
Lorry	14.9	13.4	16.1	18.3	21.5
Air	12.6	18.4	22.1	22.7	19.0
Ship Bunkers	10.4	9.6	11.3	13.6	17.2
Van	7.9	8.2	8.6	8.3	7.3
All other	10.3	6.7	6.1	5.7	6.0

We need hardly stress that none of these growths are likely to occur *unless* conservation efforts are made for all vehicles on the scale we have assumed.

REFERENCES

Advisory Council on Energy Conservation (1977) *Road Vehicle and Engine Design: short and medium term considerations,* Energy Paper 18.   London: HMSO.
Advisory Council on Energy Conservation (1978) *Energy for Transport: long-term possibilities,* Energy Paper 26.   London: HMSO.
Advisory Council on Energy Conservation/Department of Energy (1977) *Freight Transport: short and medium term considerations,* Energy Paper 24.   London: HMSO.
Allen, J.E. (1977) Have energy, will travel, in *Proceedings of 15th Anglo-American Aeronautical Conference.*   London: Royal Aeronautical Society.
Anon. (1976) *The Guardian,* 10 May.
Anon. (1977a) Special report on economy driving. *What Car?,* July.

Anon. (1977b) Coal makes a comeback on the rails. *New Scientist*,
  1 December.
Anon. (1978a) *The Times*, 8 June.
Anon. (1978b) Why lorry driving is a drag. *New Scientist*, 12 January.
Anon. (1978c) *The Times*, 7 August.
Atkinson, J. and Postle, O. (1977) The effect of vehicle maintenance
  on fuel, in Blackmore, D.R. and Thomas, A. (eds.) *The Fuel Economy
  of the Gasoline Engine*. London: Macmillan.
Basile, P.S. (ed.) (1976) *Energy Demand Studies: Major Consuming
  Countries*. Cambridge, Mass: MIT Press.
Bayliss, D. (1977) Electric vehicles – can they be fitted into urban
  Britain?, in *Proceedings of International Conference on Electric
  Vehicle Development*. London: Electric Vehicle Development Group.
Beale, J.R. *et al.* (1976) Stored energy transmission for
  road vehicles. Paper presented to the Institution of Electrical
  Engineers Conference on Automobile Electronics.
Blackmore, D. (1977) Principles governing fuel economy in a gasoline
  engine, in Blackmore, D. and Thomas, A. (eds.) *The Fuel Economy
  of the Gasoline Engine*. London: Macmillan.
Blackmore, D. (1978) Personal communication.
Blackmore, D. and Thomas, A. (eds.) (1977) *The Fuel Economy of the
  Gasoline Engine*. London: Macmillan.
British Railways Board (1978) *Railway Electrification*. London:
  British Railways Board.
Burt, R. (1977) The measurement of fuel economy, in Blackmore, D. and
  Thomas, A. (eds.) (1977) *The Fuel Economy of the Gasoline*
  London: Macmillan.
Chapman, P. *et al.* (1976) Future transport fuels. Transport and Road
  Research Laboratory, SR251.
Cohn, C.E. (1975) Improved fuel economy for automobiles. *Technology
  Review*, February.
Department of Employment (1977) *Family Expenditure Survey 1976*.
  London: HMSO.
Department of Energy (1977) *Energy Hints 9: Economical Motoring*.
  London: Department of Energy.
Department of Energy (1978a) *Official List of Results of Fuel
  Consumption Tests on Passenger Cars*. London: HMSO.
Department of Energy (1978b) *Energy Forecasting Methodology*, Energy
  Paper 29. London: HMSO.
Department of Transport (1977) *Transport Statistics Great Britain
  1965-75*. London: HMSO.
Department of Transport (1978) Interim memorandum on national traffic
  forecasts. Department of Transport, London, unpublished.
Electrical Vehicle Development Group (1977) *Proceedings of Inter-
  national Conference on Electric Vehicle Development*. London:
  Electric Vehicle Development Group.
Freight Transport Association (1977) Costs and Rates Service Report
  23. Tunbridge Wells, Kent: FTA.
Grey, J. *et al.* (1978) Fuel conservation and applied research.
  Science, 200, pp. 135-42.
Hewish, M. (1978) Aero engines climb towards better fuel efficiency.
  New Scientist, 11 May.
Leach, G. *et al.* (1979) *A Low Energy Strategy for the United Kingdom*.
  London: International Institute of Environment and Development.

Padmore, E.L. (1977) The effect of transmission lubricants on fuel economy, in Blackmore, D. and Thomas, A. (eds.) *The Fuel Economy of the Gasoline Engine.* London: Macmillan.

Porter, J. (1978) Personal communication.

Porter, J. and Fitchie, J.W. (1977) Energy for road transport in the United Kingdom. Transport and Road Research Laboratory, SR 311.

Rigby, J.P. (1977) An analysis of travel patterns using the 1972/73 National Travel Survey. Transport and Road Research Laboratory, LR 790.

Webster, F.V. (1977) Urban passenger transport: some trends and prospects. Transport and Road Research Laboratory, LR 771.

Weeks, R. (1978) A refuelling infrastructure for electric cars. Transport and Road Research Laboratory, LR 812.

Wickens, E.H. (1977) Future propulsion techniques for group transport. Research and Development Division, British Rail.

Wilson, D.G. (1978) Alternative automobile engines. *Scientific American,* 239, pp. 27-37.

Energy costs and public transport

PETER ENNOR

Crude oil, being a finite resource, will become progressively more
scarce in the foreseeable future. In democratic Western countries,
rationing of fuel is unlikely to be acceptable except in the short
term, so price is likely to remain the major long-term regulator of
demand. If the world supply of oil at a given price outstrips the
world's collective ability to pay for it, governments will use taxation policies to bring down demand. In other words, liquid fuels
for transport will become more expensive in real terms, although this
may well occur in a cyclical manner if, as seems likely, each fuel
price rise is followed by a bout of inflation.

As this happens, pressure will increase to reserve mobile fuels
for transport purposes and to improve the fuel performance of
vehicles. It will become worthwhile to exploit more expensive
sources of oil such as the more difficult undersea oilfields and the
shale oil deposits of Canada. Alternative mobile sources of energy,
such as hydrogen or various types of battery, may well be developed.
A well-developed scenario on fuel sources and supply is presented
earlier in this volume (Leach 1981).

1. PUBLIC VERSUS PRIVATE TRANSPORT COSTS

On the face of it, since fuel forms a much lower proportion of public
transport's costs than private motoring costs, particularly if only
perceived costs are taken into account, a rise in fuel costs might be
expected to make public transport more competitive. Many people,
including the present author, expected this to be the result of the
1973-74 fuel crisis. However, this failed to take into account the
indirect effects on inflation and wage rates which in the end led to
public transport prices going up rather more than the cost of
motoring. Increasing real incomes and reduced productivity resulting
from more restrictive regulations on drivers' hours have compounded
the problem. Wages of all employees typically constitute up to 70
per cent of total bus operating costs (the drivers' wages alone
accounting for about 45 per cent), whereas fuel is less than 10 per
cent. For private motorists, fuel is the major element of cost,
there are no direct wage costs but instead the value of time to
consider.

Motoring by private car is undertaken for many reasons: to travel
to and from work; go about personal business; go shopping, take
children to school; to make 'social' trips for entertainment, visiting
friends and going on holiday; and to carry goods. Neither local
business trips nor the carriage of goods are likely to switch to bus
public transport as fuel costs rise, although there is obvious scope
for some transfer to British Rail on longer journeys. Faced with
higher fuel costs, the housewife is as likely to consolidate her
weekly supermarket trip by car into a monthly visit and do more in-
fill shopping locally as she is to switch to carrying her shopping
by public transport. Social trips are possibly the most expendable.
The trips most likely to switch to public transport are those to work
or school. In some places, and for some people, there will be
suitable services with spare capacity available. Generally speaking,
however, bus public transport is ill-equipped to cope with additional
demand at peak times and places, and the average nine-to-five worker
may well find that in practice he is unable to depend on a bus being
available. To increase peak services would require additional buses
and drivers which can only be provided over a period of time and at
considerable expense. Given the highly peaked nature of travel to
work, most of these extra buses would only make one long or two short
revenue earning journeys morning and evening, and at today's typical
fares are highly unlikely to cover their costs by so doing. As an
alternative the car-borne worker or school-child may face increased
fuel costs by sharing his car, with others, perhaps on a rota basis.

Existing public transport users have less choice. As fuel cost
increases lead to wage inflation, bus fares must rise or (most
unlikely in the author's view) a continually escalating subsidy bill
must be met (Webster 1977).

Many of today's bus passengers are amongst the groups least able
to cope with inflation and, like car users, they will attempt to cut
out and consolidate journeys; the lowest elasticity is likely to be
amongst workers who travel by bus, both because they amongst bus users
are perhaps best able to pay and because they have least option but to
make ten single journeys a week. The effect will be an increased
peaking of demand for public transport as the off-peak troughs become
deeper.

2. CURRENT AND FUTURE ENERGY EFFICIENCY COMPARISONS - BUS AND CAR

Many figures are quoted for fuel consumption rates of private cars and
buses. Assume for simplicity that a double decker bus travels 10
miles per gallon of fuel while a private car travels 30 miles. (Both
figures are generous in urban conditions). Since a bus can carry up
to eighteen times the number of passengers carried by a private car,
it is sometimes argued that on the basis of seat-miles per gallon
buses are six times as efficient as cars. Of course, this argument
ignores the fact that neither the bus operator nor the motorist is
interested in moving seats alone. The current average occupancy of
all private cars is roughly of the order of 1.5 persons, giving a
figure of 45 passenger miles per gallon; in a recent year the overall
average occupancy of buses operated by one National Bus Company (NBC)
subsidiary (calculated by dividing passenger miles travelled per year
by vehicle miles operated) was actually just under 11, giving an
actual passenger miles/gallon figure of 110 or just over 2.4 to 1 in

favour of buses.

This is the current picture; as I have illustrated, a general rise in transport costs is almost certain to lead to *less efficient* use of public transport (with deeper off-peak troughs as trips are supressed coupled with increased peak movement possibly catered for in part by additional buses for which there is no practical use off-peak) but equally will lead to *more efficient* use of private cars (with fewer car journeys, but at higher average occupancies). In other words the overall fuel efficiency ratio will lower in favour of the private car. However, what really matters are not the overall fuel efficiencies but the fuel efficiencies of the more marginal activities carried out by bus and car. For a four-seat car, the load factor never falls below 25 per cent and the fuel ratio is never worse than the base figure of 30 passenger miles per gallon; for buses on some late night, off-peak or Sunday journeys, the ratio can be as low as 0 passenger miles per gallon and to better the lowest private car figure at least three passengers must be carried in each direction throughout the route.

3. IMPLICATIONS FOR PUBLIC TRANSPORT OPERATORS AND LOCAL AUTHORITIES

These arguments are viewed by some as anti-public transport. This I emphatically deny. Nothing could be more damaging to the future of public transport than a bland acceptance that public transport should and will have an assured future as transport costs rise. Evidence from before and after the 1973 crisis illustrates this. Between 1970 and 1973 car ownership in Great Britain rose by 17.2 per cent; from 1973 to 1976 the increase was 4.1 per cent. In the same periods, the number of passenger trips made by bus fell by 7.6 per cent and 7.8 per cent respectively (DTp 1979). In Oxfordshire at least, there has been a subsequent levelling-off in the number of bus passenger trips at a time when petrol costs were falling in real terms and, most recently, some evidence of a switch back to buses. But, of course, the general inflationary effects of recent fuel cost increases have yet to be felt in busmen's wage rates or bus fares.

How then should local authorities and bus operators react to recent events both in the short and long term? First, bus operators will no doubt do all they can to maintain the short-term advantage they have gained; this can only be done by *not* raising fares sufficiently to pay for increased wage costs, but by improving productivity. This will mean cutting out cross-subsidization and concentrating on those routes where bus is a truly competitive mode of travel. NBC's Market Analysis Project goes some way towards doing this, but produces a network which is still dependent on cross-subsidization. Lightly-used evening and Sunday services may well have to disappear altogether. Market pricing of individual routes should encourage more use of those routes which currently carry the burden of cross-subsidization of little-used routes and services elsewhere.

The effect of these changes should be to *increase* the average occupancy of well-used bus services and *cut out* services with low usage, thereby improving the overall energy ratio for buses. It could be argued that this will hit certain sectors of the community harder than others but in fact bus operators will be cutting down

the choice of bus services at the same time as car owners and users
are being forced to be more selective in the trips they make.

To some extent, this approach goes against the recent approach
adopted by many bus operators of trying to make maximum use of labour
and vehicles by running relatively lightly-used services at the
marginal cost of fuel and wear and tear, rather than have vehicles
and drivers idle. This may still be justified *between* peaks if the
increased marginal cost (as fuel costs rise) can be justified in
terms of the revenue generated; but in the longer term, the emphasis
should switch to more effective and flexible scheduling of crews and
vehicles to cover the peaks fully.

This leads to the second point, which is that both local
authorities and bus operators should resist the temptation to increase
peak bus services by introducing additional buses into the fleet for
which there is little demand outside the peak. The secondary energy
considerations (i.e. the energy associated with manufacturing the bus
and consumed by the staff operating and maintaining it) would suggest
that this is not a wise thing to do; operating only one or two extra
revenue-earning journeys per day, it would not cover the costs and
would need extra subsidy. There is a precedent for this in the
realization of the 1960s that it was impracticable and undesirable
to attempt to cater for the peak of private car movement in most
urban areas.

Instead, thirdly, attempts should be made to make better use of
existing vehicles. At present, as well as those going against the
peak flow, there are many buses operating empty in the peak because
they are restricted by the Traffic Commissioners from carrying
passengers. Personally I would prefer to see all quantity licencing
removed, progressively area by area, but even without this, it should
be made possible for operators to supplement the all-day services of
others by operating the occasional peak journey where vehicles are
suitably placed, if necessary on the established operator's licence.

This paper has demonstrated how pressure on individuals to
organize car sharing will increase. Local authorities could encourage
this by offering incentives to car pools through use of bus priority
lanes or reduced parking charges.

By resisting the temptation to increase peak transport capacity
local authorities will encourage the staggering of working hours. It
is within their capability to achieve a major degree of staggering at
council offices and schools, although personal experience is not
encouraging. Inevitably, as Peter Jones (1979) has shown very
effectively with HATS, there is disruption of established family
travel patterns and naturally such families complain loudly. Those
who stand to benefit may not always realize and certainly do not
speak out. One answer may be a longer day/four day week for workers,
spread over five or six days; another would be to adopt US/
continental shopping hours of later opening and closing times. The
term 'unsocial hours' should be reapplied to the nine-to-five worker
who creates fuel-burning traffic congestion or overloads peak public
transport.

Fourthly, in the longer term we need to rethink our land-use
policies. Neat and tidy zoning of industry and housing creates
travel demands. Centralization of schools, hospitals, shops, sports
centres and so on has happened with little consideration of the costs
for transport which it places on the public or private purse. Future

land-use policies should aim to minimize dependence on *all* mechanical transport, for example by encouraging development in small towns large enough to sustain most community facilities but small enough to enable most trips to be made if necessary on foot or by bicycle.

4. CONCLUSIONS

In short our present land-use and transport patterns, both temporal and spatial, have grown up in an era of cheap energy. This era is at an end and we must now adjust to take account. In this paper I have shown how this will be forced on us through market forces, especially financial considerations, and how we can help ourselves. There is plenty of scope to do so.

REFERENCES

Department of Transport (1979) *Transport Statistics 1967-1977.* London: HMSO.
Jones, P.M. (1979) 'HATS': a technique for investigating household decisions. *Environment and Planning A,* 11, pp. 59-70.
Leach, G. (1981) The implications of a low-energy strategy for transport. This volume.
Webster, F.V. (1977) Urban passenger transport; some trends and prospects. Transport and Road Research Laboratory, LR771.

The relevance of walking
to the formulation
of transport policy

MAYER HILLMAN and ANNE WHALLEY

Comprehensive surveys of personal travel reveal that in reality walking plays a major role: about one of the three journeys that people make each day are made on foot, and walks of under half a mile are alone equivalent in number to journeys by all forms of public transport combined over *all* distances. (Journeys of less than a quarter of a mile on foot exceed in number those made by rail over all distances by a factor of ten!) And although these walk journeys are generally much shorter in length than those by mechanized modes, the time spent on them represents about a quarter of the total time spent in travel.

These averages conceal wide variations. People with good levels of accessibility to the destinations they need to reach and with low levels of access to a car (such as the poor, children, women and old people) are far more likely to make a higher proportion of their journeys on foot. Thus, for instance, a pensioner in a non-car-owning household will walk on about eight of each ten journeys made; on the other hand, a young male with a car will walk on only two of each ten journeys – though even this could be considered surprisingly high in the circumstances.

However, a review of how the role of walking is treated in transport planning policy documents, in practice, and in methodology in the UK strongly indicates that it has been, if not overlooked, then at the very least inadequately recognized. Substantiation of this statement is not difficult for examples abound in nearly every sphere of activity on which transport impinges and which impinge on transport. Even though the 1972/73 National Travel Survey (NTS) and the subsequent surveys in this series have confirmed the significance of the role of walking on a countrywide basis, relatively little analysis of it has been made, and thus policy-makers still seem unaware of the actual contribution that walking makes, and the potential contribution that it could make, to the solution of many of the transport and transport-related problems currently exercising their minds.

Appreciation of the significance of walking is only apparent with respect to one aspect of this form of travel - safety. As a consequence there has been an impressive investment of technical expertise, legislation and advice aimed at establishing and then removing the causes of pedestrian accidents. But even in this instance the effectiveness of the investment in terms of actually achieving a marked and continuing reduction in the risk of people being killed or injured while walking is open to question: rather has it contained the rate of increase that was otherwise likely to occur as, over time, pedestrians have become exposed to rising numbers of what to them are potentially lethal instruments - motor vehicles.

How is it that the other two key aspects of walking - convenience and access - have received so little attention? Some explanation for this may be found in the very dearth of publically available information on the characteristics and correlates of walking.

Until late in 1979, the principal official publications on the NTS excluded journeys on foot of under one mile, though seemingly arbitrarily including these shorter journeys when made by other modes, and this has in effect resulted in the distorted image of the true patterns of daily travel being maintained. (For instance, the Report on the 1972/73 NTS states that only a quarter of all journeys were made over a distance of under two miles, whereas in reality over a half were made over this distance. It also records one in three women pensioners as not making *any* journeys in a typical week, whereas in reality few of these pensioners are housebound). This has led to a lack of awareness of the role that walking plays among both the informed public and even those charged with setting public policy. It is a fact too that the current generation of practising transport planners has been trained to view transport problems as being primarily those generated by current and forecast future levels of motor traffic. And it may be fairly stated that most of those involved in transport and land-use planning are less 'walk-oriented' in their own lives, and therefore less conversant with the reality of the travel problems that people without a car, particularly the elderly and women with young children, have to face - excessive kerb heights, too many changes of level, fear of traffic moving at high speed, inadequate road crossing times, having to carry heavy shopping by hand a long way, the discomfort of exposure to cold and rain, the declining number of local facilities, and so on.

Although examples of this oversight are easily found, but perhaps not so easily accounted for, this does not necessarily mean that the consequences are a cause for concern: a case has still to be made that oversight of this form of travel matters. This can be done from several perspectives.

First, a significant amount of travel among the great majority of the population is made on foot and it is the relatively vulnerable groups in society, including children, who most rely on travelling in this way. There can be no doubt that by overlooking the significance of walking, their needs are under-represented in transport and planning policy.

Secondly, planning and transport changes over the last twenty-five years have meant that it is becoming progressively harder for people to meet their daily travel needs on foot, with local facilities declining in number, and transport planning geared to the demands of motor traffic. Widespread planning changes have been taking place, which have channelled urban forms away from those types of development which favour walking and in which recourse to motorised modes is not so obligatory. These changes can be seen both in the rationalizing procedures implemented in the provision of shops, schools, hospitals, recreation and so on, and in the provision of low-density residential layouts in which car ownership and use are necessarily high. A long-term analysis of past trends is not possible because of the lack of data, but changes in the patterns of travel in the recent past can be observed from National Travel Surveys of the 1970s. Preliminary examination indicates a marked reduction in the proportion and number of walk journeys still made. Research has yet to establish how those who are prevented from meeting their travel needs on foot adapt, what sort of interaction is generated by a transfer to one of the motor-ized modes, whether or not the changes that are made are desirable, and whether or not they should be encouraged.

Thirdly, there is cause for concern in that, in spite of the reduction in the extent of walking journeys, comparison of their pattern in recent years with statistics on road accidents shows walking to have become more hazardous. Fourthly, the public as well as the private costs of any transfer from walking to motorized modes is manifestly expensive. In a period when there is an increasing need for economy, it is preferable that such transfers should be avoided, and certainly not made essential.

Fifthly, a strong case could likewise be made out that, as the transfer entails energy costs, the transfers should be discouraged at a time when the country is trying to adopt measures for conserving energy. Finally, from a social and environmental perspective, a reasonable claim can be made that walking is a transport mode from which the community at large benefits if its members make more rather than less use of it.

On all these counts it may be concluded that in common with other transport modes, it is desirable for all aspects of walking (and for similar reasons, cycling too) to be incorporated into the conscious-ness of policy-makers, practitioners and researchers. The role that the non-motorized modes play and could play in meeting transport needs should be comprehensively assessed. To do so requires that they are included in tests of social, environmental and financial performance and judged on the same criteria as the motorized modes.

REFERENCE

Hillman, M. and Whalley, A. (1979) *Walking* is *Transport*. London: Policy Studies Institute.

The medium is like a telephone

MELVIN WEBBER

1. THE CONTEXT

The current idiom emerging in modal choice (or travel demand) analysis derives from neo-classical economics and from its underlying notions of consumer psychology. Economists believe that consumers are economic men - that, as hedonists, they analyse alternatives available to them for the comparative pleasures and pains they are likely to yield. They then assume that consumers behave rationally, selecting that option most likely to improve their private welfares.

Much research has been carried out on the analysis of travel behaviour (for example, McFadden 1975; Ben-Akiva *et al.* 1976). Consistently, it is found that consumers of travel choose among modes according to the relative time and money costs associated with each mode. All other factors seem trivial by comparison, accounting for only modest proportions of variance.

Although I accept these findings as fact, I do not think that they are satisfactory explanations of modal choice by themselves, for these conclusions tell us little about *why* time and money costs vary so widely. They therefore tell us little about why cars have come to dominate in the Western world, and why they are likely soon to dominate over all other transport modes in the rest of the world as well. What is it about the automobile transport system that makes its time plus money costs so competitive and thus makes the car the preferred choice almost everywhere?

Thus, I should like to look behind the modal demand curves and try to see what it is that shapes them. Specifically it seems evident that the arrays of available modes and choices among them will be fundamentally shaped by societal forms, by metropolitan arrangements, and by the types of transport services the modal technologies and institutions permit. Whatever hedonic rationality consumers may then display, their choices must be fundamentally shaped by at least these three contextual conditions.

British conditions, clearly, differ from those on the west coast of North America. Because I know more about the California situation, and because it contrasts nicely with Britain's, I should like primarily to discuss that constellation of conditions.

2. THE CALIFORNIAN EXPERIENCE

California is a world of relatively recent vintage, most of the
development having happened since World War II. Growing at a pretty
consistent twenty-year doubling rate for over a century, it has
marked the growing edge of Western society - expanding with the influx
of the newest technology, the newest industries, and the most recently
emerged styles of living, religion, art, fashion, and so on.

Most striking, for our purposes here, it has developed as a
society of large scale, marked by high degrees of specialization,
extreme cultural and economic diversity, and hence extreme inter-
dependency. Having developed at the frontier of a long-term historic
trend - a trend in which both institutional and technological changes
have increasingly opened locational options - it is a society that is
locationally footloose. This is a society whose participants are
spatially separated and yet intimately interlocked in complexities of
mutual dependency.

These two traits define the paramount requirements for its systems
of transportation and communication. They call for extreme facility
of social intercourse, permitting fluid flows of ideas, goods,
services, information, and persons. This is a society whose very
existence depends upon rapid flows among virtually all establishments,
for none can long survive unless its dependencies are continuously
satisfied by nurture from all the others.

Among the historic causes that brought about so large-scale and
specialized a social economy, particularly pertinent were developments in transportation and communications systems that, having
first helped engender these social changes, then in turn became the
media through which requirements for connectivity could be satisfied.
Chief among them were the telegraph, telephone, radio, television,
communications satellite, and now the networks of data links that are
coming to interlace the world. In parallel were developments in
transport: first in river and ocean shipping, then in canals, railways, highways, streetways, subways, and now, airways. They combined
with other technological developments such as power sources that
could be easily transported (electricity most notably) with a
dramatic shift in occupational mix that also permitted labour skills
to be easily transported.

The result was a transformation in urban geography. Cities that
once relied on high density for connectivity now were dispersed in
low-density patterns over hundreds of square miles. More dramatic
still, vast sections of those cities were dispersed to other locales
thousands of miles away, but still intimately connected to the old
establishments in the mother cities - again almost as though they
were proximate geographic neighbours. San Francisco became a suburb
of New York and Washington; Berkeley became a suburb of Reading. The
contemporary geography of the global village displaced the nine-
teenth century geography of relatively independent (the so-called
'self-contained' and free-standing) cities and towns.

This much is familiar, but perhaps less well-known are the
implications for modal choice. The very viability of such a complex
social and economic system relies on interactive media that directly
connect anywhere to anywhere. The model is the telephone system: in
a place like California, virtually every building is tied into the
network, typically with numerous instruments in each building,

commonly with several instruments per person. Telephone users have
random-access to telephone users everywhere and anywhere in the world
within seconds. Although money costs are low, they are not zero; and
for many the pecuniary expenses associated with long-distance telephone use are at least a minor deterrent. For those whose employers
pay the telephone bills, those costs are effectively zero. Time
costs, are virtually zero.
     The telephone fits the interaction requirements of modern
dispersed and dependent societies very tidily, providing the standard
against which all other transportation and communication modes must
be judged. Within the transport sector, the closest analogue to the
telephone is the car; and herein lies the key, I believe, to its
success. The car is the choice for so many travellers, not because
people are 'in love with it'; not because it assigns status to its
owners, although this happens; not because it is comfortable, private
and pretty; but because the car, like the telephone, permits random
access. When origins and destinations are as scattered as they are
in the newer and low-density cities of the United States, there is no
other mode of transport that approximates the direct door-to-door
capability of the motor car.

3. THE PUBLIC TRANSPORT MYTH

That set of propositions must seem patently obvious. Yet, at the
last count, some 122 cities around the world were building or extending fixed-route public transport systems, and another half-dozen have
already done so. One such fixed-route system was built recently in
the San Francisco Bay Area. It is failing badly, largely, I believe,
because its designers have failed to understand that the consumers'
choice of transport mode depends upon spatial patterns of origins
and destinations and upon the capacity of transport systems to
approximate random access among spatially dispersed places.
     The most telling line from the original design report that
proposed the BART system reads:
     ... interurban rapid transit must be conceived as providing
     only arterial or trunk-line connections between major urban
     concentrations in the region... We are convinced that the
     interurban traveller, facing the choice between using his
     private automobile or using mass transportation, will be
     influenced in his choice more by the speed and frequency of
     interurban transit service than by the distance he must travel
     in his own car or by local transit to reach the nearest rapid
     transit station.
I suggest that this conception led to the fundamental design error
that underlay BART's failure to attract motorists in sufficient
numbers.
     McFadden's surveys of BART users and non-users (1975), which are
supported by other studies of modal choice (Daly, this volume), led
to the emphatic conclusion that travellers weigh time spent in
gaining access to the transport system as some multiplier of the
weights they apply to time spent riding in moving vehicles. Thus,
the commuter's morning trip from his front door to the corner bus
stop, then from the bus transfer stop to the door of a BART train,
was costed at 2.5 to 3.0 - in some instances up to 10 - times the
costs assigned to time riding the train. In contrast, the time

spent going from his front door to his private car is virtually zero.
Herein lies a major deterrent to train riding, for almost all would-
be BART users live at some distance from a train station, and so for
nearly all travellers, BART riding requires an onerous access trip
first. In turn, for those whose destinations are not adjacent to
BART stations, the supplementary trip from the train stop to the place
of work or other destination may also require an extended walking or
bus journey, with attendant high-valued time expenditure.

In a metropolitan area built as San Fransisco's is, at low
density with work and living places distributed over several hundred
square miles, it is only a relatively few who have both origins and
destinations adjacent to BART stations. BART's designers believed
that people preferred private cars to public transport because of
their speed advantages. The BART system was, therefore, designed to
go even faster (it can travel at speeds of 80 mph), but high speed
necessitated wide station-spacing and a large array of other design
requirements that have turned out to be problematic for the system.
The result is that, at the last count, only 2.5 per cent of trips in
the Bay Area were made by BART.

This suggests that for the time being, the car will continue to be
the dominant system. In a democratic society where consumers can
demand what they want and can afford it, they will get cars. It also
suggests that public transport systems, installed for those who do
not have discretionary use of cars, should be designed to approximate
cars as much as is technologically and institutionally possible. The
next generation of public transport modes has got to approximate
random-access capabilities. Recognition of that proposition must
surely be behind the recent flurry of interest in various modes of
para-transit (for example, jitneys, taxis, microbuses of various
types) and, eventually, personal rapid transit (PRT) built into close
geographic grids. But unless or until we can find the successor to
the car - an alternative system with superior random-access capabilities - consumers who have the choice will choose the motor car.

4.   TRANSPORT AND THE URBAN STRUCTURE

The conventional counter to that line of argument just outlined is
that the demand for car use is caused by the car-based system itself;
and that if we could but break with the causal cycle, we could
develop more intelligently designed transport systems. British
experts understand this logic. It holds that dispersed origins-and-
destinations, low-density settlement patterns and extensive intra-
metropolitan travel distances are all directly caused by the road
system. If we could install an effective and competitive system, we
could then 'redensify' these cities, induce localization and concentration of closely linked establishments, and rationalize these
runaway metropolitan settlement patterns.

I once believed all that to be possible. Indeed, those were
almost precisely the ideas behind the design of the BART system in
which I participated. But, now, having tried to reshape land-use
patterns, using a high-speed, high-capacity and high-quality
rail-transport system as the instrument for restructuring intra-
metropolitan accessibilities, and hence intra-metropolitan locational
decisions, I am compelled to conclude it will not work. BART has not
notably influenced land-use patterns, much to everyone's surprise.

And that outcome may signal a revolutionary conclusion for metropolitan planners: that it is now too late to use transport facilities
and services instrumentally as shapers of metropolitan spatial
structure. If so, modal choice will not be significantly influenced
by policy-makers who attempt to affect atomistic locational decisions
by reshaping the metropolitan-wide accessibility surface.

BART was planned in such a fashion as to make selected places
highly accessible to commuters and others. The idea was that high
accessibility at points in space would convert those places into
magnets attracting new businesses, apartment houses, offices, and so
on. In turn, once centralization and subcentralization processes had
been triggered, localization processes would generate still further
concentration at those selected places, as related and closely-linked
firms sought to join those who had arrived earlier. In that fashion,
the rapid transit system would act rather like a crystal dropped into
a supersaturated solution, triggering further crystallization. As a
result, trips formerly made to dispersed locations by car, would now
be made by train, for BART would deliver its passengers directly into
the heart of the business centre it had catalyzed. The theory was
nifty, and back in the mid-fifties it seemed guaranteed to succeed.

The mistake in the San Francisco Bay Area was the assumption that
this new rail system would make a significant change in over-all
accessibility. This is an urban region extremely well-endowed with
streets, highways, and motorways. Accessibility is extraordinarily
good. Most people can move by car from wherever their origins may be
to wherever they are bound, most of the time without friction or delay.
The accessibility isogram is remarkably level across the entire urban
region of seven or eight hundred square miles. The installation of
suburban rail stations and urban underground stations on top of so
high and homogenous an accessibility surface made only trivial
differences to the contours on that surface. That is one reason why
BART has not affected modal choice very much.

It is also the reason why it has not had much effect on land-use
patterns. Locational decisions in that metropolitan area are affected
by motor car and truck access, to the degree they are affected at all.
But the striking thing is that there is now so much accessibility
everywhere that this is no longer a determinant of locational decisions. Factories, shops, offices and residences can be placed
virtually anywhere and enjoy superior levels of random access.

BART may have had a minor influence on land use. It may have
helped generate the office-building concentration in downtown San
Francisco, but no one can prove it. It may have induced further
suburban spread, by enabling commuters to live beyond the urban fringe,
and drive to the suburban rail stations, but no one can prove that
either. The general consensus however is that land-use patterns have
been immune to BART's influence. In turn, trips that might have been
generated by concentration of jobs and residences around BART stations
have not occurred either. And this, of course, represents a further
failure in the forecasts of modal choice.

5. THE LESSONS FROM THE CALIFORNIAN EXPERIENCE

Cities like London, Paris, New York, and Tokyo are different from
Californian cities in their basic spatial structures. Built when
transport modes compelled physically adjacent locations among closely

linked establishments, each is compressed at high-density into a comparatively small area. Despite their differences from Californian metropolises, however, they share many critical traits with them.

These are all centres of high-scale societies with requirements for intimate and real-time linkages among their many specialized and interdependent establishments. Because cities like London and Paris are built around localized precincts of specialized establishments, some people use the whole city in the course of their day-to-day activities. For example they may travel from their suburban resid- encies to places such as the City, Whitehall, Bloomsbury, and, say, Chelsea, all in the course of a day's engagements. That is the sort of links-in-a-chain movement alleged to characterize Los Angelenos, rather than Londoners. Even if such travel is the habit of only a small elite group, still for such people random access is a desired attribute - even in the old cities built in the times before the car became a dominant mode of travel.

The response to demands for accessibility has been underground rail systems and bus routes that interlace London, Paris, New York, and Tokyo. High density has meant sufficient concentrations of trip ends across the cityscapes to make public transport systems feasible and capable of proving an approximation to random access, Thus they approximate the highway and freeway networks of the Californian cities. But it is evident that even the most extensive network of fixed-route public transport cannot possibly offer the quality of service that cars provide. It cannot ever completely approach the random-access and the no-wait, no-transfer, door-to-door, flexible- routing capabilities of highways and motor cars. And so, even in these well-served metropolises, a great many people are turning to the private, small-vehicle option. As they do so, congestion will increasingly affect the capacities of cars to perform to standard. If no motorways are built, the pressure will surely increase for suburban development, as centre-city establishments and residents opt for the spacious and accessible environment of low-density and auto- mobility. That seems to be the clear trend in metropolitan areas around the world, even in places where land controls are most stringent.

In sum, I am led to expect that the trend toward metropolitan spatial forms that are compatible with motor cars and trucks is probably going to continue, largely because demands for random access will continue to expand. Growing specialization and growing inter- dependence will make all of us increasingly reliant on telephones and telephone-like modes of transport. These modes are not large vehicle types.

So what is behind the economist's demand curves? Of course, consumers are alert to differences in the time and money costs, but underlying these costs are metropolitan spatial structures, trans- portation and communications technologies, and the structure and scale of the social and political economy. These are factors that have scarcely been recognized in transport modal-choice analysis, even in the most sophisticated disaggregate models. So we should look behind the demand curves, and there the model is the telephone.

REFERENCES

Ben-Akiva, M.E., Lerman, S.R. and Manheim, M.L. (1976) Dissagregate

models: an overview of some recent research results and practical applications. Proceedings of PTRC Annual Summer Conference, University of Warwick.
McFadden, D. (1975) Economic applications of psychological choice models. Working Paper 7519. Travel Demand Forecasting Project, Institute of Transportation Studies, University of California, Berkeley.

Information and Communication

This section of the book brings together a number of papers that deal, in one way or another, with unconventional alternatives to conventional transport planning problems. Two of them are concerned with the possible substitution of telecommunications for transport; another with the acquisition and use of information by passengers travelling on public transport.

Ian Young's paper deals with the impact of telecommunications on transport. He outlines some of the revolutionary new communications technologies - teleconferencing, information systems which allow access from home or other locations, videotext systems. In considering some of their likely implications for transport, he argues that it is presently difficult to predict the rate of spread of the new technologies, and hence their potential for substitution. One scenario would indicate a large-scale substitution of home work for office work, of electronic education for traditional face-to-face systems, and of electronic communication for the movement of messages. Another would suggest a general resistance to change, with little impact on home or work patterns.

David Clark's paper extends this theme by looking at the impact of of telecommunications on accessibility in rural areas. Telephone ownership has expanded extremely rapidly in recent years, but is still relatively low among poorer rural people. The spread of other services is difficult to predict. One major question is whether telecommunications will substitute for existing journeys, or stimulate new journeys. The scope for substitution appears greater for journeys that involve giving or receiving information. Much will depend on the way that service agencies exploit the new opportunities - but the existing limited use of telephones for many of these services suggest that future changes will be slow. The implications are that telecommunications are likely to have significant effects on social travel, perhaps by extending friendship networks and creating greater potential demand for social trips; and that they could be used to promote and ensure improved access to selected services - so long as policy-makers take conscious decisions to that end.

In a different vein, Peter Warman's paper shows how important it is for the bus passenger to have reliable information about the likely waiting time at the bus stop. He details an experiment for London Transport in which passengers were given information on the expected arrival time of the next bus. Warman suggests that it would be justified to develop a more comprehensive 'real time' information system, perhaps even away from the bus trip - as for instance in a shopping centre - or perhaps through some personal radio-based scheme.

One major point to emerge is the importance of integrating land-use and transport planning. A stress on smaller-scale settlements, with dispersed facilities close to people's homes, could greatly reduce dependence on mechanical transport - though in the last twenty years, planning seems to have taken us in the opposite direction with the greater concentration of facilities.

Another is the critical question of life-style. People are tending to move from urban to rural areas, but they may expect urban levels of service, which will demand increased dependence on both the car and the telephone. But at the same time, some groups were probably trapped in rural areas without access to either. This might matter more to certain groups than to others, and it seems important to discover how far different life-cycle and life-style groups need access to particular facilities either through communication or through travel.

More widely, the telecommunications issue reveals how little is known about the behavioural aspects. The new telecommunications systems tend to be limited in extent and also expensive: the branching logic system which they use might prove less efficient, for many purposes, than scanning a conventional book or magazine. Little seems to be known about how people will use the system, either in total quantity or for different purposes. This is true both for the general effects of the new information systems, and also for particular special purpose applications such as the proposed information about public transport delays. The conclusion reached is one of uncertainty about the implications of the new technology on transport: this is certainly an area where social research could usefully be initiated.

The impact of telecommunications on planning and transport

IAN YOUNG

This paper will describe technical developments and research on tele-communications in three broad areas of application: business travel; the work place; and residential communication needs. From these examples the problems associated with extrapolating trends to predict the future will be described, and finally as a tailpiece, the beloved and hated method of the futurists, the scenario, will be employed to demonstrate possible extremes of the extrapolation process for the planning requirements of the year 2000.

1. BUSINESS TRAVEL: IS IT NECESSARY?

This question, or variants of it, was the basic issue addressed by the Communications Study Group at University College London (1970-76). I will dwell on it at some length, not because it is concerned with the foremost topics in telecommunications technology, indeed most of the technology has been around for about ten years, but because the thoroughness of research methods employed have rarely been repeated, and provide a paradigm for assessing technological impacts.

Since the advent and spread of the telephone system, no business-man, civil servant, or academic would consider travelling 15-20 miles to gain a simple answer to a simple question from a colleague or client. Indeed they would rarely walk 100 yards down a corridor if there is a telephone system which enables them to establish contact and communicate quickly and effectively.

At the same time however the travelling businessman is the main-stay of certain routes on mainline railways and internal airlines, not to mention the hundreds of thousand of company cars on motorways. When telecommunications could demonstrably save both direct costs and indirect personal time costs, there should be some clear reasons why business travel is sustained at current levels, and some prospect for telecommunications developments to capture part of that travel market.

A prime reason for business travel is of course the 'business meeting' in which the number of people involved is in itself a sufficient impediment to the use of the standard telephone system.

Travel surveys of businessmen have supported the primacy of this
factor, with over 30 per cent of business travellers citing this as
the main reason why the telephone would not have been adequate.   Hence
the development of teleconferencing systems, in which groups of people
could communicate rather than just pairs, should have a ready application.   At the end of the 1960s and the start of the 1970s, there
were several such systems being developed and tested in both Britain
and America.   An example of the top end of the market is Confravision.
Developed by the Post Office, it provides full two-way interactive
audio-video communication between groups of five to six people in each
of two studios.   The service was offered as a public service, open to
any organization to book the studios in any two of the major UK cities
served.

The research programme at University College London was designed
to provide a variety of quantitative inputs to a predictive model of
the success of diverting would-be business travellers to different
types of teleconference systems.   Figure 1 shows a flow-chart of the
research stages.   It is of course slightly idealized in that it is
rarely practicable to complete one stage before progressing to the
next.   In fact the conduct of psychological experiments (stage 2) was
continued throughout the six years of research, against a series of
surveys and diary studies to elicit data on communication practices
in business.

The identification of the salient factors in business meetings
applied multivariate techniques of factor and cluster analysis to data
collected as records of meetings and communications by managerial
staff in business and government.   The records sought ratings of the
functions, activities and atmospheres of meetings.   The resulting
classifications (called DACOM - Description and Classification of
Meetings - see Pye *et al*., 1973) provided both a set of 12 underlying
dimensions of meeting activities, and a taxonomy of meetings into
discrete clusters of different combinations of these factors.

The distribution of different factors throughout meetings is
uneven, with three of the 12 factors (seeking information, giving
background information, and problem solving) each appearing in almost
half of all meetings recorded, while other factors were important
components of far fewer meetings (negotiation, 11 per cent; policy
decision making, 8 per cent; and conflict, 4 per cent).   The importance of the ubiquity of functions such as information seeking, is
that they proved to be virtually insensitive to the medium of communication used in the psychological experiments under stage 2.   Figure 2
summarizes the findings of numerous experiments in which pairs or
groups of civil servants took part in a variety of discussion tasks.
The researchers compared the performance of those tasks over full
audio-visual communication links (closed-circuit television), and
audio only systems (microphones to loudspeakers) with the same tasks
completed by participants seated face to face.

The allocations of meeting purposes or content to communication
media, stage 3 shown in Figure 2, are based on the conservative
assumption that a change in meeting outcome, which can be attributed to
the influence of the medium, indicates that the medium is not suitable
for the conduct of that meeting.   The quality of the change is not
taken into account.   So, for example, experiments demonstrated that
attitude change in negotiations was more marked in audio only communications, but the value of such a change is difficult to establish

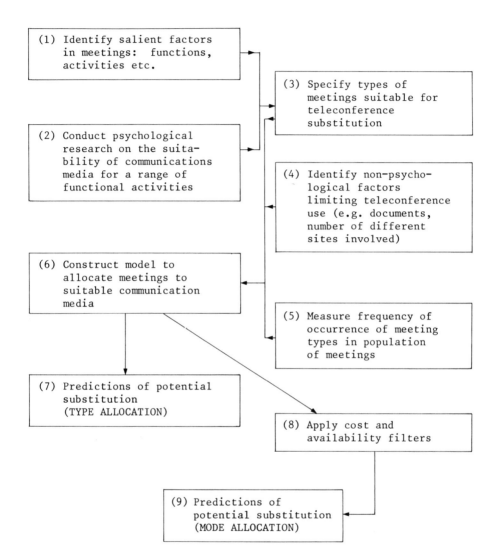

Figure 1.   Research stages for a predictive model of travel/
            teleconference substitution.

without having a vested interest in a specific outcome. Hence 'negotiation' was conservatively assigned to the 'face to face'
communication medium. A general interesting point to note from the
series of experimental studies is that the outcome of person to person
and even group communications is relatively impervious to the medium
of communication. The flexibility of people to adapt their style of
communication to suit the constraints of the medium is considerable.
    Working from the model of psychological suitability of meeting

functions for teleconference media (stage 3) two further considerations are required to progress to the next level of model. First,
additional, non-psychological, restraining factors have to be taken
into account (stage 4). On many teleconference systems there is an
upper limit on the number of possible participants, and it is impracticable to link together more than two or three sites. Meetings which
rely heavily on the discussion of diagrams or graphs are unsuitable
for audio-only teleconferences and may be difficult even over video
teleconference systems. The prevalence of these limiting factors plus
the occurrence of the psychological content factors in normal business
meetings is measured by the completion of contact record sheets (stage
5), simple check sheets completed for each meeting involving the
respondent.
    These data form the raw material for a first model (stage 6) using
suitability filters to identify the proportions of existing meetings

	Fairly definitely	Tentatively
Allocated to face-to-face	Inspection of fixed objects	Conflict Negotiation Disciplinary interview (Presentation of report)
Allocated to video	Forming impressions of others	Giving information to keep people in the picture
Allocated to audio	Problem solving Information seeking Policy decision making	(Delegation of work) Discussion of ideas

Figure 2.   Allocation of meeting functions to communication media from
            laboratory experiment data.

which could be carried by different types of teleconferencing system.
Termed the *Type Allocation Model* (stage 7), it predicts the potential
for substitution of teleconferencing for business meetings on the
grounds of the capability of the systems to handle the discussions.
The best estimated media allocation for current business meetings is
based on the records of 26,000 meetings recorded by 6,000 respondents
throughout Europe. It indicates that 53 per cent of meetings could
be substituted, without significant effect, by teleconference. Most
of these (45 per cent of all meetings recorded) could be carried by
audio-only services, with 8 per cent requiring a full audio-video
teleconference. The remaining 47 per cent of meetings are most appro-
priately required to be conducted face to face (Tyler *et al.* 1977).
    The final stages of the model (stages 8 and 9) add further
refinement to the model in terms of assumptions on the universality of
teleconference facilities (to teleconference rather than travel it is
necessary for parties at both locations to have access to teleconference facilities), and the cost trade-offs between travelling and
teleconferencing. The prescriptions for allocating the 'best mode' of

communication taking into account these additional factors are necessarily more conservative than the predictions of the 'type allocation' model, though the exact figures will be a function of the values set for the parameters of these additional factors (i.e. penetration of teleconference facilities; costs of telecommunications and travel costs).

The description just given is of a substantial research effort, but in fact it is not complete. Two major issues are left outstanding from the research paradigm presented in Figure 1. The first is that regardless of the psychological effectiveness of teleconference meetings as measured by controlled experiments, the attitudes of would-be teleconferees are important in determining the use of available systems. Early bad experiences or reports of teleconferences due to untried and untested systems can be particularly damaging to the establishment of a teleconference clientele. Similarly if, as in many companies, travel to distant branches is considered to be a 'perk' or an insignia of managerial status, then the proposed replacement of travel by teleconferencing will at best be an uphill struggle.

The second issue is that with a successful teleconference system, the volume of traffic may be greater than the straight substitution of a fixed proportion of previous meetings involving travel. Any facility which improves the opportunity to communicate may be expected to generate new communication acts as well as substitute for existing areas. Both these issues - the engendered attitudes of potential users, and the generation of new 'telemeeting' activities - are identified by the conduct of field research on actual systems implemented.

This description of a research programme is both thorough and shallow. It is thorough in that the conclusions it leads to could have been more simply stated for an audience only interested in the implications of telecommunications for planning. At the same time it is shallow for any researcher who wants to examine critically the basis of those conclusions or who wishes to adopt some of the research procedures. For those who are interested only in the implications, they are that as a substantial proportion of business meetings could be held by some form of teleconferencing, there is less requirement for companies and government offices to exist in close proximity to each other or to impose a life of 'shuttle diplomacy' on their senior management.

The emphasis on high-speed passenger trains and internal air routes may be misplaced when the potential for meetings by teleconferencing has yet to be exploited. Data from a study by the University of Newcastle on business travellers between the north-east of England and London (James *et al.* 1979) reinforces the opinions derived from the full modelling studies. It shows that 70 per cent of travellers were attending only one or two major meetings, that half of the meetings were intra-organizational and did not involve outside representatives at all, and that the main activities at these meetings were general discussions of ideas and exchanging information. All these factors favour the use of teleconferencing, though the total level of teleconference substitution of these meetings proposed by the University of Newcastle group was only 28 per cent. It is probable that different specific travel routes would yield different volumes of potential substitution, depending on the nature of the links between regional and London offices. It is also probable that in fact

the use of teleconference facilities, if they were available to compete with travel options, might reflect a strong bias of direction.
Exposing the author's personal biases, it might be presumed that
travel from regional centres to London might generally be more
attractive to potential teleconference participants than travel from
London to the regional centres.

Finally, readers with a greater interest in research methodology
than has been satisfied by this account are referred to publications
by Tyler *et al.* (1977), Williams (1978), and Short *et al.* (1976) for
more thorough discussions of the research.

2.   OFFICE FUNCTIONS: NEED THEY BE CENTRALIZED?

The preceding section has dealt with the single issue of people
travelling between offices sited at major centres. The purpose of
this section is to look at the functional operation of 'offices' and
see whether they need necessarily to exist in their present form.

A national economy is traditionally broken down into the manufacturing, agricultural and service industry sectors. This type of
breakdown though hides a commonality that they all harbour an 'office
sector' which collectively is the largest and fastest growing sector
in the Western economy. Office functions involve the storage and
retrieval of information, processing text, and manipulating symbols.
If all occupations primarily involving these functions are summated
(these would then include administrators, researchers, educators and
lawyers as well as those directly serving industry and other sectors)
they are found to occupy more than half of the workforce in both the
United States (Porat 1976) and the United Kingdom (Stamper 1977.)

The functions of the office or information sector are interesting
in that they can all exist without a singular product; the information,
text, and symbols can exist in a multitude of forms (paper-based,
magnetically encoded etc.) in a number of places at the same time.
They are indeed ripe for automation through computer-based technology
and electronic representation. To date though, the electronic thrust
into the information sector has been on a piecemeal basis. Computer-
controlled stores and accounts systems have been introduced to auto-
mate office procedures which previously invoked flurries of duplicate
forms. Word processors are beginning to replace the standard type-
writer by virtue of their greater flexibility in text manipulation,
while mainframe computers and even pocket calculators have added
speed and breadth to scientific and business calculations. But these
individual though automated functions still require the structure of
the office to which millions of workers, from clerks to managing
directors, still commute.

As the spread of office technology increases, fuelled by the
ever decreasing real costs of the microprocessor technology compared
with the increasing cost of both communication and transport alternatives (and staff time), there are initial movements towards linking
the separate components of the modern office. First within the office
itself, several of the major office technology manufacturers and
computer/business machine producers have plans or prototypes for
integrated office equipment. The keyboard that is used for producing
a draft letter, can not only correct that draft electronically, but
also file the text in a central information store, before having the
'hard copy' form of the letter produced on an output device for

despatch to the recipient. The second step in the linkage is to use telecommunications to pass this information between separated office stations and thereby remove the necessity of much of the paper flow that marks current office work patterns.

Again there are precedents for this development which reflect the piecemeal approach. The long established telex services and more recent communicating word processors provide electronic mail services with varying attractiveness of product. Remote access to computers, and data links between computers, provide powerful time-sharing computing and information search facilities from any compatible terminal attached to a telephone line.

What makes these services and capabilities of relevance to this paper is that there is no technical impediment to harnessing the capabilities of the integrated office and the telephone network as a medium of data transmission; this would permit a wide range of people to conduct their job effectively and efficiently without having to visit regularly their nominal 'office'.

As an example we can take the typical daily routine of a middle manager in a job in the information sector. The morning may start with reading incoming mail and memos, and replying to those which require it. He or she may then go on to check progress on various projects and amend timetables, perhaps give instructions to subordinates and answer their queries. The rest of the day may then be taken up with writing and correcting reports interspersed with *ad hoc* discussions of between five and thirty minutes with one or more colleagues or outside contact, and maybe one longer and larger group meeting.

Adopting the new technology approach, exactly the same operations could be conducted without the manager having to go to the central office. Incoming electronic mail and memos might be held in a central computer mail box to be accessed, with the right password, by the manager from a remote visual display unit (VDU). Alternatively they may be directed by the central computer to the manager's own local memory store for either immediate display when switching on in the morning, or if a hard copy of the letter is preferred, to be printed out at his or her local printer. Replies can be made by the more adventurous and self-sufficient manager typing in directly via the VDU to the text processing program held on the company's computer (this would automatically correct common spelling errors, provide the right format, and retrieve addresses from a memory store). The more traditional, or perhaps just more expensive, manager might alternatively dictate the first draft of the letters over the telephone to central dictation recorders. The draft would then be typed/word processed by a member of a central pool (though these could equally well be at physically separate locations), and returned to the manager electronically for corrections and authorization for despatch.

Progress on work, timetable changes etc. would all be stored and updated on the central computer to be accessed remotely, while work instructions and queries could be mainly handled by a messaging program on the computer. Likewise reports would be written directly into the computer's text processing program to permit ease of joint authorship and editing. The *ad hoc* discussions could be held over the telephone, bringing in third and fourth parties by the use of conference bridges in the telephone network. Larger, and more formal discussions or meetings would require some more dedicated teleconference equipment.

This summary description is sketchy and does not try to hide the fact that some variations in work patterns would be required to fit into this decentralized mode of operation. The level of technical capability however is continually rising and offering means of operation which are closer to existing patterns. In particular the potential stumbling block of managers developing keyboard skills are being attacked with developments such as touch sensitive screens to select options from a displayed set of alternatives, and 'intelligent' scribble pads which, used in conjunction with a VDU, can recognize many hand-written letter shapes and translate them to standard characters for use in correcting electronically-stored text. This problem could be overcome through methods which use speech recognition rather than keyboard inputs.

Disregarding for the moment the social aspects of job satisfaction and the attitudes of workers in the information sector to technology, estimates have been made that over 20 per cent of the entire British workforce (Glover 1974), or about half of the office or information sector workforce (Harkness 1977) could conduct their jobs from decentralized offices by the early 1980s.

The general formats considered for these decentralized offices have usually been of two types. First, the working from home option, with all the necessary technology provided in the home of the worker; and second, in the Neighbourhood Work Centre (NWC) where an office block would be occupied not by a single company but by a number of companies all renting small areas or offices, plus the necessary communications terminals. In either case the distance between the residence of the information worker and the nominal place of employment would become irrelevant. In the NWC concept there would be some daily travel involved between place of residence and the nearest NWC, but no general trend for travel into major conurbations.

Bird (1979) identifies some probable implications to arise from the widespread adoption of the working from home and NWC practices, at levels of the individual and his or her job, the company, and the broader society. Some factors − such as increases in office rents, the greater number of dual career families, and higher expectations from leisure time activities − are likely to foster more rapid development of decentralized office work. Others − such as the loss of personal contact with colleagues and reduced powers of management and supervision − may be expected to create pressure in the opposite direction. However, scepticism that neither model of decentralized office functions is practicable has already been overtaken by events.

In Britain a major computer software house, originally established to provide greater employment opportunities for housebound women with precious computer skills, has operated for some years with only a fairly nominal office not capable of housing all its 300 systems analysts, programmers, and clerical staff. The majority of its workforce work from their own homes, holding all work discussions by telephone, and where appropriate using home terminals for software development. Following the Equal Opportunities Act, an increasing proportion of the workforce are men, demonstrating that the appeal of working from home is not simply restricted to mothers of young families. On the NWC approach, a Californian insurance company, faced with expansion beyond the capabilities of its existing building, recently elected to establish two small satellite offices closer to

the residential areas rather than move the whole company into larger
office premises.

In the short-term future it is probable that the less radical
alternative of the NWC will be the more prevalent form of decentralized office on simple pragmatic grounds (for example very few homes
are built with sufficient superfluous space to permit turning one
room over to function as a remote electronic office). In principle
though, either or both concepts of decentralizing offices could
progress as rapidly as social and organizational inhibitions permit.
The technical capability now exists, and the cost comparisons between
high technology and high rental and commuting charges are soon likely
to reach a cross-over point for an increasing number of organizations.

3. DOMESTIC AND RESIDENTIAL NEEDS: WHY GO OUTSIDE THE HOME?

The impact of new technology/telecommunications is not restricted to
the world of work. The domestic and leisure activities of the
population are also being catered for on an increasing scale. There
are an estimated 20,000 owners in the United Kingdom of television
sets capable of decoding and displaying the teletext information
services. These are pages of information, ranging from news head-
lines to cookery recipes, which are broadcasted in digitally encoded
form in part of the spare transmission capability of the normal
television picture signal. The services are run by the BBC (CEEFAX)
and the IBA (ORACLE) on their respective channels. The pages of
information are transmitted in a constant rapid stream. The viewer,
with a special television set incorporating a decoder and character/
graphics generator to interpret the signals, has a keypad on which he
first selects to watch teletext rather than the normal programme,
then selects a particular page number corresponding to the information he wants. As soon as that page is transmitted (usually within
seconds rather than minutes) it is captured, decoded and presented on
the screen. Unrequested pages are ignored.

With a teletext set the modern family has access to 500-600 pages
of up-to-date and changing information. They can get the latest news
and weather forecasts whenever they want; they can read reviews of
films instead of asking friends' opinions; they can check their pools
coupons without having to either wait in the local newsagent for the
first arrival of the Saturday evening newspaper, or keep the family
quiet as the results are given on the radio or television. But they
are relative 'information paupers' compared with the subscribers to
the Post Office Prestel service.

Like the teletext services, Prestel uses the domestic television
receiver to display pages of text and graphic information, with the
viewer/reader selecting the information required with a simple numeric
keypad. However the information pages are fed to the individual
receiver from a central computer store by telephone line, and are
transmitted only on request sent from the user's keypad back along
the telephone line. The power of interrogation and speed of response
offered by the use of telephone line transmission means that the user
has access to hundreds of thousands of pages rather than the hundreds
offered by teletext.

The types of information held can therefore be greatly expanded,
and currently include consumer information and legal advice, restaur-
ant, theatre and film guides, price lists of consumer items, and

games and puzzles as well as more everyday news and comment.

The database is organized in a general tree-structure which means that users should be able to find the information they require by following the appropriate branches offered at each page instead of having to know the appropriate page number at the outset. This tree-structure is sometimes used by the agency supplying the information in a particular sector, to provide the viewer with a simple route through a complex issue. So, for example, the Consumers Association provides a series of pages which will advise the viewer on whether they would be eligible under law to adopt a baby. Each page asks the viewer a simple question and offers the choice of a yes/no answer. Depending on the answer given the viewer is routed to the next appropriate question and so on until a final answer is obtained. Hence Prestel can be as interactively helpful as a knowledgeable neighbour.

There is a further significant property of the Prestel service associated with the capability to send a signal back to the computer as well as receive one. Each section of the database is input and up-dated by independent information providers (IPs). Many of these IPs are only concerned with giving information, for example government departments and the Consumers Association, but others provide a sales service as well, such as direct warehouses selling consumer durables, and wine suppliers. Some of these sales-oriented IPs are experi-menting with sales over Prestel, permitting the buyer to make a simple selection of goods and pay for them with a credit card number (the buyer's address is already held on the computer as they are a subscriber to the Prestel service).

The Prestel technology is therefore offering the capabilities of access to virtually all likely information needs, friendly counselling, and easy cost comparisons and purchasing, all from the fireside chair in front of the television set. The need to set foot outside of the front door to risk muggers and inclement weather could be substan-tially reduced.

Another major area of domestic activity is education, be it for school or adults. Here telecommunications technology already has a strong toehold. The Open University, now established over ten years, has demonstrated powerfully the use of mixed media - radio, television, print and correspondence - to provide a university education to a large number of people. It has been augmenting these well-known methods of education with teleconferencing between seminar group members in their homes or in study centres, and with exploring the use of Prestel and Prestel-like services. Indeed the educational appli-cations of teleconferencing and Prestel services have been receiving a great deal of attention in the United States and Britain, for a range of students including school-aged children as well as adults.

Given the success of the Open University and the ever-growing pressure on educational budgets, it may be reasonable to expect a steady increase in the use of the home as the classroom for a wide range of academic, professional, and technical courses. Initially the main impacts may be on the domains of the universities, poly-technics, technical and sixth form colleges, but ultimately basic schooling could also be transferred to home-based teaching.

Last but not least amongst domestic activities are the ways in which we spend our leisure time. Watching television is the most time-consuming and widespread leisure activity today, and current developments are likely to sustain its status. The majority of the population is currently able only to select between three television channels at any one time, but in the future the number of choices (if not necessarily the range of choice) is likely to be broadened considerably. Over $2\frac{1}{2}$ million homes in Britain (14 per cent) receive their television signals by a cable distribution network rather than off-air with their own antenna. A good proportion of these cable networks are able to carry far more than just three television channels, and experiments have been conducted at a number of sites in Britain to provide local community television and radio programmes transmitted over cable network (Young et al. 1979).

In the United States subscriptions to cable networks offering multiple channels including Pay-TV, have been increasing rapidly over recent years. Warner's Communications, a subsidiary of Warner Brothers, are field-testing a highly complex residential cable service called QUBE in Columbus, Ohio. The QUBE service offers relay of the American network television channels, plus local programming, educational and children's channels, and Pay-TV channels for first-run films, classic films and 'adult movies'. QUBE also provides a return-path facility such that viewers can give yes/no responses to questions posed on the local television channel by pressing the appropriate keys on a hand-held keypad. These responses are fed back to QUBE's operational computer which provides instant analysis and hence 'instant democracy', which can be used in the programme itself.

Pay-TV, the subscription to a service to view newly-released films, special concerts and sporting events at home on television, provides the financial base for extensive cable operations such as QUBE. In Britain the Home Office, which regulates broadcasting activities, has recently indicated that it is prepared to see experiments start with Pay-TV over cable networks.

Cable systems are not the only way of increasing the range of television services. Satellites can be used to provide a wide torch-like beam of television signals giving national coverage on a single transmission frequency. The use of these Direct Broadcast Satellites, as they are called, can be applied to extend coverage of existing television services, to transmit a totally new broadcast service, or to operate a Pay-TV service. The regulations covering the shape and extent of the transmission beams on the earth's surface have been derived with strong concern for ideals such as national sovereignty. But given the steadfast refusal of national boundaries to conform to the geometric shapes of transmission characteristics, and the ingenuity of entrepreneurs, there is bound to be some spillover in the signal transmissions from one country to another which could be used to increase even further the range of television transmissions which can be received in the home.

Cable television networks and direct broadcast satellites, separately or together, will enable people to spend more of their leisure time, and satisfy more of their interests, from the comfort of their fireside chairs. At the simple level there will be less boredom with television if it offers a greater range. There will be no point in going to the cinema if the same films can be seen on television (teenage couples may be an exception to this rule). Special minority tastes can be catered for, giving more opera, ballet, rock concerts, sports coverage or adult education. And in the event of QUBE-like systems even party-political broadcasts might be made enjoyable if the standard appeal to the nation could be voted on instanteously.

In total, telecommunications technology is bringing just as big
an impact to domestic life as to the work environment. Increased
leisure interests, information sources, and educational opportunities
available to all (who pay the subscriptions) in their own homes, plus
the prospect of remote shopping and voting.

4. DERIVING IMPLICATIONS FOR PLANNING AND TRANSPORT

The preceding sections have broadly outlined trends and capabilities
in telecommunications technology which in my consideration may
fundamentally influence the direction of transportation and planning
research and practice. The technologies discussed are not from
science fiction, but from the present day. All that is missing is a
high degree of penetration of the technology described and the actual
integration of the facilities they offer. Hence the questions that
need to be addressed are not those that start with 'if', but those
prefixed with 'when' and 'how many'. However the quantification of
even these much less imponderable questions is not a simple or
straightforward procedure. The research programme on business travel
and teleconferencing described in section 1, while thorough, multifaceted, and taking scores of man-years of research, could only
reliably reach the point of indicating which existing meetings could
be held by teleconferencing. The next step of predicting the general
impact (how much and when) of teleconferencing on existing business
travel patterns had to involve some degree of speculation.

There are two clear problem areas which impinge on the validity
of any future predictions:
1.   social limitations on introducing new technology;
2.   the adequacy of a model which simply substitutes new tele-
     communications acts for old behaviour patterns.
The first of these is the issue which has so far been deliberately
skirted in this paper. Conservatism and resistance to change are
powerful enough factors in their own right, but in addition there is
always the prospect that some incidental component of present activities is in fact a strong and rational disincentive to adopt the new
technology. The business trip may hide any number of additional
bonuses such as free lunches, an opportunity to pick up incidental
gossip, or to make one's presence felt. Asking a neighbour for advice
might often be best done over a pint of beer, while the evening class
can be an excellent means of gaining a night out as well as learning
something substantial.

The balance between the benefits and disbenefits of the *status quo*
against those of the new technological methods, is often difficult to
assess. Additionally the method of introducing a new technology, early
experience of it, and the availability of escape to previous methods
of operation, can be critical factors in determining whether a new
approach is accepted or rejected.

The second problem area is an intricate spider's web. It is
usually inappropriate to assume that there will be a straight swop
between existing activities and those conducted via telecommunications.
For example to state that 100 business journeys taking place now would
be replaced by 40 teleconferences and 60 residual journeys may be far
too simplistic. It is more likely that they would be replaced by 50
teleconference and 70 journeys. The improved ease of communication in
this example is assumed to have resulted in 20 per cent increase in

meetings though a 30 per cent decrease in travel.

The complexity of the spider's web for assessing the impact of teleconferencing on business travel is illustrated in Figure 3 where + indicates a positive stimulus, and - an inhibiting factor.

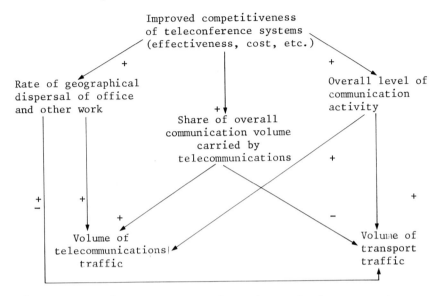

Figure 3. The impact of teleconferencing on business travel.

Given these complexities and uncertainties in the powers of prediction, it would be inappropriate and misleading to make a single statement on the likely implications of telecommunications developments for planning and transport. Instead I propose to draw up two extreme scenarios about how the developments outlined will affect our lives by the year 2000, and what implications they might have.

A technology-driven future
This assumes that the technical capabilities will provide the push to get themselves accepted, and that they will be exploited to the full:

The office - the majority of office work (a large proportion of all occupations) will be conducted from either Home Units or Neighbourhood Work Centres.

Business travel - most business communication will be held by the telephone, teleconferencing and electronic mail.

Domestic activities - shopping conducted electronically, including the selection of best items and payment by electronic funds transfer. Secondary and tertiary education conducted from the home. Subscription to Pay-TV service bringing new films and sporting events to the home provides main form of leisure activities. Residential information services replace the need for easily located information and advice centres.

Implications – the journey to work is made redundant for a significant proportion of the workforce, enabling the expansion of residential areas into places currently underpopulated and not served with good support services such as fast road or rail commuting services. Town centres become less important with remote shopping capabilities, and schooling for children over 11 years of age being conducted in the home. Increased leisure time from reduction in commuting to work, will in part be taken up by greater use of television. The main purpose of travel will be the delivery of goods in the daytime, and recreation in evenings and at weekends.

The resistance to change future
This alternative scenario is proposed from the premise that people respond to change more slowly than the changes in technology. They will only take from the new telecommunications options offered what they find useful to extend their existing life patterns.

The office – office technology will continue to be introduced in a piecemeal fashion to aid and speed present work functions. The central office will remain as it represents a focal point for work, and management patterns are not suited to individual self-discipline.

Business travel – teleconferencing and electronic mail will be used, but overall will stimulate more business travel as people call meetings to compensate for the 'depersonalization' of telecommunications.

Domestic activities – electronic media such as Prestel will be adopted for their games capabilities and for limited information functions. Travel though will be stimulated by the greater awareness of recreational possibilities.

Implications – current trends in work centres, residential areas and leisure requirements will continue. Travel will be stimulated rather than reduced by telecommunications developments.

    In drawing these two alternative pictures of the future I have side-stepped the official requirements of the outside expert, but hope to have drawn attention to the need for research on planning and transport that will incorporate reference to telecommunications.

REFERENCES

Bird, E. (1979) Future work patterns resulting from advances in
    telecommunication. Paper presented at the International Tele-
    communications Union's World Telecommunications Forum, Geneva,
    September 1979.
Glover, J. (1974) Long range social forecasts: working from home.
    Long Range Intelligence Bulletin 2. Post Office Telecommuni-
    cations, London.
Harkness, R. (1977) *Technology Assessment of Telecommunications –
    Transportation Interactions, Vol. 1.* California: SRI Inter-
    national.
James, V.Z., Marshall, J.N. and Walters, N.S. (1979) Telecommuni-
    cations and Office Location. Unpublished Report of the Centre
    for Urban and Regional Development Studies, University of
    Newcastle.

Porat, M. (1976) The Information Economy. Unpublished Ph.D. dissertation, Institute for Communication Research, Stanford University, Stanford, California.

Pye, R., Champness, B., Collins, H. and Connell, S. (1973) The description and classification of meetings. Unpublished report of the Communications Studies Group ref. P/73160/PY.

Short, J., Williams, E. and Christie, B. (1976) *The Social Psychology of Telecommunications*. London: Wiley.

Stamper, R.K. (1977) Formal information systems – their role in the economy and in society. Unpublished paper, Department of Computer Science, London School of Economics.

Tyler, M., Cartwright, B. and Collins, H.A. (1977) Interaction between telecommunications and face-to-face contact: Prospects for tele-conference services. *Long Range Intelligence Bulletin 9*. Post Office Telecommunications, London.

Williams, E. (1978) Research at the Communications Studies Group 1970-1977. *Long Range Research Report 14*. Post Office Telecommunications, London.

Young, I., Pye, R. and Thomas, H. Evaluation of Channel 40 – Community cable television in Milton Keynes Vol. 1 – Overview, Summary and Conclusions. Unpublished report of Communications Studies and Planning.

Telecommunications and rural accessibility: perspectives on the 1980s

DAVID CLARK

1. INTRODUCTION

Difficulties of providing effective links between scattered village populations and centralized urban activities have long existed in rural areas. Traditionally, this rural accessibility problem was defined in terms of physical access to employment, services, and acquaintances, and attention focused upon movements of people and goods, and upon the rural transport system. The development of new and improved telecommunications services has, however, given rise to speculation that telecommunications could influence the demand for travel. As telecommunications become more sophisticated and enter into more widespread use, so many more exchanges in rural areas could take place by non-physical means. By overcoming distance and time barriers to interaction, telecommunications could offset or compensate for difficulties of physical movement in rural areas.

Telecommunications services provide an electronic means of exchanging, storing, and processing information. Although the range of services is broad, a basic distinction may be drawn between broadcast and wired services. Broadcast services include television, radio, and television-based information services such as the BBC's Ceefax and IBA's Oracle. Television and radio broadcasts are the most widely available telecommunication service and can be received in over 95 per cent of households in the United Kingdom. Wired services are those which make use of the public switched network of telephone lines. Telegram, telephone, telex, and Datel services are familiar examples, but a wide range of new and improved peripheral devices has been developed which can be connected via the telephone network (table 1). These new media include facilities for electronic meetings linking remote locations ('teleconferencing'), the preparation, editing, filing, and movement of documents ('facsimile transmission', 'electronic mail', and 'office automation'), and the electronic distribution and display of textual and graphical information of

Table 1. New telecommunications services.

Service	Description	UK example	Status
Teleconferencing			
Conference calls	telephone calls linking more than two locations	Post Office conference call	Post Office provided
Loudspeaking telephone	desk-top audio-only system	Post Office 'Orator'	experimental
Studio based tele-conferencing	audio-only conferencing system	Plessey Telecommuni-cations 'Remote-conference'	in use with the Civil Service Department
Studio based tele-conferencing	audio-visual conferencing system	Post Office 'Confra-vision'	available in five major cities in the UK
Computer conferencing	computer exchange of text messages and graphics	Infomedia's 'Planet'	operational on an experimental basis
Mobile telecommunications services			
Private mobile radio	car paging and message transfer service	Air Call	operational
Radio telephone	mobile telephone using radio to link into main telecommunications network	Post Office radio-telephone	in widespread use
Electronic mail			
Facsimile transmission	remote copying service	Plessey Tele-communications 'Remotecopier'	commercially available
Communicating typewriters	remote typewriting service	Enhanced teletext	experimental
Electronic publishing			
Specialized information distribution services	'host' service providing access to computer databases	British Library's BLAISE	operational
Videotex services	interactive information display service	Post Office's 'Prestel'	launched commercially 1979

general interest ('electronic publishing' systems such as the Post
Office's Prestel). They could make remote working, remote shopping,
and remote service access commonplace activities by the end of the
century.

Although an increase in levels of remote access could have far
reaching implications for rural travel, telecommunications services
have as yet received little attention from planners. There is even
less recognition that telecommunications could be used as a positive
policy instrument to bring about desired changes in the ways in which
services are accessed. The 'communications' objectives of structure
and strategic plans are typically defined in transport terms in which
the main aim is to provide an adequate road and rail system for the
expected movements of passengers and commodities. For example, the
Somerset and the Gloucestershire structure plans (Somerset County
Council 1977; Gloucestershire County Council 1978) focused upon
journeys to work, to school, and to shop, but no mention was made of
the possible effects upon these flows of developments in the telecommunication. Similarly, in Choices for Cumbria (Cumbria County
Council 1976), the possibility of the remote provision of the service
needs of isolated communities was ignored. Both the Strategic Plan
for the South East (HMSO 1971) and Strategic Choice for East Anglia
(Department of the Environment 1974), drew attention to the potentials
of telecommunications, but no major regional planning document has
attempted to incorporate telecommunications in a strategic planning
framework based upon a detailed analysis of the total communications
facilities and requirements of the region.

This neglect reflects the current status of research into telecommunications services in which most of the literature is concerned
with technical rather than with social and economic aspects. It means
that planners and policy-makers have been given little guidance as to
the expected chronology and direction of telecommunication effects.
Although there may be important long-term implications for transport,
the impact of telecommunications over the next ten years is likely to
be diminished by diffusion, travel effect, and management considerations. One important constraint will be the pace of market
penetration of services, a second will be the suitability of telecommunications for handling those transactions which the rural
population wishes to make, while a third will be the attitude towards
telecommunications of those responsible for providing rural services.
This paper evaluates these constraints in the context of existing
research into telecommunications and travel. Specifically it is
concerned with the likely effects and policy implications of developments in telecommunications for rural transport over the next ten
years.

2. TELECOMMUNICATION SERVICES IN RURAL AREAS

The most basic questions about telecommunications impacts concern the
expected pattern of spread of new services. Much of the current
interest in telecommunications reflects the rapid pace of technical
innovation in the communications industry which means that services
such as teletext, which were barely discussed in surveys of future
telecommunications services written a decade ago, are now entering
into commercial use (Cowan 1969; Whyte 1969). But although the time
separating invention and manufacture has been reduced, the lag between

first introduction and complete market penetration remains substantial. One reason is the initial high cost of equipment and services, another is the need to demonstrate the value of services to potential customers, while a third is the natural reluctance of people to purchase services which at least in the short term provide links with only a small number of other users. A final reason is that the mere existence of a service is by no means a guarantee of its acceptability - as the failure of the Bell Telephone's Picturephone service demonstrated (Dickson and Bowers 1973).

Despite the proliferation of new telecommunications services, the most striking feature in recent years is the comparatively recent expansion and current rapid rate of growth of the telephone service. Although the telephone has been in use in the United Kingdom since 1876, the really large absolute increases have occurred in the last twenty years, at a time when inland telegram traffic has declined, and inland mail traffic has levelled off (Clark 1973). Much of this growth can be attibuted to increases in residential exchange connections. In 1960 less than 20 per cent of households had a telephone, in 1970, penetration was a little over 30 per cent, while the 1980 statistic is around 65 per cent. Despite this level of current availability, the average residential subscriber makes only three calls a week.

These national statistics conceal some marked variations in levels of penetration by different types of household and from place to place. An important characteristic of the telephone service is that levels of residential penetration in rural areas are below the national average and are substantially lower than in prosperous urban centres (Clark 1979). Moreover the high correlation between telephone ownership and social class means that access to telephones is lowest among low-income households in rural areas. For example in central Lincolnshire, 37 per cent of households of which the head is employed in semi-skilled or unskilled occupations were on the telephone in 1978, as opposed to 87 per cent of professional and managerial households (Clark and Unwin 1980a). Over the last twenty years, enhancements in the basic telephone service such as Subscriber Trunk Dialling (STD) and International Direct Dialling (IDD) have been introduced hierarchically, although the telephone service in many rural areas remains to be upgraded. The launching of Prestel in London in 1979 to be followed by Birmingham, Manchester, and Edinburgh in 1980, and later by Liverpool, Cardiff, Leeds, Cheltenham and Bristol and Nottingham, suggests that this pattern will be repeated in the future. The last beneficiaries of new and improved telecommunications services are therefore households in rural areas, especially low-income households.

The pattern of spread of business services is more difficult to predict. Services such as the telephone, telex, and Datel are already in widespread use, and the major implications for the structure and organization of business over the next ten years are likely to arise from 'stand alone' mini-computers and word processors, which although products of new technology, are not, strictly speaking, telecommunications services. Although much has been made of the possibility of holding remote meetings, doubts must be raised concerning the value of teleconferencing to small-scale industry in rural areas, especially as services such as confravision have yet to be widely accepted by big business. The paradox with telecommunications is, therefore, that it is the old rather than the new services that have the greatest

implications for the next decade. A continued growth of residential
exchange connections can be predicted by extrapolating current trends,
and most of this growth will take place in rural areas where penetration rates are presently lowest. This means that telephones will be
available for the first time in low-income households, many of which
contain individuals who experience severe problems of physical accessibility. Major consequences for rural transport will arise from the
opportunities this affords to provide services, especially personal
and domestic services, remotely.

3.   TELECOMMUNICATION-TRAVEL EFFECTS

Having reviewed the pattern of innovation and expected market penetration, it is now possible to evaluate the likely impacts of
telecommunications services upon rural travel. Research workers
interested in telecommunications-travel interaction have identified
three major types of effect: *substitution*, in which telecommunications lead to a reduction in movement; *stimulation*, where additional
traffic is generated; and *modification*, where new and different
patterns of travel demand arise (Tyler 1979).
    Substitution assumes that demands for travel are fully realized
and that telecommunication services will absorb some of this demand:
an example is within-work travel, where face-to-face meetings between
executives could be performed remotely. Movements which involve the
carriage and shipment of goods, and which must involve the movement
of people – such as visits to the hairdresser – cannot be substituted,
but many trips take place in rural areas to make exchanges of a non-
physical nature, which could be acceptably, economically, and usefully
replaced by telecommunications. Examples might include visits to
banks, building societies, advice and information agencies.
    Stimulus effects arise when the improved contact made possible by
telecommunications gives rise to an increased demand for travel.
Thus regular telephone conversations with friends and relatives might
make visits to see them more likely. Telecommunications could however
have important indirect effects by changing the location or nature of
activities which give rise to travel. Movement patterns would be
dramatically modified if, for example, the widespread adoption and
use of teleconferencing services enabled a set of centralized office
functions to disperse to a non-urban location.
    As telecommunication effects are likely to be highly variable, it
is useful to establish the relative importance of different types of
movement. Table 2 presents a general classification of trip purposes
in Great Britain based upon National Travel Survey data (Department
of Transport 1979). Although only 10 per cent of trips arise during
the course of work, it is these movements which have been analysed in
most detail by research workers interested in telecommunications-
travel interactions. Empirical surveys of business contacts have been
combined with the results of tests of attitudes towards business
communications services, to form the basis of estimates that up to
60 per cent of within-work movements could be substituted (Christie
and Elton 1979). Despite the importance of these findings, the
characteristics of the research design – and in particular, the types
of organization studied – suggest that the results have most relevance
to communications-intensive blocks of work within urban office
complexes. They provide little guidance to the likely effects of new

Table 2. Travel mileage: mode of transport by journey purpose, 1975-76.

Journey purpose	Per cent
To and from work	23
In course of work	10
Education	4
Shopping and personal business	16
Entertainment, sport, eating and drinking	8
Personal social travel	18
Other personal travel (holidays, pleasure etc.)	21
All purposes	100

Source: National Travel Survey (Department of Transport 1979).

telecommunications services upon the within-work movements of small manufacturing units and labour-intensive primary sector enterprises that are typically found in rural areas.

A more detailed breakdown of trip purposes in rural areas was provided by some recent research (Clark and Unwin 1980a). Part of this work involved asking a random sample of village residents in rural Lincolnshire to complete contact diaries recording details of all trips undertaken over a five-day survey period. The diaries were restricted to non-work movements, so that the data provide, in effect, a breakdown of the two-thirds of all trips which the National Travel Survey suggests involve non-work purposes. As well as recording the general purpose of each trip, the diaries requested information on the types of transaction undertaken. In this way it was possible to separate those trips upon which telecommunciations are likely to have limited effects from those which could be stimulated, substituted, or modified.

The 979 trips reported to destinations outside the local area gave rise to 1015 transactions (table 3). An important characteristic is that very nearly three-quarters of these trips involve the carriage of goods or the necessary movement of people for participation or involvement in recreational, sporting, entertainment or educational purposes. Although telecommunications have implications for some of these transactions, the overall travel effects are likely to be marginal. For example, telecommunications are likely to influence teaching practices within schools over the next decade, although the journey to school is itself unlikely to change. Similarly, despite the expected growth in home entertainment services, it could be argued that the major effects of telecommunications upon travel to entertainment, as seen in falling cinema attendances, have already taken place (Smith 1979). However, around one-quarter of all non-work trips involve transactions of a kind that could in theory be performed remotely. By far the most numerous are visits which simply involve conversation and chatting. Visits for these essentially social purposes have no explicit information content and do not involve the getting or giving of advice and information. Almost all take place with friends and relatives and involve the discussion of personal matters. In contrast to these social visits, the getting or giving of advice or information, ordering and booking, paying bills, filling in forms, and other information transactions are all comparatively

Table 3. Non-local*, non-work trips in rural areas: nature of
transactions performed.

Transaction	Percentage of 1015
Information transactions	
General conversation/having a chat	18.3
Getting/giving advice or information	4.4
Paying bills	1.4
Ordering goods, making bookings or appointments	1.2
Filling in forms	0.3
Other	1.4
Sub total	27.0
Transportation transactions	
Buying and collecting goods and services/ keeping appointments	41.9
Trip to recreation/sport/entertainment	16.6
Giving a lift to someone	12.8
Trip to school, college or work**	1.7
Sub total	73.0

* Non-local trips are those to destinations outside the home, and
immediately adjacent villages.
** Journey to work trips only included when combined with trips for
other purposes.
Source: Clark and Unwin 1980b.

minor reasons for movement in rural areas.
     The relative importance of these different kinds of information
transactions, combined with the continued expansion of residential
telephone penetration, suggest that the major implications for rural
transport are likely to be determined by the effects of telecommunication on social travel. One possibility is that, as the telephone
facilitates regular and immediate personal contact between friends and
relatives, it reduces the need for visiting; so that telecommunications provide an alternative to face-to-face communication for social
purposes. The other is that by enabling distant friendships to be
maintained on a more immediate, direct, and personal basis, the
likelihood of a visit is increased. In contrast to the study of business applications, social aspects of telecommunications have received
comparatively little attention so that these alternatives cannot be
systematically assessed. More detailed analysis of the contact data
suggests that additional social journeys are likely to be stimulated
by rising telephone ownership but that this is likely to generate
further accessibility problems (Clark and Unwin 1980b). One reason
is that the greatest demand for social travel arises in the five or
six hours in the middle of the day when the demand for travel to work
and to school is least, and when the private car is unlikely to be
available for home-based journeys. The other is that as telephone
ownership is rising fastest in non-car-owning households, any
increased demand for social travel is likely to come from those who
are least mobile. Substantial further research is necessary before

realistic estimates of the effects of telecommunications on social travel, and thus upon overall movement patterns in rural areas, can be provided.

The impact of telecommunications services upon journeys to information services has been examined in more depth. Getting and giving advice and information, ordering goods and making bookings and appointments, paying bills, and filling in forms are all activities which can be transacted remotely, and developments such as teletext, remote meter readers (Short 1979), remote shopping (Edwards 1979), cashpoints, and electronic funds transfer (King and Kramer 1978), mean that the effects of telecommunications are likely to be substantial. The contact diary data show that nearly 10 per cent of all movements outside the local area involve these transactions, but as nearly half of these information service visits are combined with shopping, recreational, sporting, leisure, and lift-giving purposes, the replacement effect of telecommunications is likely to be much reduced. Ordering and booking, filling in forms, paying bills, and other information service transactions are, in any case, numerically minor reasons for visiting and so substitution would make little impact upon overall patterns of movement.

The scope for replacement is greatest with journeys which involve the getting and giving of advice and information. Agencies providing these services are typically widely scattered in rural areas and so are associated with particular difficulties of physical accessibility (Richardson 1979). Visits to seek information and advice are the largest class of information service visits and the factual data sought are well suited to transmission by telecommunications, especially if networks of communications centres - as envisaged by the East Anglia Regional Strategy Term - are established in rural areas (Department of the Environment 1974). Telecommunications, however, are only one mode of delivery, and are perhaps best viewed as extending the options which already exist with peripatetic, town-based, and intra-village services (Clark and Unwin 1979).

Telephone access to advice and information is already commonplace, but an analysis of existing patterns of contact with agencies suggests that the telephone is used very much in a directional and signposting capacity to find out what services are available, who to contact, and how, with people still making visits to access the service (Clark and Unwin 1980a). Some visits for information and advice getting purposes will of course always be required as they involve face-to-face counselling, or the consultation of confidential documents, but these represent only a very small minority of visits to information services. Major travel effects are, however, unlikely until systems of information service delivery are developed in rural areas in which the information service iteself, and not just information about the information service, can be accessed remotely.

4. TELECOMMUNICATIONS AND SERVICE PROVISION

Important implications for travel are therefore likely to arise as a result of management decisions as to how services are made available to the public. Patterns of access are in large part prescribed by the location and modes of operation of services. For example, Electricity Board offices, where people can go to pay bills, are to be found in most market towns; but remote payment is also possible by

post, and through banks and post offices. Conversely, most social
security services must be accessed by visiting local Department of
Health and Social Security (DHSS) Offices although benefits such as
Family Income Supplement are provided remotely. Some services involve
visits; others can be provided by post or telecommunication; but for
the majority, both physical and non-physical modes of provision are
appropriate.

Telecommuncications offer managers the increased opportunity to
make services available remotely and so reduce the need for travel.
Consumers could be encouraged to access services by telecommunications, and administrative and office practices could be changed so
that remote access was convenient, effective and acceptable. This
could involve the introduction of sufficient exchange connexions to
cope with the demand for telephone access, the provision and training
of staff to deal with remote inquiries, and the advertising and promotion of services by radio, television, and teletext. Agencies could
benefit by a reduction in operating costs and higher levels of business, whereas consumers would enjoy access to a wide range of services
without the need for difficult, expensive and time-consuming travel.

Examination of information service agencies, however, suggests
that the extent to which telecommunications services will be encouraged as a mode of information service provision is likely to be highly
variable. Banks and building societies, which are traditionally among
the leaders in technological innovation, are especially likely to be
influenced by future developments in telecommunications and office
services. Indeed, the rapid growth in credit systems of finance,
based upon telecommunications technology, which has reduced the need
for visits to banks, is a major area of potential travel substitution.
More profound changes in the ways in which people organize their
finances can be expected in the near future as cashpoints, charge
cards, and remote funds transfer become commonplace, and the
locational and transport implications represent an important but
neglected research area.

In contrast, there are many areas of service provision where the
widespread use of telecommunciations services seems remote. Telecommunications services could be of benefit in the provision of
information services concerned with transport, social security,
housing, rates, health and taxation; but the limited use which is made
of existing telecommunications services in these areas suggests that
'over the counter' modes of provision, which require travel by
consumers, will be continued. One reason is the generally low
priority given to the information service component of services;
another is the lack of coordination between agencies which is necessary for telecommunications services, such as Prestel, to be
effective; while a third is the perceived suitability of telecommunications as a mode of provision to all potential customers for a
service. These constraints upon telecommunications use, and hence
travel implications, were illustrated by a detailed analysis of
passenger transport information services and social security services
in rural Lincolnshire (Clark and Unwin 1980a).

Passenger transport information services in the area are provided
by transport operators and by local travel agents. Information about
fares and timings of services is straightforward, factual and non-
confidential and so could easily be made available remotely. Most
contacts with providers are made by telephone, but difficulties in

identifying local transport operators, delays in being answered and
the restriction of the service to office hours are common. Particular
problems face the prospective traveller wishing to plan multi-mode or
multi-company journeys, especially if these involve the use of independent bus company, community bus, or post bus services, as
comprehensive information about rural transport is difficult to
acquire. There are further difficulties in finding out about delays
or cancellations to services. At first glance this seems to be an
area of provision where telecommunications services, and especially
teletext, could be of enormous benefit; but the low level of coordination and integration of transport and transport information services,
which is a characteristic of rural areas, is likely to reduce the
effectiveness of Prestel. Deficiencies in existing information
services could as easily be overcome by ensuring that adequate provision is made to deal with telephone inquiries and that timetable and
fares information is widely posted in railway stations and bus
shelters, and on public noticeboards in the area. The compilation
of comprehensive timetables for transport services in the area is an
important step in this direction (White 1977). The absence at
present, of passenger transport information services using ansaphones,
pre-recorded announcements and FREEPHONE facilities – all of which
have been long available, and are in wide use elsewhere – suggests
that the early development of systems based upon telecommunications is
unlikely.

Examination of the services provided by local Department of Health
and Social Security Offices indicates that the scope for telecommunications provision is similarly limited. Unlike passenger transport
information which is provided to help people consume a physical
service, DHSS offices – being responsible for administering contribu-
tory, non-contributory and means-tested benefits – are exclusively
concerned with information provision. DHSS benefits are inherently
complex, and as entitlements depend upon National Insurance contributions or an individual's personal circumstances, the process normally
involves inspection of confidential documents, and interviewing of
clients. Some benefits (such as Child Benefit) are consumed by a
wide cross-section of the population, but much of the work of offices
involves dealing with people who are experiencing acute personal,
social and financial hardship, who are likely to be unfamiliar with
the practices and language of bureaucracy, and who therefore might be
expected to be at least able to afford and make full use of telecommunications mode of access. For these reasons, administration of
benefits normally requires, and is likely to continue to require
attendance at local offices. Telecommunications could provide a
valuable means of advertising and publishing services, as the
Inverclyde welfare benefits information project has shown (Adler and
de Feu 1975), but the complexities of benefits and the characteristics
of clients suggest that telecommunications are inappropriate as a mode
of direct provision of social security services.

Passenger transport and social welfare agencies are only two
examples of agencies which provide information and information
services. The promotion of services by telecommunications, especially
Prestel, could be of considerable benefit in rural areas but the most
likely consequence would be an increase in the demand for travel.
Experiences are likely to vary widely, but the range of services
provided, and the receptiveness of clients, suggest that the adoption

of telecommunications as a mode of provision - at least on a scale
sufficient to reduce significantly the demand for physical accessibility - is an unlikely development over the next decade.

5. TELECOMMUNICATIONS AND POLICY PLANNING

This paper has examined the constraints which are likely to condition
the impact of telecommunication services upon travel in rural areas
over the next decade. Three major points have emerged. The first is
that the main consequences are likely to arise out of the spread of
established services, such as the telephone, as these have progressively been introduced into (and used by) households - especially
low-income households - in rural areas. The increased opportunity for
remote contact that will result, suggests that significant travel
substitution could occur. But as telecommunications access is appropriate for only a small percentage of transactions which give rise
to physical movements, notably those of a social or information-
seeking nature, overall travel effects will be small. Such effects
will be further constrained by the willingness or ability of agencies
to make services available to the public in a form suitable for
telecommunications access; and this is only appropriate, or is only
likely to occur, in a limited number of servicing areas. Two major
conclusions follow from these arguments. One is that telecommunications are likely to have significant - but largely spontaneous -
effects upon overall volumes of social travel; the other is that they
could be used as a means of promoting and ensuring improved access to
selected services or aspects of services in rural areas.
    The effects of telecommunications in these areas have contrasting
implications for transport and public policy planning. Rural
transport studies have traditionally been concerned with journeys to
work, to shop, and to recreation, but the contact diaries suggest that
social movements are of equal importance and merit equal attention.
In theory, communication by telephone could replace many of the 18 per
cent of all non-local visits which take place for social purposes,
although remote contact is unlikely to be an acceptable and effective
alternative to the face-to-face exchanges upon which most social
relationships are based. The more likely consequence is that by
extending the spatial extent of friendship and kinship networks,
telecommunications will lead to an increase in the demand for physical
movement, and may heighten an appreciation of isolation and remoteness
which is a commonly-cited reason for migration out of rural areas.
Social aspects of telecommunications use have only recently emerged as
an important research area, although the historical perspective of
most published work means that it provides only limited assistance in
evaluating these alternatives (de Solla Pool 1978). This paper,
therefore, merely draws attention to the likelihood of significant
effects of telecommunications for social travel. A more detailed
analysis of social exchanges is necessary before transport policy
implications in this particular area can be determined.
    In contrast, both important and immediate implications for policy
arise out of the opportunities which telecommunications afford to
access and provide services, especially information services,
remotely. Telecommunications are likely to have spontaneous and
largely unexplored effects upon social travel as decisions as to modes
of contact are taken by private individuals, but patterns of access to

services are in large part determined by, and so can be manipulated by, those who provide services. The central question with rural policy is, therefore, not what impact telecommunications will have, but what impact the policy-maker would want them to have. It is to ask how telecommunications services can be used, alongside, and not necessarily in place of transport services, to improve the scope and standard of servicing in rural areas.

Despite the severity and persistence of the rural servicing problem, analysis of patterns of daily telephone contacts, and of selected agencies, suggests that there is as yet little evidence that the telephone and telecommunications have been adopted widely in areas of information service activity where they could be an appropriate and beneficial means of access and provision. Examples of services based wholly or substantially upon telecommunications access do exist, such as airline passenger information services, Surrey County Council's 'Box 99' consumer advice (Kilsby 1974), services provided by the Samaritans, and telephones for the elderly schemes (Gregory 1973); and these are pointers to the types of developments that could be usefully developed in rural areas. A necessary first step is for research to identify the services or parts of services which are most appropriate for telecommunications access and provision. Mere recognition of potential and applicability is, however, insufficient, and there is a clear need for the value of telecommunications to be demonstrated to users, and the use to be encouraged, especially in areas like passenger transport information provision where present services are fragmented and incomplete. Without such 'intervention' it is unlikely that the full potentials of telecommunications for rural servicing will be achieved.

New telecommunications services are currently receiving much publicity, and it is not difficult to envisage a rural future in which a large number of activities, which today involve physical movement, were transacted remotely. A New Rural Society, of the kind that is envisaged by Goldmark (1973), is technically feasible, but consideration of servicing needs and problems in rural areas suggests that telecommunications are best seen as supplementing and widening existing access and delivery options. This means that telecommunications could be given equal attention with the car, the bus, and the train, in the modal allocation stage of the transport planning process. In place of a rural transport policy, there is a need for a comprehensive rural accessibility policy, which seeks to make best use of all forms of communication, both physical and non-physical, in rural areas.

REFERENCES

Adler, M. and de Feu, D. (1975) *A Computer Based Welfare Benefits Information System: the Inverclyde Project.* Peterlee: IBM Ltd.
Christie, B. and Elton, M. (1979) Research on the differences between telecommunication and face to face communication in business and government, in *Impacts of Telecommunications on Planning and Transport.* London: Departments of the Environment and Transport, pp. 55-84.
Clark, D. (1973) Urban linkage and regional structure in Wales: an analysis of change, 1958-68. *Transactions Institute of British Geographers,* 58, pp. 41-58.

Clark, D. (1979) The spatial impact of telecommunications, in *Impacts of Telecommunications on Planning and Transport*. London: Departments of the Environment and Transport, pp. 85-128.

Clark, D. and Unwin, K.I. (1979) Community information in rural areas: an evaluation of alternative systems of delivery, in Shaw, J.M. (ed.) *Rural Deprivation*. Norwich: Geo-Abstracts Ltd.

Clark, D. and Unwin, K.I. (1980a) *Information Services in Rural Areas: Prospects for Telecommunications Access*. Norwich: Geo Abstracts Ltd.

Clark, D. and Unwin, K.I. (1980b) Telecommunications and travel: potential impacts in rural areas. *Regional Studies, 14*, forthcoming.

Cowan, P. (1979) Communications, *Urban Studies, 6*, pp. 436-46.

Cumbria County Council (1976) *Choices for Cumbria*. Carlisle: Cumbria County Council and Lake District Special Planning Board.

de Solla Pool, I. (1978) *The Social Impact of the Telephone*. Cambridge, Mass.: M.I.T. Press.

Department of the Environment, (1974) *Strategic Choice for East Anglia*. London: HMSO.

Department of Transport (1979) *Transport Statistics Great Britain 1968-78*. London: HMSO.

Dickson, E.M. and Bowers, R. (1974) *The Video Telephone: Impact of a New Era in Telecommunications*. London: Praeger.

Edwards, M. (1979) Service provision via local communications centres, in *Impacts of Telecommunications on Planning and Transport*. London: Departments of the Environment and Transport, pp. 245-66.

Gregory, P. (1973) *Telephones for the Elderly*. London: Bell.

HMSO (1971) *Strategic Plan for the South East*. London: HMSO.

Kilsby, R.E. (1974) 'Box 99': the provision of consumer advice in Surrey. Guildford: Surrey County Council.

King, J.L. and Kramer, K.L. (1978) Electronic funds transfer as a subject of study in technology, society and public policy. *Telecommunications Policy, 2*, pp. 13-33.

Gloucestershire County Council (1979) *County Structure Plan; Draft Report of Survey, Technical Volume No. 10*. Gloucester: Gloucestershire County Council.

Goldmark, P.C. (1973) *The 1972/3 New Rural Society Project: Report to the U.S. Department of Housing and Urban Development*. Fairfield Connecticut: Fairfield University.

Richardson, B. (1979) Some innovations of a rural community council, in Shaw, J.M. (ed.) *Rural Deprivation*. Norwich: Geo-Abstracts Ltd.

Short, J. (1979) Residential telecommunications applications; a general review, in *Impacts of Telecommunications on Planning and Transport*. London: Departments of the Environment and Transport, pp. 23-54.

Smith, R.C. (1979) Telecommunications technology: current trends, in *Impacts of Telecommunications on Planning and Transport*. London: Departments of the Environment and Transport.

Somerset County Council, (1977) *Consultative Report of Survey*. Taunton: Somerset County Council.

Tyler, M. (1979) Implications for transport, in *Impacts of Telecommunications on Planning and Transport*. London: Departments of the Environment and Transport, pp. 129-168.

White, P. (1977) Timetable of independent bus and coach services in Lincolnshire and South Humberside. London: Polytechnic of North London, mimeo.

Whyte, J.S. (1969) Telecommunications in the next thirty years, in Jones, D.S. (ed.) *Communications and Energy in Changing Urban Environments*. London: Pergamon.

'Real time' information and the bus traveller

PETER WARMAN

1. THE IMPORTANCE OF BUS RELIABILITY

For the foreseeable future, the scheduled bus service will have a dominant role in providing public transport for urban, inter-urban and certain rural operations in the United Kingdom. This is determined largely by the size and distribution of existing settlements and the planned segregation of housing areas from the range of high-order facilities associated with employment, education, shopping, health care and recreation.

However, the scheduled bus is generally regarded, at best, as an adequate method of travel, and if fare levels are considered high and performance unreliable, passengers are likely to feel disadvantaged when totally dependent on it. If, in the passenger's experience, the bus service is unreliable, other improvements will not compensate for this.

The main causes of unreliability have been found to be bus and staff shortages, traffic congestion and supervision problems. The complex interaction of these factors, together with other effects caused by the variations in passenger loadings along the route and throughout the day, combine to make the objective of greater reliability difficult to achieve.

Because of these complexities and the costs associated with removing the causes of unreliability, it is important to be clear what the passenger means by the term 'a reliable bus service'. Improvements in reliability, to be effective, must be perceived by the passenger. Such assessments of reliability are related to the comparison between the anticipated waiting time at the bus stop and the perceived actual waiting time. It can be hypothesized that where the perceived time equals the expected time, the service would be regarded as reliable. This raises the question of how does the passenger derive an estimate for the anticipated waiting time and subsequently perceive the actual waiting time at the bus stop?

2. THE ANTICIPATED WAITING TIME

Perceived unreliability is a manifestation of a form of frustration arising from a sense of dependence and a felt inability to predict. Because there is a wide range of characteristics which make up a bus passenger's journeys, the manifestations of unreliability are equally varied. One such example occurs when a journey is planned as part of a sequence to participate in a tightly timed event, and success is contingent upon the scheduled bus service actually operating at a particular time. The consequences of failure could include missing a train, an appointment or the beginning of an activity. A journey of this character is obviously different from one in which people, who have a concept of frequency, arrive randomly at a bus stop expecting to have a wait for no longer than a certain time before a bus arrives. Normally, such journeys have a frame of reference related to how long the end to end journey is likely to take. There is no precisely timed target arrival time except that it should not be later than a threshold; for example, start time for work, closing time for shops, and so on. Other categories of journeys could be described, but it is important to note that although the causes and triggers of anxiety vary according to the nature of the journey, the resolution of the problems could be achieved by a single technique.

The main sources of information for anticipated bus departure times are the published timetable, previous experience gained from using the bus service, and knowledge obtained from other people. Some passengers, who plan carefully for a particular service at a defined time, could have an anticipated waiting time approximating to zero. For people who arrive randomly, expected waiting time will be related to a developed feel for what is 'reasonable'. In the nature of events, sometimes waiting time will be zero, but given a combination of experience and a perceived headway, a norm will be erected and anxiety ensues after the norm has been exceeded. As the actual performance of the bus service becomes more erratic, the determination of the norm becomes more difficult, and the accurate monitoring of waiting time is less likely because of the anxiety generated; this leads to an increased perception of unreliability.

Moreover, unless passengers travel regularly on the same service from the same stop, it is unlikely they will memorize exact arrival and departure times even given a reliable service. Thus, the estimate of the anticipated arrival time of the bus is inexact not only because of operational factors but also the limitations of a passenger knowledge and memory of the timetable. Even where a printed timetable is displayed at the bus stop, research (WYTCONSULT 1977) suggests that people can still have difficulty interpreting when the next bus is due. The use of the 24-hour clock and the apparent complexity when faced with a mass of figures (where columns of print are closely spaced) are the two most commonly reported difficulties.

Passengers' unfamiliarity with the timetable may be attributed to various causes: their inability to interpret it, the lack of availability of timetables, or merely passengers' incredulity about printed timetables. Whatever the cause, the fact that they do not know the timetable, means that they are unlikely to time their arrival at a bus stop to minimize waiting time. Nor will they be able to make confident estimates of how long they expect to wait.

3. PERCEPTION OF THE ACTUAL WAITING TIME

Time perception studies show that passengers have a tendency to
exaggerate the length of time spent waiting for a bus, and that the
level of inaccuracy increases with time. This over-estimation of
time is partly explained by experiments conducted by psychologists
(for example, Loehlin 1959); the less interesting a task, the more
the tendency to perceive it as taking longer; the interval of time may
lack in variety of content (probably due to greater attention given by
the person to the passage of time during such periods); and the fact
that the person is in a passive state (for example, listening, watching) rather than an active state. Waiting at the bus stop is usually
perceived as boring since it means standing in a queue (passive state)
acutely aware of time; even five minutes can seem 'an age'. Research
also suggests that the uncertainty of waiting time more than the
waiting time itself is felt by the traveller. If the time spent
waiting for a bus is perceived to be longer than it actually is, then
the level of service and reliability will probably be judged as worse
than it is in reality.

Thus not all passengers perceive their waiting time as longer than
the actual time waited; it will depend on the state of mind and
characteristics of the person. However, the stress of the waiting
situation can be reduced, with a possible reduction in the perceived
time, if some realistic guide to length of time required to wait is
given. An example to illustrate this might be the lift with the
illuminated floor numbers showing the present position of the lift to
potential users at other floors.

Ideas about the level of reliability of a particular bus service
are usually based on memory of different occasions of waiting at the
bus stop. There is a strong tendency to remember the more extreme or
unusual situations when the perceived time was very different from the
expected time. Additionally, a person does not easily distinguish the
times waited at this stop from those at other bus stops. He may also
wish to justify his complaints about the service. This tends to
exaggerate the unreliability associated with the particular bus
service.

In a survey conducted by the author (Warman 1971) people at a bus
stop were questioned as to how long they normally waited for the bus
at that stop. Over 50 per cent of respondents said they normally
waited longer than 15 minutes for the bus. However, both the scheduled bus frequency of every ten minutes and the observed frequency
suggested that an average wait of five minutes would be a more realistic estimate. So, whatever the reason or combination of reasons, it
seems that perceived reliability of the bus services is likely to be
worse than actual reliability.

In more recent exploratory research for London Transport, Warman
(1979) has suggested that unless the traveller is trying to meet a
tight deadline, on arriving at the bus stop he does not appear to be
particularly conscious of the time. As one respondent put it: 'You
begin to count the minutes after about five minutes, don't you?'. In
other words, there is an initial period when the person hopes/expects
the bus will arrive soon and can easily be pre-occupied with other
things/thoughts. The exceptions to this are when either no other
people are waiting at the stop (and the presumption is made that a
bus has just gone), or the queue is longer than usual and the

assumption is made that the bus has been delayed. In both these
circumstances, the person is alerted to the passing of time from the
start.

However, unless the great majority of waiting periods a person
experiences at a particular stop (about 90 per cent) are less than
five minutes, there appears to be a tendency to exaggerate the
'expected' waiting time. This may be as a result of longer waits
forming a more dominant, memorable experience. For waits of over ten
to 15 minutes, it is also likely that the perception of time by the
person waiting is also exaggerated. Unpleasant weather conditions or
pressing deadlines appear to make a person more conscious of time and
so increase the tendency to exaggerate estimates of waiting time.
Apart from referring to their watch when they become particularly
conscious of the passage of time, people do not explicitly know hcw
they make a judgement of how long they have waited. Yet they do make
estimates and tend to believe them.

4. 'REAL TIME' INFORMATION - WILL IT HELP?

The imperfect knowledge of the expected waiting time, the tendency
to exaggerate the actual time spent waiting and the tendency to
recall more readily the extreme situations experienced in a bus queue,
all tend to downgrade people's perceptions of the level of reliability
actually achieved by the bus service.

With an appreciation of these problems, it is understandable that
some operators are experimenting with methods for transmitting 'real
time' information to passengers waiting at bus stops. Two such
experiments are the Mississauga Transit Demonstration (Canada) (Green
1979) and the work sponsored by the United States Department of
Transportation (Transportation Systems Center) in Los Angeles (Blood
et al. 1979). Both systems base their predictions on the expected
bus arrival time at particular stops by using information from
'automatic vehicle monitoring' systems on board each bus. Vehicles
are periodically interrogated by a radio signal from a central
computer to determine the location and progress of the bus along the
route. The estimated 'real time' prediction can be transmitted to an
electronic display at the bus stop as shown in figure 1. Alternatively, as in the Mississauga project, the waiting passenger can
telephone the central computer and receive the information from an
'automatically composed voice message'. Both systems form part of a
transportation management system designed not only to assist the
public but also to monitor the performance of the bus system and the
use made of it by the passengers. A simpler passenger information
system has been developed in Tokyo, whereby, when a bus leaves a
stop, a signal is transmitted to the next stop to inform people waiting of its imminent arrival (Richards 1976).

These experiments suggest that the technology to provide 'real
time' information for passengers is being developed. There is
increasing interest in employing electronic aids to improve the
efficient operation of buses. The value of two-way radio to link
bus drivers with a central control is generally accepted, and experiments with automatic vehicle monitoring systems can be traced back to
the late 1950s.

However, whilst it is easy to become fascinated with new technology, more fundamental research is needed to establish whether the
operator can justify the investment in the control technology. A

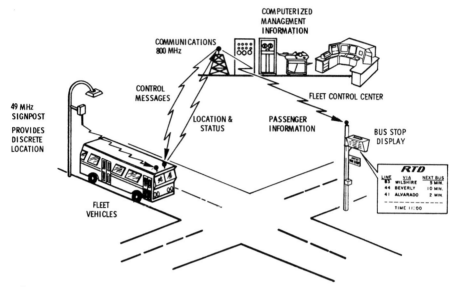

Figure 1. Automatic vehicle monitoring system (US Department of Transportation, Transportation System Center (Blood *et al.* 1979)).

central question is whether management can make use of such continuous 'real time' information to improve bus operations in a manner perceived by the public. Even more difficult to predict is how the public will respond to being informed with 'real time' information.

In 1971, the author conducted a small pilot study for London Transport to test the response of the public to providing a 'real time' 'bus arrival countdown indicator' at a bus stop (Warman 1971). By placing two observers up-route in radio contact with a controller at the bus stop, it was possible to set a 'countdown prediction' on a portable electronic display set up at the bus stop. Even with this rather simple method of monitoring, it was possible to predict the arrival of buses over the section of route in question to within one minute for 90 per cent of the bus arrivals. The error of the remainder was less than two minutes. As a small pilot study, the countdown system was tried out on the public for only three weekday afternoons. When people standing at the stop were asked about their reaction to the idea of being shown the length of time before the next bus, 61 (90 per cent) replied that they thought it was a good idea. Fourteen of these qualified their answers by saying a 'good idea if you can believe it' and the remaining 49 replied enthusiastically (for example, 'excellent, stops frustration', 'extremely useful', 'very nice to know'). It could be argued that the enthusiasm was partly due to the novelty of the indicator. Of the seven replies (10 per cent) which did not react particularly favourably, four said they 'had to wait anyway', another two said they had not noticed it, and the other person said he wanted another bus instead of the indicator.

When the countdown indicator was proved right with the arrival of the bus, there were expressions of disbelief and a certain degree of jubilation. Others expressed their feelings with accusations of 'it's a fix'. Because it was the first occasion the respondents had seen the countdown indicator operating, it was not possible to gain more than their initial reaction to it.

Informing passengers of the expected arrival time of the next bus should not only reduce uncertainty but allow them to engage in other activities besides anxiously looking for the bus. The bus user could return to the stop nearer the time of arrival, or if the length of time is excessive, he can contemplate alternative courses of action (for example, walk to the next stop or transport interchange, hail a taxi, etc.). Certainly, the frustration of the bus user would be reduced, and this, it is thought, might have a long-term benefit on the user's perception of the bus service. If the bus is about to arrive other people may be encouraged to wait for it instead of walking or going by an alternative mode of transport. It seems that the overall effect of indicating the length of waiting time would present the bus passenger with a higher level of reliability, and this would increase the status of the bus service in the eyes of potential users. However, these conclusions can only be substantiated through the operation of the countdown indicator over a period of time.

5. HOW MUCH WILL IT COST?

In the work for London Transport, Warman (1979) examines the cost of relaying 'real time' information from a central control computer to individual bus stops. It suggests a capital cost of £3000 per bus stop display and an annual maintenance and running cost of £450 per year (1979 prices) per stop. Discounting the capital cost over a three-year period it would be necessary to have an average net increase of 36 passengers a day to cover the cost solely through additional fare revenue. This would be roughly equivalent to one extra passenger boarding each bus (say 20-minute frequency) arriving at the stop with the 'real time' display.

In the estimates given above no account has been taken of the generalized cost savings that might accrue to passengers through reducing the length of time spent waiting in the queue. This reduction would occur if people were able to use the period before the bus was due by pursuing some 'useful' activity. Generalized costs would also be reduced if the arrival pattern of the queue changed such that when long waits were predicted, some people opted for other means of travel, whereas when buses were about to arrive, other people were encouraged to wait who otherwise would not have waited. However, the validity of these calculations assumes knowledge on how displays would influence queue behaviour and whether justifiable monetary values can be placed on waiting time.

The above calculations suggest that it would feasible to imagine a sufficient increase in patronage to pay for the marginal costs of providing real time bus arrival indicators. As some bus operators have decided to invest in vehicle monitoring equipment for use solely to help manage their bus operations, it is felt justified not to include the total costs for installing and operating the vehicle monitoring system. However, it would be possible to

estimate the net increase in fare paying passengers required to pay
for the complete control system if bus stop information display was
its primary function.

6.   WHAT NEXT?

If 'real time' passenger information systems are developed, there is
no reason why the information should only be displayed at the bus
stop. It is conceivable that displays could be located where people
congregate, such as large shopping precincts, offices, or educational
establishments. Estimated bus arrival times would take account of
walking time to the nearest bus stop. If radio reception proves
acceptable, a personal receiver similar in size to a pocket calculator might be all that is needed for a person to check when a
particular bus service is due to arrive at a nearby stop.

Such proposals always raise more questions than the researcher
at present is able to answer. Will the bus system be able to cope
with the demand? Will the displays be vandal-proof? Are the factors
affecting the progress of buses along a traffic route sufficently
understood to make predictions? Will the predictions be sufficiently
accurate? What is the level of accuracy required for the public to
believe them? Will the bus crews want such systems to be developed?
The necessary technology has been developed during the 1970s and
these questions will require answers during the 1980s.

REFERENCES

Blood, B. *et al*. (1979) Automatic Vehicle Monitoring Systems.
       US Department of Transportation, Transportation Systems Center.
       Paper presented at the APTA Annual Meeting, New York, September.
Green, L.E.S. (1979) The Mississauga Transit Demonstration of the
       Automatic Bus Passenger Information Concept. Paper presented
       at the Automatic Vehicle Monitoring Symposium, Dublin, May.
Loehlin, J.C. (1959) The influence of different activities on the
       apparent length of time. *Psychological Monographs,* 73 (4).
Richards, B. (1976) *Moving in Cities*. London. Studio Vista, p. 88.
Warman, P.R. (1971) Time Wasted in Travel. Unpublished MSc Thesis,
       Imperial College of Science and Technology, London.
Warman, P.R. (1979) Exploratory research – public behaviour and
       attitudes at bus stops which would be influenced by real time
       information displays. Martin and Voorhees Associates,
       unpublished.
WYTCONSULT (1977) Methodology and detailed studies for medium and
       long term planning in the free standing towns, West Yorkshire
       Transportation Studies, Document 436.

The Distributional Effects
of Transport Decisions

In this section, the concepts of distribution and equity are
introduced. The first four papers report on empirical analyses of
the variations in expenditure on transport, and the spatial variations within the urban and the rural environment. The next two
papers cover some of the social problems with the definition of needs
and a welfare perspective on transport. The section concludes with a
paper which examines the contribution of the social services to
transport planning, and forms a link with the methodological issues
which are covered in part 2 of the book.

Susan Carpenter and Ian Heggie look at the distributional impact
of expenditure on transport. They conclude that transport spending
may well not grow in the future as in the past. They conclude further
that it is very difficult to measure the social impacts of transport
spending in any systematic way. It is true that higher-income households spend more on rail public transport but not on bus. But is not
certain that the poor benefit from public transport subsidies, because
of difficulties of measurement. In particular, the figures are
confused because they do not take proper account of variations in
household structure, numbers of employed adults and other factors.
For the future, analysis must be based on a much finer definition of
the household.

Derek Wagon's paper on changing markets for London Transport
describes methods of market analysis developed in recent years, and
uses them to analyse recent changes and future prospects. Overall,
population has fallen but car ownership levels have risen; the result
is that the numbers of cars in London has remained static while the
numbers living in non-car owning households are declining rapidly –
and this could continue in the early 1980s. The resulting changes in
trip patterns suggest that the traditional markets of London Transport will continue to decline but that – due primarily to the
increase in tourism – central area demand may well rise.

Malcolm Moseley's paper deals with patterns of accessibility and
inaccessibility in rural areas. It discusses ways of achieving the
three principal planning goals of low cost, high accessibility and

wide geographic coverage. It argues for an approach drawn from
developments in related urban research, with a new stress on the
study of the powerful decision-makers and the ways they had taken
their decisions - often in an ill-coordinated way, with objectives
other than accessibility in mind. The study should go beyond the
public sector to look at decision makers in the private sector and the
quasi-independent executive bodies.

Following on this, Poul-Ove Pedersen's paper assesses alternative
public transport systems for low-density rural areas, looking at both
direct and indirect consequences. Under the direct heading, it
considers costs, revenues and accessibility. Under the heading of
indirect consequences, it considers changed locations of activities,
resource costs and environmental effects. It concludes that so-
called demand-responsive travel models do not function very well in
many rural circumstances.

Writing as a philosopher, David Wiggins raises some difficult
and disturbing questions about the nature of the need for transport.
People's desires to move around may conflict with other objectives,
and there is no easy way of reconciling them. Revealed preferences -
a traditional assumption in transport planning - may be misleading,
and the total effect of incremental 'improvements' may be to produce
a state worse than previously. He proposes a rigorous definition of
'needs' and on that basis develops a list of basic needs.

Mary Benwell's paper looks at questions of access to activity,
need and welfare. It develops a theoretical structure based on
mobility, preferences and supply characteristics - of which the last
is the best developed and most familiar. In contrast, relatively
little is known about preferences and motivations. She suggests a
list of priorities for future research; the development of measurements
of accessibility and their relevance to behaviour, the improved understanding of constraints in mobility and the development of techniques
to determine preferences and perceptions of subjective need or demand
for access.

In the final paper, Kit Mitchell discusses some applications of
the social sciences to transport planning. Two in particular are at
the base of many people's concern about transport, yet they have been
as yet hardly researched: first, the extent to which people forego
activities because of problems of access; second, the ways in which
life-styles are affected (if at all) by transport availability.
Perhaps, Mitchell suggests, these may be topics not easily amenable to
quantitative research. He argues that there is a need for more study
of opportunities created or suppressed, or the values of activities
that are changed, as a result of transport changes - something that he
believes could be incorporated into travel surveys. He advocates an
approach to transport planning based on meeting objectives defined in
terms of accessibility. More conventionally, it would be a great
advance to be able to predict better the demand for transport in
relation to variations in policies - but this is difficult because
people are good at adapting to change.

The difficulties of identifying the distributional impacts of
transport are apparent, particularly as the available data are limited.
The problems are twofold; first we have to define the target groups
which may be affected by decisions, and secondly the impacts have to be
measured. Although research into these issues is being initiated,
there is considerable scope for further analyses which appreciate the

complexities of the problems, rather than studies which take accepted social groups, such as those based on one variable (for example income, car ownership). The conclusions reached often depend on the assumptions made, and they may only give a partial view of the whole picture.

In the paper dealing with London, the main topic of discussion is the 'uniqueness' of the Greater London conurbation. The problems specific to London include congestion, the trend towards the increased use of the small car and the taxi, and the institutional constraints on solutions. Additionally, there is the difficulty of forecasting whether the recent rapid changes - the decentralization of the population, and the changes in the urban and population structure - will continue. All these difficulties lead to an emphasis on incremental, short-term planning.

The problems of rural accessibility seem to centre on the relations between travel demand and the location of jobs and services. People might adapt in anticipation of a change rather than as a result of it: thus they might buy a second car before the bus service declines, and that might in fact lead to a decline. It seems difficult to investigate such issues through research: specific case studies could be used to monitor the effects of particular changes, but it might not be clear that a particular policy in one area has any application elsewhere. Perhaps, one answer lies in adopting an historical perspective and then looking at social and geographical change over time. But again, it is not entirely clear what conclusions ought to be drawn from a study of movement patterns - particularly since life-styles could adapt.

With more particular reference to public transport in rural areas, it seems clear from Danish work that for non-car-owners the choice lies between staying at home, taking rides in cars and using buses. If resources are used to increase bus services, then people might simply divert from going in other people's cars; they might also travel further to shops and other services, to the detriment of local services and of possible long-term accessibility overall. But a change in transport facilities could only be marginal, and what is finally important is the whole relationship between people and the services they need.

The definition and the measurement of needs have always raised many questions. Should needs be based on the planner's judgement, or on some survey base? Are the expectations of individuals fixed? Do needs change over time? Can needs be identified in terms of the response of individuals to changes in transport services? Alternatively, can they be defined in terms of the set of opportunities to which some fixed proportion of the population has access? Would it be possible to ask local communities to vote resources for improving public transport? Is is possible to avoid an explicit statement of what is meant by transport needs?

A further theme concerns the role of different kinds of institutions in transport research. Government centres such as the Transport and Road Research Laboratory (TRRL) are mainly concerned with either descriptive social research that could influence policy in the medium to long term, plus specific attempts to answer questions of interest to government. University researchers on the other hand are more concerned with innovative research including social and welfare objectives, and with theoretical or speculative longer-term research.

Consultant research is mainly concerned with large-scale survey work, together with the application of fairly well-tried analyses. In each case different institutions are best suited for particular types of research and their functions are complementary. These points are again returned to in the conclusions to the book.

The distributional effect of transport expenditure

SUSAN CARPENTER and IAN HEGGIE

The main issue discussed in this paper is who benefits, by how much and at whose expense. This raises two fundamental questions. First, how do we define those people who are affected by changes in expenditure on transport and secondly, in what way do we measure the distributional impacts on these people?

1. PROBLEM DEFINITION

Defining those involved
Conventionally we tend to talk in terms of the temporal, spatial and social impacts of transport expenditures and we measure their incidence in terms of their effect on different households, usually classified by household income. But as we hope to show during the course of this discussion, this definition based on households is often ambiguous and leaves a great deal to be desired. The following analysis concentrates on temporal and social effects.

Measuring distributional impacts
Which measures are we to use to record the impacts of transport expenditure? This is a more straightforward issue, but is not without its pitfalls. We are here referring to benefits which may well appear as one of three distinct types:
  (a) reduced expenditure (for example reduced vehicle operating costs);
  (b) increased income in kind (for example savings in travel time);
  (c) increased opportunities (for example a new road for those with access to a car or the provision of a new out-of-town shopping centre).
  The first two effects are relatively straightforward, given the problem of marginal tax rates which always tend to bias benefits at the margin. The third is more intractable because there is no well-established way of discovering the equivalence between £x of financial benefit/the value of a car, or of its unrestricted use/the value of a new road opening up the possibility of new consumption activities

159

(whether realized or not). In the present context however it is
intended to set these problems aside and to concentrate on the key
questions of who loses and who gains. Let us start with the conventional wisdom on this subject.

2. TEMPORAL EFFECTS

It is commonly assumed that transport expenditure is growing and will
continue to do so in absolute terms and as a proportion of total
expenditure. The clearest manifestation of this belief is seen in
car-ownership forecasts which always continue to point upwards no
matter how often they are revised nor how much running costs are
assumed to increase. But will car ownership and use continue to
increase, implying indefinite growth in car traffic and the demand for
new roads? The facts are illustrated in table 1. From 1968 to 1972,
household expenditure on travel increased in real terms at about 4 per
cent p.a., and then decreased at a slightly faster rate until 1976.
The trend for the last three years is still unclear. However, the proportion of household expenditure spent on travel remained fairly
stable across the whole period. Variation in expenditure appears to
be correlated with income, so slower growth in income will lead to a
reduced rate of growth in demand for travel and increased road space.

There are several reasons for the reduction in expenditure on
transport from 1972. First, there was the energy crisis in 1973 which
made people more aware of the need to economize on fuel and this was
accompanied by an increase in real prices. The underlying pattern of
land use had also changed considerably with the growth of suburban
housing and changes in the retail sector. These had more or less
worked themselves out by the early 1970s so that the pressure to
increase travel expenditure had been diminished. Finally, the higher
cost of travel was made more acute by the lower growth and, in some
years, the decrease in personal income which started to show itself
from 1975 onwards.

It is interesting to note how the years 1972/73 were a key. They
represented the turning point in increased fuel prices and, most
importantly, they signalled a halt to the rapid changes in land use
which had been a common phenomenon during the later 1950s and 1960s.

It could be argued that increasing company support for travel has
resulted in a decrease in household travel expenditure. Figure 1
suggests that this is not the case, at least with respect to expenditure on motoring. There has indeed been a substantial increase in
company expenditure on motoring since 1975, but the level of household motoring expenditure from 1976 is more likely to be due to the
decrease in personal disposable income, rather than an indication of
a substitution effect.

3. SOCIAL EFFECTS

These have received more attention than the purely temporal effects.
There are two principal sources of analysis on this subject. The
first is Webster (1977) in his Transport and Road Research Laboratory
report on the future of bus travel, the second is the 1976 Green Paper
(Department of the Environment 1976) which had a special appendix
chapter devoted to the distributional impact of transport expenditure
(volume 2, paper 2). The Webster thesis is illustrated in figure 2.

Table 1. Household expenditure on transport (average £/week at 1970 prices).

	1968	1969	1970	1971	1972	1973	1974	1975	1976	1977	1978
All household expenditure	27.98	27.82	28.58	28.32	29.90	30.81	31.06	29.60	28.71	28.85	29.77
All travel and transport	3.67	3.89	3.91	3.89	4.24	4.20	4.17	4.09	3.79	3.90	4.04
Net purchase of motor vehicles, spares and accessories	1.37	1.44	1.38	1.41	1.67	1.66	1.39	1.36	1.23	1.35	1.48
Maintenance and running of motor vehicles	1.51	1.61	1.64	1.58	1.67	1.70	1.94	1.91	1.75	1.80	1.74
Rail fares	0.16	0.17	0.20	0.18	0.19	0.19	0.18	0.19	0.18	0.18	0.19
Road public transport fares	0.44	0.41	0.43	0.45	0.43	0.39	0.34	0.34	0.36	0.33	0.33
Percentage of household expenditure on travel and transport	13.1	14.0	13.7	13.7	14.2	13.6	13.4	13.8	13.2	13.5	13.6

Source: Department of Employment (1979) and Annual Abstract of Statistics (1979).

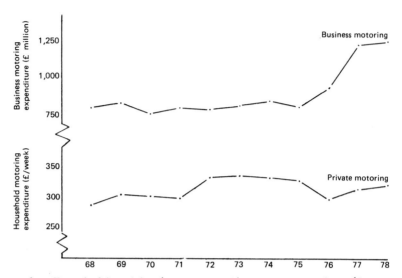

Figure 1. Household and business expenditure on motoring. (Sources: Department of Employment (1979) and Transport Statistics 1968-78.)

He interprets this in the following terms '... using data from the national travel survey, it was found that, for households with no car available, the higher the household income the more bus trips were made ... Some of the effect may be due to the fact that higher-income households tend to have more workers in them...'.

It is interesting to see in figure 2 the wide variation in this pattern between households with no cars (where the Webster trend is most obvious), households with one car and those with two or more cars. In the latter case the trend is almost non-existent with the bus trips per person per week remaining relatively constant across a wide range of income. This points to a major difficulty with this type of analysis. Income is highly correlated both with age and with household size. Webster rightly recognized the importance of this latter factor. It tends to be the case that the low-income households are those consisting of retired persons or young people who have only just started work, whilst the high-income households tend to be households in which there are several employed adults. The varying proportion of such households in any sample could clearly lead to quite a significant bias. This will be most acute in the case of those households with no cars. This group will include a large number of elderly persons, many young people who are only just starting off on their working career and large, poorer households. This will be less true in the case of one-car households and households with two or more cars. These households will tend to be far more homogeneous as a sample and this is reflected in the fact that the variation across income is very much less than it is with the heterogeneous group which comprises the households with no cars.

Moving on to the Green Paper, table 2 shows that the use of stage bus services is fairly evenly spread across households, although it increases slightly as income rises. A rather different picture

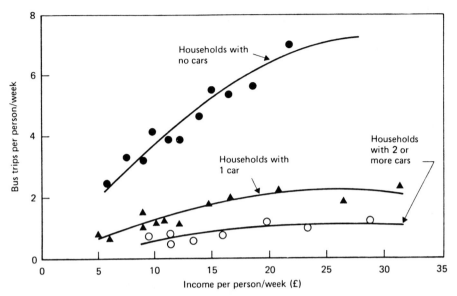

Figure 2.   Effect of income on trip-making by bus.   (Source: Webster (1977).)

emerges when car ownership is taken into account.   Expenditure on bus travel increases with income for both car owning and non-car owning households.

Table 2.   Expenditure propensities for bus travel.

Adjusted household income group	% of non-OAP households in each group	Expenditure propensities*		
		non-car owning households	car owning households	all households
1	14	1.20	0.25	0.95
2	16	1.33	0.57	1.06
3	23	1.70	0.64	1.04
4	23	1.88	0.73	1.22
5	24	2.00	0.58	0.75

* Expenditure propensities are derived by dividing the percentage share of expenditure by the proportion of households in each income group.

Source: Department of the Environment (1976, volume 2).

The procedure used in the Green Paper analysis adjusts household income to reflect the number and ages of children, and excludes old age pensioners.   However, it does not allow for different levels of employment within households in the same income category.   Therefore, as recognized in the Green Paper, many of the results may be due to the varying structure between the households.

What if household structure is included in the analysis? Let us
now examine some of the graphs prepared from the Family Expenditure
Survey, adjusting as far as possible for differences in household
structure.

The first problem is that of correlation: household income is
highly correlated with the number of employed persons. This is
clearly shown in figure 3. In order to disentangle the various causal
processes one must prepare special tabulations which control for
household structure and the number of employed persons. Indeed, the
ideal classification is to have a given household, say husband and
wife and two children, with a given number of employed persons. This
unit is then compared across various categories of income where variations in income reflect changes in the wealth of the standard
household rather than variations in the structure of the household and
number of employed persons.

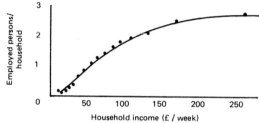

Figure 3. Household employment and income. (Source: Department of
Employment (1977).)

What if we then allow for variations in the household structure
as systematically as is possible from published tables in the Family
Expenditure Survey? Appreciable changes in expenditure patterns emerge
if income per employed adult (figure 4) is used instead of gross
household income (figure 5). The use of the former variable allows
for differences in household employment structure, and may be seen as
a proxy for the stage in the family life-cycle. In households with
children, those with a low level of income per employed adult are
mainly younger families with pre-school or school children, where the
wife (or secondary worker) has not returned to work. Households with
a high adjusted income per employed adult are generally older
families, where the secondary worker has a full-time or part-time job,
and there are also young people under 18 who are employed and still
living at home. The importance of the family life-cycle variable has
been demonstrated in an analysis of the National Travel Survey by the
Department of Transport (Hayfield 1978).

Referring to the figures, various distinctive patterns emerge:

(a) Figure 4 shows that as levels of employment and income rise, the
rate of increase in expenditure on transport is the same for Groups I
and II, i.e. households without children. Expenditure on travel
increases more rapidly when children are present. The people who
benefit from general transport subsidies are therefore those in households with one or more children, with high levels of employment and a
high household income per employed adult. Thus they do not correspond
to the conventional definition of 'poor' households.

(b) Expenditure on bus and coach travel increases with household size (figure 6). However, there is no obvious relationship between expenditure and adjusted income, although less is spent in the highest adjusted income bracket. This finding suggests that households of the same structure make a more or less fixed outlay on bus travel, and consequently, that subsidies, particularly in the form of general revenue support, may benefit all income groups equally.

(c) With car users (figure 7) expenditure increases with income. The low level of expenditure in single person households (Group I) reflects the low level of car ownership in this group.

(d) There is an even stronger correlation between adjusted income and expenditure on rail fares (figure 8). The presence of children leads to a lower level of expenditure than in two person households.

(e) In terms of the socio-economic group of the household, as measured by the occupation of the household head (figure 9), the only trend appears to be that the lower rate of increase in expenditure of self-employed households may be partly due to the receipt of business expenses for travelling.

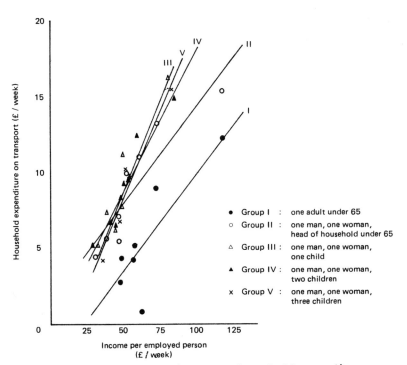

Figure 4. Effect of adjusted income on household expenditure on transport. (Source: Department of Employment (1977).)

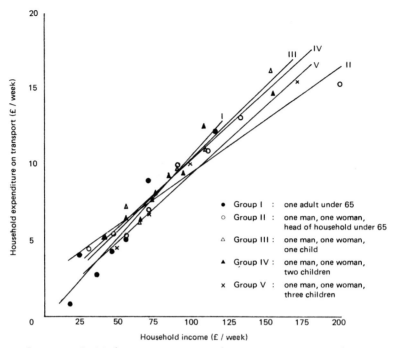

Figure 5. Household income and expenditure on transport (Source: Department of Employment (1977).)

4. CONCLUSIONS

In conclusion one can draw out a number of important themes. First, the idea that transport expenditure, and thus travel, will continue to grow in the future in the way that it did in the 1960s is not borne out by the figures. It is also interesting that the most recent National Travel Survey shows an increase in trip rates of only about 2 per cent between 1972/3 and 1975/6. This was accompanied by an increase of about one-third in trips of less than two miles, but a reduction of about 10 per cent in trips of between two and ten miles (Department of Transport 1979). Secondly, it is immensely difficult to measure the social impact of transport expenditure in any systematic way. When differences in household size and levels of employment are taken into account, the conventional wisdom which implies that high-income households spend more on public transport is confirmed for travel by railway, but not for bus and coach travel. The assumption that the poor benefit from public transport subsidies is likewise not as straightforward as it seems. The conventional wisdom seems to fall down for the following reasons:

(a) The classification of households does not allow effectively for differences in household structure, or more to the point, for stages in the family life-cycle,

(b) There is insufficient allowance made for the number of employed

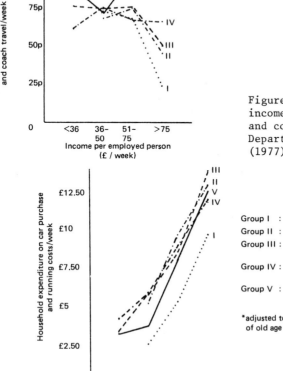

Figure 6. Adjusted household income and expenditure on bus and coach travel (Source: Department of Employment (1977).)

Group I   :   one adult*

Group II   :   one man, one woman*

Group III :   one man, one woman, one child

Group IV :   one man, one woman, two children

Group V   :   one man, one woman, three children

*adjusted to account for high incidence of old age pensioners

Figure 7. Adjusted household income and expenditure on motoring. (Souce: Department of Employment (1977).)

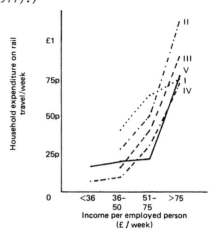

Figure 8. Adjusted household income and expenditure on rail fares. (Source: Department of Employment (1977).)

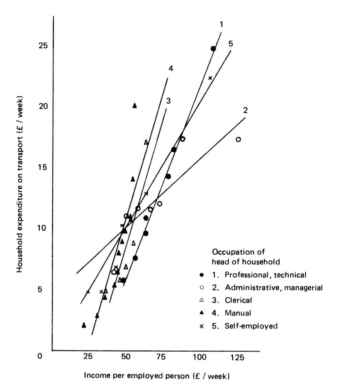

Figure 9. Effect of adjusted income and occupation of household head on household expenditure on transport. (Source: Department of Employment (1977).)

adults, whether this be husband and wife or grown-up children, and their effect on household income, however this is measured.

(c) The tabulations are often confused by the incidence of old age pensioners. The Webster diagram shows this quite clearly, and one would expect the varying incidence of OAPs in different income groups to distort quite badly the relationship between income and transport expenditure.

The general conclusion is thus that the analysis of transport expenditure must be based on a much finer definition of the household so that differences in patterns of travel can be associated more specifically with changes in richness or poorness rather than being confounded by variations in household structure, number of employed adults, and a number of other factors as well.

NOTE

This paper was written by Susan Carpenter, based on notes and diagrams from the verbal presentation given to the SSRC seminar by Ian Heggie.

REFERENCES

Department of Employment (1977, 1979) *Family Expenditure Survey 1976,
    1978*. London: HMSO.
Department of the Environment (1976) *Transport Policy: a Consultation
    Document*. London: HMSO.
Department of Transport (1979) *National Travel Survey 1975/6 Report*.
    London: HMSO.
Hayfield, C. (1978) *The Travel Patterns of Family Structure Groups*.
    Department of Transport, unpublished.
Webster, F.V. (1977) Urban Passenger Transport: Some Trends and
    Prospects. Transport and Road Research Laboratory, LR 771.

London's changing transport markets

DEREK WAGON

1. MARKET ORIENTATION

No product can be sold effectively without an understanding of its
market. This is as true for the sale of public transport seat miles
as it is for the sale of cosmetics or soap powder. Indeed, in one
sense it is much more critical. For more durable products the costs
of misunderstanding may merely involve short-term misallocation –
excess stocks in one place, shortage in another. Public transport
seat miles are, however, an immediately perishable good. If a seat
mile is not bought – it never can be. Failure to understand markets
and to respond sensitively to their changing needs can accordingly
lead to low sales and low average load factors. Thus the need for
strong market orientation is evident.

Such a market orientation is not, of course, new to public transport. However, during recent years when car-ownership levels have
been increasing and public transport's stable markets have been
declining, the accusation of being production oriented rather than
market oriented could be made with some justification. During this
period of contraction the emphasis tended to be on service economies
to match budgets which automatically lead to a production orientation.
More recently, however, the objectives of public transport organizations are beginning to be expressed more in terms of maximizing
patronage within budget constraints. In this situation it becomes
crucially important to understand the markets within which public
transport operates and the way in which these markets change with
time.

An important feature of this understanding is that it must cover
the whole of the travel picture – car, bus, rail and even walk – and
must include an awareness of the sensitivity of markets to policy
changes. Finally, it must embrace the longer-term trends which are
underlying service catchment areas. Thus, in London, the decline of
the more stable captive commuting markets, arising jointly from the
decreasing population and increasing car ownership, will inevitably
imply a tendency for markets to become more sensitive. The operators
response to this must be to ensure that service quality remains high
and that they vigorously market the products they are trying to sell.

2. ANALYSIS METHODS

In this paper on London's changing passenger transport markets an
attempt will be made to describe:
- (a) the present share of markets between modes;
- (b) the changing structure of London, its population,
       employment, car ownership etc.;
- (c) the sensitivity of markets to alternative policies;
- (d) the next few years.

This is a formidable list of topic areas and it cannot be claimed
that we have a complete understanding of the present structure of our
markets let alone their future composition. However, techniques of
market analysis have advanced a long way in the last ten years and it
is now possible to paint a much clearer canvas. So far as transport
statistics in London are concerned, we are perhaps fortunate in that
an extensive data source exists in the Greater London Transportation
Study undertaken in 1971/72. However, such sources do not of themselves provide all the answers we need. The data have first to be
aggregated into sensible units which, on the one hand, are not too
large to obscure important differences but, on the other hand are not
too small to be subject to random fluctuations. Thus the approach to
statistics has to be imaginative and flexible and different decisions
will have different data needs.

However, perhaps more important than the statistics themselves is
an understanding of the factors that are influencing our travel
markets. Thus we require a dynamic picture of what is going on - not
a static one. The data we have available are based in 1971/72 and
are really only a snapshot of the travel situation. What has changed
since then? Certainly the population of London has declined. Car
ownership on the other hand has increased. Inflation has meant that
the price of goods, including public transport fares, has more than
doubled. In London, the relativity of bus and rail fares has altered
a great deal. So where, after all this, is our photograph of travel
patterns taken back in 1971? How useful is it to us? The answer is
that, on its own, it is not too useful. It also happens to be an
extremely expensive photograph to take - more than £1 million at 1971
prices - and a lot more analysis undertaken since then. So we cannot
afford to use this particular camera too often. What we need therefore are ways of turning this static picture into a dynamic and
changing description of what is going on.

To achieve this understanding a synthesis of two different
approaches is required. The first approach is based upon the methods
that have been used in the many land use-transportation studies that
have been undertaken throughout the United Kingdom over the last ten
to twelve years. The other is based upon econometric studies of the
factors affecting London Transport's (LT) receipts and passenger
miles. The former methods allow a detailed picture to be drawn of the
travel choices that confront people and the way in which they make
decisions. The latter methods, on the other hand, gain in that they
measure directly the effect of changes and thus, for example, the
effect of a fares increase or a service level change can be measured
rather than inferred.

In London Transport a computer program (The Scenario Model) has
been developed which is a synthesis of these two approaches. It takes
as its starting point a description of the market shares as they were

in 1971, broken down by mode of travel, journey purpose and distance travelled. These market shares are then rolled forward from year to year adjusting them to allow for the effects of population change, car-ownership increases etc., and also for other factors that will have influenced travel patterns such as fares, service levels, etc. These latter adjustments are made using the 'models' of peoples' choice of mode which were developed in land use-transportation studies. Once this system has been developed, it is then possible to use it to see how well it estimates travel pattern changes since 1971. As a result a direct comparison can be made with the actual changes which have occurred. Further 'calibration' can then be undertaken to tune the model to give the best fit. When all of this had been done the model gave a good representation of the changing markets (Fairhurst *et al*. 1977). The results quoted in the following sections of this paper have used this analysis method to define the changing travel markets of London.

3. LONDON 1978

The table below indicates in broad terms the current shares of London's transport markets between the available motorized modes of travel. Excluded from this table is any mention of walking trips – simply because the problems of definition result in some of the data being suspect. The forecasting model itself, however, includes walking trips because, for a lot of journeys, they are an important option.

Table 1.   1978 trip patterns (million trips per annum).

	Car	Taxi	Bus	LT rail	BR rail	Total
Central	86(17%) 2.7	94(18%) 1.4	127(25%) 1.2	205(40%) 2.0	2(-) –	514(100%) 1.8
Radial	162(23%) 6.9	10(1%) 2.1	174(24%) 2.6	211(29%) 7.7	159(22%) 10.2	716(100%) 6.8
Suburban	2527(68%) 3.1		979(26%) 1.8	105(3%) 4.6	98(3%) 4.6	3708(100%) 2.8
Totals	2879(58%) 3.2		1280(26%) 1.8	521(11%) 4.9	259(5%) 8.3	4939(100%) 3.3

Percentage figures in brackets refer to modal shares. Figures below main numbers refer to average journey length in miles.

Central trips are defined to be all of those which remain completely within an area approximately bounded by the Circle Line. The map (figure 1) shows the extent of this area. As there is a tendency to think of London's transport problems in terms of the Central Area alone, it is worth noting that some 75 per cent of all trips occur wholly outside this area. Within the centre the largest market is LT rail (40 per cent) with bus carrying only some 25 per cent. Cars and taxis with their low average loads carry some 35 per cent shared in approximately equal proportions. One important feature of the Central Area is that the average journey lengths are

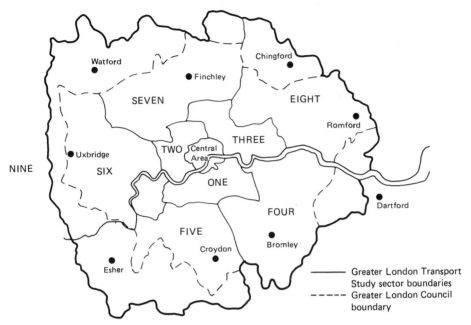

Figure 1.   The Central Area and The GLTS sectors

all relatively short, and perhaps more important are similar to each other. This represents *prima facie* evidence of significant competition between the modes, the most obvious example of this being the competition between taxi and bus with average journey lengths of 1.4 and 1.2 miles respectively. It is also of note that there is less evidence of competition between LT rail and bus, where journey lengths are significantly different.

The radial market is defined as all those trips which begin or end in the Central Area, but are not wholly contained within it. Thus, this market is dominated by the highly tidal commuting patterns. For these trips, table 1 indicates that there are remarkably equal shares between the modes, although it must be noted here that the figures are a little misleading as British Railways trips from outside the Greater London Council boundary are excluded. Onward journeys from the London rail termini are, however, included in the Central Area statistics. Perhaps the most significant feature of the radial market concerns the wide disparity in average journey lengths. These range from the relatively short journeys of bus and taxi of between 2 and 3 miles, up to BR rail trips which, even when non-GLC residents are excluded, average 10.2 miles in length.

The suburban market consists of all the remaining trips which at no point cross the Central Area boundary. Of these 68 per cent are undertaken by car and 26 per cent by bus, leaving only a mere six per cent to be carried by the rail modes. Clearly the only significant public transport penetration into the suburban market is therefore that of the buses. Another point of interest is that some 77 per cent

of total bus trips are wholly contained in this suburban area.   The
average journey length of bus and car trips appear different but these
averages may well be concealing a significant overlap.   Thus, undoubtedly, there is a degree of competition between the two modes in
serving suburban town centres, for example.

In table 2 the market shares of each of the modes are cross referenced according to the journey purpose of the trips involved.   The
figure in the top right hand corner of each square represents the
market share by mode for each journey purpose whereas the figure in
the lower corner indicates the journey purpose composition of each
mode.

Table 2.   Market shares by journey purpose (based on number of trips
made).

	Car	Taxi	Bus	LT rail	BR rail	Total
Journeys to and during work (share)	45%	0%	28%	15%	11%	100%
Journeys to and during work (composition)	24%	1%	32%	41%	64%	29%
Adult non-work (share)	68%	1%	21%	8%	3%	100%
Adult non-work (composition)	58%	23%	39%	34%	23%	48%
Tourist (share)	0%	32%	23%	44%	2%	100%
Tourist (composition)	0%	75%	4%	20%	2%	5%
Senior Citizens (share)	36%	0%	54%	4%	6%	100%
Senior Citizens (composition)	5%	1%	15%	3%	9%	7%
Children (share)	74%	0%	23%	1%	1%	100%
Children (composition)	13%	0%	9%	1%	2%	10%
Total (share)	56%	2%	26%	11%	5%	100%
Total (composition)	100%	100%	100%	100%	100%	

Journey purpose composition for each mode	Market share by mode for each journey purpose

From this it is evident that the major proportion of car use is for non-work purposes, whilst for public transport the work purpose is more important. Public transport penetrations are high in the tourist market, where rail achieves 44 per cent and taxi 32 per cent. For senior citizens the bus achieves the highest market penetration of 54 per cent. Elsewhere car achieves much the largest share – even for the work journey which is traditionally viewed to be public transport's main market. Here the dominance of the car (with a share of 46 per cent) arises from the very high car usage in the suburbs. No doubt this result would be very different if the radial market were isolated. The same point arises for LT rail trips. Here the journey to work proportion, at 41 per cent appears low. However, in the radial market the proportion rises to 58 per cent, and would be even higher in the peak.

4. LONDON CHANGES: 1971 to 1984

Before looking at the changes in travel patterns that are occurring in London, it is worth first considering the underlying changes that are taking place to London itself.

The first such change is population. Since 1972 this has decreased by 7 per cent over London as a whole, but for the Inner London boroughs the decline has been over 11 per cent. Associated with this has been some surprising changes in the population mix. Perhaps the most surprising is that the number of children (0 to 13 years old) has dropped by 13 per cent overall, and by 20 per cent in Inner London. Senior citizens (defined as those over 65) have declined by much less – about 2 per cent over London as a whole.

The next important change to consider is that of car ownership. Between 1972 and 1978 the proportion of people living in car-owning households rose from 59.5 to 64 per cent. Taken in conjunction with the decline in population, however, this has resulted in the number of people in car-owning households remaining virtually constant – a finding which is at variance with some of the more sensational reports made by transport experts! However, before environmentalists, and public transport operators in particular, rejoice at this minimal increase in car use, we should also remember that the corollary of this is that the number of non-car-owning families has dropped very steeply – in fact by some 18 per cent throughout London. The implication of this is that the market which is usually assumed to be 'captive' to public transport is declining very rapidly. In practice, of course, the 'captive' public transport market is wider than this. It includes for example, all those who do not necessarily have access to the family car, even if the household itself owns one. However, here again, the declining population of children in London, and the increasing likelihood of households owning more than one car, all suggest that even if the definition is widened, nevertheless the 'captive' public transport market is still declining rapidly. This particular feature of the changing character of London needs to be quantified further and more research undertaken into the changing composition of households and their related car-ownership patterns.

Looking now to the next five years, it is likely that the downward trends in population will continue although the latest GLC forecasts suggest that this will be at a moderated rate. Such forecasts are subject to quite wide uncertainties given the difficulty in estimating

future fertility and migration rates. However, the present work
assumes that by 1984 the population will have declined by 7 per cent
over London as a whole, and 10 per cent in Inner London. Once again
it is the child population that is likely to fall most steeply.
However, this particular decline is likely to moderate by the end of
the period as the proportion of women of child bearing age rises
again.

The proportion of the population living in car-owning households
will also continue to rise from 64 per cent to a figure of nearer
68 per cent. However, once again, given the declining population, the
total number of car-owning families will remain virtually constant or
at worst increase by about 1 per cent. However, once again the proportion of non-car-owning households will drop dramatically (by 15
per cent) making a decline over the period (1971 to 1984) of some 30
per cent. Another interesting feature concerning non-car-owning
households is that their composition is changing with the changing
structure of population. In 1972 only some 32 per cent of car-owning
households were senior citizens, by 1978 it was about 38 per cent,
and by 1984 it will be nearer 42 per cent. Over the same period the
number of children in non-car-owning households will drop by about 50
per cent. Thus, the captive public transport market will be more and
more dominated by the aged — a fact which clearly should have implications for the pattern of services and indeed for the design of buses.

The other major change in London to be considered concerns the
changing pattern of employment. Between 1972 and 1978 this declined
reasonably uniformly throughout London by 6 to 7 per cent. However,
within this there were significant compositional changes. The most
important of these concerned the decline of manufacturing employment
from Inner London areas which was partly replaced by new office
employment. Over the next five years the pattern is likely to be much
the same with a further decline of some 6 to 7 per cent.

5. THE CHANGING PATTERN OF TRANSPORT MARKETS 1971 TO 1978

Between 1971 and 1978 patronage (measured in terms of passenger miles)
dropped by 19 per cent on the Underground and by 4 per cent on buses.
However, before jumping to conclusions concerning the decline of these
markets, a number of factors have to be taken into account which have
given rise to the specific changes noted over this period. A list of
the factors to identify would include:
    (a)   the effect of population changes;
    (b)   the effect of employment changes;
    (c)   car-ownership changes;
    (d)   real income changes;
    (e)   changes in bus and rail fares and their relativities;
    (f)   the increasing attractiveness of London as a tourist centre;
    (g)   free travel for senior citizens.
The change in the first three factors has been described in the
previous section, and it is relatively easy, using the Scenario Model,
to take account of the effect of these changes. Over the period
1971-78 real incomes only changed marginally and, therefore, had
relatively little effect on trip making. A much more important
determinant of the pattern of travel was the change in the relative
bus and rail fares over the period. For a variety of reasons, some of
which will be discussed in the next section, rail fares were increased

more than bus fares over this period, and as a result there was a
significant diversion of travel from the LT rail system to the bus
system. In fact if the effect of such changes is removed then it is
likely that the underlying trend on bus services lies somewhere
between −1 and −2 per cent per annum whereas on rail services it is
virtually zero.

Using the Scenario Model the change in trip making between 1971
and 1978 can be summarized in table 3.

Table 3. Percentage change in trips 1971-78

	Car	Taxi	Bus	LT rail	BR rail	Total
Central	−3.6	+24.4	−3.7	−2.4	−	+0.9
Radial	−1.8	+25.0	−4.5	−16.1	−14.5	−9.5
Suburban		−1.8	−4.9	−24.8	−20.7	−3.1
Total		0.0	−4.8	−13.3	−16.7	−2.7

From this it is evident that the suburban sector has experienced a
substantial decline in public transport usage − particularly on the
railways (although this is a decline in an already small market). In
the Central Area, however, both bus and rail demands have remained
much more buoyant − a feature which arises principally as a result of
the effect of tourism. However, perhaps more important than this is
the increasing use of taxis over the period. The market share of
taxis (18 per cent) in the Central Area is now beginning to get
significantly nearer to that of the bus services (25 per cent). This
increase in taxi usage has arisen primarily as a result of the
increases in tourism.

Before going any further it is perhaps worth saying a little more
about the increase in tourism. Between 1971 and 1977 the number of
nights which overseas tourists spent in London increased from 45m to
61m. UK tourists on the other hand have remained virtually constant
in number. The effect that this increase in tourism has had upon LT's
receipts has been the subject of some debate, however, it is currently
estimated that tourist expenditure on ordinary tickets has risen from
£16m in 1971 to approximately £41m in 1978. On top of this an extra
£4m is now collected from the sale of Go-As-You-Please tickets. The
main impact of all this growth has been in the Central Area and the
average journey lengths involved are quite short. As a result the
effect on total passenger miles has been relatively low (+3 per cent
on the LT rail +1 per cent on buses).

6. THE SENSITIVITY OF TRANSPORT MARKETS

Having looked a little at the changes in trip making that have
occurred over recent years, it is now useful to see how sensitive
transport markets are to change. In order to explore this area
further, two concepts are useful:
1. Elasticity − this is a term much loved of economists which
expresses the ratio of the percentage change in one variable to
another. Thus a fares elasticity of −0.3 would imply that for every

10 per cent increase in fares there is a patronage loss of 3 per cent.
2. Gearing - this is a concept used to indicate the extent to which
a company's sales are dependent upon a few of their customers. Thus,
if 50 per cent of sales go to 2 per cent of customers, then that
particular firm is very sensitive, and indeed vulnerable, to the
behaviour of that 2 per cent of customers.

Of the two concepts elasticity is the more basic. No matter how
high the gearing is, if the elasticity is low - i.e. customers are
committed to use the product and are unlikely to change - then the
markets are not vulnerable in the short term. If, however, both
elasticities and gearing are quite high we may have a problem. Here
again, however, the seriousness of the problem will depend upon the
exact circumstances. Indeed, it is quite possible that a sensitive
market is one which if properly marketed will yield more sales than a
stable market. Thus, the 'problem' of vulnerability can also turn out
to be an opportunity.

The study of elasticities is essentially one of understanding how
sensitive our markets are to change, and as such the most direct way
of measuring them is to analyse how total receipts or passenger miles
have varied from week to week. Such figures are, however, inevitably
subject to large variation due to seasonal and other factors. The
starting point in the analysis is therefore to remove the influence of
such factors. This has been done in London Transport by undertaking
an analysis based upon comparing one week's receipts with those of a
year previously. Having done this it is possible to perform analyses
which allow us to isolate the effects in which we are most interested.
The techniques are, however, complex and will not be described here
(Rendle, Mack and Fairhurst 1978). However, some of the results will
be described below.

Fares elasticity

	Bus	Rail
Peak	−0.27	−0.10
Off-peak	−0.37	−0.25
Average	−0.33	−0.16

These results indicate clearly that the off-peak bus market is
the most sensitive and the peak rail market the least. More generally
it is perhaps saying that the off-peak market as a whole is more
sensitive to fares policy, since during these times passengers have
more discretion whether to travel or not. During the peak, however,
the dominance of the journey to work suggests that in the short term
at any rate the market is much more stable. The less sensitive nature
of the rail market is probably also accounted for by the longer
average journey lengths involved. Thus, on longer trips there are
fewer options for choice. Conversely we also know that the highest
elasticity market of all is that for short distance bus trips where
the walking mode is an obvious alternative.

The above analysis shows some of the reasons why rail fares have
been increased more than bus fares at recent revisions. However, such
changes did bring to light the sensitivity of our market to transfers
between rail and bus. Thus for every 1 per cent change in rail fares
over and above bus fares a 0.2 per cent transfer of rail patronage to

bus was noted.

Service elasticities

It is also possible to measure in the same way the effect of a 1 per cent increase or decrease in service levels. The results, however, are much more variable and depend upon the way in which the service level change comes about. Thus, if it arises as a result of a schedule change the results are quite different than if the mileage is lost due to, for example, staff shortage. However, we believe that a 1 per cent increase in bus miles arising from a scheduled change increases our receipts by between 0.1 and 0.4 per cent. If, however, it arises as a result of a drop in lost mileage then it is believed that the increase in receipts lies between 0.2 and 0.5 per cent. Whereabouts it actually lies in these ranges depends mainly upon the frequency of the services.

Inflation and wage increases

Over the last few years the effects of inflation upon receipts have been very significant. It is important, however, to distinguish carefully the components of the changes that have occurred. Thus, if wages and prices rise together it is likely that patterns of expenditure will remain the same. Hence, people will continue to buy washing machines, go to Spain for their holidays, and use public transport to the same extent. The corollary of this is that if fares are held constant during a period of inflation, then this is equivalent to an effective fares decrease. Thus, one might expect that at constant fares a 1 per cent increase in level of inflation would lead to approximately a 0.3 per cent increase in trips. This indeed is precisely the result that the analysis described above had identified.

The effect of wage increases, however, when they are not in line with inflation, that is real incomes either rise or fall, is not so easy to establish. However, results do tentatively suggest that a 1 per cent increase in wages over and above the general level of inflation leads to a 0.6 per cent increase in rail usage and a 0.1 per cent increase in bus usage. Thus, levels of expenditure on public transport do indeed rise, but they rise less in proportionate terms than expenditure on other commodities.

Remaining trends

Once all the above factors have been taken into account, there remains the effects of all the other factors which are affecting London, many of which have been described earlier in this paper (e.g. population change, car-ownership levels etc.). Results suggest that this underlying trend is between -1 and -2 per cent on the buses, and more or less zero on the rail services. This is an important difference and one which it is important we should be able to explain - perhaps a little better than we can at the moment. It is likely to arise from the continuing shift in population from the Inner London boroughs to the Outer London boroughs giving rise to longer journey lengths. It also arises as a result of increased car ownership in the suburban markets which, so far as public transport is concerned, are dominated by bus usage. Finally, over recent years, the stability of the rail market has arisen in large part from the increase in tourism concentrated in the Central Area.

Moving on now to the 'gearing' concept it must be conceded that this is one which has not yet been researched in depth, but it does

contain some intriguing possibilities. Some recent consultancy work
done for London Transport Executive (Shires 1978) has compared the
characteristics of bus and rail users with those of the population as
a whole. More important perhaps it has started to identify those
sections of the population which make the most intensive use of LT's
services. It notes, for example, that 16 to 34 year olds represent
only some 20 per cent of the population, but they account for more
than 70 per cent of Underground trips and about 30 per cent of bus
trips. This could be taken as *prima facie* evidence that the LT rail
market is vulnerable to the behaviour of this particular group of the
population.

However, before taking the analysis too far, it should be noted
that the concept of 'gearing' is not quite the same as that used by
other undertakings. Normally, it is the proportion of sales that are
accounted for by a relatively small proportion of customers that is
used. In this case, we are assuming that the whole population of
London can be considered our customers. However, it is evident that
public transport services have over the years grown up to serve very
specific needs. Thus the rail market is highly radially oriented and
the LT rail system itself covers by no means all of London. Thus,
one of the reasons for the high gearing of rail users may be that it
specifically provides services for this particular section of the
community. In this way, one could argue that the existence of a high
gearing is an indication of the way in which services have been
tailored to meeting the needs of the community over the years.

Indeed, all the previous analyses have suggested that in elasticity terms the rail market is the least sensitive and it is the bus
market about which we should be most concerned. The new analysis is,
however, interesting and throws some light on the relationship between
population structure and public transport usage which will have to be
analysed further.

7.   THE FUTURE

Having described the way in which London and its transport markets
have changed and are continuing to change, we are now in a slightly
better position to peer just a few years into the future. Obviously
one of the reasons for producing a computer system like the Scenario
Model is to make such a forward look possible. There are, however,
dangers in assuming that the forecasting problem is now solved. This
would be very rash as the understanding that the system is based upon
can only be a partial one - no model can ever represent diversity of
customer choices in a market like that of London's travel. On top of
this we still do not know whether some of the assumptions about, for
example, the future population of London will be correct. It
only requires a brief examination of the way in which such forecasts
have been wrong in the past, to indicate the need for caution now.
What we can do, however, is to put together on the basis of our understanding and of some assumptions about the future of London, a
consistent picture. It may not turn out to be the right one, but at
least it will be consistent.

For the purpose of these forecasts it has been assumed that over
the next five years:
   (a)   population will continue to decline, but at a lesser rate
         than in the last six years and employment levels will

follow population levels;

(b) car ownership will increase from 64 per cent to 68 per cent of the population;

(c) all prices (petrol, fares etc.) will remain constant in real terms;

(d) public transport service levels will remain the same;

(e) tourism will rise by 3 per cent per annum for foreign market and by 1 per cent per annum for the domestic (UK) market.

On the basis of these assumptions it is believed that the change in trip making will be as shown in table 4 and the market shares as shown in table 5.

Table 4. Percentage change in trips 1978-1984.

	Car	Taxi	Bus	LT rail	BR rail	Total
Central	+11	+9	+2	+5	–	+6
Radial	+12	+14	–9	–3	–4	–1
Suburban	+1		–8	–8	–7	–2
Total	+2		–7	0	–5	–1

Table 5. Trip pattern 1984 (million trips per annum).

	Car	Taxi	Bus	LT rail	BR rail	Total
Central	93(17%)	103(19%)	129(24%)	216(40%)	2(0%)	543
Radial	182(26%)	12(2%)	159(22%)	205(29%)	152(21%)	710
Suburban	2558(70%)		897(25%)	97(3%)	91(3%)	3643
Total	2948(60%)		1185(24%)	518(11%)	245(5%)	4896

The main features that seem to stand out of this picture are as follows. First, it would appear that the Central markets are relatively buoyant and all modes show a continuing increase. This is no doubt sustained by the assumed increase in the number of tourists – a forecast which is based upon the British Tourist Board's assumptions. Secondly, taxi use continues to increase, but interestingly the biggest change is in the Radial market. This trend to more taxis outside the Central Area has been commented on by other observers. Thirdly, the biggest decline in public transport markets appears to be occurring in the suburbs where bus usage continues to decline.

Overall, the results bear out our earlier findings that so far as public transport is concerned LT rail is a relatively stable market and it is the bus market which is declining by about one or two per cent per annum. The results for BR rail, upon which I have commented little in this paper, are perhaps not so well established and should be viewed with more caution. It is hoped that as time goes by it will be possible to improve the representation of BR rail trips in this system.

8. CONCLUSIONS

This paper has indicated the kinds of methods which have been developed over the last few years to enable public transport management to
understand its passenger markets better. No claim is made that these
methods are in any sense final. No doubt in ten years time they
themselves will appear naive and over simplified. However, the
methods are a step forward, representing as they do an attempt to
make our understanding and our forecasting consistent. It is hoped
that the preparation of this paper will further advance discussion of
the issues that such methods raise, and encourage this more consistent
approach to forecasting.

REFERENCES

Fairhurst, M₀ *et al.* (1977) London Transport's Scenario Model. London
    Transport Economic Research Report R229.
Rendle, G., Mack, T. and Fairhurst, M. (1978) Bus and underground
    travel in London: an analysis of the years 1966-1976. London
    Transport Economic Research Report R235.
Shires, P. (1978) Private communication.

The supply of rural (in)accessibility

MALCOLM MOSELEY

1. INTRODUCTION

Concern for inadequate levels of personal accessibility in rural areas mounted in Britain through the 1970s. (By 'rural' I mean those areas where the demand for services is sufficiently scattered to ensure that indivisibilities in the supply of services render that supply sporadic or uneconomic. By 'accessibility' I mean the ability of people to reach or be reached by the services or activities they require.) This rise of concern reflected in part the socially uneven increase in car ownership with its tendency to undermine public transport and village services, and in part the growing responsibilities placed upon the local authorities to mitigate the worst effects of this deterioration. In consequence a considerable amount of research was undertaken by academics and practitioners on the nature of the problem and of possible policy responses (see Moseley *et al.* (1977 volume 2) for a comprehensive bibliography to 1977, and Moseley and Packman (1980) for a review of more recent material). The present paper argues that a new thrust in research direction is needed if significant further understanding is to be achieved.

The point is that the research to date has focused almost exclusively on the 'demand' or 'need' side of the problem. It has been concerned with the consumers not the producers of inaccessibility. Using data for individual households (from social surveys) or for aggregates of households (from the census or similar sources), researchers have built up a clear picture of who suffers what and where. Such research has included studies of certain social groups, such as the elderly (for example Garden 1978); of small areas and specific transport routes (for example Halsall and Turton 1979); and of different modes, such as community transport (for example Department of Transport 1978). Other work has tried to define the social and spatial distribution of accessibility (for example Moseley *et al.* 1977) and to set this particular concern in the context of other rural problems (for example Shaw 1979). But still the spotlight has rested on the sufferers and on their immediate problems such as closed village shops, lack of a car and withdrawn bus services. There has been relatively little attention paid to the business of devising and implementing policies to alleviate those problems, much less to the super-structure of political and economic forces which surrounds the sufferers, their problems and those policies.

2. THE DEVELOPMENT OF POLICY

Let us take the first of these criticisms - the limited amount of
research on policy formulation and implementation. It is clear that
the 'shopping list' of possible policies is a long one. Even
restricting ourselves to transport options, the list includes bus
subsidies and the better use of existing transport services (school
buses, mail vans, etc.) Casting the net beyond passenger transport,
it is clear that mobile services, telecommunications, land-use
planning policies, etc. can all alleviate, or worsen, the rural
accessibility problem. But the point is, how can all these elements
be fashioned into a coherent and effective policy package within
specific rural areas?

I have suggested elsewhere (Moseley 1979, Chapter 8) that the
planning problem is effectively one of reconciling three conflicting
goals: low cost, good levels of accessibility, and wide geographical
coverage. What we have to consider is how this reconciliation might
best be achieved within specific counties - because it is undoubtedly
the county councils, following the legislation of 1972 and 1978, that
are at the centre of the stage. A number of issues would repay careful research:

1. How far is it useful to set 'accessibility standards' to which the
council would be committed; for example, all villages above a certain
size being assured a certain quality of service? (It is interesting
that one long-established standard - that school children living over
3 miles from school have a right to free transport to school - is
currently at risk.) In setting such standards how should weights be
applied to certain areas, needs, client groups, etc.?

2. What is the role of public participation in devising policy? How
are surveys of opinion and of behaviour (for example the behaviour of
car-owning compared with non-car-owning households) useful in setting
objectives? How do people trade-off the ills of rural isolation
against the advantages of rural life? What is the perceived relative
severity of inaccessibility within the broader field of 'rural
deprivation'?

3. How far can alternative strategies be comprehensively costed? Can
non-transport costs be brought into the analysis, relating for example
to the operation of village schools and post offices and to the scale
economies of concentrated residential development?

4. How effectively can policies be implemented which involve agencies
other than the county council, for example the district councils,
the health authorities, the Post Office, etc.?

5. What may reasonably be expected of volunteers and the 'informal
sector'? Why does 'community action', for example taking over the
village pub or operating a minibus service, flourish in certain
places and fail elsewhere?

6. In monitoring the impact of policy and of other changing
circumstances, what are the 'key indicators' or 'warning lights' that
should be carefully watched, for example the level of attendance of
the elderly at day centres? What information network is needed to
gather this data?

7. How will developments in the 1980s modify the context? Three
examples might be posed. Will technological developments (in tele-

communications, energy supply, etc.) promote a wider scatter of the population? Will further economies of scale in retailing, hospital provision, etc. accelerate the demise of rural services? Will a combination of high unemployment, shorter working hours, early retire- ment and a predilection for alternative life-styles increase the potential rural supply of 'community resources'?
8.   In sum, can the county councils shift their concern in the 1980s from 'transport coordination' to 'accessibility management', with all that the latter term implies for breadth of concern and for systematic action?

It was with questions such as these - questions of planning and management - that the present author concluded his recent book on 'rural accessibility' (Moseley 1979). They remain important, but what increasingly seems even more important is the wider political and economic context within which the problem lies. In short, improved 'system control' can achieve only so much if this wider context is not understood.

3.   THE POLITICAL CONTEXT AND THE RESEARCH PARADIGM

Let us widen the debate by considering what was happening in another discipline, urban geography, during the 1970s. A number of over- lapping phases, involving different research paradigms, might be distinguished:
1.   *Quantitative model-building*, in which statistical relationships were sought to 'explain' aggregate spatial patterns and processes, such as the distribution of ethnic minorities or journey-to-shop behaviour.
2.   *'Behaviouralism'*, in which detailed examinations of individuals' attitudes and behaviour were linked to those patterns and processes.
3.   *'Managerialism'*, in which attention was directed to the working of urban institutions and people who effectively act as 'gatekeepers' in the allocation of resources such as housing and jobs.
4.   *'Political Economy'*, an overtly radical approach in which attention was directed to the link between the economic and political structure of society and the various urban phenomena of interest.

In applauding the shift in urban housing research (broadly in the mid-1970s) from (2) to (3) and (4), Robson observed that recent work has been 'emphasizing the importance of constraints rather than choice in access to housing; illustrating the role of conflict rather than consensus in the goals and interests of the groups involved and... arguing that class interests lie at the base of much of the system through which housing is produced and distributed' (Robson 1979, p. 71).

Another stimulating way of summarizing the shift from (2) to (3) to (4) is that it amounts to a shift of focus from bottom dogs to middle dogs to top dogs (a metaphor due I think to Pahl). What we have to consider is whether, given a concern to help the rural deprived (unmistakeably 'bottom dogs' in this context), the balance of advant- ages lies with further studies of them, or alternatively with a shift of focus to the 'middle and top dogs' who, it may be argued, control the parameters of their behaviour. In the rural accessibility context who and what are the 'gatekeepers' equivalent in function to the building societies, estate agents and local authority housing managers explored in urban housing research? How do they operate? How do

decisions taken by the national and international financial institutions and by national and international government agencies affect the
mobility and accessibility of the rural deprived?

There is an obvious danger of over-generalizing, but I would
suggest that both 'rural studies' and 'transport studies' have in the
1970s tended to avoid these questions: they have been concerned much
more with paradigms (1) and (2). Even the burgeoning rural deprivation literature has been concerned chiefly with the experience of low
incomes, insufficient jobs, unobtainable housing, etc., in short with
'the powerless rather than the powerful, and the propertyless rather
than the propertied', to paraphrase Newby *et al.* (1978). Yet do not
the activities of those with power and property fashion the life-
chances of the rural disadvantaged, for example, by not building
council houses or by fostering private transport? Similarly, much of
the transport literature - as other papers in this book may affirm -
reflects a growing search for sophistication in the comprehension and
modelling of 'bottom-dog' behaviour, rather than with understanding
how agencies and organizations reach decisions which indirectly
fashion, or at least constrain, that behaviour.

4.   WHO ARE THE 'GATEKEEPERS'?   HOW DO THEY OPERATE?

If we keep our focus firmly within the rural areas, who effectively
decides whether people without cars should have access to the things
they need? Work in Norfolk by the author and his colleagues (Moseley
et al. 1977) suggested a long list of relevant public-sector bodies
(table 1 sets out the principal ones).

A cursory consideration of the roles played by these agencies
pointed to a number of conclusions. First, some of them are important
because they affect the *need* to travel (for example by closing
village post offices, choosing villages for residental expansion);
others do so directly by affecting the *ability* to travel. Secondly,
even given the Public Transport Plans, (PTPs) which county councils
are required to produce annually, the consultation and coordination
that occurs between these bodies is often minimal. Thirdly, accessi-
bility-relevant decisions are often taken with *other* objectives more
firmly in mind; the Post Office, for example, is in business to
collect and deliver mail not to run a passenger transport service.
Fourthly, ripples of effects pass readily through the system, with
other agencies often becoming unwittingly involved: closing village
schools, for example, has obvious transport implications. Fifthly, no
single agency is empowered to coordinate all of the relevant decisions,
though since the 1972 Local Government Act and the 1978 Transport Act
the county council comes nearest. Sixthly, little is known about *how*
such bodies reach their decisions: how county councils, for example,
decide on *x* per cent of their transport budget going to public
transport support or how the Post Office decides to close, or reprieve,
this or that village outlet.

It would be a useful step forward to examine the reasons for the
extremely variable reaction by county councils to their new responsibility of preparing county-wide 'Public Transport Plans'. Some
councils have been luke-warm or even antagonistic to this task. For
example, the chairman of the Norfolk County Council Transport
Committee considers the preparation of PTPs as 'a public relations

Table 1. Some public-sector rural agencies relevant to personal accessibility.

Agency	Some fields of actions
County Council Surveyor's Department	preparing Transport Policies and Programmes and Public Transport Plans, allocating transport resources between mode and area
County Council Planning Department	long-term influence on location of residents, services, jobs
County Council Social Services Department	specialist transport to day-centres etc; assistance with telephone installation etc.
County Council Education Department	size and location of schools; provision of schools' transport
District Council	operating some bus services; amount and location of council house building
Regional Health Authority	location of hospital and other health services; discretionary transport
National Bus Company	operating majority of rural bus services; deciding networks, frequencies, fares
British Rail	operating majority of rural rail services; deciding networks, frequencies, fares
Traffic Commissioners	road service licencing
Post Office Corporation	rural 'sub-post offices'; scope for post buses

exercise and a waste of time and money'. One county surveyor, to take another example, is known to feel that the only public expenditure in the field of rural transport which helps the national economy (and is therefore justified in his eyes) is the maintenance of roads for use by farm vehicles. How attitudes such as these arise, persist and find expression is an area which would repay research. A study of more ambitious and committed county councils might seek to establish the legal and *de facto* boundaries of their 'action-space', relating for example to the municipalization of village shops or to conflicts with the Traffic Commissioners over route licensing.

Examples from outside the county council also illustrate the point. The Post Office probably has more vehicles in rural Britain than does any other agency. Its sub-post offices and staff not only provide a 'commercial' service by selling stamps, paying pensions etc. but they constitute an important element in the 'information network' of rural areas. Little or nothing is known about *how* decisions are reached on the deployment of these vehicles, outlets and personnel. Yet such decisions clearly impinge on the rural accessibility situation. So too do decisions by the regional, area and district health authorites regarding the development of the hospital service (one district general hospital or several community hospitals?) or the operation of transport services for patients, visitors and staff.

The net, however, should be cast more widely so as to embrace decision-makers outside the public sector and outside the immediate rural area in question. Decisions taken by national, international or essentially 'aspatial' bodies may have just as fundamental consequences for rural accessibility as do those taken by National Bus Company subsidiaries and county council committees regarding the future of specific bus routes.

The corporate plans of large retailing companies and vehicle manufacturers, the strategies of quangos such as the Manpower Services Commission and the Development Commission, even the decisions of international bodies as disparate as OPEC and the EEC – all may be hypothesized to have a real, if distant impact upon elements of the rural accessibility problem. These impacts need to be clarified. So does government policy in such fields as central-local government financial transfers and the balance between public expenditure and private taxation. In short, a shift from behaviouralism to managerialism must be followed by a wider analysis of the whole political and economic context. The problem will be to define a manageable research programme – but that is no excuse for continuing to imagine that the problems of the rural deprived are best understood by studying the rural deprived.

REFERENCES

Department of Transport (1978) *A Guide to Community Transport*. London: HMSO.

Garden, J. (ed.) (1978) *Solving the Transport Problems of the Elderly*. Keele: Department of Adult Education, University of Keele.

Halsall, D. and Turton, B. (eds.) (1979) *Rural Transport Problems in Britain*. Keele: University of Keele.

Moseley, M.J., Harman, R.G., Coles, O.B. and Spencer, M.B. (1977) *Rural Transport and Accessibility*, 2 vols. University of East Anglia: Centre of East Anglian Studies.

Moseley, M.J. (1979) *Accessibility: The Rural Challenge*. London: Methuen.

Moseley, M.J. and Packman, J.P. (1980) Planning for rural transport: a review of recent literature, in Gilg, A.W. (ed.) *Countryside Planning Yearbook*. London: Dawson.

Newby, H. *et al.* (1978) *Property, Paternalism and Power: Class and Control in Rural England*. London: Hutchinson.

Robson, B.T. (1979) Housing, empiricism and the state, in Herbert, D.T. and Smith, D.M. (eds.) *Social Problems and the City: Geographical Perspectives*. Oxford: Oxford University Press.

Shaw, J.M. (ed.) (1979) *Rural Deprivation and Planning*. Norwich: Geo Books.

Assessments of public transport systems for low-density areas

POUL-OVE PEDERSEN

1. INTRODUCTION

Assessment of a public transport system can take place at different levels. First, different systems can be compared on the basis of *technical standards*, as for instance frequency, geographic coverage, bus quality, walking distances or fare levels.

However, especially in low-density areas the technical standards tell very little about the resource use of the system, because that depends on how the different parts of the system are coordinated; they also tell little about the accessibility the system offers and about the number of passengers it will attract, because that will depend on how well the system is coordinated with the location and opening hours of the travel destinations it should serve.

Secondly, therefore, the different transport systems should be compared with respect to what might be called *the direct consequences:* (1) use of resources or costs; (2) passenger traffic generated or attracted from other transport modes; and (3) accessibility to services, jobs and other potential travel destinations offered to the population in the area served by the public transport system.

But the public transport system can also have more far-ranging consequences for other sectors of the society. Improved public transport might reduce car traffic and thereby reduce the costs in the road sector and improve the physical environment; it might also lead to changed use of public and private services and lead households to change their choice of dwelling and job location, and thus lead to a changed travel pattern. Such *indirect consequences* should also be assessed.

The main thrust of this paper is to discuss these direct and indirect consequences of improved public transport. However, the potential consequences mentioned above will only be realized as positive benefits if the public transport planning is coordinated with other sectoral and urban-regional planning. Therefore, public transport systems should be assessed in relation to the planning and administrative systems.

2. TECHNICAL STANDARDS OF THE PUBLIC TRANSPORT SYSTEM

The quality of the public transport system can be changed by changing
any of a host of parameters or technical standards. A list of the
most important of these is given below:
   Vehicle quality and size
   Frequency of departure in peak hours, weekdays, evenings and
   weekends
   Degree of demand responsivity
   Fare level and structure
   Level and structure of direct and indirect subsidies
   Net structure:
      Geographic coverage
      Number of transfers necessary
      Degree of coordination with other transport systems, for
      instance long-distance transport, school buses and social
      transport systems
      Degree of coordination with opening hours of services and
      working places
   Overall speed
   Walking distances and pedestrian area quality
   Waiting area quality
   A given transport system represents a given combination of such
technical standards. Of course not all combinations are equally
feasible, and many of the standards are interrelated. If, for
instance, geographical coverage is increased, walking distances are
likely to go down, and if costs are not allowed to increase, frequency
and/or overall speed are likely to fall.
   Some of the technical standards can be decided upon by the
transport operator, for instance choice of bus and frequency; others
require collaboration with other authorities, for instance the quality
of the pedestrian and waiting areas, and the coordination of the public
transport system with other transport systems and services. The
choice of such standards, therefore, will depend on the structure of
the public administrative system and on the place of public transportation in that system.
   If public transport is organized at the communal level, coordination with school buses and local service facilities is eased,
while coordination with long-distance transport might be more difficult.
If public transport is organized at higher levels in the administrative
system, the opposite might be true.
   Some of these coordination problems might be solved by a
hierarchical organization of the public transport system in two or
more levels of trunk lines organized at the country and county level
and a system of feeder services organized at the communal and local
level. Such a hierarchical network is well fitted to the administrative system, but it might result in a large number of transfers
at the longer travel distances, and it might not lead to an optimal
transport system. For instance, when each level of the hierarchy is
rationalized independently of the other levels, the problems of
reduced services in the low-density areas, created by centralization
of the route network, tend to be shifted from the higher to the lower
levels of the hierarchy. At the lower levels the problems must be
solved by creating publicly-financed specialized school bus and social
transport systems, or expensive dial-a-bus systems.

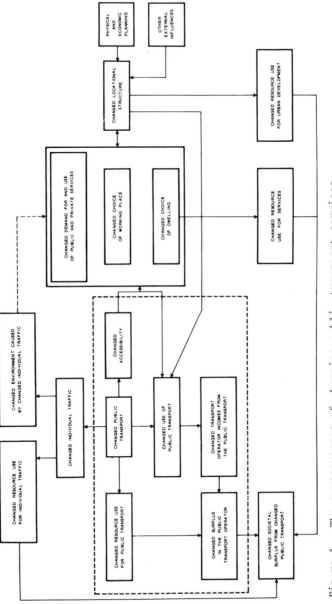

Figure 1. The consequences of changing public transport services.

3.   THE DIRECT CONSEQUENCES OF CHANGED PUBLIC TRANSPORT

In the flow diagram in figure 1 we have attempted to show the
consequences of changed public transportation. The part of the
diagram enclosed by a dotted frame represents the direct consequences;
outside the frame the indirect consequences are shown.
      The direct consequences of changed public transport consist of a
changed resource use for public transport; a changed number of
passengers transported; and a changed accessibility, defined as the
possibilities for the inhabitants to reach potential travel destinations by public transport even if they do not use the possibilities.

Costs
A main feature of the cost structure of public transportation is that
the labour cost constitutes a very sizeable part of the total costs,
generally in the range of 40 to 70 per cent of the total costs. Hence,
a main trend in public transport has been to increase the size of the
vehicles so that each driver could produce more seat miles. Such a
policy is of course only sensible when the demand is large enough to
fill the increased number of seats. Therefore, generally the costs
per passenger or seat-mile decrease when the demand increases.
      The cost curve is steeper the larger the vehicles used. Thus it
is steeper for ordinary fixed-route buses, less steep for demand-
responsive systems and almost flat for conventional taxi services (see
figure 2). This means that for very low traffic densities, taxi
services will be cheaper than both demand-responsive and fixed-route
buses, while fixed-route buses will be cheapest for very large traffic
densities.

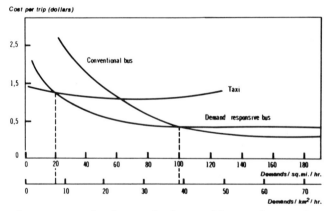

Figure 2. Costs per trip for taxi, bus and bustaxi as a function of
the demand density.
Source: Saltzman (1973).

      The traffic densities at which one should shift from one system to
another will vary from case to case, depending for instance on the
degree to which the demand is concentrated in time and space. Based
on simulation results, Saltzman (1973) concluded that at traffic
demand below 5-10 trips per km^2 per hour taxi services would be

cheapest, while fixed-route buses would be cheapest when the demand
becomes larger than 35-40 trips per km^2 per hour.

Demand and revenue
The revenue of the public transport system depends on the demand and
the fare. The demand in general will increase with the population
density and the level of service, but it will also depend on the type
of trips which are served.

In very low-density areas with equally low service level public
transport generally has not been able to compete with the car. The
new public transport trips resulting from improved public transport
have largely been either trips which were not carried out before, or
which were carried out on foot, on bicycle or as a passenger in
someone else's car. Only in the case of very long trips, or trips to
large urban centres with serious traffic and parking problems has
improved public transport attracted car drivers. As a result most
public transport passengers are people without access to a car, either
because there is no car in the household, because the person has no
driver's licence, or because someone else is using the household car.

The interrelationship between the level of service and the demand
is not very well understood. In a study of the relationship between
the daily frequency of bus departures and the generation of bus trips
per capita in a Danish rural county, where the number of daily departures ranges from one to twelve departures per day, it was found that
the number of bus trips per capita, apart from school trips, increased
proportionally to the number of daily departures. In suburban areas,
where the frequency varied from one to four departures per hour, the
number of trips per capita increased somewhat slower than proportionally to the frequency (see figure 3).

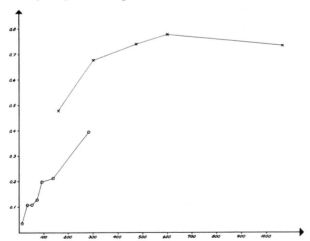

Figure 3. Passenger generation per inhabitant as a function of
departure frequency in public transport.
Source: Johansen, Krogh and Pedersen (1979) and Pedersen (1980).

In another county (Sønderjyllands amt), the public transport
system has been improved and coordinated, and the traditional distance-
dependent fare structure has been substituted by a zonal fare

structure with fares which at the long distances are only one-half
to one-third of the former level. As a result of these changes, the
traffic has increased so much that the total revenue has remained
constant even though fares have been reduced drastically. A detailed
analysis of the increase in demand has not yet been carried out.

As a final example should be mentioned the improvements carried
out in the town of Roskilde with about 50,000 inhabitants. Here four
circular routes within the town centre, running every half hour, and
two routes from the town centre to nearby villages, running every
hour, were substituted by seven direct routes running every half hour
between the town centre and the periphery or villages outside the
town. Distance-dependent fares were substituted by fixed fares. As
shown in table 1, there was no effect of fare decreases, while increased frequency and regularity led to increases in demand varying
from 38 per cent to 260 per cent.

Table 1. Bus passengers in Roskilde before and after service
improvement.

Number of passengers arriving in or departing from	Before change	After change	Percentage change
The town centre:	5555	5951	7
Other parts of the town with			
unchanged service	1403	1331	5
improved service	2153	2771	29
Nearby villages where the service has been changed from:			
1 bus/hour to 1 bus/$\frac{1}{2}$ hour	694	955	38
Good rural bus service to fixed schedule with 1 bus/ $\frac{1}{2}$ hour	528	813	54
Bad rural bus service to fixed schedule with 1 bus/ $\frac{1}{2}$ hour	98	354	260
Service unchanged, but fare reduced	317	317	0

Source: Kommunernes Landsforening (1978).

Accessibility
Even if the demand for a given public transport system is not large
enough for the revenue to cover the costs, the system might still be
worthwhile because of the accessibility it creates. This allows
those without cars access to services and jobs which they could not
otherwise reach: and for car-owners, who do not usually use the
public transport system, it provides an assurance that they can
reach their travel destinations even when the car is used by others,
or is being repaired.

Improved access to services and jobs can be achieved not only by
better public transport, but also by establishing new service outlets

and jobs in low-density areas. In many cases, such a policy might be
preferable. The interplay between service location and public transport has been studied in detail by Moseley *et al.*(1977) in a study on
rural transport and accessibility.

4. INDIRECT CONSEQUENCES OF CHANGED PUBLIC TRANSPORT

Figure 1 distinguishes between two sets of indirect consequences of
changed public transport: those related to changes in the individual
car traffic, and those related to changes in the choice of location
and travel destinations.

Savings due to reduced car traffic
To the extent improved public transport leads to reduced car traffic,
this might reduce resource use (to run the private cars, to repair
old roads and to construct new ones) and improve the environment with
reduced noise and pollution.

These effects, however, are not likely to be very important in
low-density areas; first, because most experiences seem to indicate
that only a small proportion of the new passengers travelling with
an improved public transport system are former car drivers; most of
the new passengers are carless, who make trips which were not made
before or were made on foot.

Secondly, the road wear of an extra bus is likely to be larger
than the wear of the cars it substitutes, even if all its passengers
were former car drivers, because the road wear increases with the
fourth power of the vehicle weight. Only where there are capacity
constraints on the road system, will the consequences for the road
costs be important. This is not likely to be in the low-density
areas themselves, but in the nearby town centres to which the traffic
flows; thus improved public transport in the low-density areas might
lead to a decrease in the demand for new road and parking space in
the town centres.

Also the environmental effects are likely to be negligible in the
low-density areas themselves, while they may be of some importance in
the neighbouring towns. However, even here, the noise effect will be
small, while some reductions in air pollution (especially of lead
and carbon monoxide) can be expected (Andersen 1975).

The reduction in energy consumption as a result of the improved
public transport will depend on the vehicle productivity, and on the
size and type of vehicle. In conventional taxi services, the efficiency is so low that energy consumption will be almost twice as high
as in car traffic. Also, in most demand-responsive bus services,
the efficiency is so low that energy saving on the bus service itself
must be very limited. However, where the demand-responsive service
increases the utilization of suburban trains or express buses, the
effect might be important. Only large fixed-route buses are likely
to lead to important energy savings. This energy saving will of
course only be a real saving if all the new passengers are former car
drivers and their passengers. If, as is often the case, the passengers
are former pedestrians or car passengers but not drivers, it is
questionable if one can talk about energy savings at all.

Changes in locations and travel destinations
The second set of indirect consequences of changed public transport
are those related to changed accessibility. Changes in accessibility

might lead to changes in people's choice of service facilities and
jobs, and ultimately to changes in the location of dwellings, jobs
and service facilities. Such locational changes will in turn influence the demand for transport.

This feedback effect is generally not likely to be very strong
because the location and urban development processes are much more
influenced by physical planning measures, the development of the
individual traffic, and many other factors varying from sector to
sector. In some cases, however, the feedback might be very important.
In the Copenhagen area, for instance, improved public transport to
the city centre is argued to increase the pressure on land development in the central parts of the city, and thus to work against the
redevelopment of dwelling areas here.

As another example, a Danish rural commune found that the cost of
providing a free bus route from the hinterland to the centre serving
a new swimming pool was more than covered by the decrease in the
deficit of the pool resulting from an increase in the visits to the
pool, so that the establishment of the bus route was beneficial to
the communal economy. In other cases, when it is the use of a free
public good which is increased by improved public transport, the
costs of course might rather go up, but the distribution of the
services will be more just.

Introduction of demand-responsive transport services is likely to
reduce the impact of the transport system on activity location.

While the feedback effect of public transport on land development
especially in the low-density areas will be limited, the opposite
effect of physical planning on the economy of the public transport
system is much more important. By coordinating the route network of
the public transport system and services and job location, it is
possible to reduce the cost of providing an intensive public transportation.

5. ASSESSMENT OF DIFFERENT PUBLIC TRANSPORT SYSTEMS

In a total assessment of a public transport system, it is important
that both the direct and the indirect consequences are considered.
Clearly it is not possible here to make a generally applicable
assessment of different proposed public transport systems, because
such an assessment will depend on the specific conditions under which
the sytem should be implemented.

Which combination of standards should be chosen in any specific
case must first of all depend on the structure and size of the
demand. Where the demand is so large that a relatively dense network
of fixed-route buses (less than 400 m to the bus stop) and a service
frequency of two to three departures per hour or more can be maintained, interview investigations indicate that this will be preferred
to an ideal demand-responsive system operated with ordinary bus fare
and an overall travel time below two to three times car travel time
(Vilhof 1976).

When the distance to the bus stop increases above 400 m, and the
frequency becomes one departure per hour or less, the ideal demand-
responsive system is preferred. However, Canadian experience
indicates that it seems difficult to keep the high standard of the
demand-responsive systems. Fares are often kept at twice the
ordinary bus fare, and travel times of between three and ten times

those by car seem to be realistic. This of course means that the frequency of a fixed-route service should be below one departure per hour before a demand-responsive service would be preferred (Suen and Lehnen 1978).

The reason for the rather poor performance of many demand-responsive systems is that the costs of operation increase when the travel time is reduced below two to three times car travel time (Wilson *et al.*1970, 1971). For the same reason, the service level of the demand-responsive system decreases very rapidly when the demand increases above a certain level. It is therefore not well suited to serve peak demands and must be supplemented with a fixed-route service or specialized buses during peak hours.

On the other hand, when the demand becomes very low, chances are small that trips which can be combined into shared riding will occur at the same time. In such cases conventional or route-based taxis should be preferred to demand-responsive systems.

The feasibility of demand-responsive systems also depends on the structure of the road network. In areas with many culs-de-sac, as exist in many rural areas, and in many traffic-differentiated suburban areas it will be difficult to run door-to-door services.

REFERENCES

Andersen, T.V. (1975) Er kollektiv trafik miljøvenlig? In *Kollektiv Trafik i byer, forsteder og landdistrikter*, Copenhagen, pp. 37-43.

Johansen, C.U., Krogh, F. and Pedersen, P.O. (1979) *Kollektiv trafik i tyndt befolkede områder - Udvikling, struktur og planlægning*. Sydjysk Universitets-forlag, Esbjerg.

Kommunernes Landsforening (1978) *Kollektiv trafik*, Kommune-information nr. 14, Copenhagen.

Moseley, M.J. *et al.* (1977) *Rural Transport and Accessibility*. Centre of East Anglian Studies, University of East Anglia, Norwich, UK.

Pedersen, P.O. (1980) A demand model for public transport in rural areas. *International Journal of Transport Economies*, 7, forthcoming.

Saltzman, A. (1973) Para-transit: taking the mass out of mass transit. *Technology Review*, July/August pp. 46-53.

Suen, L. and Lehnen, A. (1978) An overview of para-transit activities in Canada. Working paper, Urban transportation research branch, CSTA Transport, Canada.

Vilhof, P. (1976) *Kollektivtrafik - specielt med henblik på Københavns omegn*. IVTB-rapport nr. 2, Lyngby.

Wilson, N.H.M. *et al.* (1970) Simulation of a computer aided routing system (CARS). *Highway Research Record*, 318, Highway Research Board, Washington DC. pp. 66-76.

Wilson, N.H.M. *et al.* (1971) Scheduling algorithms for a dial-a-vide system. *USLTR-70-13*, Cambridge Massachusetts: MIT.

Public rationality, needs
and what needs are relative to

DAVID WIGGINS

1. THE CONCEPT OF A NEED, AND THE PLACE OF THE CONCEPT IN THE
POLITICAL FRAMEWORK WITHIN WHICH TRANSPORT STUDIES ARE CONTAINED

1.1. I begin with five recent occurrences of the work 'need', taken
almost at random:

(i) 'This paper defines Transport Studies as the scientific discipline underlying the professional practice concerned with the movement
of goods and people and with the social, economic and environmental
effects of such movement. It is thus equally concerned with the
'need' to take part in activities in other spatial locations, the
engineering and technological means for accomplishing these changes,
as well as the implications - interpreted in the widest sense - that
such changes imply for those either directly or indirectly involved
or affected by it' (Heggie 1977a).

(ii) 'M3 Inquiry Will Continue: A motorway inquiry is to continue at
Winchester despite protests that there are no powers to divert a canal
in order to build the road. "I must decide first on the need for the
motorway and then the route", Major-General Raymond Edge, Inspector
for the Department of the Environment, ruled yesterday'. (The Times
1977).

(iii) In the White Paper on Transport Policy (Department of Transport
1977), one of the three main objectives was 'to meet social needs by
securing a reasonable level of personal mobility, in particular by
maintaining public transport for the many people who do not have the
effective choice of travelling by car' {1}.

(iv) 'However the concept of minimum need may be used in social
security arrangements, it is a poor guide to consumer behaviour,
whether at the minimum income or other levels, and whether in an
advanced or primitive society. The particular purchases made by a
family reflect not only their immediate tastes such as a liking for
warmth, bright colours, and tinned fruit, but also their spiritual

life and fantasy world — the stone fireplace as a safe stronghold in
a morally insecure world, the Jaguar car to release frustration or
bolster a waning virility, the tingling toothpaste as a ritual purifi-
cation. Far from being a matter for ridicule, consumer choice is
something to nurture, cultivate and protect' (Bray 1970) {2}.

(v) 'The minister decided not to reopen the inquiry, and in his decision he said that he had taken into account the general changes
relating to design flow standards and traffic forecasts since the
inquiry, and he was satisfied that they did not affect the evidence on
which the inspector made his recommendation. He was convinced the
schemes were needed and the road should be constructed' (*The Times*
1977b).

1.2. Unless these examples are very atypical, they suggest something
that is highly arresting but rarely remarked. Make for yourself the
experiment of replacing 'need' in (ii), (iii) and (v) by some supposed
equivalent like 'want' or 'very strongly desire', and then perceive
the effect. In each case plausibility, point and coherence are
replaced by feeble inconsequentiality.
    By the end of the account of needing that I shall offer, I hope
that an explanation will begin to emerge for this apparent irreduci-
bility of the idea of a need; and I believe that it will be clearer
why (in spite of all the discredit that the devisors of rigid and
costly minimum standards have brought upon it) the concept is actually
indispensable to the social and political framework within which
transport studies have (at the level of prescription obviously, but
equally at the level of observation and understanding) to be contained. But the framework itself is so important to an understanding
of the nature and promise of the concept of need that I shall not
try to engage with the question of what needs are or why we cannot
always settle for some weaker claim than the claim that a thing
is needed (sections 5.2–7.2) until I have located within it some of
the conflicts that are so conspicuous a feature of the scene that the
student of transport has to survey.

1.3. Like every other aspect of land use, transport has always been
the scene of conflict. But few dispassionate persons will deny that
in the twentieth century, a century of unparalleled human aspiring,
the motor vehicle first, and then the great increase in car ownership,
have heightened this conflict to an extent that is simply unprecedented in history. There is conflict *between people* (sections 2.1–
2.3) and there is also what one might denominate conflict *within
people,* or real value conflict (sections 3.1–4.3). These conflicts
are of equal importance. But I shall begin with the first, because
it is there that it is most manifest that the notion of need has some
role to play in arbitration and rational compromise and that our
rationality has to wait on our conceptual understanding.

2. CONFLICTS BETWEEN PEOPLE: AND HOW TO GET THE WORST OF BOTH
CAPITALISM AND SOCIALISM

2.1 Consider the notorious and self-perpetuating conflict between
cars and buses on urban roads; or the equally familiar conflict
between the interest that car and bus users taken together have in an

increase of road capacity {3} and the contrary interests of bicyclists
and pedestrians, whom larger roads endanger or obstruct; or the
conflict between the interests of people who live in a place and the
interests of people who want to go through or past it at high speed;
or the conflict between the interests of intercity railway travellers
in a hurry who also owned cars and the interests of poor or middle-
income people in the nineteen sixties who were carless or lived in
places severely exposed to the effects of increasing road traffic and
would have been served best (if statesmen had realized what will seem
far more obvious to the hindsight of a historian living in the twenty-
first century) by a private or nationalized railway that answered to
their need for a *dense, medium-speed* network of near universal passenger access. (A possibility all the more interesting if the system
could have been in active competition, with the help of cybernetics
and other modern technology, for the freight whose transfer to road
has consigned to fading memory the stillness and relative safety of
the streets that we now wonder at in old and not so old photographs
of, say, Islington or Hackney.) Consider finally the present
conflict between the interests of motorized persons, who wish to carry
their patronage to shops and all sorts of other facilities located at
all sorts of distance in all sorts of direction from where they live
or work, and the interests of those who are seriously threatened by
the continuing shift towards this new pattern of retailing and provision of services – that is persons heavily dependent on public
transport and better served by a more numerous array of smaller scale
facilities, less centralized, less concentrated, and situated near
their home, near their work place, or along the *corridors* of public
transport along which so many people still like (in the manner so
characteristic of the settlement patterns of the earlier twentieth
century) to live, work and find the facilities they have a routine or
everyday need for.

2.2. It will serve our main purpose to embark here on a brief
excursus about the last of the several interpersonal conflicts just
enumerated, which is the conflict we may yet find to be the most
ruinous conflict of all. Opinions will differ about how important it
is that the conflict supervenes on a process that has already made
comprehensive public transport coverage nearly impossible. What will
force everyone to agree that this conflict is ruinous will be what
happens if the said process continues to rearrange {4} people and
facilities in such a way that *even as fossil fuels become unprece-
dently scarce*, individual car travel needs are maximized (compare this
with the U.S.A. now), and the economy can scarcely function at all
without freight ton-*miles* increasing more quickly than tons consigned
(a sinister trend already in evidence).
     Now some will suggest that here, as so often, we must acquiesce in
what is happening and see it as inevitable (or, more metaphysically,
as 'society's choice'). But, before one does acquiesce, one should
ask the question how much it contributes to this process that not all
the present and future costs to the public that are created or transferred by the rationalizations now being attempted by retailers,
manufacturers, education authorities, hospitals, doctors, dentists or
whomever are charged to the rationalizers. Neither are they charged
to the particular classes of people whose patronage large concentrated
facilities are attracting from the older smaller scale facilities.

These costs are not even reckoned. Still less then do they impinge
on the decision process by which these locational changes are made.
The result is scarcely atypical of the province of transport. It
seems that *those who are disadvantaged by the majority of the changes
that now take place get the benefits neither of socialism nor of
capitalism.*

Capitalism, at least as J.S. Mill and his liberal successors have
sought to justify it {5}, would have required the operation of a
mechanism or agency which would identify the costs just mentioned
within however approximate limits and visit them upon those actually
responsible or benefiting. Had this happened at each stage, and had
road provision been correspondingly costed in all relevant respects,
I submit that we should have had less road space at some points, a
larger and more extensive public transport system than we now have,
and much better fit between that system and the settlement pattern.
Paradoxical as it may seem at a time of heavily subsidized public
transport, those who still depend upon it have suffered far more from
the ruination of the price system and our incapacity to set sensitive
accurate prices in the transport sector than any other single group.
(Note that this claim stands or falls as a statement of fact, counter-
factual though it is. It does not stand or fall with the separable
question whether, for example, we *ought* now to institute road pricing.)

A socialist, on the other hand, (if we have any idea what a socialist is) would have to regard the protection of public transport users
as of paramount concern – and for two reasons, of which one is
actually uncontentious. The uncontentious reason is that among these
people you will find those who are most disadvantaged in almost every
other way. The more contentious reason is that the form of life of
these people represents, in respect of transport and settlement
pattern, the one and only form of life not open in a crowded land to
a socialist criticism to which the newly emerging pattern (in which
the Department of Transport has long since acquiesced, in spite of its
being the most expensive settlement pattern in respect of both private
transport *and* subsidies to public transport) is profoundly vulnerable.
The criticism is that, if or when most people come to live by this
pattern, then it will be markedly worse for most people than it would
be for them if each of them, in company with most other people, lived
his life by another pattern of home, travel and work {6}. We now have
at hand many of the legal, statutory and fiscal instruments of socialism, and they have contributed their full share to the collapse of the
price system. But the principal effect of their becoming available
has not been the identification of such coordination problems, but to
hasten the corruption of capitalism by capitalists who have found ways
to avail themselves (knowingly or unknowingly) of the instruments of
socialism in order to enhance their competitive position in a way
radically inconsistent with the theoretical and moral justification of
capitalism. (If this is obscure, consider what Mill or Schumpeter
would say about a state of affairs in which, without doing anything
corrupt or illegal, a city council can pull down housing in its inner
area to construct at public expense a shopping centre plus parking and
give the lessees of the complex a significant advantage over shop-
keepers in other cities within the region, indeed bankrupt some
rivals, while even the financial return to government and city funds
from the complex is inadequate to defray a commercial interest on the
capital cost of the construction. It is well worth noting that one

typical result of this being done is that, having gained a commanding position in this way, the regional centre then has to increase its accessibility from outside by building roads across its own areas of light industry and working-class housing, using as always - wholly legally - its statutory powers to raise taxes and make compulsory purchase of land.)

2.3. Liberal pluralists and adherents of compromise must be grateful that, here and now and as matters stand, we have neither pure capitalism nor pure socialism {7}. But there is benign compromise, and there is compromise in the disreputable sense. For a transport minister or transport planner with seemingly open ended responsibilities, working along the small space that he can find between vocal pressure groups and special interest groups, the path of least resistance cannot help but be a quite special temptation. Often it may seem to be the only path there is. But much too often what this path leads on to are the disadvantages of both capitalism *and* socialism without the advantages of either.
   There is another sort of compromise of course. There is compromise in the good sense, that is creative or constructive compromise. Being liberal and pluralist, this tries to secure some of the distinctive advantages of both systems. But being strenuous both practically and conceptually, it is this conception of compromise that most urgently requires a fresh understanding of the difference between a need and a more *desideratum* {8}. Such compromise is not to be implemented by translating every substantive problem into a simple proposal that the more powerful parties in conflict should get together and settle their differences. For they may settle these differences to the disadvantage of a party less ably or vocally represented, or in defiance of all economy and common sense. This is one of the most pressing problems of our times. I wish I thought that the exploration of the concept of need was more than one small part of the theoretical part of the solution to it.

3. CONFLICT WITHIN PEOPLE, AND CONFLICT BETWEEN VALUES THEMSELVES

3.1. Let us take stock. Sections 2.2 and 2.3 were a digression arising from the description of conflict between people or classes of people; the description itself being an attempt to suggest the shape of the conceptual lacuna that the notion of needing might, if only we understood needing, help to fill. In these conflicts, classified as I have classified them, it will often happen that one person is on both sides. What I am now to progress to is the kind of conflict where this holds from the nature of the case. These are conflicts where the satisfaction of some of a man's wants or desires is inconsistent with the satisfaction of other wants or desires of the same man. Men wish to travel as fast as possible from any place they happen to be in to the next place they want to be in, for instance. Some at least of these men wish, at the moment of starting the journey at least, that a large fast road should exist to link these two particular points. But they also desire *equally or more strongly,* even if there be no equally manifest way open to them of registering some behavioural expression of the fact   all sorts of other things which are logically inconsistent with a declared and consistent public policy that would make general provision for the satisfaction of this kind of desire. I

mean that such men may care about the preservation of architectural
beauty or rural peace, or that they may want solitude (which may have
been the object of the journey at the moment we began by considering),
or city streets in which one can walk without fear of being run over,
or lower income tax or lower vehicle taxation. Again, they may hanker
after certain aesthetic, economic and social features of the more
self-contained settlement pattern of the pre-automobile age. (There is
even a trace of this in behaviour; men in motor cars seek out remorse-
lessly the places where these features have not yet been obliterated.)
Or it may be that if they were consulted, they would wish to see
modern architects explore afresh the possibilities of close knit urban
forms that present regulations for vehicle access and parking
virtually exclude (even if the client's brief does not exclude them).
There does not necessarily exist any outlet for the expression of
such a wish.

3.2. There is a danger that the familiarity of truistic character of
the example will distract you from the less familiar main point I am
now preparing to make. *Most people desire inconsistent things.*
Economists are apt to dismiss this as irrationality, and then temper
the hardness of this hard saying by adding that their's is a technical
sense of 'rational'. But here, as so often in matters of the mind,
I should hold that they are marching on the spot.
     There is no justifiable conception of rationality that makes it
irrational to have conflicting desires. It is of the essence not of
irrationality but of rationality to give hospitality to many multi-
various concerns that logically or economically compete with one
another for realization. Incompatible desires are in fact the
rational response - on the level of deliberation, and appreciation
(though not of course action *per se*) - to the irreducible plurality of
mutually incommensurable human goods. Everything that is true of the
world has to be consistent with everything else that is *true of it*.
But not all the claims of all rational (or even of all moral) concerns
that the world *should be* thus or so can be expected to be reconcilable.
Indeed there is every reason to expect them not to be completely
reconcilable. And the rational man is the man who takes these
competing concerns or desires for what they are, and then focuses in
the circumstances upon a subset whose realization will make his life
practicable and invest it with meaning. When he arbitrates between
his competing concerns, ordinary prudence will constantly suggest to
him, among many other questions, the question 'What, in the most basic
and most inescapable ways, do I need?'. Before he asks it, the degree
to which he wants a thing will sometimes be pretty indeterminate.
Nor, if a thing wanted loses out here and now to its competitors is
that simply the end of it. It may still exert an unseen influence on
the man's overall value scheme and affect the question of what
structural changes the man might wish for and what real choices he
would like to be offered. (This is a real fact about him, even if it
is virtually inaccessible to direct behavioural test, except the test
of his answering questions or speaking aloud in the course of a
discursive debate. One of the important points in favour of a
defensible capitalism would be its provision of a market place and
forum in which this very difficulty was diminished.)

4. REVEALED PREFERENCE THEORY AND SOCIETY'S CHOICE

4.1. At this point, before I develop any further the consequences of
real value conflict, I have to dispel two potential misunderstandings.
I have not wanted to suggest that the primacy of need is some *magical*
principle of arbitration of inner conflict, still less that it can
amicably resolve all outer conflict. The reader may have thought he
detected underlying the claims so far advanced some fundamental
opinion of mine that a sensible decent twentieth century society is
one that *first* seeks to counter all actions or events that threaten
the inescapable needs of anyone; *second,* brings it about that
socially coordinated action attend positively to the basic inescapable
needs of citizens who will not otherwise have a way to satisfy them;
and *third* (if its citizens will not allow government to stop at the
second stage) attends positively to certain distinctive desiderata
that will not otherwise be secured (remembering *not* to undo at the
third stage what has been achieved or guaranteed at the first and the
second stages). This would be a large and highly discussable view of
social justice, or of the proper view for the *State* to take of social
justice. Perhaps some such conviction affects my view of the question
of transport policy. But it presupposes a careful reconsideration of
something that lies outside my present scope - the proper province
in general of government. My subject here is only the *claim* that
needs would make upon the transport policy of a government that
distinguished needs from other desiderata. And the most that I am
contending is first that in a world, constrained by scarcity, and by
the logic of *one man one life,* needing is one crucial idea in the
process of arbitration of conflict; and second, that my findings
about rationality, motivation and choice ought to be enough to
disturb those who construe the proper province of government as wider
than I think it is, believe that the proper end of public policy is
maximal desire satisfaction, and seek to apply revealed preference
theory to questions of transport policy. I say that the theory
cannot provide what they seek.

4.2. Revealed preference theorists are right no doubt to be discontent
with the mere assertions that people make about what matters to them.
But, if behaviour is not only founded in indifference to costs that
are not reflected in prices, and not only in partial ignorance (this
everyone knows), but founded also in an inconsistent set of desires,
then it follows that interpretation of individual behaviour is more
difficult than has been candidly acknowledged, and that the interpretation of the aggregated behaviour of individuals is even more
difficult. I would add here that in practice this problem is
inextricably bound up with another problem. The *specificity* of a
behaviour pattern associated with a desire (and transport behaviour,
in particular, is very specific in appearance) ought not to be
confused with what must in theory be distinguishable from specificity,
namely the importance or urgency or high ranking of that desire. Why
should anyone suppose these to be the same? Contentment is very
important, or so it is said. But the search for contentment is not
behaviourally specific. If behaviourally specific desires always
claim pride of place in the ratiocination of planners just because
they are manifest, and if policies are always designed to satisfy the
behaviourally most manifest wants, it is certain that in the longer

term these wants will tend to displace all desires and needs which are
behaviourally less specific. This will happen regardless of the
others' importance. But I ask you: is everything that you value
highly something that there is a specific and unambiguous way of
showing in behaviour that you value?

4.3. So much is more than enough, I hope, to suggest how complex a
painstaking account of the phenomenology of individual choice would
have to be, and how relevant this phenomenology would have to be to a
planner who saw his role as promotion of desire satisfaction, rather
than as the prevention of certain specific sorts of evil and deprivation. But the phenomenology of individual choice is a simple matter
when compared with the attempt to envisage a full dialogue between a
large number of people who were not only aware of the indeterminacy
and conflict of their own inward desires but also aware that by no
means all possible resolutions of their own internal conflicts of
desire were compossible with other persons' resolutions of their
internal conflicts of desire. The coordination problem here is so
complex, and so many perversities can operate (think, apart from the
relatively recent breakdown of the price mechanisms of the market
place, how many variants there must be here of Kenneth Arrow's voting
paradox), that I am amazed that anyone can speak seriously of 'society
having made a choice', and mean by this more than that what has
happened has happened (see Independent Commission on Transport 1974,
Chapter 5). Still less could anyone speak of society having made a
sequence of choices such that each consequential state of transport
and land use has seemed to society better than *all* its predecessors in
the sequence, and not merely better than its immediate predecessor.
(For a simple counterexample to the claim that this can be regularly
expected see Mishan 1967.) Yet this is nothing less than a precondition, of our claim to enjoy a state of public rationality.

5. PUBLIC RATIONALITY: FOUR REQUIREMENTS

5.1. Thus I arrive at the ideas of public rationality and irrationality. Nobody can surprise anybody else by declaring that what we
shall need for public rationality in transport is a concerted attack
by the most economical and modest means thinkable on the coordination
problems of transport and land use, these being considered as a problem of finding the best constructive compromise and of making the
best use of existing assets. But the gloss I wish to put on this
claim may be more contentious. Nothing will turn out any better than
it has so far if the attack is not undertaken in the conscious understanding that, unless we arrange our deliberations to make the
relation *x appears to us and continues to appear to us better than y*
transitive in the domain of the states of transport and land use that
society plans at each stage to bring about at the next stage, then the
relation will *not* be transitive. We shall continue to do what we do
now, combining the disadvantages of laisser faire and interventionism.
What we do now is to move through a sequence of steps by which each
coming stage of transport and land use holds out the *prospect* of being
something better than the stage it will replace; yet, when it comes,
it is seen by many (even in the end by some who favoured the change)
as worse in its actuality than its *pre*-predecessor - or its *pre-pre*-
predecessor - which may still be only ten years back.

I do not doubt that it is some perception of such problems as
this that motivates the call for more dynamic policy intervention,
and more research, and more resources for research in transport.
Writing with the special authority and the special ignorance of a
disinterested outsider, I shall list four of what seem to me the most
neglected requirements upon public rationality in transport planning.

In the first place conceptual problems must be seen for what they
are, and they should not be delegated to those who prefer technical
or surrogate notions of *need, rationality, interest, cost, good, evil,
harm,* or who pretend that the proper treatment for the political
rhetoric of transport planning is to ignore it completely and replace
it with technical language. The proper treatment of the language of
transport politics is to take it on its merits, see what it means, and
(where it means something) try to ascertain whether what is being said
is (approximately) true or not. There is no other route to anything
we can recognize as human rationality. It is in this area that these
inadequate reflections are meant to belong. If we understand needs
better, for instance, then we may understand better *one* of the several
elements that go to make up the judgement by which some observers are
tempted that the overall pattern of transport and land use has either
deteriorated between 1960 and 1977 or not benefited in proportion to
what has been spent in trying to improve it.

Secondly, transport planners must place a higher premium on discursive description in the ordinary terms of the social historian and
economic historian.

Third, a dangerous but indispensable thought, suggested by the
dangerous and indispensable art of medicine: sometimes one can
identify a necessary condition of somethings' happening without
knowing the complete explanation of its happening, or without knowing
in better than anecdotal terms why it happens. The necessary condition may give a planner some control of the phenomenon, even though
the academic theorist declares the phenomenon to be in many respects
ill-understood or unexplained. Provided the second requirement is
needed (and provided the faculties of imagination and perception are
not allowed to wither away), the planner may have no rational alternative but to take advantage of his control over the necessary
condition. And research into such controlling factors can be organized, not only by the desire for theoretical understanding, but also
by our interest in finding those controlling factors with the smallest
or most benign side-effects.

Fourthly, transport planning must be brought into a saner and more
self conscious relation with what human knowledge is.

6. THE FIRST REQUIREMENT ON RATIONALITY AND A SPECIMEN CONCEPTUAL
PROBLEM - NEEDING

6.1. Needing is a problem of conceptual understanding. Needing may
seem to be like wanting, but a simple test shows that it is not at all
like it. If I want x, and $x = y$, then I do not necessarily want y.
(The prospective Mrs. Crippen wanted to marry Dr. Crippen: but she
did not wish to marry *her future murderer*). But it can only be true
that I need x if anything identical with x is something that I need.
What I need (contrast desire) depends not on thought (or not only on
thought), but on how the world is. (In philosopher's language,
needing is not an intensional or purely intensional phenomenon in

Brentano's sense.) This point applies equally to what I shall call
unconditional needs and to needing *for an end or purpose*. Unconditional needs (needs *tout court*) are the sort of need we are principally
interested in here; and the whole rhetoric of the passages (ii) (iii)
and (vi) that I began by quoting depended on our idea of an unconditional need. But, as Sira Dermen has demonstrated, the unconditional
kind can be analysed via the conditional or instrumental kind. So
I will start with these.

Someone may say 'I now need to have £100 to buy a certain suit'
- or, speaking elliptically or allusively, 'I need £100' or 'there's
something I need £100 for'. It may well be true that to *buy that
suit* he needs £100. If he can't get that suit (or any passable
substitute) for less than £100, then I should say here that we have
a true statement of *instrumental, conditional* (or one might say *pro
tanto forsakeable*) need. For, if there is nothing like that suit to
be had for less than £100, things being what they are, then the
following temporally indexed necessity holds:

Necessarily at *t* (if the man has the suit then the man
had £100).[9]

This form is what I should propose as the outline analysis of what is
said by a statement of instrumental need. (In this case the need is
instrumental with respect to having the suit.) According to this
analysis or elucidation, the claim does *not* entail that the man
unconditionally or unforsakeably needs a suit - or that he has any
unforsakeable or unconditional need. He may or he may not. The
sentence under analysis says nothing of that at all. He may need
£100 to buy the suit, but not need £100 (because he doesn't *need* the
suit). But now, using the schema

Necessarily at *t* (if_____ then.....),

we can define unconditional need in terms of instrumental need.

We arrive at the case of unconditional need, and at the special
and central sense of the word, if we supply to the antecedent of the
foregoing schematic conditional something that is *itself* unforsakeably or unconditionally needed, or is instrumentally needed for
something unforsakeable (or instrumentally needed for something that
is instrumentally needed for something unforsakeably needed...).
Thus we have

Necessarily at *t* (if *x* (which is unforsakeable) is to be then
-----).

Here I am deeply indebted to Aristotle's definition of what he
recognizes as a special sense of necessity at *Metaphysics* 1015a20
following and yet more deeply indebted to Sira Dermen (formerly of
University College, London, and now Warden of Holly House, Richmond
Fellowship, London), who is the first person I know of to have
identified this modality of Aristotle's with needing (Aristotle has
no special word for it), and to have seen that unconditionally
needing can be defined in terms of instrumental needing.

What counts then as unforsakeability for the purposes of this
analysis? Aristotle suggests that the relevant question is 'whether
The Good is to be'. But let us say more realistically that a person
needs unconditionally those things *without which he is bound to live a
maimed or wretched life*. It is convenient however to have something

less diffuse and less exigent to insert into the antecedent of the
schematic conditional and, following Sira Dermen, one can make
'flourish' the hostage here. (As we shall shortly see, it is no more
than a hostage.) Thus we have

> N at t needs x unconditionally or unforsakeably
> if and only if
> Necessarily at t (if N flourishes then N has x).

6.2. It is sometimes said that needs are relative. This analysis
displays at least three things that might be meant by this.

First, the definition reveals or makes explicit a hidden parameter
always latent in the ordinary notion of unconditional needing.
'Flourishing' or 'not living a wretched life' is our hostage for that.
Indeed it is well worth noting here that the effect of relativizing
the explicit content of a sentence is usually to *derelativize* the
notion of truth. An analogy may be useful. Historians and philosophers of science tell us that Newton gave laws of motion which he
supposed to be the laws of absolute space and time. Following
Leibniz, Mach smoothed the road to the Special Theory of Relativity
by making length, duration and motion relative concepts and then
relativizing Newton's laws to the reference frame of the observer who
makes measurements and all reference frames in uniform motion with
respect to him. Later it became possible to supply from the Special
Theory certain stipulations whose explicit introduction suffices to
restate the Newtonian laws (suitably restricted) in a form in which
they are *absolutely true*. The question the analogy prompts is: Can
we hope to achieve the same for needing by making its situation-
relativity explicit? This brings me to the second relativity.

The second and distinct sense in which needing emerges as
relative may seem fatal to the hope that the first sense might
inspire. The second sense in which needing is relative is that what
constitutes or *counts* as flourishing or not living a wretched life is
an essentially contestable matter, both in respect of definition and
in respect of content. It is not merely *anthropocentric*, but *etho-
centric* or *epochocentric* (relative to a culture or an age, that is).
There is a great deal more to be said. But in the present context
the best thing to do with this second sort of relativity is to
concede it. For it shows nothing about the inutility for us here or
now of the notion of a need. What we have to confront is how *we*
determine needs, not how a Hottentot would. The urgent question one
might say is whether the Department of Transport have grasped *our*
conceptions. For as regards a considerable number of needs our
culture is already in a much more impressive state of reflective
equilibrium (John Rawls' phrase) than it is with regard to a large
number of economic and medical questions. And even when due latitude
is allowed for disagreement about what is implied by the antecedent of
the 'flourishes' conditional and the instability is conceded of the
opinions that our culture has now reached about needs in the serious
sense, what a 'needs' sentence claims is still something extremely
strong. It may also be decidable. I shall come back to that. But
first let me accommodate explicitly a third relativity. This is
relativity to time.

When we make a claim of the form *Necessarily at t if such and such
then so and so*, where t is a moment for which this *necessarily* is
temporally indexed, when we confine our consideration to *all alter-*

native futures from t onwards. We are saying that every alternative
in which such and such holds is one in which so and so holds. But if
'need' is the modality we are interested in, then the only futures of
any concern to us for such conditionals are futures in which we do not
envisage ourselves as bringing about morally or socially unacceptable
variations in the arrangements of society and which do not violate
what is physically, psychologically and economically conceivable.
(Note that we relied on the former of those ideas at the outset when
we allowed that N needed £100 to buy a suit. The fact that there is
a future in which he has a suit without paying £100 because he steals
one, say, did not count against the claim.) I take this opportunity
to declare that a great deal of open disagreement about need reposes
on latent disagreement and/or misunderstanding about the relevant set
of futures or about the length of time span to be considered. But,
once they are identified, these are points one can argue about.

6.3. The definition we now arrive at is this: A person needs x with
respect to timespan t if and only if, no matter what morally and
socially acceptable variation and no matter what psychologically and
economically possible variation be brought about within the t timespan, the person would not flourish – *or* the person's life or
activity would be blighted – unless he had x. (It will make a
difference that I do not explore here which of these two variants we
prefer.)

A full account would have to make room for certain obvious and
essential refinements: (1) under what conditions one can detach 'with
respect to timespan t' from 'person p needs x with respect to timespan
t'; (2) the measure of how badly and urgently a thing is needed; and
(3) which may vary independently from (2), the measure of *how basic*
any need is for something. The question of badness or urgency is a
question of how much a person will suffer without x. The question of
basicness is a question of the conceivability or difficulty, human
nature being what it is, of arranging or re-arranging matters so that
a person can dispense with x and use something else instead without
his life or activity being blighted. An adequate treatment that
measured up to the requirements of arbitration would also require
other refinements: an account of the sensitivity of a need claim to
discovery of alternatives that could be adopted within the specified
timespan, for example; an account of the relevant sensitivity to
variation in the selected timespan; and some proper provision for the
substitutability of certain things by other things and the *entrench-
ment* of extant arrangements (which create definite requirements in
the short term, but may not in the longer term). These further
problems lie in the intersection of political theory, social philosophy and semantics. (An under-cultivated area, because, unluckily,
most political philosophers now prefer untrammelled invention over the
discovery *malgré nous*, of what we mean by what we say.)

6.4. To say that someone cannot flourish without something is to make
a very strong statement. Perhaps not very many sentences of this form
are true, though some are. But the reason for the failure of so many
claims of need to be properly true is not some hopeless feebleness in
our ideas of what it is for a life to be blighted or some semantic
impotence in 'need' sentences which is consequential upon that. The
real situation is quite the reverse. In practice the truth-condition
for a sentence of unconditional needing – the requirement, that is,

that the person who needs x *cannot* flourish without whatever the thing
is - is so clear that it is tantamount to a challenge to the imagination to find an alternative future in which he does flourish without.
The result of the challenge may be to weaken the specification of the
thing - 'He will only flourish if he has x *or* y *or* z'. This is a very
familiar move. But there are cases where what survives it is still a
very strong statement indeed. In spite of the exigency of the truth-
condition, for instance, one can certainly generate, simply on the
basis of our most commonplace ideas of human life, the following list
of *basic needs* (given here in order of ascending contestability):
air, food, shelter, sleep, a measure of security, self-respect, love
or at least acceptance, work or occupation, space about one in which
one is free from let or hindrance, education up to the minimal norm
of the society in which one lives, certain freedoms to come and go
(somehow) and to pursue other needs. Then, in the presence of a
determinately given social and economic framework, these basic needs
will generate in their turn more specific *standing needs:* for example
- again in order of ascending contestablity - adequate protection
from winters of such and such a prevailing temperature, reasonable
peace and quiet during night hours, and environment in which a child
can go about without fear, access to the place of work or school or
shopping, an environment that does not preclude community, a system
of schooling, accessibility between a person's home and other places
besides work, school and shops, and so on. I hope this seems quite
boring. If so, the definition is generating the right list. Obviously the more specific standing needs result from the interaction of
human constitution and our particular economic and cultural circumstances.

7. NEEDS CONTINUED. NEEDS IN THE FIELD OF TRANSPORT; AND FREEDOM,
EQUALITY, ETC.

7.1. Here at last we reach the transport field. If you take any of
these needs as so far specified, there will usually be more than one
way of satisfying it. The descriptions have to be rather broad and
unspecific, *because overspecificity in a need sentence falsifies it.*
'Mobility', in particular, does not figure as a more specific standing
need (though mobility now and in the short term is a need relative to
some settlement patterns and relative to any settlement pattern cum
pattern of facilities that cannot function at all unless most households have motor cars). What *underlies* the demand for mobility is
indeed a need, perhaps a basic need. But this basic need itself is
for something far less specific. At most it is the need for access
or for the mutual accessibility of dwellings, work-places, and everyday facilities. And such accessibility can be secured either by the
said dwellings, work places, shops, recreation etc., being placed
close together and by multiplying such functions, or by making good
transport communications between a smaller number of facilities. The
need as such for access also leaves open the *mode* of such communications. The mode can be determined by reference to other potentially
competing needs.
    One might think that a public policy founded in human needs would
have to take account of all the basic needs that are incontestable
within the given society. Accessibility is but one of these. Given
that needs often make apparently conflicting demands in the public

sphere, it seems that a needs-based policy must take maximum advantage of the existence of all alternative ways of satisfying needs to get the best overall solution to the problem of meeting or safeguarding all of them. For such a policy the more plastic needs must accommodate to the less plastic, and (what is different) the less urgent must give way to the more urgent. This is the public counterpart of what is called in the private case common prudence or good sense. (For suggestive sociological work in this area, showing little disagreement about the relatively low rating of certain over-specific transport desiderata, see Willmott and Young 1970.)

So far as I can envisage such a policy (and the difficulty of doing so relates to the unfinished business alluded to in section 4.1), it would be rather different from what we have had over the last twenty years, and a great deal less expensive for government and taxpayer.

7.2. It may appear to an irascible or precipitate reader that by preparing the way for a needs-orientated public policy to be described, or by articulating the notion of need that figures in some criticisms of the effects of present policies, I am preparing some brief to deprive various people of certain of their freedoms. If it were the case that I was preparing to do such a thing, I suppose that I could retort that I was preparing equally to restore freedoms to other people. But how can I be preparing to do either of these things when I am simply clearing the ground for the determination of the extension of the concept of need as it applies in the field of transport? What practical effects such a determination would have depends on two further and interrelated questions: first, the proper province of government in the transport field (should all road building and maintenance really be the business of government; and how can present institutions and practices be brought into conformity with a defensible political theory?), and second, the nature of the political principles of need that will regulate government intervention in the transport field. A principle that would certainly deserve scrutiny is that, so far as public intervention is concerned, anyone's needs of any sort have a *prima facie* title to precedence over anyone else's mere desires. But, whatever improvement this may represent over other and sillier principles of equality, I am not on this occasion engaged in arguing about equality or justice. I am only arguing about what needs are. What is more, if someone claims that there are other criteria of excellence in a transport policy beside its answering to needs, I shall be the first to agree. If he urges that maximal desire satisfaction is a better criterion, well, I doubt that that statement is quite right, but the only thing I have *said* here against it is that it faces an interpretation of enormous complexity. What would really mystify me - except that Sira Dermen's analysis of 'need' reveals one part of the secret of the *magic* of the word (one can only flourish if one's needs are satisfied) - is its being said by someone who wanted a transport policy based simply on desire-satisfaction that it was wrong for me even to speculate about the title that needs have to consideration within transport policy; or his claiming that my speculating about this was itself an assault on freedom. For I myself think that freedom is a need. And even if I were wrong about that, there would be no contradiction between my saying what a need was and my saying what freedom was, or my thinking both very important.

8. CODES OF MINIMUM STANDARDS, AND THE DISCREDIT THEY HAVE BROUGHT
ON THE CONCEPT OF NEED

8.1. The idea of a human need obviously played a very important part
in early twentieth century attempts to specify standards for sani-
tation, safety, public health and building. These humanitarian
efforts have been responsible for much of the improvement that has
been experienced in the living conditions of twentieth century
cities. No one can safely criticize the improvements that have been
brought about without taking considerable precautions not to be misunderstood. To say that these improvements were not as good as they
could have been is not to say that they were not good. But it might
be to say that, in excesses of visionary fervour and hatred of the
old, many marvellous opportunities have been missed, and that in
many cases the cost, both economic and human, has been excessive
relative to the actual improvements - or that, at least where new
building is concerned, less megalomaniac planners could have done
more good more quickly. Very likely it is also to criticize the
architectural and environmental standards of that which has replaced
the city of factories and slums. And here the building regulations
and the rigid standards that were fondly supposed to protect the
disadvantaged (but have in practice been so disturbingly efficacious
in squeezing the housing stock actually available for habitation)
have much to answer for. Those who devised these things should no
doubt have remembered that standards and zoning, restrictions will
always be enforced by some people who are both unimaginative and
stupid. They should also have remembered that it is a pity if
building standards are so detailed and exigent that for a large class
of sites they leave room for only one architectural solution, and
would exclude many that we admire in the architecture of the past.
But it is not enough to say this. And I have to admit that here I
find myself in what you may regard as a paradoxical position. I
side unashamedly with those who have attacked all the idiocies that
have been committed in the name of zoning, minimum standards and the
rest. Yet I want to retain the concept of need that inspired these
things, thinking it would be a pity if it were held to blame for all
the absurdities that their inflexibility and stupidity have inflicted
upon us.

Surely the resolution of the difficulty is this. As we have
analysed need, one who claims that something is needed claims, not
only something universal or general (having to do with the conditions,
economic, social, human etc. that issue in the necessity), but also
something particular and special to the particular circumstances of
the person or persons who will not (here and now, placed as they in
particular are placed) flourish without the thing stated to be needed.
The rigid standard institutionalizes the neglect of this crucial
distinction. But this is precisely the area in which one must
distinguish extremely carefully between statements of basic need,
that is statements of a rare and special kind which are not sensitive
to variations in anything except human nature, and statements of the
form 'It is necessary (at t) that if A, placed as he is at t,
flourishes at t then A has x at t'. Both kinds of statement are
readily analyzed by our schema. But they are different, and it is
the latter that bear more closely on public health and safety.

9. HAPPINESS

9.1. Before I take leave of the concept of need and return to the
three other things I have represented as requirements of public
rationality, I shall venture two further observations concerning the
substantive content of the idea of a need.

The first is that a planner who sees it as his role to promote
human happiness positively (remember that I am not saying that is his
role) would do well to speculate more often about the thoughts and
feelings that lie behind the desires that lie behind the choices that
lie behind behaviour. As I have already stressed, much behaviour is
given its determinate shape by arrangements which individual people
have to accept, but would not themselves have chosen, or which *nobody*
has chosen (or which were only chosen, where they were chosen, through
the failure to comprehend or solve a coordination problem). The
desire for mobility *per se*, taken neat, may be a relatively uncommon
thing. But where we have the appearance of it, it may well conceal
something much more interesting – even the desire to escape from
terrible surroundings that the promotion of mobility itself has made
more terrible (or blighted by indecision concerning plans which almost
always have road-building among their most controversial feature), or
the desperate desire to find something to find satisfaction in.
Desires themselves need explaining. Sometimes they can be traced back
to needs which are unsatisfied. What needs are at present unsatisfied
then? A way has to be found for people themselves to articulate their
own answer to this question in speech and in behaviour. But in the
meanwhile I leave the last word on this particular point with a poet
(W.H. Auden) 'Distrust the man who says, "First things first! First
let us raise the material standard of living among the masses, and
then we will see what we can do about the spiritual problems." In
accomplishing the first without considering the second, he will have
created an enormous industrial machine which cannot be altered without
economic dislocation and ruin'.

The second valedictory point is this. Mill predicted (1874, p.
489) that the religion of the future would rest on the idea of each
man doing his share of what was required to realize humanity's
destiny and the victory of good over evil. This is where he saw life's
meaning. The consciousness that we are squandering natural resources
aimlessly quite certainly undermines this aspiration. A planner who
discounts the future at too steep a rate may not be doing the favour
that he supposes he is doing to the generations he professes to be
concerned with. He may create not happiness but, amid affluence,
despair. Planners and politicians who are seen by the public as
discounting the future destroy many peoples' sense that their lives
mean something.

10. THE SECOND AND THIRD REQUIREMENTS OF PUBLIC RATIONALITY

10.1. I return now to public rationality. I claimed in section 5.1
that the planner and statesman should not despise description. In a
way none does. Yet I think that the folk memory of recent history on
which so many of them rely stands in need of *amplification* and by
'amplification' I mean something that goes beyond the Department of
Transport's careful concentration on questions that can be directly
attended to in policy, and its statesmanlike agnosticism about the

errors that were committed in the past. If we are to understand what
I referred to as the problem of intransitivity (sections 4.3 and 5.1),
for instance, then what we require among other things is a wide-
ranging description of the costs and the benefits of the last twenty-
five years of change on the transport scene. Economists have refined
ways of measuring the time saved by certain new transport developments.
But we are not as a nation short of time. And, even if we were, it
would be necessary to inquire more carefully than our economists have
so far about the tendencies which have increased the number and
frequency of the journeys that have under the new pattern to be undertaken, whether or not the journeys are desired for themselves. In
any case the real question which economists do not answer is whether
these transport and land-use changes have in any way promoted wealth
in the pretheoretical, genuine and interesting sense of 'wealth'.
What is really required is surely a description of the present and
recent past, not in the bloodless vocabulary of economics, but in the
ordinary anecdotal language of economic history and social history
(not without arithmetical stiffening). This language is not value-
free. In many cases, genuinely evaluation-free description would be
unintelligible to us as a description of what interests us (or, where
intelligible, irrelevant). But the only purity the describer need
aim for is freedom from *prescription*. And the ordinary language of
'good' and 'evil', 'harm' and 'benefit', understood literally in the
way it is understood by ordinary educated men who are not destroyed by
philosophy or social science, has just this purity. If nothing is
said about 'must' and 'must not' or 'ought to be' or 'ought not to be'
then this is language with the same aspirations to objectivity as any
other anthropocentric description. Which, I ask you, is more
question-begging as a description of a state of affairs? A behavioural
description which rigorously excludes all sentences that are inter-
pretation-dependent and says on the basis of some doctrinal cum
methodological censorship 'this is all there is to the matter'. Or
one which evaluates without prescribing (as in the best work of Mayer
Hillman and Anne Whalley) and invites complementation by further
description and further evaluation - that is a description which
freely acknowledges that respecting any particular situation there is
usually much that is good and much that is bad about it? Surely it is
much more important for the student of transport to enumerate goods
and evils than to claim any finality for his overall appreciation of
the scene he surveys or the advice that he gives.

10.2. There is another impurity in which I would urge workers in the
field simply to acquiesce. This is the fact that events often happen
more quickly than they can be described in the language of the text-
books; and that they often have a much more complicated causal
ancestry than our theories are capable of retracing in any detail or
fully explaining.

     I venture to think that something like this holds of many issues
of settlement pattern and of the whole problem of the rational anticipation of energy shortage in the year 2000, plus or minus. Nobody
who looks at them can fail to be struck by the contrast between the
carefully qualified geographical language employed in the works
detailed in the bibliography appended to Peter Hall's paper (which is
earlier in this volume) and the following description of some of the
same things.

'Responding to the freedom and the new opportunities that
road transport has given it, industry has moved steadily away
from locations near to railheads, ports or inland waterways
and has evolved a new, more dispersed approach to Land Use
than was evident in the 19th Century with its emphasis on
consolidation in metropolis and conurbation. Much new light
industry is situated either on industrial estates on the out-
skirts of established towns, or in new towns. Warehouses in
which goods are prepared for final delivery are often located
in rural or semi-rural areas where land prices are lowest and
supplies of labour are still reasonably consistent and of
quality. Research into this area consistently underlines and
reflects the irrefutable hold which road transport now has
secured over the channels of supply, illustrated by the
Mercedes Blue Book and the FTA handbook and studies in my own
organisation, and the ever increasing and well justified need
for road infrastructure as a pre-requisite for growth...
There can be little doubt that growth will continue and, while
it will extend the pleasures of increased affluence to more
sections of the population, it will also make more pressing
the problems that affluence brings, and highlight the less
attractive aspects of the road transport industry as it
responds to the increase demands made on it'.
   'We must give a great deal more thought and determination to developing the concept of the dispersed society,
one which in both its appeal to individual liberty and
mobility and its use of land is more attuned to the motor car
and the lorry responding to individual needs than the concentration and conurbation developments of the 19th Century
dependent on and conditioned by the railways, providing for
the pattern of supply in commodity terms to the population
en masse'.(Pettit 1975).

Am I alone in thinking that, for purposes of making a policy, it is
as important for a civil servant or planner or academic to read such
statements as these, conceived not as propaganda but as descriptions
of the perceptions and intentions of one powerful sector of commerce,
as it is for him to read the careful description of academic persons
more bent on understanding than either promoting or diverting these
tendencies?{10}

11.   HUMAN KNOWLEDGE AND THE FUTURE

11.1.   The fourth prerequisite to an improvement in our public rationality is, I believe, a reappraisal of our relation to the future.
But at a moment when the vicious circularity has at last been
recognized of allowing policy and prediction to reinforce one another
in justification of what is always the continuation of more or less
the same policy (meeting foreseen demand without even putting a price
on it).   I can content myself perhaps with less than would have
needed to be said as little as two or three years ago.
   My first remark is that the economists - if you call F.P. Ramsey
and J. Von Neumann economists - have something to teach us here. In
considering unpleasant things which may happen and assessing their
importance we should take into account not only their *improbability*

but also their *nastiness if they happen*. Transport economists have
been conspicuous among those who disregard this economist-originated
injunction, and in laughing to scorn the laymen who would have had us
pay regard to it in matters of energy conservation.

Second, in 1990 or 2000 we shall not, most likely, be amongst the
richest of nations. What other expenditure on other ends shall we
have foregone, in our continuing awe of car-ownership forecasts, to
achieve an expensive and arbitrary compromise between a predominantly
private and a predominantly public transport policy? Could a needs-
based policy find a different compromise from that which was envisaged
in the Department of Transport's White and Green Papers on Transport?
(Department of Transport 1976, 1977).

11.2. Fifteen years ago the anthropologist Margaret Mead opened a
remarkable speech in London at the Bartlett School of Architecture
with the words:

> 'I want to start by discussing the current tendency to treat
> whatever is going on as 'evolution'... When one asks why
> {something} is inevitable, one is told "this is evolution" or
> "this is history". What happens is that we first invent "forces"
> by making statistical studies – studies that are neither very
> careful nor very extensive, *though they may be very detailed*
> – and then, reapplying the forces which we have invented, we
> treat them as inevitable and evolutionary – as something that
> must be accepted. This viewpoint has a resemblance to other
> deterministic theories of history, in which the only thing
> human beings can do is to alter the pace, but the course is
> predetermined... the statement that megalopolis, for instance,
> is inevitable is based on the experience of a very short
> period in the history of the human race... As such, it should
> be re-examined dispassionately for its defects and its virtues
> without the added burden of the statement that, because it has
> occurred recently, it is an evolutionary process' Mead (1964-65).

Notice that Margaret Mead presciently abstained in her speech from
denying that men with a mistaken notion of what is inevitable can, in
pursuit of that notion, do much to make that very thing come to pass.
But if they do, we may justifiably resist their claims to any monopoly
in the understanding of rationality, human needing, or human history.

12. POSTSCRIPT

12.1. All of this was written in 1977, before the publication of the
Leitch Report, and before energy prices reached 1980 levels. And so
of course were the words I have quoted from Margaret Mead.

NOTES

{1} At the time of speaking in Reading University (December 1977)
this objective was due to be realized by legislation, namely the 1978
Transport Act. Clauses 1 to 3 of the Bill dealt with county transport
planning. Clause 1 re-enacted with amendments Section 203 of the
Local Government Act 1972, which placed on non-metropolitan county
councils in England and Wales a duty to develop policies to promote a
coordinated and efficient system of public transport *to meet the*

county's needs. Clause 2 required these county councils to prepare
and publish annually a five-year public transport plan reviewing
existing services *in relation to need* and showing how they intended to
carry out their duties under clause 1.   The county councils were to
afford consumer organizations (and any others appearing to the councils
to be specially concerned with public passenger transport matters) an
opportunity to comment on a preliminary draft of the plan and to make
representations with respect to its contents.   Clause 3 of the Bill
required county councils to enter into agreements with public passenger
transport undertakings to provide financial support for services which
were required by the plan but would not otherwise be provided.
{2} Note that Bray says this not only in the name of liberty or
diversity, where I agree with him (even if I should put the point in
more sober terms), but also on the grounds that individual consumers'
decision processes are 'not wholly rational in the economic sense',
and on the grounds that anyone who *either* thinks there is room for
reason in this sphere *or* sets much store by the concept of need must
be preparing to deny freedom.   Yet it seems to me that one can think
liberty is a good thing, and also think that satisfaction of need is
a good thing, and one can then give priority to the former, to the
latter, or to neither.   No reason has been given to be uninterested
in what the satisfaction of need exactly amounts to.
{3} This is not of course an interest of bus passengers taken by
themselves, except on the feeble-minded assumption that there exists
no reasonable way at all to reduce car traffic or total traffic
volumes in cities.
{4} As it does. 'As car ownership spreads' the 1976 Green Paper
(DoE 1976) says 'schools become larger, hospitals regionalized, out
of town shopping centres multiply, and council offices are sited
further away'.   The document does not say what it is in the power of
the authors or anybody else to do about this for the benefit of those
for whom it here expresses concern.   What *is* going to happen next may
possibly be divined from an advertisement, on which my eye lighted
while writing this paper, in *Times Business News* December 1977.   This
was an advertisement by Sainsburys' advertising for large plots of
land for larger scale retailing developments.
{5} Or as John Rawls does in our own times (1971) 'Once a suitable
minimum is provided by transfers, it may be perfectly fair that the
rest of total income be settled by the price system, assuming that it
is moderately efficient and free from monopolisitic tendencies, and
unreasonable externalities have been eliminated'.   I should add that
neither Rawls nor modern market economists have thought very practically what would have been required at each stage to adapt market
mechanisms to the unprecedented political and technological circumstances of the second half of the twentieth century.   (One example
will suffice; it is all very well to propose road pricing, but
imagine a public debate on what should be done with the revenues.)
{6} I hope that in a place such as this I can put forward a
proposition of this last form without misunderstanding.   It is to be
understood and judged not as a prescription but a statement of probable
fact.   It involves evaluation, but it does not say what should be done
about what is evaluated.   If the bare prediction that it involves is
correct, then the truth of the rest of what is involved by the
proposition is not very sensitive to disagreements in standards.
{7} I do not imply that there is another country in the world where

we shall see even an approximation to capitalism in the pure sense (or capitalism tempered by the alleviation Adam Smith envisaged of extreme poverty).

{8} It is hard to believe that the Department of Transport would have received between 1000 and 2000 replies to the Green Paper (Department of Transport 1976) if the general public were satisfied that the Department has a coherent understanding of constructive compromise; or that it grasps the difference between what can and cannot be sacrificed to motor car mobility; or that it has any sense at all (best derived perhaps from a reading of Mill (1848)) that the only compelling reason for our having such a Department at all concerns the need for an agency which can solve problems of rationality and coordination that citizens and entrepreneurs and groups of citizens cannot from the nature of the case solve for themselves by negotiation in the market place. If the public's view of the Department is just, perhaps the Department's systematic degradation of the concept of a need is one part of what makes the view just.

{9} We should add here perhaps "and having a suit is of concern to him". The addition will be superfluous, however, so soon as we supplant "has a suit" by a sentence representing something he cannot help being concerned with. (See the sequel in the text.) That is the unconditional needing case.

More fully, the form that we require is:

(It is necessary (relative to t and relative to the t - circumstances c) that   if (_____ at t'') then (----- at t'))

The three time variables t, t', t'', are all needed in the full form of the need sentence without ellipse or abbreviation. But in a full semantics it will be evident that they do not vary entirely independently.

{10} I take the opportunity to make a remark about explanation which will be as unwelcome to a large number of people in my own discipline as it certainly will be to those in the social sciences who have schooled themselves to think that nothing is explained unless, after the fashion of the idealized physicist, we identify a set of conditions C and a law L such that the conjunction C and L logically implies the explanandum sentence. There is no reason why any social science should be able to produce explanations better than an historian finds. And an historian very often contents himself with explaining not why some explanandum *had* to happen but how it was *possible* for it to have happened. One way of doing this is to identify a condition which was *in the historical circumstances* all or most of what was missing for the explanandum to occur (or all or most of what was required for it to become probable that the explanandum would occur). The connexion of this kind of explanation and questions of control is very obvious. If one accepts that there is a kind of explanation that singles out one feature (the difference from what *might* have been that made all the difference to what was), one will very likely be prompted by the first excerpt from Sir Daniel Pettit to ask whether the largest single factor in the whole process of disorderly dispersion has been the failure of society to make the externalities attendant upon such dispersion register upon the price mechanism. Indeed by building roads to accommodate foreseeable demand and charging all users indifferently, instead of arranging to charge more to those who act in such a way as to maximize traffic-volumes,

society has done precisely the opposite of what theoretical
defenders of capitalism should in all consistency have urged upon
society. (Socialists had a quite different responsibility towards
the problem. See section 2.2.)

REFERENCES

Aristotle, *Metaphysics*, Book V, chapter 5.
Bray, J. (1970) *Decision in Government*. London: Gollancz.
Department of Transport (1976) *Transport Policy: A Consultation
    Document*. London: HMSO.
Department of Transport (1977) *Transport Policy*, Cmnd 6836. London:
    HMSO, para 9.
Heggie, I. (1977) Transport studies research at UK universities.
    Transportation, 6 (1), pp. 19-44.
Hillman, M., Henderson, I. and Whalley, A. (1976) *Transport Realities
    and Planning Policy*. Political and Economic Planning Broadsheet
    567.
Independent Commission on Transport (1974) *Changing Directions*.
    London: Coronet/Hodder.
Mead, M. (1964-65) Megalopolis: is it inevitable? *Transactions of the
    Bartlett Society*, 3, pp. 23-41.
Mill, J.S. (1848) *Principles of Political Economy*, Book V.
Mill, J.S. (1874) Three essays on religion, Works X, p. 489.
Mishan, E.J. (1967) A note on the interpretation of the benefits of
    private transport. *Journal of Transport Economics and Policy*,
    1 (2), pp. 184-9.
Pettit, D. (1975) The role of the truck. Paper presented at the
    Mercedes Benz Conference, Eastbourne, 18-20 June.
Rawls, J. (1971) *A Theory of Justice*. Cambridge, Mass.: Harvard
    University Press.
The Times (1977a)
The Times (1977b) Law report. 10 December.
Willmott, P. and Young, M. (1970) How urgent are London's motorways?
    New Society, 10 December, p. 703-6.

Access to activity, need and welfare; towards a fuller view of transport demand

MARY BENWELL

1.   SOME UNDERLYING ASSUMPTIONS

In this paper, three basic assumptions are made, and it is felt that
they will be accepted by those working in transport policy making and
research. They are:
1.   That the analogy of the pure rational model of decision-making
(Dror 1968) is, and should be, applied to transport planning and
policy-making, albeit at times in an adapted form more akin to a
mixed-scanning approach. Transport planning is, then, characterized
here as a goal-achieving and problem-addressing activity into which
research, if it is to be relevant, must ultimately feed an understanding of the processes at work, as simply and rigorously stated
as possible.
2.   That transport planning is now accepted to be an inevitably
discriminant activity, which confers differential costs and benefits
between groups and between locations, and that demand for transport is
conflict-inducing. Thus, if a rational approach is to be adopted, the
planner needs a fuller comprehension of the nature of demand. This
will enable deliberate, explicit and justifiable choices to be made
between the competing claims on resources, and a clearer understanding
of the likely impacts of the options open for action.
3.   That changes in transport planning over the last decade have
resulted in a need for certain changes in technique. There is also a
sense of urgency for the development of appropriate new approaches so
that this information can be input to policy-making.

2.   THE CHANGING INFORMATION REQUIREMENTS IN TRANSPORT PLANNING

Under what can be designated a traffic-functional approach to transport, we have developed a range of sophisticated techniques which
enable us to predict effective demand for movement (e.g. Williams in
this volume). These techniques continue to be relevant in a context

where policy is concerned with strategic changes in aggregate demand. But the associated methods of data collection, underlying concepts, and analytic techniques associated with them do not enable us to address some of the questions of welfare which we are now being asked. This is because the disaggregate and distributional effects of policy were not formerly construed as an issue or problem in a formal sense. For example, the situation could exist and never be identified or questioned, whereby certain sub-groups might be allocated an increasingly unfavourable pattern of service provision because their effective demand, or their capacity to vote-by-movement was initially low within the existing system. This we have come to regard as unacceptable.

In the terms of Friedman and Abonyi (1976), policy-makers and policy-related researchers in transport are, within their separate domains, currently in the process of redefining the 'theory of reality' which underpins their choice of policy. In such a situation, any conflict between the traditions of scientific enquiry within the academic domain and the requirement for information in the domain of tight decisions and critical pay-offs of the decision-taker or practitioner may be exacerbated.

Thus transport planning now finds itself at a point where a lead time of perhaps a decade may be required for the rigorous development of new techniques related to a thoroughly developed theory. Yet, in the meantime, transport planning decisions will continue to be made. During this period, researchers in transport must be concerned to adopt frameworks which enable a common language and perspective to develop at both the operational and theoretical level. This paper suggests one possible framework which may serve the purpose, and attempts to demonstrate its relatedness to some current policy questions.

3. MOBILITY AND WELFARE − A CENTRAL QUESTION

A key question facing researchers in transport is that of the relationship between mobility and welfare. This is an area of considerable confusion. The 1977 White Paper on Transport Policy gives one objective as

The meeting of social needs by securing a reasonable level of personal mobility. (Department of Transport, 1977, para 9) thereby appearing to imply that it is possible to identify, and plan for, some welfare-associated minimum level of movement. This tends to obscure the question of what transport provides and is contrary to our understanding of transport as a derived demand. For transport must be seen as facilitating not simply movement, but participation in other activities. This is not a purely pedantic point, as it underpins the way in which we structure our 'theory of reality' within the research process, and dictates the discipline areas from which we should seek relevant concepts and theories.

4. THE ACTIVITY PERSPECTIVE AND THE QUESTION OF WELFARE

Within recent research and model-building in transport there has been an emerging emphasis on the examination of activity and accessibility rather than mobility (Mitchell and Town 1977; Jonès 1979). This is a logical way of attempting to improve our understanding of demand, which itself derives from peoples' need to, or wishes to, participate in activities. We must begin to think of individuals or households not as generators of n trips of x type per unit of time, but as participants in a range of activities distributed across different locations, and accessible within constraints of, for example, mode, time and cost. Transport serves as the potential integrator or disintegrator of the desired activity system, and it is this function which imbues it with welfare significance. As Hägerstrand (1970), among others, has noted, mobility is like income; it is a means of gaining access. Unlike income, mobility does not occur in readily definable units, and it has little direct relevance to welfare when considered in conventional units such as trips.

If we accept such a view of transport and welfare, then the academic researcher faces the task of building an understanding of activity systems and action spaces, while the transport planner must identify and implement the most efficient or effective means of facilitating participation in activities. The definition of which activities are accessed, and at what level and cost, remains the political component of policy-making.

This constitutes an ambitious redesignation of the 'theory of reality' underpinning transport planning. In designing and monitoring transport policies, the planner requires a general framework that enables him to consider those components which, taken together, constitute the need/demand for access to activity opportunities. Such a framework must, it is suggested, enable us to specify the information needs of policy-makers in terms of a set of four questions (questions which articulate the phases of the rational model of decision-making).

1. Given a hypothetical situation in which the full range of potential activities were readily available, what *is* that group of activities that any sub-group in question would choose to take part in, and with what frequency?
2. What appears to be the set of constraints operating to inhibit or prevent those activities being engaged in?
3. How do these constraints arise? (e.g. through the land-use system, cost, vehicle design, time-related aspects?)
4. What instruments of policy are available to the decision-maker and to what extent could action employing those instruments be expected to remove constraints and improve access to the desired activities?

The goals which the transport planner addresses, and the indicators through which policy analysis and design take place can all, it is argued, be set within the activity perspective. If we focus on mobility alone, it is argued that we are in danger of adopting indicators which are conceptually unrelated to the real function of the system we are planning for. (This is a problem familiar in other policy areas, for example housing, Carlisle 1972).

5. NEED AND TRANSPORT

The 1977 Transport White Paper uses the term 'need' in relation to mobility and the term also appears in a number of other transport planning contexts (for example in the legislation relating to the Transport Policies and Programmes system). While the measurement of 'need' may be a fairly new problem within transport, it has a longer history in other areas of public policy, for example in the health service (Bradshaw 1972) and in housing (Knight 1974).

As has been noted above, the conceptual structure to which a measurement system relates is highly relevant to policy design. Yet, even if the activity system is accepted as the appropriate conceptual structure, we are still faced with choices of definition of terms like 'need'. Referring to medical care, Bradshaw has suggested that there are three potential sources of definition: the normative, the comparative, and the subjective. *Normative* definitions rest on the postulation of a standard below which no one should fall, as, for example, Rowntree's income standards. (These, incidentally, were based on what must be acquirable and thus have close parallels with the concept of an activity budget as implied above.) The *comparative* approach uses the standards pertaining to another group as a design target. An example would be the use of car owners' behaviour to set standards for individuals to whom a car is not available. *Subjective* need, which may be felt or expressed need, rests on the other hand, on an individual's own judgements and desires and will reflect his own norms and expectations rather than those of others.

The way in which we arrive at the standards for policy design is likely to range across all of these sources of definition. However, a key problem in our analysis and design should be seen as that of considering access to activity rather than movement as the key to our measures and indicators.

6. A POTENTIAL LEARNING FRAMEWORK

So far this paper has set out one particular 'theory of reality' within which transport planning and policy-making now operate. In this section, the paper discusses the development of relevant research strategies.

Since we are here concerned with the role of transport policies as welfare policies, it may be helpful to attempt to relate what we know of the operation of transport demand to welfare theory. This can be done at a simplistic level by taking the simple welfare model (figure 1).

$$\text{Utility} = f \frac{(I, \; P, \; S,)}{D}$$

and expressing it in the following form:

Figure 1. The relationship of transport demand to welfare theory.

From such a model it becomes possible to show how welfare is determined in terms which relate to the activity system and to transport. Such a translation into transport-relevant variables then enables us to produce a framework relevant to the discussion of policy research in transport (figure 2). An examination of this framework then enables us to assess which areas of existing knowledge are relevant to our changed 'theory of reality', and which require future development.

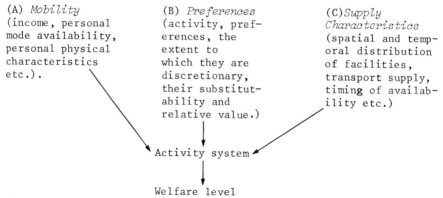

Figure 2. Welfare levels as determined by the activity and transport systems.

Of the three components cited here, the spatial interaction component (C), suggested under the term 'supply characteristics', is undoubtedly the best developed and the most familiar. The Hansen type accessibility models and their adaptations enable us to describe the spatial distribution of opportunities in terms which link land-use patterns and transport provision. This component alone can provide a means of evaluation of transport and location policies (Wachs 1973; Martin and Dalvi 1976). Personal mobility or potential mobility (component (A) in the framework) is also an area about which we have a great deal of information. In this instance, the knowledge is derived from the movement-focussed studies of transport from a previous period. However, the actual relationship between movement levels and person characteristics has often been inferential with the consequent absence of a conceptual link. Nevertheless, there is a reasonable base suggested here within which this explanation can be developed.

Component (B) (figure 2) forms the set of factors about which the present state of understanding is limited. The reason for this is that this group, expressing preferences and motivations, constitutes the most distinctive component of a welfare perspective on transport as opposed to one based in revealed demand. This requires an understanding of both the contents of the activity budgets of individuals and sub-groups, and of the ordering of their priorities and their trade-offs among these activities. In particular, an examination of any systematic patterns of association between preference patterns and more visible indicators is essential.

The general model presented here might tend to imply that we can examine the factor-sets independently. One of the problems that we have to face is the complex interactions which exist between the separate components in figure 2 (for example, the lowering of expectation which occurs among populations with low levels of fixed facilities provision, a variable developed by feedback between components (B) and (C)).

A number of important functions can be claimed for this framework, given the current state of knowledge:
1. By disaggregating the components of welfare in transport-relevant terms, the formulation is highly suggestive both of general

research areas and of particular research designs. It highlights the
need for control of potentially intervening variables, both within
one factor set and in their across-set interactions.
2. It provides an integrative framework (albeit at present at far
too general a level) against which to appraise existing areas of
knowledge, and to specify future research needs in relation to that
knowledge.
3. In relation to policy design, it enables us to take account of
the fact that transport-relevant policies may operate at the level of
the individual, the household, or the transport-land use system.
Indeed, it may not necessarily fall within a 'transport' remit in
terms of relevant policy instruments.
4. The framework can also constitute a common conceptual base for
both researchers and practitioners in policy-making, and allow a
dialogue to take place.

7. WHERE DO WE GO NEXT?

The very general formulation presented earlier now enables us to
propose a number of short-term developments which may enable us to
provide decision-makers with an information base more closely related
to the questions now being asked.
      Within this framework we can also begin to specify priorities for
transport research in the social sciences:
1. The adaptation and testing of various constructs of physical
accessibility and an examination of their relevance to observed
behaviour.
2. The improvement of our understanding of the ways in which
constraints on mobility operate at the individual and household level
(e.g. Jones 1979; Benwell and White 1979).
3. The development of techniques which will enable us to determine
the preferences and perceptions which determine subjective need or
demand for access to particular activities.
      This rather personal statement of a conceptual framework is not
intended to suggest that the objective of future developments should
be to produce one complex model to answer all questions. The
intention is to suggest how various strands of current research fit
together and relate to a new 'theory of reality' in transport policy-
making. What we must recognize is that within such a framework, there
can exist a variety of models of differing levels of complexity which
can be applied to different levels and kinds of decision. But, while
it may be wrong for us to aspire to the production of a single complex
model, it *is* necessary for us to see quite clearly how simpler models
and questions relate to one another. This paper suggests one way in
which, at least at the conceptual level, such integration may be
sought. A pragmatic structure is outlined which may both contribute
to the emergence of a more rigorous analytic framework, and form a
'bridge' until such a framework is developed.

8. THE FRAMEWORK IN PRACTICE - TWO ILLUSTRATIVE CASE STUDIES

This final section briefly discusses two recent pieces of policy
research carried out by the author, and places them within the framework presented above.

The Harlow concessionary fares study

The problem with the concessionary fares study was to decide how to maximize the benefits from a budget (funded by the Harlow Council for Voluntary Services) which was bound to decline in real terms. Harlow District Council commissioned a study which would provide an information base against which to evaluate future options, and a 1 in 6 (17 per cent) (n = 350) survey of the elderly was undertaken to provide that information (Benwell 1977).

Concessionary fares policies have a general welfare objective. Consequently, 'need for' or 'dependence upon' buses must be adopted in some appropriate form as a design criterion. This relates back to questions discussed earlier in this paper as to whether the Local Authority should be concerned with adopting policies which have increased or maintained trip-making as a goal, or should the concern be with the role of public transport within the patterns of access to activity within the sub-group in question?

The survey provided four main pieces of information at a crude level:

1. a picture of absolute frequencies of travel by mode and purpose;
2. a more detailed account of bus use in relation to total travel;
3. a comparison by neighbourhood of different measures of bus dependence;
4. a base for a cost-effectiveness assessment of full-fare and half-fare policies.

Even at a crude level the data set enables the researcher to highlight conflicting aspects of the different options available; whether the local authority is interested in buying trips (and increasing 'value' for its money?). If so, does it matter that some of the target group can derive little or no benefit from a bus pass? How far do certain residential locations or particular physical conditions lead to a greater need for, or dependence upon, the public transport system?

In the analysis, current behaviour (bus use) was examined in relation to access to local facilities, peoples' interest in having a bus pass (Harlow, uniquely, offered other options in its place), their stated ability to walk, and the structure of households. Figure 3 provides a brief summary from the report to the local authority, showing how different parts of the town compared.

One obvious problem to emerge from the survey was the difference between the objective and the subjective measures of level of facility. (One 'well-provided' neighbourhood centre was particularly disliked and unattractive.) Another problem was that a potentially large proportion (up to 40 per cent) of the elderly did not necessarily get improved access to activities by the single policy instrument of the bus pass in its current form. A broader view of 'transport' may allow us to be more aware of how non-transport policy instruments can relate to welfare (e.g. home location and fixed facilities provision).

The Carrick Study

The research project OPTIC (Operation Public Transport in Carrick) was undertaken during 1978. This research had the objective of providing information against which the passenger transport network

Figure 3. Harlow - An inter-neighbourhood comparison of some measures of trip-making.

	who cannot walk to shops		who can walk to shops but do so less than once a week		total by neighbourhood in these two categories		who make one trip or less per week by bus		mean distance (km) from nearest neighbourhood centre	mean distance from the central shopping area (km)
	No.	%	No.	%	No.	%	No.	%		
Old Harlow	4	6.6	14	22.9	18	29.5	15	24.6	0.4	3.3
MK Hall North	2	9.1	4	19.0	6	28.1	3	13.6	0.4	2.2
MK Hall South	2	4.0	8	16.0	10	20.0	9	18.0	0.6	2.0
Netteswell	2	3.5	20	35.1	22	38.6	15	26.3	0.5	0.9
Little Parndon	17	41.5	10	24.4	27	65.9	11	26.8	–	0.9
Hare Street	4	15.4	5	19.2	9	34.6	10	38.4	–	0.6
Potter Street	3	6.5	20	43.5	23	50.0	10	21.7	0.3*	3.0
Brays Grove	4	16.7	4	16.7	8	33.4	1	4.2	0.5	2.0
Tye Green	5	9.6	13	25.0	18	34.6	4	7.7	0.5	1.5
Latton Bush	6	17.6	7	20.6	13	38.2	3	8.8	0.4	2.4
Passmores	10	26.3	10	26.3	20	52.6	6	15.8	0.5	1.6
Great Parndon	11	29.7	5	13.5	16	43.2	6	16.2	0.9	1.8
Stewards	6	16.2	7	18.9	13	35.1	4	10.8	0.7	2.2
K'moor	4	30.8	1	7.7	5	38.5	0	0	0.5	
All Harlow	80	14.9	128	23.8	208	38.7	97	18.11	2.4	

*Sub-neighbourhood centre. Becomes 1.3 if Bush Fair is regarded as neighbourhood centre.
Per cents are of the total sample in each row.

in part of rural Ayrshire could be designed to optimize user benefits under a reduced public transport subsidy. Once more, the concept of need is inherent in the analysis and interpretation, since section 151 of the 1973 Local Government (Scotland) Act mentions 'the needs of an area' as a design criterion for subsidy allocation. An on-vehicle survey, a household travel survey and an attitudinal survey of the 'bus dependent' were all carried out to collect information on bus use, travel patterns and attitudes to current services. Bus dependence was defined in terms of belonging to one of the following groups, namely a member of a non-car-owning household, a non-licence holder in a car-owning household, or a licence holder in a car-owning household to whom the car is not normally available.

The use of an attitude survey was a device for introducing the concepts of accessibility and the activity system into the analysis. The survey was conducted on 246 bus-dependent individuals as a follow-up to the main household survey. The research was designed

to yield data on the following points:
1. a ranking of different activities in terms of the
    importance attributed to public transport for their
    fulfilment;
2. a rating of the current bus service in terms of its
    usefulness to the respondent for accessing different
    activities;
3. a rating of the salient attributes of the service (as
    determined in earlier in-depth interviews);
    additionally a number of 'softer' questions were asked
    about activities and destinations which could not be
    accessed and about possible objectives to be pursued
    under a changed system.

In the analysis, differences in attitudes and expectations were
examined in relation to settlement type (i.e. level of local facilities) and person-type (Benwell 1978). From the responses it was
possible to provide a picture of those activities to which the bus
system provides a less-than-desired level of access, and of those
attributes of the system which, in the individual's view, are felt to
be the main constraint on participation.

The attitude study pointed out a number of issues not highlighted
in conventional surveys, such as which groups and which activities are
poorly served at present and in what ways, where 'satisfaction thresholds' may be identified in existing arrangements (especially timing
and frequency) and which destinations are most valued and by whom. No
attempt was made to predict likely user levels on a changed system.
The research did however produce pointers towards a 'needs' or user
perspective on the existing system's attributes.

These two examples of small-scale policy research have been
referred to in order to underline the assertion that the framework
presented in this paper can encompass a 'theory of reality'. This
approach is appropriate equally to short time-based policy decisions
and to the longer-term emergence of frameworks for academic research.

REFERENCES

Benwell, M. (1977) An examination of the extent and welfare
    implications of bus use by Harlow's elderly. Cranfield Centre
    for Transport Studies Research Memo No. 22, produced for Harlow
    Council.
Benwell, M. (1978) Attitudes to public transport in a rural area (A
    consultancy report to Greater Glasgow PTE). Cranfield Centre for
    Transport Studies Report No. 14.
Benwell, M. and White, I. (1979) Car availability and transport need.
    Traffic Engineering and Control, 20 (8), pp. 410-8.
Bradshaw, J. (1972) A taxonomy of social need, in McClachlan G. (ed.)
    Problems and Progress in Medical Care. Oxford: Oxford University
    Press.
Carlisle, E.M. (1972) The conceptual structure of social indicators
    in Schonfield, A. and Shaw, S. (eds.) Social Indicators and
    Public Policy. London: Heinemann.
Department of Transport (1977) Transport Policy, Cmnd 6836. London:
    HMSO.
Dror, Y. (1968) Public Policymaking Re-examined. London: Leonard
    Hill.

Friedman, J. and Abonyi, G. (1976) Social Learning: A Model for
    Policy Research. International Institute for Applied Systems
    Analysis, Research Memorandum 76-26 Laxenburg, Austria.
Hägerstrand, T. (1970) What about people in regional science?
    Regional Science Association Papers, 24 (1), pp. 7-21.
Jones, P. (1979) 'HATS'; a technique for investigating household
    decisions. *Environment and Planning A*, 11 (1), pp. 59-70.
Knight, T.E. (1974) A conceptual background to the use of social
    indicators for identification of areas of urban deprivation.
    Department of the Environment. Economic and statistical note
    No. 21 (1).
Martin, K.M. and Dalvi, M.Q. (1976) The comparison of accessibility
    by public and private transport. *Traffic Engineering and
    Control*, 17 (12), pp. 509-15.
Mitchell, C.G.B. and Town, S.W. (1977) Accessibility of various
    social groups to different activities. Transport and Road
    Research Laboratory, SR 258.
Wachs, M. and Kumagai, T.G. (1973) Physical accessibility as a social
    indicator. *Socio-Economic Planning Sciences*, 7 (5), 437-56.

An application of the social sciences to transport planning

KIT MITCHELL

1.   INTRODUCTION

Many of the criticisms of current methods of transport planning are
concerned with their lack of social content; for example, that they
have been too much concerned with vehicles and too little with
people, that they have not been equitable, and simply that they are
incapable of describing the complexities of real life and predicting
the consequences of many of the changes that may occur. Much social
research on transport has been and is being done; some, particularly
in the field of economics, is incorporated into operational transport
planning techniques. But it is by no means clear how the branches of
social science other than economics can best be used to improve
transport planning. This is the subject that this paper addresses.

It is common to think of social science as meaning those studies
directly concerned with people's behaviour and problems and decisions
in their normal lives, but this is too narrow, as it really only
includes sociology, geography and perhaps social psychology, and
excludes branches such as philosophy. So this paper will consider,
first, the range of transport questions to which the social sciences
could be applied, and the ways they are being applied at present;
second, possible ways of putting the social sciences into operational
planning methods; and finally, suggestions of the ways in which we
might go next.

2.   POSSIBLE APPLICATIONS OF THE SOCIAL SCIENCES

The range of possible technical ways in which the social sciences
could be applied to transport planning is enormous. A list, probably
incomplete, in rising order of complexity might be as follows:
  (1) improvements to conventional demand analysis by market
      segmentation and attitudinal techniques;
  (2) improving demand analysis by considering constraints on
      behaviour (use of HATS, or differences between car users
      and car non-users);
  (3) identifying access patterns to different types of activity;

(4) identifying travel requirements and problems of various social groups;
(5) quantifying the extent to which opportunities are restricted for particular groups of people by difficulties of reaching the opportunities;
(6) quantifying the extent to which activities are foregone because of difficulties of access;
(7) developing a theory to represent the ways in which life-style (residential location, type of job, pattern of activities, pattern of friendships) is affected by transport availability (if at all).

The first three of these applications are relatively routine today. The fourth and fifth are topics of current research, and the last two have hardly been touched. While it is clear that these last are at the basis of many of the worries people have over changes in transport provision, it is by no means obvious that they are topics that are amenable to quantitative research. This paper will not touch on social studies of the workings of institutions and the processes of taking decisions, though there appears to be useful work that could be carried out on these topics. Similarly, a general review of current applications of social research to transport planning is given in two working papers issued by LTR1 Division of the Department of Transport (Martin and Voorhees Associates 1978a and b).

In addition to the different technical applications of social sciences listed above, it is important to distinguish between a number of different ways in which the results are used.

Most social research studies end with a report which describes and perhaps explains what is happening in some group or area, and which improves the understanding and the quality of decisions of those who read it (see, for example, Hillman *et al.* 1973). The effect of such work on either policy or specific planning is indirect, but appears to be quite powerful.

When a piece of research has been completed, and particularly if it has produced a data bank that can be interrogated, the researchers are in a position to answer specific questions raised by admini-strators. For example, the National Travel Survey makes it possible to give quantitative answers to questions such as the social characteristics of bus users, the role played by public transport in rural areas, what journey purposes cars are used for, and how travel differs between car-owning and non-owning households. Because existing data are used, answers can be given very quickly, which is necessary if the results are to be made available in time to help with specific decisions. This kind of activity seems to be appreci-ated and certainly can improve the quality of decisions by ensuring that they are made in the fullest possible knowledge of both the current situation and of any constraints that will affect the outcome of the decisions. However, although the use of existing data is valuable in answering general policy questions, it is rarely possible to use existing data to plan specific changes to transport systems or to answer specific questions relating to particular localities.

To date, the use of social research in operational planning is relatively limited. In the marketing field, social segmentation of

potential markets is used to improve estimates of demand for new
services. The current trend to disaggregate analysis of survey data
is a step towards the routine use of the approach of the social
scientist. It is fairly common to use a range of the non-structured
survey techniques of the social scientist to decide on the general
ways in which services are to be developed, but usually without being
able to make confident numerical predictions of the effects of the
developments. If these techniques are used to derive objectives for
transport plans, the derivation is done intuitively, rather than by
any formal method. It may well be that there cannot be a formal
method, as the development of objectives involves weighting the
attitudes and requirements of different groups of people and this is
properly a political process. However, the fact remains that to date
it has rarely proved possible to use social science directly in
detailed operational transport planning (for an exception to this,
see Benwell 1978). Until this can be done routinely, the social
sciences will remain somewhat on the sidelines of transport planning.

3.   THE USE OF THE SOCIAL SCIENCES IN TRANSPORT PLANNING

At present transport planning is based on one of three approaches.
The first of these is the identification of existing or predicted
problems, such as congestion, frequent accidents, or environmental
intrusion, and the subsequent elimination of the problems by
improvements to infrastructure or the introduction of traffic management schemes. The second, mainly applicable to freight or public
passenger transport, is the commercial appraisal of investment to
produce a financial profit. The third is the appraisal of expenditure on transport provision in order to produce social benefits.
     The appraisal of an investment is almost always made using a
conventional demand analysis for the users of the changed or new
transport system, possibly including costs or benefits to travellers
on other modes due to changes in congestion, and to local residents
affected by environmental side-effects. No value is put on opportunities created or suppressed, or on the values of activities that are
changed as a result of the change to the transport system, or on the
changes to the pattern of land-use development that are induced.
     One relatively straightforward use of the social sciences would
be to include in travel surveys questions on travel problems and
frustrated or impracticable trips, and so identify any area or groups
in which or for whom opportunities are abnormally low. This could be
a relatively simple extension of the existing disaggregate, or
market segmentation, approach to the analysis of travel surveys.
     A more radical approach would be for local authorities to
consider the quality of access to a small number of key activities
(work, shopping and medical care, for example), and to use conventional transport planning methods to determine the extent to which
some given level of accessibility could be achieved without wasteful
provision of transport. Before this approach could be used it would
be necessary to establish measures of accessibility that do predict
whether or not people feel that they are able to reach activities,
and how the values of these measures vary for different activities
and for different types of people. It would be desirable to measure
how people's participation in different activities changes as access
to them becomes more difficult, and possibly also to try and measure

the level of accessibility that is necessary before people feel an opportunity to participate exists, even if they choose not to do so. A review of accessibility measures has just been completed at the Transport and Road Research Laboratory (Jones 1980).

This approach would put a different emphasis on transport planning. It could well better reflect the feelings of the people for whom the transport system was being planned and demonstrate directly the equity or otherwise of particular proposals. A system designed to meet objectives defined in terms of accessibility would not maximize social benefit or financial profit, but there would be nothing to stop the social and financial balance sheets for systems being calculated. Indeed, if this approach were to be followed it is likely that the final system chosen would achieve as much of the accessibility required within constraints on social benefits and financial budgets, rather than completely achieve the objectives regardless of cost and social benefits. On the other hand, setting rigid standards could lead to resources being employed inefficiently to provide public transport services that few people used. However, the accessibility approach to transport planning has been used successfully in a major transport study for West Yorkshire (Cooper *et al.* 1979).

Reverting to the more conventional transport planning, there is a distressingly long list of practical conditions under which we cannot predict the demand for transport. We cannot with confidence predict the transport effects of parking policies, traffic restraint, staggering of school or work hours, fuel price or availability, or major changes in the rate of economic growth. The reason for our inability to predict the effects of such changes or policies is that travel is only a reflection of the complex pattern of household activities. People are remarkably good at adapting to change, and the process of adapting can lead to results that conventional transport models could not predict. The Oxford HATS simulation looks at household constraints and the process of adaptation (Jones 1979), but even conventional travel surveys such as the County Surveyors' Trip Rate Data Bank will yield extremely detailed pictures of household behaviour. If sufficient detail is available, the reasons for peoples' behaviour often become self-evident, and indeed the household's probable behaviour under new circumstances may be predictable. If the gulf could be bridged between analysis and prediction for individual households, and that for complete cities, many of the difficulties of transport modelling would disappear.

4. WHERE DO WE GO NEXT?

Social research in transport must be a balance between improving the things we can already do and which are at present useful, and working towards new methods of including social factors in transport planning. In practice it is often possible to do both. For example, studies TRRL has done of the mobility problems of particular groups of people also include questions on how participation in activities changes with ease of access to them. In this way, while doing studies that are useful in themselves, we are developing the background data for a possible accessibility approach to transport planning. In a study we are making of the effects of the Tyne and Wear Metro we are looking at changes in accessibility, perceived changes in opportunity, changes

in travel behaviour, changes in participation in activities, and
changes in land-use development (Miles and Mitchell 1979). The
study could well provide the necessary background for the testing of
an operational measure of accessibility, and thus lead to methods of
transport planning that begin explicitly to take account of social
factors that we can only include intuitively at present.

REFERENCES

Benwell, M. (1978) Operation of public transport in Carrick; the
    attitude survey. Cranfield Centre for Transport Studies, CTS
    Report No. 14.
Cooper, J.S.L., Daly, P.N. and Headicar, P.G. (1979) West Yorkshire
    Transportation Studies: 2. Accessibility analysis. *Traffic
    Engineering and Control*, 20 (1), pp. 27-31.
Hillman, M., Henderson, I. and Whalley, A. (1973) *Personal Mobility
    and Transport Policy*. Political and Economic Planning Broadsheet
    542.
Jones, P.M. (1979) 'HATS': A technique for investigating household
    decisions. *Environment and Planning A*, 11 (1), pp. 59-70.
Jones, S.R. (1980) Accessibility measures: a literature review.
    Transport and Road Research Laboratory. Report in preparation.
Martin and Voorhees Associates (1978a) Social research techniques:
    a manual. Department of Transport. LTR1 Working Paper 5.
Martin and Voorhees Associates (1978b) A review of social research
    techniques and some applications to transport planning.
    Department of Transport. LTR1 Working Paper 4.
Miles, J.C. and Mitchell, C.G.B. (1979) The Tyne and Wear Public
    Transport Impact Study. Paper presented to the PTRC Annual
    Summer Meeting, University of Warwick.

© Crown Copyright 1981. This paper expresses the personal views of the
author, which are not necessarily those of the Department of the
Environment or of the Department of Transport. The paper is published
by permission of the Director, Transport and Road Research Laboratory.

PART TWO

Methods of Survey
and Analysis
in Transport

Survey Methods: an Investigative Tool in Transport Research

The papers in this part of the book form a major review of the current state-of-the-art in the theory and practice of survey and analysis methods in transport. The first section covers the ways in which different survey methods can be used in identifying and under-standing selected transport issues; the second section examines the methodologies available, starting with the aggregate models and then covering the disaggregate, behavioural and attitudinal methods, ending with the most recent developments in psychometrics and activity-based analyses; in the third section, the theoretical approaches are contrasted with a particular case study where the methods have been implemented, and the section concludes with the questions: What do we want from travel demand analysis? Can any lessons be learnt from the parallel developments in urban systems analysis?

The context of the survey as an important method for highlighting particular transport issues is introduced by Barry Hedges; here some of the aspects of sample surveying are outlined. The concepts of response errors are commented on, together with the necessity for a robust sampling framework. Once these problems have been overcome, the researcher must then decide how he wants to describe and explain travel behaviour, as this may involve different approaches to data collection; whether it is essentially a quantitative, fact-finding exercise or whether it is a qualitative, attitudinal survey. Some of the problems and pitfalls are covered, and the paper concludes by offering some guidance to those investigating transport issues.

In the second paper, Frank Sando describes the National Travel Survey and Long Distance Travel Survey. These are the two major surveys organized by the Department of Transport and are carried out on a regular basis (for example, the NTS data are collected every three years). The main purpose of these surveys is to provide background information on personal travel in Great Britain, and this forms an essential data base against which secular changes such as those in

car ownership and population can be compared. The sampling base, the
types of information selected, and response rates are all covered,
together with comments on the problems of organizing such large-scale
data collection exercises, the difficulties of interpretation, and
the use to which the information is put by decision-makers from the
government downwards.

The final paper in this section complements the other two in that
it traces the development and application of social research methods
in transport. In this essentially personal perspective, David
Hollings comments on the problems which have been encountered in the
use of such survey methods, particularly those which enable inter-
disciplinary research teams to communicate with both planners and
transport operators. Wherever possible, the principal phases in
development are illustrated with actual examples of how research
methods have evolved in response to the changing demands of decision-
makers.

In the past the importance of questionnaire and interview design
has tended to take second place to technical research. It is
essential that this imbalance should be redressed. Different survey
methods have much to offer, from the structured national survey down
to the highly personal unstructured in-depth survey. The collection
of data should be problem specific with an explicit statement on the
limitations, and perhaps more important, the purpose of the survey
should be comprehensible both to the policy-maker and the public.
The availability of time series data now makes analysis of change
possible and this may lead to a new set of techniques which emphasize
dynamic rather than static processes.

Certain other broad issues seem to suggest themselves: whether
for instance data collection should focus on trips as the unit of
study or activities so that sequences of events can be investigated;
whether observation may offer a more accurate representation of
behaviour than interview, as the latter is fraught with inaccuracies
in recall on the part of the respondent. Perhaps small-scale
highly-structured surveys might give as accurate results as a much
larger-scale exercise. It seems that transport surveys are large
enough compared with other surveys, but the degree of certainty which
can be placed on the output is low. All these points raise further
questions on methodology, but the basic dilemma is to establish the
purpose of the survey; should it be to inform people of what is
happening or is it more important to understand how issues are
articulated? The conclusion seems to be that the purpose of surveys
should be to provide information which - although it may be approximate - is reliable, rather than information which claims to be
precise but is wrong.

An introduction to some aspects of sample surveying

BARRY HEDGES

This paper is primarily concerned with providing an introduction to structured quantitative sample surveys and the collection of data by personal interview. Mention is also made of the role of qualitative survey methods, and the final section draws out some of the issues with respect to research on transport.

1. SAMPLING

As is well known, a sample is a kind of miniature model of its parent population. The larger the sample, the greater the resemblance between sample and population, and the greater the precision with which any population characteristic can be estimated from the sample. It is often not appreciated that the proportion the sample forms of the population is not normally a factor of much importance: in most surveys it is the absolute sample size that primarily determines sampling error in samples of a given population.

But if there is *bias* in the design or execution of the sample, estimates of population characteristics will be wrong however large the sample may be. Error from samples can be considered as comprising two components, sampling error and bias. Sampling error can be reduced to any desired magnitude (given sufficient resources) simply by increasing the sample size, but bias will be unaffected by this: thus, the larger the sample, the greater the relative importance of the bias.

Bias can arise in sample selection in various ways. The sampling frame, for example, may be deficient in its coverage of the population. Or the design may have features that give unequal selection probabilities to members of the population. Bias can also arise through failure to achieve the selected sample, principally through non-response. Typically, about 20 per cent of a selected adult population sample in Britain do not respond. This percentage varies from case to case, but non-response in London tends to be particularly high. The evidence suggests that in most household surveys non-response does not introduce large biases (though there are some established tendencies, for example for larger households to have a

greater propensity to respond than smaller ones). But this should
not permit the dangers of non-response to be underestimated; it is
often troublesome and can lead to serious bias in certain instances.

The fact that larger samples tend to have smaller sampling errors
should not lead to the uncritical acceptance of size as an indicator
of sampling error magnitude. Multi-stage (clustered) designs are
in common use in survey research because of their cost-efficiency
(though not for transport surveys of the standard type, where their
use is precluded by the need for fine zonal data for modelling
purposes). In a multi-stage design, sampling errors are normally
larger than those for simple random sampling by a factor known as the
'design effect'. Thus a sample which has a small design effect may
yield estimates with smaller sampling errors than those of a larger
sample which happens to have a large design effect. In practice, the
choice of sample size is determined primarily by the level of
disaggregation likely to be required in analysis and by available
resources. The choice usually involves a compromise.

Sample design and, particularly, sample size are important
determinants of survey costs, but if costs are left aside, the
problems sampling presents tend to be less difficult to solve than
many of the others connected with surveys, such as questionnaire
design. In some surveys, sampling is especially difficult, but for
most of the choice of design is a tactical question of cost-efficiency
and does not raise fundamental issues.

2. NON-SAMPLING ASPECTS

If sampling error and sampling bias are assumed not to exist (if,
for example, we assume that we survey the entire population), what
are the characteristics of the other aspects of the survey?

Its prime function is to *describe* the population: What do its
members do? What are their circumstances? What, as far as we can
discover them, are their mental processes? It can be stated that
surveys have special functions, such as their role in experimentation
or in monitoring, but these also are essentially descriptive. It is
also the survey's aim to explain, even to predict, but explanation
and prediction will normally be analytical processes firmly founded
on good descriptions.

'Facts'

It is convenient to regard data collected by surveys as comprising
either 'facts' or 'attitudes'. 'Facts' are involved in response to
the first two of the three questions posed above. It is widely
believed that it is easier to collect valid factual data than valid
attitudinal data. This is a crude generalization, but can be taken
as broadly true. Factual data are capable, at least in principle, of
verification. Although the number of surveys that have directly
verified their collected 'facts' at the level of the individual
sample members is small, there has been a good deal of aggregate
verification of one kind or another, for example comparing sample
data with the census or other sources.

Simple, accessible, current facts (like the respondent's age) are
usually not difficult to establish.

Sometimes the requirement is for complex *sets* of facts (for
example all journeys made in the past week, or net housing costs).

The problems of ascertaining good factual data are well documented.
They include such matters as memory error, a tendency to think events
more recent than they actually were, lack of knowledge, responses
biased towards the socially acceptable and so forth. One difficulty
in public policy surveys is that respondents may not have a particular
concept that policy-makers have evolved: for example, a recent survey
to establish the use of legal services had to disaggregate this
concept, which had no clear identity to respondents, into separate
items that did; these were then used to provide the required synthesis.
An example of the same kind of problem is encountered in coding journey
purposes, since respondents are unfamiliar with this particular
categorization.

'Attitudes'
This term is used loosely here to describe any kind of mental set or
process, and includes not only attitudes but awareness, perception,
belief and feelings. Psychologists have attempted to define an attitude, but there is no clear, universally accepted definition.
Attitudes are studied both as policy objects in their own right and
(more often) because they help to explain behaviour. The minimization
of subjectively experienced environmental disturbance is an example of
the first kind (we are using the term attitude in a broad enough sense
to include sensations of disturbance).

A major problem of attitude research is the lack of external
validation. Although attitudes are linked to behaviour, the link is
normally not close enough for behaviour to serve this purpose. The
type of verification in aggregate that provides much of our knowledge
of the way factual questions operate is not available for attitude
questions.

More than factual questions, attitude questions tend to lack
robustness in the face of question form or wording differences. This
does not necessarily mean that attitudes themselves are unstable, but
it certainly makes them more difficult to study. Question wording
experiments in the 1940s and 1950s showed this, but researchers tended
to fall back on the untested assumption that *relationships* were stable
in form even if marginal totals were not, or on batteries of items
which performed a kind of averaging and stabilizing function. One
approach to attitude measurement is to regard the attitude as a
probably complex, multi-dimensional composite; rather than squeeze it
with difficulty into uni-dimensional format, it may be better to bring
out its multiplicity and try to reconstruct it inductively from its
varied manifestations in responses to a wide range of questions. It
would be more convenient if an attitude could be located somewhere on
a simple bi-polar scale (for example from 'favourable' to 'unfavourable'), but if that is not an adequate description of the attitude in
question, convenience must be sacrificed.

3. QUALITATIVE WORK

In studying attitudes, the rigid boundaries of quantitative techniques
are often too limiting. The researcher then has recourse to a variety
of other methods ranging from the semi-structured interview to the
informal 'depth' interview or group discussion. These methods have a
vital role in the opening stages of a research programme, key elements
being quantified in later stages. But sometimes they are incapable

of, or do not need, quantification. In such contexts qualitative
methods have great potential value, but also potential for misuse.
They are much more influenced by the researcher's subjective viewpoint: quantitative surveys are also influenced by this, but the
extent of influence is much more clearly discernible by others.
Qualitative surveys are almost always based on small and unrepresent-
ative samples. This does not matter in some circumstances, but it
does in others. Finding the right balance between qualitative and
quantitative is a major target of research programme design: too
little qualitative work is likely to result in lack of understanding
and sensitivity; too little quantitative work may result in undisci-
plined speculation and viewpoints of which the bias may remain
unperceived.

4. DATA REQUIREMENTS IN TRANSPORT

Establishing the facts about patterns of travel does not in
principle pose particularly acute problems. Requirements for disaggregation however, tend to be greater than in many other fields,
leading to large sample sizes. This is particularly so with surveys
intended to provide data for transport modelling purposes, for which
a network of fine zones is the basis; for these, it is often not
possible to take advantage of the scope afforded in other contexts
for using multi-stage designs to improve efficiency.

Travel behaviour is also very varied, and there are advantages
in studying each respondent's trips over a period of at least a
week. But this is likely to require recourse to diary methods, since
recall without such an aid is insufficiently reliable. This, coupled
with the large sample size, tends to make major fact-gathering
studies expensive, and it is particularly important to use cost-
effective designs. A good deal remains to be done on the basic
methods; for example, the travel diary appears to be subject to an
element of respondent 'fatigue', in that fewer trips tend to be
recorded later in the diary than at the beginning (starting days are
varied between sample members to minimize such effects).

Attitudinal work was for a long time not well-developed in the
transport field, even when large sums were being spent on studying
travel behaviour; more recently, however, it has come to play an
important role. The central question - why people choose the travel
modes they do - seems at first sight to be simple to answer, but in
fact has proved curiously intractable. The various factors involved
can be discovered reasonably easily (reliability, frequency, comfort,
cost, privacy and so forth), but measuring them is more difficult,
since in dealing with decision-making it is necessary to be concerned
with perceptions rather than with the objective facts of, say, cost
structures. It has, for example, been shown that motorists do not
have an accurate idea of the cost of motoring, and that they tend to
underestimate it. Other variables, such as comfort, are based
largely or entirely on subjective perceptions, for which there is no
objective criterion. In any case, people do not appear to optimize
in their decision-making to the extent that is implied by models
derived from economics. Instead of performing the complex calcula-
tion (at the very least, a weighted sum of variables) with which a
mode decision confronts them, they may simplify by repeating yesterday's behaviour, or may use another mode 'for a change'.

Modelling has played a larger part in transport than in most other fields of social research, and has had a good deal of success. This very success has, however, had an unfortunate side-effect: it seemed so promising an avenue of exploration that more conventional research approaches have been undervalued. In most research fields, a good basic description of patterns of behaviour and attitude is regarded as a necessary, if not a sufficient, condition of informed decision-making. Yet few of the large-scale transport surveys that have been done in Britain have led to descriptive or analytical reports: the data set has been used solely as an input to modelling.

It is perhaps significant that the results of the 1975/76 National Travel Survey (NTS) were only published as a general report in July 1979. The purpose of the NTS is in fact mainly descriptive, and its primary role is as a data set to be consulted by administrators and others in relation to specific problems that arise. Some of these issues are taken up in the next two papers which examine in greater detail the functions of the National Travel Survey, the Long-Distance Travel Survey and other social survey methods. The development of modelling techniques and their capabilities are extensively covered in the eleven other papers in this part of the book. However, it should be remembered that, whatever theoretical advances are made, there will still be a considerable demand both for the collection of reliable primary data and for the greater utilization of existing sources of secondary data.

The role of survey methods in transport research

FRANK D. SANDO

1. INTRODUCTION

This paper discusses briefly the conventional structured survey as a means of providing background information on the personal travel of residents of Great Britain. This data base is useful as an investigative tool in transport research. The main objectives are as follows:

1. to provide estimates of the general levels and trends in personal travel;
2. to investigate interurban travel and its relationship to demographic, socio-economic and other variables;
3. to estimate the distribution of car ownership and car utilization, and their dependence on demographic, socio-economic and other factors;
4. to estimate personal and household travel generation rates and their dependence on demographic, socio-economic and other variables;
5. to investigate the modal split for journeys of different types;
6. to investigate the competitiveness of public and private transport;
7. to investigate any seasonal variations;
8. to fill gaps in national transport data; taxi and car-hire usage; ownership and usage of two wheeled vehicles; and the distribution of expenditure and mileage on private and business travel;
9. to provide a basic framework for further research using either the data in the survey itself or using the survey as a reference point for other surveys within and outside central government.

The Directorate of Statistics of the Department of Transport currently has two surveys in the field collecting information on personal travel patterns. They are the National Travel Survey (NTS) and the Long-Distance Travel Survey (LDTS).

2. NATIONAL TRAVEL SURVEY

This survey collects data on personal travel patterns and relates
them to both household and individual characteristics and to types of
residential areas. When the survey was introduced in 1964 it was
envisaged that it would be carried out at regular intervals in order
to provide an up-to-date source of personal travel data. The first
survey in 1964 was a pilot survey followed by a major survey in 1965
and a smaller one in 1966. Further surveys were carried out in
1972/73 and 1975/76 and most recently in 1978/79. Prior to 1964 a
number of surveys on private motoring were carried out by the
Government Social Survey (Gray 1969). Although the data from each
travel survey relate only to a single twelve-month period, the series
of surveys enables changing patterns to be identified and thereby
provides a basis for future travel forecasts.

As the National Travel Survey is household interview based, data
on all travel modes including journeys by walking are obtained from
the one source together with household and personal characteristics
for both travellers and non-travellers. The survey data are used in
conjunction with data from British Rail, bus operators, traffic
censuses, roadside surveys and other central government surveys such
as the General Household Survey, the Family Expenditure Survey and
the Census of Population.

General approach
In the 1978/79 survey about 15,000 households were approached by
personal interview throughout the twelve-month period from May 1978
to April 1979. At a first interview information was collected on the
characteristics of (i) the household, (ii) each individual member,
and (iii) the household vehicle(s). A travel diary which acts as an
aide memoire was left with each individual for the purpose of
recording all journeys travelled during a prespecified seven-day
period, together with a car diary for each car available to the
household for recording its movements over a three-week period.
Unlike the travel diary, the car diary recorded the origin and destination of journeys. On the seventh and final day of the travel week,
respondents recorded all walk journeys over 50 yards, whereas for the
previous six days the recording of walk journeys was limited to those
of one mile and over.

At a second visit shortly after the seven day travel period was
completed, the interviewer returned to the household and transcribed
each individual's journeys on to specially prepared journey sheets
and checked the first week of the self-completion car diaries. The
remaining two weeks' car diaries was returned by post.

The survey methodology was piloted and found practicable whilst
the response rates were improved by the payment of incentives to
respondents. In general the survey provided reliable and consistent
results.

Sampling
A three-stage stratified sample is used whereby parliamentary constituencies are taken as the primary sampling units. The constituencies
are stratified by (i) standard regions, (ii) electoral population
density, and (iii) an economic indicator based upon household car
availability rates. For 1978/79, the sample consisted of 240
parliamentary constituencies, three wards in each constituency and

twenty-one addresses in each ward. This clustering helps to reduce interviewer travelling costs. At each stage in the sampling process, a constituency or ward has a probability of selection proportional to the electorate size. The actual addresses are selected using the 'firsting rule' from the electoral register with special rules for dealing with multi-household addresses. Institutions are excluded. The 240 constituencies are divided into four subgroups of sixty, each group being representative of the regions of Great Britain. These subgroups are allocated to the four quarters of the twelve months of the survey. Wards are selected to represent the different population densities and each ward is surveyed for one month. The twenty-one addresses are divided to give three 'travel weeks' starting on each possible day of the week and these are distributed over the month. In this way each day of each month is equally represented in the sampling scheme and thereby a balanced picture of travel throughout the survey period is obtainable.

Response rates
The NTS is a voluntary survey but good response rates have been obtained. In 1975/76 there were 15,120 addresses issued to inter- viewers which resulted in 14,677 households being in scope, that is after allowing for derelict dwellings, institutional addresses, etc. and for 254 extra households found. Of these, 68 per cent were fully productive, 8 per cent provided some travel data, and a further 9 per cent were partially productive without travel data. The other 15 per cent were mostly refusals and non-contacted households.

'Fully productive' does not mean that absolutely every question was answered. The main exception is income: in the 1975/76 survey some 24 per cent of individuals, to which the question applied, did not provide details of their income. In 1975/76 this question was asked in bands using a show card but in 1978/79 a direct question 'What is your income?' was asked with a follow-up question using a show card for those who demurred.

The 1975/76 survey did not include the three-week car diary which was introduced in 1978/79 to meet the monitoring requirements of the Regional Highway Traffic Model. To improve response because of this new part of the survey, incentives are being paid to respondents for each set of weekly journey details provided. Pilot work carried out during 1977 showed this incentive payment to be cost effective.

Type of information collected
The survey collects information on household income, which is considered one of the main determinants of non-work journeys, together with information on journey purposes, distances travelled, time taken and modes of travel, the occurrence of journeys by time of day, by day of week, and the costs of public transport journeys. These journey patterns have been analysed by age and sex of respondents and by household characteristics such as income and family composition (DTp 1979a).

The distribution of the number of cars, motor cycles and bicycles available to households is obtained together with estimates of annual vehicle mileages for motorised vehicles. Average occupancy rates of private passenger vehicles can be derived for the different travel purposes.

3. LONG-DISTANCE TRAVEL SURVEY

The incidence of long-distance journeys, by definition over 25 miles, is rare and therefore ways of supplementing the data from the NTS have been investigated. The current NTS design collects on average only one and a half long-distance journeys per responding household.

Development
Various methods were tried without success to obtain additional data on long-distance journeys. Questions were asked on various commercial omnibus surveys (1970/71) and on central government's General House-hold Survey (1971). Screen-line surveys were not practicable because of the problems associated with stopping motorists on motorways. A selected panel of individuals classified as frequent, not so frequent and less frequent travellers, was set up in 1967. However, it was disbanded because of the difficulty of classifying travel frequency, the high drop-out rate of those initially selected, and the difficulty of maintaining a representative sample as regards household and travel characteristics.

Current methodology
The method that has proved most successful is a postal survey technique and this has been used on a continuous basis since mid-1974. Names and addresses are selected annually from the electoral rolls and allocated to twenty-six fortnightly periods; allowance is made for the fact that the electoral roll published in February becomes progressively more out of date as the year proceeds.
After selecting a name, an introductory letter outlining the purpose of the survey and requesting the respondent's cooperation is forwarded to the address. The questionnaire and a covering letter are despatched, asking respondents about their long-distance journeys in the previous fourteen days before delivery. In order to maintain the response rate a first reminder is posted four days after the period ends and a second reminder, together with a duplicate questionnaire, seven days later. A felt-tipped pen is enclosed with the questionnaire to encourage immediate completion, and the covering letter explains that respondents will receive an address book on receipt of the completed questionnaires. The use of these incentives, felt-tipped pen and address book, have helped to maintain a response rate of around 70 per cent.
Throughout the year about 2000 non-respondents to the postal questionnaire are contacted by personal interview and this both increases the overall response rate and from the data obtained enables estimates for all non-respondents to be made. Addresses of 16- and 17-year olds, whose names are not on the electoral roll, are obtained from respondents, and these people then complete questionnaires which are collected and given appropriate weightings before incorporation into the data bank.
Frequent travellers, that is those persons making more than six journeys in the two weeks, are visited also to check on their under-standing of the questionnaire. Further details are collected of the extra journeys as only details for six journeys can be recorded on the questionnaire, although the total number of journeys in the fortnight is requested. Refinements to the methodology have improved the quality of the data. Experience shows that because of memory failure, week-end journeys are not as fully recorded as week days,

necessitating adjustment of the data, and that the classification
details need to be simple and clearly defined for any self-completion
questionnaire.

4. USES OF SURVEY DATA (NTS AND LDTS)

Some major departmental uses of the data have included:
1. General background information on travel for input to
    transport policy documents (for example, DTp 1976a, 1977a
    1979b).
2, Public transport: detailed use of different modes and the
    expenditure on each by different income group and household
    composition (DTp 1976b).
3. Traffic forecasts: data are provided on car availability
    associated with such factors as household income and popul-
    ation density and car trips by length and purpose.
    Development work on forecasting models has required data
    relating car traffic volumes to factors like car availability
    and income (DTp 1977b)
4. Business and private motoring: data are provided on the
    subsidization of motoring costs relevant to transport
    taxation policy.
5. Road accident analysis: background information is provided
    on the exposure to risk of different groups of people both by
    age and sex. When linked with road accident data, accident
    rates for these different groups can be determined (DTp
    1978).

5. PROBLEMS OF INTERPRETATION

One of the difficulties with large-scale multi-stage stratified
samples is that estimates of the sampling errors are not easy to
compute. NTS is such a case and there are the additional complications of the clustering of individuals within households, and the
fact that neither journeys nor journey stages are independent events.
Work is being carried out to rectify this position based on a paper
by Kish and Hess (1969). The exercise will not only give an idea of
the precision of the estimates, but also indicate whether differences
between results, either within or between surveys, are significant.
This work will also contribute to the discussion on the sample sizes
of any future surveys.
    There are known biases occurring in the survey other than the
statistical sampling errors. When non-response arises it is difficult
to determine the reason, but it may be that frequent travellers are
not available or too busy or that elderly ladies, probably non-
travellers, may be too timid to respond. In the 1978/79 survey, for
example, it may be found that car owners do not respond because of the
three-week self-completion car diary, although this was not apparent
in a pilot survey.
    Any question on income, assuming it can be adequately defined,
causes problems since people in higher-income groups are more likely
to refuse to give this information in particular, and to respond to
the survey in general. This bias in response reduces the sample
sizes and limits the usefulness of some of the main analyses.
    Bias can also arise from differential response in certain areas,

for instance response rates for London and other urban areas are
usually relatively low. The response rate for Scotland is often poor.
Depending on the required analyses it may be advisable to re-weight
regional figures before presenting the national picture.

Although in NTS the data are recorded, using a diary as an aide
memoire, over a seven day period, there has been a tendency for the
average daily trip rates to fall off as the period progresses to day
six. However, on the seventh day there is an up-turn possibly because
respondents are aware that they have to do something different, that
is to record all walks over 50 yards, and possibly because of the
improved recall of events nearest to the time of the second interview.

The best data on purposes are probably those on journeys to and
from work and, for children, to and from school since these journeys
are made regularly. Therefore, journeys to and from work could be
more fully represented in the results than other journey purposes.
Long-distance journeys also may be well recorded, but as they are
comparatively rare events, the random sampling errors associated with
any estimates tend to be large. The recording of holiday journeys is
probably low because of non-response caused by the household being
away from home or being reluctant to take the burden of recording a
diary while away on holiday.

Journey lengths are estimated by respondents and this could
clearly provide scope for errors. More work needs to be done in this
field, but available evidence from a pilot survey in 1977 suggests
that the distances estimated by respondents, when averaged, are only
about 3 per cent different from objectively measured distances.
Respondents also make their own (subjective) estimates of annual
vehicle mileages, journey times and motoring costs which are all prone
to error. It appears that in relative terms people can estimate
longer distances better than short, and that motoring distances are
more reliable than the other modes.

In analysing the travel data there are difficulties in choosing
the count variables - journeys, journey stages, mileages, time or
expenditure. Clearly, care has to be taken in constructing the
hypothesis to be tested. Both journeys and journey stages will be
recorded, but the mileages and durations recorded will not be as
accurate nor the expenditure in the case of public transport. It is
important to ensure that like is being compared with like when using
tabulations prepared from the travel survey data base. In comparing
the results of surveys, whether spatially or temporally, it is
essential to reconcile any differences in definition used. Unfortunately any interviewer differences both within or between surveys have
to be tolerated hence the importance of good interviewer training,
briefing and control.

When comparing with other sources of passenger travel data it is
important to allow for the fact that the NTS is household-based and
limited to British residents, and does not include institutions and
foreign visitors who are included in passenger figures published by
transport operators. Similarly road traffic figures cannot
distinguish between private and non-private motoring nor between
private cars and hire cars (taxis).

Analyses using the income variable, or expenditure figures, are
difficult to interpret because the data are collected over a twelve-
month period and their values can vary greatly in times of inflation;
for example incomes recorded at the beginning of the period are not

strictly comparable with those recorded at the end.

6. POSSIBLE DEVELOPMENTS

Using the current methodology the NTS is very time consuming and takes on average between two to three hours of the interviewer's time if the entire household responds. Consequently the survey has high unit costs and is a considerable burden on both respondents and interviewers. Although ways of streamlining the survey and reducing costs are being explored it is unlikely that the length of the interview can be shortened.

One way of reducing costs would be to use the postal survey technique. Experience with the Long-Distance Travel Survey has shown that it is difficult to get detailed household and personal characteristics, particularly income, and it is unlikely that self-completion of journey details would obtain reliable information on distances and times taken. A seven-day period would not be practical with the postal technique and recourse to a one or two day re-call method would be necessary.

One day re-call could be used on the household interview method with possibly a diary for unusual trips, but to obtain adequate coverage, the sample size would have to be increased. It may also have to be based on individuals instead of households, since it is unlikely that all members of the household will be present at the same time on a random visit. There would be a requirement to get an even spread of interviews over the seven days of the week, which would have to be incorporated into the sampling scheme. There is need for live surveys such as on-train, on-bus and roadside interviews, but these have limitations if valid comparisons are to be made and the characteristics of non-travellers determined. Improved distance estimates for local journeys (short) could be obtained by the interviewers using maps to trace the journeys and could thereby reduce dependence on subjective estimates.

A further problem is to decide the optimum size and frequency of the survey. For practical purposes, both in the fieldwork and for office coding, a continuous survey would be easier to manage since the staff could be engaged permanently on the project. Other users suggest the frequency could be about every five years with an increased sample size. The work on standard errors will be relevant here.

NTS seeks only factual information and has avoided attitude questions, *inter alia* on public transport and roads, since it is misleading to the respondent to imply that their replies will directly affect local conditions. Also hypothetical questions on marginal motoring costs have been avoided. There is scope for specialist surveys on these subjects, as well as more analysis of both reasons for travel and reasons for not travelling, the use of the telephone instead of transport, travel by tradesmen, and other topics.

Various pilot surveys have led to a refinement in the use of the survey as an investigative tool, although it is more accurate to conclude that the pilot surveys have helped to maintain the position against an increase in demand for a more lengthy questionnaire. Nevertheless, there is scope for more detailed analysis into the relative merits and validity of the other alternatives; because continuity is extremely important for comparability, changing to a completely new methodology would need a few surveys to overcome any teething troubles.

REFERENCES

Department of Transport (1976a) *Transport Policy. A Consultation Document*, Volume 1. London: HMSO.

Department of Transport (1976b) *Transport Policy. A Consultation Document*, Volume 2, Paper 2. London: HMSO.

Department of Transport (1977a) *Transport Policy*, Cmnd 6836. London: HMSO.

Department of Transport (1977b) *Report of the Advisory Committee on Trunk Road Assessment*. (Chairman: Sir George Leitch). London: HMSO.

Department of Transport (1978) *Road Accidents in Great Britain 1977*. London: HMSO.

Department of Transport (1979a) *National Travel Survey: 1975/76 Report*. London: HMSO.

Department of Transport (1979b) *Transport Statistics Great Britain 1968-1978*. London: HMSO.

Gray, P.G. (1969) *Private Motoring in England and Wales*, Social Survey Report 329. London: HMSO.

Kish, L. and Hess, I. (1959) On variances of ratios and their differences in multi-stage samples. *Journal of the American Statistical Association*, 154 (286), pp. 416-46.

© Crown Copyright 1981. This paper expresses the personal views of the author, which are not necessarily those of the Department of the Environment or of the Department of Transport.

The evolution of transport policy and planning and the development of applications for social investigation

DAVID HOLLINGS

1. INTRODUCTION

Over the past twenty years there have been substantial changes in planning techniques and the associated research methods. The character of these changes has tended to obscure the somewhat surprising fact that the main issues about which planners are concerned have not changed at anything like the same pace. For example, the problems which generated the impetus for the formation of the Development Commission in the early part of the century provides a catalogue of the main topics of concern in contemporary rural affairs. Reference to the development plans which stemmed from the 1947 Town and Country Planning Act will show that they embrace most of the issues embodied in the recently evolved structure plans.

It is worth recalling also the intensive nature of much of the survey data which were collected in the late 1940s and 1950s in pursuance of the statutory responsibilities to prepare development plans. Whilst much of the data were oriented to the emphasis on physical planning and land-use classification, considerable effort was devoted to quality of life issues ranging from housing stock, through employment and shopping opportunities and choices to leisure facilities. Indeed a great deal of the planning and research activity was inspired by the political and social goal of creating and implementing standards. Here is another contemporary pre-occupation.

Most of the problems arising from the pressures of population movement and the effects of improving infrastructures in some areas and of declining ones in others were identified. What infects hindsight with poignancy were the prevailing faiths that both mechanics and economic resources would be available to secure the implementation of planning policies. Britain's postwar balance of payments problems

and the economic stringency brought about by the Korean war were soon
to be reflected in statements about the need to trim public expenditure budgets. But aspirations have not only been tempered by
resource difficulties. It was increasingly recognized that planning
powers were more easily utilized to prevent a certain limited number
of things happening than to ensure that desired goals were achieved.

It seems helpful to generate a simple historical perspective of
planning evolution before focusing upon transport and transport
planning and research. Transport has an abstruse role in the general
planning context. There is no question that in the immediate postwar
era its importance was felt, if not fully comprehended, and this
emotion provided the stimulus for substantially expanding the degree
of public ownership of operating concerns. In theory, the ownership
of operators allied to the existing central and local government
responsibility for road construction and maintenance created an almost
perfect mechanism for ensuring that transport could be exploited as a
creative instrument in support of planning policies. In practice it
was far from perfect. Some of the possible reasons are elaborated
upon in the following paragraphs. Central however to the argument is
that policy could hardly be effective in the absence of a good understanding of the interaction between transport systems and the public.
It is fundamentally to this gap in knowledge that so much research has
been directed at a host of levels including the marketing of services,
the design of new facilities, the analysis or avoidance of social
conflicts and the importance of transport as an influence upon settlement patterns and social deprivation.

The inhibiting stresses on transport policy
The continual modification of the structure of the public ownership
and control of the transport industry is a manifestation of the social
dissatisfaction with the performance of the industry. Whilst part of
the dissatisfaction is attributable to the scale of financial losses
which began to emerge during the late 1950s, disquiet was also occasioned by the fact that the rail and bus industries appeared to gear
their investment programmes less to the circumstances resulting from
increased car ownership and commercial vehicle operation than to
internal self-created goals. In fact the interaction between planners
and the public transport industry was minimal.

Some of the explanation is that, in general, the industry was
operationally rather than commercially oriented. But it was also due
in some measure to the fact that planners had little practical understanding of transport operations and lacked the facility to
communicate effectively with transport managements whom in any event
they believed would have a good understanding of the nature of demand.
Not only was this untrue, but increasingly transport managements
became pre-occupied with the financial pressures arising from falling
ridership. No longer was it possible to maintain the basic character
of historically-evolved networks through a process of cross subsidization.

The absence of congruency in policies led to the legislation of
which the 1968 Transport Act was the most significant. At this time
were established the Passenger Transport Executives (PTEs), the
concept of the 'socially supported railway', and the requirements for
local authorities to generate transport plans in parallel with
structure plans.

The relationship between planners and operating enterprises was

not the only one in which poor communications had a deleterious
effect. The inequality in the respective responsibilities of engineers and planners both in local and central government was inimical
to the development of a creative relationship. The executive
authority of engineers for the design, construction, maintenance and
control of road networks had no parallel within the planning profession.

With respect to roads, county and city engineers were pursuing
activities for which their basic training had equipped them, and in
which their motivations were re-inforced both by an awareness of
technical competence and by physical manifestations of their achievement. The strength of the profession at local level was in turn
reflected in the national administrative structure by central government activity in respect of trunk roads and motorways. Given the
level of direct responsibility placed upon the engineer, it would be
surprising if he were able to be creatively receptive to many of the
less tangible concepts of planners or to feel other than that public
transport managements were another group of competent professionals
who should determine their own practices.

From a sociological stance it can be seen that the combination of
roles and authorities and rewards could hardly be propitious for the
effective generation and execution of broad transport planning
policies regardless of the aspirations and injunctions incorporated in
legislation. Indeed, the narrowness of interpretations and the lack
of a comprehensive collective understanding is echoed in the sub-title
of a report prepared for the Bedfordshire County Council, 'Public
Transport in Bedfordshire - A Study of Viewpoints' (Voorhees and
Associates 1974). This study included an additional dimension which
was that of public attitudes and concepts. The addition served to
illustrate further the great diversity of perceived priorities within
the overall context.

The major innovation of the 1960s in the field of transport
planning and policy was the introduction of urban and regional transportation studies. They rested on the, now, somewhat questionable
assumptions that large population and employment growths coupled with
rising car ownership would create substantial pressures on transport
infrastructures and that public funds would be available to undertake
major investments.

Although it can be argued that historically the basis of the
transportation/land-use study was to develop understanding of the
impacts upon transport of alternative land uses, in practice,
techniques were applied in order to help engineers recognize the
effectiveness of alternative transport schemes. It is perhaps not
unfair to observe that the role of the planner was frequently to do no
more than generate a single land-use pattern in respect of which
engineers could then devise a range of transport options. In mitiga-
tion it could be argued that at the time there appeared to be more
practical options in respect of transport systems than there were in
land use.

The transportation studies
It is too early to judge the real nature of the impact and influence
of the transportation studies. In the perspective of the matters this
paper is addressing, noteworthy features of the studies were the very
large data collection and compilation processes. To capture an image

of the movement generated by a conurbation there were in most cases, at least: cordon counts and surveys; screen line counts and surveys; parking counts and surveys; public transport counts and surveys; employment surveys; household surveys; commercial vehicle counts and surveys. Great quantities of information about a part of human behaviour were transcribed on to tapes and then fed into a computer within which the very individualistic communications patterns of cities were portrayed by the clinical simulation of zones, nodes and links.

Because of its scale, the process acquired a self-perpetuating momentum and the mathematical modelling and simulation exercises developed their internal language. Journey origins and destinations became trip ends, journey patterns became trip matrices and data manipulation was pre-occupied with stages in simulation known as distribution, assignment and modal split. The transportation study industry spawned new professions, people attracted titles such as network coder or public transport analyst. At the heart of it all were the computer programmes, the logic of which was created by another set of specialists.

The juxtaposition of skills and scale created an activity which in totality was actually beyond the comprehension of most of the participants. It was therefore also technically beyond the grasp of most of the local authority officials and elected representatives whom in theory the tool was supposed to be serving.

The problems were exacerbated by three factors. The transportation study in effect represented a portable kit which presupposed that every city could be studied in exactly the same way. Pressure from central government favoured a level of uniformity in approach because this provided a seductive method for determining how to allocate transport resources in an equitable fashion. Finally, it could be argued that the transportation study provided an orderly mechanism for determining the interactive relationships of transport systems on a conurbation-wide basis and that this was beyond the comprehension of any given set of individuals.

Each of the three concepts has persuasive merit. However, in being attached to transportation studies, they perhaps invested too much confidence in what was in fact a cumbersome and insensitive tool. The studies were, it now transpires, over obsessed with the problems of growth in population, income, employment and car ownership. The techniques were much better at forecasting aggregate volumes of movement than area to area flows; they were better attuned to determining the effects of road traffic schemes and alternative alignments than they were at predicting the results of investment in public transport; and they could not accommodate satisfactorily the differences between rail systems, rapid transit systems, buses and innovatory modes.

In fact, one of the major flaws in the whole process was that scheme generation remained vested in the qualitative judgements of the study participants and their views of which problems it was most important to solve. Predominant amongst these was the peak hour journey to work, particularly in the future, where the vision was dominated by the pressures of high car ownership and decline in public transport. The vision itself was not wholly spontaneous. It was greatly influenced by the fact that the techniques of the transportation study were very much oriented to these issues. Transportation studies could test the impacts of different types of peak hour

transport facilities. They could in no way as easily examine the
impact of alternative fares policies, staggered hours, fuel tax
changes,major pedestrian schemes, or high-price parking policies.

Technically and mechanically transportation studies were concerned
with issues of movement and they essentially adopted an implicit
scale of unchanging social values derived from an analysis of movement. The data actually processed from the huge collection exercises
were directed to establishing how cities and citizens should adapt to
movement demands. The theme was, of course, well enunciated by the
Buchanan team in *Traffic in Towns* (Buchanan 1963).

New Pressures
While the paraphanalia of the transportation study was evolving its
greater complexity, the planning environment was being changed as new
forces gathered impetus within it. In the United States there was a
developing focus upon minority groups, the handicapped and the urban
poor. Planners and politicians gave attention to the decline in city
cores. In these, North American pre-occupations, not for the first
time, anticipated a shift of emphasis in the UK planning climate. It
is interesting to note that with the awakening recognition of the
manifestations of the interaction between transport facilities and
various social groups, together with the impact of changes, has come
also better understanding of the role of transport in maintaining the
vitality of cities. Applications of the advanced technology Downtown
People Mover Systems are designed for much more than moving people to
and from work. They are concerned with the promotion of all manner
of social interactions within the city. These include visits in the
course of work, lunching or dining, shopping, culture and leisure.
Regardless of whether or not advanced technology is involved, here is
evidence of visions of transport incorporating wider perceptions of
the movement rhythms of human activity.

The greater levels of enlightenment which exist today are not,
however, wholly attributable to the endeavours of planners and
researchers. Some of it is due to the shock effects of the reaction
to the alienation between the planners and the planned. During the
1960s in the United Kingdom (and elsewhere) emerged the pressure and
action groups and the concepts of community politics. Not only were
planning assumptions and values challenged but often the techniques
as well. Local communities mastered many of the skills of persuasion
necessary to prevent policies being implemented or to secure ends they
regarded as important. The postponement of the development of a Third
London Airport for twenty years is perhaps the spectacular example.
But there are numerous others relating to mineral workings, the establishment of tips and reservoirs, and in the urban context of
resistance to housing schemes or local development policies. In a
more creative mood, law abiding citizens took to direct action as an
effective means to generate pressure to obtain the provision of
pedestrian crossings, footbridges or subways.

It was earlier recognition of the uneasy relationship between
policies and the aspirations of the various communities which led to
the 'Skeffington Act' which placed a statutory requirement on planners
for public participation and consultation (HMSO 1969). Its provisions,
however, did not embrace transport nor the transportation studies. It
is often said of this Act that it was a classic example of Parliament
willing the end but not the means in the sense that it gave little

guidance on how to create an effective communication between planner
and public. A similar observation could be made about the intentions
underlying the formation of the Public Transport Authorities. The
belief was that the PTAs and the control of the metropolitan
counties would generate more responsive local transport systems thus
effectively achieving a measure of democratisation. In practice, in
most cases, it is the theoretically subordinate bodies, the Passenger
Transport Executives, which have the dominant role.

In terms of transport strategy the US citizen has perhaps a
stronger position than his UK counterpart. In at least two American
cities highway-oriented strategies were rejected by direct vote and
similarly, locally, supported transit systems are made the subject of
individual mandates. However, self-evidently this does not preclude
a divergence between the directions in which planners move and the
views of the local populations.

The changing policy emphases
It is necessary to conclude this review of the very difficult pattern
of relationships in the administrative structure of transport policy,
planning and operation and the interface with communities by making
brief reference to two contemporary aspects.

First, the major emphasis in transport policy has shifted much
more towards the short term. Both the present government and its
predecessor appear committed to the belief that the proportionate
call by transport upon national resources should be reduced. Moreover it is improbable that very large investments in single schemes
will be undertaken. The theme of policy is likely to be to maximize
the benefits obtainable from existing infrastructure but to be
prepared to make modest investment where it is clearly in support of
strategic overall planning policies. Energy conservation factors
too, sooner or later, are likely to generate policy requirements
which may involve some significant behavioural changes.

The second issue is that public transport is likely to continue
to suffer from cost inflation and the possibility of a continued
deterioration in performance. The implications for transport
planning and research are very significant. It has, for instance,
to develop many more economic methods for assessing the impact
of possible major policy changes including high prices for public or
private transport, restriction or high pricing of parking, vehicle
speed restrictions or of any other mechanisms directed at reducing
the demand or supply of transport facilities. Other parallel
desirable developments would be provision of good analytical aids to
the public transport industry, particularly the bus industry. This
development is already being undertaken in the United States where
transportation planners and modellers are, under Department of
Transport auspices, producing manuals to enable bus operators to
improve their scheduling and reliability with the aid of no more
sophisticated equipment than desk calculators. But with the development of the microprocessor there are great gains to be made in the
field of operational control also.

Finally, there is the issue of standards. If public transport is
to be operated with minimum investment and at as low a cost as is
reasonable, it is desirable that it should be oriented to a publicly
acceptable level of service. Without such a level social conflicts
will develop. An important role for transport research therefore is

the development of consumer-oriented standards which can be incorporated in a practical way into the operating criteria of the transport
undertaking.

All these objectives for transport planning have some requirement
for social research. The remainder of this paper is directed to a
review of some of the historical applications and comments on the
current state of the art. The topic of social research is the
relationship between transport systems and policy and the public.
That does not and should not exclude the analysis of sociological and
psychological stresses within the administrative structure itself.
It is hoped it is recognized that the preceding sections attempt
partially to meet that criterion.

2. APPLICATIONS OF SOCIAL RESEARCH METHODS IN TRANSPORT

Some early examples from the railways
Marketing of transport probably has an earlier origin than the words
which describe it. Evidence of aggressive sales techniques can
easily be gathered from the archives of transport museums and indeed
they were inseparable from the entreprenurial spirits which laid the
foundation of the modern transport industry. The marketing edge was
blunted by the cumulative effects of amalgamations which took place
in the bus and rail industries, and the notions of public service
which were assumed during the Second World War and carried forward
into the postwar era. Much of the stimulus for marketing was absent
also because of the relatively low perceived level of competition and
the regulation of fares policies. There was an implicit goal of
maximizing service rather than profit.

In the field of data collection, the railways did take some very
significant steps. In the 1950s, large surveys were conducted in
respect of both passenger and freight traffic. These were part of
the very important traffic costing studies initiated by Sir Reginald
Wilson and Alick Tait. Whilst they were intended to facilitate a flow
of management information they also provided a very natural foundation
for the development of demand-oriented research. The basic form of
the statistics in association with census data made it possible to
generate greatly improved forecasts for the London commuter services
and for schemes such as the electrification of the Bournemouth route.

The 1960s was a decade of furious research activity in the railways which was hardly paralleled in the bus industry. But of course
the latter lacked the impetus of major technological change represented by the conversion from steam to diesel and electric traction,
the development of new products such as the inner-city network and
the torrid wave of rationalization introduced by Dr. Beeching. The
fact remains, however, that British Railways, albeit ten years later
than British Airways, developed a market research function in the
1960s and drew substantially upon it for the formulation of its
subsequent commercial and planning policies. The basic groundwork
and the inherited data base had been earlier prepared by the Traffic
Costing Service.

Much of the market research was of conventional survey form
concerned with determination of market shares and with market segmentation. Some of it was of a very different character. One example
concerned the relative merits of electric versus diesel traction for
commuter services. Statistical evidence had suggested that at

comparable service levels electrified services attracted greater
levels of patronage than diesel services. The evidence was not
conclusive but the issue mattered because in some cases a higher
level of patronage might justify the additional investment outlay on
electrification. This was clearly not a matter which could be explored with basic survey methods even utilizing attitudinal techniques.
So qualitative research was enlisted. A range of depth interviews
was conducted on and off trains in a number of locations. It was
established that, at a level of abstraction, electric traction was
associated with a number of positive features such as cleanliness
and reliability, but that, at the practical level, there were a
number of circumstances which actually would generate a preference
for a diesel train. These could be observed to be operating on
routes where a choice of traction was available. Moreover there was
not, on a day-to-day basis, necessarily an active or accurate perception of the traction form. However in tracing through the decision
process to commute by rail and the locations in which homes were
sought, it became clear that an electrified service had a greater
attraction. The image conveyed by electrification was that the
frequency would be adequate and the service, because it was electrified, would be of an assured, stable and permanent form. Thus the
traction form, although for some people critical to an initial
choice, was not subsequently retained in consciousness as experience
developed.

The other example is of a much less specialized character.
Following the conversion from steam to diesel and the improvement of
the schedule, traffic failed to develop as had been anticipated on
the Norwich-London route. A major market research project was undertaken followed by a marketing experiment. Both in terms of type of
research undertaken and in terms of the direct management action
taken as a result of it the project represents a milestone
(Hollings 1970).   What is worth recording here is the range of
techniques employed, the management action developed, and the
subsequent monitoring.

There were three basic aspects to the research. One was the
establishment of a large behavioural data base concerned with social
and demographic comparisons between the existing rail service patrons
and the characteristics of the catchment areas for it. Another was
attitudinal research on and off the trains to develop an understanding of contrasting feeling and beliefs about the service. The third
facet was concerned with motivations for travel and the attractions
of the places it served. Much of the research was undertaken concurrently so that initial qualitative research could also serve as an
input to survey questionnaire design.

It can be seen that the philosophy of the research programme was
to draw as heavily as possible upon the techniques of sociological
and psychological research, with the twin objectives of generating a
good quantitative data base and also developing an understanding of
the interaction at various levels between the transport system and
the population it potentially served. A small but integral aspect
was the study of the attitudes and beliefs of railway managers and
staff about passengers and potential.

So many conclusions were reached that it is too demanding to
summarize them all. The most significant findings were that there
were strong kinship links with London and the South East, that trip

making propensities were much higher from areas of developing population and highest of all amongst migrants to the area. The users
of the improved rail service had very positive attitudes to it except
in relation to the undoubted complexity of the reduced rate fare
structure. This was so complicated that even railway personnel found
it difficult to memorize. It was designed to protect full fare
revenue, and in that sense represented a logical application of sound
economic principles. But it resulted in a tariff which was difficult
for the railway to promote and advertise and nearly impossible for
the public to understand. Indeed it was interpreted by the traveller
as a near conspiracy to hold out a promise of cheaper travel, obtaining a commitment to a rail journey, and then to extract the full fare
for it. However, with this issue aside, rail travellers were well
satisfied with the new services and regarded them as a great improvement on the previous ones.

It became clear however that the public at large had no knowledge
or awareness of the type illustrated above with respect to rail
travellers. Indeed, much of the general public image was retained
from wartime and postwar experience. Moreover, many branch line
closures in Norfolk had created a wide impression that the railway
system was contracting and quality was declining. There was in fact
a slightly hostile climate towards the railway system as a whole.

Therefore, despite the fact the users of the service recognized
the improvements, there had been no corresponding development in
general public knowledge and awareness. British Rail's own marketing
effort had been relatively low key, a large proportion of it being
through handbills and posters. Arousal and interest was inhibited
also by the complications with fares.

One of the effects of residing in a relatively isolated area from
which long-distance travel was perceived as being difficult was that
the population became defensively introverted. It was only the
relatively intensive psychological research which was able to establish that, given improved accessibility to London by rail, especially
for day trips, there could be quite substantial trip generation.

Trip motivation by itself is not translated into action without
planning, and the psychologists also established that a key in the
process was the possession of factual information about schedules and
fares. People who understood little of timings and frequencies really
needed a reference source which would enable them to see what types
of journeys were possible.

The response of British Rail management to the research was
remarkable and rapid. The conclusions were translated into an action
plan for marketing the service. The fares structure was dramatically
simplified and liberalized. Most restrictions on the use of trains
for reduced rate travel by time and by day were lifted. The advertising agents were presented with a brief which identified the target
markets by profile and location. Travel motivations were defined and
they were provided with a campaign budget which enabled television to
be employed for the projection of motivational themes and descriptions
of service quality. Newspapers and posters were employed to communicate factual data about frequencies, speeds and fares, and this was
re-inforced in turn by a house-to-house distribution of train service
cards in particular areas.

The experiment was not merely ambitious in marketing terms; it
was also organized in such a way as to ensure that there could be

very careful monitoring of the results. It was a success in generating
revenue and travel, and also, because of the investment in monitoring
and in post-experiment research, it was possible to demonstrate
conclusively the effectiveness of marketing in certain areas and its
ineffectiveness in others. Many of the original hypotheses about
how, where, and why travel might be stimulated were established
because of the controls built in to the marketing programme and
coverage.

    The value of the broad approach in the use of techniques was amply
confirmed. But the limitations of the mental perceptions of researchers were also revealed. The entire campaign was directed to
optional travel. The business market was assumed to be well informed
and relatively inelastic. In the event, business was a significant
extra source of increased travel. Because the day trip to London
was, as a result of the campaign, seen to be both feasible and cheap,
the practice of inter-office visits also expanded quite substantially.

    It should be recognized that this project was significant not only
because it was innovatory in research and action terms and was
successful but also because it occurred at a time when British Rail
was technically reforging a major product. These were reasons therefore why the management climate was receptive to new ideas and had an
understood need to develop them.

    There is hardly an aspect of British Rail's passenger activity
which has not been subject to market and social research, from catering
to car parking, from reservations to headrests, and from frequencies
to family fares. Some of it has been in support of marketing, much
of it supporting investment proposals, some of it to establish
consumer-oriented design criteria and latterly to determine consumer-
oriented operating standards. The stream of research provides an
opportunity to witness the constancy of some public attitudes and
values and the dynamic and changing nature of others. What will
change can only partly be predicted and to some extent this is due
to the fact that any piece of research examines only part of an
acitivity or relationship. It is due also to a reaction by people to
externalities which the research cannot embrace and also the practical difficulty of estimating how strong a stimulus may be. A good
example is the passenger patronage of all night services on Tyneside.
They were part of a marketing package for the local rail services.
The research team was correct in its belief that daytime patronage
would expand greatly. It was wrong in assessing that late night and
early morning services would not be successful.

    However good the research may be and however sophisticated the
techniques, the factors which shape human behaviour are in practice
so complex that only an improved level of understanding can be
achieved. Whilst this should provide reassurance to those people who
have a fear of the employment of sociological and psychological
research techniques because of the opportunities for 'manipulation',
it should also sound a cautionary note for those enthusiasts who
look to social research for total rather than supplementary information.

    In concluding this section, it is fair to observe that by the
close of 1970s nearly all transport operators were converts to the
principles of marketing and marketing research. Railway examples
have been described because British Rail started sooner, and because
it provides the greatest range of case studies and some of the

most interesting applications.

Some early examples from transport planning

In a previous section on transportation studies, there was some discussion of the dehumanization of the analysis and forecasting practices. This was hardly ameliorated by the importation of quantitative devices which created only the illusion of a reflection of social values. The concepts of the value of time, perceived costs, generalized costs and the application of social cost/benefit analysis all used values which were either derived within mathematical exercises or from choosing factors which were amenable to measurement. In themselves, of course, the techniques possess great merit. The danger lies in developing conclusions and policies which are based on what is only a partial analysis of the character of movement and the effects of a need for mobility. What is excluded from them is any sense of local communities, their orientations and the perceptions of locality. It is recognized that the strategic planner is often confronted with similar needs to examine problems at the macro-level, but he tends to retain some sense of the specialness of areas. The transport planner generated techniques which presumed similarities.

The first major transportation study in Britain was the London Transportation Study conducted by Freeman Fox and Associates and Wilbur Smith and Associates. As a result of the remarkable vision of Brian Martin and Tony Ridley, then of the Highways and Engineering Department of the LCC, it was successfully suggested that a programme of social research was undertaken in parallel with the transportation studies.

The programme of social research extended over four years and in many respects provided a fundamental basis and an impetus for subsequent studies. This is not surprising for so many different topics of prime interest were covered. In listing the topics, it will be apparent that it is not feasible to summarize the conclusions nor to elaborate greatly on the techniques employed. There were ten major studies, but many of the topics were the subject of focus in more than one. The topic list is as follows:

(i)   public attitudes to the planning process;
(ii)   public attitudes to transport operators;
(iii)   the changing roles and perceptions of individuals as pedestrians, drivers and public transport patrons;
(iv)   factors influencing location of residence;
(v)   factors influencing car ownership;
(vi)   perceptions and influence of traffic congestion;
(vii)   perception of and attitudes to modes;
(viii) knowledge and information sources about public transport modes;
(ix)   factors affecting satisfaction with various modes;
(x)   factors affecting choice of route and choice of mode;
(xi)   spatial distribution of activities;
(xii)   transport facilities and life-style;
(xiii) attitudes to traffic restraint;
(xiv)   the characteristics of and attitudes to 'park and ride'.

The techniques employed included counts, observations and surveys, and analysis of census, transportation study and public transport operators' data. However, this basic framework of behavioural data was developed in a number of different ways. A correlation matrix was

produced which examined the association between a range of social
variables and transport variables. A typology was produced utilizing
similar variables to allocate each of over one hundred traffic
districts (comprising numbers of zones) to one of nine groups or
types. Using journey-to-work surveys, involving over 10,000
questionnaires which included attitudinal questions, a discriminant
analysis was conducted employing the programmes previously developed
by David Quarmby, but taking into account the attitudinal variables.

The employment of these statistical and mathematical techniques
was at the time thought desirable for four reasons.

(i)   to see if it was possible to extend the relationship
        between social and transport variables beyond those
        previously derived from transportation studies;

(ii)   to provide inputs in respect of human behaviour and
        values to refine some of the crude assumptions employed
        in transport modelling, for example about waiting times,
        about how far people will walk, and about whether various
        forms of public transport were different in their
        attractiveness;

(iii)   to provide a broad sampling frame for more qualitatively-
        oriented research;

(iv)   to produce generalized statements about an area so vast
        and heterogeneous as London.

So far as the motivational studies were concerned, the
behavioural research was integrated with the qualitative approaches
of the professionally-qualified sociologists and psychologists. These
field researchers, who conducted depth interviews and acted as group
discussion leaders, were initially drawn primarily from the University
of Brunel and the Tavistock Institute. Their prior knowledge of
transport was exclusively related to personal experience and they had
no understanding of the mechanics of transport planning.

The briefing of this team involved directing its attention to the
issues which were of concern to transport planners. In turn the de-
briefings concentrated upon matters which could have an impact on the
transportation study. In effect, the researchers became an intermediate link between the planners and the public but on terms of
reference determined by the planners. This was a natural outcome of
the logic of the situation - but it established a confined role for
social research from which it has only comparatively recently been
freed. In the context of a strategic planning study there was a
natural focus on vehicular movement, on the journey to work, on the
most frequent journeys and on journeys to the central area, and on
possible reactions to alternative types of strategy.

In predetermining the topics the planners, in practice, were pre-
empting the type of interaction they were able to have. Determining
the relative importance of certain types of issues is not the same as
determining whether they are important at all or whether they are
necessarily the right issues. The impact of transport facilities
upon the individual or household has a very wide range of references.
Transport may have a very low saliency. It may have a high saliency
but related to travel rhythms which are not overtly recognized by the
data collection techniques which are oriented to an inventory of one
day's journeys. In other words the factors concerning mobility which
matter to people are not necessarily those with which the transport
planners are concerned.

The latter are pre-occupied by the transport system stresses
which are generated by volumes of movement. This is not an improper
concern but its emphasis can be limiting upon the character of social
research and the feedback from it. The results of the social
research which can be assimilated by the planner are mainly those
which are of direct assistance for the formulation of plans to resolve
those issues which have already been identified as the most important.
The impact on social research particularly during this pioneering
phase was that it had a peculiarly interpretative role. It had
initially to absorb planning concepts and to translate them into
terms which enable them to be explored with members of the public.
Having obtained results, these had to be translated into formulations
with meaning to the transport planners. In this context the expression 'planners' also embraces transport economists who have a view of
human behaviour which, however valid it is for economic analysis, is
considerably at variance with that which is understood by sociologists
and social psychologists.

This theme has been developed at some length because the initial
relationship between the disciplines of social research and of
engineering, economics, modelling and planning was quite a difficult
one and it will be referred to again. There were a number of lessons
which were understood as a result of the motivation studies within the
London Transportation Study, On the negative side, it became clear
that social research could contribute very little to an already
defined modelling process. It could, however, have a useful input
into some of the conceptual aspects of scheme generation influencing
the form of the transport measures which could be devised for testing.
Further, it could be of help in assessing the 'reasonableness' of
some of the qualitative judgements which lead to the creation of the
'preferred scheme'.

The studies produced interesting and useful insights into some
policy issues such as the most acceptable forms of traffic restraint.
They illustrated that different standards governed the basic acceptability of the various public transport modes and that, even then, the
highest priority for bus services was improved reliability. They
showed that if cars were available, mode choice was much more
profoundly influenced by the acceptability of the car journey and
assured parking than it was by the quality of the alternative public
transport service. They revealed that rail commuting was often more
of a life-style than a modal choice. They suggested that public
transport interchanges did not always impose penalties. They began
to unravel some of the awful complexities associated with generating,
receiving and processing information about public transport
schedules. They showed that lack of confidence could influence some
people's choice of mode. They began to tease out the taboo subject
of safety both in respect of accidents and personal security. They
demonstrated that public transport was felt to be safer than cars,
that pedestrian and cycle conflict with cars could be a physical as
well as an environmental issue. They showed that buses with
conductors were felt more likely to guarantee freedom from assault or
intrusion of privacy than were trains.

The correlation matrix gave evidence that people did not invest in
private vehicle ownership until they had achieved a minimum standard
of household amenities. The studies established that the motivations
for the initial acquisition of a car were significantly related to a

desire to maintain social intercourse but that once acquired, unless
the work journey was to central London, its predominant use would be
for the work journey. They also revealed that unskilled manual
workers would acquire vehicles in order to maximize their earning
capabilities, enlarging on the range of places which were accessible
by public transport. Interesting in the context of transport planning
is the fact that such workers would carefully trade off transport
costs against earnings and that they had a low proclivity to use the
car for other than work journeys.

More significant from the social point of view was the attachment
to their neighbourhoods and the strength of the extended family.
Also revealing, in respect of unskilled working wives, was the indication that they might not work if employment was not available within
walking distance. Evocative of the low level of job satisfaction
was the comment made to psychologist Sheila Stark by one young wife,
'Well, I walk to work, but I run home'.

Finally, on the topic of walking, the comprehensive study which
was carried out in one traffic district, selected because it was the
closest of all to the norm for the whole study area, provided the
information that walking (or cycling) accounted for:

    25 per cent of work journeys;
    32 per cent of employer and personal business journeys;
    66 per cent of shopping journeys;
    33 per cent of other journeys.

In each case, walking journeys outnumbered those by any other mode.

This account of some of the techniques and the results of this
first social research programme will provide a flavour of the base
from which future applications and studies could be launched. Together with the earlier marketing work for British Railways, it helped
to establish some of the technical forms for undertaking the research
and provided a demonstration of the value of the findings in enlarging
understanding and in informing judgement.

The technique of the social typology was subsequently employed for
British Rail to provide a classification of over 400 station catchment
areas, and by Peter Warman in his Rural Studies for WYTCONSULT – the
joint consultancy of Halcrow Fox and Associates and Martin and
Voorhees Associates, undertaking the West Yorkshire Transportation
Study (WYTCONSULT 1977a). In this application it was used to classify
over 300 rural communities into a number of groups for which, in
association with other data inputs, relevant action plans for rural
transport could be developed.

Qualitative social research techniques have, of course, also had
many applications in rural transport studies. The connection between
the metropolis of Greater London and rural studies may not be
immediately obvious. However the facts that some of the more affluent
describe London as a series of villages, that the historical origin of
urban London was due to the expansion of villages, and that there is
a fairly highly developed sense of local community in most parts of
the London area, says something about the sense of scale with which
people can identify. Most activities of households take place within
a fairly limited radius. Moreover, some of the differences and even
conflicts in the scales of values between the members of older
established elements of local communities and the newer migrants were
originally detected in the London research. This particular issue
has been seen to be of significance in the rural context over

and over again.

The justification, therefore, for giving an extended attention to work undertaken a decade and a half ago is that it provided the foundation for much of what has subsequently been achieved. A great deal is owed to the people who originally commissioned it. In a sense they are also responsible for the continuity of social research in transport planning and for the development of very experienced practitioners. The next section considers the adaptation of transportation studies to a greater level of social research.

The transportation studies – later developments
The Sheffield–Rotherham Land Use Transportation Study incorporated what is believed to be the first community involvement programme. There were basically three streams of involvement. One at least, had little to do with the principles of social research. It consisted of a number of activities designed to publicize and promote the transportation study. The study team was particularly committed to being seen to be conducting an open study and certainly sought a lively interaction with the public.

The second form of involvement consisted of orderly consultations with a range of organizations, specialist associations, action groups, pressure groups, special interest groups and community groups and associations. This was the mechanism for taking soundings of organized opinion and also for communicating some explanations about the planning process and some facts about the costs of providing various forms of transport. In fact, if organizations wished to use it they had a kit which enabled them to generate within the overall investment constraints their version of what the 'plan' should be. In a sense this was a variation on the planning games which had been developed in other contexts.

It raises, however, the major question of how far any organization or individual remains representative of the public after going through the education of learning how to play and then playing a planning game. It is obviously important to consult with voluntary or specialist interest organizations at the positive level to receive informed and helpful views and, at the very least, to avoid the penalties of the distrust, suspicions and hostility which arises from lack of consultation.

At the same time it could be observed that the role reinforcement which occurs in organizations tended towards the projections of views on behalf of an organization which were narrower or more partial than the views of any individual who was a member of it. Similarly, it was noted that the person who attended the meetings with the study team subsequently, whether willingly or not, became the 'transport expert' of the group of association.

The third stream of involvement or participation was through the medium of social research. Some attitudinal questions were added to the household survey; group discussions were employed both as a preliminary to develop some knowledge of the role of transport in everyday life in the study area and at other times in the study to examine specific topics in particular locations. An innovatory research method was a three-stage set of interviews with selected families. The first round was designed to create an understanding of the life of typical families in the study area, the type of community orientation and constraints and opportunities conferred by transport

facilities. The second phase involved reactions to the options
devised for the transportation study and assessment of the potential
local impact. The third phase related to the preferred scheme which
combined some features from each option. Simon Coventry and John
Wicks have outlined the Community Involvement Programme in an article
(Coventry 1977), and they describe the effect which it had on the way
in which the Study developed.

Later transportation studies, for example Bedford/Kempston and
West Yorkshire, utilized broadly similar programmes. In West Yorkshire, however, a large number of semi-structured interviews were
undertaken in pursuit of the identification of very local transport
problems or issues. Significantly, these had the greatest direct
impact on schemes developed for some of the smaller towns or urban
complexes in West Yorkshire. They formed part of a comprehensive
assembly and analysis of issues most of which could be assimilated
into schemes which were capable of being examined without going
through a modelling process. Here then is a much greater affinity
between the public and the planner because the scale and effect of
movement and the requirement for mobility can be more easily perceived
at a common level. Social research of a higher qualitative form was
undertaken in a number of rural areas after a very large data bank
had been assembled for each community in order to test, in the field,
hypotheses which had been generated about the possible character of
transport differences or to establish whether relative isolation did
in fact represent perceived deprivation.

Finally, the opportunity arose during the course of the study to
undertake a before-and-after social research study of the effect of
heavy goods vehicle intrusion into differing types of residential
areas. Some innovatory techniques were employed and from the research
it was possible to develop new forms of assessments of the effects of
HGV intrusion, adding to the quantitative measures which had previously been arrived at as a result of the work of Imperial College and
others. In somewhat oversimplified terms, the actual experience and
perception of intrusion could be seen to be related to the qualities
attributed by its inhabitants to a neighbourhood. A later section
will show that this concept can also be of relevance for improving
assessments of the impact of new road schemes.

The West Yorkshire Study was notable also for the development of
accessibility measures as a basis for evaluating the impact of
transport measures. Some rural transport studies have also taken
quantified accessibility as a means of comparing transport or activity
opportunities and developed it also as a basis for determining
standards or policy goals. The role of social research in a number
of these exercises has been somewhat unclear. It has certainly been
enlisted as an aid to establish what sorts of access may be given
high priority, for example to choice of work opportunities or to a
pharmacy. Whether, however, accessibility *per se* has value beyond
description to serve as a standard is open to some doubt. Peter
Warman felt that the results from social research in the rural areas
of West Yorkshire suggested that it was not useful as a standard
because expectations and aspirations were so much tempered by the
experience of living in rural areas (WYTCONSULT 1977b).

In practice, what seemed to matter more were relative changes to
accessibility rather than any absolute levels. However, as an
element in an analytical framework, it could be useful both for

providing a prior indication of the types of adaptation which were likely to be occuring in rural areas and also for measuring some of the effects of making changes in transport facilities. There was, however, no *prima facia* reason for assuming that changes should be made solely on the basis that accessibility happened to be low.

Similar conclusions were reached in a study conducted concurrently with the West Yorkshire Study for the Transport and Road Research Laboratory and the Department of Transport, and which was concerned with the withdrawal of rural bus services. The study pointed out that many communities and settlements had never been directly served by public transport and that it was not therefore a condition of life support. The importance of accessibility could be seen more in terms of its social impact upon the composition of village populations. The immediate impacts of changes were moreover not primarily economic in character but were of a sociological and psychological form. With reduction in facilities, certain activities were curtailed or had to be abandoned and opportunities for privacy and the exercise of choice were diminished. The effect is that at the personal level quality of life is adversely affected. The longer-term effect was most probably, either a population decline, or an exchange of populations between urban and rural areas, the urban migrants arriving with the built-in accessibility of the private car.

The West Yorkshire Transportation Study, although the largest conducted in the United Kingdom, took place late enough for there to be an increasing recognition that growth in population was not going to pose major problems and that economic constraints would severely limit the availability of investment funds. There was a greater concentration on short- and medium-term measures. Some of the social research was concerned with the impacts of relatively new issues such as the effect upon travel demand of sharply increasing public transport fares and of the problems of vandalism and violence in some of the urban areas. Some effort was also directed to certain minority groups such as cyclists, and teenagers in rural and some urban areas. Pedestrian safety and ease of movement was also given a much higher overt recognition as a result of the data obtained from the semi-structured interviews. In many ways therefore, the study had a much greater level of input of social values and aspirations than did many of its predecessors.

Certainly the transport planning assessment of the free standing towns incorporated a much greater range of viewpoints than had been normal in the past. For the study as a whole it can be said that data collection techniques were much less exclusively oriented to the facts of movement.

Other developments in the application of social research to transport planning

The mathematical models employed in transport planning have been implicitly criticized for being somewhat mechanical in the choice of the variables employed. There are a number of examples where social research was initially conducted to help in informing the assumptions built into the modelling process. In the South-West Corridor Study conducted for CIE in Eire (Martin and Voorhees Associates 1977), which was related to rail investment, preliminary social research was initiated to obtain an understanding of the competitive status of the rail services, to establish something about the nature of

journeys made by rail, to learn about the characteristics of the rail
travellers and to gauge the possible influence of speed or frequency
improvements. This work was undertaken before the model was formulated.

In a rail strategy study (Martin and Voorhees Associates 1978a,
undertaken for the PTE and the Greater Manchester County Council,
social research was conducted to determine what commuters and off-
peak travellers would regard as significant in respect of improving
the quality of service provided by the rail network. This included
issues such as rolling stock quality, station environment and information as well as speeds and frequencies. The package of improvements
incorporated into some of the options produced were therefore directly
derived from the potential patrons. The estimation of off-peak
revenue was based on the social research and involved no modelling at
all.

Similarly, in the context of the possible development of a large
transport interchange for the centre of Dublin, observational and
interview data formed part of the basis of the criteria of the design
of the facility.

These are just three examples to illustrate how capabilities of
social research have been progressively exploited over time as
planners, architects and engineers have become more aware of its
potentiality for reducing the areas which doubt or uncertainty (or
prejudice) previously occupied.

Social research and innovatory modes
This is a vast subject but one in which, *faute de mieux*, social
research has been directed for many years. Public reaction to new
modes is obviously a difficult area to research. It is made more
acute by the problems of communicating what new modes will be like.
Visual aids are helpful but the visions of designers are not always
well attuned to realities of systems experienced by users. Moreover,
respondents who do not perceive the relevance of a system, or who are
resistant to its concepts, have a tendency to attack the technical
feasibility rather than explore its ramifications. This is a reaction
understandable to psychologists, but very inhibiting to the conduct
of useful fieldwork. This was a problem Sheila Stark had to overcome
in her research into traffic restraint where the presence of a meter
in a car was regarded as an intrusion into privacy.

One early successful example of research was on the subject of
hovertrains designed to operate at speeds at 300 mph or so between
cities. British Petroleum, who were associated with the project,
produced a film using an existing train but increasing the rate of
movement to the appropriate speed so that the impression likely to be
generated by such high-speed ground passage could be perceived in the
context of a familiar experience. The social scientists who conducted
the research concluded that confidence could be placed in the findings.

A more recent example concerns the novel application of old-
established transport modes. There have recently been installations
of aerial cable cars in a number of cities where the system is
designed to fulfil a public transport function. Major uncertainties
which inhibit planners from considering such systems are doubts about
whether they will be thought safe or comfortable or basically acceptable to the public.

Because a system is installed in so unlikely a place as Manhattan,

an opportunity existed to examine the behaviour and attitudes of its
users. The following consists of abbreviated extracts from the
Report:

'1. *Introduction*. The aerial tramway connects Manhattan to Roosevelt
Island. Roosevelt Island is virtually car-free, special permits being
required and issued only on proof of need to drive around the Island,
and consequently the streets are very safe for those handicapped who
are mobile. The housing accommodation is in the form of flats or
apartments. The school is divided into several units which are
located at the ground level of the apartment blocks.

There is a very strong and vibrant sense of community among the
residents, and there are many active groups catering for different
elements of the community.

2. *Safety*. Commuters were clearly embarking upon a fear-free
experience. During the course of the Study there were no manifestations of the anxiety which is sometimes occasioned by sudden or
unfamiliar noises or arrests of progress which occur on subways,
trains, buses or aeroplanes. Whereas anxiety can be generated by a
normal journey on other modes it would appear that the tramway ride
contains perhaps fewer unassimilable signals than other transit
modes.

Casual users revealed an initial anxiety that others would be
fearful and "leaders" of sections and groups did attempt to impart
reassurance to others. Little of the anxiety was sustained throughout
the course of the journey. Visual interest supplanted the initial
anxiety input and the most normal conduct was the progressive trans-
ference of attention from the system to external objects. So total
was the transfer that return journeys were almost entirely devoted to
the view potential or even to the next event in the itinerary.

There was some evidence that while familiarity and practice
rapidly generate an almost total sense of security, people initially
approach the system with some latent or subdued anxiety. This was
interestingly manifested by some children who did assert that they
were slightly nervous when they made their first unaccompanied
journeys.

3. *Comfort*. There was no rush for seats on the tramway, although
provision was made for only ten seated passengers. In practice,
while no-one actively preferred to stand, it was perceived as a
standing mode. Seats were not necessarily occupied by the first ten
passengers. The shortness of the journey, together with its outward-
looking nature, was quite consonant with standing, and it was not
thought that a lack of seating contributed to a sense of discomfort.
There was no expectation or perceived need for more seating provision.

A comparison with the subway illustrates cogently the acceptable
and even, for some people, the enjoyable nature of the tramway transit.
"On the subway, you're looking in at yourself, or you have to look at
other people" {Respondent illustrated with hunched, closed body
language} "Whereas here {open, expansive gesture} you're looking out,
there's a view, it's all open".

4. *Comparison with other modes*. Because it is a different form of
mode which provides a relatively gentle transit it attracts positive
comparisons with the subway and buses and a sense of "advantage" is
felt over people who have to use the other modes.

There is further re-inforcement in that it is thought that it is
a form of transport consistent with the atmosphere and ethos of

Roosevelt Island. In fact there is often significantly hyperbolic language employed. People were heard to remark "we do *love* our tramway" which compares with the more normal expression e.g. "Yes, we like our minibuses or local drivers".

The emotional commitment has to be viewed in the context of a high practical level of dependence but whatever degree of discounting might be employed there can be little doubt that the transit ride is basically attractive and fully acceptable to the residents.

The other points on the continuum are represented by those who have no basic vested interest in the system. These are the employees commuting on to the Island, visitors, tourists and sightseers. Interviews with the employees indicate an acceptance of the transit ride and a view that it is superior to other forms of public transport for the sort of journey it accommodates.

Visitors, tourists and sightseers provide plain evidence that the facility is thought to be a novelty. One positive feature is that it clearly does generate some trips and there were examples of people who were sufficiently strongly motivated to experience it that they made a public transport trip instead of an automobile trip.
General conclusion. In special circumstances the acceptability of this form of transit as opposed to others can operate at a very high level. It is likely to be regarded as an unusual and novel form of transport facility by the general urban public. However the quality of the transit creates positive acceptance of it as a rational method of urban travel.' (Martin and Voorhees Associates 1978b) .

This study was undertaken by a very experienced psychologist and the report apart from having intrinsic interest and usefulness also displays the value of a continuity of such experiences of transport research within a social researcher. The inter-modal comparisons, for example, are particularly important.

It provides the opportunity to raise the point that social research can be abortive if the people who undertake it are involved in transport for the first time and are not properly oriented or alerted to some of the basic parameters which have previously been established. Briefing must incorporate some guidelines about the nature of perceptions about transport.

Evaluating social impact
Environmental impact evaluations have historically, perhaps for defensive reasons bearing in mind the numeric orientations of transport planning, been primarily directed to the use of numeric or economic measures. Severance has been recognized but has been somewhat difficult to define. Qualitative research has been distrusted because it is somewhat difficult to assimilate and is not easy to handle.

Quite recently, one of the Lancashire Boroughs commissioned a study to examine the social impact of two proposed urban highway alignments. The Borough accepted the proposition that social research should be a principal component of the study. The Department of Transport, the highway sponsers, had already conducted an environmental impact assessment which was primarily concerned with physical issues. The Borough's interest was in determining in the widest sense the effect of either route on people living close and on the communities as a whole. It wished to know the impact of the changes which would be imposed and also which route would be reluctantly preferred.

The significance of the study from the social research viewpoint was in the issues that were studied and in the fact, because the results were required for a planning enquiry, that the disciplines of social research were accepted in their own right as having an independent valid professional status in the planning context. One major effect is that it requires that other professions have to understand the method of approach of the social researchers and the basis on which they approach the study of people. The extracts below give a brief review of the factors taken into account, descriptions of the types of psychological costs involved in a change such as the construction of a motorway and the nature of the responses which can be expected.

Most social research is undertaken in order to focus on specific issues. Cognition of these issues is rarely identical between the instigators of the research, the people who undertake it and the people who are its subject. Two examples will illustrate. The issue of traffic congestion is understood by planners in mathematical terms with such variables as throughput and capacity have also economic and environmental expressions. The driving citizen interprets congestion primarily as a series of impediments to personal progress with the major variables being time and frustration.

Similarly, the recurrent problem of public transport reliability is understood by an operator, mainly in technical terms related to crew and vehicle rosters, maintenance, standby capacity, control and monitoring systems and traffic congestion. For the passenger reliability relates to expectation, trust, commitments and personal planning.

The absence of commonality is clearly inconvenient for the planning process insofar as the desire exists to incorporate social value scales into planning objectives. In particular, it makes it very difficult to generate standards by which alternative planning schemes can be compared within a framework which is wider than the purely technical. That is to say whilst planners may consider the technical efficiency of alternative highway alignments, the incorporation of social impact in an unconstrained form tends to disorder because the conceptual framework of the public is so widely divergent from that of the planners. Moreover the public does not have a homogeneous set of value scales.

The conclusion reached is that the ultimate decision has to be based on informed judgements. It is improbable that it could be assisted by a constrained process such as social cost/benefit analysis or a "planning balance sheet" type of approach.

There are, no doubt, many planning decisions which have to be made on this basis. Perhaps one intrinsic feature of the relationship between planners and the public is that the former make decisions now on the basis of their view of the future, where the public reaction is related to their experience of the present and their personal plans for the future. Because the visions may be different, the actions of the planner may be thought by the public to have a negative impact on past decisions and present aspirations.

One reason for the potential for conflict is derived from the fact that the planner, because of his training and professional responsibility, focuses upon a particular issue such as transport about which he is both expert and disengaged. A member of the public, however, develops awareness and attitude, and accords it a level of importance only in the context of its direct personal relevance. Their attitudes are shaped by the decisions they have made, the responsibilities they accept and the activities they pursue.

It is not surprising, therefore, that a gulf exists between the two conceptual frameworks. Social research can aid the decision process by helping to reveal some of the social value scales which might be taken into account when reaching a decision. Particular topics were chosen for study:

    (i)   the concept of the house or home;
    (ii)   perceptions of area;
    (iii)   attitudes to change.

The importance of the topics is that some reference to them provides a guide to understanding and interpreting attitudes which will be displayed to a new feature such as a motorway. The background is the fact that motorways can lead first to the generation of resistance and then to adaptation. The purpose of the review was to examine the anxieties which are involved and what adaptation entails.

The house or home. The first consideration is what a house or home actually represents to people. Whilst home-owners may vary in the importance they accord to it, they do feel that their homes communicate images about themselves to other people. To recognise this concept and its implications is to accept that esteem, whether it be self-esteem or accorded esteem, is a factor which will influence the reaction to the reality or probability of a motorway. People will not initially, because of their emotional investment, accept (unless there is overwhelming evidence to the contrary) that they will be personally affected negatively by a new highway. The reason is that moving house is the most tenable response and there may be a host of emotional and practical reasons why this is seen as an extreme option. People are, therefore, motivated to believe, for example, that it would be 'too far away to affect them personally' or 'unlikely to happen'. Nonetheless it should be recognised that this motivation is itself partly a compensation for the anxiety they feel.

The tangible and sometimes measurable expressions of the effects of anxiety are embraced in the term 'planning blight'. The existence of blight which is an extreme consequence of uncertainty can have paradoxical effects. People who live in an affected area may have already embarked upon the process of adaptation, either because they feel they would be economically disadvantaged by the blight or because they have other reasons for remaining which are more important than the expected impact of the motorway. There will also be some new entrants who feel they can opt into a house in the area. They are also motivated by the expected benefits to discount the disadvantages of living adjacent to a motorway. Both these occurrences will tend to depress reaction to motorways which are *a priori* viewed as negative rather than positive attributes of a residential location.

Perceptions of area. The second topic relates to perceptions of area. There are two rather different aspects to this:

    (i)   definition of territory and the limits of awareness;
    (ii)   sense of locality.

The boundaries of the home or the house are legally circumscribed but concepts of territory extend beyond these. For many people there is a wider physical area, the driveway or the road space in front of the house which becomes perceptively involved in the notion of territory. On a different plane, the territorial concept also embraces shared areas such as the immediate neighbours and "our part of the street".

There is also a proprietory sense about things or features which, in fact, clearly do not belong to individuals but are thought of in association with the home. These include such obvious features as streetlights, pillar or telephone boxes, trees and vegetation and open spaces. These are all part of a repetitive home oriented experience or vista.

It is not relevant to speculate on the reasons for the value placed upon vegetation and open spaces. However, in the context of social impact, it does seem reasonable to take into account the almost universal attraction they have for people.

Territory related to the house is not easily, therefore, delineated on a purely geographic or spatial basis. It can exist as an extension of a home-based experience. Alternatively, it can be related to senses, of sight or hearing, rather than of movement. It is also often quite limited. Even within the very local area people may not ever explore the whole of it.

In psychological terms, distance assumes another form of dimension. Places close but not visited in effect seem further away and more remote. But experience of places which are felt as part of the territory do not have to be physically visited. Space or trees viewed from the home are part of territory, although not owned and not necessarily visited.

It can be seen, therefore, that the value derived from aspects of a local environment cannot necessarily be fully determined by measuring the volumes of people who visit them or examining the activities pursued in them.

The other aspect of the topic of area is that of the concept of locality. Understanding lies in the answer to the question "what sort of a place is it in which we live?" Viewed from the stance of a social scientist the answer is very complex. It is obviously bound up with the various levels of sense of identity which people have. These strata can be family, neighbourhood, community and wider references such as town or country.

There can be no absolutes in description of the behaviour of people or in their attitudes. Sense of area is not always associated with a high environment. It may be related to quality of people or as some studies have shown with a highly valued opportunity of choice of work. The fact remains, however, that social research in the particular study area indicated that choice of house was heavily associated with the character of the area and that the character of the area was a well-developed proposition in the minds of the people who live there. This conclusion leads naturally to the final topic which is that of attitude to change.

Attitudes to change. A large proportion of human activity involves a high proportion of routine. Indeed, routine is a pre-requisite of orderly social and economic relationships. Nonetheless, change is another important factor in human existence. Nearly all changes involve amending old routines and adopting new ones. Psychologists reveal that for the individual the 'change of set' is not without its problems.

Although planning is an interventionalistic activity, many of the acts which are related to preservation may attract no more than passing and passive notice. Acts related to innovation may arouse emotion because they involve a behavioural change from people. Thus, town centre redevelopments are often disturbing for people. The old and familiar is changed and the new opportunities have to be learned and exploited.

A sequence of changes can be disorienting rather than disturbing. People may be unconfident of their ability to make effective decisions or of the possibility of securing the style of life to which they aspire. Essentially, therefore, there are reasons why people might be expected to incline towards being conservative rather than innovatory. Adaptation normally involves going through a minimum process of adjustment in order to accommodate a change. Here then lies the explanation of a high level of resistance to change followed, by a muted expression of the impact of change once it has occurred.'

Social research and standards

Another notable development of recent years has been the growing desire by consumers, operators and manufacturers, and governments to generate sets of standards which are highly attuned to the needs of the public. Partly related to the idea of fairness or to rights of redress they are also sponsored by a belief that product composition should be as relevant as possible to the needs of the consumer.

This might be thought to be a natural field for market research, but the market research industry has largely devoted itself to discovering what makes products sell, particularly in competitive environments. A somewhat differently ordered form of research is required to determine what sort of internal targets and priorities should be erected within operating concerns both in terms of day-to-day performance and also in respect of investment priorities and criteria. When Sir Peter Parker embarked on his plans for a Commuters' Charter he recognized that, like the world, British Railways' performance would often be less than perfect. What was needed was an understanding of what things were most important to commuters so that, wherever it was possible to give practical recognition to these in terms of operating performance, the providers generated a service as closely as possible attuned to the accommodation of the needs. Underlying the standards in the Commuters' Charter was a rapid programme of new social research and a huge background of previously compiled studies (British Railways 1979).

Within the study which generated the consumer standards, which in turn were translated into operating standards, were set out some critical issues which described the commuters' approach to the work journey and influenced the interpretation of shortfalls in system performance. Some selected extracts are shown below.
'Issues critical to the development of standards:

(i) Commuters display a mental attunement to a very highly repetitive journey to work within which they attempt to plan within very fine limits.

(ii) The "plan" involves a predetermined access to the station, processing through it, minimum waiting time for a train, positioning on platform to optimize travel objectives and an expectation of the objectives to be executed whilst travelling.

(iii) Whenever it is practically sensible to do so commuters identify with a particular train from the particular station they use. The sense of local identify creates the conditions for extreme levels of satisfaction and dissatisfaction.

(iv) Levels of satisfaction therefore are very highly related to the efficiency with which people feel they are able to execute this plan. These considerations transcend many objective criteria, such as running speeds, quality of rolling stock, frequencies (above a minimum level) and range of amenities on and off the trains.

(v) If the basic expectation is normally adequately fulfilled there are much higher levels of tolerance of some features which can generate dissatisfaction, e.g., low environments and service disruptions.

(vi) The journey from work for commuters tends to be less finely tuned because there are more factors which complicate planning. Returning commuters are interested in more options and have some different qualitative expectations in respect of the stations at which they re-enter the railway system.

(vii) Standards for commuter services, whatever their operational focus, should in part be derived from the efficiency criteria within which commuters judge their particular journeys.

(viii) It should be recognized that the railway, rightly or wrongly, is regarded as a satisfier of other than travel needs, e.g., toilets, newspapers, cigarettes and sweets, refreshments, telephones and car parks. People do have a sense of scale which is related to how 'important' the station is.

(ix) The closer to London and the higher is the level of service provision the greater is the perception of the railway as a metropolitan transport system accommodating large numbers of travellers and the lower is the perception of it as a local facility providing a personalized form of service. When people actually conceive of the railway system as moving very large volumes then they have a different set of criteria by which they judge it, e.g. in relation to expectation of seat, and rolling stock design characteristics.

(x) The locally oriented commuter because of his regularity seeks and responds to recognition. In general this need is being accommodated by local station staff and by the confidence with which commuters are able to use the local station. It is not well satisfied at the Central London Terminals; nor is there the same expectation of recognizing other local people on the journey home until the local station is reached. All other users of the train are actually perceived as people who are intruding by making use of the service. Despite the practical problems of attempting to cater for the need for personal recognition of groups of people from different stations who have a latent antipathy towards one another it is important to try to do so because of the satisfaction which it creates.

(xi) For the locally oriented commuters there are two inextricable priorities. These are punctual morning departures and the availability of a seat. They are directly connected with the aspiration that the rolling stock should have at least a neutral environmental quality, e.g. interior and windows should not be perceived as dirty, and that the quality permits reading, conversation and does not induce fear through vibration or lurching.

(xii) Whilst it is possible for the operator to generate a rough order of priorities for the operation of commuter service, commuters are better understood by accepting what they are trying to achieve and recognizing that some service characteristics act as 're-inforcers' or 'motivators' and others generate dissatisfaction.

(xiii) It should be recognized that if the commuter's basic

criteria are not met then he/she will tend to find sources of dissatisfaction in nearly all features of the service and importantly very
strongly in respect of fares. But dissatisfaction can also be evinced
about rolling stock, station amenities, staff and information facilities. On the other hand if the basic criteria are met, then
commuters will have a much higher tolerance of features which appear
to generate large degrees of dissatisfaction in other circumstances.

(xiv) It should also be recognized that not all the commuters'
criteria can be accommodated in practice. The commuting process
potentially gives rise to conflict because:

(a) Commuters feel they are in competition for the use of
trains with people who join them or leave at other
stations.

(b) The sheer scale of the operation of most of the Central
London terminals is such that the individual recognizes
that he/she is involved with a very large system. The
individuals have to take the initiative to process themselves effectively. The experience, however, inevitable
it may be, is essentially negative.'

It is easy to underestimate the actual impact that the adoption of
standards might have on a transport undertaking. The call on management resources can be substantial, the need for new types of
monitoring practices may be very demanding and the maintenance of an
operating standard or raising it closer to a consumer standard may
involve very substantial investment. However, the adoption of
consumer-oriented standards can also be very highly motivating for
staff and management. In the case of London and the South-East it
could also create in the minds of central and local government a new
series of guidelines for the development of transport policies.

3. CONCLUSION

This paper has attempted to trace the developing application and use
of social research in respect of the changing needs of transport
policy and planning, and operating. It has discussed its role in
relation to other disciplines and referred to some of the practical
problems of relationships within the various planning professions as
well as those which exist between the transport systems and the
public.

Social research by its nature is inexact and great emphasis has
been placed on the need to reinforce it with conclusions arrived at by
other methods. It is not a universal problem solver. In isolation,
it often has substantial limitations, particularly for predictions.
In the sphere of transport operation it has not so far effectively
successfully explored the real ramifactions of three major questions:

what is reliability?

what is cleanliness?

what information is most helpful?

these together with other issues of the importance of travel stress
may not in the end be answerable by social research.

On the other hand it is probable that social research will have a
growing role in respect of the new policy challenges facing transport
planning and will continue to have progressive applications, without
the need for new techniques, in reducing the potential for social
conflict.

REFERENCES

British Railways (1979) Statement on the Commuters' Charter. December.
Buchanan, C. (1963) *Traffic in Towns*. London: HMSO.
Coventry, S. (1977) Sheffield and Rotherham Land Use/Transportation
    Study: 2 Strategy development. *Traffic Engineering and Control*,
    18 (9), pp. 408–13.
HMSO (1969) *Planning for People*. Report of the Committee on Public
    Participation (Chairman: Skeffington). London: HMSO.
Hollings, D. (1970) Impact of information and environment on inter-
    urban flows. Two case studies. PTRC Symposium on Models of
    Traffic outside Towns, Amsterdam.
Martin and Voorhees Associates (1977) Rail Investment in the South-
    West Corridor. Report for CIE, Eire.
Martin and Voorhees Associates (1978a) Greater Manchester Rail
    Strategy Study. Report for the PTE and the Greater Manchester
    County Council.
Martin and Voorhees Associates (1978b) Urban Applications of Passenger
    Ropeway Systems. Phase 1 Report for the Transportation Division
    of Von Roll Ltd., Berne, Switzerland.
Voorhees, A.M. and Associates (1974) Public Transport in Bedfordshire:
    Facts, Views, Issues, Options. Report for the Bedfordshire County
    Council.
WYTCONSULT (1977a) Rural Typology Study. West Yorkshire Transpor-
    tation Studies, Document 803.
WYTCONSULT (1977b) Social Research in Rural Areas. West Yorkshire
    Transportation Studies, Document 804.

Theoretical Developments
in Transport Research

The changes in survey methods have been accompanied by major changes in theory, and although there is considerable overlap between the different approaches to analysis, this group of papers is presented in an order which reflects the development of the theme. Huw Williams introduces an extensive review of the theoretical development of travel forecasting models, with particular emphasis on the contribution of British research. As well as outlining the principal problems which researchers have faced, the paper explores the different means by which problems can be resolved. The considerable progress - made over the last ten years - particularly in the dominance of entropy maximizing models and the emergence of random utility theory, suggests a fairly buoyant picture. But in the concluding section on future prospects, a more sombre point is made: as to whether behaviour can ever be successfully examined within the conventional mathematical paradigm.

This theme is taken up again in the following paper where Andrew Daly gives an overview of the development of disaggregate demand modelling, with particular reference to its application. Most of the theoretical problems have been overcome, and limited application seems to indicate that the methods are both flexible and give plausible results. It is suggested that behaviour can be represented as a process of choice within the framework of utility maximization, but the main disadvantage seems to be in the lack of available expertise for implementation.

Complementing some of the themes covered in the first two papers, Jeffrey Johnson introduces the concepts of Q-analysis and their application to transport systems. He argues that most transport analysis offers only a partial view of the system, and that a holistic approach is required to understand the relationships within transport, and between transport and (say) land-use. Q-analysis attempts to overcome this limitation by making an explicit statement of the structural relationships between transport and the environment. The principles introduced are extensively illustrated with examples, and the conclusion is drawn that Q-analysis could offer a prescription for integrated planning.

The problems of implementation are a particular concern in David Hartgen's paper, as he has been involved in both the development and the application of behavioural models. The history and potential for these methods in transport, as developed in the United States since the late 1960s, are assessed and critically commented on. Disaggregate and attitudinal models have posed particular implementation problems as they have not lived up to their capabilities, and there has been some institutional reluctance to take on the new ideas; suggestions are made on how further progress can be achieved. Household-based activity structures on the other hand appear to hold promise, but assessment is difficult as they are so recent.

Attitudinal models, mentioned in the previous paper, are further covered in the contributions by Peter Stopher and Kerry Thomas. In the first of these two papers, an extensive review of the current state of attitudinal modelling is made, together with comments on their advantages and disadvantages; the application of attitude measurement and modelling is still in the infancy stage, but certain future issues are identified. These include the use of attitudinal data for diagnostic purposes and in short-term forecasting. In the longer term, their use as modelling methods in their own right poses certain unanswered questions on the prediction of attitude-based measures and their relationship to physical attributes. However the future of attitudinal modelling seems to rest on the establishment of firm links between behaviour and attitudes.

This particular theme is taken up by Kerry Thomas who examines one particular attitudinal model and its contribution to the debate, namely the expectancy-value model. This approach, which seems to have considerable potential in survey-based research, is then contrasted with the application of other attitudinal research to policy making in general. The conclusions reached are that these approaches require extensive in-depth sampling, and that one has to decide whether the wealth of qualitative and quantitative data are usable in the policy process in anything other than descriptive terms.

The contributions of psychology to travel demand modelling are covered in Martin Dix's paper. Here, with respect to attitudinal models, it is suggested that a number of conceptual and methodological problems have yet to be overcome, thus confirming the conclusions reached from the previous three papers, but from a different starting point. The recent renewed interest in methods of social-psychological investigation is discussed together with selected applications to the question of choice, but again the conclusions are cautious. The reaction against regarding choice as a static process has led to approaches which involve the understanding of travel behaviour and change. This has generated an increased interest in interactive role-playing methods which attempt to understand the decisions made within the household; the conclusion is optimistic, thus confirming the final comments made in David Hartgen's paper.

The final paper in this section on theory examines the time-geographic approach developed in Sweden. The simulation model, which uses both time and space as constraints, determines whether certain activity programmes are feasible within the constraints imposed. Locations are classified according to whether they are accessible or not, and a wide range of policies (for example, transport, locational

and temporal) can be tested. Bo Lenntorp illustrates the conceptual
part of the paper with examples taken from the dairying industry in
Sweden and selected activity patterns for household members in the
city of Karlstad.

In this extensive section on theory, a comprehensive coverage of
the current position in transport research is presented. The
theoretical points are illustrated wherever possible: the aim has
been to identify where research is current, and to indicate which
directions are likely to be the most fruitful for further inquiry.

The main debate which has arisen from the section of techniques
is whether the extra effort involved in calibrating disaggregate
models is worthwhile. Practice is still heavily reliant upon the
aggregate methods of travel demand analysis, as it is possible to
give a system-wide assessment. The more recent developments in
techniques are problem specific and their application seems to have
been restricted primarily to mode-choice and inter-city travel
demand. Their advantages include the efficient use of data and their
claimed behavioural structure, but on the debit side the main problems
seem to be their use for prediction and the expertise necessary for
their implementation. Even among researchers, the case is not proven,
and there are distinct 'camps' of aggregate modellers and disaggregate modellers.

Although modelling is primarily concerned with consistency and
curve fitting, there has been a significant change in direction from
description of travel demand to the understanding of behaviour. This
move is best illustrated with respect to the modal choice question,
where the individual is no longer assumed to be a 'rational optimser'
of his choice decisions, but a 'satisficer'. Attitudinal studies
have played a key role in the understanding of behaviour, in
particular those who have a choice and under what conditions a choice
is made. The emphasis here is on choice as a process rather than
choice as an event.

However attitudinal research seems to pose as many problems as it
resolves, in particular the relationship between attitudes and
behaviour. The link is still unclear as to whether it is in one
direction or the other, or whether it is mutually reinforcing.
Perhaps one could avoid attitudes altogether and look at particular
situations.

This possibility is covered in the final set of techniques which
include explicitly time and space as constraints within which activities take place. The interactions within households and between
transport and land use are made explicit, and the techniques developed
have included interactive gaming methods and simulation; it may be too
early to assess this latest generation of models. However, one can
conclude that with respect to these methods, as with other disaggregate methods, evaluation is particularly weak. Only recently has
sensitivity analysis, together with the notion of uncertainty, been
explicitly included in analysis.

This conclusion relates to the essentially reactive nature of
models. Although their main function is to inform decision-makers on
the outcomes of particular policies, the output from models tends
to specify the well-known, even reinforcing the present system. This
relationship between policy and modelling works well as policy is
itself essentially incremental and not radical. However, there is
some uncertainty over whether models can accommodate the unexpected.

It is in this area that planning becomes more politicized as the circumstances in which certain decisions are made become more important than the decisions themselves.

Travel demand forecasting: an overview of theoretical developments

HUW WILLIAMS

1. INTRODUCTION

It is commonly remarked that the approach to travel demand forecasting inherited from the pioneering Detroit and Chicago studies,
which was to become institutionalized in the early 1960s, was
essentially descriptive. It was sought to *describe* the variability
in travel behaviour rather than *account for* observable patterns.
Indeed, it was not until the mid-1960s that specific theoretical
perspectives began to assert themselves. Whether it be considered a
science or an art, travel forecasting has, since that time, been the
subject of an invasion by theoretical constructs from disciplines
traditionally associated with other paradigms. The ideas borrowed
from information theory, statistical mechanics, economics, and
psychology come immediately to mind. These have provided frameworks
within which formal problems have been posed, data collected and
solutions sought. The exponents of each particular perspective have
sought to provide insights into the nature of topical issues, and
have, in turn, by the very nature of their 'world view' been subject
to limitations in the interpretation and analysis of behavioural
response.

A very considerable number of models have now been proposed and
implemented in various studies, and several classification schemes
have been put forward (see, for example, Manheim 1973; Brand 1973).
The classes themselves are often the product of theoretical innovations with the result that what is deemed to be a significant
classification is a function of the progress made in problem solving.
Many of these theoretical issues with which the travel forecaster
becomes pre-occupied are, as Alan Wilson has pointed out, often
associated with different manifestations of the aggregation problem.
I think this is particularly true of recent times in which the prime
distinctions between models have been associated with the way in which
a model interfaces with survey data - at an aggregate (grouped) or
disaggregate (individual) level - and with the process of aggregation
over travel related substitutes. The debate over the adoption of
'simultaneous' or 'sequential' model structures relates to this latter

issue and is fundamentally associated with the relationship between behavioural hypotheses and the analytic structure of the model itself.

The purpose of this paper is to review the theoretical development of travel forecasting models with particular emphasis on British experiences, to examine the problems which have been overcome and those which currently confront us, and finally to offer some views on future prospects.

Many of the criticisms of models relate to very basic issues concerned with the manipulation of data, and the generation of forecasting assumptions in conjunction with the analysis of statistical variance in travel patterns. In section 2 some such aspects relating to the aggregation problem will therefore be discussed. Ultimately *theories* of travel demand, as distinct from the technical process of analysis of variance, are concerned with the *interpretation* of this trip dispersion as perceived, by an observer - the modeller. Theories of dispersion are thus the subject of section 3. The extension of simple dispersion theories to accommodate choice contexts involving many 'complex' alternatives is examined in section 4. We discuss how an interpretation of the distinction between the traditional 'simultaneous' and 'sequential' travel demand model structures may be shown to relate to the perceived similarity between travel substitutes.

An important line of theoretical enquiry addresses the implementation and refinement of specific demand models, and in particular those currently adopted in transportation studies. In section 5, some theoretical issues concerned with the requirements of internal consistency and the 'goodness-of-fit' of models are considered.

In section 6, a number of topics relating to the evaluation of transport/land-use strategies are reviewed. We discuss the search for mutual compatibility between the demand model as a predictor of *response*, and corresponding measures of welfare change. This search has shed light on both the interpretation of benefit expressions, and on the derivation of alternative model structures.

In a final section, a general overview is given of issues relating to the state of the art, and problems and prospects are discussed.

It is not easy to present in a few thousand words a well balanced view of the many theoretical issues which have emerged in recent years and indeed are currently emerging, and at the same time provide a non-parochial view of British research. Limited by space, and, as ever, by an author's individual perspectives, the material is inevitably selective. The work may be seen as complementary to Neuberger's (1973) review and to the paper by Wilson (1973a).

2. INFORMATION, MODELS AND THE AGGREGATION ISSUE

If the classification process tends to emphasize the *distinctions* between travel forecasting models, it is important to emphasize at the outset that the overwhelming commonality of those implemented in Transport Studies has been their construction with data collected at one snapshop moment of time - the base year. The reliance on cross-sectional information alone has rather significant implications for theory development - the equifinality issue - as we shall note in later sections.

The very possibility of forecasting in the cross-sectional approach - with no other information available than that obtained from traditional surveys - ultimately depends on the ability to associate with a policy, a set of (objective) variables which may be shown to contribute statistically to observed variability in behaviour, and the will to attribute to this correlation a causal association. Having specified and estimated travel demand models on the basis of statistical criteria in conjunction with hypotheses and a miscellany of assumptions, the focus of attention changes to the elasticity parameters - essentially the first derivatives of the demand function with respect to policy variables. The model is converted into a stimulus-response relation.

With the restrictions on available data, it is not perhaps surprising that modellers have resorted so readily to the classical notion of equilibrium in the transport and activity systems. Although many dynamic models have been proposed which may be calibrated with two or more cross-sectional data sets (see, for example, Wilson 1974) very few structures have reached an operational stage. The dynamic disequilibrium models developed at Cambridge (Echenique and de la Barra 1977) and Leeds (Mackett 1977) which incorporate the mutual interaction between the land use and transport systems are two exceptions. In this representation the causal structure of the model may be unambiguously defined.

The cross-section may be 'probed' for information on the attributes of 'spatial actors' - individuals, households and firms - and for their *association* with activity-transport options. The variability in behaviour, manifested in a data set, is crucially dependent on the definition of states and categories. In turn, the series of transformation on data between the raw state and travel forecasts - which constitutes the modelling process itself - inevitably involves many simplifications, and it is a matter of concern that the approximations currently adopted prevent the process from exceeding a threshold of relevance. These aspects are closely related to the aggregation issue itself, and we can point to: the conventional treatment of individual decision units within wider organizational units (individuals within households); the treatment of linked trips; the *definition* of routes, modes, location, etc., as increasingly studied areas in which grouping may, and usually does, imply a loss of information crucial to the understanding of behaviour. It cannot be emphasized too strongly how basic data processing and state definition (together of course with specific modelling assumptions) may immediately present limitations on the range of behaviour a model can address. Indeed, at the preliminary stage of state specification possibly more than any other, the observer (modeller) can impose his perceived model of behaviour on the interpretation and analysis of response. We shall return to these issues in section 7.

Much of the (current?) euphoria which has been associated with the 'second generation' modelling framework relates to the successful marriage of microeconomic theory with an efficient process of information analysis, advances in sampling theory and econometric methods of model estimation. (Later it will be important to distinguish carefully between these aspects in dealing with criticisms raised against the state of the art.) In the early 1960s there was concern that the aggregate approach simply did not exploit the full

range of statistical variability in a data set and was, at best,
inefficient. The specification of appropriate units of analysis has
long been the subject of interest both from the viewpoint of analysis
of variance and with the problem of interfacing with the representation specific behavioural or forecasting assumptions. Wootton and
Pick (1967) and Fleet and Robertson (1968) clearly showed, in the
context of trip generation, how to exploit a greater range of
variability in a data set by avoiding an initial aggregation to the
zonal level. The work reported by the Coventry Transportation Study
(1973) and by Lawson and Mullen (1976) (see also Dale 1977) on trip
generation models based on the individual can be seen as a natural
extension of these earlier studies both from the viewpoint of
statistical efficiency and in coming to grips with the analysis of
household interactions, which are now the subject of so much interest
(see section 7).

Ultimately *theories* of travel demand are concerned with an
explanation of the influence of policy variables on both the 'natural'
processes of development of decision units and the dynamics of their
association with activity/travel options. In the case of households,
in contrast to many businesses and firms, transport and location
variables are not considered to have a significant direct influence on
life-cycle dynamics, and theories have traditionally addressed the
problem of association. Now, *current* patterns of association may be
attributed to individual decisions made at some previous point in
time, and the cross-section itself may be viewed in terms of a
compression of the processes giving rise to observable aggregate
patterns. In section 3 we shall examine two theoretical approaches to
the problem of aggregation over the decisions made at a micro-level
and the treatment of association.

Before proceeding to these aspects it is useful to comment briefly
on some general characteristics of model specification. In the
formulation of a model three types of formal entity are encountered:
endogenous variables which will, in general, be implicit or explicit
functions of time and policy variables; *exogenous variables* which will
be a function of time but not policy variables; and *parameters* or
constants which are assumed to be dependent on neither. Models differ
very significantly according to the classes in which particular
entities are to be found. A whole range of criticisms directed at
models may be traced to these distinctions. In table 1 we note the
typical classification involved in strategic transportation studies.
Those studies which embrace models of the activity system clearly
include certain land use variables in the endogenous set.

Table 1. Classification of selected variables in conventional
transport studies.

Endogenous variables	*Exogenous variables*	*Parameters or constants*
demand for travel	planning variables	peak hour factors
over space (distrib-	zonal population,	trip rates
ution function)	employment, etc.	'elasticity parameters'
mode shares	income	β, λ, δ etc.
route shares	value-of-time	
etc.	car ownership	

It would be desirable in a number of study contexts to specify additional endogenous variables. These might include, for example: car availability; car ownership; car occupancy; trip rates; peak rates; peak hour factors; stock supply functions, etc. The subtle relations between many of these variables and transport system attributes have long resisted satisfactory identification. In the last five years considerable progress has been made in this task by using disaggregated data sets. Indeed dissatisfaction with the use of car occupancy factors and the requirement to test car pooling schemes has, in the United States, greatly contributed to the acceptability of the micro-analytical approach (Spear 1977), in which multiple occupancy has been interpreted in terms of a choice process.

3. THEORIES OF DISPERSION AND THE POLICY-MODEL INTERFACE

In the absence of specific theoretical considerations it was perhaps inevitable that the traditional components of trip modelling – generation, distribution, modal split, and assignment – should be seen as such distinct areas of study. One of the tasks of the theorist is to present a unified account of the dispersion existing in observed patterns of movement. This dispersion is, as we have stressed, identified in terms of the occupancy of *pre-specified* states or categories. Both entropy maximizing and random utility maximizing methods which embody the notions of probability distribution likelihood and choice between discrete alternatives, respectively, may be abstracted from specific choice contexts (frequency, location, mode and route) and can thus address all these contexts (though of course this does not guarantee satisfactory models).

It may in fact be partly due to the simultaneous emergence of the much heralded generalized cost concept (developed in the micro-statistical studies of Warner (1962) and Quarmby (1967)) and its incorporation into the entropy maximizing models introduced in the SELNEC study (Wilson *et al.* 1969) that the methodology which generated these models (Wilson 1967, 1969) had such an immediate impact and profound influence on British transportation research and practice. Here was a *statistical* interpretation of trip dispersion; a flexible, easily applied and systematic way of generating models, which were *typically* expressed or converted into multinomial logit form, consistent with any relevant information available to the analyst. The method was deemed to generate models with the minimum number of *a priori* assumptions. It brought internal consistency to more highly disaggregated models (which involved improved market segmentation on 'trip-end' variables) and allowed new structures to be proposed. Indeed, its role in model generation has been nothing short of spectacular in the wider context of urban research in which complex phenomena and 'inter-locking' systems demand that models be underpinned by a rigorous accounting framework (for recent references see Macgill and Wilson 1979; Wilson and Macgill 1979).

While there are at least four interpretations of the entropy maximizing method (Wilson 1970) it is perhaps unfortunate, though natural, that the physical analogy should be primarily recalled. Recently the generalization of the approach to include Kulback's information measure (Kulback 1959) has found application in minimum information adding contexts (Batty and March 1977; Snickars and Weibull 1977).

Wilson has expressed the view that aggregation over preference relations at the micro-level may be performed only under unacceptably restrictive assumptions. He has, however, envisaged the formulation of models using entropy maximizing methods in conjunction with utility maximizing principles (Wilson 1973b). Southworth (1977) has implemented such a model which involves elastic trip frequencies and expenditures, and which provides a link between the trip generation and distribution stages of the strategic transport model.

The micro-approach beckoned not only because of the potential for greater statistical efficiency, the *possibility* of increased policy sensitivity, and the greater likelihood of parameter transferability, but also because of the possibility of combining these facets with a 'first principles' attack on the aggregation problem, which the 'behavioural school' finds a desirable prerequisiste to the satis-factory *explanation* of macro-behaviour. It is most important in a consideration of random utility theory of probabilistic choice models to distinguish between those assumptions which express the basic philosophy of the approach and those 'secondary' assumptions which are invoked to produce 'workable' models.

Among these 'secondary' assumptions are included the following:

(1) that the multiple objectives of each individual may be resolved in the formation of (net) utility functions, linear in attributes, which are used to record preferences;

(2) interpersonal variation of characteristics (e.g. values of travel attributes and *unobserved* attributes) may be introduced by means of random parameters or 'stochastic' residuals in this linear function, the distributions of which are prespecified by the modeller;

(3) each individual decision-maker scrutinizes all alternatives and selects that which offers the highest net utility;

(4) under changed conditions individuals reassess their choice contexts.

It should be stressed that the uncertainty which requires the introduction of random variables is a characteristic of the observer (the modeller) who invokes this device to account for dispersion – the fact that some people with identical *observable* characteristics select different alternatives. The decision-maker himself is, in this theory of rational choice, considered to choose optimally and consistently within his own utility frame of reference.

The probability that an individual with particular characteristics (drawn randomly from a population with similar *observable* character-istics) selects a given alternative, may now be formally expressed as the probability that the net utility associated with that option is the maximum associated with the set of alternatives. An analytic expression for the choice probabilities in terms of the choice and individual characteristics will result if certain specialized distributions are assumed for the random utilities.

If identical and independently distributed Weibull functions are assumed, then the multinomial logit model may be derived. Similarly, if normal distributions are assumed, then simple probit models can be generated.

Policies are directly interpreted in terms of changes in the attributes incorporated in generalized cost functions which are essentially the linear utility functions discussed above. One of the merits of the random utility approach was that it provided a unifying behavioural context for earlier studies on the value of travel attributes (see the discussion by Daly (1978)). In British studies it has become the widespread practice to *input* a *given* generalized cost function estimated from disaggregate data external to the model (as for example, that recommended by McIntosh and Quarmby (1970)) with the possible 'tuning' of the coefficients. The generalized cost function is scaled in spatially aggregated expressions by parameters (β and λ in conventional notations) and their estimation, together with such factors as modal penalties, forms the basis for model calibration. (A more rigorous and consistent approach is available to the aggregation and estimation procedures as for example outlined by Domencich and McFadden (1975); and Ben Akiva *et al.* (1977)).

The generation of identical model functions from alternative theoretical standpoints - the equifinality issue - has been recognized for some considerable time. The interpretation of such a model - in this case the multinomial logit model - does however depend on the theoretical notions assumed to underpin it, and this is particularly true of the embedded parameters. Take, for example, the λ and β parameters which appear in association with generalized and composite costs in the modal split (choice) and distribution (location) models. Now, we can seek to interpret these parameters through an examination of the model properties, and indeed they may be seen to be prominent in dispersion, moment (e.g. mean cost) and elasticity (response) relations (Thrift and Williams 1980). On the other hand, each has an additional and distinct interpretation dependent on the underpinning theory. In entropy maximizing models the parameters correspond to Lagrange multipliers associated with the change in likelihood of observing a given allocation (share) pattern (probability distribution) with respect to incremental changes in system trip cost measures. In random utility theory, however, the parameters are inversely related to the standard deviation of the utility distributions from which the choice model is generated.

These general comments are equally true for the interpretation of the 'balancing factors' or 'shadow prices' which are associated with constrained gravity models. Indeed, one of the interesting byproducts of the equifinality issue is the elaborate correspondence between the partition (generator) and potential functions associated with the model in its statistical mechanical interpretation and the various cost related value indicators in the economic interpretation (Williams and Senior 1978; Leonardi 1978).

4. MODEL STRUCTURES AND THE TREATMENT OF SUBSTITUTES

Did the theoretical constructs above extend to an arbitrary number of substitutes of differing character? Here there was certainly need for clarification. In a multiple-mode context involving, for example, car, bus and rail, should a three movement multinomial logit structure be adopted or should a hierarchical structuring be developed which entailed an initial division of appropriate trips between private transport and a public 'composite' mode, followed by a sub-split between bus and rail. These 'simultaneous' (or 'joint choice') and 'sequential' (or 'recursive') representations can be pictorally represented as in figure 1.

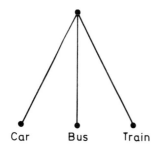
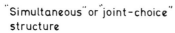
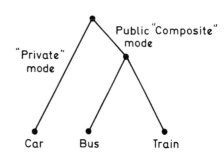

"Simultaneous" or "joint-choice" structure

"Sequential," "cascade" or "recursive" structure

Figure 1. A representation of alternative demand model structures for the choice between car, bus and train.

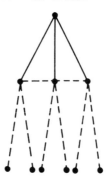
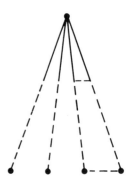

MS/D structure   D/MS structure   D-MS structure

– – – Model dimension

——— Location dimension

Figure 2. A representation of alternative model structures for the choice between mode-location combinations.

Many such dilemmas presented themselves in different modelling contexts which included mixed-modes, multiple routes and mode-route combinations. Perhaps the most obvious example of structural ambiguity, however, related to combinations of choice 'dimensions' involving frequency (G), location (D), mode (MS), and route (A), which were employed in the strategic transport planning models. With regard to the location and modal combinations in particular, should 'sequential' or 'simultaneous' models be developed as in the traditional pre-distribution (MS/D), post-distribution (D/MS), and joint distribution-modal split (D-MS) structures represented in figure 2? How were the D and MS 'submodels' to be interfaced in the MS/D and D/MS structures, and what was the significance of the composite costs used for this purpose? Were they subject to restrictive properties? Could we appeal to theory to ratify the general model structures, and indeed to discriminate between them?

On the question of interfacing the distribution (location and modal-split models) the entropy maximizing method could not give unambiguous guidance because it did not involve any unifying statements or hypotheses linking these segments. Nevertheless Wilson discussed in detail the simultaneous and sequential (nested logit) structures and proposed a series of possible composite costs to transmit modal information to the distribution model in the D/MS system (Wilson 1969). This important paper introduced several innovations which were to be implemented in the SELNEC model (Wilson et al. 1969) and more recent transportation studies.

In the early 1970s the question of model structure came into sharper focus. Three American studies by Manheim (1973), Charles Rivers Associates (1972) (see also Domencich and McFadden 1975) and Ben-Akiva (1974) were to have considerable influence on theoretical and practical developments. The developments of Charles Rivers Associates (1972) and Ben-Akiva (1974) were concerned with the implementation of micro-models for shopping trips involving the combination of frequency, location and mode, and with the rationalization of model structures from behavioural principles of utility maximization.

Ben-Akiva strongly recommended the simultaneous structure - and the multinomial logit model in particular - both because the latter was assumed to embody faithfully a simultaneous consideration by decision-makers of the mode-destination combinations, and because there was, it was argued, no a priori reason to choose between the alternative orderings D/MS and MS/D which were demonstrated to yield different values for the elasticity parameters.

In other modelling contexts however, particularly those involving multiple modes and mode-route combinations, it was becoming increasingly clear that the multinomial logit model could not be indiscriminately applied. The model suffered a well known restrictive property of cross substitution, quaintly termed the independence from irrelevant alternatives characteristic (IIA), rendering it highly suspect in those cases in which a subset of options were more 'similar' than others. The dangers implied by the IIA property were epitomized by the red-bus/blue-bus conundrum (Mayberry 1970) which was a whimsical but important example, characterizing a whole class of problems to be resolved in theoretical developments designed to account for the 'similarity' between alternatives. It was soon recognized that the multinomial logit model, which results from the assumption of equal and uncorrelated Weibull distributions, was often applied in conjunction with utility functions which themselves manifested natural correlation. In other words the model was, in general, inconsistent with the form of utility function assumed to generate it.

The injection of correlation between the random components of utility functions took a number of forms. Williams (1977a) showed that the introduction of stochastic components which corresponded to the form of certain additive separable utility functions, resulted in the natural formation of 'structured' or 'hierarchical' models. Further, just as Strotz (1957) had shown in his treatment of commodity grouping in classical theory, the random utility theory of choice between discrete alternatives allows composite options and suitably defined composite costs or index prices to be defined, and this enables the consistent integration of partial models in hierarchical structures. One special member of this class of models – the nested or hierarchical logit form – was independently shown by Williams (1977a) and by Daly and Zachary (1978) to be generated from random utility maximizing behaviour. The latter implemented the structure in the Huddersfield Bus study. McFadden (1978) in turn showed that the nested logit model was a special case of a class of general extreme value (GEV) models.

In essence this line of theoretical research has indicated the conditions under which the nested logit and similar structured models can be generated from random utility theory, and more specifically has shown that:
(1)   one interpretation of the distinction between the 'sequential' and 'simultaneous' forms shown in figure 1 can be traced to the existence of correlation or similarity between alternatives. In the absence of this similarity one structure will transform into the other, D/MS, MS/D → D-MS;
(2)   in the structured logit model the underpinning require-ment of rational choice behaviour imposes two particular restrictions on the resulting model relating to:
    A   the form of the composite cost (utility) which is unique (up to an additive constant)
    B   a relationship between certain elasticity parameters characterizing the partial shares of the hierarchy.
If either of these conditions is violated the model will not be consistent with utility maximization.

It is disturbing to note that in those British transport studies employing the (aggregate) nested model structure G/D/MS/A, one or other, and usually both, of these conditions has been violated, and this can be shown to result in highly unrealistic response character-istics in common policy testing contexts (Senior and Williams 1977; Williams and Senior 1977). The source of these pathological results for the calibrated D/MS structure has recently been attributed by Hawkins (1978) to the coarse market segmentation and the treatment of short trips usually adopted in transport studies (again aspects of the aggregation problem).

An alternative attack on the correlation problem has been made by adopting multinomial probit models (derived from normal distributions for the random utility components) for the multi-modal problem both in particular, and in a general form with arbitrary variance-covariance matrix (Domencich and McFadden 1975; Langdon 1976; Haussman and Wise 1978). The recent implementation of the Clark approximation (Clark 1961) by Daganzo, Bouthelier and Sheffi (1977) has extended the possibility of applying this very general model in arbitrary choice contexts beyond the few alternatives (four or five) achieved by direct numerical integration.

In spite of advances in the generalized probit field there appears to be a need for a compromise between the generality afforded by this model and the computational tractability of simpler models, for example, the nested logit model which incorporates a more restricted form of 'similarity' between alternatives. McFadden's general class of extreme values models (McFadden 1978) is one such possible research direction. Another *ad hoc* model is the cross-correlated logit model D*MS, proposed by Williams (1977a), which contains the two structured logit (D/MS, MS/D) and multinomial logit (D-MS) forms as special cases.

A further line of enquiry, which is increasingly adopted for model implementation and in testing the theoretical accuracy of models involving approximations in their derivation, is the use of Monte Carlo simulation. Here sampled 'individuals' are confronted by choice contexts (Albright, Lerman and Manski 1977; Ortuzar 1978, 1980; Robertson 1977; Robertson and Kennedy 1979). Using this method Williams and Ortuzar (1979) have recently examined the accuracy of the multinomial, nested logit and cross-correlated logit models in two-dimensional contexts (say D and MS). Their results suggest that the practice suggested by Williams and Senior (1977) and Ben-Akiva (1974, 1977a) of employing the multinomial logit model and alternative forms of hierarchical structure (and be guided by the size of the 'similarity coefficient') is not likely to result in substantial error, when compared with more general structures.

5. ISSUES IN MODEL DEVELOPMENT AND IMPLEMENTATION

The development of the subject is closely associated with the more efficient and satisfactory implementation of particular demand models chosen for trip forecasting. Perennial concerns of both theorists and practitioners are with the appropriate level of parameter classification, estimation procedures, the production of acceptable goodness-of-fit measures, and with the achievement of consistency between the measures of transport service (times and costs) incorporated in different parts of the model. With the exception of a very few models, developed in a research context (see the reviews by Wigan (1977)) the approaches adopted in British studies for the achievement of equilibrium have been *indirect* - the submodels are calibrated independently and the output of one fed into the next, with a limited degree of 'feedback' between the segments.

The recognition that certain common models corresponded to the optimal solution(s) of particular mathematical programs has had a number of practical implications. First, it allowed certain algorithms and solution procedures to be subject to formal scrutiny and their convergence properties assessed. Secondly, in those cases for which the programs may be underpinned by some theory of behaviour at the macro- or micro-levels, the dual variables have usually had some very relevant significance to the evaluation problem and could furthermore be exploited in model solution. While primal variables tend to have a 'stock' or 'flow' interpretation, duals could be interpreted in terms of 'prices' or 'value differentials'. Thirdly, the properties of the models themselves could be elucidated through an examination of the structure of the mathematical program. Fourthly, it has allowed demand models to be integrated into consistent frameworks of analysis including those embodying demand-supply equilibria.

That the double constrained gravity (distribution) model could be generated from extremal principles was recognized by Murchland (1966) and Wilson (1967), and the dual properties of this program have been examined by Evans (1973a) and Wilson and Senior (1974). It has been shown that its limiting form corresponds to the optimal solution of the corresponding transportation problem of linear programming (Evans 1973b). Murchland (1977a) has formally examined the convergence properties of the doubly constrained gravity model balancing equations and proposed a termination criterion, while Champernowne *et al.* (1976) have solved the dual program through direct minimization to produce simultaneously the 'deterrence parameter' and balancing factors. Evans and Kirby (1974) have furthermore indicated how the conventional iterative approach to the balancing of the model with an empirically derived deterrence function could be formally examined in terms of a three-dimensional Furness procedure.

It has long been known that the Kuhn-Tucker conditions (Kuhn and Tucker 1951) of a program introduced by Beckmann *et al.* (1956) corresponded to the Wardrop network equilibrium conditions for congested assignment (Wardrop 1952). Murchland's elegant exposition of Rockafellar theory (Murchland 1969) has provided the basis for the construction of algorithms for computing solutions for congested assignment models with elastic demand and the rigorous analysis of convergence. This work has been extended and elaborated by Evans (1976) and others in combining distribution and assignment models and more recently incorporating modal split (Florian 1976). The comparison of heuristic approaches to the achievement of equilibrium with rigorous methods remains an important line of research (see, for example, Murchland 1977b; Van Vliet 1977).

The work described above is concerned with the properties and implementation of models which can be shown to have a programming derivation. But what of their ability to adequately correspond, in a statistical sense, with base year travel patterns? Some recent British concerns include studies on the design of appropriate zoning systems for the analysis of interaction data (see the collection of papers in the special issue of *Environment and Planning, A.* Vol. 10, 1978); the fine disaggregation of distribution and modal split model parameters by Southworth (1977) using the relative likelihood approach developed by Hathaway (1973, 1975) and Ian Williams (1976) to investigate the *significance* of segmentation; and the influence on modal-split parameter values of alternative methods of estimation (Senior and Williams 1977). Recent work at University College London has examined in considerable detail the statistical issues involved in calibrating gravity models (Kirby 1974; Leese 1977; Kirby and Leese 1978) and a new test for its acceptance or rejection has been proposed.

We shall return in section 7 to reconsider the role which the analysis of variability and 'goodness-of-fit' plays in the concerns of model validity.

6. THE DEMAND MODEL-EVALUATION INTERFACE

Although forecasts of travel demand are seldom ends in themselves, they have traditionally dominated those parts of the planning process implemented in transport studies. While the scope of transport strategy appraisal has broadened considerably since the early 1960s (Dalvi and Martin 1973; Bayliss 1977) the computation of so-called 'user benefits' associated with a policy remains a central feature of scheme evaluation.

In this section I shall comment briefly on certain aspects of the relation between the demand model as an instrument of *response prediction* and corresponding *measures of welfare change* implied by that response. Five specific areas have recently attracted attention:

(1)   the possibility of obtaining exact nonmarginal measures
      of user benefit;
(2)   the generation of mutually consistent models and
      evaluation measures within the framework provided by
      random utility theory;
(3)   the accuracy of the so-called 'rule-of-a-half'
      consumer surplus measure;
(4)   the disaggregation and interpretation of spatial benefit
      measures;
(5)   the broadening of the evaluation framework to embrace
      arbitrary changes in the land-use (activity)-transport
      system, and in particular the establishment of links
      with urban economic theory.

Since the mid-1960s the change in consumer surplus arising from
the introduction of a scheme has become a standard measure of user
benefit, and the 'rule-of-a-half' (ROH) introduced in the London
Transport Study Phase III (Tressider *et al.* 1968) has served to
relate such changes in welfare to the demand response. This marginal
expression was initially proposed as an *ad hoc* extension of the
Marshallian (area under a demand curve) trapezium equation and, as
such, it was recognized that there were certain problems in accounting
for the 'shifting' demand curve phenomenon accompanying simultaneous
changes in the perceived generalized cost of travel substitutes.
Elaborate arguments were put forward to suggest that such effects were
small and could for all intents and purposes be safely ignored.

By appealing to the generalized measure of consumer surplus
proposed by Hotelling (1938) - a natural extension of the Marshallian
framework which embraced the full range of substitution accompanying
demand response - Neuberger (1971) noted that for the multinomial
logit model (in fact the singly constrained gravity model) an exact
measure of benefit could be obtained. This result was to be recon-
structed within the framework of random utility theory by Koenig
(1975) and Cochrane (1975). It was further recognized (Williams
1976; Champernowne *et al.* 1976) that the ROH itself resulted from a
particular method of evaluating the line integrals which were central
to Hotelling's scheme of welfare measurement.

It was natural to enquire whether exact measures could be generated using Hotelling's method for the more complex models involved in
transport studies, and under what conditions were such measures
compatible with the models derived within the framework of random
utility theory. These questions were addressed by Harris and Tanner
(1974), Williams (1977a, 1977b) and by Daly and Zachary (1978). In
contrast to the common method of extracting user benefits *after* the
forecasting process, it was found that the condition of optimality
which underpins the behavioural models allowed the economic measures
to be extracted directly from the calculations performed during model
implementation. For *suitably specified* urban transport planning
models this distinction is between the assessment of benefits at the
trip generation stage rather than *after* the assignment submodel.

With the provision of exact measures of consumer surplus it has
been possible to test the accuracy of the 'rule-of-a-half' in policy
analysis. Except in those cases for which the ROH is known to be
inapplicable - as, for example, may happen in the introduction of new
options or the suppression of existing ones - the marginal approximation has been found to be in error typically by less than 5 per cent

(Neuberger 1971; Williams and Senior 1977) and does not affect the
ranking of schemes.

It should be emphasized that the main value of these exact
measures is not therefore in their numerical or computational significance, but in the provision of new perspectives on the evaluation
problem. In particular, by focusing on the choice contexts of spatial
actors it allows a meaningful analysis of the spatial disaggregation
of benefits, and a rigorous − though not necessarily unique −
interpretation of such concepts as 'accessibility' in terms of
consumer surplus (Neuberger 1971; Koenig 1975; Cochrane 1975; Williams
1977a; Williams and Senior 1978; Ben-Akiva and Lerman 1979).

It has been shown that these exact measures may be extended to
embrace arbitrary changes in the transport *and* land-use (activity)
system, in cases for which the resultant (derived) demand for travel
may be considered to result from rational choice behaviour (Neuberger
1971; Williams 1976; Williams and Senior 1978). This provides a basis
for the generation of activity patterns themselves from programming
frameworks which embrace the transport related options available to
producers and consumers (Coelho and Wilson 1976; Coelho 1977; Coelho
and Williams 1978), and thus establishes a link with urban economic
theory in the tradition of Alonso (1964) and Herbert and Stevens
(1960). To derive meaningful measures of locational benefit in cases
for which the 'stock' of houses and employment locations changes
slowly, it is necessary to underpin appropriate spatial interaction
models with an economic rationale (Beckmann and Wallace 1969; Cochrane
1975; Champernowne *et al.* 1976; Williams and Senior 1978; and
Brotchie 1979). Total benefit is now apportioned between the demand
and supply sides in housing, job and land 'markets'. The nature and
determination of urban rent is now central to the computation and
distribution of benefit.

The results of these analyses on the mutual interaction of the
transport and activity systems are, I believe, not solely confined to
academic interest. Who *does* benefit from the introduction of a
transport policy? What portion of the benefit ultimately will
percolate into the activity system and manifest itself in changes of
rent differentials? What are the distributional implications of these
changes? In the final analysis the answers to these questions will
depend on the model of the urban economic system proposed and the
mechanism assumed to be embedded in it (Scott 1978; Williams and
Senior 1978).

7. PROBLEMS AND PROSPECTS

It is not infrequently argued that the modelling experience over the
past twenty years has contributed significantly to our understanding
of traveller behaviour. Purists might well argue that this rather
optimistic perspective is at best misplaced, and would point to a
desirable distinction between our knowledge of current patterns of
movement (a question of information, which though still limited, few
would deny has greatly increased) and our understanding of, and
ability to predict realistically, the *response* of travellers to
proposed changes in the activity-transport system. They might indeed
question what *can* be known about some future state from observations
on cross-sectional information alone.

Pragmatists on the other hand, who view the holding of absolute

standards as an ultimate luxury, accept incomplete knowledge as a
natural state of affairs and look to the evolutionary upgrading of the
technical process for improvement in the forecasting method. They
would point to the conventional stage of the problem solving paradigm
- generalized sensitivity analysis - as the appropriate means for
handling the many uncertainties involved in modelling response. That
the practitioner is invariably placed under severe implementation
constraints of costs, times, and existing software is widely appreciated. Where practicalities come into conflict with strict theoretical
integrity, the compromise is not surprisingly in favour of the former
as the more candid technical reports reveal.

It is against such a background of conflicting attitudes and
changing requirements of the planning process, that innovations and
the state of the art are judged. Inevitably *theoretical* debate
however focuses on three generations of model development: the first
involving the so-called aggregate models; the second, the disaggregate
perspective based on analytic probabilistic choice models: and the
third, the activity frameworks in which social roles emerge as a
theme of prime significance. In this context it is worth remarking
that for many years the models in Britain have been of hybrid form
and if classification were demanded it would be somewhere between
first and second generations. By incorporating the household-based
category analysis, and embedding generalized and composite costs
(with micro-parameters) within the framework provided by entropy
maximizing models, the SELNEC and later studies (though deficient in
many known respects) could I believe be defended from the more severe
forms of censure reserved for American transportation study practice
in the late 1960s and early 1970s, as for example discussed by Barker
(1973), Ben Akiva (1973) and Domencich and McFadden (1975).

So, what of the contribution of theory? Did theoretical innovations consolidate, or provide a *post hoc* rationalization of existing
practice? Did they deal hammer-blows to widely held beliefs? What
new interpretations, concepts, or suggestions emerged? Some of these
questions have been addressed already in sections 2 to 6. A few more
comments are in order.

We noted above the dominance of the entropy maximizing models
(and therefore presumably the acceptability of the method) in British
practice. If we take the SELNEC model (Wilson *et al.* 1969) as the
first practical expression of the approach it clearly built on and
consolidated existing G/D/MS/A models. The method did in turn inspire
the detailed specification of many subsequent models including those
applied in the most recent (1977) West Yorkshire (G/D/MS/A) and
Greater London (G/D-MS/A) Transportation Studies.

Random utility theory too provided a rationalization of existing
model structures, modifying them to be consistent with the notion of
travel as a derived demand. By showing how alternate structures
could be derived, it uncovered an interpretation of the theoretical
distinction between them. It further indicated how general structures
could be formulated which embodied many existing models (e.g. D/MS,
MS/D, D-MS) as special cases. A solution was found to the red-bus/
blue-bus, and related, problems which in turn allowed insight into the
nature of travel options themselves. Indeed the hypernetwork concept
discussed by Sheffi (1978) and others may be seen in terms of a
generalization of the abstract mode concept introduced in the mid-
1960s. The framework also provided a basis for the construction of

consistent evaluation measures.

The theory of course is not without its critics (I have myself heard it described by a seasoned North American transport planner as a 'load of statistical junk'!) and some of these have been anticipated in sections 2 and 3. As with all 'first principles' approaches, the formalism does provide a basis for its own self examination, and most importantly reveals the extent to which the modeller imposes *a priori* assumptions on the analysis.

It is argued that the current generation of models 'pay lip-service to behaviour' (Burnett and Thrift 1979) and involves 'more of a caricature than a true description' (Heggie 1978). How can the subtleties of adaptive behaviour involving complex trip linkages be portrayed by choice models? How can the framework accommodate the detailed constraints in time and space under which individuals find themselves, and how can the detailed interactions within and between households be incorporated? How do we account for limited and often heterogenous information in choice contexts, and the how do we incorporate habit, learning and satisficing behaviour on the part of the decision-maker? (Heggie 1978; Banister 1978; Heggie and Jones 1978; Burnett and Hanson 1979).

With an appropriate definition of states and market segmentation, and the relaxation of the 'secondary restrictions' involved in the formation of random utility models, many'of the above facets of choice contexts could in principle be accommodated within the existing theoretical framework, and some progress has been made in these directions (see for example, Adler and Ben-Akiva 1979; Goodwin 1977; Hensher 1975; Ben-Akiva 1977b; Gaudry and Dagenais 1979; Williams and Ortuzar 1979). Of more profound importance, however, is whether a satisfactory empirical basis for the implementation and validation of such models is available!

Such fundamental questioning of the tenets of choice models based on random utility theory has been accompanied by the call for new approaches to the study of activities within a space-time framework originally conceived by Hägerstrand (see, for example, Jones 1977; Carlstein *et al.* 1978; Burnett and Hanson 1979). Heggie (1978), in advocating the use of gaming techniques, has expressed doubts whether behaviour can ever be successfully examined within the conventional mathematical paradigm. Such a gaming approach has found expression in the HATS technique developed at the Oxford Transport Studies Unit in which the individual, within a family context, may determine preferable courses of action and resolve any conflicts which these imply (Jones 1979).

The extension of this approach to formal modelling on a computer (if indeed it is sought) will be aided by the development of an appropriate state-attribute representation. It may well be that the list processing device employed by Orcutt *et al.* (1961) and Wilson and Pownall (1976) in conjunction with Monte Carlo simulation will prove a useful step in this direction. A similar type of micro-simulation study has been developed in a car-pooling model by Bonsall (1979) in which transfer pricing methods were adopted in the estimation of model parameters. This procedure of processing individual decision units within an extended micro-representation using Monte Carlo methods is currently being applied in Leeds in the examination of a broader range of urban phenomena (Wilson and Pownall 1976; Clarke, Keys and Williams 1979, 1980).

Although considerable progress may be claimed in the development
of models since the mid-1960s, particularly in relation to the use of
micro-data, a variety of problems remain as the weight of the above
criticism implies. What successes may be claimed in relation to
solved problems have taken typically five to ten years to bring to
fruition. It is sobering to think, for example, of the alternative
and possibly more realistic explanations of model structure based on
satisficing behaviour which awaits full development (Brand 1973;
McFadden 1975; Williams and Ortuzar 1979; Richardson 1978). What
then of the status of generalized cost and separability?

Ultimately we seek the invariants in traveller and location
behaviour, and this was of course one of the prime incentives for the
development of the disaggregate approach. The issue of transferability of model parameters in space and time appears now however to
be a much more controversial issue than it was five years ago
(Southworth 1978; Kirshner and Talvitie 1977). It remains to be seen
how successful hypotheses based on time budgets will prove.
Hypothesis generation and testing remains a most fundamental concern,
and progress here is hampered by the lack of available data, and the
recognition that the cross section alone will often prevent discrim-
ination between competitors.

I believe that one of the most significant classifications of
formal models will in future be not on the basis of their structure
but on their calibration procedures - whether they will be implemented
on the basis of *stated* or *revealed* preferences. That is, whether some
indication of *response* is sought (through, for example, transfer
pricing methods) or whether *currently observed* behaviour is thought
to be the most reliable indicator of *future* actions. In the case of
'new modes', for example, the 'abstract mode' concept was indeed
attractive, but to the extent that success in the public transport
field is sought in unconventional concepts, it will be necessary to
rely more heavily on attitudinal data and stated preferences.
Finally, the much called for distinction between demand and need must
here be fully recognized in examining the implications and possible
biases of models calibrated on the basis of observed behaviour.

But what now of the practitioner, who usually works in an
environment of competing models and theories? He must be guided by
the theorist's understanding of their differences and the circumstances under which such differences would be important (if these are
known). He might take some comfort in the equifinality issue which
would imply that the ultimate validity of a model (to be judged *post
hoc*) is *not necessarily* dependent on a discredited or 'unrealistic'
theory. Sensitivity analysis of parameters, structures, aggregation
procedures, etc. will remain his indispensable tool (Bonsall *et al.*
1977; Ben-Akiva 1973; Senior and Williams 1977; Southworth 1978). As
ever the choice of model and indeed method of forecasting will depend
on the questions asked and the nature of the answers sought.

REFERENCES

Adler, T. and Ben-Akiva, M.E. (1979) A theoretical and empirical
model of trip chaining behaviour. *Transportation Research*, 13B
(3), pp. 243-257.

Albright, R.L., Lerman, S.R. and Manski, C.F. (1977) Report on the development of an estimation program for the multinomial probit models. Prepared for the Federal Highway Administration, by Cambridge Systematics, Inc.

Alonso, W. (1964) *Location and Land Use*. Cambridge, Mass.: Harvard University Press.

Banister, D.J. (1978) The influence of habit formation on modal choice: a heuristic model. *Transportation, 7*(1), pp. 5–18.

Barker, W.G. (1973) *The Use of Models in Urban Transportation Planning*. Report prepared for the U.S. Department of Transportation.

Batty, M. and March, L. (1977) Dynamic urban models based on information-minimising, in Martin, R.L., Bennett, R.J. and Thrift, N.J. (eds.) *Dynamic Analysis of Spatial Systems*. London: Pion Press.

Bayliss, D. (1977) Priorities in urban transport research, in Bonsall, P., Dalvi, Q. and Hills, P.J. (eds.) *Urban Transportation Planning: Current Themes and Future Prospects*. Tunbridge Wells: Abacus, pp. 349–62.

Beckmann, M.J., McGuire, C.B. and Winsten, C.B. (1956) *Studies in the Economics of Transportation*. Cowles Commission monograph. New Haven: Yale University Press.

Beckmann, M.J. and Wallace, J.P. (1969) Evaluation of user benefits arising from changes in transportation systems. *Transportation Science, 4*(4), pp. 344–51.

Ben–Akiva, M.E. (1973) Structure of Passenger Travel Demand Models. Unpublished PhD dissertation, Department of Civil Engineering, Massachusetts Institute of Technology.

Ben–Akiva, M.E. (1974) Structure of passenger travel demand models. Transportation Research Record 526, pp. 26–42.

Ben–Akiva, M.E. (1977a) Passenger travel demand forecasting: Applications of disaggregate models and directions for research. Paper presented at the World Conference on Transport Research, Rotterdam.

Ben–Akiva, M.E. (1977b) Choice models with simple choice set generating processes. Working Paper, Department of Civil Engineering, Massachusetts Institute of Technology.

Ben–Akiva, M., Adler, T.J., Jacobson, J. and Manheim, M. (1977) *Experiments to Clarify Priorities in Urban Travel Demand Forecasting Research and Development*. Summary report, US Department of Transportation.

Ben–Akiva, M. and Lerman, S. (1979) Disaggregate travel and mobility choice models and measures of accessibility, in Hensher, D.A. and Stopher, P.R. (eds.) *Behavioural Travel Modelling*. London: Croom Helm, pp. 654–79.

Bonsall, P.W. (1979) Microsimulation of mode choice: a model of organized car sharing. PTRC Proceedings, Summer Annual Meeting, University of Warwick.

Bonsall, P.W., Champernowne, A.F., Mason, A.C. and Wilson, A.G. (1977) Transport modelling: sensitivity analysis and policy testing. *Progress in Planning, 7*(3), pp. 153–237.

Brand, D. (1973) Travel demand forecasting: some foundations and a review. *Highway Research Record* Special Report 143, Highway Research Board, Washington, DC, pp. 239–82.

Brotchie, J.F.   (1979)   A model based on non-homogeneity in alloc-
    ation problems, in Hensher, D.A. and Stopher, P.R. (eds.)
    Behavioural Travel Modelling. London: Croom Helm, pp. 355-77.
Burnett, P. and Hanson, S.   (1979)   A rationale for an alternative
    mathematical paradigm for movement as complex human behaviour.
    Paper presented at the Transportation Research Board Meetings,
    Washington, DC, January.
Burnett, P. and Thrift, N.   (1979)   New approaches to understanding
    traveller behaviour, in Hensher, D.A. and Stopher, P.R. (eds.)
    Behavioural Travel Modelling. London: Croom Helm, pp. 116-34.
Carlstein, T. Parkes, D. and Thrift, N. (eds.) (1978)   *Timing Space
    and Spacing Time,* Vol. 2: *Human Activity and Time Geography.*
    London: Edward Arnold.
Champernowne, A.F., Williams, H.C.W.L. and Coelho, J.D. (1976) Some
    comments on urban travel demand analysis, model calibration, and
    the economic evaluation of transport plans. *Journal of Transport
    Economics and Policy,* 10 (3), pp. 267-85.
Charles River Associates (1972) *A Disaggregate Behavioural Model of
    Urban Travel Demand.* Federal Highway Administration, US Depart-
    ment of Transportation, Washington, DC.
Clark, C.E.   (1961)   The greatest of a finite set of random
    variables. *Operations Research,* 9, pp. 145-62.
Clarke, M., Keys, P. and Williams, H.C.W.L. (1979)   Household
    dynamics and economic forecasting - a simulation approach. Paper
    presented at the European Congress of the Regional Science
    Association, London. Also as Working Paper 257, School of
    Geography, University of Leeds.
Clarke, M., Keys, P. and Williams, H.C.W.L.   (1980)   Micro-analysis
    and simulation of socio-economic systems: progress and
    prospects, in Bennett, R.J. and Wrigley, N. (eds.) *Quantitative
    Geography in Britain: Retrospect and Prospect.* London:
    Routledge and Kegan Paul.
Cochrane, R.A.   (1975)   A possible economic basis for the gravity
    model. *Journal of Transport Economics and Policy,* 9(1),
    pp. 34-49.
Coelho, J.D.   (1977)   The use of mathematical optimization methods in
    model based land use planning. Unpublished PhD Thesis, School of
    Geography, University of Leeds.
Coelho, J.D. and Williams, H.C.W.L.   (1978)   On the design of land
    use plans through locational surplus maximization. *Papers of the
    Regional Science Association* 40, pp. 71-85.
Coelho, J.D. and Wilson, A.G.   (1976)   The optimal location and size
    of shopping centres. *Regional Studies,* 10(4), pp. 413-21.
Coventry City Council (1973) Coventry Transportation Study, *Report
    on Phase Two:* Technical report, Parts i and ii.
Daganzo, C.F., Bouthelier, F. and Sheffi, Y.   (1977)   Multinomial
    probit and qualitative choice: A computationally efficient
    algorithm. *Transportation Science,* 11(4), pp. 338-58.
Dale, H.M.   (1977)   Trip generation: what should we be modelling?
    in Bonsall, P., Dalvi, Q. and Hills, P.J. (eds.) *Urban Trans-
    portation Planning: Current Themes and Future Prospects.*
    Tunbridge Wells: Abacus Press, pp. 23-9.
Dalvi, M.Q. and Martin, K.M.   (1973)   Urban transport evaluation
    procedures. Working paper 23, Institute for Transport Studies,
    University of Leeds.

Daly, A.J. (1978) Issues in the estimation of journey attribute values, in Hensher, D.A. and Dalvi, Q. (eds.) *Determinants of Travel Choice.* Farnborough: Saxon House, pp. 187-202.

Daly, A.J. and Zachary, S. (1978) Improved multiple choice models, in Hensher, D.A. and Dalvi, Q. (eds.) *Determinants of Travel Choice.* Farnborough: Saxon House, pp. 335-57.

Domencich, T. and McFadden, D. (1975) *Urban Travel Demand - a Behavioural Analysis.* Amsterdam: North Holland.

Echenique, M. and de la Barra, T. (1977) Compact land-use transportation models, in Bonsall, P., Dalvi, Q. and Hills, P.J. (eds.) *Urban Transportation Planning: Current Themes and Future Prospects.* Tunbridge Wells: Abacus Press, pp. 111-25.

Evans, S.P. (1973a) The use of optimization in transportation planning. Unpublished PhD dissertation, University College London.

Evans, S.P. (1973b) A relationship between the gravity model for trip distribution and the transportation problem in linear programming. *Transportation Research,* 7(1), pp. 39-61.

Evans, S.P. (1976) Derivation and analysis of some models for combining trip distribution and assignment. *Transportation Research,* 10(1), pp. 37-57.

Evans, S.P. and Kirby, H.R. (1974) A three dimensional Furness procedure for calibrating gravity models. *Transportation Research,* 8(2), pp. 105-22.

Fleet, C.R. and Robertson, S.R. (1968) Trip generation in the transportation planning process. Highway Research Record 240, Highway Research Board, Washington DC, pp. 11-26.

Florian, M. (1976) A traffic equilibrium model of travel by car and public transport modes. Report No. 32, Centre de Recherche sur les Transports, Université de Montreal, Canada.

Gaudry, M.J.I. and Dagenais, M.G. (1979) The DOGIT model. *Transportation Research,* 13B (2), pp. 105-12.

Goodwin, P.B., (1977) Habit and hysterisis in mode choice. *Urban Studies,* 14(1), pp. 95-98.

Harris, A.J. and Tanner, J.C. (1974) Transport demand models based on personal characteristics. Transport and Road Research Laboratory, SR 65UC.

Hathaway, P.J. (1973) Some statistical problems associated with trip distribution models. Proceedings of PTRC Summer Annual Meeting, University of Sussex.

Hathaway, P.J. (1975) Trip distribution and disaggregation. *Environment and Planning A,* 7(1), pp. 71-97.

Hausman, J.A. and Wise, D.A. (1978) A conditional probit model for qualitative choice: discrete decisions recognizing interdependence and heterogenous preferences. *Econometrica,* 46(2), pp. 403-26.

Hawkins, A.F. (1978) Some anomalies due to misspecification in transport models. Proceedings of PTRC Summer Annual Meeting, University of Warwick.

Heggie, I.G. (1978) Behavioural dimensions of travel choice, in Hensher, D.A. and Dalvi, Q. (eds.) *Determinants of Travel Choice.* Farnborough: Saxon House, pp. 100-25.

Heggie, I.G. and Jones, P.M. (1978) Defining domains for models of demand. *Transportation,* 7(2), pp. 119-25.

Hensher, D.A. (1975) Perception and commuter modal choice: an
    hypothesis. *Urban Studies*, 12 (1), pp. 101-4.
Herbert, D.J. and Stevens, B.H. (1960) A Model for the distribution
    of residential activity in urban areas. *Journal of Regional
    Science*, 2, pp. 21-36.
Hotelling, H. (1938) The general welfare in relation to taxation and
    of railway and utility rates. *Econometrica*, 6, pp. 242-69.
Jones, P.M. (1977) Travel as a manifestation of activity choice:
    trip generation re-visited, in Bonsall, P., Dalvi, Q. and
    Hills, P.J. (eds.) *Urban Transportation Planning: Current Themes
    and Future Prospects*. Tunbridge Wells: Abacus Press, pp. 31-49.
Jones, P.M. (1979) 'HATS': a technique for investigating household
    decisions. *Environment and Planning A*, 11(1), pp. 59-70.
Kirby, H.R. (1974) Theoretical requirements for calibrating gravity
    models. *Transportation Research*, 8(2), pp. 97-104.
Kirby, H.R. and Leese, M.N. (1978) Trip distribution calculations
    and sampling error: some theoretical aspects. *Environment and
    Planning A*, 10(7), pp. 837-51.
Kirshner, D. and Talvitie, A. (1977) Specification, transferability
    and the effect of data outliers in modelling the choice of mode
    in urban travel. Working Paper SL-7701, Department of Economics,
    University of California, Berkeley, California.
Koenig, J.G. (1975) A theory of urban accessibiltiy: a new working
    tool for the urban planner. Proceedings of PTRC Summer Annual
    Meeting, University of Warwick.
Kuhn, H.W. and Tucker, A.E. (1951) Non-linear programming, in
    *Proceedings of the 2nd Berkeley Symposium on Mathematical
    Statistics and Probability*. Berkeley: University of California
    Press, pp. 481-92.
Kulback, S. (1959) *Information Theory and Statistics*. New York:
    John Wiley.
Langdon, M. (1976) Modal split models for more than two modes.
    Proceedings of PTRC Summer Annual Meeting, University of Warwick.
Lawson, G.P. and Mullen, P. (1976) The use of disaggregate modelling
    techniques in the Telford Transportation Study. Proceedings of
    PTRC Annual Summer Meeting, University of Warwick.
Leese, M.N. (1977) A statistical test for trip distribution models.
    Paper presented at the 9th Conference of the Universities
    Transport Studies Group, January.
Leonardi, G. (1978) Optimum facility location by accessibility
    maximizing. *Environment and Planning A*, 10(11), pp. 1287-305.
Macgill, S.M. And Wilson, A.G. (1979) Equivalences and similarities
    between some alternative urban and regional models. *Urbani
    Systemi*, 1, pp. 9-40.
Mackett, M.L. (1977) A dynamic activity allocation transportation
    model, in Bonsall, P., Dalvi, Q. and Hills, P.J. (eds.) *Urban
    Transportation Planning: Current Themes and Future Prospects*.
    Tunbridge Wells: Abacus Press, pp. 95-110.
Manheim, M.L. (1973) Practical implications of some fundamental
    properties of travel demand models. Highway Research Record 422,
    Highway Research Board, Washington, DC, pp. 21-38.
Mayberry, J.P. (1970) Structural requirements for abstract-mode
    models of passenger transportation, in Quandt, R.E. (ed.) *The
    Demand for Travel: Theory and Measurement*. Lexington, Mass:
    Lexington Books, pp. 103-25.

McFadden, D. (1975) Economic applications of psychological choice
    models. Working Paper 7519, Travel Demand Forecasting Project,
    Institute of Transportation and Traffic Engineering, University of
    California at Berkeley.
McFadden, D. (1978) Modelling the choice of residential location, in
    Karlqvist, A., Lundqvist, L., Snickars, F. and Weibull, J.W.
    (eds.) *Spatial Interaction Theory and Planning Models.* Amsterdam:
    North Holland.
McIntosh, P.T. and Quarmby, D.A. (1970) Generalized cost and the
    estimation of movement costs and benefit. MAU Note 179,
    Department of the Environment, London.
Murchland, J.D. (1966) Some remarks on the gravity model of trip
    distribution and an equivalent maximising procedure. Mimeo,
    LSE-TNT-38, London School of Economics, London.
Murchland, J.D. (1969) Road traffic distribution in equilibrium,
    in *Mathematical Methods in the Economic Sciences.* Matematisches
    Forehungsinstitut Oberwolfach, West Germany.
Murchland, J.D. (1977a) Convergence of gravity model balancing
    operations. Proceedings of PTRC Summer Annual Meeting, University
    of Warwick.
Murchland, J.D. (1977b) Constructing congested assignment test
    problems with a known solution, in Bonsall, P., Dalvi, Q. and
    Hills, P.J. (eds.) *Urban Transportation Planning: Current Themes
    and Future Prospects.* Tunbridge Wells: Abacus Press, pp. 129-46.
Neuberger, H.L.I. (1971) User benefit in the evaluation of transport
    and land use plans. *Journal of Transport Economics and Policy,*
    5(1), pp. 52-75.
Neuberger, H.L.I. (1973) Travel demand models. *Economic and
    Statistical Notes, No. 14,* Department of the Environment, London.
Orcutt, G., Greenberger, M., Korbel, J. and Rivlin, A.M. (1961)
    Microanalysis of Socio-Economic Systems: A Simulation Study.
    New York: Harper and Row.
Ortuzar, J.D. (1978) Mixed mode demand forecasting techniques: an
    assessment of current practice. Proceedings of PTRC Summer Annual
    Meeting, University of Warwick.
Ortuzar, J.D. (1980) Testing the theoretical accuracy of travel
    choice models using Monte Carlo simulation, Working Paper
    (Forthcoming), Institute for Transport Studies, University of
    Leeds.
Quarmby, D.A. (1967) Choice of travel mode for the journey to work:
    some findings. *Journal of Transport Economics and Policy,* 1(3),
    pp. 273-314.
Richardson, A.J. (1978) A Comparative analysis of transport choice
    models. Working Paper 78/11, Civil Engineering Department,
    Monash University, Australia.
Robertson, D.I. (1977) A Deterministic method of assigning traffic
    to multiple routes of known cost. Transport and Road Research
    Laboratory Report LR757.
Robertson, D.I. and Kennedy, J.V. (1979) The choice of route, mode,
    origin and destination by calculation and simulation. Transport
    and Road Research Laboratory Report LR877.
Scott, A.J. (1978) Urban transport and economic surplus: notes
    towards a distributional theory, in Karlqvist, A., Lundqvist, L.,
    Snickars, F. and Weibull, J.W. (eds.) *Spatial Interaction Theory
    and Planning Models.* Amdersterdam: North Holland.

Senior, M.L. and Williams, H.C.W.L. (1977) Model based transport policy assessment, 1: the use of alternative forecasting models. *Traffic Engineering and Control*, 18 (9), pp. 402-6.

Sheffi, Y. (1978) Transportation network equilibration with discrete choice models. Unpublished PhD thesis, Department of Civil Engineering, Massachussetts Institute of Technology.

Snickars, F. and Weibull, J. (1977) A Minimum information principle-theory and practice. *Regional Science and Urban Economics*, 7, pp. 137-68.

Southworth, F. (1977) The calibration of disaggregated trip distribution and modal split models: some comparisons of macro- and micro-analytic approaches. Unpublished PhD Thesis, School of Geography, University of Leeds.

Southworth, F. (1978) Modelling the changing relationship between travel demand and land use. Working Paper 225, School of Geography, University of Leeds.

Spear, B.D. (1977) Application of new travel demand forecasting techniques to transportation planning: a study of individual choice models. US Department of Transport, FHWA Office of Highway Planning.

Strotz, R.H. (1957) The empirical implications of a utility tree. *Econometrica*, 25(2), pp. 269-80.

Thrift, N.J. and Williams, H.C.W.L. (1980) On the development of behavioural location models. *Economic Geography* (In press).

Tressider, J.O., Meyers, D.A., Burrell, J.E. and Powell, T.J. (1968) The London Transportation Study: methods and techniques. *Proceedings of the Institute of Civil Engineers*, 39, pp. 433-64.

Van Vliet, D. (1977) An application of mathematical programming to network assignment, in Bonsall, P., Dalvi, Q. and Hills, P.J. (eds.) *Urban Transportation PLanning: Current Themes and Future Prospects*. Tunbridge Wells: Abacus Press, pp. 147-58.

Wardrop, J.G. (1952) Some theoretical aspects of road traffic research. *Proceedings of the Institute of Civil Engineers*, part II(1), pp. 325-61.

Warner, S.L. (1962) *Stochastic Choice of Mode in Urban Travel: a Study in Binary Choice*. Evanston, Illinois: Northwestern University Press.

Wigan, M.R. (Ed.) (1977) *New Techniques for Transport Systems Analysis*. Special Report Number 10, sponsored by the Australian Road Research Board and the Bureau of Transport Economics.

Williams, H.C.W.L. (1976) Travel demand models, duality relations and user benefit measures. *Journal of Regional Science*, 16(2) pp. 147-66.

Williams, H.C.W.L. (1977a) On the formation of travel demand models and economic evaluation measures of user benefit. *Environment and Planning A*, 9(3), pp. 285-344.

Williams, H.C.W.L. (1977b) Generation of consistent travel-demand models and user-benefit measures, in Bonsall, P., Dalvi, Q. and Hills, P.J. (eds.) *Urban Transportation Planning: Current Themes and Future Prospects*. Tunbridge Wells: Abacus Press, pp. 161-76.

Williams, H.C.W.L. and Ortuzar, J.D. (1979) Behavioural travel theories, model specification and the response error problem. Proceeding of PTRC Annual Summer Meeting, University of Warwick.

Williams, H.C.W.L. and Senior, M.L. (1977) Model based transport
    policy assessment, 2: Removing fundamental inconsistencies from
    the models. *Traffic Engineering and Control*, 18(10), pp. 464-9.
Williams, H.C.W.L. and Senior, M.L. (1978) Accessibility, spatial
    interaction and spatial benefit analysis of land use - transport-
    ation plans, in Karlqvist, A., Lundqvist, L., Snickars, F. and
    Weibull, J.W. (eds.) *Spatial Interaction Theory and Planning
    Models*. Amsterdam: North Holland, pp. 253-87.
Williams, I. (1976) A comparison of some calibration techniques for
    doubly constrained trip models with an exponential function.
    Transportation Research, 10(2), pp. 91-104.
Wilson, A.G. (1967) A statistical theory of spatial distribution
    models. *Transportation Research*, 1 (3), pp. 253-69.
Wilson, A.G. (1969) The use of entropy maximizing models in the
    theory of trip distribution, mode split and route split. *Journal
    of Transport Economics and Policy*, 3(1), pp. 108-26.
Wilson, A.G. (1970) *Entropy in Urban and Regional Modelling*.
    London: Pion.
Wilson, A.G. (1973a) Travel demand forecasting: achievements and
    problems. Highway Research Record, Special Report 143, Highway
    Research Board, Washington, D.C.
Wilson, A.G. (1973b) Further developments of entropy maximizing
    transport models. *Transport Planning and Technology*, 1(3),
    pp. 183-93.
Wilson, A.G. (1974) *Urban and Regional Models in Geography and
    Planning*. London: John Wiley.
Wilson, A.G., Hawkins, A.F., Hill, G.J. and Wagon, D.J. (1969)
    Calibration and testing of the SELNEC transport model. *Regional
    Studies*, 3(3), pp. 337-50.
Wilson, A.G. and Macgill, S.M. (1979) A systems analytic framework
    of comprehensive urban and regional modelling. To be published
    in *Geographica Polonica*. Also Working Paper 209, School of
    Geography, University of Leeds.
Wilson, A.G. and Pownall, C.E. (1976) A new representation of the
    urban system for modelling and for the study of micro-level
    interdependence. *Area*, 8, pp. 246-54.
Wilson, A.G. and Senior, M.L. (1974) Some relationships between
    entropy maximizing models, mathematical programming models and
    their duals. *Journal of Regional Science*, 14(2), pp. 207-15.
Wootton, H.J. and Pick, G.W. (1967) A model of trips generated by
    households. *Journal of Transport Economics and Policy*, 1(2),
    pp. 137-53.

Behavioural travel modelling: some European experience

ANDREW DALY

1. INTRODUCTION

It should be clear from the outset that a 'behavioural model' cannot exist. A model, by its nature, implies a simplification, an abstraction, and we cannot expect to represent more than crudely the full range of human behaviour by simple mathematical formulae. The term 'behavioural modelling', however, indicates an objective, an approach to predicting the particular aspects of travellers' behaviour most relevant to the planning of transport facilities.

The approach has two key premises. The first is to recognize that the observed aggregate-travel phenomena – passenger car units on a highway link, for example – are the result of disaggregate decision-making by a large number of individuals. The second premise is that this disaggregate behaviour can best be studied and understood by considering the options open to each traveller and the factors influencing his or her decision. These premises are easy enough to accept in isolation, the difficulty is to accept that they are relevant to the prediction of total usage of our transport systems, since we are ultimately concerned with totals of travellers, not with the behaviour of any particular individual.

The relevance of disaggregate analysis is established in two ways. First, we can obtain from a study of individuals' behaviour considerable insight into the factors influencing that behaviour. This insight is of direct value in indicating the criteria that travellers themselves consider most important in making their choices. Concrete expression of this type of information is given by the numerical 'trade-offs', the marginal value ratios for the various factors. The most commonly-required trade-off, and historically the most important, is the 'value of time', the trade-off ratio between time and money. Perhaps the more important application of disaggregate behavioural analysis, however, is as a basis for aggregate forecasting. Providing the technical statistical problem of aggregation can be overcome, the advantages of disaggregate analysis in flexibility and efficiency can be exploited to improve aggregate forecasting.

The analysis of individual behaviour of any kind requires a

framework by which the observed facts may be interpreted. The
framework most readily available for quantitative analysis of travel
behaviour is that suggested by microeconomics: that individuals
('consumers') act so as to maximize some benefit or 'utility'. As we
shall see, this concept of behaviour has proved extremely productive
for travel modelling. The possibility remains, of course, that some
other discipline, such as psychology, will suggest a framework that
will prove equally or more useful. So far, however, most of the
studies that have been developed from a theoretical basis have taken
that basis from economics.

In this framework of utility maximization, the individual is
represented as exercising his choice over the full range of options
available to him, limited by his constraints of money and time. In
the economic literature, the choice is usually represented as being
among continuously divisible commodities for consumption. In travel
modelling, we tend to be concerned more often with choice between
discrete, exclusive alternatives – bus or car for the journey to
work, for example, or zonal alternatives for the destination of a
shopping trip. This feature means that the models developed in
transportation planning tend to appear rather different from the
usual economic models, and it is occasionally difficult to relate the
transportation models back to the economic framework in which they
are set.

In the following section of this paper, I describe the studies of
mode choice and value of time with which behavioural travel modelling
was initiated in Britain. By the early 1970s there was a clear
methodological separation between the studies attempting to predict
aggregate demand, such as the modal choice work, and those that tried
to predict travellers' trade-off values, as done in value-of-time
studies. This separation was reconciled around 1975 by the development of utility maximization theory, which is described in the third
section of the paper. This theory, developed by several workers in
Britain, was also developed in parallel and approximately simultaneously in the United States by at least two groups. The fourth
section is concerned with applications of disaggregate analysis. For
applications on a large scale, we have to look outside the United
Kingdom, particularly to the United States and the Netherlands, and it
is the Dutch studies that will be taken as examples. Finally, we draw
some conclusions about the value of this work, the problems still to
be overcome, and the possibilities for implementation of disaggregate
analysis in Britain. A fairly extensive bibliography is also given.

2.   MODE CHOICE AND VALUE-OF-TIME STUDIES

The publication in 1970 of the justly famous M.A.U. Note 179
(McIntosh and Quarmby 1970), 'Generalised Costs and the Estimation of
Movement Costs and Benefits', gave a clear expression of the advanced
state of British methodology at that time. The Note lays down an
evaluation procedure which has been heavily and often correctly
criticized since, on the grounds that the evaluation procedure is
unsound. The procedure is, however, based on an understanding of
traveller behaviour and shows a clarity of approach that have been
sadly lacking in many more recent studies. The Note is so well known
that it provides a most useful starting point for our discussion of

the developments of the 1970s.

The Note itself had been strongly influenced by Quarmby (1967) in his earlier work, which was the first in this country to work systematically with the notion of generalized cost incorporating both cost and several separated components of time. An important following study was that by Rogers, Townsend and Metcalf (1970) who applied Quarmby's technique of discriminant analysis to investigate the transferability of mode choice models between British cities. This latter study also showed the consistency of discriminant analysis with the logit model of mode choice, which by that time was beginning to be used widely for aggregate planning studies (Wilson *et al*. 1969).

The Note assigned an important place in the evaluation procedure to the value of time, and this imposed an obligation on the government to make available reliable numerical estimates. The studies that the government commissioned to meet this obligation, however, found theoretical difficulties with the discriminant analysis technique. The study by Davies and Rogers (1973) for example, returned to the much earlier technique of Beesley (1965) in estimating time values so that a maximum number of travellers' choices were consistent with the estimate. This intuitively simple concept was subsequently studied in detail by Manski (1975) who termed it 'score maximization', a kind of democratic estimation.

Meanwhile, in aggregate forecasting work, the logit model was coming to be the standard procedure, as in the Department's COMPACT program, for example (Mackinder 1973). The reasons for this substitution were that the logit formula was easier to use, and could readily be extended to cover choices from more than two modes, although statistical estimation of the parameters of the model remained a problem.

This dichotomy of methodology between the applied mode choice forecasts and the value of time estimations using mode choice data was unsatisfactory in itself, since it suggested an inconsistency in the theories of traveller behaviour. Moreover, workers in both separate fields were beginning to find difficulties with the separate approaches. For example, in mode choice studies, the application of the simple extension of the logit formula to choices from more than two modes required assumptions of equality in the cross-elasticities that were difficult to justify: the extreme example of this is the notorious red-bus/blue-bus anomaly. Similarly, although Manski had shown the score maximization technique to be sound for large data sets, he had also indicated that it would be inefficient for small sets. The time was clearly ripe for a broad advance in theoretical understanding that would reconcile the methodology and suggest means for dealing with the outstanding problems in each field. This advance was given by the development of the utility maximizing models.

3. UTILITY MAXIMIZATION MODELS

In the value-of-time study of Davies and Rogers, it was clearly formulated that a traveller in preferring one mode to another is revealing a preference for the chosen combination of cost, time and other attributes over the alternative combination. In other words, the combination of cost, time and whatever else is seen as some

rudimentary utility that the traveller is trying to maximize. I
shall defer discussion of the economic interpretation of this
'utility' to a more appropriate juncture, and concentrate meanwhile
on the development from this simple model of behaviour.

The crucial step, from which all else follows, is to recognize
that it is not possible to measure exactly all of the criteria
relevant to an individual's choice, nor to determine exactly the
weights that he attaches to those criteria. The best we can hope
for is to derive some measures that represent the relevant criteria
correctly for a hypothetical 'typical' traveller, and treat the
actual behaviour of real individuals as being small deviations from
that average. The most useful way of doing this is to treat the
individuals as being randomly sampled from the total population of
travellers, so that their weights for the criteria are randomly
distributed about the overall average.

The advantage of this step of postulating a random distribution
of weights is that we can then *derive* the probability that a given
individual will make a given choice. We can measure the average
utility of each of the choices open to him, and then predict from
the postulated distribution of the weights how likely it is that
any of the available choices will actually have the highest utility.
Of course the choice with the highest average utility will in
general be chosen most often, but other choices will be made by a
minority of travellers. The derivation of measures of average
utility for each choice is then a statistical problem of finding a
best fit to the observations in a data set. This step of deriving
probabilities from a postulated distribution of weights was the
basis of the theoretical study of Harris and Tanner (1974) and the
value-of-time work of Daly and Zachary (1975). Parallel work was
done in the United States a little earlier (Ben-Akiva 1973; McFadden
1977).

This step of postulating a distribution of weights (and, hence,
utilities) in the population had the advantage of reconciling the
two opposing methodologies. As presented here, the approach is
clearly consistent with the value-of-time estimations. For these
estimations, this development represents a generalization of the
framework of analysis, in which the existing techniques could be more
properly evaluated. On the other hand, as shown by Daly, (1976b) not
only the logit formula but also the other mode choice models (including the probit or normal model and the linear probability model) can
be derived from the premise of utility maximization.

The work of Domencich and McFadden (1975) which concentrated on
the logit formula, extended beyond mode choice to develop models of
trip distribution or 'destination choice', as did that of Cochrane
(1975) and Koenig (1975). These models took the same general form as
the entropy maximizing models of Wilson (1967) showing that these
models too were consistent with the utility maximizing framework,
at least in this early stage of its development. In my opinion,
there remain even now some outstanding duality problems concerning
the relationship of utility and entropy maximizing models.

Given this reconciliation of approaches, it was now possible to
turn the powerful insights given by utility maximization to the
problem of constrained cross-elasticity in the logit formula, which
I mentioned above. The problem is interpreted in utility terms as a
need to assume that the actual utilities are distributed about their

averages with distributions that are independent and identical.
This assumption is clearly implausible whenever some of the choices
available have closer relationships (e.g. more features in common)
than some of the others.

The solution to this problem is in principle clear, and has
occurred to nearly all the workers who have used utility maximization
as an approach (e.g. Daly and Zachary 1975; Hawkins 1978). The
real difficulty, however, was to find suitable functional forms to
express the predictive formulae in cases of choice from more than two
alternatives. This problem was by 1975 under intensive study in
America (McFadden 1975), and in 1976 three separate solutions were
published by British workers (Andrews and Langdon 1976; Daly and
Zachary 1976; Williams 1977). It is very striking that largely the
same solutions were developed in the United States at exactly the
same time, also in simultaneous work by different groups (Ben-Akiva
and Lerman 1977; McFadden and Train 1977).

The solution adopted by Andrews and Langdon (1976) was to assume
a normal distribution in the utilities, thus deriving normal or
probit formulae for the choice probabilities. These formulae
presented analytical problems with which they were able to make some
progress in the three-mode case. Subsequent American work has derived
useful approximations for these complicated formulae, but their
complexity remains a barrier to the effective use of probit formulae.
More technical reasons also argue strongly for the use of the logit
formula in preference.

The logit formula was preferred by Williams (1977), Daly and
Zachary (1976), and by the American workers. The crucial generalization of the simple logit formula was the definition of groups of
closely-related choices, and allowing different cross-elasticities
for choices within and outside the groups. Williams drew attention
to the possibility of this structure for modelling jointly mode and
destination choice, treating modes to the same destination as a
closely-related group. He also noted the important consequences of
this methodology for simplifying evaluation. Daly and Zachary derived
a test that could be applied to any given prediction formula to test
its consistency with utility maximization. They also showed in this
paper the significant improvements that the improved models could give
in practical application, a point confirmed by Senior and Williams
(1977).

By the time of these studies, it was clear that the theoretical
developments had run somewhat ahead of their implementation. In the
next section I consider the practical results obtained from models of
this type, finding that most of the examples come from abroad.

4. APPLICATIONS OF DISAGGREGATE METHODS

The model structures developed in the studies described in the
previous section give the analyst great freedom in specifying the
models he wishes to study. Relative to the conventional approaches,
they also offer improved accuracy, both in predicting demand in
evaluation, and can reduce the cost of both data collection and the
evaluation of alternative policies. We should therefore expect to
see a wide implementation of these ideas, but in Britain this is
not the case. The two largest recent British studies, the Regional
Highway Traffic Model (Bridle 1978) and the West Yorkshire

Transportation Study, have both explicitly required a conventional approach. For proof of the practicality of the disaggregate approach we must look elsewhere.

As indicated in the introduction, application of disaggregate analysis can be of value in two situations. One of these is its use to derive information about individuals trade-offs, and it would therefore be natural to find a number of value-of-time studies that exploited the new methodology. But again we know of no recent behavioural studies of the value of time. Values of time have been derived by other studies, but these have been incidental to the main purposes of those studies, and the time values have been less accurate than those we could obtain from a specific study.

Aggregate forecasting using disaggregate models requires in general an adjustment of the models to avoid 'aggregation bias' (Daly 1976a; Koppleman 1976; McFadden and Reid 1975). In many ways, the best such procedure is 'sample enumeration', a technique invented and developed in the United States (Ben-Akiva and Atherton 1977) which has been inadequately used in Britain. The technique works by considering the impact of each policy on each individual in a real or artificial sample. The literature gives the statistical background establishing the efficiency and reliability of the technique.

Sample enumeration was the basis of the Daly and Zachary study (1977a) of free public transport in England, but so far as I know no other British study has used the approach. This study developed logit models of car ownership, car availability and mode choice for a sample drawn from several cities and which included public transport employees paying no fare for their journey to work. Sample enumeration was then used to estimate the effect on the remainder of the sample of the extension of these concessions to them. This study also, and incidentally, estimated values of time, which are more recent and based on a larger sample (2000-odd cases) than other British studies I know.

The other application of disaggregate models we could seek is as a basis for aggregate forecasting. The parallel in the United States is the study by Domencich and McFadden (1975), which went on from theoretical development to apply the models to a practical study of Pittsburgh. This stream of work was continued in the massive Urban Travel Demand Forecasting Project (Ruiter and Ben-Akiva 1977). Nearly all the British studies described in the previous section, however, were purely theoretical. Daly and Zachary (1976) applied their new models to the Huddersfield Bus Study, but none of the other studies had a practical intent. Senior and Williams (1977) tested their theories with practical data, but their work was not applied for local planning.

A few studies have used disaggregate methods, and the Telford Transportation Study (Mullen, Bursey and White 1976; Mullen and White 1977) is a good example. The papers referenced show simple and effective use of the advantages of disaggregate technique, but they do not involve the large-scale model systems applied in the United States nor even the realistic small-scale structure used by Daly and Zachary (1976).

In the Netherlands, by contrast, there has been a much greater application of this type of modelling. The first significant study in the field was for Eindhoven (Richards and Ben-Akiva 1976), a study which applied disaggregate modelling to develop mode and distribution choice models, but which did not incorporate any sophistications of structure. Subsequently, a much more ambitious project was undertaken by the Ministry of Transport and Public Works, through consultancy with the Institutes of Economics and Transport and with Cambridge Systematics (Ben-Akiva *et al.* 1978; Netherlands Ministry of Transport and Public Works; van der Hoorn and Vogelaar (1978). This study set up a complete set of linked demand models, covering generation, distribution and mode choice for most trip purposes. These models are now being applied in policy planning for the Amsterdam region.

A further study is now in progress in the Netherlands, this time focussing on the Zuidvleugel (Rotterdam) area (Daly 1978). Again these models will form a complete forecasting set, extending to predict time-of-day choice. Forecasting will be available using both sample enumeration and a more conventional aggregate forecast system, following an aggregation procedure.

One of the strengths of disaggregate models is that they can be extended to cover a very wide range of household and personal decisions. In relation to travel, this means that we are also able to use disaggregate methodology to cover transport-related choices as well as the direct demand decisions discussed so far. For example, we have already mentioned the subject of car ownership, which has been developed much further in the United States than anywhere in Europe, and is now able to consider the combinations of types of cars that households may own, not just the total number (Manski, Sherman and Ginn 1978).

Another field that can be investigated very profitably by the use of disaggregate choice models is that of household mobility and its relationship to workplace changes. Work in this field is not as yet very well advanced, but the outlines for progress are clear (Lerman 1976), and work is in hand in the United States and in the Netherlands.

5. CONCLUSIONS AND RECOMMENDATIONS

From the discussions of the previous section it is clear that applications of disaggregate techniques have been more numerous and ambitious in other countries than in Britain. It seems reasonable therefore to assess the advantages and disadvantages of these techniques, and to draw some conclusions about their applicability in Britain.

The chief advantages of disaggregate methods, I believe, are in flexibility and plausibility. The main disadvantage is that they make demands for expertise that is not always available.

The models are flexible because they can readily be adapted to deal with a particular problem at hand. Both the traveller choices represented and the variables by which they are influenced may be selected specifically for a specific policy analysis. The forecasting time frame, the spatial scale and the level of detail of the modelling may be set as required. Important policy variables are not excluded by structural rigidity. Data may be collected in the most cost-effective manner for the given study.

The technique of sample enumeration gives a special advantage for disaggregate modelling, since it gives the capability for very quick evaluation of a policy - one or two days is typical, but this can be

reduced. However, as indicated above, more conventional forecasts may
also be produced if required, after the application of an aggregation
procedure.

These models also have the advantage of plausibility, in that the
theories on which they are based are at least common-sense. Discussion
of their compatibility with the economic theory of consumer choice has
not been entirely conclusive. It is, however, clear that there is a
fundamental consistency, and all that is necessary is for the theory
to be clearly set out, along the lines started by Train and McFadden
(1978).

More important than consistency with economic theory is the fact
that the clear basis on which utility maximization sets the modelling
gives an equally clear basis for formulating and testing hypotheses
about travellers' behaviour. Statistical tests may be conducted in
circumstances which leave little doubt about their meaning, and the
whole study of traveller behaviour can be placed on a more scientific
basis. Moreover, sophisticated statistical techniques can be
developed to deal effectively with special situations, such as with
biased (Lerman, Manski and Atherton 1976) or deficient (Daly and
Zachary 1977b) data.

Against the approach it must be said that it requires a deeper
level of understanding than would be needed for a routine exercise of
the conventional procedures. Typically, issues are posed that require
a good knowledge of statistics to understand, and effects are revealed
that require considerable imagination to model properly. On reflection, however, it seems that the disaggregate approach is just
bringing into better focus the true issues of demand forecasting, and
that the difficulties that arise are caused by the very real complexities of the true issues.

For application in Britain, the problem of expertise should prove
far from insuperable, for, as we saw, British workers were able to
make significant contributions to the theoretical development. It is
likely, however, that we suffer from a lack of software and practical
computation techniques, so that the initial studies could be aided by
importing this expertise.

In conclusion, it appears that this area of work has not been
explored sufficiently empirically in the United Kingdom to convince
decision-makers of its value. The evidence from abroad suggests
strongly that disaggregate studies can give significant improvements
in the effectiveness of travel demand analysis, and I therefore
conclude that pilot studies should be undertaken forthwith in Britain.

REFERENCES

Andrews, R.D. and Langdon, M.C. (1976) An individual cost minimising
    method of determining modal split between three travel modes.
    Transport and Road Research Laboratory LR 698.
Beesley, M.E. (1965) The value of time spent travelling: some new
    evidence. *Economica*, 32, pp. 174-85.
Ben-Akiva, M. (1973) Structure of passenger travel demand models.
    Transportation Research Record 526, Transportation Research
    Board, Washington D.C., pp. 26-42.
Ben-Akiva, M. and Atherton, T. (1977) Methodology for short range
    travel demand predictions: analysis of car pooling incentives.
    Journal of Transport Economics and Policy, 11 (3), pp. 224-61.

Ben-Akiva, M. and Lerman, S.R. (1977) Disaggregate travel and
    mobility choice models and measures of accessibility. Papers
    presented to the Third Conference on Behavioural Travel
    Modelling, Tanunda, Australia.
Ben-Akiva, M., Kullman, B.C., Sherman, L. and Daly, A.J. (1978)
    Aggregate forecasting with a system of disaggregate travel
    demand models. Proceedings of PTRC, Summer Annual meeting,
    University of Warwick.
Bridle, R.J. (1978) A general framework for trunk road appraisal.
    Proceedings of PTRC, Summer Annual meeting, University of Warwick.
Cochrane, R.A. (1975) An economic basis for the gravity model.
    Journal of Transport Economics and Policy, 9 (1), pp. 34-49.
Daly, A.J. (1976a) Modal split models and aggregation. Local
    Government Operations Research Unit, Transportation Working Note
    6.
Daly, A.J. (1976b) Issues in the estimation of journey attribute
    values. Local Government Operations Research Unit. Transportation
    Working Note 12.
Daly, A.J. (1978) *Zuidvleugel Study Report 1: Proposed Model
    Structure*. Netherlands Ministry of Transport and Public Works.
Daly, A.J. and Zachary, S. (1975) Commuters' value of time. Local
    Government Operations Research Group, Report T55.
Daly, A.J. and Zachary, S. (1976) Improved multiple choice models.
    Proceedings of PTRC, Summer Annual meeting, University of Warwick.
Daly, A.J. and Zachary, S. (1977a) The effect of free public
    transport on the journey to work. Transport and Road Research
    laboratory, SR 388.
Daly, A.J. and Zachary, S. (1977b) Appendices to Transport and Road
    Research laboratory
Davies, A.L. and Rogers, K.G. (1973) Modal choice and the value of
    time. Local Government Operations Research Group, Report C143.
Domencich, T. and McFadden, D. (1975) *Urban Travel Demand: A
    Behavioural Analysis*. Amsterdam: North Holland.
Harris, A.J. and Tanner, J.C. (1974) Transport demand models based
    on personal characteristics. Transport and Road Research
    Laboratory, SR 65UC.
Hawkins, A.F. (1978) A micro-analytic approach to mode choice and
    route choice, PTRC, Proceedings, Summer Annual meeting,
    University of Warwick.
Koenig, J.G. (1975) A theory of urban accessibility. Proceedings
    of PTRC, Summer Annual meeting, University of Warwick.
Koppelman, F. (1976) Guidelines for aggregate travel demand fore-
    casting using disaggregate choice models. Transportation
    Research Record 610, Transportation Research Board, Washington
    DC., pp. 19-24.
Lerman, S.R. (1976) Location, housing, automobile ownership and mode
    to work: a joint model. Transportation Research Record 610,
    Transportation Research Board, Washington DC., pp. 6-11.
Lerman, S.R., Manski, C. and Atherton, T. (1976) Non-random sampling
    in the calibration of disaggregate choice models. Federal
    Highway Administration.
Mackinder, I.H. (1973) COMPACT: a simple transportation planning
    package. *Journal of the Institute of Municipal Engineers*,
    August.

McFadden, D. (1975) Report of the workshop on model structure. Paper presented to the Second Conference on Behavioural Travel Modelling, Asheville, USA.

McFadden, D. (1977) Quantitative methods for analysing travel behaviour of individuals: some recent evidence. Paper presented to the Third Conference on Behavioural Travel Modelling, Tanunda, Australia.

McFadden, D. and Reid, F. (1975) Aggregate travel demand forecasting from disaggregated behavioural models. Transportation Research Record 534, Transportation Research Board, Washington DC, pp. 24-37.

McIntosh, P.T. and Quarmby, D.A. (1970) Generalised costs and the estimation of movement costs and benefits. MAU Note 179, Department of the Environment.

Manski, C.F. (1975) Maximum score estimation of the stochastic utility model of choice. *Journal of Econometrics,* 3(3), pp. 205-28.

Manski, C.F., Sherman, L. and Ginn, J.R. (1978) *An Empirical Analysis of Household Choice among Motor Vehicles.* Cambridge Systematics Inc.

Mullen, P., Bursey, N.C. and White, M.T. (1976) Telford transportation study 2: new techniques in modelling trip generation and modal split. *Traffic Engineering and Control,* 17(3), pp. 106-9.

Mullen, P. and White, M.T. (1977) forecasting car ownership: a new approach - 2. *Traffic Engineering and Control,* 18(9), pp. 422-8.

Netherlands Ministry of Transport and Public Works (1978) SIGMO Study Reports 1-5. Projectbureau IVVS.

Quarmby, D.A. (1967) A choice of transport mode for the journey to work: some findings. *Journal of Transport Economics and Policy,* 1(3), pp. 273-314.

Richards, M.G. and Ben-Akiva, M. (1976) *A Disaggregated Travel Demand Model.* Farnborough: Saxon House.

Rogers, K.G., Townsend, G.M. and Metcalf, A.E. (1970) Planning for the Work Journey. Local Government Operations Research Group, Report C67.

Ruiter, E.R. and Ben-Akiva, M. (1978) A System of Disaggregate Travel Demand Models. Metropolitan Transportation Commission.

Senior, M.L. and Williams, H.W.C.L. (1977) Model based transport policy assessment. *Traffic Engineering and Control,* 18(9), pp. 402-6.

Train, K. and McFadden, D. (1978) The goods/leisure trade-off and disaggregate work trip mode choice models. *Transportation Research,* 12(5), pp. 349-53.

Van der Hoorn, A. and Vogelaar, H. (1978) SIGMO: Disaggregate models for the Amsterdam conurbation. Proceedings of PTRC, Annual Summer meeting, Universit̩ of Warwick.

Williams, H.W.C.L. (1977) On the formulation of travel demand models and economic evaluation measures of user benefit. *Environment and Planning A,* 9(3), pp. 285-344.

Wilson, A.G. (1967) A statistical theory of spatial distribution models, *Transportation Research,* 1(3), pp. 253-69.

Wilson, A.G. Hawkins, A.F., Hill, G.J. and Wagon, D.J. (1969) Calibration and testing of the SELNEC model. *Regional Studies,* 3(3), pp. 337-50.

Research on Q-analysis and transport

Jeffrey Johnson

1. INTRODUCTION

This paper is divided into two distinct parts. The first serves as
an introduction to the principles and some of the notation involved
in Q-analysis, and the second demonstrates the application of the
technique to a variety of transport problems. The case is presented
for a general audience unfamiliar with the subject, either at the
conceptual level or at the practical level. The methodology suggested
in this paper arises out of a concern about the adequacy of existing
theory, which has failed to establish a framework within which to
analyse the structural relationships between transport and the urban
environment. The importance of a holistic approach to the analysis of
social dynamics is widely accepted, and Q-analysis provides a single
description of transport in the context of its environment, and in
conclusion, it is proposed that this methodology could offer a
prescription for integrated planning.

2. THE CONCEPT OF Q-ANALYSIS AND THE FRAMEWORK FOR ANALYSIS

The Concepts

Most people would agree there is a transport problem, but it is
doubtful there would be agreement on its technical definition. It is
possible to be side-tracked into problems of technical representations
and the real problem can still remain intractable, even after the
technicalities have been exhaustively researched. 'Simplifications' or
'approximations', which stray too far from the substantive problem, make
it possible for the researcher to devote his energies to abstract
problems. At best, such work is irrelevant, at worst it may provide
a theoretical justification for unsound policies and expensive
mistakes.

The first stage in addressing any problem scientifically is the
accurate formulation of a description of the universe under investigation. This stage must precede the formulation of theories, however
interesting these may be. The work which applies Q-analysis to
transport has been restricted to the problem of description since

formulating 'theories' as such would have been premature; the initial
belief that transport could be better organized was more a matter of
intuitive observation and optimism than theoretical insight. Nonetheless, a good description may make certain relationships clearer and
the clear statement of these may be thought of as a *post hoc* theory.

For some time there has been a typically Anglo-American attitude
to transport analysis. The time has come for us to extend our
horizons beyond a mechanistic and behaviourist approach towards the
actual people who have need to make trips, a view of the world more
common on the European Continent (e.g. Matzner *et al.* 1976). Transport exists as an essential part of the social environmental whole,
and transport research has been impaired by addressing artificial
problems or taking too narrow a view of the problems. The fundamental
problem transport researchers should be addressing is the formulation
of an accurate and integrated description of this whole, and this is
where Q-analysis may have a role to play.

A fundamental concept in Q-analysis is that of hard data defined
as the result of observing set-membership in well-defined sets (Atkin
1974a, 1977a, 1977b). In practice this resolves itself into collecting (weighted) relations between hierarchically organized sets or
assigning numbers to elements of the sets to define mappings.

Usually the hierarchy must be defined using the concept of a
cover of intersecting sets since the special case of the pigeon-
holing tree-hierarchy associated with partition is too gross a
distortion of reality (Johnson 1978). Relations between sets give
rise to structures called simplicial complexes, while the numbers
assigned to set elements (viewed as simplices) give rise to dimen-
sionally graded mappings called patterns. The set of simplicial
complexes under study is called the hierarchical backcloth. Patterns
and changes in pattern (t-forces) are given the collective name of
traffic on the backcloth. In general the properties of the traffic
are intimately related to the structure of the backcloth, an idea
analogous to the importance of the structure of time and space in
relativistic physics (Atkin 1974a). This technical use of the word
traffic is compatible with the concept of traffic flow when applied
to transport analysis (Johnson 1977b).

The mathematical basis for Q-analysis
The usual description of the road network involves a set of nodes, a
set of links with routes between pairs of nodes defined as sets of
links.
Let R be a set of routes and L be a set of links for a road network.
The relation

$$\lambda \subseteq R \times L$$

is defined as

$$R_i \text{ is } \lambda\text{-related to } L_j \text{ iff } R_i \text{ traverses } L_j$$

Each route can be thought of as the set of links it traverses.
This can be represented schematically as

$$R_i \longleftrightarrow \{L_{\alpha_0}, \ L_{\alpha_1}, \ \ldots, \ L_{\alpha_p}\}$$

where this particular R_i traverses all of the L_j for $j = \alpha_0, \alpha_1, \alpha_2,$
$\ldots, \alpha_p$. Each link can be thought of as a vertex of a polyhedron in

multidimensional space. Thus if route R_i traverses the four links $\{L_{\alpha_0}, L_{\alpha_1}, L_{\alpha_2}, L_{\alpha_3}\}$ it would be represented as a three dimensional polyhedron (tetrahedron) in a three dimensional space (figure 1).

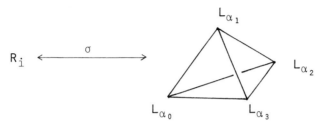

Figure 1. A route represented by a 3-simplex.

If R_i traverses one link it is represented by a point, for two links it is represented by a line, for three links it is represented by a triangle, for four links a tetrahedron, for five links a 5-hedron and so on. The polyhedra, otherwise called simplices, can be thought of as solid multidimensional objects determined by their vertices. They are given a pictorial representation in figure 2, and while the first few can be drawn quite convincingly on a piece of two-dimensional paper, the picture gets more stylized and less satisfactory as the dimension increases.

The polyhedron defined by R_i will be denoted $\sigma_p(R_i)$, which is also written as $\langle L_{\alpha_0}, L_{\alpha_1}, \ldots, L_{\alpha_p}\rangle$ when it is desired explicitly to list the vertices. The number p is the dimension of the polyhedron $\sigma_p(R_i)$ which is also called a p-simplex.

In common speech we refer to the 'triangular faces of a tetrahedron', which can be rephrased as 'the two-dimensional faces of a 3-simplex'. This is generalized by saying the simplex σ_p is a face of the simplex σ_q if $p \le q$ and every vertex of σ_p is also a vertex of σ_q. This is written as $\sigma_p \stackrel{\sim}{\cdot} q$, and in Figure 1, $\langle L_{\alpha_2}, L_{\alpha_3}\rangle$ is a one-dimensional face of $\langle L_{\alpha_0}, L_{\alpha_1}, L_{\alpha_2}, L_{\alpha_3}\rangle$.

A set of routes R determines a set of simplices of varying dimensions, one for each route $R_i \in R$. This set of simplices together with all their faces is called a simplicial complex and it will be denoted by $KR(L,\lambda)$.

In simplicial complexes the simplices are connected according to the faces they share, and this idea of connectivity is fundamental in Q-analysis. For example in figure 3, σ_a shares a triangle (2-simplex) with σ_b and they are 2-near. σ_b is 2-near σ_c and, although they share no vertices, σ_a and σ_c are 2-connected through σ_b. In general simplices are referred to as q-near and q-connected.

The roles of R and L can of course be reversed with the former as vertices and the latter as simplices. The link L_j can be written as

$$\sigma_r(L_j) = \langle R_{\beta_0}, R_{\beta_1}, R_{\beta_2}, \ldots, R_{\beta_r}\rangle$$

NUMBER OF VERTICES	DIMENSION	SYMBOL AND COMMON NAME	GEOMETRIC REPRESENTATION
1	0	σ_0 point	
2	1	σ_1 line	
3	2	σ_2 triangle	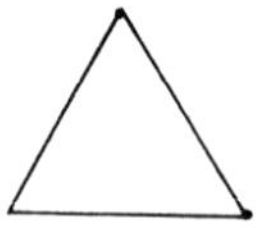
4	3	σ_3 tetrahedron	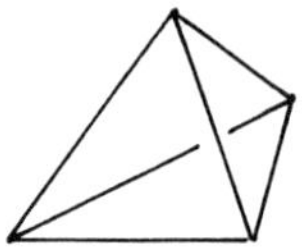
5	4	σ_4	
6	5	σ_5	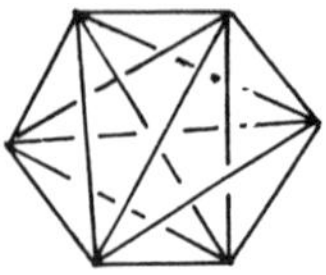

Figure 2. The geometric representation of some lower dimensional simplices

where L_j is λ-related to each R_{β_k} . This set of simplices is written

$KL(R,\lambda^{-1})$ and is also a simplicial complex (called the conjugate complex).

2-dimensional
shared faces
(triangles)

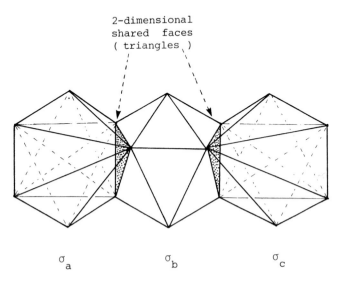

$$\sigma_a \qquad\qquad \sigma_b \qquad\qquad \sigma_c$$

Figure 3.   2-connected simplices.

In this simple example $KR(L,\lambda)$ and $KL(R,\lambda^{-1})$ form a backcloth for traffic patterns: the mappings

$$f:R_i \longrightarrow \text{the traffic flow on } R_i$$
$$F:L_j \longrightarrow \text{the traffic flow on } L_j$$

generate the traffic flow patterns

$$F:KL(\mathbf{R},\lambda^{-1}) \longrightarrow \text{traffic flow}$$
$$F:\sigma_p(L_j) \longrightarrow \text{traffic flow on } L_j$$

Since the simplices are graded by dimension we can write F as a graded pattern.

$$F = F^0 + F^1 + F^2 + \dots$$
$$\text{with } F^p(\sigma_q) = F(\sigma_q) \text{ for } p = q$$
$$= 0 \qquad \text{for } p \neq q$$

Then we have $f = F^0$ with

$$\hat{\Delta}^p \; F^0 = F^p$$

by using the coface operator $\hat{\Delta}$ which is defined with reference to the structure of the backcloth (Atkin 1977a).

3.   THE APPLICATION OF Q-ANALYSIS TO TRANSPORT PROBLEMS

In the previous section, a basic introduction to Q-analysis has been
outlined, and in this section, a wide range of actual applications
are presented. These include both the static and the dynamic processes
of traffic assignment, trip generation, trip distribution, activity
location and the costs of transport. First, we cover these five
applications within a static framework, and then the scope is widened
to include the dynamic elements of each of these applications.

Traffic assignment and road intersection
In the notation above, the traffic assignment problem involves finding
the values of F (which has a unique solution) by consideration of f
(which does not have a unique solution). An algebraic assignment
procedure based on Q-analysis has been devised and this could be of
practical use in day to day traffic management (Johnson 1977b).

Road intersection 'experiments' are a familiar part of the scene
in Britain and they certainly seem to work. As a scale down analogue
of the previous example, pieces of the intersection can be considered
as 'links'. 'Routes' through the intersection will then be sets of
these links. It has been shown that it is an advantage for the links
of intersections to have the smallest dimension possible and to be as
disconnected as possible, and the same remark applies to the routes.
A dramatic example of this concerns the A41 junction at Hemel
Hempstead where the Plough roundabout was redesigned to carry two-way
flow as illustrated in figure 4.

Q-analysis shows that the dimension of the links decreases from
$q = 11$ to $q = 8$ and they are significantly disconnected by the
experiment. Likewise the highest route dimension is decreased from
$q = 12$ to $q = 8$ and these routes are also significantly disconnected.
From theoretical results this allows the intersection to carry a
greater flow (increases its capacity), and indeed this was the case
in practice (Johnson 1976b).

Hägerstrand's space time approach
The space-time model of trip generation (Hägerstrand 1970) concept-
ualizes transport in an interesting way; it literally affects the
variety and dimension of the activity space in which people live their
lives. If the usual space-time description is rewritten in terms of
Q-analysis it gives an even richer picture of the relative advantage
of the mobile over the immobile (Johnson 1976a). These latter can be
thought of as having their human dimension crushed due to their
immobility confining them in a low dimensional cage. The location-
activity backcloth is not equally available to everyone, and some
people cannot realize the high dimensional traffic to which they
might aspire. In terms of policy, this immediately gives meaning to
the alternatives of relocating people or activities, or improving
mobility by changing the transport structure. These observations
illustrate the argument that transport policy cannot be properly
formulated in the absence of a policy for structuring the activity-
location backcloth.

Trip distribution
Entropy modelling has allowed new approaches to the problem of
combining some of the generation/distribution/modal split/assignment
aspects of the transport model, and it provides a theoretical background to the empirically-determined gravity type models (Wilson 1970).

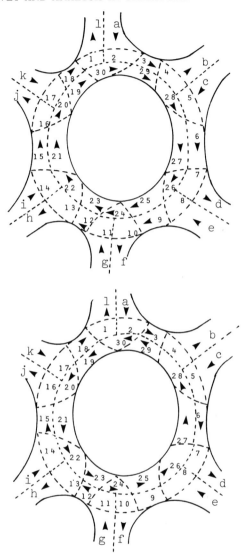

Figure 4. Experimental layout of the Plough roundabout at Hemel
Hempstead. (Top: pre-experiment; bottom: post-experiment.)

However, it can be argued that entropy modelling involves hierarchical pattern aggregation over the location-activity structure which
assumes all destinations are accessible from all origins. This last
consideration is equivalent to assuming that the origin-destination
structure is totally connected, i.e. there are no structural
disconnections in the backcloth (Johnson 1975; Atkin 1977c). In
practice there will be disconnections; for example, some villages
have only one bus per week into the local town, which effectively
does not exist during the rest of the week for bus-using villagers.

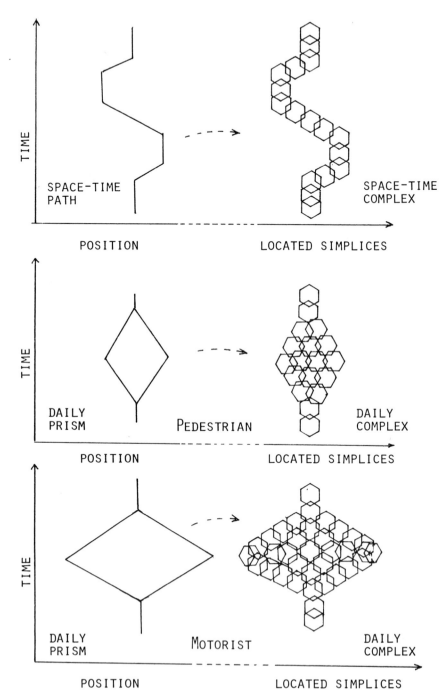

Figure 5. A multidimensional interpretation of the space-time model.

The origin-destination access structure is indeed an individual thing
and it certainly varies from day to day and season to season for us
all. Even the motorist who usually does have an adequately connected
structure may find that persistent traffic jams induce temporary dis-
connection in his structure. When these structural disconnections
exist, techniques such as entropy maximizing (which effectively
assumes the possible existence of very many micro-structures and
counts them) must be carefully used to embrace the real world disconnections which have real implications for the existence of
micro-states.

Activity location

It is reasonably assumed that people travel to avail themselves of
activities at their destination. A person's activity needs can be
thought of as an abstract simplex of activities, and his trip as an
attempt to find a location with activity simplex matching his activity
needs. There are two possible problems here; the first occurs when a
person cannot find his desired activity simplex within his mobility
range, and the second involves too many people travelling at the same
time and getting in each other's way. Solutions could be cheaper and
more frequent buses and trains, wider roads, more flyovers, etc. They
could also involve relocating activities or changing the location-
activity structure. If I have a teletype in my house attached by
telephone to a computer, I effectively have a computer in my house,
and I do not need to make a trip to access the computer. If I can
telephone my grocery order, I effectively have a grocery shop in my
house and do not need to go shopping if I know what I require and what
it will cost. It is clear that telecommunications can increase the
dimension of our favoured location and make our spatially distant
homes and offices very highly connected. Thus we could have the flow
of ideas and information as traffic on this structure without requiring ourselves to carry the ideas through a relatively disconnected
'physical space structure'. This situation may apply to a great
number of commuters who all contribute to the 'specific problem'. Of
course people involved at the hard end of manufacturing industry
cannot at present access their machines and raw materials from their
homes, or can they?
     Telecommunications cannot carry all our social traffic and
sometimes we like to see each other face to face. However, if it is
necessary for me to drive three miles to the shops in order to chat
with people, it raises the question as to why I cannot chat with my
neighbours? Similarly if I have to travel sixty miles to go to get
the comradeship of the office, it raises the question as to why the
intermediate social vacuum should exist?

Costs of transportation

It can be argued that transportation costs will be inequitable so
long as social costs are ignored. If I drive my car down your street
at 1.00 a.m. and wake you up it costs me nothing. If too many people
wake you up it could cost you your health. That these costs are very
real can be seen from the furore following the suggestion that traffic
should be directed along certain residential streets. The residents
argue that they will be subjected to an increase in noise, fumes and
traffic accidents, and so they will. If the scheme goes through, the
value of the houses may drop as the area becomes less desirable; who
pays? If they argue well, the residents might get their rates reduced

but will probably not be compensated for any loss of capital value.
Out of equity, should not full compensation be paid out of road
traffic taxes? If lorries and buses were taxed accordingly to their
noise and fume level, we might reduce the enormous environmental
damage they do. Again, this emphasizes the need for an integrated
approach to planning, administration and transport policy and
practice, and again Q-analysis may provide one such method for
integration.

Dynamic micro-theory versus static macro-theory
Although eminently reasonable, Wardrop's hypothesis is essentially
static in its statement of route choice (Wardrop 1952), and this has
led to much of the subsequent research on road transport being
static. The consequent static macro-theory is totally incompatible
with the dynamic wave theory at the micro-level (Lighthill and
Whitham 1955), so that transport theory does not fit together. The
micro-theory has good agreement with observation and proven practical
use (e.g. in the Lincoln Tunnel, Eddi and Foot 1961), and this
suggests attention must be given to making the macro-theory dynamic.

   The dynamic practicalities of macro-traffic flow are clear when
one considers the traffic-helicopter used by police and local radio
stations in the United States: here indeed is a continuous source of
data at the macro-level. It is possible that every city could build
an analogue computer with an electronic network representing its road
system. Land use-transport data could be incorporated into the system
(and the quality of these data might finally have to be admitted), and
special conditions could be simulated (e.g. roadworks here, traffic
lights not working there, accident here, rain everywhere, etc).
Algebraic principles could make very fast and cheap minute-by-minute
assignment possible which would be of great potential value in traffic
management. If the simulation showed an expected congested flow, it
might be possible to redirect traffic, find the best detour, alter
traffic light settings (how annoying it is to be stuck in a traffic
jam because the lights are set in a way inappropriate to conditions),
warn people by radio how to time their trips, temporarily forbid
parking, etc. Unless we intend to demolish our towns and cities in
the attempt to get into or through them, a dynamic macro-theory must
be the goal, thus enabling us to make better use of the existing
hardware of roads.

   It has been shown that the dynamics of road systems depend on the
connectivity of the backcloth (Johnson 1977b), and changes in pattern
values are literally transmitted from one simplex to the next by
virtue of their q-connectivity.

   This is illustrated in figure 6 where we might suppose that roadworks on L_2 make the route between A and C more difficult to travel.
If this depresses the demand to travel R_1, the traffic on links L_5,
L_6, L_7 will be lighter making them easier to travel, and making R_2
between B and C easier to travel. If more people then travel R_2 this
means then links L_8, L_9, L_{10} become more congested and difficult to
traverse. In turn this makes R_3 between B and D more difficult to
traverse which may result in less people travelling this route. In
this example, the traffic pattern change on R_1 has been transmitted
through the structure to R_3 although R_1 and R_2 share no links. The
transmission occurs by virtue of the shared two-dimensional faces and
this is an example of q-transmission through the structure (Johnson

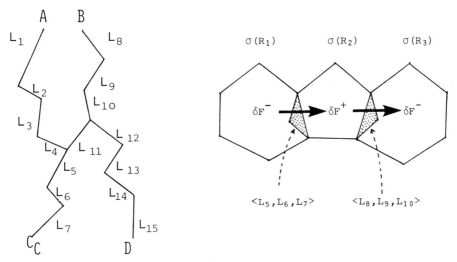

Figure 6.   Q-transmission through the road network.

1976b, 1979).

    As this kind of transmission occurs at both macro- and micro-
levels, it is very real and has very significant effects on the
performance of road systems. It is of course necessary that road
systems be sufficiently highly connected to make places accessible.
However, if they are too highly connected they become liable to
problems of q-transmission. For example, the Colchester by-pass of
the 1950s can be shown to be of high dimension and to be highly
connected to the town network structure. Small wonder that it was
subsequently thought necessary to build a by-pass to by-pass the by-
pass, where this new by-pass is of low dimension, and only 0-
connected to the town centre network by its access (Johnson 1977b).

    A relation can be defined between locations according to their
travel cost separation by mode. Slicing this by what people can
afford for a mode, we obtain a structure which reflects (otherwise
is) the perceived spatial separation. It is clear that certain
policies will change this structure (e.g. on the building of a new
road the dimension of some areas will change). If it is assumed that
travel cost along a piece of road increases with the number of
vehicles on that road, a high dimensional connectivity between areas
can be disconnected as more and more people attempt to travel. Thus,
as more people attempt to travel, the more difficult it gets, or as
the traffic increase on the backcloth, the less able is the backcloth
to support it. When we get stuck in a jam, we know the structure has
collapsed and we have ceased to be the traffic we wanted to be; the
level of traffic has literally caused the backcloth to disintegrate.

    This last consideration again highlights the fundamental question
as to whether we should be making trips? Might it be better for a
person to be unemployed for some time and then get a job closer to
home, than to take the first job going at a more distance place?

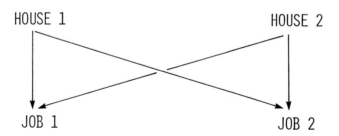

Figure 7. Selecting job locations can reduce travel demand.

Clearly it is better for everyone (not gaining any intrinsic
benefit from the trip to work) if we all live close to our workplace.
As we can see from figure 7, the total distance/travel cost will be
much lower and we will not get in each others way so much.

Some businesses have decided that it is not necessary to be
located in the centre of large cities and have moved themselves and
their workers to less congested (more highly connected areas). And
what of the so-called 'inner city problem'? This problem reflects the
demolition of houses close to workplaces thereby making many commuting
trips necessary. Such unwise destruction of the land-use backcloth in
the 1950s, 1960s and 1970s leaves the inner city areas desolate and
inhuman; the structure cannot support the rich traffic of human
relations that once existed. The protesters wanting 'houses not
roads' are presumably attempting to arrest this disintegration of the
land-use backcloth with the logical argument that, if workers can
live close to their work/leisure/shopping place, they will not need
new roads to make long trips to access these activities. Thus planning for the traffic may be unnecessary if we can plan the backcloth to
eliminate as much 'unecessary' travel as possible.

4.   THE RELATIONSHIPS BETWEEN TRANSPORT AND LAND USE

Urban structure and transport
Q-analysis has already been applied in this area for studies in both
Lavenham (Atkin 1972) and Southend (Atkin 1973). In Southend it was
possible to consider the land-use structure which supports various
retail, leisure and work patterns. Furthermore, it was possible to
see how road traffic within the area significantly disconnected the
pedestrian's structure in the residential and public garden area.
This study monitored a theoretical development such as might be submitted to the council by a property developer, and showed that
significant changes (t-forces) would result. Interestingly, a similar
proposal was submitted to the council after the study, and Q-analysis
was able to show how the visual structure of the area would be
changed (Atkin and Johnson 1974).

Regional structure and transport
As a natural extension of the work on urban structure, Q-analysis has
been used to study the structure of the East Anglia Region. This
study showed how the land-use backcloth is fundamental to proposed

changes and policies as presented in the structure plans (Atkin 1977b). Also, it is clear that transport plays a fundamental role in determining the regional structure available to support various traffic such as population, employment, industrial production etc. It is possible to use the same sets of zones for both the usual planning functions and transportation analysis, and it is suggested this could be done in a well organized way for the entire country (Johnson 1977b).

5. CONCLUSIONS

Academic arguments are not necessary to show that transport theory and management are far from perfect. The advocated use of Q-analysis marks a methodological shift and a difficult challenge to practitioners and researchers. The general argument for Q-analysis has been conducted by illustration and those reviewed here are documented in greater detail in the references (e.g. Atkin 1980; Johnson 1977a). Transport problems are but part of the greater malaise of environmental planning problems, an area which also has a considerable Q-analysis based literature. Q-analysis offers a means of combining the parts into a logically consistent description of the whole for those really wanting to address the real problem.

REFERENCES

Atkin, R.H. (1972) Research Report I. Urban Structure Project, University of Essex.
Atkin, R.H. (1973) Research Report III. Urban Structure Project, University of Essex.
Atkin, R.H. (1974a) *Mathematical Structure in Human Affairs*. London: Heinemann Educational Books.
Atkin, R.H. (1974b) An approach to structure in architectural and urban design. I. Introduction and mathematical theory. *Environment and Planning*, 1 (1), pp. 51-67.
Atkin, R.H. (1974c) An approach to structure in architectural and urban design. II. Algebraic representation and local structures. *Environment and Planning*, 1 (2), pp. 173-91.
Atkin, R.H. (1975) An approach to structure in architectural and urban design. III. Illustrative examples. *Environment and Planning*, 2 (1), pp. 21-58.
Atkin, R.H. (1977a) *Combinatorial Connectivities in Social Systems*. Basel: Birkhauser Verlag.
Atkin, R.H. (1977b) Methodology of Q-analysis, Research Report X, A Study of East Anglia 6, University of Essex.
Atkin, R.H. (1980) *Multidimensional Man*, Harmondsworth: Penguin.
Atkin, R.H. and Johnson, J.H. (1974) A Report on Proposed Developments in Southend-on-Sea. Mimeo. University of Essex.
Eddi, L.C. and Foot, R.S. (1961) *Experiments on Single-Lane Flows in Tunnels*. Proceedings of Symposium on Theory of Traffic Flow, General Motors, Michigan. Amsterdam: Elsevier.
Hägerstrand, T. (1970) What about people in regional science? 9th European Congress of the Regional Science Association, *Papers of RSA*, 24, pp. 7-21.
Johnson, J.H. (1975) A Multidimensional Analysis of Urban Road Traffic. Ph.D. Thesis, University of Essex.

Johnson, J.H. (1976a) The methodology of Q-analysis in planning and transportation. *Proceedings of IFIP Workshop*, Technical University in Vienna.

Johnson, J.H. (1976b) The Q-analysis of road intersections. *International Journal of Man Machine Studies*, 8, pp. 531-48.

Johnson, J.H. (1977a) An Introduction to Q-analysis and Related Topics, Part I of 3, Mimeo. University of Essex.

Johnson, J.H. (1977b) A Study of Road Transport. Research Report XI. Regional Research Project, University of Essex.

Johnson, J.H. (1978) Describing and classifying television programmes: a mathematical summary. International Television Flows Project. Discussion Paper 4. Department of Geography, Cambridge University.

Johnson, J.H. (1979) Q-transmission in simplicial complexes. International Television Flows Project. Discussion Paper 10. Department of Geography, Cambridge University.

Lighthill, M.J. and Whitham, G.B. (1955) On Kinematic waves. II. A theory of traffic flow on long crowded roads. *Proceedings of the Royal Society A*, 229 (1178), pp. 317-45.

Matzner, E., Henseler, P. and Rüsch, G. (1976) Theoretical frame of references to the planning of urban commuter traffic. *Proceedings of IFIP Workshop*, Technical University in Vienna.

Wardrop, J.G. (1952) Some theoretical aspects of road traffic research. *Proceedings of the Institute of Civil Engineers*, part II (1), pp. 325-61.

Wilson, A.G. (1970) *Entropy in Urban and Regional Modelling*. London: Pion.

Behavioural models in transport: perspectives, problems and prospects

DAVID HARTGEN

1. INTRODUCTION

One of the most important trends in United States transport analysis in the last decade, and one of the most frustrating for practitioners, has been the development of a class of methods loosely called 'behavioural' in nature. Evolving on several more or less independent themes, these procedures have been hailed as circumventing and/or eliminating many distasteful characteristics of older more traditional procedures developed in the 1950s and 1960s: the so-called Urban Transportation Planning System-based methods. These techniques' most salient attributes are purported to be that they are based on *individual-level* data rather than on aggregates of individuals (i.e. disaggregate); that they contain a *causal* structure; that they are sensitive to *policy options*; that they are amenable to *qualitative* inputs; that they are capable of addressing the requests of *particular traveller groups*; that they are *data-efficient*; that they are *mathematically tractable* and well grounded in the theory of choice; that they are sensitive (more recently) to *constraints*; that they are capable of treating *family* travel patterns; that they are easy to *calibrate* (estimate coefficients); and that they are *simple* to understand and describe to decision-makers. Interest in these techniques, recently characterized as a 'back-to-basics' movement in transportation analysis (Hartgen 1978), has increased rapidly in recent years, particularly in academic circles, where the main research has been conducted. But despite these advantages, progress in the application of such tools has been slow and the results often disappointing. Although there is still a certain amount of uncertainty, the following reasons are suggested as some of the factors which are combining to produce the poor results: first, the above *claims turn out to be overstated* in practice; secondly, the realities of planning practice do *not reward* such innovations; thirdly, the values placed on such techniques do not reflect the *views of practising planners;* fourthly, *habit* breeds reluctance to change; and fifthly, the methods are *difficult to operate.*

In the remainder of this paper, these issues are addressed, not in a critical sense – indeed, some people view me as one of the strongest proponents of them – but as a planner concerned with the implementation of these methods.

2. PERSPECTIVES

There are three groups of 'behavioural' methods used in transport analysis: the 'disaggregate' models; the attitudinal models; and a recent group of studies, too formative to be termed 'models', dealing with household-level travel patterns.

The first group, disaggregate models, evolved from the literature on consumer choice theory in the late 1960s. While originally formulated in aggregate terms with emphasis on functional form (e.g. Stopher 1969), they were rapidly converted to disaggregate (i.e. individual trip level) models, and subsequently tied to consumer and economic choice theory (Stopher and Meyburg 1975; Stopher 1971). The thrust of these techniques is the use of *individual-level trip data,* rather than aggregates of observations, as the basic building blocks of model construction (note however that other forms of aggregation were retained, Hartgen and Wachs 1974); the use of *specialized calibration methods* unfamiliar to most planners; and the use of *specific functional forms* (for example, logit).

The mathematical evolution of these methods rapidly outstripped their applications; several recent reviews from the sequence of conferences on travel behaviour (for example Brand 1973; Ben-Akiva and Koppelman 1974; McFadden 1976; Westin and Manski 1977; Daganzo 1979) reveal heavy emphasis on mathematical structure and extensions. One review of applications (Spear 1977) found most studies in mode choice, while other research has reported numerous conceptual and practical problems with the techniques (Charles Rivers Associates 1976).

Attitudinal models have likewise had a mixed history. Model techniques (apart from pure polling methods) have evolved from the so-called Fishbein models of attitude structure. Early examples can be found in Hartgen and Tanner (1970); Golob (1970) and Sommers (1970), and a fairly thorough review (Hartgen 1970) produced only a handful of studies.   But research in this area also expanded rapidly in the early 1970s, building on the following concepts: (1) use of *individual-level data,* as above; (2) *perceptions* of alternatives as reported by individuals and scaled by a variety of procedures taken from the literature on attitude measurement and psychometrics; (3) treatment of a wide range of *qualitative attributes;* (4) detailed *attitudinal models for separate individuals* using conjoint and functional measurement models.

A number of extensive reviews of this literature have recently been made and alleviate the need for detailed description here (for example Golob and Dobson 1974; Dobson 1975; Louviere *et al.* 1977; Tischer 1979; Fried and Havens 1977; Charles Rivers Associates 1978a, b; and Talvitie and Morris 1979).

Finally, a very recent trend focusing on household-level travel behaviour has also emerged. While it is too early to assess its impact accurately, interest is great. Although certain earlier studies (for example Hartgen and Tanner 1970a, 1970b; and Aldana 1973)

described portions of this, the new trend is generally unrelated to
this earlier work. It focuses primarily on four main types of
approaches: first there are the attempts to integrate certain
concepts of household structure from sociology and psychology
(particularly family decision making, role allocation, lifestyle and
lifecycle; (for example Fried and Havens 1977; Charles River
Associates 1978b; and Damm 1979); secondly, there has been the development and applications, primarily in England, of small group (e.g.,
family) *games* to investigate family decision making and response to
changes in activity patterns and/or transportation systems (for
example Jones 1979; Burnett *et al.* 1978); thirdly there has been
very recent work on household travel time and cost *budgets* and their
use as constraints on travel (for example Zahavi 1978; and McLynn
and Spielberg 1978); and finally several analyses of *learning and
adaptation* processes and their relationship to transportation have
been initiated (for example Fried and Havens 1977; Hartgen 1974)
(these studies are only generally related to the above, and have been
oriented to individual travel).

3. PROBLEMS

Characteristics versus capabilities
One of the early bones of contention surrounding disaggregate and
attitudinal methods was the great confusion over the characteristics
of such tools versus their capabilities. For instance, in retrospect,
the following are known to be characteristics of such methods, namely
that they use individual-level data; they are amenable to qualitative
inputs; they are data-efficient; and they are mathematically tractable.
    However, the following capabilities are open to conjecture,
namely that they extract causality (whatever that means); they are
policy-sensitive; they are user group-sensitive; they analyse family
patterns; they are easy to calibrate; and they are easy to understand.
In particular, consider disaggregate models. Early claims for
these tools centred not on their primary advantage (data efficiency)
but on the assertion of their ability to extract causality and their
policy-sensitiveness. The difficult problems in model calibration
(primarily unavailability of an easy-to-use maximum likelihood
calibration for logit models) were minimized by proponents, or
asserted to be solvable. But experience proved otherwise because
planners working with such tools found inconsistencies in the model
structures, such as the Independence from Irrelevant Alternatives
(IIA) property (Charles Rivers Associates 1976), and problems in
calibration increased. After great effort, the Travel Demand Forecasting Project at Berkeley ended with a cumbersome tool, deemed
unsatisfactory by its clients and this resulted in the group being
subsequently disbanded.
    The few successful non-academic model-builders, as perhaps best
represented by my own group at the New York State Department of
Transportation (NYSDOT), felt compelled to demonstrate the effectiveness of these procedures against conventional methods (for example
Liou *et al.* 1976; Liou 1974) *even though* significant savings in data
collection were readily apparent. Such activities consumed much time
and were seen as dead efforts given the obvious justifiability of such

procedures on data-collection groups alone. Given that such tools
used precisely the same data as did conventional methods, it was
difficult to argue that they were more causal in structure or more
policy-sensitive. After much thought we decided in 1976 to avoid
such claims, and the technical jargon associated with them. The use
of such procedures within my agency has subsequently increased
markedly (with far less pain!) albeit under a different, more
straightforward jargon.

Attitudinal models seem to have suffered a similar fate. Early
arguments about scaling methods have died away leaving a hollow
emptiness about the tools generally: to my knowledge no United States
agency or company is at present pushing these methods. Current work
in this area focuses on comparisons on conjoint and functional models.
Household-focused methods have so far escaped; whether by later birth
or greater skill is unclear.

Reward for innovation

The analysis above does not mean that the blame rests only at the feet
of model 'developers' since it should be noted that most transport
planning agencies - federal, state, and local - are not at present set
up in such a way to reward innovations. To see this we need to review
briefly the evolution of transport planning over the last few years.
In the 1950s and 1960s transport planning was oriented to issues of
accessibility, and models were the bread-and-butter of analysis and
plans. But the last decade - with its emphasis on constraints
(financial, energy, and political), impacts on non-users and environment, and non-auto modes - has seen a slowdown of highway construction
and parallel decline in the use of such tools. Professional transport
planning now consists of significantly more rule-conforming and
administrative behaviour (in themselves behavioural processes, of
course) than in the past, and much less analysis. The successful
planner is often not the one who plans best but the one who works
best through federal and state policy to provide adequate transport
services to all groups in society at reasonable cost, minimal impact,
and with provision for uncertainty (Schofer and Stopher 1979). There
is little time for analysis, let alone modelling, except as it
facilitates that end. While it is clear that new tools have a key
place, perhaps even an essential one, in such an environment, I am
much less sure what characteristics or capabilities they should have,
nor am I sure how to build them from the ashes of Urban Transportation Planning System (UTPS).

Views of values

Further, it is currently fashionable among transport decision-makers
to look askance at complicated analytical procedures for modelling
travel. More often than not it has been suggested that planners -
and of course their models - are generally 'in the way' of transportation actions. Their sole and most valuable function, it is said,
is to maintain certification of urban and state planning processes
so that federal dollars for a multitude of transportation projects
will not cease. In other words, the appropriate function of planning
is process, not product. In such a context we should be amazed if
all models - but particularly innovative approaches - were not
treated with great scepticism and some cynicism. It is without
question unfortunate that behavioural techniques were developed at
precisely the time when the gears of transport planning were shifting

to this new style.

Resistance to change
A subtle but critically important set of factors influencing the use
of new methods is the degree of investment in agency skill and
resources already made in traditional methods (Liou and Hartgen 1976).
Most state and local urban transport planning agencies use an assign-
ment-based system of forecasting travel. In the United States such
systems. with few exceptions, follow the four-step process (generation,
distribution, modal choice, assignment) embedded in the federal Urban
Transportation Planning System. The amount of effort required to
gear up this system and to put it into operation is not insignificant,
requiring upwards of 15 person-years in data collection, analysis and
other steps.

Once developed, these methods were then used to prepare forecasts
of travel which formed the basis of long-range plans. Agency
positions were thus established on projected travel and actions
necessary to serve it. To ensure consistency with these forecasts,
many agencies have been reluctant to introduce new methods, as the
results may differ from those of previous work. This reluctance is
perhaps understandable since it has recently become apparent that
these newer methods are not necessarily 'better', more accurate, or
more policy-sensitive.

Another factor inhibiting innovation of new methods is the skill
level of available personnel. Generally, it is observable that the
same individuals who would be responsible for such development within
an agency are also in short demand for other work. The plethora of
studies required by federal legislation on a continuing and once-for-
all basis precludes the possibility that such individuals will have
much time available for development work, without sacrificing 'production' work. Given this choice, it is not surprising that most
agencies - particularly the smaller ones - opt for the *status quo*.

Complexity
In spite of the recent availability of computer programs to conduct
disaggregate and attitudinal studies, special knowledge and training
is required to calibrate and use such methods. I believe that such
methods, while not intrinsically difficult, are probably less well-
understood than conventional methods and do in fact require knowledge
that most transport analysts do not possess. The need for specialized
data sets (for attitudinal modelling), and complex calibration methods
compounds the problem. It is also clear that such methods are generally more difficult to present clearly to non-technical planners,
officials, and the public at large.

4.   PROSPECTS

The present status of new modelling approaches in transport planning
in the United States may therefore be summarized in table 1. Generally disaggregate model theory and mathematics have been extensively
developed and the method has become bogged down at the 'testing'
stage. Since an earlier assessment of disaggregate models was made
in 1975 (Liou and Hartgen 1976), not much progress has been made in
application. Attitudinal models have not seen applications or trials
and household structures are in the formation stages.

Table 1. Present status of behavioural models in transport planning.

	Disaggregate models	Attitudinal models	Household structures
Theory development	*e*	*s*	*s*
Mathematical representation	*e*	*s*	*p*
Preliminary tests	*m*	*p*	*M*
Trials	*p*	*M*	
Demonstrations	*p*	*M*	*M*
Widespread application	*M*	*M*	*M*

M = minimal; *p* = partial; *m* = modest; *s* = substantial; *e* = extensive.

Generally, the development and application of these methods at the New York State Department of Transportation (NYSDOT) has been ahead of other states. This trend is the result of a combination of factors. First, a *large planning group* at NYSDOT (375+ persons) is responsible for all modes and scales of transportation planning. The group requires continuing evolution of present and new procedures. Secondly, the issues addressed by this group are many, and continue to change; thus new procedures are continually required. Thirdly, NYSDOT has set up a *separate developmental group*, the Planning Research Unit, to conduct such work on a continuing basis; other groups are generally responsible for 'production' work and day-to-day planning. While a certain portion of its effort is in short-term studies and 'firefights', it presently spends about one-third of its efforts on developmental work.

This structure obviously facilitates developmental studies, but since not all agencies can collect such resources, it is probably not a generally viable approach.

Disaggregate models
The prospects for the continued expansion of applications and the use of these techniques are largely dependent on the availability of software and stronger support for the method at the federal level. Both are likely to happen. But the gap between theory and practice is large and widening; it seems likely that it will continue to widen for the foreseeable future, since mathematical extensions will continue to evolve and outstrip practice. Such a trend is not necessarily bad; at worst, it is probably irrelevant since it does not influence practice materially. Criteria for the selection of these tools will continue to revolve primarily around administrative factors, with data collection considerations a secondary but important factor. Arguments for 'behaviouralness' or causality embedded in these tools are likely to carry little weight with those concerned with implementation.

The prospect for *rapid* implementation however, is not good. Already these methods are advanced far beyond current practice, and implementation will be even more difficult as they become more complex. Implementation will be *measured* and *even*, lagging behind theory by perhaps five years. To speed adoption we need to push ahead on two fronts: theory and practice. While a great deal is known about the structure of disaggregate methods, gaps remain in our knowledge. The following are developments that would be of great use in understanding: (1) a disaggregate method that does not incorporate the IIA property but allows for *differential competiti-veness* among alternatives; (2) models extracted from causal structures; (3) models which are developed for *each individual* rather than for assumed homogeneous groups; short of that, (4) a definitive statement on clearly delineated *groups*, perhaps through lifestyle or other social concepts (see below); (5) *calibration methods* that are simple.

In practice advances can also be made, perhaps even more rapidly. In particular, we need: federally sponsored *demonstrations* of these methods, that are simple and convincing; *syntheses* of experiences that are *issue*-oriented not method oriented; *training* in the use of procedures on *a formal basis;* tests of the empirical usefulness of different *stratification groups;* and examples of applications in areas outside urban modal split.

Attitudinal models
Work in transport attitude structures, never particularly extensive, seems now to be carried on by a handful of individuals in the academic community. Yet while a vast body of literature on attitude scaling exists (recently summarized by Tischer 1979), few people in transport planning are seriously applying it. It is not clear if the recent work on conjoint and functional models will fare much better.

I am tempted to call for a major 'push' by the federal government to get recent studies put into general practice, but similar calls in other areas (for example disaggregate models) have not been particularly successful. Further, there appears to be a number of very real problems inhibiting adoption that are not likely to be solved overnight. These include the facts that first, no clear link has as yet been established *between attitude structures and behaviour* of individuals confronted with choices. Secondly, *attitude measure-ment techniques* have not yet been applied in convincing manner so that the transport analyst sees their value. Thirdly, no methods of *predicting attitudes* have yet been developed. At best, it is a job far more difficult than predicting demographics or system variables. Fourthly, few links between various attitude or perceptual measures and *physical levels* of a transport characteristic have been establi-shed. Fifthly, *market segmentation* by attitude structure is a nascent activity, but is essential for empirical progress. Lastly, the ability of *attitudinal models* to handle *policy issues* better than conventional models has not been established.

Basic research in all of these areas would ultimately be of great value in developing these tools. Meanwhile, a good part of the work to date can be extended into applications. To further this, the following must be available: federal-level promulgation of *computer programs* for simple attitude scaling; guidelines on how to use them; and support in getting programs operational; *syntheses of applications* at present being conducted, with evaluation of what procedures work best with what kinds of problems and contexts; federally-supported *trials and demonstrations* of the most viable methods; and *workshops and training* for state-level and local-level analysts.

Household structures
There is little evidence at present available on which to judge the prospects for this newest trend in behavioural models of transporta-tion. Initial work generally went unnoticed, but much interest has been expressed in academic circles about the newer approaches, parti-

cularly games. The interest coincides with a growing realization that
much travel behaviour is not individual but interactive, and that
changes in family group structure and operation are likely to have an
important influence on tomorrow's travel patterns.

The prospects for success are therefore, good, but hinge on
advancements in several areas. These are: demonstrations of a *strong
tie* to sociological and psychological theory; clear *linkage* to present
transport planning, via trip generation for instance, as well as
making use of existing data sets; operational versions which are *data-
parsimonious*. (In fact, one of the many outstanding issues in this
area is the nature of the data and encoding process); *federal support*
and dissemination of research results; and *tests* which show the
superiority of these methods over conventional approaches in understanding travel behaviour (for example Jones 1979).

Current federal-level research in the United States on household
roles, life-style and other concepts (Charles Rivers Associates 1978b)
also shows promise. Its emphasis is on the application of *existing*
sociological principles to transportation and it is not oriented
towards theoretical developments.

5. CONCLUSION

Almost five years ago, this author was asked to assess the issues in
implementing disaggregate travel demand models (Liou and Hartgen 1976).
It was concluded:

> To put it bluntly, it is time to stop talking among ourselves
> about the advantages of such procedures, and to move quickly
> and decisively to encourage the practising profession to
> implement them. If we do not move ... we will have only our-
> selves to blame if five years from now we are still at the
> present state of implementation.

We have made some progress - but not much. Disaggregate and
attitudinal models are pretty much at the stage of implementation
they were at five years ago. In retrospect perhaps no more could
have been expected.

The diffusion of an innovation is itself largely a social process
and likewise the diffusion of behavioural models through the transport profession is itself a behavioural phenomenon. Rogers (1962)
describes it as a five-step process: awareness, learning, evaluation,
trial, and adoption or rejection. The evidence strongly suggests
that disaggregate models are in the 'evaluation' stage, attitudinal
models are in the 'learning' stage, and household structures are in
the 'awareness' stage.

This assessment of behavioural models in transportation in the
United States may therefore be viewed as lukewarm. There has been
extensive theoretical development, but little application, and very
few convincing arguments for the value of most of the work. Yet, for
all these shortcomings, these methods hold much promise for transport
planning. Consequently, I will continue to use them whenever possible,
and I believe that they will eventually become widely accepted
methods.

REFERENCES

Aldana, E., DeNeufville, R. and Stafford, J. (1973) Micro-analysis of
    Urban Travel Demand. Highway Research Record 446, Highway
    Research Board, Washington DC, pp. 1-11.
Ben-Akiva, M. and Koppelman, F.S. (1974) Multidimensional Choice
    Models: Alternative Structures of Travel Demand Models. Trans-
    portation Research Record SR 149, Transportation Research Board,
    Washington DC, pp. 129-143.
Brand, D. (1973) Travel Demand Forecasts: Some Foundations and A
    Review. Transportation Research Record SR 143, Transportation
    Research Board, Washington, DC, pp. 239-82.
Burnett, K.P., Hanham, R.Q., and Cook, A. (1978) Choice and
    Constraints Oriented Modeling: Alternative Approaches to Travel
    Behavior. Paper prepared for the US Department of Transportation.
Charles River Associates (1978a) On the Development of a Theory of
    Traveler Attitude-Behavior Interrelationships. Final Report to
    the Transportation Systems Center.
Charles River Associates (1978b) New Approaches to Understanding
    Travel Behavior, Phase II: First Interim Report, 'Behavioral
    Science Concepts for Transportation Planners'. Prepared for
    NCHRP Project 8-14A.
Charles River Associates (1979) Disaggregate Travel Demand Models,
    Project 8-13: Phase I Report. Prepared for the National Cooper-
    ative Highway Research Program, Cambridge, Mass.
Daganzo, C. (1979) Calibration and Prediction with Random Utility
    Models: Some Recent Advances and Unresolved Questions. Paper
    presented at the Fourth Conference on Travel Behavior Modeling,
    Germany.
Damn, D. (1979) Toward A Model of Activity Scheduling Behavior.
    Unpublished Ph.D. dissertation, MIT.
Dobson, R. (1975) Uses and Limitations of Attitudinal Models. Paper
    presented at the Second Conference on Travel Behavior Modeling,
    Asheville, North Carolina.
Fried, M. and Havens, J. (1977) Travel Behavior: A Synthesized Theory.
    Final Report prepared for the National Cooperative Highway
    Research Program, Project 8-14.
Golob, T.F. (1970) The survey of user choice of alternative transport-
    ation modes. *High Speed Ground Transportation Journal,* 4 (1),
    pp. 103-16.
Golob, T.F. (1973) Attitudinal Models. Highway Research Record SR
    143, Highway Research Board, Washington DC, pp. 130-45.
Golob, T.F. and Dobson, R. (1974) Assessment of Preferences and
    Perceptions Towards Attributes of Transportation Alternatives.
    Transportation Research Record SR 149, Transportation Research
    Board, Washington, DC, pp. 58-84.
Hartgen, D.T. (1970) Mode Choice and Attitudes: A Literature Review.
    NYSDOT, Preliminary Research Report No. 21.
Hartgen, D.T. (1974) A dynamic model of travel mode switching
    behavior. *Transportation,* 3 (1), pp. 45-58.
Hartgen, D.T. (1978) Applications of Behavioral Sciences to Issues in
    Transportation Planning. Paper presented at the Conference on
    Applications of Behavioral Science to Transportation, Charleston,
    South Carolina.

Hartgen, D.T. and Tanner, G.H. (1970a) Behavioral Model of Mode Choice. NYSDOT. Preliminary Research Report No. 19.

Hartgen, D.T. and Tanner, G.H. (1970b) Individual attitudes and family activities: a behavioral model of traveler mode choice. *High Speed Ground Transportation Journal*, 4 (3), pp. 439-65.

Hartgen, D.T. and Tanner, G.H. (1971) Investigation of the Effect of Traveler Attitudes in a Model of Mode Choice Behavior. Highway Research Record 369, Highway Research Board, Washington DC, pp. 1-14.

Hartgen, D.T. and Wachs, M. (1974) Disaggregate Travel Demand Models for Special Context Planning: A Dissenting View. Transportation Research Record SR 149, Transportation Research Board, Washington DC, pp. 116-28.

Jones, P.M. (1979) A Methodology for Assessing Transportation Policy Impacts. Paper presented at the 1979 Meeting of Transportation Research Board.

Liou, P.S. (1974) Comparative Demand Estimation Models for Peripheral Park-and-Ride Service, NYSDOT, Preliminary Research Report No. 71.

Liou, P.S. and Hartgen, D.T. (1976) Issues for Implementing Disaggregate Travel Demand Models, in Stopher, P.R. and Meyburg, A.H. (eds.) *Behavioral Travel Demand Models*. Cambridge, Mass: Lexington Books.

Liou, P.S., Cohen, G.S., and Hartgen, D.T. (1976) A Systems Level Planning Application of the Disaggregate Modeling Technique. Transportation Research Record 534, Transportation Research Board, Washington DC, pp. 52-62.

Louviere, J.J., Wilson, E.M. and Piccolo, J.M. (1977) Psychological Modeling and Measurement in Travel Demand: A State-of-the-Art Review with Applications. Paper presented at the Third International Conference on Behavioral Travel Modeling, Australia.

McFadden, D. (1976) The mathematical theory of demand models, in Stopher, P.R. and Meyburg, A.H. (eds.) *Behavioural Travel Demand Models*. Cambridge, Mass: Lexington Books.

McLynn, J.M. and Spielberg, F. (1978) Procedures for Demand Forecasting Subject to Household Travel Budget Constraints. Paper prepared for the Federal Highway Administration, Washington, DC.

Rogers, E.M. (1962) *Diffusion of Innovations*. New York: Free Press.

Schofer, J.L. and Stopher, P.R. (1979) Specifications for a new long-range urban transportation planning process. *Transportation*, 8 (3), pp. 199-218.

Sommers, A.N. (1970) Towards the theory of travel mode choice. *High Speed Ground Transportation Journal*, 4 (1), pp. 1-8.

Spear, B. (1977) Application of New Travel Demand Forecasting Techniques to Transportation Planning: A Study of Individual Choice Models. Federal Highway Administration, Office of Highway Planning, Washington DC.

Stopher, P.R. (1969) A Probability Model of Travel Mode Choice for the Work Journey. Highway Research Record 283, Highway Research Board, Washington DC, pp. 57-65.

Stopher, P.R. (1971) Transportation analysis methods: unpublished notes. Department of Civil Engineering, Northwestern University.

Stopher, P.R. and Meyburg, A.H. (1975) *Urban Transportation Modeling and Planning*. Cambridge, Mass: D.C. Heath and Co.

Talvitie, A.P. and Morris, M. (1979) Attitudinal Models: A Literature Review. Paper prepared for the US Department of Transportation.

Tischer, M.L. (1979) Attitude Measures: Psychometric Modeling.
    Paper presented at the Fourth International Conference on
    Behavioral Travel Modeling, West Germany.
Westin, R. and Manski, C. (1977) Theory and Conceptual Development of
    Demand Models. Paper presented at the Third Conference on
    Travel Behavior Modeling, Australia.
Zahavi, Y. (1978) Travel Over Time. Prepared for the Office of High-
    way Planning, Federal Highway Administration, Washington, DC.

Attitudinal modelling and measurement in travel behaviour: some observations

PETER STOPHER

1. THE CONTEXT

Attitudinal modelling and measurement are relatively new to transportation, the first major attempts to use such procedures appearing in
the late 1960s (McMillan and Assael 1968; Mahoney 1964; Paine et al.
1969; Sommers 1969). From that time, one can see three basic themes
of interest emerging as transport planners and researchers began to
become aware of the potentials of using methods from psychology and
marketing. The earliest studies exemplify the first theme - that of
measuring attitudes as a means to develop an improved understanding of
traveller responses to the transport system and to various policies
and investments. It is interesting to note that the idea of measuring
attitudes seems to have surfaced at about the time the first attempts
were being made to develop travel-forecasting techniques based on
individual travel behaviour (Stopher 1967). Stated simply, the first
theme was concerned with the basic idea behind marketing: the development of an understanding of the attitudes of people to a particular
product - in this case, urban transport. It is assumed that such an
understanding may provide certain diagnostic information, on the basis
of which either features of the product can be changed or information
can be provided that changes the perceptions that people have of the
product (i.e., their attitudes can be changed).

The second theme in transport applications arose directly out of
the emerging area of individual-choice modelling of travel decisions,
and is concerned with various aspects of improving the modelling of
travel decisions. The earliest form of such attitudinal measurement
was raised by both Quarmby (1967) and Stopher (1967) in the opening of
the debate over the use of so-called perceived, reported, or engineering values for system variables in these models. As individual
-choice models began to be developed, a second sub-theme emerged in
the notion of using attitudinal measurement to enrich the set of
level-of-service variables that could be used in the models. In mode
choice, this included measuring a variety of notions such as comfort,

convenience and reliability (Hartgen and Tanner 1971; Nicolaidis 1975;
Spear 1976; Stopher *et al.* 1974), which had previously been considered
important but unmeasurable (Claffey 1964). Subsequently, attitudinal
measurement has been seen as the enabling process for destination
choice (Burnett 1975; Koppelman and Hauser 1978; Stopher 1977a, b),
where the characterization of the attractiveness of alternative
destinations has long been a problem for transport planners {1}.
Finally, the most recent element of this theme has been the use of
attitudinal measurement as an aid to segmentation of the population in
order to improve the power of forecasting models, as well as to assist
in identifying target or affected population subgroups (Dobson and
Kehoe 1974; Dobson and Nicolaidis 1974; Dobson and Tischer 1976; Ergün
and Stopher 1979). While much of the earlier work in segmentation
concentrated on socio-economic descriptors as segmentation variables,
the relevance of such variables to segmenting people on the basis of
their tastes was called into question with increasing frequency
(Hensher 1976; Louviere *et al.* 1976). It was from this concern that
the idea of using similar attitude groups and – more recently –
personality measurements as a basis for segmentation has arisen.
     The third major theme is that of direct attitude modelling. In
the preceding two approaches, attitude measurement was used either
directly as a diagnostic tool or in conjunction with some form of non-
attitudinal modelling. While the separation of this third theme may
seem questionable to some, it appears to this author as a substan-
tively different use of attitude measurement. Specifically,
attitudinal modelling has been concerned with attempts to develop
direct relationships between attitudes and the occurrence of a phenomenon, principally choice or behaviour, and builds on a number of areas
of psychometrics. There are a number of useful summaries of this work
in transportation, including those by Tischer (1979) and Louviere, *et
al.*(1979). Within this theme has been work aimed at developing a
better understanding of the importance of various transport-system
attributes (Costantino *et al.* 1974; Dobson 1974; Golob and Dobson
1974), and the development of models linking attitudes and behaviour
(Golob, Horowitz and Wachs 1979; Hensher and Louviere 1979; Levin
1979; Louviere *et al.* 1979; Tischer and Phillips 1979). These latter
models have also provided a basis for introducing some new notions
into travel forecasting, such as information-integration theory
(Louviere and Norman 1977) and cognitive dissonance (Golob, Horowitz
and Wachs 1979), as well as suggesting new techniques for analysing
attitudinal information and its potential linkages to behaviour
(Dobson 1976; Tischer 1979; Tischer and Phillips 1979).
     After fifteen years of research and development of attitudinal
measurement and modelling in transport planning, it seems to be
appropriate to raise some questions about this work. First, most of
the work cited above has taken place in the research community. One
of the obvious questions to raise is to what extent the work has found
its way into practice. Second, there may be some minor issues that
need to be resolved in the short run that would affect measurably the
extent to which attitudinal work would be used in practical transport
planning. Third, there are some longer-term research needs that
promise considerable potential for improving both the understanding
and quality of models of travel behaviour, and the development and
implementation of a variety of transport policies. This paper seeks
to explore some of these issues, albeit from the specific perspective

of a travel demand researcher.

2. CURRENT AND NEAR-TERM USES IN TRANSPORT PLANNING

Hartgen (this volume) suggests that attitudinal work has largely
remained in the research community for a variety of very cogent
reasons. Nevertheless, there are at least two aspects of attitudinal
work that are finding a place in current applications. Both of these
are aspects of attitudinal measurement, and are the collection of
attitudinal information for diagnostic purposes and the collection of
perceived values of transport-system characteristics for travel forecasting.

There is a growing acceptance that there is value in collecting
information on attitudes, particularly to various aspects of transport
service {2}. A number of examples of the collection of such information within more or less conventional transport studies in the United
States can be given. These include a survey in Dallas-Fort Worth in
1974 (Haynes *et al*. 1977), a major portion of the 1976 Los Angeles
Area Regional Transportation Study (LARTS) survey (Davis 1976), a
number of surveys by the New York State Department of Transportation
(Hartgen 1977; Weiss and Neveu 1977), a survey for designing a local
transit system in Schaumburg/Hoffman Estates, Illinois (Pfefer and
Stopher 1976), and surveys by Cleveland (Northeast Ohio Areawide
Coordinating Agency 1977) and various studies on carpooling (Dueker
et al. 1978; Stormes and Molinari 1977; Tri-Met 1979). There are also
proposals to undertake attitudinal surveys in Dade County, Florida
and in the state of Wisconsin, among others. The National Passenger
Transportation Survey of 1977 also designed and developed a major
attitudinal section that was to have been administered to a subsample,
but was not implemented because of a cost overrun on the main survey.
These various examples, more of which could be found relatively
easily, seem to provide reasonable evidence that the value of collecting attitudinal information is gaining reasonably wide acceptance
in the transport-planning community in the United States.

A number of the same studies, together with others such as
Minneapolis-St. Paul (Spear 1977), have also collected information on
traveller perceptions of travel times and travel costs. In some
respects, this represents a more major acceptance of attitude measurement, because of the traditional position of transport planners in
using network travel times and often ignoring travel costs altogether.
Given some of the problems outlined by Hartgen (this volume) for
accepting and implementing new ideas in transport planning, particularly where those new ideas demand replacement of older notions or a
change of thought on an issue, this change takes on a greater
significance. After all, the inclusion of attitudinal data alone
could, cynically, be suggested to be a low-cost, superficial nodding
at innovation, with little significance to changes to any aspect of
the planning process. Indeed, one has to acknowledge that there is
still some lack of any substantial documentation of the results of
the attitudinal data collected.

Finally, it is interesting to note that the transport planning
courses run by the U.S. Department of Transportation do now include
one lecture that deals with attitudinal information (U.S. Department
of Transportation 1979). While this lecture does not seek to provide
information on how to collect and process such data, it does seek to

generate an awareness that such data can be collected as a part of
transport planning studies, and effectively provides an official
endorsement of their use.

In effect, however, this is the extent to which attitude measurement and modelling has found practical acceptance in transport
planning, to date. Hartgen (this volume) suggests a number of reasons
for this and some possible ways to change it. One of the major
reasons for the lack of practical applications, however, is that
transport planning has succeeded in attracting too few behavioural
scientists to assist in the development of good procedures. To a
large extent, a review of the recent literature on attitude measurement and modelling in transport planning shows transport researchers,
trained in other areas than behavioural sciences, proceeding through
a lengthy learning process about techniques and approaches, and only
discovering the appropriate literature in social and behavioural
sciences at a rather slow pace. As a result, transport planners have
progressively met with a whole series of problems and issues in
attitude measurement and modelling that they have set about to try to
solve, eventually discovering sophisticated behavioural-science
literature that shows these same problems and issues to have been
recognized and either fully or partially solved or circumvented. As
a result, it is also quite possible that the suggestions made here for
advances in knowledge of attitude measurement and modelling may prove
to be redundant, because they are available but currently unknown to
the transport-research community.

At present, there appears to be a reasonably high probability that
attitudinal measures can be used for various aspects of mode choice
and particularly for investigating response to less usual modes, such
as carpools and vanpools (Margolin *et al.* 1976). For such applications to be made, two things are desirable. First, some clear
direction needs to be given on the appropriate techniques for collecting data on attitudes to alternative modes. There are several
aspects to this need:
(1) What are the most useful attitudinal measures to collect –
importances, satisfactions, perceptions, etc. – and how is each used
for diagnostic procedures?
(2) For any given type of attitudinal information, what is the best
method to use for collection – for example, semantic scales, Likert
scales, paired comparisons, etc.? {3}. For any given method, there
still remain further questions on how to collect the information. For
example, should attitudes be obtained by asking for ratings on all
attributes one mode at a time, or by asking for ratings on all modes
one attribute at a time? Also, how should the context of the rating
task be described? {4}.
(3) Perhaps the most important need is to generate an item pool for
attitudes to travel modes. That is, there needs to be some agreed-
upon set of attributes on which attitude questions would be asked, or
from which a subset could be chosen. Preferably, this item pool
should be structured into a set of concepts that have been shown to be
valid and useful for diagnosing mode use and response.
(4) What are the appropriate analytical techniques to use on these
data? First, it is necessary to provide a relatively simple differ-
entiation between situations where the measurements are of a single
dimension and those where there are many dimensions. For each of
these situations, a variety of methods exists for analysis. While the

researcher may use several methods in a search for convergent
validity, the transport planner must generally seek a single method
that provides the required diagnostic information {5}.

While a number of other issues can almost certainly be identified
- and Hartgen (this volume) suggests a number of practical steps
needed that complement the above needs - these at least serve to highlight the types of issues that need to be addressed, rather than
merely recognized. Also, all of these needs seem reasonable to meet
in the short run, thereby providing a more propitious environment for
practical use of attitude measurement.

3. LONGER-TERM ISSUES

The preceding section has concentrated on some limited aspects of
attitudinal measurement. For several reasons, these seem to define
the most likely areas for short-run implementation. Among those
reasons are that these are the aspects of attitudinal measurement
that have been in use the longest in transport planning; that they
are relatively simple and explicable; and that they have fairly
obvious policy pay-offs, in the sense of providing transit operators,
planners and decision-makers with information about the way in which
the transport system is perceived to perform, the levels of information people have about the system, and qualitative information on
certain aspects of design that can direct future system and technological improvements. However, this makes use of only a relatively
small segment of the potential of attitude measurement and modelling
in transport planning. There are some longer-term needs for basic
research and development that may have considerable benefits to offer
to transport planning.

Hartgen (this volume) identifies two of these areas as being the
prediction of attitudes and the link between attitudes and physical
(or physically measurable) characteristics. In terms of prediction,
one can identify two specific research areas immediately. First,
there is a need to know how to predict changes in attitudes that come
about over time. For example, it is clear that satisfactions with
various attributes of transport systems are dependent upon expectations. As various aspects of lifestyle change over time, so do
expectations. Thus, lifestyle changes can be expected to precipitate
changes in satisfactions with any given level of transport service.
Unlike transport-system characteristics, attitudes cannot be considered to be fixed values over time.

Second, there is a need to be able to predict changes in attitudes
consequent upon physical or policy changes within the transport
system. This element of prediction is concerned with the second area
identified by Hartgen (this volume). Given a change in a transport-
system characteristic, we need to be able to predict how attitudes
will be changed and for which groups of the population. This assumes
that there is a relationship between the physical characteristics of
the transport system and individual (or group-average) attitudes. So
far, little work has been done to find such links. Without them,
attitude measurement has relatively little to offer as a predictive
tool.

Another major area for longer-term research is to explore more
carefully and more fully the link between attitudes and behaviour.
As noted by Louviere *et al.* (1979), behavioural scientists have, in

general, cast considerable doubt on the existence of such a link, or
suggest that it may exist only with respect to 'a number of related
behaviours', rather than to any single action such as choice of travel
mode on a particular day for a specific trip. A number of the early
attempts to find such a link in transport choices seemed to produce
either failures or rather equivocal results (Golob 1973). There may
be several reasons for such failures or unconvincing results. First,
recent work (Dobson 1979; Dobson et al. 1978; Tardiff 1977; Tischer
and Phillips 1979) has suggested that the link is not a simple unidir-
ectional one in which attitudes affect behaviour in some manner.
Rather, evidence is being accumulated that behaviour influences
attitudes which, in turn, influence future behaviour. It seems likely
that these linkages may include the process of resolving cognitive
dissonances (Golob, Horowitz and Wachs 1979), as well as learning
procedures and other forms of linkage (Stopher 1979). Clearly, more
research is needed in this area.

Second, it has been suggested that the apparent failures may stem
from the use of the 'wrong' model structure. Louviere et al. (1979)
report strong findings from the use of information-integration theory
and a variety of nonlinear models, quite unlike the logit model with
its traditional linear utility function. Similarly, Recker and Golob
(1978) report greater success by investigating non-compensatory
models, as compared to the almost total concentration in the past on
compensatory models.

A third reason for past failures almost certainly stems from the
short-run issues already identified with respect to measurement. A
key area here has been the over-reliance on analyst-generated lists of
attributes (Neveu et al. 1978; Nicolaidis 1975; Spear 1976).
Generally, the set of attributes used is limited in size and scope, is
inadequately pretested, and reflects a rather narrow view of salient
attributes. It seems probable that this has led both to equivocal
results in relating behaviour and attitudes, as well as to conflicting
results on the structure of salient concepts (for example, Neveu et
al. 1978; Transport Consultancy Services 1978). In place of this,
there is a need to use the more formal process of concept identification, item listing, pretesting of items through cluster and factor
analysis, reliability and validity testing, etc. (Ergün 1979; Ergün
and Stopher 1979; McKechnie 1974a,b; Tischer 1979). This demands research on identifying relevant concepts for a variety of travel
choices and travel behaviours and the development of suitable item
pools for these concepts. An issue of considerable importance here is
to try to ensure that items are unidimensional to respondents. It is
disturbing to note the frequency with which items such as comfort,
convenience, and reliability appear as single items in attribute lists,
notwithstanding research that has shown these to be multidimensioned
concepts (Nicolaidis 1975; Prashker 1978, 1979; Spear 1976) that may
be perceived differently by different segments of the population and
under various different situations (for example, for access modes and
main modes of travel). It is clear that the use of such items will
result in extremely questionable results from any analytic process and
may well lie at the root of many of the conflicting results and failures to produce good results from attitudinal modelling and
measurement.

A fourth major area for research is that of population segmentation for analysis of travel behaviour and attitudes. Much has been
written on segmentation recently (Dobson 1979; Heathington and Barnaby

1979; Hensher 1976; Louviere *et al.* 1976; Nicolaidis *et al.* 1977;
Stopher 1977; Stopher and Meyburg 1974; Stopher and Ergün 1979; Tye
1979; Tri-Met 1979), but little progress seems to have been made in
achieving satisfactory segmentations. There are two roles for segmentation. First, segmentation may be used to define or identify target
groups or impact groups for various policies and investments (Hensher
1976). For example, current concerns in the United States with
providing equitable transit service to the elderly and handicapped
demands that one can identify that target population and then predict
how members of the target group will respond to different schemes.
Similarly, many projects in developing countries are financed on the
assumption (proved, it is hoped) that they will provide major benefits
to those of the population who are least economically developed or
have the lowest access to jobs and opportunities. In this use of
segmentation, segments are often defined by policy and the analyst's
task is to define procedures to identify members of the appropriate
segments and determine the likely behavioural reactions of members of
those segments. In many respects, the research needs relevant to
attitude modelling and measurement are rather minimal here, except to
provide better information to decision-makers and policy-makers about
groups in the population that are sufficiently homogeneous to be
relevant for such exercises {6}.

Second, segmentation may be used to improve behavioural and
attitudinal models, where identifiable groups have different perceptions, tastes or decision processes. As noted in most earlier work,
this segmentation has relied largely on socio-economic variables,
despite the general recognition that these variables are unlikely to
be good determinants of homogeneous population groups, with respect to
travel behaviour. There are several reasons for this continuing use
of socio-economic variables. First, they are relatively easily
measured, and have been included in most travel questionnaires.
Second, data on these variables are available from such sources as the
decennial census, thus providing an easy basis for sizing each segment
within a given population. Third, *a-posteriori* segmentation on similarity of attitude ratings or behaviour has not been very successful,
both because such groupings have generally failed to show useful
similarity on other measures that would allow the groups to be named
in some way, and because the need, in many cases, is to identify the
segments prior to – not after – data collection. Fourth, apart from
a-posteriori segmentation, there has been a singular lack of practical
suggestions of variables to use for segmentation.

An emerging area of research that may be useful in segmentation
is the measurement of certain personality traits that appear to affect
tastes and choices in travel. In this case, personality is being used
in a strict psychological sense as a measurement of certain predis-
positions and values held by individuals (Hollander 1971; Pervin 1975;
Wiggens 1973). Of specific interest to personality research are
individual differences among people that may give rise to different
behaviours under some given set of circumstances. Personality
research is not new in psychology, the first clear exposition of a
theory of personality having been put forward by Hippocrates in about
400 B.C. However, application of personality theory to travel and
related choices is new. The nearest related work is probably that of
McKechnie (1974a,b) with respect to outdoor recreation activities.
Most recently, Ergün (1979; Ergün and Stopher 1979) has examined the

possibility of a relationship between personality and both perceptions and choices of recreation activities. In this exploratory work, personality traits that have obvious relationships to travel and recreation activities have been found to provide a substantial increase in understanding of perceptions and choices, and also to provide a potentially useful and theoretically sound segmentation base. This appears, then, to be a potentially fruitful direction for research.

Whether personality measurement succeeds in providing a useful basis for segmentation directly or through correlation with more easily measured socio-economic or other variables, research is clearly needed on appropriate ways to segment and the relative worth of segmentation. Without question, segmentation adds significantly to the costs of data collection (larger samples are needed) and data analysis (separate relations are required for each segment). Such costs can be justified only if it can be shown that failure to segment will lead to erroneous results of a magnitude sufficient to degrade seriously the decision-making process.

Many other issues for long-term research can be identified; however, this section concludes with one further issue: data collection and analysis methodology. In this broad area, there are a number of specific issues that require research of a fairly basic type and a number that simply require transport researchers to become more familiar with established results from the behavioural sciences. A few of these issues are mentioned here for illustration.

There is considerable debate upon the issue of including a mix of reported values (for example, times and costs) and psychologically-derived values (for example, reliability, comfort) in the same mathematical choice model. Some members of the research community consider that these two types of values cannot be used together, while others customarily mix them. There is a clear need to understand the implications of building such mixed models, both conceptually and statistically.

As mentioned under short-run issues, there is much disagreement on the use of multidimensional scaling procedures and factor analysis. In many respects, the current trend by transport researchers to use factor analysis is based on pragmatic reasons: lower computer costs; wider availability of computer programs; need for fewer stimuli or potential of recovering more dimensions from a given set of stimuli; and significantly less limitation on sample size (c.f. INDSCAL, with a maximum sample of 100 individuals, and IDIOSCAL, with a maximum of 20), *inter alia* (Koppelman and Hauser 1978). A better understanding is clearly needed of the conceptual and statistical differences between these methods. The principal basis on which this needs to be done is with respect to the scale properties assumed by each method and the reasonableness and sensitivity of those assumptions with standard rating-scale data.

Transport planners have experimented briefly with a wide variety of methods for requesting attitudinal information. First, there is the basic issue of interview versus self-administered surveys. Given realistic response rates for each type, the reliability of data from each has apparently not been determined for attitudinal data on travel. Second, there is the form of question itself, including a variety of direct scaling procedures (semantic differentials, Likert scales, Guttman scales, etc.) and indirect procedures (pair comparisons, method of triads, etc.). None of these has been tested in a scientific manner to determine their degree of substitutability, comparative reliability (for example, test-retest), etc. Tischer (1979) notes that behavioural scientists are not agreed on the relative merits of these different methods. Research is needed also on the number of scale positions to be used. Many behavioural scientists seem to feel that five points provide the optimal design (Jenkins and Tabor 1977; Tischer 1979). On the other hand, some researchers have used the notion of allocating 100 points among a set of attributes, and others request respondents to mark an unmarked line of predetermined length. There is also division of opinion on the use of even-numbered scales and odd-numbered ones, where the latter provide an option for indifference, while the former tend to force respondents towards one or other pole of the provided scale.

Finally, there appears to be a serious lack of statistical tests for the results of most attitudinal measurement. For example, if segmentation is carried out, there are no accepted and available statistical tests to determine if perceptual or preference spaces, derived through factor analysis or multidimensional scaling, are significantly different between segments. Hence, many hypotheses of behaviour become extremely difficult to test scientifically.

4. CONCLUSIONS

In common with the statement made by Hartgen (this volume), this paper has concluded that there is relatively little being done in the application of attitude measurement and modelling in practical transport planning. In the immediate future, the principal applications seem likely to be limited to the use of attitudinal data for diagnostic purposes in assessing aspects of transport service and the motivating characteristics for travel, together with the use of perceived or reported system values in choice models. Even here, a number of issues require resolution before such applications seem likely to be widely accepted and used.

There are two main uses of attitudinal methods in policy analysis. The first is to enrich the decision-making process from the diagnostic uses, and the second is to improve the quality of short-term forecasting from the use of perceived or reported system values. In the case of the former, this enrichment comes about through improved understanding of how people view or react to various qualities of the travel environment, many of which may be important in design. For example, it may be possible to assess the value of providing air-conditioning on buses, shelters at bus stops, cross-platform interchanges, etc., by comparing certain attitudinal ratings of such items against others such as fare, travel time, and headway changes.

In the longer term, this paper has identified a variety of issues in attitudinal measurment and modelling, most of which are somewhat farther removed from policy implications. Some fundamental questions need to be answered with respect to: predicting attitudinal-based measures; relating these measures to physical attributes that would be used in design and implementation; determining the relationship between attitudes and behaviour; investigating the value of, and appropriate processes for, segmentation; and a number of methodological issues relating to attitude measurement.

From a policy viewpoint, prediction of attitudinal variables is a necessary precondition to their use in travel-forecasting models. It seems fairly certain that travel-forecasting models containing attitudinal variables will remain of interest to researchers alone until those variables can be projected under various conditions. Similarly, attitude variables suddenly become much more interesting to the policy-maker when they can be related to physical attributes used in design. However, neither of these uses will be effective unless clear links can be established between behaviour and attitudes. Upon the clear establishment of this linkage rests the entire future of attitudinal modelling and measurement in transport planning. Finally, it seems appropriate to re-emphasize the need for well-qualified behavioural scientists to become involved in transport planning research and applications. Unless this takes place, it seems inevitable that transport researchers and planners will continue to stumble over various issues relative to attitudinal processes, often 're-inventing the wheel' or following outdated and unproductive directions. Furthermore, in the process of doing so, there are real dangers that interim results and wrong directions will so discredit the concept of attitudinal measurement and modelling in the eyes of the practising transport planner that these techniques will lose their credibility for potentially enhancing the planning, policy- and decision-making process.

NOTES

{1} It is interesting to note that travel-forecasting models have continually hit up against the problem of relative attractiveness of destinations. The earliest forms of destination-choice models - the growth-factor models (Stopher and Meyburg 1975) - begged the question by assuming simply that attractiveness changes were directly proportional to growth, and thereby avoided having to describe attractiveness. The gravity model has generally used a similar subterfuge by equating attractiveness to total trip attractions obtained from a trip-generation model. The intervening-opportunity model raised the question more directly, but circumvented it through the assumption that every destination considered was equally attractive. That this assumption is unacceptable is shown by the majority of applications of this model, in which various justifications are provided for assigning a variety of values to the probability of accepting a destination. However, these values are found empirically as those that provide the best fit to observed data, and the segmentation to different values has been done without seriously confronting the issue of relative attractiveness.

{2} There has been a reasonable level of acceptance of gaining attitudinal information for marketing purposes, both for marketing a specific transport service and for 'marketing' the acceptance of a local tax or other fund-raising effort that may be used to provide some transport service. These activities are not included in this discussion, largely because they have been handled (more often than not) by marketing and public-relations experts, rather than by transportation planners.

{3} This is one area where the behavioural-science literature is not as helpful as it might be. Several writers (for example, Nunnally 1967; Triandis 1971) claim that Likert scales (agree-disagree with an even-numbered set of categories) are superior to other methods. However, Tischer (1979) points to other studies that show a high degree of interchangeability between the various methods. Thus, it seems there is some disagreement among behavioural scientists in this area, and transport planners certainly need guidance on the methods to use.

{4} Much experimental work in psychology has focused on laboratory situations, in which the analyst/experimenter can control the context more or less completely. Applications in transport planning are much more likely to take place in field conditions where the planner has little or no control, and must therefore specify the rating context very closely to ensure comparability of ratings from different individuals.

{5} Again, there is lack of agreement among behavioural scientists on analytic methods. Early work in transport planning used multidimensional-scaling methods (Nicolaidis 1975), but these were later rejected in favour of the older factor-analysis methods (Koppelman and Hauser 1980; Peterson *et al.* 1979; Stopher *et al.* 1977). Tischer (1979) points out that the merits and demerits of both classes of analytic technique are still being debated actively by behavioural scientists.

{6} In this respect, some current research (Sternthal and Phillips 1977) has shown that the elderly and handicapped consist of several highly heterogeneous groups with respect to needs for transport, attitudes, and behavioural reactions; hence, it is not appropriate to identify the elderly and handicapped as a single target group. Failure to recognize this is likely to lead to the promulgation of inappropriate measures for providing transit service, and may well lie at the root of the failure of many special services for the elderly and handicapped in the United States today.

REFERENCES

Burnett, K.P. (1973) The dimensions of alternatives in spatial choice processes. *Geographical Analysis,* 5(3), pp. 181-204.
Claffey, P.J. (1964) User criteria for rapid transit planning. *Journal of the Urban Planning and Development Division,* Proceedings of the American Society of Civil Engineers, 90 p.5 et seq., September .
Costantino, D.P., Golob, T.F. and Stopher, P.R. (1974) Consumer preferences for automated public transportation systems. Transportation Research Record 527, Transportation Research Board, Washington DC, pp. 81-93.
Davis, M.B. (1976) *The 1976 Urban and Rural Travel Survey: Volume 1 Background and Description.* Los Angeles: Los Angeles Regional Transportation Study.

Dobson, R. (1974) On the assessment of attitudinal and behavioral responses to transportation system characteristics. Proceedings for Conference on the Design of Procedures to Evaluate Traveler Responses to Changes in Transportation System Supply, U.S. Department of Transportation, Federal Highway Administration, Washington, DC.

Dobson, R. and Kehoe, J.F. (1974) Disaggregated behavioral views of transportation attributes. Transportation Research Record 527, Transportation Research Board, Washington DC, pp. 1-15.

Dobson, R. and Nicolaidis, G.C. (1974) Preferences for transit service by homogeneous groups of individuals. *Transportation Research Forum Proceedings*, 15, pp. 326-35.

Dobson, R. (1976) Uses and limitations of attitudinal modelling, in Stopher, P.R. and Meyburg, A.H. (eds.), *Behavioral Travel-Demand Models*. Lexington, Mass.: Lexington Books, D.C. Heath and Co.

Dobson, R. and Tischer, M.L. (1976) Beliefs about buses, car pools, and single-occupant autos: a market segmentation approach. *Transportation Research Forum Proceedings*, 17, pp. 200-9.

Dobson, R. and Tischer, M.L. (1977) Comparative analysis of determinants of modal choices by central business district workers. Transportation Research Record 649, Transportation Research Board. Washington DC, pp. 7-14.

Dobson, R. (1979) Market segmentation: a tool for transport decision making, in Hensher, D.A. and Stopher, P.R. (eds.), *Behavioural Travel Modelling*. London: Croom Helm, pp. 219-51.

Dobson, R. *et al.* (1978) Structural models for the analysis of traveller attitude – behaviour relationships, *Transportation*, 7(4), pp. 351-63.

Dueker, K. *et al.* (1978) *Ridesharing Demonstration Project: Davenport, Iowa, Final Report*. Center for Transportation Studies, Institute of Urban and Regional Research, University of Iowa.

Ergün, G. (1979) Effects of Personality on Recreational Travel Behavior. Unpublished Ph.D. dissertation, Department of Civil Engineering, Northwestern University.

Ergün, G. and Stopher, P.R. (1979) The effects of personality on recreation travel demand: some preliminary findings. Paper presented to the International Conference on Environmental Psychology, Guildford, England, July.

Golob, T.F. (1973) Resource paper on attitudinal models. Highway Research Record SR 143, Highway Research Board, Washington DC, pp. 130-45.

Golob, T.F. and Dobson, R. (1974) Assessment of preferences and perceptions towards attributes of transportation alternatives. Transportation Research Board Special Report 149, Transportation Research Board, Washington DC, pp. 58-81.

Golob, T.F., Horowitz, A.D. and Wachs, M. (1979) Attitude-behaviour relationships in travel-demand modelling, in Hensher, D.A. and Stopher, P.R. (eds.), *Behavioural Travel Modelling*. London: Croom Helm, pp. 739-57.

Hartgen, D.T. and Tanner, G.H. (1971) Investigation of the effect of traveler attitudes in a model of mode choice behaviour. Highway Research Record 369, Highway Research Board, Washington DC, pp. 1-14.

Hartgen, D.T. (1977) Ridesharing behavior: recent studies. New York State Department of Transportation, Report PRR 130, Albany, NY.

Hartgen, D.T. (1980) Behavioral models in transportation: perspectives, problems, and prospects. This volume.

Haynes, J.J., Fox, J.N. and Williams, B.T. (1977) Public attitudes toward transit features and systems. Transportation Research Record 649, Transportation Research Board, Washington DC, pp. 42-8.

Heathington, K. and Barnaby, D.J. (1978) Market segmentation in behavioural travel modelling. In Hensher, D.A., and Stopher, P.R. (eds.), *Behavioural Travel Modelling*. London: Croom Helm, pp. 252-61.

Hensher, D.A. (1976) Use and applications of market segmentation, in Stopher, P.R., and Meyburg, A.H. (eds.) *Behavioral Travel-Demand Models*. Lexington, Mass.: Lexington Books, D.C. Heath.

Hensher, D.A. and Louviere, J.J. (1979) Behavioral intentions as predictors of very specific behavior. *Transportation* 8(2), pp. 167-82.

Hollander, E.P. (1971) *Principles and Methods of Social Psychology*, New York: Oxford University Press.

Jenkins, G.D., Jr. and Tabor, T. (1977) A Monte Carlo study of factors affecting three indices of composite scale reliability. *Journal of Applied Psychology*, 64(4), pp. 392-8.

Koppelman, F.S., Prashker, J.N. and Bagamery, B. (1977) Perceptual maps of destination characteristics based on similarities data. Transportation Research Record 649, Transportation Research Board, Washington DC, pp. 52-8.

Koppelman, F.S. and Hauser, J.R. (1978) Destination choice behavior for non-grocery shopping trips. Transportation Research Record 673, Transportation Research Board, Washington DC., pp. 157-65.

Levin, I.P. (1979) The development of attitudinal modelling approaches in transportation research, in Hensher, D.A. and Stopher, P.R. (eds.) *Behavioural Travel Modelling*. London: Croom Helm, pp. 758-81.

Louviere, J.J., Ostresh, L.M. Jr., Henley, D.H. and Meyer, R.J. (1976) Travel demand segmentation: some theoretical considerations related to behavioral modeling, in Stopher, P.R. and Meyburg, A.H. (eds.), *Behavioral Travel-Demand Models*. Lexington Books, D.C. Heath.

Louviere, J.J. and Norman, K.L. (1977) Applications of information-processing theory to the analysis of urban travel demand. *Environment and Behaviour*, 9(1), pp. 91-106.

Louviere, J.J., Wilson, E.M. and Piccolo, M. (1979) Applications of psychological measurement and modelling to behavioural travel-demand analysis, in Hensher, D.A. and Stopher, P.R. (eds.) *Behavioural Travel Modelling*. London: Croom Helm, pp. 713-38.

McKechnie, G.E. (1974a) The psychological structure of leisure: 1. Past behavior. *Journal of Leisure Research*, 6(1), pp. 27-45.

McKechnie, G.E. (1974b) *Manual for the Environmental Response Inventory*. Palo Alto, California: Consulting Psychologists Press.

McMillan, R.K. and Assael, H. (1968) *National Survey of Transportation Attitudes and Behavior: Phase 1, Summary Report*. Washington DC: Transportation Research Board, National Cooperative Highway Research Program Report No. 49.

Mahoney, J.F. (1964) *A Survey to Determine Factors Which Influence the Public's Choice of Mode of Transportation.* Boston: Joseph Napolitan and Associates.

Margolin, J., Misch, M. and Dobson, R. (1976) Incentives and disincentives to ride-sharing behavior: a progress report. Transportation Research Record 592, Transportation Research Board, Washington DC, pp. 41-4.

Neveu, A., Koppelman, F.S. and Stopher, P.R. (1978) Perceptions of comfort, convenience and reliability for the work trip, New York State Department of Transportation, PRR 143, August.

Nicolaidis, G.C. (1975) Quantification of the comfort variable. *Transportation Research,* 9(1), pp. 55-66.

Nicolaidis, G.C., Wachs, M. and Golob, T.F. (1977) Evaluation of alternative market segmentations for transportation planning. Transportation Research Record 649, Transportation Research Board, Washington DC, pp.23-31.

Northeast Ohio Areawide Coordinating Agency (1977) *Analysis of Air Quality and Transportation-related Questions in the 1977 Cleveland Area Survey.* Cleveland, Ohio: Northeast Ohio Areawide Coordinating Agency.

Nunnally, J.C. (1967) *Psychometric Theory.* New York: McGraw-Hill, p. 531.

Paine, F.T., Nash, A.N., Hille, S.J. and Brunner, G.A. (1969) Consumer attitudes toward auto versus public transport alternatives. *Journal of Applied Psychology,* 53(6), pp. 472-80.

Pervin, L.A. (1975) *Personality Theory Assessment and Research.* New York: John Wiley.

Peterson, G.L. *et al.* (1979) Prediction of Urban Recreation Demand, Final Report to National Science Foundation. Department of Civil Engineering, Northwestern University.

Pfefer, R.C. and Stopher, P.R. (1976), Transit planning in a small community: a case study. Transportation Research Record 608, Transportation Research Board, Washington DC, pp. 32-41.

Prashker, J.N. (1977) Development of a 'Reliability of Travel Modes' Variable for Mode-Choice Models. Unpublished PhD. dissertation, Department of Civil Engineering, Northwestern University.

Prashker, J.N. (1979) Mode choice models with perceived reliability measures. *Transportation Engineering Journal,* Proceedings of the American Society of Civil Engineers, 105 (TE3), pp. 251-62.

Quarmby, D.A. (1967) Choice of travel mode for the journey to work: some findings. *Journal of Transport Economics and Policy,* 1(3), pp. 273-314.

Recker, W.W. and Golob, T.F. (1978) A non-compensatory model of transportation behaviour based on sequential consideration of attributes. Paper presented at the Transportation Research Boards 57th Annual Meeting, January.

Sommers, A.N. (1969) Survey data collection for urban systems analysis. Paper presented at 6th Space Congress, Cocoa Beach, March.

Spear, B.D. (1976) Generalized attribute variable for models of mode choice behavior. Transportation Research Record 592, Transportation Research Board, Washington DC, pp. 6-11.

Spear, B.D. (1977) *Applications of New Travel Demand Forecasting Techniques to Transportation Planning.* Washington DC: U.S. Department of Transportation, Federal Highway Administration.

Sternthal, B. and Phillips, L. (1977) Age differences in information
    processing, *Journal of Marketing Research*, November.
Stopher, P.R. (1967) Choice of Mode of Travel for the Journey to Work.
    Unpublished Ph.D. dissertation, University of London.
Stopher, P.R. (1977) Towards market segmentation in destination
    choice. Transportation Research Record 649, Transportation
    Research Board, Washington DC, pp. 14-22.
Stopher, P.R. (1979) Preference models and destination choice. Paper
    presented to the PTRC Annual Summer Meeting, University of
    Warwick, July.
Stopher, P.R. and Ergün, G. (1979) Population segmentation in urban
    recreation choices. Paper presented at the Transportation
    Research Boards 58th Annual Meeting, January.
Stopher, P.R. and Meyburg, A.H. (1974) The effect of social and
    economic variables on choice of travel mode for the work trip, in
    Buckley, D.J. (ed.) *Transportation and Traffic Theory*. Sydney,
    Australia: A.H. and A.W. Reed.
Stopher, P.R. and Meyburg, A.H. (1975) *Urban Transportation Modeling
    and Planning*. Lexington, Mass.: Lexington Books, D.C. Heath.
Stopher, P.R., Spear, B.D. and Sucher, P.O. (1974) Toward the
    development of measures of convenience for travel modes. Trans-
    portation Research Record 527, Transportation Research Board,
    Washington DC, pp. 16-32.
Stopher, P.R., *et al.* (1977) *A Method for Understanding and Predicting
    Destination Choices*. Evanston, Ill.: Final Report to U.S.
    Department of Transportation, Office of the Secretary.
Stormes, J.M. and Molinari, J. (1977) *Study of Public Opinion Surveys
    Regarding Transit and High Occupancy Vehicle Programs in Los
    Angeles, Ventura, and Orange Counties: Final Report*. Sacramento,
    Cal.: Caltrans.
Tardiff, T.J. (1977) Causal inferences involving transportation
    attitudes and behavior. *Transportation Research*, $\underline{11}$(6), pp. 397-
    404.
Tischer, M.L. (1979) Attitude measures: psychometric modeling.
    Resource paper for Fourth International Conference on Behavioural
    Travel Modelling, Eibsee, West Germany, July.
Tischer, M.L. and Phillips, R.V. (1979) The relationship between
    transportation perceptions and behavior over time.
    Transportation, $\underline{8}$(1), pp. 21-36.
Transport Consultancy Services (1978) *Randburg/Sandton Bus Study:
    Final Report*. Pretoria, South Africa: National Institute for
    Transport and Road Research, Council for Scientific and Industrial
    Research.
Triandis, H.C. (1971) *Attitude and Attitude Change*. New York: John
    Wiley.
Tri-Met (1979) *Carpool: Attitude and Awareness Study*, Portland,
    Oregon: Tri-Met.
Tye, W.B. (1979) Consumer segmentation, in Hensher, D.A. and
    Stopher, P.R. (eds.) *Behavioural Travel Modelling*, London: Croom
    Helm, pp. 262-78.
U.S. Department of Transportation (1979) Introduction to urban trans-
    portation systems analysis - course notes. Urban Mass
    Transportation Administration and Federal Highway Administration,
    USDOT, Washington DC.

Weiss, D. and Neveu, A. (1977) Attitudes toward transit service
    improvements in seven small urban areas. New York State Depart-
    ment of Transportation, Report PRR 119, Albany, NY.
Wiggens, J.S. (1973) *Personality and Prediction: Principles of
    Personality Assessment.* Reading, Mass.: Addison-Wesley.

An evaluation of attitude measurement as an aid to consumer-orientated policy formulation

KERRY THOMAS

1. INTRODUCTION

In this paper I describe and evaluate a formal survey technique
designed to measure attitudes, contrasting this approach in terms of
its aims, practical difficulties and conceptual problems with less
structured survey research and open-ended interviewing. I raise
issues about the applicability of attitude research to policy making
in general, using transportation problems as illustrations rather
than critically reviewing attitude research in the transportation
literature. Throughout the paper I make the assumption that transport planning is more or less consumer-oriented. By this I mean that
policy decisions are made in the light of the needs and preferences
of the public (or publics); and that the aim of the planner, given all
the usual constraints of finance, technology and conflicting
interests, is to provide services which please as many people as
possible, thus facilitating public acceptance of planned environments
and maximal use of services.

Let me begin with a simple statement: the choice of survey
methodology must be rigorously examined in relation to the question
the planner is trying to answer. Too often surveys are initiated as
little more than vague exploration and frequently the 'mysteries' of
attitude research are invoked unnecessarily. I have used the word
'mystery' deliberately for two reasons: first, there is still much
confusion about what attitude research is and hence the kind of
information it can provide. Secondly, even in the more formal (or
perhaps I should say academic) use of the term, the conceptual status
of 'attitude' and its relation to other cognitive and motivational
constructs is still unclear. The terms 'opinion', 'belief', 'values',
'attitude', etc. are frequently used loosely and interchangeably.
Where lines *are* drawn between them, the distinctions usually centre
on: (1) the definition of 'attitude'; (2) on the nature of its
relation with overt action/behaviour; and (3) the mathematical form

of the relation between attitude and the beliefs (information) and values from which it is derived. In this paper I adopt a particular theoretical approach, an expectancy-value model, which at present seems the most powerful empirically, and the most straightforward (if over-simple) conceptually.

2. AN EXPECTANCY-VALUE MODEL

Attitude is treated here as an individual's overall favourable or unfavourable feeling toward an object, where 'object' refers to any discriminable aspect of the individual's world including his own behaviour. There is little disagreement in the literature that an individual's attitudes are in some way dependent upon his 'beliefs'. In the attitude model described here (Fishbein and Ajzen 1975), belief is defined as the individual's subjective probability that an attitude object is characterized by a given attribute (or in the case of behaviour, the subjective probability that performing a behaviour will lead to a given consequence). The association between an object and its attributes, or between a behaviour and its consequences, are assumed to be learned, either indirectly or directly through inter-action with the environment. An attitude toward an object (behaviour) is then construed as the sum over the *evaluations* of the attributes (consequences) associated with that object (behaviour). The model is expressed formally as follows:

$$A_o = \sum_{i=1}^{n} b_i e_i \qquad (1)$$

where
A_o = the attitude of an individual toward the object 'o';
b_i = the strength of his belief which links the attitude object to attribute, i;
e_i = his evaluation of attribute i;
n = the number of salient beliefs, i.e. those currently within his span of attention.

   Since an individual can only process a limited amount of in-formation at a given time (Miller 1956), attitude is thought to be determined by just those beliefs ($n = 7 \pm 2$) which are within the span of attention at that time. These are known as the *salient* beliefs. In practice, using a suitable form of words, it is possible to elicit the salient beliefs held about some object (behaviour) by a sample of individuals and, provided that the sample is homogenous, a list of the ten or so beliefs which are most frequently elicited can be constructed. These are known as the *modal salient beliefs,* and can be used in a closed questionnaire format to measure:
   1. The strength of each belief (b_i) in probability terms (that is the strength of the learned association between the attitude object and that attribute). This is done by having the respondents rate the belief on a seven-point scale labelled from likely to unlikely (see note 1).
   2. The evaluation of each attribute (e_i), using the semantic differential technique (Osgood, Suci and Tannenbaum 1957).
   This model, by multiplying belief strengths (expectancies) by values, is similar to many other motivational 'theories' in psychology (for example, Feather 1959; Rosenberg 1956; Vroom 1964) and also has

much in common with formal decision theory (von Neumann and Morgenstern 1947), in particular with multi-attribute decision theory (Edwards 1978; Keeney and Raiffa 1976). However, Fishbein has extended the simple expectancy-value model when applied to predictions of behaviour by introducing the concepts 'intention to perform a behaviour', and 'normative influence'; thus an intention to behave in a particular way is seen as being dependent upon both attitude and normative influence. The concept 'intention to behave' is introduced with the explicit recognition that overt behaviour may be determined by other, unanticipated factors, especially when the measurement of intention and behaviour are separated in time. The mathematical statement of the model for the prediction of an individual's intention to behave (and hence his behaviour) is given below:

$$B \approx I = (A_B)_{W_1} + (SN)_{W_2} \tag{2}$$

$$\text{or} \quad B \approx I = \left(\sum_{i=1}^{n} b_i e_i \right) W_1 + \left(\sum_{j=1}^{n'} Nb_j m_j \right) W_2 \tag{3}$$

where

B = his overt behaviour;
I = his intention to perform behaviour B, measured as his belief that he intends B;
A_B = his attitude toward performing behaviour B;
SN = his belief in the existence of a generalized norm with regard to behaviour B;
W_1 and W_2 = empirically-determined weights;
b_i = his belief that performing behaviour B leads to outcome e_i;
e_i = his evaluation of outcome i;
n = number of his salient beliefs about the performance of behaviour B;
Nb_j = his belief in a normative prescription about behaviour B perceived as originating with referent j;
m_j = his motivation to comply with referent j;
n' = number of his relevant referents.

Both the simple and extended versions (equations (1) and (3)) enable the researcher to estimate attitude from a set of beliefs; and this overall attitude is thus an *evaluative summary* of the beliefs. The important point, from the policy-maker's perspective, is that the model permits an understanding of the beliefs that underlie some preferred object or chosen course of action. This means that the planner is potentially in a position to appreciate the cognitive elements which differentiate the preferences of different individuals. Clearly this gives him some degree of flexibility which simple preference rankings and overall measures of attitude lack. I will return to this below.

A considerable amount of successful empirical work has now accumulated using these relatively simple and easily operationalized concepts and relations. Both versions of the model have been used in experimental studies (for example Ajzen 1971; Ajzen and Fishbein 1969, 1973); in the marketing and advertising area, the behaviour prediction model has been used to investigate brand choice and buying behaviour (Bruce 1971; Cowling 1973); and Tuck (1971) has applied and

extended the techniques involved. Other applications of the models
in a fieldwork context include a series of 'cross cultural' studies
of 'family planning' intentions (Fishbein and Jaccard 1973), studies
of voting behaviour and party identification in both the United States
(Fishbein and Coombs 1974) and United Kingdom (Fishbein, Thomas and
Jaccard 1976), and in transportation research (Thomas, Bull and Clark
1977; and Thomas 1976).

Having described in some detail the concepts and methods of a
relatively successful attitude model, let us now turn to the problems
of using attitude research in practice.

3. THE APPLICABILITY OF ATTITUDE RESEARCH

There are two inter-related uses to which the planner can put attitude
research: (1) he can predict the behaviour of individuals given
different policy options X, Y, Z etc.; (2) he can attempt to measure
the overall attitudes of the affected public(s) toward policy options
X, Y and Z, perhaps with the intent of maximizing positive attitude.

If the policy-maker is primarily concerned to predict what the
consumer will do when provided with alternatives X, Y and Z, then the
attitude model described above has relatively good predictive
efficiency, although this varies with the *suitability* and *specificity*
of the behaviour(s) selected for study. 'Suitability' is a term which
can cover a multitude of problems, particularly in complex planning
systems. For example, it is not easy to decompose a planning problem
and isolate simple choices which can be put to the public in
questionnaire form. These choices have to be relevant to actual or
possible alternatives, within the public's understanding, and not too
time consuming to administer. At the same time the 'suitable'
questions must provide data which are capable of re-synthesis in manner
which contributes to the original 'systems' problem. As far as
'specificity' is concerned, behaviour (or intention to behave) must
be tied to a particular target (for example, a particular transport
mode), to place (for example, particular journeys) and to time (for
example, in a particular season). In general, the more specific the
behaviour studied the better the predictive power of the model and
vice versa; in practice this may require a compromise between accuracy
of prediction and the relevance of the information.

In summary, what attitude research can offer is a way of predicting (specific) behaviours; and perhaps more importantly, it
provides a method for 'unpacking' the beliefs that underlie attitudes,
enabling the policy-maker to compare and contrast different individuals and/or groups.

With respect to point (2) above, it would seem reasonable to
suggest that a planner should select the policy which maximizes
'positive attitude', given the way the model has been formulated.
Other maximands such as minimization of negative attitude or a Pareto
criterion are also possible. Using these terms we are clearly close
to the problems of utility maximization so central to welfare economics.
However, for the policy-maker to use the model in this way one would
have to assume that the belief-based estimate of attitude provides a
cardinal measure and permits intersubjective comparisons (a Pareto
criterion would only require an ordinal measure). That is, one would
have to assume that both belief strength and evaluation themselves
fall on cardinal scales, although clearly this is not the case. There

is some evidence to suggest that belief strength measures (subjective probability) are better than ordinal measures, although the measurement of evaluation using the semantic differential is more controversial. In practice, however, given the algebraic form of the model, this assumption is made. In these respects, the use of attitude suffers from the same problems as all measures of subjective utility (von Neumann and Morgenstern 1947) and developments thereof (for example, Luce 1958; Luce and Kranz 1971).

The measurement problems inherent in attitude and utility thus constrain intersubjective comparisons and limit the formal social welfare aims of the policy process. Measurement-theoretic utility may be the least restrictive in this respect, but it is certainly impracticable for public surveys (at present). When multi-attribute utility techniques are used on a large scale, the axiomatic measurement basis is ignored leaving a survey technique which, for practical purposes, is virtually identical to the attitude model described above. In theory, however, the multi-attribute utility technique has the advantage over attitude methods in that it can be validated by comparing the results of the survey with those obtained on a subsample of the same individuals in a more demanding, measurement-theoretic laboratory experiment. Where this has been done virtually the same results have emerged from the two methods (Edwards, private communication).

The current vogue for attitude research in certain areas of policy making marks a loss of confidence in (or even the failure of) these formal techniques of utility measurement. Since it is virtually impossible to use them on a larger scale, formal analysis (decision-theoretic) of the policy-making process has tended, insofar as public preferences are incorporated at all, to use experts' judgements as a proxy. Increasingly this is becoming politically unacceptable. The less demanding attitude approach enables the policy-maker to assess public attitudes, although the basic measurement problems remain, and at the end of the day the judgements and values of the policy-maker (and to some extent the survey researcher) are still crucial. But the fact that these judgements can be made in the light of richer data (that is, determinant beliefs) means that in theory at least, the planning process can be 'opened up' to public participation.

Given this somewhat optimistic view of the value of attitude research I think it is worthwhile considering some of the more specific problems of attitude research in the planning context. I have selected a few such problems for more detailed discussion in the sections below, referring to the attitude model described above in order to illustrate some of the points.

4. ATTITUDE RESEARCH AND POLICY FORMULATION: SOME PROBLEM AREAS

The search for determinant beliefs
If one wants to delve beneath the level of attitude and examine the beliefs that underlie differences in attitude and/or behaviour, then it is necessary to apply some criterion for the selection of those beliefs which really contribute to, or (as a set) are determinants of, attitude. The attitude model described above differs from most attitude approaches in that it formally states a relation between an individual's attitude and a set of *determinant* beliefs, i.e., salient

beliefs (operationally defined as those most easily elicited as free
responses to the attitude object). This relation is expressed as an
algebraic function which is assumed to represent the process by which
the beliefs (i.e., their strengths and evaluations) are combined 'in
the individual's head' to give rise to his attitude. Given this
relation, it might appear that the model is open to falsification and
is thus of more worth both theoretically and in practice than methods
which are more loosely formulated. For example, there is the common
technique of choosing 'attributes' of an attitude object from a
variety of sources including the literature and the researcher's
intuition, and then obtaining measures of the consumer's agreement with
statements which relate these attributes to the attitude object.
Often, in the absence of a conception of 'salience', the subjective
'importance' of the attributes is measured, or in other cases the
attributes (or clusters of them obtained from factor analysis) are
combined in a multiple regression equation, and 'importance'
estimates are thus derived from the β weights. But the concept of
salience, on which 'determination' depends, has no independent
criterion of validity. It follows that in this respect the accuracy
of the model cannot be demonstrated; and can only be achieved in
direct proportion to the time and effort put into the elicitation of
salient beliefs.

The problem of selecting 'salient' beliefs is compounded by the
fact that validation of the model (that is by correlating $\Sigma b_i e_i$ with
either an independent measure of attitude or of behaviour) is not a
critical test, since beliefs which are not salient can correlate more
highly with an independent measure of attitude for reasons other than
their status as determinants. These correlations may occur either
because the beliefs are merely representative of the general affective
tone of the individual's beliefs about the object (or behaviour), or
because they are novel ideas; in this case, in the absence of any real
knowledge, the individual may scale a belief item in accordance with
his attitude, i.e., the direction of causality is reversed (Thomas
and Tuck 1975).

The relative importance of beliefs
In general, to arrive at an overall measure of attitude using
determinant beliefs, it is necessary not only to select the correct
belief items, but also to know the appropriate weighting for each
belief, i.e. its contribution to attitude relative to the other
beliefs. Clearly this weighting or 'importance' can also add to one's
understanding of the attitude, although it should be noted that
'importance' is open to many interpretations (for example, Darlington
1968).

The model described here simply adds over the products of belief
strength evaluation for each of the set of salient beliefs, thus
giving each product equal weight. During the development of this
model it was specifically suggested that the simple summation rule
represented the internal psychological process. But even if this were
the case, the test of the combination rule (the correlation with an
external criterion) is a statistical test whereas the model was
formulated at the level of an individual. It may well be that
different combination rules are used by different individuals, or that
these rules may be a function of the substantive content of the
beliefs themselves. Coombs *et al.* (1978), for example, have suggested

that positive attributes or consequences satiate, whereas negative
ones escalate. In other words decreasing and increasing marginal
affect is contributed by positive and negative beliefs respectively,
implying complex non-linearity. Clearly, if this is the case, it
could be an important consideration for those who make policy decisions
in order to maximize benefit and minimize disbenefit.

If one rejects the major assumption of the model, namely equal,
linear weights for each $b_i.e_i$ product (assumed to be 1) then the obvious
alternative is some form of regression model. But there are practical
difficulties with the use of more complex models. Frequently,
multi-collinearity will exist between attributes leading to high
standard errors and instability of β weights. Further, unless samples
are virtually homogenous, β weights will be unstable in the sense
that if such samples are split, quite different profiles of
'importance' (if indeed β should be equated with importance) are
found. For these reasons it has been suggested that in practice one
might as well start by weighting each $b_i.e_i$ product equally; certainly
it has been shown empirically that this procedure gives as good if
not better predictions. But prediction *per se* is not always the
goal. It could be argued that a marginally less good prediction,
achieved using a regression technique which retains more of the
structure in the data (i.e. the importance of items in terms of their
ability to predict the criterion), is more useful than the *a priori*
summation rule which loses the possibility of this information, and
can only treat 'importance' as the absolute magnitude of the
contribution (belief strength x evaluation) of each belief.

So there are at least two problems here: the 'correctness' of the
model as a representation of the psychological processes of individuals, including the importance they attach to different attributes,
and the practical need for a model which aggregates individuals (who
are different to a greater or lesser extent), and derives some
statistical indication of the 'importance' of attributes. These
points may seem a little abstract but the literature on the practical
application of attitude research (and this includes transportation
research, see Thomas (1976)) is full of references to the relative
'importance' of different attributes; I merely want to emphasize that
the meaning of 'importance' and its assessment are controversial
issues.

Equivalences between belief profiles
One of the advantages of the model described here is its ability to
provide detailed information on what underlies an attitude. As
noted earlier, this can increase the planner's flexibility. Consider
a situation where the planner wants to know the relative public
acceptability of three planning options, X, Y, and Z. Traditionally
he might ask a suitable sample of the public for their preference
rankings on X, Y and Z; and with this information (the Arrow paradox
apart) he could choose a policy to maximize acceptance. However,
this would not take account of the complexity of cognitive structure
which might underlie the ordered preferences. If the planner, rather
than asking for rankings of X, Y and Z, instead measures the attitudes, attribute evaluations and beliefs associated with each option
(thus comparing X, Y and Z on $\Sigma b_i e_i$), he is then in a position to
determine what contributes to each person's ranking of the options.

It should be clear that an individual's attitude toward an option may vary for any one of the following reasons: (1) the content and number of salient beliefs (see note 2); (2) the strengths of these beliefs; and (3) the evaluations of the associated attributes. I refer to these three aspects of cognitive structure as 'belief profile'. The planner, by examining the individuals' belief profiles, can begin to understand why preferences differ. In many cases this information will enable him either to provide different options for different groupings (i.e., those groupings with sufficiently similar belief profiles) or to suggest alternative options apart from X, Y or Z which somehow provide the characteristics which the individuals regard as important. The planner is thus, potentially, in a creative role *vis-à-vis* the initially formulated policy options.

These advantages are, however, to some extent offset by technical problems. Both the strategies described above mean that the planner must be able to impose equivalences on individuals in terms of their belief profiles. These equivalences may be created on any one, or any combination of the three aspects of 'belief profile'. In practice this is difficult to do. Methods exist but they require a substantial element of 'judgement', perhaps the biggest problem being the initial choice of criteria on which the equivalences are to be formed.

There is a further reason for wanting to create equivalences on individuals in terms of belief profiles. In much research on environmental and transportation issues, the planner is interested in differences between groups which can be defined in broadly demographic terms. When hypotheses relate such demographic variables to overall attitude, the planner may fail to recognize that individuals (or groups) can have the same overall attitudes but as a consequence of very different belief profiles. Creating equivalence classes (which can then be related to demographic/geographic variables) in terms of belief profiles provides considerably more information and permits the testing of more detailed hypotheses. But again, in practice, there are potential difficulties, this time with sampling: the more complex the criteria on which the equivalence classes are constructed, then, in order to test such hypotheses, the more extensive the sampling will have to be, and this may be an even greater constraint when the research is exploratory.

Defining the attitude object or behaviour
This topic was raised earlier and here I merely want to underline one aspect which is particularly relevant to choice situations. In many cases the sort of questions to which planning and transportation research will be directed will be concerned with choices between options. It is important to realize that the attitude of the consumer toward a given option *in isolation* need not necessarily be the same as his attitude toward the same option when it is presented as a choice. Where underlying belief profiles are studied then the salient beliefs may relate not only to the alternatives themselves but to the alternatives *in the context of the choice process*.

The manner in which the range of alternatives in a choice situation may affect an individual's salient beliefs and values about any one option is an area that has not been studied in the context of the attitude model described here. However, decision theorists have recently become more concerned with descriptive aspects of the choice process; for example, the work on 'elimination by aspects' (Tversky 1972).

Non-attitudinal constraints on behaviour

This is not the place to review the controversies about the relation
between attitude and behaviour; the model described here has had a
reasonable degree of empirical success in predicting behaviour, but
this is in part attributable to the inclusion of a 'normative' term
alongside attitude as a potential co-determinant of behaviour. It
has been shown empirically that many behaviours are largely under
attitudinal control, but others may be determined by apparently
normative considerations (for example, choice of toothpaste depends
to a large degree on the advice of the dentist). It is worth noting,
however, that the normative component as formulated here, is not
necessarily normative in the usual sense of the word. The example
above, for instance, is less 'normative' than informational, i.e.,
making use of the professional knowledge of one's dentist. It appears
that the normative component of this model can act not so much as an
indicator of the prescriptions of relevant others but as a mirror in
which relevant others reflect knowledge and realistic constraints on
the behaviour in question. These constraints may be too obvious to
be elicited as salient beliefs. It may prove possible to exploit this
more general, informational function of the normative component to the
advantage of the policy-making process. But, again, it is worth
noting that the role which a truly normative (prescriptive) component
should play in the deliberations of the policy-maker is not at all
clear.

5. CONCLUDING REMARKS

I have outlined a model which has been relatively successful in
exploring consumer behaviour in marketing and in relation to certain
policy questions (for example, Otway, Maurer and Thomas 1978; Thomas,
Swaton, Fishbein and Otway 1980). It is based on an expectancy-value
notion in common with other attitude approaches and formal decision
theory. I have raised issues which demonstrate its considerable
potential, and its practicability in survey research as compared with
decision theory. However, I hope I have also made it clear that if
this sort of attitude research is to contribute to the solution of
complex planning questions, then these questions have to be formulated
in a rigorous way which takes account of the limitations of the model.
In evaluating this kind of research the most important problems are:
whether it is feasible in practice to sample extensively and in
sufficient depth to fully exploit the real advantages of the approach;
and, if one does accept these costs, one has to decide whether the
wealth of qualitative and quantitative data is usable in the policy
process in anything other than descriptive terms.

Notes

1. (a) Operationally, this measure of belief strength is not a
probability measure. (b) The beliefs are not treated as a
partitioned event space where probabilities would sum to 1. (c) By
using a bipolar (+3 to -3) scale it is possible to encompass levels
of probability that the attitude *is* and *is not* associated with the
attribute in question.

2. This first aspect of a belief profile (the salient beliefs) can only be established by interview, a costly procedure if carried out for the entire sample rather than a representative subsample.

REFERENCES

Ajzen, I. (1971) Attitudinal vs normative measures: an investigation of the differential effects of persuasive communications on behaviour. *Sociometry*, 34 (2), pp. 263-80.

Ajzen, I. and Fishbein, M. (1969) The prediction of behavioural intentions in a choice situation. *Journal Experimental Social Psychology*, 5 (4), pp. 400-16.

Ajzen, I. and Fishbein, M. (1973) Attitudinal and normative variables as predictors of specific behaviours. *Journal Personality and Social Psychology*, 27 (1), pp. 41-57.

Bruce, J. (1971) First experiences with Fishbein theory and survey methods, in Proceedings of ESOMAR (European Society of Market Research) seminar on advertising research. Madrid.

Coombs, C.H., Donnell, M.L. and Kirk, D.B. (1978) An experimental study of risk preference in lotteries. Unpublished manuscript, University of Michigan, Ann Arbor.

Cowling, T. (1973) Determining and influencing consumer purchase decisions. *European Research*, 1 (1), pp. 26-31.

Darlington, R.B. (1968) Multiple regression in psychological research and practice. *Psychological Bulletin*, 69 (3), pp. 161-82.

Edwards, W. (private communication) Public values: multiattribute utility measurement for social decision making.

Feather, N.T. (1959) Subjective probability and decision under uncertainty. *Psychological Review*, 66 (3), pp. 150-164.

Fishbein, M. and Ajzen, I. (1975) *Belief, Attitude, Intention, and Behaviour: An Introduction to Theory and Research*. Reading, Mass: Addison Wesley.

Fishbein, M. and Coombs, F.S. (1974) Basis for decision: an attitudinal analysis of voting behaviour. *Journal of Applied Social Psychology*, 4, pp. 95-124.

Fishbein, M. and Jaccard, J.J. (1973) Theoretical and methodological issues in the prediction of family planning intentions and behaviour. *Representative Research in Social Psychology*, 4, pp. 37-52.

Fishbein, M., Thomas, K. and Jaccard, J.J. (1976) Voting behaviour in Britain: an attitudinal analysis. Occasional Papers in Survey Research, 7 Social Science Research Council Survey Unit, London.

Keeney, R.L. and Raiffa, H. (1976) *Decisions with Multiple Objectives: Preferences and Value Trade-Offs*. New York: John Wiley.

Luce, R.D. (1958) A probablistic theory of utility. *Econometrica*, 26, pp. 193-224.

Luce, R.D. and Krantz, D.H. (1971) Conditional expected utility. *Econometrica*, 39, pp. 81-97.

Miller, G.H. (1956) The magical number seven; plus or minus two: some limits on our capacity for processing information. *Psychological Review*, 63 (2), pp. 81-97.

Osgood, C.E., Suci, G.J. and Tannenbaum, P.H. (1957) *The Measurement of Meaning*. Urbana: University of Illinois Press.

Otway, H.J., Maurer, D. and Thomas, K. (1978) Nuclear power: the
    question of public acceptance. *Futures*, 10, pp. 109-18.
Rosenberg, M.J. (1956) Cognitive structure and attitudinal affect.
    Journal of Abnormal and Social Psychology, 53 (3), pp. 367-72.
Thomas, K. (1976) A reinterpretation of the 'attitude' approach to
    transport-mode choice and an exploratory empirical test. *Environ-
    ment and Planning A*, 8 (7), pp. 793-810.
Thomas, K., Bull, H.C. and Clark, J. (1977) Attitude measurement in
    the forecasting of off-peak travel behaviour, in Bonsall, P.,
    Dalvi, Q. and Hills, P.J. (eds.) *Urban Transportation Planning:
    Current Themes and Future Prospects*, Tunbridge Wells: Abacus
    Press.
Thomas, K., Swaton, E., Fishbein, M. and Otway, H.J. (1980) Nuclear
    energy: the accuracy of policy makers' perceptions of public
    beliefs. Research Report RR-80-18, Laxenburg: International
    Institute for Applied Systems Analysis, in press.
Thomas, K., and Tuck, M. (1975) An exploratory study of determinant
    and indicant beliefs in attitude measurement. *European Journal
    of Social Psychology*, 5 (2), pp. 167-87.
Tuck, M., (1971) Practical frameworks for advertising research, in
    Proceedings of ESOMAR (European Society of Market Research)
    seminar on advertising research. Madrid.
Tverskey, A. (1972) Elimination by aspects: a theory of choice.
    Psychological Review, 79 (4), pp. 281-99.
von Neumann, J. and Morgenstern, O. (1947) *Theory of Games and
    Economic Behaviour*. Princeton, NJ: Princeton University Press.
Vroom, V.H. (1964) *Work and Motivation*. New York: John Wiley.

Contributions of psychology to developments in travel demand modelling

MARTIN DIX

1. INTRODUCTION

This paper reviews applications of attitude research – and more generally, psychological methods – towards a number of research and policy objectives. It draws mainly from work reported in the transport literature in the United Kingdom and United States.

Much of this was stimulated at first by the move from aggregate to disaggregate economic models of travel demand: the drive from the 'first generation' towards the 'second generation' approach, as described in Manheim (1976). Attitude research, it was envisaged, would complement the new econometric models by allowing 'psychological variables' to be taken into account. In particular, measures of generalized cost might be refined and extended. Research is still active in this area, but a number of conceptual and methodological problems have yet to be overcome, and increasingly, applied psychology is being aimed at modified or new objectives.

This review outlines the mainstream approaches, together with research outside the second-generation framework. Some reactions against individual-choice concepts are then noted. Recent, renewed interest in methods of social-psychological investigation is discussed, and finally, possible roles are considered for applied psychology within third-generation approaches: towards 'understanding' travel behaviour and change.

2. RESEARCH ON EXTENDING SECOND-GENERATION MODELS INTO THE SUBJECTIVE DIMENSION

Most of the early attempts to incorporate psychological variables into the second-generation demand models focused on the mode choice submodel, for two main reasons.

First, the mode choice problem appeared particularly amenable to attitude modelling. It seemed reasonable to say that, before

choosing between the modes, travellers weigh up what the
alternatives offer in terms of comfort, convenience and other
aspects of the subjective 'image' of each. On the other hand,
decisions whether to generate trips, for example, were viewed as
being determined by the individuals' socio-economic characteristics
rather than choice factors.

Secondly, the key policy issue from the mid-1960s onwards was how
to attract urban car-users on to public transport. If attitudes
influenced choices, then by effecting a change in attitudes,
behaviour could be changed. A quantified understanding of relationships between attitudes and choice behaviour would therefore
considerably assist effective investment decisions. We would know,
for example, the relative payoffs from higher bus frequencies, or
improved seating comfort.

This policy question, of course, is still very much alive today.
The way it was approached in the 1960s and 1970s, in the United
States especially, was through 'attribute-utility' measurement, with
a view to incorporating results into the emerging second-generation
models.

Attribute-utility approaches
This approach suggests that the individual evaluates the expected
utility attached to all perceived attributes (travel time, parking
cost, feeling of safety, and so on) of each option. He chooses the
option – the mode – offering maximum net utility. A theory to link
the attribute-utility models with econometric models of choice has
been developed (Stopher 1976, with reference to classical decision
theory; Edwards 1954). In fact the difference between the two
models is primarily in procedures, rather than in concepts.
Psychological measurement procedures follow these steps:
   (a) We try to identify an attribute set. This will be much wider
   than that in the econometric model, which includes time and cost
   attributes alone.
   (b) We measure subjective evaluations of the attributes of given
   options. This is where attitude surveys come in. Attitude
   measures should give results close to measures of expected
   utility. The convention adopted for this was to measure each
   respondent's 'satisfaction' with the attributes in the questionnaire, weighting these values with additional scores for
   attribute 'importance'.
   (c) We should calibrate the model against a measure of the
   dependent variable, e.g. which mode is actually chosen – or
   considered most likely to be chosen – by the sampled individuals.
   The earliest applications of the approach preceded the theoretical rationale. It had already been common practice to estimate
coefficients for dummy variables representing modal bias (marked
preferences for one mode unexplained by time and cost factors alone:
Bock 1968; Lave 1969; Watson 1971). Work aimed at measuring
subjective factors soon followed. Brunner (1966) had produced a
list of some forty attributes which a sample of travellers judged to
have some importance for their mode choice decisions. Other
researchers made efforts at task (b) above. Some drew from Brunner's
list in compiling attribute lists, others prepared lists of items on an
a priori basis. The work met with mixed success, and re-appraisals
(McFadgen 1974) showed that there was a confusion about the concept

of attributes.

The problem was this. For planners, design engineers, and others concerned with influencing public preferences, results are best expressed in terms of policy-sensitive or system variables: tangibles like service frequency, transfer times, options for vehicle air-conditioning, and so on. It is entirely possible to ask respondents to consider and evaluate system variables, and this was often done. But the shortcoming is that although this may say how much the public would like or approve of each feature, we gain no direct understanding of how system variables affect behaviour (i.e. how important they are for modal split). To avoid that problem, we can choose to think of attributes as purely psychological constructs, collecting evaluations of concepts like 'comfort', 'convenience' and other subjective yard-sticks (Sommers 1969; Sherret 1971).   Ratings of these dimensions were considered more closely linked to decisions, but the disadvan-tage is not directly knowing their sensitivity towards changes in the system variables. Hence, an understanding of 'psycho-physical correspondence' - the connections between perceived and system attributes - was soon seen to be essential to further progress.

Work by Hensher et al. (1975), Spear (1975), Nicolaidis (1975) and others acknowledged this requirement. Hensher used attribute-utility survey procedures broadly as before, but now in two stages: measuring strengths of association between perceived attributes (like convenience) and system variables (like service headways), before estimating the importance of the former for mode choices.

So, by the mid-1970s, much progress had been achieved. Indeed, stated research objectives now extended to constructing general models of mode choice incorporating demand-and-supply relationships and couched in abstract-mode terms, so that mode shares might be estimated for redesigned or innovative systems. Work at General Motors Research Laboratories perhaps went furthest in this direction. However, as results of further studies became available, some inconsistencies were apparent. There was particular controversy over the question of why studies like those by Dobson and Tischer (1977) showed subjective (non-time, non-cost) variables to be much more important than did results from Hartgen's (1974) work, for example. One answer to this was found, at the cost of relaxing an important implicit assumption. This assumption was that the importances of a given mode's attributes have absolute values. Instead, it was now evident that the effects of 'soft' variables on mode choices vary according to the *relative* values of the attributes of competing modes. Improved comfort levels, for example, would only attract drivers to bus use if travel times and costs for the two modes were made closely similar (which they were in Dobson and Tischer's corridor study, but not in Hartgen's network-wide analysis).

The implications of this for empirical model building proved quite damaging. They pointed to a complexity of data requirements surpass-ing the limitations of cross-sectional surveys. Requirements now included (Spear 1976):

- measuring the real values for each relevant system variable, together with the individuals' evaluations of these;
- establishing one-to-one correspondences between perceived and system variables;
- measuring attribute utility over a wide, and in effect controlled range of values of every system variable.

This formidable re-specification of the research problems actually
raises issues for travel demand modelling generally, not just its
extensions into the subjective realm. As far as psychological
research work was concerned, the attribute-utility techniques subsequently seem to have been employed for different and more *ad hoc*
purposes – such as problem recognition, and as an input to local
transport management and marketing plans. In these fields, certain
other technical problems, specific to the objective of contributing
to second-generation models, do not arise. These include:
- the controversy about how successfully importance-and-satisfaction
  scores serve as a proxy for the concept of utility (Wilkie and
  Pessemier 1975); and
- the difficulty in fitting values from psychometric and econometric analyses to a common (money or time-equivalent) scale,
  given that attitude measuring scales yield interval-level but
  not cardinal-level data.
So it seems, from the published literature, that interest in using
attribute-utility techniques for general model-building waned, and
certain other research objectives became advocated instead.

Segmentation by psychological criteria
The most important change of objective, in the United States
particularly, was to emphasize using attitudinal techniques as a means
of segmentation. Improving the behavioural content of second-generation models remains the overall aim, but the approaches are different
and more indirect. By dividing the population sample into 'psychologically similar' groups, a series of models (i.e. standard multinomial
logit models) can be estimated and operated independently for each
(Stopher and Watson 1975; Stopher 1977). The expected advantage is
an improvement in the models' statistical fit, which should be greater
than if more arbitrary or non-behavioural classifications are used.

Attitudinal segmentation has, as before, been directed at the
mode choice submodel, although not exclusively. Stopher (1977)
selected choices of (shopping) destination in a recent study which
well illustrates the approach. It shows that the work actually
produces two kinds of output.

The first is information on individual perceptions. In this case,
the important subjective dimensions of the attractiveness of competing
shopping centre locations were identified: items like quality of
merchandise, free parking, prestige of store and others, clustered
into three dimensions of quality and convenience, price and expedience.
The relative importance of these could be quantified. However,
subjective dimensions are unlikely to replace the conventional,
although crude indices of attractiveness, such as zonal retail employment or floor area, because these clearly can be more readily predicted
when considering future-year trip attraction models. So the problem
again arises of a need to establish psycho-physical correspondence.
Without this, a feedback of information to existing models is blocked.

The second kind of intended output is information on the socio-
economic characteristics of population groups (segments) found to be
similar in terms of their perceptions and evaluations of destination
attributes. Bróg (1978) argued that no theoretical reason could be
advanced for the hypothesis – which is an implicit assumption of the
approach – that socio-economic or demographic characteristics will
act as determinants of perceptual structure, or even as proxies. This

concern seems to be borne out, because no attempt at classifying
segments has as yet produced clear results.

So it seems that neither segmentation nor the attribute-utility
approach has made the contributions to second-generation modelling
that were wished for, although both have led to gains in our qualitative understanding of some aspects of travellers' decisions.

3. PSYCHOLOGICAL RESEARCH OUTSIDE THE 'SECOND-GENERATION' FRAMEWORK

Work along the lines outlined above is continuing, and recent papers
by Michaels (1980), Dix (1980) and Tischer (1980) provide reviews of
more detailed issues yet to be tackled, and further work proposed.
Different, more *ad hoc* uses of possible psychological approaches in
transport research have probably been more influential in modifying
our theoretical understanding of travel demand. This is true of a
general and somewhat disparate body of research which can be called
the 'interest in concepts from psychology'.

Interest in concepts from psychology
Work within the second-generation context uses techniques of
psychological measurement for primarily economic models. A different
research activity is to look for concepts in the psychological
literature, then to identify possible implications for our models or
understanding or travel behaviour. Some examples are these:
- habit formation, used to modify 'trading' assumptions in
  mode choice (Banister 1978);
- learning theory, applied to spatial choice models (Golledge
  and Brown 1967);
- cognitive dissonance theory, proposed for diagnosis of attitude-
  behaviour relationships, especially in mode choice (Horowitz
  1978);
- satisficing - as distinct from optimizing - and non-compensatory
  decision-rules as an alternative to utility-maximization
  (Foerster based on Wright 1972);
- arousal, or curiosity-seeking, again as alternatives to utility-
  maximization (Scitovsky 1976; Sheth 1975);
- psychological response thresholds, for models incorporating
  discontinuous demand functions (Goodwin and Hensher 1978);
- selective attention, and the notion of attaching economic costs
  to information acquisition (Heggie 1978a);

Not all of the above have been put into empirical operation, but
they have all informed theories of travel behaviour and enlightened
our view of behaviour-change. Some attempts have however been made
to adapt purely psychological theories of individual choice into free-
standing travel-demand models (Ewing 1973; Thomas 1976).

Experiments with psychological individual-choice theory
Thomas (1976 and this volume) provides a good example of attempts to
use psychological choice theory - in this case Fishbein's (1975)
expectancy-value model - as a complete alternative to the economic
approach. Again looking at choices of mode, Thomas criticized
attribute-utility approaches, reviewed earlier, in which attributes of
objects (i.e. characteristics of alternative transport modes) are
specified by the researcher and then passively evaluated by respondents. Fishbein's theory directs us instead towards finding out what
the individual believes will be the direct personal consequences of

using each option. Loosely speaking, the emphasis switches from the
image of transport modes, to their perceived values-in-use. The
latter are considered the stronger causal determinants of mode choice
decisions.

Procedure is two-stage. First, depth-interview sessions seek to
establish what consequences would be anticipated in the actual use of
each alternative. Matters of interest include both behavioural
consequences (like more or less time to do shopping) as well as the
purely psychological (whether friends would approve of either option).
A list of the items mentioned most frequently is then compiled - these
represent 'salient beliefs' in the theory - and standardized
questionnaires are constructed. Among a larger sample, importances of
each item and feelings towards these are rated, and results trans-
formed according to an explicit formula to provide a prediction of
behaviour.

The empirical test was prediction of mode choice for a future
shopping trip, where destination and time were specified. Actual
behaviour was measured in an after-survey.

Results were successful, but did not entirely recommend the
approach. Three subsamples had been included, two consisting of bus-
captive individuals and those with cars-exclusively-available. The
model did successfully predict - or confirm - each group's choice of
mode, but correlations between predictions and outcomes were lower
than 0.75 in both cases, and the model's independent variables
accounted for only half the variation in 'after' behaviour (R^2 =
0.53).

The example is included because it illustrates a problem quite
fundamental both to psychological and economic models: the inability
to distinguish a person's preferences, and his ability to convert
these into action. Attitude models require that a choice postulated
by the researcher is considered by the respondent, even though the
respondent's behaviour may be constrained to one alternative only.
Although all respondents in the example were entirely able to imagine
the consequences and desirability of using both alternative modes,
some were (almost by definition) simply in no position to choose.

It is no coincidence that Fishbein's choice model has worked well
where individuals are genuinely free to translate their preferences
into action: the best example being voting behaviour in a democratic
election system (Fishbein and Coombs 1974). The conclusion must be
that individual-choice models, originally developed to explain
consumers' or voters' choices, will not necessarily prove appropriate
to travellers' decisions. Heggie (1978b) has argued this theme
vigorously. Thomas's work is important because it draws attention to
this fact. It is also notable for its concern with validating the
model by means of an independent 'after' survey: much travel choice
theory remains to be validated by means other than checks of goodness-
of-fit with the original data set (again, see Heggie 1978b).

4. REACTION AGAINST INDIVIDUAL-CHOICE MODELS

One of the attractions in applying purely psychological choice models
was the hope that restrictive assumptions of the economic model -
including some which the attribute-utility approaches were intended to
lift - could be avoided. Experience with the psychological models,
however, suggested that these may simply re-introduce limiting

assumptions, or replace one set with another. Some implicit limitations of individual-choice models - typified by psychological choice models - are set out here. They have attracted increasing concern with the growing emphasis on methods of 'understanding' travel behaviour and change.

The static nature of psychological measurement models

Hartgen (1974) reviewed a mass of evidence showing that proposed public transport innovations were being highly rated in detailed surveys of local attitudes, only to be underutilized on implementation. This drew his attention to the idea that mode-switching should not be seen as a set of simultaneous judgements, or snap formations of attitude, which precede and determine a change of behaviour. This is the view we are forced to take in adopting the attribute-utility framework within cross-sectional survey procedures. Instead, we should view choosing as a constrained process involving several distinct stages of psychological and behavioural adjustment. Rogers, (1962) identified the following five main stages.

On becoming aware of an alternative to his current travel option, the individual judges its relevance. Certain attributes will be considered here (e.g. is the destination relevant?) while others (will the ride be comfortable?) are irrelevant at this stage. If key attributes are judged to be both relevant and satisfactory, information on others is then sought in pre-trial evaluations. Try-out may then follow. Only after experience in use and subsequent re-evaluation are subsidiary features (like comfort, perhaps) taken into account. Finally, the individual makes a choice between adopting and rejecting the option, after which behaviour becomes inertial and insensitive to marginal changes in the system of either mode.

The snapshot interview procedures in conventional attitude surveys cannot, of course, simulate such a process. Their tendency to overestimate seriously the extent of mode-switching (as reported by Hartgen in the United States, and by Heggie (1977a) with reference to the United Kingdom) suggests that they work at the level of initial impressions only; they merely capture the pre-trial evaluations. Hierarchical relationships among different attributes are collapsed by the presentation of attribute lists which implicitly assume items are equally relevant.

Hartgen discussed the use of correction factors to allow for bias, and certainly, the extent of intrinsic error warrants close investigation. For research purposes, however, we should note that cross-sectional surveys can be fundamentally ill-suited to understanding travel choices which occur naturally over time.

Narrow focus on isolated aspects of choice

For theoretical reasons (Fishbein and Ajzen 1975) predictions of behaviour from attitudes must be more accurate when the researcher specifies alternative options narrowly and precisely. Thomas (1976) took note of this when she chose to examine choice between two modes, among homogeneous groups, for a specified trip purpose, destination and time.

Reviews of research over recent years indicate two trends: increasing data requirements, and despite this, an increasingly narrow focus on specific choices isolated within the spectrum of individuals' everyday travel decisions. This seems to be forcing a trade-off between accuracy, and the general usefulness of results. Attempts to

examine in equal depth every decision which – in transport modelling
terms – an individual is said to make over the day would meet the
impracticable data-collection problems.

More fundamentally, however, the treatment of trip decisions in
isolation, as if these are independent psychological entities, may
itself run the risk of imposing false assumptions. Do people in
fact categorize everyday trip decisions as the modeller does, or are
these inter-linked within some broader plan governing their routine
behaviour? (Dix 1976). This larger question is returned to later.

The diminution of the respondent's role
Consider the following assumptions. These are implicit within the
'behavioural travel demand model' specifications which the large-
scale attitudinal surveys, reviewed earlier, complemented.

- decisions are made autonomously by the individual;
- the individual makes each decision independently of all other
  decisions (except that an overall budget constraint may operate);
- decisions are based upon minimization of travel disutility.
  Relevant utilities (operationally, degrees of satisfaction and/or
  importance) only consist of those attached to trips (usually
  differentiated with respect to trip purpose);
- utilities are estimated on the basis of full knowledge of all
  attributes of every (objectively available) option;
- preferences are based upon utility maximization and are
  synonymous with action;
- all the characteristics of transport supply are perceived and
  evaluated continuously. Changes to any perceived attribute of
  any alternative item change the total utility attached to that
  item, and behaviour is changed directly and simultaneously.

Few of these assumptions are tenable in terms of psychological
theory, many are intuitively unlikely, and none is supported without
qualification by work reviewed later in this paper. Why, then, did
widespread applications of sophisticated psychometric methods of
enquiry leave these assumptions largely unchallenged, producing data
quite consistent with them?

Inspection of the nature of the respondents' role in many
conventional attitude surveys quickly reveals some of the reasons.
All too often the respondent's task is entirely passive, involving no
more than, for example, repeated indications of whether a pair of
given statements is similar or not. A movement towards the disintegration of research questions into a series of simplistic, mechanical
questionnaire judgements has grown up alongside the development of
increasing mathematical sophistication within data processing methodology, particularly following the innovation of multidimensional
scaling procedures. This movement has led logically to another; an
increase in the extent to which *a priori* conceptions influence or
determine the eventual output and conclusions.

The result is a methodology which enables, in fact compels
respondents to make judgements that are consistent with a model, but
which may be quite inconsistent with their own decision-making
behaviour. The only means by which a respondent can indicate an
awareness of his own non-conformity with the model is by indicating
'not relevant', *if* the questionnaire provides this option. This
action is however unlikely. Respondents are seldom informed about
the researcher's assumptions concerning their own behaviour, nor are

they often invited to comment on these.

The concern with the respondent's role has more than just academic or ethical importance. An extreme example of the degeneration of questionnaire design is given in figure 1. This shows how it is possible for the researcher to be led into constructing quite meaningless tasks for the respondent, and thus undermining the validity and purpose of the empirical exercise itself.

Please read the feature enclosed in the box at the top of this page. Then read each feature listed below it. If you feel the two features are alike "X" the "yes" box. If you feel the two features are not alike "X" the "no" box. Please "X" either "yes" or "no" for every feature listed below.

Is | BEING ABLE TO GET WHERE I WANTED TO GO ON TIME | like:

WHETHER THIS IS LIKE THE FEATURE ABOVE:

Having my own private section in the vehicle...................... yes☐ no☐

Having short travel times... yes☐ no☐

Having a short waiting for a vehicle............................... yes☐ no☐

Having low fares.. yes☐ no☐

Having a comfortable ride in a quiet vehicle...................... yes☐ no☐

Having a driver instead of a completely automatic system.......... yes☐ no☐

Being safe from harm by others and from vehicle accidents......... yes☐ no☐

Having room for strollers or wheel chairs......................... yes☐ no☐

Being able to get to many places in area

     using a guideway.. yes☐ no☐

Having refreshments and newspapers................................. yes☐ no☐

Figure 1. '...How is it possible for the researcher to be led into constructing quite meaningless tasks for the respondent...'. An extract from a questionnaire designed around a multidimensional scaling model of attribute 'similarity'.

5. RENEWED INTEREST IN 'SOFTER' METHODS OF SOCIAL-PSYCHOLOGICAL INVESTIGATION

'Softer' methods of social-psychological enquiry have attracted increasing attention recently, and this reflects a reaction against some of the hazards which can accompany the use of highly structured data-collection techniques.

Instead of focusing a model on a selected 'decision' in order to understand this, the concern is with experiencing the 'rich picture' of choices and constraints which travellers in their real-life environment face, *before* prescribing any more specific models of behaviour change. The value of qualitative interviewing approaches has of course long been recognized (a useful reference manual for social-research techniques in transport is provided by Martin and

Voorhees (1978)). It is the inter-linking of qualitative with larger-scale quantitative approaches which is the key feature of renewed interest in the former. The value of largely unstructured, in-depth interviewing methods in exploratory stages of research is discussed by Dix and Spencer (1979). Important methodological features of the approach are:

- the respondents' role is active;
- interviewers introduce themes, but are non-directive, and interpretations of respondents' statements are offered back for correction;
- the researchers do the interviewing;
- all interviews are tape-recorded;
- analysis is based on summaries from tapes, card-indexed for cross-reference;
- hypotheses from interviews are tested, wherever possible, using larger-scale quantitative data sources: conclusions may follow several stages of hypothesis-modification.

Reports on two major projects embodying this approach will be available shortly (Transport Studies Unit 1980). Further examples of uses of in-depth interviewing are provided by Brög and Schwerdtfeger (1977) and Heggie (1976).

Brög and Schwerdtfeger developed a useful model of mode choice, for predicting response to marginal system changes. An unusual feature was that constraints on mode-switching behaviour were defined, and several different categories of 'non-trading' travellers identified. The survey used to quantify the model was structured around insights gained in an earlier, in-depth study. If Brög had relied upon conventional wisdom and adopted individual choice assumptions, then no indication would have been given of the most significant findings. These were that 32 per cent of car-using individuals were 'materially constrained' from using an alternative, half of the others had no information about transit routes, times or costs, and the proportion conforming to trading criteria was only 16 per cent of the total.

Heggie (1976) was concerned to examine the effectiveness of vigorous policies of car restraint upon commuter mode choice. During his semi-structured household-interview survey, however, the frame of reference became extended. The work provided classic illustrations of how the household may substantially restructure its existing pattern of travel behaviour, when adapting itself to a changed environment within a pattern of constraints. Individual decisions to change mode for particular journeys had triggered changes in the frequencies, destinations, modes and timing of other journeys including those made by other members of household. Reallocations of activities between household members were also noted. Adaptations like these had not come to light during more structured surveys concerned with monitoring restraint policies elsewhere, as for example in Nottingham (described by Collins 1975), where decisions to count only peak-hour trips were taken in advance. Their importance was underlined by the finding that many adaptations ran counter to policy intentions: for example, some responses to car restraint involved a doubling of vehicle trip rates.

Complex adaptations like these cannot be understood or predicted by our existing individual-choice models, including sophisticated psychological models of behavioural intention. Improvements to these

can nevertheless be envisaged. For example, Golob,Horowitz and
Wachs (1979) have suggested adding questions on the constraints
individuals perceive to diaries or questionnaires. This would
assume, however, that individuals will know within what constraints
they are free to adapt. This is doubtful when responses may depend
on the decisions of others - on the outcome of negotiations about use
of the family car, for example.

Not all adaptations to policy measures are complex ones, of
course: the problem of prediction is knowing when they will be, and
when not. Heggie and Jones' (1978) work on 'domains' of response
provides a classification of response types set broadly in terms of
their complexity. Identification of the domain in which responses to
a given policy proposal will be made, can help the practitioner
determine with what confidence available alternative models can be
used. This means carrying out a pilot study using methods of measurement *not* restricted to particular domains. Here, social-research
techniques can be exploited to special advantage, and in particular,
the Household Activity-Travel Simulators ('HATS') device can be a
powerful supplement to an in-depth survey.

6.   THIRD-GENERATION APPROACHES TOWARDS UNDERSTANDING TRAVEL
BEHAVIOUR AND CHANGE

Studies using 'HATS' can also represent one example of attempts to
meet the requirements of 'third-generation' models of travel
behaviour, as discussed by Manheim (1976) and summarized by Heggie
(1977b) thus:
   'A realistic interactive model.....of travel choice, should
   contain at least six principal ingredients:
   (i)   It must involve the entire household and allow for interaction between its members
   (ii)   It must make existing constraints on household behaviour
   quite explicit (i.e. it should not use hypothetical sums of
   money or blocks of time)
   (iii)   It must start from the household's existing pattern of
   behaviour
   (iv)   It must work by confronting the household with realistic
   changes in its travel environment and must allow it to respond
   within a framework that makes the household's aspirations, its
   knowledge and spatial awareness of alternatives, and all the
   other constraints on behaviour quite explicit
   (v)   It should provide for the influences of long-term adaptation
   and experience
   (vi)   It should be able to tell the investigator something more
   fundamental that he did not know before (i.e. the model should
   not be a rigid formalisation of existing knowledge).'
'HATS' can cope with most of these requirements, except for the fifth
(long-term adaptations).

The Transport Studies Unit Household Activity-Travel Simulator (HATS)
'HATS' studies involve the use of display equipment for in-depth
interviews with each household in a selected sample. Activity-travel
diaries, completed for a specified period beforehand, are translated
into physical representations of a given day as shown in figure 2.
Each household member builds a detailed picture of how and where time

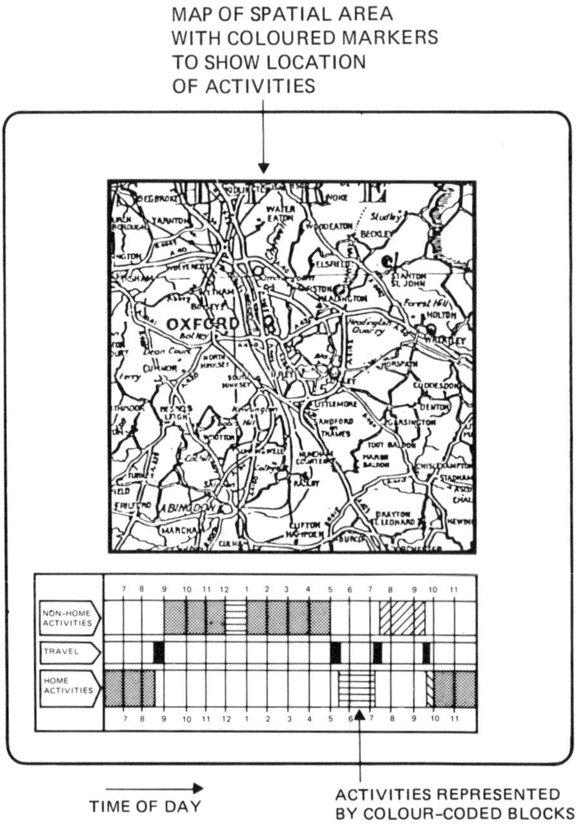

MAP OF SPATIAL AREA
WITH COLOURED MARKERS
TO SHOW LOCATION
OF ACTIVITIES

TIME OF DAY

ACTIVITIES REPRESENTED
BY COLOUR-CODED BLOCKS

Figure 2.   'HATS' representation of a person's day.

is spent through the day, distinguishing travel as a special linking
activity.   Stages of the interview procedure are outlined in figure
3 (reproduced from Jones 1979); the emphasis on different stages
varies according to the application.

Generally, respondents start by describing the pattern of the
day, how this varies, and also perhaps how present behaviour patterns
were built up in the past.   A special focus is on the nature of
constraints (e.g. times and places of work, and how flexible these
are; needs for fitting in shopping; for being home at certain times;
for having a car on certain days- etc.) and inter-personal linkages
(e.g. lift-giving arrangements; different drivers' claims on the
family car; all persons being home for joint activities like meals
etc.).   In other words, the aim at first is to gain general insights
into decision rules underlying each household's day-to-day behaviour.

Latent demands may be considered next: certain activities may be
desired but unattainable, and locations attractive but inaccessible.
In exploring these questions, which relate to the concept of accessi-

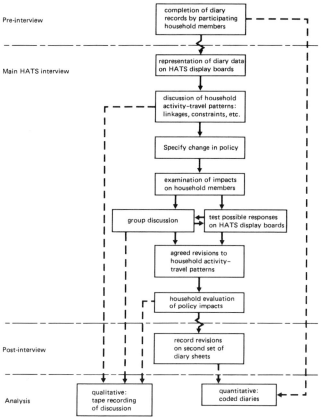

Figure 3. Stages of typical 'HATS' interviewing procedure.

bility in its broadest sense, time-geographic, social, and psychological constraints can each be distinguished in the 'HATS' interview.
     Where a specific policy is under study, tentative individual
responses to the proposal are set up on the 'HATS' board and immediate
consequences of the choice appear visibly as shown in figure 4. In
exploring reactions to proposed new opportunities (such as an urban
rail-transit scheme, Jones and Dix 1979), the technique is able to
assess perceptions and feelings concerning the mode itself together
with - but distinct from - its relevance-for-use. This is because
explicit checks can be made of such critical factors as the accessibility of the new service to home; whether it serves appropriate
destinations between appropriate times; what activities can be realistically sacrificed in order to make 'generated' journeys; and whether
any indirect problems will be encountered through the medium of inter-
personal or spatio-temporal linkages. Any re-evaluations of the
initial response - in the light of simulated experience - are noted,
and re-adjustments may be tried. At each stage, possible repercussions for other household members are identified and their reactions
to these probed. Infeasible options are thus rejected, and feasible
alternative patterns are identified (their number is usually in fact
very small, which itself reflects the importance of patterns of
constraints in a family's day).

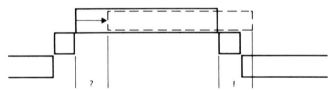

(a) CHANGE OF WORK/SCHOOL TIMES ('HATS' format reveals overlaps, unaccounted for periods of time, and other infeasibilities; e.g. being in two places at once)

(b) BUS WITHDRAWAL ('HATS' shows secondary repurcussions of a change in activity-travel patterns through the day)

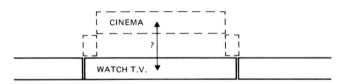

(c) ACTIVITY TRADE-OFFS (explaining trip generation or suppression)

Figure 4.   Tracing impacts of policy: some logical checks in 'HATS'.

The group then determines the most probable adaptation, according to its own rules. Often, the revealed rules demonstrate the importance of non-transport 'attributes' in determining how travel patterns are adapted towards the policy change (for example, will mother be at home before her children, will the family breakfast routine need to be changed?). Detailed considerations like these, of course, cannot be considered in 'snapshot' attitude-survey procedures. At the conclusion of each interview session, the simulated 'after' activity-travel pattern is coded onto new diaries which, together with the tape recordings of discussion, form the outputs for analysis.

Potential applications of 'HATS' are numerous, the chief limitations on its use being that: (a) surveys are necessarily limited in scale to sample sizes typical of depth interview surveys; (b) long-term responses to policy are beyond reach, because reliance is upon current knowledge of alternatives, and therefore results of job or residential relocation cannot be anticipated; (c) a financial budget is not incorporated explicitly. It is implicit to the judgement of alternatives by participants, but money-cost changes are not represented physically in the way that time changes are.

7. CONCLUSIONS

At present, work within 'the second-generation' approaches –
especially concerning the incorporation of psychological variables
into the disaggregate, economic, demand-model – is primarily a
feature of research activity rather than application in the field.
This review has identified a number of conceptual and methodological
issues which need to be resolved if this situation is to change.

At the same time, interest in the philosophy and techniques of
possible 'third-generation' approaches is increasing. The paper has
set out some reasons for this, viewed from the researcher's standpoint. These approaches, too, have yet to see widespread application,
although interest from practitioners does appear to be fast growing.
Now that social-psychological approaches are coming under close
scrutiny, it is important to be clear about their role.

What needs to be stressed is that they should not be viewed (or
offered) as alternatives to other aspects of transport planning
methodology, nor judged in isolation. Their potential contributions
really depend on their inclusion with other ways and means of
problem-solving, in both the research and applied areas. In fact this
is central to the 'third-generation' philosophy. Linked with
quantitative planning data available on a large scale, for example,
and perhaps with *ad hoc* use of regular econometric techniques for
modelling specific aspects of behaviour change (response domains
having first been identified), they can take on an important role –
perhaps a key role – in assessing the effects and impact of
alternative policy proposals, and assisting with the policy-generation
stage itself. Where the effects of a policy are found likely to
involve complex adaptations – beyond the scope of existing models –
techniques like 'HATS' may also be useful in a predictive role. This
should not be seen as their primary purpose, but in such circumstances
they are likely to produce results which, although approximate, are
reliable. This reliability would be compared with the output from
other methods which would be precise but wrong.

NOTE

The development of 'HATS' forms part of an SSRC-sponsored project on
travel choice behaviour begun in 1974. The manufacture of the
equipment is the subject of UK Patent Application No. 45433/76 held
jointly by the National Research Development Corporation, M.C. Dix
and P.M. Jones.

REFERENCES

Banister, D.J. (1978) The influence of habit formation on modal
    choice – a heuristic model. *Transportation*, 7 (1), pp. 5-18.
Bock, F.C. (1968) Factors Influencing Modal Trip Assignment. Highway
    Research Board NCHRP Report No. 57, Washington DC.
Brög, W. (1978) Behaviour as a Result of Individual Decisions in
    Social Situations. Proceedings of Conference on Mobility in
    Urban Life, Arc-et-Senans, France.
Brög, W., and Schwerdtfeger, W. (1977) Considerations on the Design
    of Behavioural Oriented Models. Proceedings of the World
    Conference on Transport Research, Rotterdam.

Brunner, G.A. *et al.* (1966) User-Determined Attributes of Ideal
    Transportation Systems: An Empirical Study. Department of
    Business Administration, University of Maryland.
Collins, B.T. (1975) Transportation developments in Nottinghamshire,
    Transport, 36 (10).
Dix, M.C. (1976) Applications of In-depth Interviewing Techniques to
    the Study of Travel Behaviour. Proceedings of the UTSG
    Conference, Aston; and Working Paper No. 9, Transport Studies
    Unit, Oxford University.
Dix, M.C. (1980) Structuring our understanding of travel choices: the
    use of psychometric and social-research techniques, in Stopher
    P.R. (ed.) *New Horizons in Travel Behaviour Research*. Lexington,
    Mass: D.C. Heath.
Dix, M.C. and Spencer, M.B. (1979) Car Use Study: Report of Pilot
    Survey. Working Paper No. 34, Transport Studies Unit, Oxford
    University.
Dobson, R. and Tischer, M.L. (1977) Comparative Analysis of
    Determinants of Modal Choices by Central Business District
    Workers. Transportation Research Record 649, Transportation
    Research Board, Washington DC. pp. 7-14.
Edwards, W. (1954) The theory of decision making, *Psychological
    Bulletin*, 51, pp. 380-417.
Ewing, R.H. (1973) Psychological theory applied to mode choice
    prediction. *Transportation*, 2 (4), pp. 391-410.
Fishbein, M. and Ajzen, I. (1975) *Beliefs, Attitudes, Intention and
    Behaviour: an Introduction to Theory and Research*. Reading,
    Mass.: Addison-Wesley.
Fishbein, M. and Coombs, F.S. (1974) Basis for decision: an
    attitudinal analysis of voting behaviour, *Journal of Applied
    Social Psychology*, 4 (1), pp. 95-124.
Golledge, R.G. and Brown, L.A. (1967) Search, learning and the market
    decision process. *Geografiska Annaler*, 49 (2), pp. 116-24.
Golob, T.F., Horowitz, A.D. and Wachs, M. (1979) Attitude-behaviour
    relationships in travel demand modelling, in Hensher, D.A. and
    Stopher, P.R. (eds.) *Behavioural Travel Modelling* London: Croom
    Helm, pp. 739-59.
Goodwin, P.B. and Hensher, D.A. (1978) The transport determinants of
    travel choice, in Hensher, D.A. and Dalvi, M.Q. (eds.) *Determinants
    of Travel Choice*. Farnborough: Saxon House, pp. 1-65.
Hartgen, D.T. (1974) Attitudinal and situational variables influencing
    urban mode choice: some empirical findings, *Transportation*, 3 (4),
    pp. 377-92.
Heggie, I.G. (1976) A Pilot Study of Travel Behaviour in Oxford.
    Working Paper No. 21, Transport Studies Unit, Oxford University.
Heggie, I.G. (1977a) Consumer response to public transport improve-
    ments and car restraint: some practical findings. *Policy and
    Politics*, 5 (1), pp. 47-69.
Heggie, I.G. (1977b) Socio-psychological models of travel choice.
    Traffic Engineering and Control, 8 (12), pp. 583-85.
Heggie, I.G. (1978a) Behavioural dimensions of travel choice, in
    Hensher, D.A. and Dalvi, M.Q. (eds.) *Determinants of Travel
    Choice*. Farnborough: Saxon House, pp. 100-25.
Heggie, I.G. (1978b) Putting behaviour into behavioural models of
    travel choice. *The Journal of the Operational Research Society*,
    29 (6), pp. 541-50.

Heggie, I.G. and Jones, P.M. (1978) Defining domains for models of travel demand. *Transportation*, 7 (2), pp. 119-35.

Hensher, D.A., McLeod, P.B. and Stanley, J.K. (1975) Usefulness of attitudinal measures in investigating the choice of travel mode. *International Journal of Transport Economics*, 2 (1), pp. 51-75.

Horowitz, A.D. (1978) A Cognitive Dissonance Approach to Attitudinal Modelling in Travel Behaviour Research. Proceedings, Transportation Research Board, 57th Annual Conference, Washington, DC.

Jones, P.M. (1979) 'HATS' - a technique for investigating household decisions. *Environment and Planning A*, 11 (1), pp. 59-70.

Jones, P.M. and Dix, M.C. (1979) Household Travel in the Reading Area: Report of a Pilot Study using 'HATS', Technical Report No. 4, Transport Studies Unit, Oxford University.

Lave, C.A. (1969) A behavioural approach to modal split forecasting. *Transportation Research*, 3 (4), pp. 463-80.

Manheim, M.L. (1976) An overview of some current travel demand research, in Matzner, E. and Ruesch, G. (eds.) *Transport as an Instrument for Allocating Space and Time - A Social Science Approach*, Report 11, Institute of Public Finance, Vienna Technical University.

Martin and Voorhees Associates (1978) Social Research Techniques: A Reference Manual. LTR 1 Working Paper No. 5. Department of Transport, London.

McFadgen, D.G. (1974) Attitudes and Behaviour: A Current Review of the Consistency Question. Working Paper No. 7406. Institute of Transportation and Traffic Engineering, University of California at Berkeley.

Michaels, R.M. (1980) Workshop Chairman's Report: The Role of Psychometrics, in Stopher, P.R. (ed.) *New Horizons in Travel Demand Research*. Lexington, Mass.: D.C. Heath.

Nicolaidis, G.C. (1975) Quantification of the comfort variable. *Transportation Research*, 9 (1), pp. 55-66.

Rogers, E.M. (1962) *Diffusion of Innovations*. New York: Free Press.

Scitovsky, T. (1976) *The Joyless Economy*. New York: Oxford University Press.

Sherret, A. (1971) Structuring an Econometric Model of Modal Choice. Unpublished Ph.D. Thesis, Cornell University, Ithica, New York.

Sheth, J.N. (1975) A Psychological Model of Travel Mode Selection. Discussion Paper, University of Illinois.

Sommers, A.N. (1969) Expanding Nondemographic Factors in Modal Split Models. Paper presented at the Operations Research Society of America, November.

Spear, B.D. (1975) The Development of a Generalized Convenience Variable for Models of Mode Choice. Unpublished Ph.D. Thesis, Cornell University, Ithica, New York.

Spear, B.D. (1976) Attitudinal modelling: its role in travel demand forecasting, in Stopher, P.R. and Meyburg, A.H. (eds.) *Behavioural Travel-Demand Models*. Toronto: Lexington.

Stopher, P.R. and Meyburg, A.H. (eds.) (1976) *Behavioural Travel-Demand Models*. Toronto: Lexington.

Stopher, P.R. (1977) Development of market segments of destination choice. Transportation Research Record 649, Transportation Research Board, Washington, DC. pp. 14-22.

Stopher, P.R. and Watson, P.L. (1975) *Destination-Choice Modelling: An Application of Psychometric Techniques.* Chicago: American Psychological Association.

Thomas, K. (1976) A reinterpretation of the attitude approach to transport mode choice and an exploratory empirical test. *Environment and Planning A*, 8 (7), pp. 793-810.

Tischer, M.L. (1980) Attitude measures: psychometric modelling, in Stopher, P.R. (ed.) *New Horizons in Travel Demand Research.* Lexington, Mass.: D.C. Heath.

Transport Studies Unit (1980) Understanding Travel Behaviour (SSRC) and Car Use Study (Department of Transport): Project Reports, in preparation.

Watson, P.L. (1971) Problems Associated with Time and Cost Data used in Travel Choice Modelling and Valuation of Time. Highway Research Record 369, Highway Research Board, Washington DC. pp. 148-158.

Wilkie, W.L. and Pessemier, E.A. (1975) Issues in marketing's use of multi-attribute attitude models. *Journal of Marketing Research,* 10, pp. 428-41.

Wright, P.L. (1972) Consumer Judgement Strategies: Beyond the Compensating Assumption. Proceedings of the Third Conference for Consumer Research.

A time-geographic approach
to transport and
public policy planning

Bo Lenntorp

1. INTRODUCTION

The paper contains two sections. The first provides a general background to the research and an analytic framework. The second mainly
consists of some detailed, empirical studies. There are some links
missing between the two levels, but this is seen as a challenge rather
than a drawback.

Perhaps I should point out that transportation is not the main
focus of research in our group {1}, although we have considered
transportation or movement of goods and people in many of our studies.
Our main area of interest is the allocation of time, space and
resources between simultaneously competing demands. And within this
context transportation is an extremely interesting phenomenon.

Modern society can be characterized by a profound functional
division in its organization. The earlier, predominantly agrarian,
society - which is not too far distant - relied on a vertical relationship, as seen geographically, between people and the soil. The
changes or structural transformations, which have been imposed upon us
mainly for economic reasons, have been achieved with the aid of
intensive private and public planning largely divided up on a sectoral
basis. (I have explictly focused on the economy because I think we
should incorporate the characteristics of our economic system into
models in the transportation field to a greater extent than we do at
present.) The economic and technological development, which has
created a high degree of specialization in the population through the
division of labour has also had important repercussions in the field
of transport.

In a society where the division of activities is markedly
functional, while planning is sectoral and focused on current
critical problems, it is hardly surprising that certain questions -
consistently ignored by researchers, planners and politicians - are,
to a great extent, those of an intersectoral nature. This implies

that future research will have to include this intersectoral
character, and this presents a challenge to researchers as well as
planners. New or complementary conceptual frameworks, theories and
models will all be needed. If we neglect these new areas, we leave
the field wide open to unplanned and unforeseeable actions, which
might have severe negative repercussions.

Transportation is one vital area with a key role in our society.
The functional division has led to an increasing amount of transport
for both individuals and goods. To a large degree the transportation
field is *dependent* on the development in other sectors, sometimes even
to the extent that transport planners have 'to tidy up' after changes
in other sectors. The primary task of this 'tidying up' has been to
deal with the consequences of development, that is to alleviate the
negative repercussions and to tackle specific questions - often
described as 'bottlenecks'. This bottleneck-strategy is, of course,
by no means confined to the transport section - it is in fact a
general characteristic of our research and planning. A great deal of
research work carried out today is involved in the analysis of such
consequences.

However, transport has more than a dependent role. Decisions and
changes in the transport sector are also made independently of other
sectors, and transport is therefore active in creating movement
possibilities and distributing them within a population. This aspect
of transportation makes the sector extremely important and this must
be made explicit, as Hägerstrand (1973) has pointed out.

2. DIRECTIONS FOR INTEGRATION

The complexity of our society calls for a broader perspective and for
approaches which can deal with transport and non-transport questions
simultaneously. To achieve this we must begin to integrate in two
ways.

First, we have to evolve concepts and techniques that can project
societal arrangements on to the individual level, so that we can carry
out analysis in terms of individual experiences, attitudes, images of
environment, and so on. Every individual decision is based on
experiences of society, and so it is important to trace historically
these experiences which lie behind any decision.

Secondly, we have to evolve concepts and techniques that will
enable us to grasp the interplay between individual activities and the
organization of production, distribution and consumption on a macro-
level in our society. It is on this level that the general decisions,
which govern or determine micro-situations, are taken.

These two propositions highlight the fact that we are not dealing
with movement activities in isolation, but as one class of activities
that has to be explicitly related to stationary activities. These two
methods of integration are being followed by our research group and
they are also behind our conceptual and analytical framework. The
framework for analysis presupposes that individuals are kept separate
from activities, an abstract distinction which has value in many
contexts.

A population is regarded as a set, with individuals as its
elements. The biological, social and other relationships between the
individuals enable us to refer to a population system. Similarly, all
the activities of a population - during a given time-interval - are

regarded as a set, and the mutual relationships of its elements (that is the activities) describe how these are linked to particular individuals or to collective projects. The total number of activities for a specific population also forms a system. (These two systems could be supplemented with other sets or systems comprising of, say, tools, vehicles or other objects.)

Social research, planning and policy is geared to analysing and regulating each of the two systems, as well as the distribution of activities over the population. The latter aspect is perhaps the most relevant one when analysing transportation, although an enormous variety of influences governs this distribution.

Linking individuals to activities amounts to tying elements together in time and space. Physically, each individual constantly requires space and describes an unbroken life-line over time. Activities in turn are tied in specific ways to space-time. Some activities, for instance, are bound to certain spatial localities by, say, the existence of premises with certain machines or other equipment. Moreover, many activities have to be arranged in specific sequences because they represent single steps in a larger project.

It can be concluded from this introduction that there are two main levels of restrictions on linkages between the two systems. One is the physico-geometric level at which fundamental characteristics of space-time have to be respected. Objects occupy space and activities take time; individuals are indivisible and so in a sense are certain activity sequences. This is a type of absolute constraint, which, though seemingly trivial, must be taken into account. A representation is feasible and, once certain fundamental restrictions have been established, it can serve as a platform for further discussion. The other, overriding level has to do with aspects of control and regulation, for example, what to produce and how to produce it.

We turn now to the discussion of more concrete questions using, as a spring-board, an individual's everyday life. Figure 1 shows how an individual in the course of a day is involved in numerous activities, often of a wide variety. The unbroken path is on the left side of the diagram and is drawn in space as well as in time. Movements are schematically displayed by changing location along the one-dimensional space-axis. Connected to this path - or rather to the individual - is a set of activities (encircled with lines) which have been performed during the day. These activities are to a great extent regulated and controlled by different institutions in society, as indicated on the right in the appropriate box. The relevant subject areas and academic descriptions are also displayed in boxes.

A few comments on figure 1 may clarify some general points made earlier. First, it is important to consider the individual's complete day and not just parts of it. It is especially dangerous to separate movements from stationary activities. This point of view has now been widely accepted within the field of activity research, where a full day is taken as the unit of time in which to study the interdependence of decisions. I would go somewhat further and state that it is also necessary to look at the day as a part of a longer perspective. The experiences and attitudes of an individual are formed over a life-time, and we therefore have to be very careful when we observe, for example, similarities between individuals. This perspective can be clarified by linking activities directly to the physical individual

time

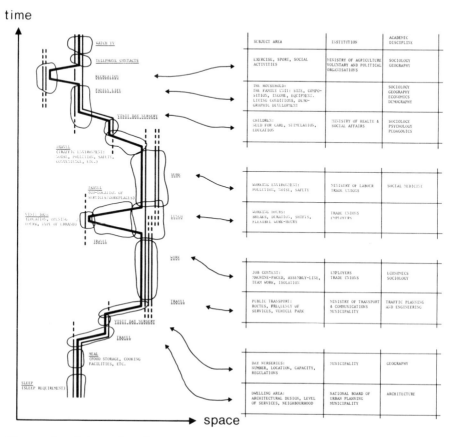

SUBJECT AREA	INSTITUTION	ACADEMIC DISCIPLINE
EXERCISE, SPORT, SOCIAL ACTIVITIES	MINISTRY OF AGRICULTURE VOLUNTARY AND POLITICAL ORGANISATIONS	SOCIOLOGY GEOGRAPHY
THE HOUSEHOLD: THE FAMILY UNIT: SIZE, COMPOSITION, INCOME, EQUIPMENT, LIVING CONDITIONS, DEMOGRAPHIC DEVELOPMENT		SOCIOLOGY GEOGRAPHY ECONOMICS DEMOGRAPHY
CHILDREN: NEED FOR CARE, STIMULATION, EDUCATION	MINISTRY OF HEALTH & SOCIAL AFFAIRS	SOCIOLOGY PSYCHOLOGY PEDAGOGICS
WORKING ENVIRONMENT: POLLUTION, NOISE, SAFETY	MINISTRY OF LABOUR TRADE UNIONS	SOCIAL MEDICINE
WORKING HOURS: BREAKS, DURATION, SHIFTS, FLEXIBEL WORK-HOURS	TRADE UNIONS EMPLOYERS	
JOB CONTENT: MACHINE-PACED, ASSEMBLY-LINE, TEAM WORK, ISOLATION	EMPLOYERS TRADE UNIONS	ECONOMICS SOCIOLOGY
PUBLIC TRANSPORT: ROUTES, FREQUENCY OF SERVICES, VEHICLE PARK	MINISTRY OF TRANSPORT & COMMUNICATIONS MUNICIPALITY	TRAFFIC PLANNING AND ENGINEERING
DAY NURSERIES: NUMBER, LOCATION, CAPACITY, REGULATIONS	MUNICIPALITY	GEOGRAPHY
DWELLING AREA: ARCHITECTURAL DESIGN, LEVEL OF SERVICES, NEIGHBOURHOOD	NATIONAL BOARD OF URBAN PLANNING MUNICIPALITY	ARCHITECTURE

space

Figure 1.   Schematic diagrams of how an individual in the course of the day is involved in many activities, which are handled by different institutions in society and belong to various academic and scientific disciplines (Lenntorp 1978a).

through life-lines or trajectories.
     Another important point concerns the sectoral construction of our society. Such a division of policy making, planning and research often appears rational in isolation, but when projected on, for example, an individual's everyday life, where effects are combined and where solutions to different problems are interrelated, then it may well have strong negative repercussions which could hardly have been foreseen at the planning stage. The effects of a combination of actions on individuals form an area where we have mutual responsibility; we cannot limit ourselves to analysing specific activities and hope that our results or recommendations will fit in with others, more or less by chance.
     There are, however, at least two main directions we can take. The first is to start from the viewpoint of population and to analyse activity patterns of individuals and households. The second is to

start from the viewpoint of activities and to analyse how they are
scheduled - not as a result of individual choices - but as a result of
the organization of production, distribution and consumption, which in
turn is determined by the institutional and organizational framework
of the society.

The first approach is linked to time-use studies, and behavioural
modelling, and is predominantly micro- or individual-oriented. The
second approach deals particularly with the societal dimension and
is more feasible or convenient to connect to macro-observations of
(for example) the economic system. One might also say that the first
approach emphasizes individual choice aspects and the second one
societal constraint aspects.

These two approaches are illustrated in figure 2. Each of the six
sub-figures consists of an upper time-space and a lower cartographic
representation. In accordance with the analytical framework, the
figure is divided into a population side and an activity side. On
the population side (left) the daily paths of a single household at
three different points in time are illustrated as an example. On the
right side are the activities described, here illustrated by a single
plant or station. The thick bars inside the plant illustrate the
demand for individual time during a day. The long-term perspective
in the figure shows how demand for individuals in a production process
has changed over time and perhaps will change again in the future.

3.   THE CASE STUDIES

The dairy farming industry
In the first study we took production as the starting point. We
wanted to see whether it was possible to describe methods of production in terms that could be linked to studies of time-use of
households and their activity scheduling. If we could describe, for
example, the demands that production processes make on individuals and
on their time, we could extend our activity analysis to determine what
happens inside the plants. It would then also be possible to analyse
how changes in production technique cause changes in travel pattern
and in activity scheduling.

As a case study we selected dairy farming in a particular area
and we made a very detailed analysis of the daily production at
different points in time, from the end of the last century up to the
present (Ellegård and Lenntorp 1980). The economic and technological
development in this century has radically changed dairying. Specialization, division of activities and scale advantage have gradually
reduced the number of dairies in the region from about 300 in 1900 to
about 75 in 1955, and to just one single unit today. The development
towards highly routinized activity programmes that can be observed
today is in fact shaped by the way we produce things, and it is not an
option for single-individual decisions on a daily basis.

Some researchers in the transportation field have pointed out the
importance of looking not just at outdoor activities but also at
activities within households. This concept could be further extended,
in the light of the dairying case study, to stress the importance of
looking at activities inside the factories, offices and other places
of work. Economic and technological development have had a tremendous
effect in shaping the transport pattern. If we want to foresee
changes in transport patterns, we have to follow the changes in the

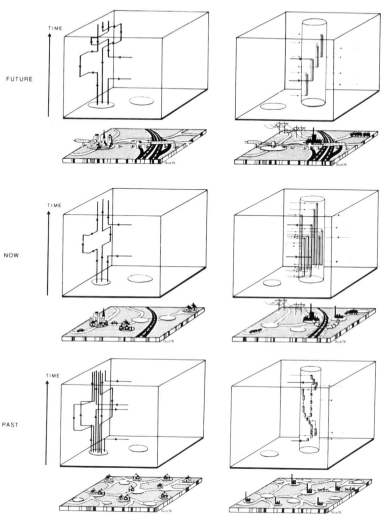

Figure 2. Schematic diagram of households and production processes in a long-term perspective. It shows how the development of production processes (right) changes over time and influences the pattern of movements and the everyday lives of households (left) (Lenntorp 1978b).

production of goods and services very carefully, as these issues lie close to the roots of our economic system. Planners and researchers need not only to look more carefully at this area but also to react to changes much earlier and faster than they do today.

Individual travel sequences in Karlstad
The second study concerns the household (the focus is on the left side of figure 2). As mentioned earlier, our studies in the research

group have been focused not on behaviour but constraints on possible behaviour. This approach based on the assumption that even if we now have a solid background of empirical studies of individual behaviour and activity patterns for individuals as well as for households, it is not a very promising undertaking to predict future behaviour on the basis of observed, past behaviour. We believe that it is much more fruitful to focus attention on the ways in which limits to freedom of action are created (Hägerstrand 1975).

With this in mind, ten years ago, a simulation model was created which estimates the number of alternatives open to an individual in a specific situation; that is when he or she has to perform a whole sequence of activities in a certain environment (Lenntorp 1976b). The model simulates an individual's possible behaviour, not his probable future behaviour. A primary intention behind the model is that it should serve to reproduce the structure of physical constraints and limits for an individual's activities. The applications so far have been in the daily perspective, which is a time perspective of great relevance to transport planning.

The model is a prototype or a concrete means of demonstrating an approach. There is no supposition that one has to work with this exact model when applying the approach, nor that one is limited to a specific scale in time and space. The model operates with two main elements:
(1) The activity programme contains information about where activities are to be undertaken, how long they are to last, when they can start and by which modes the individual can move between points in space.
(2) The individual's environment contains stationary elements. These comprise different stations or supply points, with specific spatial locations and times when they are accessible. The environment also comprises a set of transport systems, by which movements are regulated in principle in one of three ways:
- freely over space at any 'time (for walking movements);
- only along given tracks in space at any time (for car drivers and cyclists);
- only via given points in space at given times (for travel by public transport).

The model simulates individual-trajectories that comply with the conditions in the activity programme and the space-time structure of the environment. The simulation generates possible ways in which the individual can perform the programme. These are created by (i) permutating the sequence of activities (i.e. permutation of activities over time); (ii) testing different stations in the path (i.e. combinations of paths in space).

The simulation model can be demonstrated by a simple example. The activity programme is as follows: travel to full-time work and visits to day-care centre before and after observed hours of work. The maximum time permitted for travel and visits is 40 minutes each way. The programme is simulated in the city of Karlstad in central Sweden, which is approximately 7 × 5 km in size, with 75 000 inhabitants. Figure 3 gives the location of the six existing day-care centres and of six major places of work. Locations of dwellings are represented spatially aggregated within a regular lattice (62 sample-points).

The outcome of the simulation for a person travelling by public transport was as follows:

Figure 3. The city of Karlstad - the test area. The figure gives
the location of all six existing day-care centres, six major places
of work and the sample of dwellings plus the existing public transport network. (Lenntorp 1976a).

from 8 sample-points	5 work-places were within reach
" 16 "	4 " "
" 4 "	3 " "
" 19 "	2 " "
" 7 "	1 " "
" 8 "	0 " "

In another test the trip density was improved. All lines which
originally had only two or three starts per hour were now given four.
In general, the overall improvement in terms of widened access was
insignificant. The number of work places within reach increased from
ten sample points by one. In another test a new, tangential bus-
line was added. The new line was assumed to have four starts per
hour; otherwise, the situation in the first test was maintained.
Again the degree of improvement was very small: access to work-places
increased from four sample points only. One reason for this small
increase was that service on this line had to start at 7 a.m.,
according to the local authorities - the same time as most of the
workplaces start in the morning (Lenntorp 1976a, 1978c).

As background information, it is worth pointing out that a car
driver could carry out all mathematically possible combinations of
work places and day care centres. Thus the difference in terms of
physical freedom of action between different mobility groups - that
is, between a person with an available car and a person who has to
rely on public transport - is very great. The figures for this

specific activity programme, expressed as a percentage of the maximum number of possible combinations, are:

Car	100%	
Walking	19%	
Public transport		
observed		43%
improved service		46%
new bus-route added		44%

Even through this simple exercise with the simulation model, one can get a fairly good idea of how the number of possible activity programmes is affected by a combination of factors:
- the organization of transportation;
- the location of stations (dwellings, supply points etc.);
- the hours of access to activity centres.

The capacity of activity centres (for example day-care centres) is one aspect which was not taken into account, but from the simulation one could easily calculate demand. Another way in which this type of exercise can be made more sophisticated is by connecting specific programmes to various groups or household types, and then to introduce some procedure to weight the different programmes so that a given level of accessibility can be obtained for different areas and groups.

4. CONCLUDING COMMENTS

At present there are many problems in transport which require a rapid solution, and so have to be tackled within the transport sector itself. In many instances this means that, as a major problem is dealt with, one or more minor problems spring up because all solutions tend to have side-effects. While these may arise in the transport sector itself, they can equally well affect conditions outside it, and thus escape the notice of transport researchers and planners. It therefore seems reasonable to demand that greater efforts should be made to develop and evaluate techniques and measures at a more general level, and implicitly this is of a more intersectoral nature. It is not necessary that this process should hinder work in the conventional field.

One way to achieve this more general level of intersectoral scanning is to avoid a single large complex model, and instead to establish a collection of models which could be used in such a way that a model could benefit from the output of others. However to establish such a collection means that many problems have to be overcome, such as conceptualization, model building and the interdisciplinary character of the models.

The emphasis should not be exclusively on the development of quantitative models, but on a mixture of both quantitative and qualitative models. The implementation of methodology does not mean that actual numbers have to be presented in all cases, as this often means a distortion of reality. A standard argument in politics and policy making is that there is a need for numbers. Mathematics is too precise and exact to describe a complex society. What we must do as researchers and planners is to set up a problem-structure for politicians, and then to develop a collection of suitable models – this task cannot be achieved at random. There has to be a theory construct behind it; the content of such a construct is at present open for discussion and opinions on it are profoundly different.

Transport researchers and planners will have a very important role to play in discussions concerning our future, provided that they can broaden their horizons. They must be able to relate transport to non-transport problems, and to look upon decisions in this area as far reaching choices between different directions of *societal* change.

Note

{1} The Research Group for Process and Systems Analysis in Human Geography at the University of Lund is directed by Torsten Hägerstrand.

REFERENCES

Ellegård, K. and Lenntorp, B. (1980) On the connection between technological development in production and the everyday life of households and individuals. Forthcoming.

Hägerstrand, T. (1973) The impact of transport on the quality of life. Paper presented at the Fifth International Symposium on Theory and Practice in Transport Economics, European Council of Ministers of Transport, Athens.

Hägerstrand, T. (1975) Space, time and human conditions, in Karlqvist, A., Lundqvist, L. and Snickars, F. (eds.) *Dynamic Allocation of Urban Space*, Farnborough: Saxon House. pp. 3-12.

Lenntorp, B. (1976a) A time-space structured study of the travel possibilities of the public transport passenger. Rapporter och Notiser, 24. Lund: Department of Social and Economic Geography.

Lenntorp, B. (1976b) Paths in space-time environments: A time-geographic study of movement possibilities of individuals. *Lund Studies in Geography*, Series B, 44. Lund: Liber.

Lenntorp, B. (1977) A time-geographic approach to individuals' daily movements. Rapporter och Notiser, 33. Lund: Department of Social and Economic Geography.

Lenntorp, B. (1978a) The time-compact society and its representation. Rapporter och Notiser, 49. Lund: Department of Social and Economic Geography.

Lenntorp, B. (1978b) Physical movement as part of life: a conceptual framework for analyzing the distribution of movement possibilities in a population, in *Mobility in Urban Life*, Proceedings International Conference, Arc-et-Senans. Arcueil: Institut de Recherche des Transports, pp. 147-164.

Lenntorp, B. (1978c) A time-geographic simulation model of individual activity programmes, in Carlstein, T., Parkes, D. and Thrift, N. (eds.) *Timing Space and Spacing Time*, Vol. 2: *Human Activity and Time Geography*. London: Edward Arnold. pp. 162-80.

Lessons from Experience

The concentration on theory in the previous section should not imply disregard of the fundamental purpose of analysis, namely to help the decision-maker formulate policies which are both well thought out and backed up by empirical evidence. In this section, therefore, a particular case study is outlined to highlight the relationships between theory and practice; this is followed by a paper which addresses itself to some likely future developments in analysis methods. Finally, the problems of transport research are contrasted with the somewhat similar development of methodology in urban systems analysis to see whether any comparisons can be drawn.

The case study taken is London, and Paul Prestwood-Smith draws comparisons between the three main transport studies carried out: the London Traffic Survey (1964), the Greater London Development Plan (1970) and the Greater London Transportation Study (1977). By focusing on the main exogenous variables (population, employment and car ownership), the analysis demonstrates that prediction never matched the actual changes that took place. The effects that these inaccurate estimates of travel demand have had on policy are outlined, and some insight is given into the likely changes that will be taking place in the future. The cautious conclusion is that understanding of the underlying relationships determining travel demand has improved considerably, and that there is now an institutional framework available which can more readily adapt its policies to cope with change.

The second paper emphasizes the shortcomings of aggregate demand analysis techniques, and stresses the necessity to look at alternative means by which particular transport problems can be resolved. On the theoretical side, the previous section has indicated some of the responses from researchers, and in his paper Marvin Manheim asks the critical question - what do we want from travel demand analysis? First, he outlines the changing environment of transport analysis, and draws the implications for planners. This essentially personal view is continued with a summary of the available techniques; the conclusion is that there is a necessity to develop small-scale

problem-specific models which can be programmed on to portable
computers and used in the field to give a quick, responsive analysis.
The development of these techniques may circumvent the present
difficulty of the time gap between the results of basic research and
their implementation by practising professionals.

The focus on the detailed implementation issues is contrasted by
the final paper in this section which attempts to develop a perspective
through which the nature and role of systems analysis in urban policy
making and planning can be viewed. In his paper, Michael Batty
suggests that the experience of using such analysis is one in which
knowledge always appears inadequate in relation to the policies
required, but can never be abandoned due to the necessity for attempting problem-solving. Hence the experience is dominated by recurrent
cycles of action and reaction. To explain this, the nature of social
problem-solving and the role of theory and practice, science and
design as essential constructs of the planning activity are presented.

Where the techniques have been applied, the results seem to have
been disappointing, either because the predictions have not been
sufficiently accurate, or because the nature of travel behaviour has
not been well understood. The response to significant advances in
theory has been cautious and this may in part be due to uncertainty
within the research fraternity. It may also be due to the absence of
large-scale resources for investment, but probably the main reason is
the lack of expertise to apply the techniques. To many practitioners,
the methods used may seem irrelevant and not addressed to the problems
on which they have to advise. The danger may be that one set of
techniques will replace another without significantly adding to an
understanding of the processes under study. Perhaps there is scope
here for a new flexible approach that examines alternatives on the
spot - a specific method will be used to analyse a specific problem -
and an evaluation can take place that summarizes the key points together with an explicit statement of the consequences for all parties.

This close involvement of research, planning and decision making
is necessary so that new ideas and methods can be disseminated
together with a clear indication of their advantages and disadvantages.
In this way a meaningful dialogue could be established so that the
general resistance to change could be overcome. There would be an
incentive to learn new skills so that the best available method would
be used for the analysis of a particular problem.

The papers comprising the second part of the book give the overall
impression that we are faced with 'digesting an iceberg', and we are
just beginning to look at what is actually going on under the surface.
The fundamental questions range from issues such as whether we ought
to be using trips or activities as the basic unit of travel demand
to whether the present set of techniques do in fact help policy-makers
to make more rational decisions. But across the whole spectrum,
uncertainty is evident: whether one should collect quantitative or
qualitative data; whether description and explanation are more useful
than understanding; whether there is any future in disaggregate
methods; whether the time-space methodology is more than description;
whether policy conclusions can be drawn from activity-based
approaches; whether models should be based on simple explicit
assumptions, on simulation, or on better analytical techniques;
whether models have to predict accurately or not; whether there is
a consistent relationship between attitudes and behaviour; and whether

one can in face apply precise methods of analysis to imprecise social situations.

Despite this uncertainty, transport analysis methods are at present in the process of reassessment, and a crossroads has been reached. There has recently been a decline in modelling activity, but the methods used have been remarkably resistant to change. The conclusion is that the various approaches should be viewed as complementary and not competing; each set of methods has both strong and weak points, and so the key question is first to identify the problem and then to select the best available method for analysis.

There are three main conclusions reached here: first, the scope for transport analysis should be broadened. Secondly, no single method of survey and analysis should be used; rather, different complementary approaches should be employed. Thirdly, research should not concentrate on the development of any one method to the exclusion of the others; even though fashion may exert a short-term influence, the objective must be to ensure a continuous generation of new ideas and processes.

Theory and practice:
the London experience

PAUL PRESTWOOD-SMITH

1.   INTRODUCTION AND BACKGROUND

The development of transport planning as it is currently understood is relatively recent; in fact much of it has taken place over the last twenty years. The first studies of travel demand in Britain were in the late 1950s and early 1960s, and followed the earlier American work in this field. Projects such as the first South East Lancashire and North East Cheshire (SELNEC) study and the Leicester Study were essentially simple assignment exercises of existing and future road traffic based upon the simplest of growth assumptions. These early studies were carried out by the more enlightened local authorities lucky enough to have staff with a knowledge of the American work in this field, or in the case of the larger metropolitan areas by the Department of Transport on behalf of the county authorities.

But it was not until the London Traffic Survey (LTS) of 1962 that full advantage was taken of the American work and the funda-mental relationship between land use and traffic was recognized (Greater London Council 1964, 1966). These later studies, such as the LTS, were carried out by American, or American and British consultants, who were able fully to utilize the American technology and implement it in a British context. These studies were largely concerned with the potential growth in car ownership and long-term large-scale road network solutions. While the concepts and assumpt-ions on which these studies were based were relatively simple compared with the more detailed assumptions that are made today, they set the framework within which subsequent development has taken place. The 1960s were probably the most productive time in transport planning and led not only to considerable technical development but also to its rapid spread throughout the United Kingdom.

Until the 1960s transport planning, and many other aspects of town and country planning, had been conducted on a fragmented basis. For example in 1917, the planning of the Western Avenue in London involved consultation with no less than twenty-three authorities. Proposals for a unitary authority with responsibility for transport planning were first made by Rees Jeffreys to the Royal Commission on

London Traffic in 1905. Competition and free market forces led to the combination of public transport operators, and in 1933 the London Passenger Transport Board was set up in London to coordinate and operate most of the public transport services. However the first move towards a unitary authority was not until 1963-65 when the Greater London Council (GLC) was instituted, with powers of strategic planning and of the Highway Authority for London. These powers were extended in the Transport (London) Act 1969 when the Council was then required to develop policies, to encourage, organize and where appropriate carry out measures which would promote the provision of integrated, efficient and economic transport facilities and services for Greater London.

By the late 1960s, while most travel demand studies were still being carried out by consultants, the initiative for research and development - in the case of London, practice - was passing to local authorities. At this time the output of the Mathematical Advice Unit (MAU) of the Department of Transport (DTp) was beginning to have a significant impact on transport planning while the GLC was totally occupied with assembling the Greater London Development Plan (GLDP). The relationship between land use and transport had been formally recognized by the requirement for the publication and public scrutiny of structure plans, the first of which was the GLDP. The public inquiry into the GLDP and the subsequent publication of the reports of the inquiry Panel marked the end of an era in UK transport planning.

By the early 1970s, while there was some concern as to the results of analytical transport planning, the scene was quite firmly set for the developments which took place in the remainder of the decade. Comprehensive transport planning models, while criticized for their forms and function, were formally established and more widely known and used. They provided a common framework for discussion, and they led to better understanding: 'of the relationship between land use, public and private transport; of the effects of road network capacity restraint; and of those factors which might be used in evaluation. Where quantification could be accepted, they served to qualify subjective judgement. Much had been learnt about data collection techniques so that where the results of comprehensive transport models were less useful, separate independent analysis and modelling could be used.

Following the GLDP inquiry much more attention was paid to the detailed development of transport policy. Planners were less concerned with the large-scale strategic road network solutions to the growth in car use. They became more concerned with the impact of the car and new roads upon the environment, controls over the use of the private car, the role of public transport, and the identification of those who would gain and lose through the transport proposals. While research continued into the detailed aspects of the modelling of travel demand, the greater emphasis in transport planning was upon the analysis and review of transport objectives and the continuing development of transport policy.

During this period of time local government outside London had been reorganized (1974) along the lines of the GLC, thus giving strategic planning and transport responsibilities to the shire and metropolitan county authorities. Passenger Transport Authorities (PTAs) were set up in 1968 to coordinate public transport services and plan improvements jointly with the metropolitan authorities; and the Transport Policies and Programmes (TPP) system was established in 1974, thus constituting a proper financial framework for the development of national and local authority transport. At the same time the setting of the main guidelines for longer-term development in the form of structure plans and their examination through public inquiry procedures became established practice.

Studies in the 1960s were based upon simple assumptions about future trends of such factors as population, employment, incomes and car ownership and use, and development concentrated on techniques relating these factors to future travel demand. Structure plans had a definitive view of future development, derived from these deterministic basic assumptions, and transport plans were equally inflexible. Throughout the 1970s there was an increasing need to revise these basic assumptions with corresponding reviews of forecasts and policy, and the future looks more uncertain. The earlier blueprint-style structure plans could not cope with these uncertainties, yet it is difficult to draw up a new style of structure plan that can deal with uncertainty without undue ambiguity and vagueness. This presents a new challenge to planners to adapt to the new situation by developing techniques and policies flexible enough to cope with a wide range of possible futures. 'Transport in London - A Longer Range View' is an interesting example of this more flexible approach (Greater London Council 1977). It is a form of 'scenario writing' in which different levels of usage of the transport system are postulated and - given various assumptions on availability of funds - different policy packages are examined.

2.   PLANNING FACTORS AND TRAVEL DEMAND

Population forecasts

In the early 1960s in spite of losses of population from inner city areas, losses which actually had been occurring since the first census in 1890, it was still confidently expected that redevelopment plans and planning permissions, already granted in the euphoria of rebuilding post war Britain, would lead to an increase in population in urban areas. In London taking an area bounded by the London Traffic Survey and Greater London Transport Survey (LTS GLTS cordons), it was expected that population would increase from 8.8m in 1964 to 9.1m by 1981, an increase of some 3.6 per cent. Employment in London, closely linked to population, was also expected to increase slightly from 4.8m to 5.3m (+11.4 per cent) while the central area would maintain its dominant role, growing from 1.4 in 1964 to 1.6m by 1981.

It had become clear by the late 1960s, however, that these estimates of urban population would not be achieved. In London, although population expectations were repeatedly re-adjusted downwards during the GLDP inquiry, it was still thought that by 1981 the population would be some 8.1m and would stabilize at this figure down to 1991. It had also been recognized that central London employment since 1964/66 had begun to decline with considerable implications for the planning of bus and rail services. Central area employment was expected to fall from 1.4m in 1964 to 1.2m by 1981/1991, while overall employment would fall from 4.8m to 4.3m.

Throughout the early 1970s, as understanding of demographic forecasting and monitoring of population levels through mid-year estimates improved, forecasts of urban population, particularly in metropolitan areas, were repeatedly revised downwards. Assumptions concerning birth rates however are crucial, and following more recent information in this respect, present expectations of future urban population are now slightly higher than before, but show a widening range. Expectations for London suggest some 7.8m by 1981 while estimates for 1991 vary from 7.5m to 7.8m (table 1).

Table 1. London (GLTS area) - population projections (in millions)

Projection date	1962	1971	1981	1991
1964 (LTS) *	8.8	-	9.1	-
1970 (GLDP) +	8.8	-	8.1	8.1
1977 (GLTS) †	8.8	-	7.8	7.5 - 7.8

* London Traffic Survey
+ Greater London Development Plan
† Greater London Transportation Study

Employment forecasts

While the changes in population are better understood, the general understanding of the economic base of the city and the cause and effect of the changing pattern of employment remains depressingly poor. Improved census statistics on migration and journeys to work allow improved estimates of employment to be made from demographic projections. Inevitably however, they reflect the changes predicted for population. By 1977 the GLTS (Greater London Transportation Study) forecast for London was some 3.9m jobs by 1991 with some 1.0m jobs in the central area (table 2).

Table 2. London (GLTS area) - employment projections (in millions)

Projection date	1962	1971	1981	1991
1964 (LTS)	4.8	-	5.3	-
(Central area)	(1.4)		(1.6)	
1970 (GLDP)	4.8	-	4.3	-
(Central area)	(1.4)		(1.2)	-
1977 (GLTS)	4.8	-	4.1	3.9
(Central area)	(1.4)		(1.1)	(1.0)

Car ownership forecasts

Throughout the 1960s estimates of future car ownership were directly related to changes in household income. In the early part of the decade growth rates of over 3 per cent per annum were expected in incomes, giving rise to an expected car population of some 2.5m by 1981. By the time of the GLDP the favoured figure was around 2.3 per cent giving rise to a car population in London of 2.4m by 1981 and 2.9m by 1991.

At that time the effects of changing car prices, the relationship between Gross Domestic Product (GDP), household income and disposable income had all been included in the car ownership model and subsequent projections. However, changed expectations throughout the 1970s again influenced the projections of car ownership. Incomes are not expected to grow by more than 16 per cent from 1971 to 1981; and since 1973/74 the prices of cars, instead of falling at a rate of some 2 per cent per annum as they did before 1971, have begun to rise at an average rate of something less than 1 per cent per annum. The picture of car price changes is made more complex by the changes in the average life span of cars, the changes in the average size of cars, and (more recently) increasing company car ownership. A factor which has further complicated the picture has been decreasing household size, which in terms of total cars owned has tended to offset the effects of lower income growth. Most recent estimates for car population in London are 2.0m for 1981 and some 2.3m by 1991 (table 3).

Table 3. London (GLTS area) - projections of the number of cars owned (in millions).

Projection date	1981	1991
1964 (LTS)	2.5	–
1970 (GLDP)	2.4	2.9
1977 (GLTS)	2.0	2.3

Projections of the number of households with cars give a first indication of how changes in population, households and incomes may affect projections of travel demand (table 4).

Table 4. London (GLTS area) - numbers of households with cars (in millions)

Projection date	1961	1971	1981	1991
1964 (LTS)	1.2	1.7	2.1	–
1970 (GLDP)	1.2	1.5	1.9	2.2
1977 (GLTS)	1.2	1.5	–	1.9

Total travel demand

Since the early 1970s, planners have recognized and begun to understand the effects of other factors on travel demand such as public transport fares and petrol prices. The effect of these factors on journey length and mode of travel are now included in conventional transport models. Petrol prices and fares however also influence the total number of journeys made but are not as yet well enough understood to be included as part of trip generation models. However it is instructive to look at demand forecasts in terms of total vehicle journeys (i.e. excluding effects of fares and petrol prices) to see how changed expectations of population, employment and income growth have affected projections of total travel demand.

Table 5 illustrates that while the earlier forecasts expected a considerable growth in total journey demand, more recent estimates suggest that the future total demand for travel will be little different from that experienced today, clearly demonstrating the importance of the assumptions made.

The breakdown of these journeys by mode of travel provides a much more important set of statistics in terms of the development of public policy. Table 6 gives the number of journeys by London

Table 5. London (GLTS area) – Total journey demand by residents (million of journeys per average weekday).

Projection date	1962	1971	1981	1991
1964 (LTS)	11.3	–	16.7	–
1970 (GLDP)	11.3	–	14.9	16.6
1977 (GLTS)	11.3	12.6	–	12.4

residents for a typical weekday as reported in the London Traffic Survey in 1962 and the changes that were then expected by 1971 and 1981. Revised assumptions in population, employment and growth in car ownership had given the GLC cause to revise the forecasts for the GLDP; in addition, a further comprehensive survey of travel was carried out in 1971 (Greater London Council 1974).

Table 6. London (GLTS area) – Journey demand by mode of travel (millions of journeys per average weekday).

	Mode	1962	1971	1981	1991
1964 (LTS)	Car driver	4.1	6.6	9.0	–
	Public transport	5.9	5.0	4.4	–
1970 (GLDP)	Car driver	4.1	5.2	–	–
	Public transport	5.9	5.0	–	–
1977 (GLTS)	Car driver	4.1	–	–	5.9
	Public transport	5.9	–	–	4.0

The 1971 survey showed that there had been considerable growth in car use, but not quite as much as expected. The decline of the use of public transport had continued, but there had been a greater decline in the use of the bus system than had been expected. Rail and underground, on the other hand, had maintained their market share but rail travel to central London had shown a small fall. The distribution of these changes over London was also some cause for concern. In inner London the demand for car travel had remained relatively constant but falling population and employment had led to a large fall in bus travel. In outer London, in the more stable areas, public transport patronage had fallen by some 25 per cent but car travel had increased considerably.

Although the future is much more uncertain, current forecasts based upon more recent estimates of population, employment, incomes and car ownership suggest that the trends emerging throughout the 1970s are likely to continue in the future (table 6). The main lessons to be learnt from these trends are clear.

Growth in car ownership and use is still expected to continue but with a falling population, much slower income growth, and increasing petrol prices, future usage will be less than previously expected; again, in the inner areas there will be little change with the main growth in car use occurring in outer London. The decline in public transport usage is expected to continue, in particular with respect to bus use in outer London. Rail travel to the central area may also be expected to show a slow but steady decline.

Such views of the future have persuaded central government and

metropolitan areas to revise regional policies in order to encourage
population and employment back to the inner cities. Increases in the
cost of travel may encourage these policies; on the other hand,
public expenditure cuts could work against them. If these policies
are successful they could have a marked effect on the future distribution of population and employment and subsequently on travel
demand patterns.

3.   THE DEVELOPMENT OF PUBLIC POLICY

In the 1950s and 1960s public policies were mainly concerned with
measures to cope with the increasing demand for road space. The more
immediate increase in provision of road space was achieved through
local improvements, traffic management and traffic control, while
longer-term planning was concerned with the development of comprehensive road networks, a hierarchy of roads and standards of
operation. The forecasts which formed the basis of longer-term plans
were principally concerned with growth of car ownership and use, and
where public transport journeys were forecast, they were usually a by-
product of the trip end estimates. Separate distribution and
assignment to the public transport network was rarely undertaken. The
assignment of projected growth in car use to the longer-term strategic
road networks gave considerable cause for concern. The proposed networks were not capable of absorbing the projected growth in traffic
and would have required roads of dimensions quite out of scale with
the urban structure. Forecasting techniques were reviewed, with more
attention paid to public transport journeys and the possible
restraint of car journeys compatible with the capacity of the road
network. Economic evaluation, which began with the assessment of
inter-urban road schemes, became more widely used in an urban context
and was extended to cover transport solutions which included both
road and public transport networks. In London, by the time of the
GLDP, the longer-term plans included the role of public transport and
anticipated restraint of car traffic possibly through parking
controls. It also included a preferred road plan which had been
selected on operational planning and economic criteria and which,
though considerable in scale and in terms of investment, represented
a feasible construction proposition, if society was prepared to pay
the price.
      Over this period of time, falling bus patronage had been accommo-
dated by service reductions and fare increases in order to preserve
the broad objective that the revenue from fares should match the cost
of operation of public transport services. Rail services had also
been following the changing distribution of population, with service
reductions in the inner areas and preferential fares for the longer-
distance commuter. The potential for increasing road capacity through
traffic management measures was limited, with traffic control schemes
providing some breathing space but not a long-term solution. In the
late 1960s the unhappy experience with the construction of urban
motorways, planned in the 1950s and early 1960s without due attention
to the urban environment, had begun to call into question solutions
based on large-scale urban motorway networks. The public inquiry
into the Greater London Development Plan provided the impetus for a
complete review of transport objectives in the early 1970s (Greater
London Council 1970, 1973).

There was broad agreement that the objectives for transport
planning, previously expressed simply in operational and commercial
terms, should now be expressed in terms of more general economic
criteria. Moreover, it was agreed that because an effective pricing
system could not be introduced for transport as a whole, in particular
for use of the road network, social benefit cost terms should be
employed. Costs would set constraints on alternative plans of
action; then, the best of the remaining alternatives would be that
showing the greatest benefit. However, technical disagreements
arose over the detailed methods, such as the use of the first year
rate of return, the precise contribution of tax benefit, the treatment of land cost and blight. Some of these initial problems were
subsequently resolved, but more basically, the overall evaluation
procedures were found to be in need of fundamental revision. First,
there was the need for a practical evaluation of possible financial,
cultural, political or practical constraints on which an alternative
might founder; for example, public attitudes to loss of housing,
practical problems of enforcement of traffic restraint and – perhaps
most important – availability of finances to fund projects. Secondly,
it was necessary to examine the effects of alternative solutions from
the points of view of those bodies with particular transport responsibilities. It might be that a solution showed an overall net social
benefit, but it could show a financial loss for the public transport
operator. Furthermore this examination should also check whether the
objectives of these various authorities were mutually consistent; for
example, were the objectives of the highway authority for roads
consistent with those of the public transport operator for the use of
roads by buses? Thirdly, there was the problem of the incidence of
benefits amongst the various categories of transport user. The
perception of the transport problem for the car driver and the rail
or bus passenger may be quite different; for example, the effects of
a poundsworth of benefit for a low-income bus passenger may be
different to those for a high-income rail traveller. Fourthly, there
was the question of how to incorporate in the evaluation those items
of account which deny quantifiable assessment; such as the promo-
tional effects of new transport facilities on land use, and in
particular the environmental effects on residents arising from
traffic noise, fumes and visual intrusion.

Public transport policy
The re-examination of objectives in the early 1970s was (as already
noted) precipitated by the public reaction to urban motorway construction, and the emphasis in transport planning turned towards
public transport as a solution to the urban transport problem. The
early steps in the argument stemmed from analysis of problems associated with travel, paricularly peak period travel, to central areas.
It had long been accepted that demand for journeys to central areas
were beyond the capacity of conceivable road plans and that future
travel to central areas would continue to rely on public transport
services. It was also recognized that increases in road capacity
through major road improvement, while easing the flow of traffic,
also brought environmental disbenefits. In inner urban areas where
car ownership was low these disbenefits were the more unacceptable.
Control of central area car travel therefore had become accepted
practice. This argument was now extended. If central area car

travel could be reduced by improvements to public transport as well as increased restraint measures, this would release road space in inner areas.   This would in turn improve operating conditions, attract more passengers to public transport services, and bring environmental relief to inner residential areas.

Many of the improvements to public transport have been made on the basis of this reasoning.   In the early 1970s the emphasis was generally on improvements in bus journey time, for example, bus lanes, bus priorities and particular traffic management schemes giving advantages to buses.   Subsequent measures to improve rail services included improved signalling and service frequencies, improved interchange facilities, park-and-ride services and new forms of ticketing. Whilst these measures have reduced journey times, the improvements have in general been marginal.   In particular, bus lanes have not led to improved bus speeds due to difficulties of enforcement.   On the other hand, they have led to improvements in reliability and retained existing levels of patronage.   In many respects reliability, not necessarily frequency of services, is the major issue in public transport operation, particularly on the lower frequency services. Many of the priorities in public transport are now aimed at operational improvements to reliability such as garage modernization, radio control of bus services, signal automation and improved bus and train design (see Warman, this volume).

In the early 1970s considerable stress was laid on new technology to improve the role of public transport.   Many of these proposed schemes were based on savings in manual operation and were designed to provide personalized services which would be more competitive with the private car than conventional forms of public transport.   However the total costs of these proposals - including the costs of vehicle manufacture, of track construction and of operation - did not justify them as viable alternatives to more orthodox use of bus and rail. The future of such unorthodox solutions to urban transport problems remains in considerable doubt; the stress has shifted on to improvements in the operation and efficiency of existing tracked systems.

Because of the wide variety of service provided by buses - including main journeys, linking of mixed mode journeys and collector services to railway stations - there was a greater opportunity to experiment with alternative forms of operation and service, for example, mini-bus services, dial-a-ride, and express bus services to supplement the radial rail network.   Some of these experiments have proved successful and no doubt others will be tried.   However, few of these experiments have escaped the general malaise of public transport: that fares revenue does not match operating costs.

In the late 1960s, when blanket subsidies were a reluctantly accepted remedy for rail deficiency, specific grants for unremunerative services were introduced following the failure of the Beeching rationalization of the railways.   In the early 1970s it soon became clear that if public transport patronage was to be maintained through improved services and reasonable fare levels, subsidies would be required to support urban rail and bus systems.

Throughout the last decade, the promotion of public transport remained a main plank in urban transport policy.   However, the considerable increases in costs of operation and increased restrictions on public expenditure have thrown into sharp relief the questions of what levels of service and what levels of subsidy are to be provided.

Central government has taken the view that its contribution to
subsidies towards urban public transport must be reduced, while local
authorities have discovered that there is some evidence to show that
subsidies should not be drawn from increased rates. The case against
the use of blanket subsidies to rail services has been made, even if
not accepted; however, the case for specific subsidies remains. While
reduced rates for the elderly and for school children are accepted
practice, there must also be a case for subsidies to urban rail
travel to reduce demands upon the road system and as part of an overall plan for urban travel. The case for subsidies to urban rail
services, however, is weakened since the main markets for rail
services are those longer-distance journeys to central areas and
strategic centres. These passengers enjoy higher-than-average income
and can bear greater increases in costs. Furthermore, should these
journeys be made by car, they are more amenable to restraint measures.

The needs for subsidies to bus services are the greater and will
become more acute. With falling population in inner city areas, it
will become increasingly difficult to maintain existing service levels
without considerable increases in subsidies or fares. The precise
solution will vary from area to area, will depend on local opinion,
and will be the subject of much analysis and deliberation. The
objective will be to balance the reductions in levels of service and
the increases in the levels of fares, so as to have the minimum
effect on patronage. They will be the more palatable if accompanied
by improvements in reliability, which should be obtainable in part by
increased efficiency on the part of the operators.

Private transport policy
Restraint on car use became a widely accepted objective, particularly
for busy areas at busy periods, in association with the promotion of
the use of public transport. Levels and methods of restraint however
proved difficult to establish and are still in the development stages.
Throughout the 1970s, the main means of restraint was through
physical measures and parking controls. Many of the traffic management measures introduced to improve bus operation or the environment
resulted in a loss of road capacity. These measures were generally
incremental in their approach and the average car traveller adjusted
to them by changing his journey routeing, his mode or his time of
travel. More radical plans for physical restraint were more
dependent upon the availability of suitable ring road capacity to
take the displaced traffic. Where introduced in British cities, as
in Nottingham, they failed to convert the motorist to park-and-ride
and the use of alternative public transport facilities; thus they did
not gain public acceptance. The greater emphasis has therefore
remained on parking controls.

Control of parking began with limitation of on-street parking
and the provision of off-street spaces, in order to improve traffic
flows. It was subsequently extended by reducing the numbers of on-
street meters, limiting off-street public spaces (including temporary
car parks) through planning control and controlling the residential
use of road space for parking by the introduction of residential
parking permits. Although not a marked problem in many cities,
control of private non-residential parking spaces in offices and
other land uses had become a major cause of concern in central London
where such spaces represent some 50 per cent of all available

parking space. In spite of these changes in parking control there remain major problems. There is the question of enforcement: the difficulties of finding the necessary manpower, the cost of yet another labour-intensive and non-productive activity, and the problems of identification and proof in the courts of law which have promoted some criticism. The keeper's liability rule and the centralization of vehicle registrations should improve legal procedures; new methods of intensive spot checking will improve enforcement; and increases in fines and towing away charges can help reduce the level of illegal parking. In spite of its inherent drawbacks, in particular the problems of enforcement, parking control is widely accepted by the public and has undoubtedly contributed to the restraint of traffic to and from central areas and other strategic centres. Nevertheless, parking control will not be able to control the volume of through traffic. Therefore, if it is deemed necessary to control traffic other than by the crude physical limitation imposed by the capacity of the network, alternative measures will be required.

Several studies have indicated the benefits to be achieved through some form of road pricing. The experience of Singapore has demonstrated the viability and practicability of such schemes as supplementary licensing, at least given the conditions prevailing in that country. However, in Britain these methods have not yet received political acceptance so there is no operational demonstration. Many arguments have been put forward in opposition to pricing as a means of restraint, such as the difficulties of enforcement, the effects on certain groups of traveller (e.g. the unsubsidized as compared with the subsidized motorist), the effects on commercial concerns, and the longer-term effects on land use. While there is limited evidence of the viability of such schemes, similar concerns that have been expressed about car-free zones have in fact proved unfounded. What is required is some suitable opportunity to test out such ideas on a small-scale experimental basis, such that if the experiment were to prove unsuccessful it could be abandoned without undue difficulty and embarrassment.

Throughout the 1970s, the promotion of public transport has remained the mainstay of urban transport policy. Oil price rises and economic recessions have interrupted the continuous growth in car ownership and use; nevertheless, with economic growth - albeit at a lower rate than had previously been enjoyed - and continued outward migration of population and employment, society has become increasingly dependant upon the private car. Most of the urban roads and street systems were built with other modes of travel in mind. They are now used for a wide range of purposes and many remain unsuitable for the heavy volumes of traffic that they are expected to carry. But with severe restrictions on public expenditure and with the public deeply conscious of the environmental impact of road construction, there has been only limited major improvements to urban road systems in the 1970s. Improvements have been restricted to local road and junction improvements, and to those major schemes where there is an overwhelming case and for which there has been considerable local support. In periods of inflation, large wage settlements and resulting increases in public transport operating costs, together with constraints on public expenditure and restrictions on public transport revenue support, the view has been reinforced that while public transport can and will continue to provide for certain patterns of urban travel, a

greater proportion has been and will be accommodated by the private
car. However, while this trend may continue, energy scarcity and the
rising cost of motoring are likely to moderate it in future.

Freight transport policy
The need for recognizable main road networks operating with consistent
standards, with properly designated secondary and local roads, has
remained and has become more widely accepted. This has been supported
by at least two lines of argument. In the latter part of the 1960s
changes in commercial and industrial operation and improvements in
commercial transport costs went hand in hand with the greater use of
larger goods vehicles. For example, while the total number of goods
vehicles operating in London remained relatively stable, the number of
large lorries (greater than 5 tons) increased by some 74 per cent.
This growth continued in the 1970s and with it public concern for the
environmental effects of these heavy goods vehicles. This concern
prompted the development of performance criteria to control noise and
pollutant emissions, research programmes into the development of
quieter and less obtrusive vehicles, and road management policies to
control the use and operation of heavy goods vehicles. Early proposals
for lorry routes were unacceptable since residents fronting on one road
did not wish to acquire the environmental problems of others. Local
bans, however, are providing much relief and, as more bans are
introduced, they are *de facto* defining a system of roads more suitable
for lorry use. Local authorities have also begun to take the
initiative in providing lorry parks to remove the irritation of overnight on-street parking and to provide office accommodation, break
bulk and vehicle maintenance facilities. As policies to control
heavy vehicles have developed, so has the recognition of the contribution that road freight traffic makes to the urban economy. It is
estimated that over 90 per cent of the volume of goods and commodities
transported in urban areas are carried by road. The argument continues that improvements in the urban economic base will follow efficient
goods vehicle operation and that this is dependent upon improved road
networks.
   The second argument follows on from the first. It is argued that
only with a sound economic base will population return to declining
inner city areas. Now that government and regional policies have
been reversed to redirect resources to inner cities, new, purpose-
designed roads can provide not only for the movement of people and
goods and the efficient operation of existing enterprises, but can
also encourage the establishment of new enterprises and promote the
regeneration of inner cities. The argument is somewhat tenuous and
has yet to be satisfactorily quantified in modelling terms but
history is strewn with examples of land development promoted by the
construction of transport facilities, and instinctively the planner
recognizes this relationship which is at the very heart of transport
planning.

4. CONCLUSION

The development of transport planning over the past twenty years has
been remarkable. While the early concepts and assumptions have formed
a framework for development, unexpected changes in technology,
planning factors, and public attitudes have produced a present
different to that anticipated. However, policies, transport systems

and urban structure have adapted to change. The future looks even
more uncertain; it will become increasingly difficult to predict the
effects of change. This will throw into sharper relief the difficulty of developing current plans and policies consistent with
longer-term aims and objectives. Here is an interesting challenge to
the planner to develop techniques and policies flexible enough to
deal with an unexpected future.

REFERENCES

Greater London Council (1964) *London Traffic Survey*, Vol. 1. July.
Greater London Council (1966) *London Traffic Survey*, Vol. II. July.
Greater London Council (1970) *Greater London Development Plan*,
     Public Inquiry, Subject Evidence. November.
Greater London Council (1973) *Greater London Development Plan*,
     Report of the Panel of Inquiry. London: HMSO.
Greater London Council (1974) *Greater London Transportation Study*,
     Initial Results, Research Report 18.
Greater London Council (1977) *Transport in London - A Longer Range
     View*. March.

What do we want from travel demand analysis?

MARVIN MANHEIM

1. INTRODUCTION

In the original invitation to prepare this paper, it was suggested
that I should give a comprehensive overview of current American
research in understanding travel behaviour. I declined, for two
reasons: first, to do a comprehensive overview is a very major task,
given the diversity and volume of research and practical applications
now going on. Secondly, and much more importantly, I do not believe
that the central message lies in the cataloguing of this research, but
in highlighting certain themes emergent in some of the current work.
For those who do feel the need for a survey, I recommend the papers
by Huw Williams and Andrew Daly in this volume; also Ben-Akiva *et al*.
(1978); Ben-Akiva, Lerman and Manheim (1976); Hensher and Stopher
(1979); and other recent conference proceedings.

In this paper, I want to give a personal position statement as
to the perspectives on travel demand modelling that I see emerging.
To do this, I will first summarize briefly today's world of transport planning and decision making. Then, I would like to examine
briefly the changed nature of transport planning and the way this
has changed our image of the role of the planner and his/her analysis
activities. Finally, I will draw some implications for travel demand
modelling.

2. THE ENVIRONMENT OF TRANSPORTATION ANALYSIS

Let me summarize today's image of transport planning and decision-
making, as I am sure we all know it on both sides of the Atlantic.
Today's situation consists of:
1. Multiple options to be implemented, ranging from new facilities,
to changes in vehicle fleet size and characteristics, to traffic
management, public transport routing and scheduling, pricing and
regulatory schemes, etc. (the whole is known as Transportation
Systems Management in the United States).
2. Multiple impacts to be considered, including not only direct
costs and revenues to users and operators, but also concerns for

mobility for a wide variety of potential user groups such as the
elderly, handicapped, low-income, non-car owning and other groups,
and a concern also with land development and redevelopment and such
environmental effects as air quality, traffic noise, disruption of
residential neighbourhoods, air pollution and energy consumption.
3. Consequent on the above, a concern for the distributional aspects
of transport system changes - the incidence of gains and losses - and
the equity issues associated with alternative distributions of gains
and losses.
4. A commitment to an open planning process, in which multiple
interest groups provide inputs throughout the process of reaching
decisions about transport projects, whether those transport projects
be major infrastructure changes, or primarily short-range policy-
oriented actions.

    Thus, today's environment of transport planning and decision-
making is a complex and multifaceted one. In this environment, for
transport decisions to be implementable and implemented, the actions
which are proposed and considered for adoption by decision-makers must
be feasible not only technically, but also politically. 'Decision-
makers' - those individuals with formal decision-making responsibility,
whoever they are - can and will take a decision only when they have
reached a point at which they understand (1) the major alternatives
open to them; (2) the major advantages and disadvantages of each
alternative, with particular attention to the incidence of gains and
losses; and (3) the viewpoints of all interests significantly
interested in or affected by the decision. Only if these conditions
are met can decision-makers take a decision with reasonable confidence
that they can implement it (Manheim, *et al.* 1975; Mannheim 1979b;
FHWA 1973; UMTA 1976).

3. IMPLICATIONS FOR ROLE OF PLANNERS

This environment implies that planners and analysts must operate as
'staff to decision-makers' in a complex institutional arena. That is,
they must operate professionally to support the information needs of
decision-makers, formal and informal. Various terms have been used to
describe the kinds of activities in which technical staff must
participate in this environment: 'catalyst', 'coordinator', 'entrepreneur', and others. These terms all suggest styles of work which
involve interaction with individuals and interest groups as well as
traditional technical work. One specific model which has been
proposed to guide this style of work is that technical staff must try
to develop 'substantial, politically-effective agreement on a course
of action which is feasible, equitable and desirable'. This objective
is proposed whether one is trying to put together a new public transport pricing policy, or to implement a major traffic management scheme
or a road project (Manheim 1979b; Manheim *et al.* 1975). Other models
might also be proposed to guide professional practice in this new
environment.

    The general image described above has had numerous practical
ramifications. For example, in public transport management, the
notion has evolved of a transport 'broker', in which a single agency
develops and implements a broad variety of service strategies. Thus,
a public transport undertaking may develop, and manage, in addition to
regular fixed-route and fixed-schedule bus services, such services as

shared-ride taxi services operated by private operators, on a contract basis or independently, car-pooling coordination services where large employers take primary responsibility for matching pool members, van-pooling programmes where large employers provide vans for employee use on a shared-ride basis, and specialized services operated by social service agencies for elderly or handicapped, or welfare-dependent services (Bradley 1979).

As another example, in urban transport planning agencies the focus has shifted from the traditional emphasis on long-range, comprehensive, area-wide planning, to development and analysis of specific near-term implementable projects directed towards specific problems or specific markets; for example, bus-lanes or car-restricted zones in central business districts, sub-regional traffic management schemes, arterial road improvements and traffic schemes in a particular corridor, specialized public transport service improvements for a particular market segment, etc.

These changes affect the role of the planner in two ways: first, the need to operate in interaction with various groups as 'catalyst', 'coordinator', 'entrepreneur', etc., as described above: and second, in the use of technical analysis.

To see the changes in the use of technical analyses, let us review the way in which travel predictions were used in the 'classical era' of urban transport planning. In this era, the primary transport planning activity revolved around the development and analysis of alternative comprehensive schemes for land use and transport, for a time horizon twenty to thirty years in the future. In this environment, while analysts did spend some time developing alternatives, the primary focus of transport planners' activities was the management of large-scale data collection efforts and the development of a set of models to be used for predicting the effects of the various land use and transport strategies. The evaluation methods used were generally economic analysis or other quantitative methods.

It appears to me that during this period there was a highly technocratic overtone to the nature of transport planning activity. That is, planners were almost wholly oriented towards the abstract intellectual activities of developing and using large-scale models and the related technical apparatus (for example, cost-benefit analysis). The whole style of analysis was that of attempting to do a relatively rational, objective and value-neutral assessment of the likely effects of alternative courses of action and to evaluate those effects with the use of evaluation methods which were nominally value-neutral. It seems to me that the implicit image of professional activity was one of aloofness from the political process, staying very far away from the value issues of conflicting goals and objectives, standing apart from the emotionally-expressed needs and desires of various interest groups. Thus, we attempted to operate as objective professionals, in a sense of proceeding deliberately and supposedly unemotionally through the steps of a widely-accepted (among professionals) technical process. This implied a personal professional style of seeking to develop predictions of consequences of alternative plans (for example, travel forecasts) on the basis of systems of models which represented high standards of technical excellence and in which the role of judgement was minimized, at least in principle.

In this style, the planner hoped to be viewed as a technical expert. His/her major political role would be to appear at meetings or public hearings or inquiries as an expert who would talk in a value-neutral way about the likely effects of various alternatives, and the reasons why a particular plan, evaluated in a value-neutral technical manner, appeared to be best for society as a whole.

In today's world, I believe that the style of the transport analyst has to be very different, if one is to survive technically and politically and if one hopes to do a useful job. In today's world, where the 'catalyst'-'coordinator'-'entrepreneur' role is an important part of our professional activity, it is very difficult for transport professionals to stay aloof, in an attempt to be wholly objective and value-neutral. Rather, they must be thoughtful, yet aggressive, interveners in the process, trying to change people's perceptions of what alternatives are available, of the advantages and disadvantages of various alternatives, and of what it is feasible to achieve technically and politically. In this function, analysis will be useful and should be used, but in a support role, not as the dominant professional activity.

In this style of work, the transport professional will rarely succeed in being wholly value-neutral and objective. Rather, the decision-makers, whether public transport system general managers or city councils or mayors or governors or ministers, will look to the transport professional (if they look to him or her at all) as an individual professional whose advice and insights they find useful. To respond effectively, the transport professional must first and foremost stand on his or her own feet intellectually and professionally. He or she must be prepared to make judgements, often with relatively little data, sometimes with more; often with relatively little time to do an analysis; often with little prior preparation (but sometimes with substantial opportunity for significant technical studies); and almost always with attention to the political aspects, especially who gains and who loses and how they feel about it; and sometimes, perhaps, also able to place equal attention on the technical aspects. In other words, transport professionals must operate first and foremost as 'professional staff', with analysis activities in a secondary 'support' role.

Perhaps a useful analogy is that of the manager of a private enterprise. He must, first and foremost, take decisions. He can use analysis support, if it can produce information which is useful and timely; but he will take decisions with or without analysis. So too with transport decision-makers.

Some would argue that supporting decision-makers in this way is not appropriate for transport professionals. I will argue that it is an appropriate, legitimate, and necessary role for transport professionals if we are to have an impact on actual transport decisions.

4.   IMPLICATIONS FOR TRAVEL DEMAND ANALYSIS

What does this say about analysis tools in general, and tools for predicting traveller behaviour in particular? To me, this says that we must have a range of techniques ready in our arsenal in our daily working environments. We will use some of these techniques to try to develop insights in each particular decision situation, and to assist us in communicating these insights to others. These techniques should include, potentially, large-scale, formal model systems such as we often developed in the past, small-scale problem-specific models implemented in computer environments, and quick and responsive analysis techniques utilizing pocket calculators or nomograms or sliderules. These 'techniques' should also include the ability to make insightful judgements, informed in some cases by economic reasoning and knowledge about such things as 'typical' elasticities, and informed in other cases from other perspectives, such as inductive case studies or surveys or samples developed from a methodological basis in sociology, anthropology, or psychology. So, to my mind, there is not one single 'best' direction for developing operationally-useful insights into travel behaviour. Rather, our attention ought to be focused on what we can learn from each of several types and levels of research into travel behaviour and how we can utilize effectively the results gained from each type of activity.

My personal judgements (or biases, if you will) are these:
1. Disaggregate econometric models are very powerful as a major advance over the traditional models, for a number of reasons: sounder behaviourial reasoning (within the context of economic theories of behaviour); much more powerful and valid statistical estimation approaches than used for traditional aggregate models; and, especially importantly, the capability for being employed for forecasting purposes in a wide range of ways. For example, in several related works (Manheim 1979b; Manheim *et al*. 1978; Daly, in this volume; Ben-Akiva *et al*. 1976), we discuss a wide range of ways in which disaggregate models can be used for forecasting, ranging from the traditional large-scale regional model systems, to short-range policy-oriented computer-based procedures, to pocket calculator procedures and manual work-sheet procedures (using only pencil and paper). The key element that excites me about disaggregate models is that they open the door to a wide variety of ways to developing insightful, valid and policy-relevant analysis techniques, for a wide variety of analysis situations and styles, as illustrated by this range of developments.
2. At the same time, we recognize the limitations of the particular economic models of consumer behaviour that underly the application of such econometric methods as disaggregate modelling (at the present state of the art). Clearly there are many insights to be gained through other social science research methods, including psychological or 'market research', and through inductive case study approaches, illustrated by the HATS techniques developed by Heggie, Jones and colleagues (Jones 1979). These classes of techniques do have major limitations, by comparison with the disaggregate econometric methods; we do not yet have practical ways of utilizing these techniques for predictions of behaviour of groups of individuals in a formal, systematic way. While this is a liability, it is counterbalanced by the qualitative insights that we can gain by these techniques.

Therefore, from my point of view, I would like to have in our arsenal a range of travel behaviour analysis methods, including formal predictive methods developed with the best state-of-the-art of econometric methods, as well as less formal methods, and insights, developed from a wide variety of different perspectives. When a transport analyst goes into a particular problem-solving situation, whether it be urban transport planning at the sub-regional scale, public transport brokerage on an area-wide or localized basis, or whatever, I would like that analyst to be able to draw on a variety of available analysis techniques and accumulated insights and to

choose from among those techniques one, or several, which would be
most useful to him or her in a particular problem-solving situation.

In some cases, it may be useful just to go out and count passengers on a couple of bus routes for two days, and interview twenty or
thirty households, perhaps in an open-ended format, or perhaps using
a more formal HATS-type simulation. Alternatively, it may be useful
to take available published census data, develop a synthetic sample
of households from such data, apply a previously-developed disaggregate demand model to that sample of households, and predict bus
passengers' responses to alternative strategies from that sample,
using pocket calculators or simple manual methods or simple computer
programs (Manheim *et al.* 1978). Or alternatively, there may be
sufficient staff resources and time available for doing analysis so
that both sets of techniques can be utilized (for example, if one is
doing this on a regular basis as staff within a public transport
organization who provide input to route and schedule changes quarter-
ly or semi-annually).

While it is useful to discuss what are the most important
directions to go in further research, I would like us also to explore
this question: to equip transport planners and analysts better for
today's role, what do we need to do to disseminate more effectively
the capability to do analysis in this range of styles? This means
we also must ask, which are the ten or fifteen most promising methodologies that we would like practicing transport planners to
understand? What are the advantages and disadvantages of each
technique? How should an analyst think through which technique(s) to
use in a particular situation?

Finally, I want to close by re-emphasizing the theme of technocratic style I raised earlier. I am glad that we are finally
beginning to admit that travel forecasts are instruments rather than
ends; that evaluation is a complex activity and not simply the
application of packaged computer programs to do packaged economic
analyses (for example, Leitch 1978); and that analysts should be useful to decision-makers. In this context, it is very important that
significant attention be given to understanding traveller behaviour
and assessing the directions of such changes. It is also very
important that some significant attention be given to shaking loose
the transport professional bureaucracies and disseminating to them
the changes in attitudes and perceptions and professional work styles,
and potential modelling approaches, that we have been discussing here
(see for example the increased professional responsibility implied by
a more programmatic planning process, in Manheim 1979a).

I do not wish to say that we should not have much more basic
research to develop a deeper understanding of traveller behaviour.
This is certainly essential: it is appalling how much money we spend
on transportation and how little money we spend on trying to understand consumer behaviour. However, while there is, in every country,
a paucity of appropriate basic research in travel behaviour, there is
also a real gap between the results of basic research and the entry
of these results into the 'pipeline'; the steps of prototypical
application, production development and dissemination to practicing
professionals in the field.

While I am not knowledgeable of what intellectual trends may be
emerging in the transportation community in the United Kingdom, I am
aware of substantial discussions of these issues in the United

States, in France and in some other countries, and I am also aware of
the difficulties of bringing about change in what transport
professionals perceive as legitimate or appropriate professional work
styles. These are the issues to which travel demand analysts should
be addressing themselves.

ACKNOWLEDGMENTS

This note draws substantially on research and ideas of many
colleagues, and most especially Moshe Ben-Akiva. In addition,
because of the vastness and diversity of work going on, I have not
endeavoured to cite references in any comprehensive way. Rather, I
have chosen simply to refer to a few selected items, primarily out of
our research group, which further amplify the themes developed in
this very brief position statement. Many of the ideas and comments
made here are expressed elsewhere in the literature, as the source
referenced in the documents cited here will indicate.

REFERENCES

Ben-Akiva, M.E., Lerman, S.R. and Manheim, M.L. (1976) Disaggregate
    models: an overview of some recent research results and
    practical applications. In Proceedings of PTRC Annual Summer
    Meeting, University of Warwick.
Ben-Akiva, M.E., Manheim, M.L. and Salomon, I. (1978) Policy-
    sensitive and responsive transportation planning: applications of
    transportation demand, performance and equilibration models.
    Paper presented at the Joint International Meeting on the Inte-
    gration of Traffic and Transportation Engineering in Urban
    Planning, Tel Aviv, Israel.
Bradley, R. (1979) Draft proposal for Urban Mass Transportation
    Administration support to the Greater Bridgeport Transit
    District. Bridgeport, Conneticut.
Federal Highway Administration (1973) *Process Guidelines (Social,
    Economic, and Environmental Effects of Highway Projects)*, Policy
    and Procedure Memorandum 90-4 (codified in Federal Aid Highway
    Program Manual as Vol. 7, Ch. 7, Section D). Washington, DC:
    Government Printing Office.
Gray, G.E. and Hoel, L.A. (eds.) (1979) *Public Transportation:
    Planning, Operations and Management*. Englewood Cliffs, NJ:
    Prentice Hall.
Hensher, D.A. and Stopher, P.R. (eds.) (1979) *Behavioural Travel
    Modelling*. London: Croom Helm.
Jones, P.M. (1979) 'HATS': A technique for investigating household
    decisions. *Environment and Planning A*, 11, pp. 59-70.
Leitch, Sir G. (1978) *Report of the Advisory Committee on Trunk Road
    Assessment*. Department of Transport, London: HMSO.
Manheim, M.L. (1979a) Towards more programmatic planning, in Gray,
    G.E. and Hoel, L.A. (eds.) *Public Transportation: Planning,
    Operations and Management*. Englewood Cliffs, NJ: Prentice Hall.
Manheim, M.L. (1979b) *Fundamentals of Transportation Systems
    Analysis; Vol. 1. Basic Concepts*. Cambridge, Mass: MIT Press.
Manheim, M.L. *et al.* (1975) *Transportation Decision-Making: A Guide
    to Social and Environmental Considerations*. NCHRP Report No.
    156. National Cooperative Highway Research Program, Transport-

ation Research Board, Washington, DC.
Manheim, M.L., Furth, P. and Salomon, I. (1978) Responsive
    transportation analysis: pocket calculator methods. Vol. 1.
    Introduction to calculator methods; Vol. 2. Examples of
    transportation analyses using pocket calculators; Vol. 3. Program
    library, part 1: using calculator programs, part 2: technical
    documentation. Working papers prepared by the Responsive
    Analysis Methods Project (RAMP), Center for Transportation
    Studies, Massachusetts Institute of Technology, Cambridge, Mass.
Urban Mass Transportation Administration (1976) *Major Urban Mass
    Transportation Investments*, Federal Register 41: 185, Part II.
    Washington DC: Government Printing Office.

A perspective
on urban systems analysis

MICHAEL BATTY

1. INTRODUCTION: A PARADOX OBSERVED

It is a common enough feature of social life that conflicts between
individuals and groups often remain unresolved despite quite strong
motivation on all sides to seek some compromise. Conflicts persist
and attempts at solution take on a perennial character, usually due
to the increasingly disparate and irreconcilable goals of the actors
involved. Yet at the same time, this type of history is characterized
by recurrent attempts to reach a compromise, thus indicating that
although actors sense the difficulties involved, some decision is
necessary simply to proceed or progress. There are many examples of
such behaviour. Political history is full of such conflicts spanning
the global-international to local-parochial scales. Although decisions are made for expediency, conflict is never really resolved. It
is more likely that changing conditions in the environment and
changing perceptions on the part of the actors lead to the conflict
disappearing as it is no longer judged to be important.

Nevertheless, when conflicts do persist, they can often be interpreted as cyclical phenomena; intense periods of attempting to resolve
conflict are followed by disillusion and disengagement from the
struggle. But reflection on the continuing need for resolution means
that the quest is never abandoned and eventually the fray is joined
once again. In a complex and uncertain world, it appears that such
behaviour characterizes the interaction between many opposed but
necessarily related actors such as trade unionists and employers,
professionals and politicians, scientists and humanists, and so on.
Conflict is the cement which ties these groups together and as Marx
would have it, such behaviour contains elements of both comedy and
tragedy.

There is a certain sense of paradox in all of this, and this is
particularly well illustrated by the recent history of professional
and technical involvement in a variety of government and public policy
making. The professional-political interface has always implied a
dilemma over questions of value, but as important is the relevance and
usefulness of the professional knowledge, brought to bear as advice on

which politicians must make decisions. In public policy making, such
advice clearly reflects a plurality of interests, and when decisions
are ultimately made this must reflect a weighting or priority ordering
of those interests. Thus the knowledge brought to bear is necessarily
partial and in the light of the action to be taken, seemingly inadequate. Yet the action must be taken, and once engendered, the results
rarely please any of those involved. Inevitably, this reflects upon
the source of the advice in the first place, and often the knowledge
and its professionalization falls into disrepute.

In few cases, however, is the knowledge ever judged to be sufficiently inadequate to be abandoned. Once the dust settles and a
broader perspective on the problem regained, the knowledge might be
used once again to attempt to resolve the conflict, perhaps from a
slightly different standpoint. Thus another cycle begins which builds
on the previous one. Indeed, government policy at a variety of
levels, certainly during the last thirty years, seems to be dominated
by such cycles of action and reaction, optimism and pessimism, engage-
ment and disengagement, and this appears to be the dominant mode in
which the world moves on.

Such an image seems to be particularly applicable to the development of new forms of theory and analysis to aid policy making and
problem solving, especially in the public sector, but to a lesser
extent at all levels of management. It is widely recognized that as
wealth has increased, the opportunities for more diverse and varied
social behaviour have also been increased, social constraints have
been relaxed, and in short, the world has become a more complex place
to understand and plan for. New forms of knowledge addressing such
complexity, have been a natural consequence. Moreover, as the opportunities for conflict have increased, this has led to a multiplicity
of problems hitherto unknown.

In an effort to tackle such problems, governments have prolifer-
ated the variety of society by increasing bureaucracy, thus adding
greater opportunities for addressing such problems, but in essence,
only adding to the problems themselves. Furthermore, the development
of a new analytic capability through the revolution in computers and
information processing rather than containing such problems, has given
complexity an added twist. A new dimension of coping with complexity
has evolved but this in turn has brought its own complexity. Thus it
is becoming widely felt that the increasing proliferation of variety
by the very instruments and organizations designed to contain it, is
one of the most insidious and difficult problems of the times (Beer
1974; Steinbruner 1974).

It is not surprising that professionals and politicians alike when
faced with such a bewildering array of problems, should turn to areas
of knowledge which have, in some sense, a proven performance in
problem solving. Science and its applied face - technology - have
dominated popular attitudes towards problem solving for fifty years,
perhaps longer. With the development of large-scale information
processing systems after World War II, the stage was reached when
scientific theory could be developed for a variety of systems and
problems, not hitherto so researched due to their complexity and
scale. Social systems were a case in point. As soon as computers
became commercially available in the early 1950s, attempts began to
develop scientific and systematic analyses of such systems using the
burgeoning power of the computer as a means for representing and

manipulating complexity. In a rather general sense, this activity
was called systems analysis, the terminology being strongly reflective
of the interest in general systems theories of all types of organized
phenomena, pioneered two decades or so ago.

Systems analysis consists of two integral phases: the representation of the system itself as a theory or model in computable,
numerical terms, and the use of that model in some applied context.
Information processing is central to the means of representation and
application centres around the process or medium of model-building.
In the urban sphere, the first attempts at such analysis were in the
area of transport modelling in the early 1950s, and these developments
were closely followed by applications to land-use location, and public
systems - urban service systems - during the 1960s. In these areas,
perhaps public systems models, with their emphasis on rather ordered
day-to-day functions of the urban system, are the best defined and
most contained, although some transport models might justify this
claim. Land-use models, on the other hand, are much broader and
abstract, and have always been more problematic. Lastly, urban
systems analysis has been applied to the wider operations of the
planning or governing agencies themselves, involving the corporate
functions of such organizations rather than their traditional planning
- problem solving-activities.

The recent history of these areas certainly illustrates the
cyclical phenomena referred to earlier and the development of these
ideas has been the subject of great euphoria and deep pessimism. This
has been particularly heightened by the apparently well-defined nature
of the analysis itself, in contrast to other areas of technical advice
such as in economic or defence policy where intuition and gut-feeling
has been given greater reign. Urban systems analysis was too easily
accepted and too aggressively marketed in the first place. Moreover,
the fact that the computer has been so essential to these ideas, has
compounded the false sense of success originally argued for in these
developments. Interestingly, the same is true of other areas dealing
with social behaviour and problems cast in a strict analytic and
computable form. In artificial intelligence and cognitive psychology,
for example, the history of claim and counter-claim, optimism and
pessimism, is as deeply reinforced as in urban systems analysis. In
one sense this is even more so for the notion of man creating a com-
mensurate intelligence, no matter how artificial, goes to the very
roots of philosophy and ethics (McCorduck 1979).

Therefore, the general quest of this paper will be to provide a
perspective for interpreting the success or otherwise of urban systems
analysis in public policy making. Due to the issues of complexity in
social life already alluded to, it is essential to have some overview
of the terrain of both systems analysis and public policy making
before attempting such an evaluation. Indeed, most evaluations so far
have been quite partial, and have sought to emphasize particular
problems of application, rather than some wider context. Given the
strictures already made however, the perspective developed here is
clearly only one from many. The purpose of this paper is not to imply
that this is *the* perspective but that perspectives are required when
attempting to interpret a phenomenon as diverse as systems analysis.
The implication here is that there is an urgent need for such perspectives in developing a critique of systems analysis, rather than a need
for this perspective *per se*.

Thus the paper begins with a brief review of urban systems
analysis and some partial critiques. Then follow two aspects of
complexity and uncertainty in social life which underpin the ideas
developed here: first, the nature of social problems is explored with
an emphasis on definition and closure, and second the constituents of
planning and policy making are described. The links between knowledge
and action in the guises of theory and practice, science and design,
are emphasized, and problem solving relating to each of these inter-
relationships is presented. Models are defined as providing the
bridge between theory and practice, and between science and design,
and it is then argued that planning or policy making is concerned with
both types of problem solving. These ideas are then used to examine
what has been learnt through the development of this field, and then
the role of fashion in these developments is presented. Finally,
future directions for the field are charted and prospects are
explored.

2. CRITIQUES OF SYSTEMS ANALYSIS

The beginning of systems analysis in government can be traced to the
early 1950s in North America, to the time when computers first became
commercially available and when the complexity of social problems and
the need for a rational attack upon them, was first perceived.
Relatively self-contained problems were handled at first – in particular, problems of transport flow and congestion, and simple analyses
of public service systems. Very quickly, these ideas were generalized
to much less constrained problems of urban policy making. Hard on the
heels of transport models came land-use models in the early 1960s
addressing much wider issues of land-use location, the interrelationship of traffic and land use, and the economic structure of urban
systems. Throughout the decade of the 1960s, operations research
techniques were applied to public systems, involving such services as
police, fire, health, refuse etc., and based upon modelling the somewhat routine operations characterizing these delivery systems. More
recent developments have extended systems analysis to the realm of
government itself; that is, in treating government agencies as public
systems in their own right, thus emphasizing resource allocation and
the budgetary process. In this sense, then, systems analysis has not
only been developed in the planning of urban systems but also to plan
the planning of those systems themselves.

All these areas have been dominated by the cycles referred to
previously and it is worth taking one of these – land-use modelling –
to illustrate the point. During the late 1950s, great euphoria
accompanied the realization in North America, that the computer could
be used as a kind of artificial laboratory in which to explore the
consequences of certain types of plan, thus opening a door to experimentation which had been undreamed of in the social sciences. The
notion that a model of the city could be designed and implemented on
a computer, thus enabling different theories to be tested, alternative
predictions to be made, and optimal prescriptions to be systematically
sought, really caught the imagination of all those who were attempting
to wrestle with urban problems (see Dyckman 1963). Moreover such
models provided order where none had seemed to exist before. As Lee
(1973) so cogently pointed out:
    'Everything seemed to be an urban problem, and everything

seemed interrelated; the whole world was a jumble of secondary and iterative side effects. Some way of integrating it
all was needed without giving anything up ... and computers
and models held out this promise.'
From 1960 to 1965 saw an explosion in land-use modelling. A
diverse selection of models appeared, motivated largely from policy
problems, and mostly developed in a practical context by government
agencies and consultants. But the euphoria was short-lived as the
immensity of the task was realized. Three key problems appeared.
First, there was considerable confusion over how resources were to be
used. In many applications, the data required, the time available,
the related computer technology, general cost, expertise and ability,
all proved insufficient. The scale of the task was totally misper-
ceived. Second, the organizational environment in which models were
built was unsympathetic. Decision-makers wanted instant answers from
instant models, and model-builders thought they could deliver. The
notion that such models provided a magic box belied the fact that
there were and are no easy answers. And lastly, the use of the models
in anything other than a limited forecasting context was not thought
through and thus when it came to making plans, the effort floundered.

Yet there appears, at least in hindsight, to be a much greater
problem which led to reaction against these ideas. The adequacy of
theory was clearly in doubt. Many of the models were theoretically
vacuous, constructed out of bits and pieces of theory but in no consistent or comprehensive manner.   What is more, basic research had
to be conducted in what was effectively a policy environment and this
led to a clash of temperaments. By their nature, model-builders were
inclined to research their models whereas the clients wanted immediate
applications. In short, these difficulties were found out only after
the effort had been started, for in no sense were they anticipated.
A reaction set in. From 1965, to 1970 at least, was a period of
massive retrenchment and disengagement, pessimistic to a degree, and
in Lee's (1973) phrase the movement went 'underground'. Indeed, Lee's
(1973) article proclaiming 'a requiem' for such work implied that the
field was now dead and buried, and many who read Lee's polemic, but
do not follow the field, still believe this.

In fact, the reaction led to reflection and by the early 1970s, a
revival of sorts was beginning. More work on theoretical models
emerged from the universities, more caution and less ambition characterized new applications in practice and in a sense, the reaction from
burnt fingers set against a continuing practical need, led to much
more sensitive applications of systems analysis. Indeed, Lee's (1973)
quote, reproduced above, not only shows why models were used but shows
why they continue to be used. As Pack (1978) has shown in the United
States, there has been an amazing proliferation of modelling applications through the 1970s. In fact, it appears that all the surveys
of model use to date indicate that upwards of 50 per cent of relevant
planning agencies are involved with using systems analysis (Batty
1979).

There is substantial evidence too, especially in the United
States, that the present second cycle of work in land-use modelling is
being deeply enriched by new theoretical work, thus representing a
diversification of the field in general. The situation elsewhere is a
little different. In Britain for example, a period of reaction still
dominates but the original work came later anyway and it is possible

that the new theoretical work emerging will give a spur to further
applications. In fact, the critiques of the experience have only
emerged in the 1970s after the deepest reaction had set in. Indeed
in the United States, the late 1970s have seen the emergence of anti-
critiques (for example, Kain 1978) which have sought to set the
experience in a wider context. In contrast to Lee's 'requiem', Pack
and Pack (1977) see a 'resurrection' of the field, and all of these
attempts demonstrate the need to see this field in wider perspective
of the kind being attempted here.

In setting the context to a perspective on urban systems analysis,
it is worth being a little more explicit about the partial, rather
restrictive nature of the existing critiques of this field. This can
be elaborated in terms of the key difficulties alluded to above,
namely scale and organization of the effort. Many of the critiques
have focused on the difficulty of developing systems analysis in
particular organizations. Brewer (1973) in his seminal book on the
horrific stories of the San Francisco and Pittsburgh Community Renewal
Program models, mainly deals with the abuse and misuse of models,
rather than use. His criticism is a poignant reminder of the exploit-
ation of mysticism which could occur in any field, but is particularly
prevalent in this one. A much less damaging but equally cogent
critique is that by Hoos (1972) whose survey of systems analysis in
military and other corporate contexts, again reveals the tendency to
'blind with science' and equally tragic, to 'want to be blinded by it'.
Perhaps the clearest evidence of genuine organizational difficulties
is that presented by Greenberger, Crenson and Crissey (1976) in their
review of the difficulties experienced by the Rand-New York City
Institute in their construction of public systems models for New York
City. In the event, it is easy to separate these difficulties from
the substance of the analysis itself and to argue that these things
happen with any applied technique. But in fact, there is a connection
for it is with techniques which are so reliant upon the experience,
wisdom even, of the expert, that such difficulties abound. And this
certainly has implications for the organization of future work.

The second set of critiques relate more to the model-building
process and how this is organized, and this involves the question of
scale. Lee's (1973) critique is the most vociferous in that he argues
that the early experience with systems analysis was blinded by scale:
models were too big, too expensive, and too blunt for the tasks
required of them. Their theoretical base was too inadequate and Lee
concludes that although right in principle, such analysis is unsuitable in practice and likely to be so for a long time to come. Similar
critiques have been developed elsewhere (see for example, Cole (1974)
in Britain), but in general, the question of scale is one which has
not halted these developments. Systems analysts have dealt with such
questions easily by adapting their models and developing a sensitivity
to the demands of the problem context.

Running through all these critiques is a rather confused notion of
evaluation which seeks to blend critique of scientific merit with
critique of instrumental merit in the policy context. Although inevitably related, there should at least be a clear distinction between
the use of analytic techniques and models in a scientific context -
to help produce a better understanding of the world, and the use of
such techniques to aid policy making - to help change the world. This
distinction revolves around the time scale involved, and the

motivations adopted. Better theory and understanding is a continuing
quest whereas policies are a product of the moment. This difference
is caught up in the cliché that policy-makers cannot delay until
appropriate theory is forthcoming.   Indeed the history of science
shows that theory can always be improved. The debate has been recurrent throughout urban modelling. An early but also somewhat
propitious exchange between two of the doyens of the urban modelling
field, Britton Harris and Ira Lowry, led Lowry (1967) to comment:
      'On reading this paper on the problem of optimal design, my
      first reflection was that if God had been exposed to Professor
      Harris' instruction, he would have postponed the Creation
      indefinitely and applied to the Ford Foundation for a
      research grant.'
In all these critiques and comments, this central distinction,
although realized, has been rarely thought through. Implicit in a
good deal of the criticism has been the notion that good theories from
a scientific standpoint imply good practice from a policy standpoint.
In fact, it is assumed that once good theories have been 'discovered',
better understanding and better prescription will go hand-in-hand.   In
other words, the cycle of action and reaction, caused by using inadequate theory to form what must inevitably appear inadequate policy,
will eventually disappear. This implication ignores the different
motivations involved in knowledge and action, science and design, and
in this thesis, it will be argued that what is required is a perspective which accepts that these differences will exist. For only by
such acceptance, can one learn to develop a balanced view of what is
possible in using systems analysis in policy making. Moreover, the
view espoused here is also tempered by the realization that any such
perspective must in itself be inadequate in some senses, for it is
built upon the critiques, the experience, the reflections on the
development of this field thus far. This is not the last word on how
to interpret systems analysis in public policy making; but it does
imply that such interpretations must always fall back on a theory of
the wider context. And it is to this that the discussion now turns.

3. ON THE NATURE OF SOCIAL PROBLEMS

The only determinate way to define a problem is in terms of its solution. It is a simple consequence of this point that the system in
which a problem and its solution are embedded must in some sense be
closed; that is bounded so that the system is potentially understandable in a total sense. Clearly, such systems only exist in the realm
of mathematics and are hence abstractions for in reality or at least
any perception of it, there is always uncertainty. The implication
of this important but brief excursion into philosophy is related to
the popular conception of problem solving and its critique in a policy
making context. As argued above, the popular conception of science is
one in which it is assumed to have produced 'successful' solutions to
important problems, and this has largely accounted for the transfer-
ence of scientific ideology to the social domain. Yet for social
problem solving to meet the 'success' of science, the system of
interest must in some sense be closed. Put in these terms, nothing
could spell greater contradictions for the nature of social systems,
and thus it is not surprising that scientific analysis has failed
to live up to the kind of 'success' it appears to have generated

elsewhere.

There are two points which flow from this argument. The first concerns the nature of social problems in terms of their closure, their tractability, and the second concerns the appropriate strategy for dealing with them, given their nature. Both will form the essence of the perspective to be developed here and each will be elaborated in the sequel. It can also be argued in science that there are no systems which meet the requirements of total closure, apart from perhaps those stationary and isolated systems such as the universe which have been shown to be closed. But even this is debatable for the argument is clearly related to the level of resolution, level of abstraction and must thus be relative like all the others.

In short, our ability to define problems at all in any total sense, in the social domain, must be highly questionable, for it is extremely difficult to identify closed social systems at any level. The way theory has developed in the social sciences is not reduction- ist as in science, but in terms of different dimensions or ways of looking at social phenomena. Economic, sociological, psychological, spatial, temporal and many other dimensions exist and in no way can these be separated from one another in seeking a comprehensive view. This is in marked contrast to physical and natural science where hierarchical structure is articulate and where it is possible to get 'useful' understanding of the phenomena from different vantage points: chemical, physical, biological and so on.

This point has rarely been appreciated by theorists in social science, by those concerned with devising theory of the social domain or by the recipients of such theory, that is those empowered to decide. Yet in the last two decades, as more thought has been given to the development of social systems theory, there has been a kind of progress. In psychological problem solving, the notion of the ill- structured problem has come to the fore (Reitman 1965), problems which can only be solved, if at all, to a degree of approximation. And considerable effort has been devoted to procedures for solving such ill-structured or ill-defined problems using heuristics. These have become the basis for research into artificial intelligence and mani- fest enormous promise (Simon 1977).

More generally, it is being recognized that the problem of closure cannot be put aside when attempting to apply systems analysis in the social domain: it must be broached directly. The problem of closure is one in which it is necessary to accept the Hegelian axiom that everything is related to everything else, and in the absence of finding a way to discriminate clearly between the importance of relationships, social problems must at least be accepted in their totality. Ackoff (1974) makes the point very cogently in his argument that systems analysts must employ a style of problem solving which deals with a *system* of ill-structured problems. In somewhat light- hearted vein, he defines a system of problems as a 'mess' and he argues that the job of system analysts is to get to grips with 'messes'. Dramatic imagery perhaps but essential in learning about the nature of social problems.

A similar imagery has been invoked by Strauch (1975) who terms the ill-defined problem a 'squishy' problem. Strauch argues that policy problems in particular are sufficiently ill-defined to admit a variety of viewpoints and one of his examples involving recognition of such a problem is so good that it is worth repeating here. He gives the example of a configuration of letters and numbers which due to the level of discrimination/observation, is ambiguous. Consider the following configuration which might be drawn using a stencil:

Dependent upon one's perspective, it is possible to see the sequence as letters horizontally, numbers vertically; that is as part of an alphabet or a number system. But it is also clear that a total understanding can only be achieved by holding both perspectives in mind together.

Social problems are very much like this: they are inadequately perceived from one perspective or another and it is necessary to look at the total context to generate any clear understanding. For example, consider the problem of inequality. From a sociological perspective, the concept of equity can be very different from the economic perspective, and they may even contradict one another. But together they can do nothing but enrich the analysis. In spatial planning for example, what might appear to be a non-problem spatially, might take on new importance when viewed in non-spatial terms, witness the problem of locating low-income housing in low-rent areas on the edge of a city. There are countless other examples in the social sciences. And one of the major dilemmas in systems analysis has been embodying these different perspectives into models which enrich rather than stultify policy analysis.

Strauch's configuration reproduced above can be manipulated endlessly to illustrate the necessity of adopting the whole set of perspectives. Alphabets are closed while number systems are open but in the overall configuration, the resulting system takes on yet another characteristic of openness. Dependent upon how such systems are partitioned, entirely different forms of system might be imagined. The totality is required for any sense to be made of the system. Artificial though these examples may be, they do give some insights into the difficulty of defining systems, and this leads directly to the difficulties inherent in the related activity of problem solving. Indeed, problems of defining the system itself, and of defining the problem of the system both form the essence of problem solving in a planning or policy context. And at this stage, it is worthwhile elaborating this point.

4. PROBLEMS OF KNOWLEDGE AND ACTION

A central tenet of planning and policy making rests on the notion that such activity is primarily about using knowledge to change the world in some way, rather than solely understand it. Knowledge and action represent two poles which are spanned by the activity of planning. The imagery of problem definition and problem solving conjured up here, is reflected in these two poles of planning. Problems of understanding and of changing the world involve processes of problem solving, and this distinction is so important to the ideas that follow, that they will be spelt out again in rather a different form.

Solving the problem of understanding concerns defining the system of interest and gaining a requisite understanding through devising theories and models. This type of problem solving is akin to the process of hypothesizing and falsifying appropriate theory and thus involves the normal scientific method. In the social sciences in general and urban analysis in particular, the system of interest – the social system or the city system – is intrinsically ill-defined in any perception and can rarely be expressed in closed form. The partiality of existing disciplinary perspectives and the difficulties over observing such systems in any detached way inevitably lead to inadequate theory.

The same dilemmas exist over solving the problem of change. The system involving the activity of planning is different from that involving understanding, and thus the problem is even more confounded. Rarely are there social problems which can be identified and solved by and for one individual; for by their nature, the problems of interest are collective, involving different interest groups, with different viewpoints and value systems. In this sense, these problems are also ill-defined. Combined with the inadequacy of theory which is relevant to defining social problems in the first place, the uncertainty about what is to be planned, why it should be, and how it should be done using systems analysis, is magnified many fold.

Indeed, it is arguable although not so relevant a pursuit here, that problem definition and problem solving in the contexts of understanding – science, and of changing – design, are so inextricably linked in social systems that it is positively misleading to emphasize these distinctions. Although this viewpoint is growing as more thought is given to the nature of social systems, these distinctions still dominate the activity of planning and policy making. Given this situation, urban social problems are never likely to be solved in any total sense, although the development of systems analysis and its application during the 1960s were implicitly postulated on the basis that such problems could be solved. An important result of such endeavours, however, through reflecting upon the difficulties alluded to above, has been the development of a much deeper understanding of social problems and possibilities for their solution. For example, Downs (1972) in discussing ecological problems such as pollution, says:

> 'The implication is that every obstacle can be eliminated and every problem solved *without any fundamental restructuring of society itself*, if only we devote sufficient effort to it. In older and perhaps wiser cultures, there is an underlying sense of irony or even pessimism which springs from a widespread and often confirmed belief that many problems cannot be 'solved' at all in any complete sense. Only recently has this more pessimistic view begun to develop in our culture.'

Attempts have been made to develop theories of planning in which the nature of this dilemma is exposed. Rittel and Webber (1973) call

such problems 'wicked' in that attempts to solve them lead to unfore-
seen consequences, often exacerbating the original problem itself.
The problems which science in its guise as systems analysis and operations research can actually solve, are those which are 'tame' or
'benign'; in short, those which are well-defined. As argued at length
already, in social systems there is no such thing as the well-defined
problem, for such systems cannot be closed in any sense. Recognition
of this point has been slow in coming but is beginning to emerge.
Webber (1978) says:

> 'Moreover, since no condition or event can be seen as iso-
> lated, every problem is but a symptom of some deeper problem
> imbedded in the next larger subsystem; and that perception
> compels a depth of humility guaranteed to turn the most
> evangelical reformer into the most cautious planner.'

A variety of commentators on the current social condition and
attempts at improving it, have echoed Webber's words. Schumacher
(1973) in his famous polemic *Small is Beautiful* makes a series of
similar points. In talking of problems of economic inequality, he
argues that present strategies by Western governments simply shift
problems from one domain to another - out of sight, out of mind, so to
speak. And the lack of any real closure in problem solving implies
that: 'As one problem is being "solved" ten new problems arise as a
result of the first "solution", (Schumacher 1973, p. 23). Furthermore
like Webber, Schumacher argues that what is required in approaching
such problems is not 'clever research' but such wisdom which can only
be acquired through experience, reflection and learning.

The implications from all these home-spun philosophies, and there
are many more not directly referred to here, are that the dilemmas of
using well-defined, but inadequate theory to inform ill-defined
problems, mean that: 'Social problems are never solved' (Rittel and
Webber 1973). They continue: 'At best, they can only be re-solved
over and over again'. Problems may also disappear or dissolve as
conditions change, as our perceptions of what is or is not important
change, or they may be absolved in that what is originally thought of
as a difficulty emerges as a positive advantage. Or they may be
unsolved in that in attempting the 'obvious' solution, the less
obvious solutions which form the glue around the original problem,
become unstuck.

5.   THEORY AND PRACTICE, SCIENCE AND DESIGN

In the previous section, the basic distinction between knowledge and
action was introduced as the guiding light in exploring processes of
both understanding and changing the world. To elaborate the framework, it is worthwhile taking the argument forward in two ways: to
make distinctions between problem solving and planning, and to explore
the role of modelling in this conceptual schema, thus providing a
clearer perspective for evaluating the contribution of urban systems
analysis. Friedmann's (1973) definition of planning as the mediation
between knowledge and action - as the process of using knowledge in
an active context, provides a useful starting point, and his definition can be elaborated in two ways.

First, it is possible to see the creation of knowledge itself as
a type of action, and this involves the distinction between theory
and practice. Second, knowledge reflects what exists in terms of
understanding - science, while action reflects what should exist or

might exist - design. When these two features of knowledge and action
- theory and practice, science and design, are put together, it is
possible to interpret science *or* design as theory *and* practice, and
theory *or* practice, as science *and* design. This picture can be
clarified as follows:

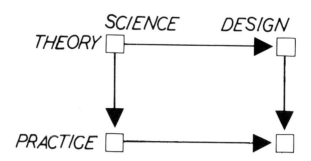

Reading the diagram in a vertical or horizontal direction implies some
process of interrelating these elements. In fact, the processes can
be interpreted as problem solving and the arrows which link and direct
these elements refer to such activities. Although the asymmetry of
the diagram might be debated, at one level of resolution it can be
argued that design requires science whereas science does not depend
upon design; and to produce good science or design, the source of
inspiration is theory or hypothesis, not practice. Clearly such
implications are contestable but a detailed discussion is beyond the
scope of this paper. Interested readers are referred to a related
essay by the author (Batty 1980).
     At this point, a new definition of planning has emerged from the
discussion and this is worthy of an explicit statement. In the spirit
of Friedmann's (1973) thesis, planning is the mediation between knowledge and action and in this perspective, it can be seen as involving
both theory and practice, science and design and the processes which
link them. Planning is about all of these; it embraces different
types of problem solving whether they be cast in a theory-practice,
science design mould. In this sense, the activity of science cannot
be separated from design as is traditionally done in planning. Such
distinctions may exist in an institutional or practical sense or in a
professional sense, but if planning, as Webber (1978) so cogently
argues, is: '... *fundamentally a cognitive style*, not a substantive
field', then problem definition and solving in generating social
knowledge, cannot be separated from the activity of using that knowledge to engender change.
     Onto this conceptual structure, it is easy to map the activities
of systems analysis and modelling. Quite clearly, these activities
characterize modes of problem solving in general, and thus analysis

and modelling can be seen as mediums through which theory is linked to practice, science to design. Indeed, the confusion of definitions over what constitutes a model, can be directly clarified from this discussion. Some researchers working in the field have defined models solely in their theory–practice role. For example, Harris (1966) defines a model as: 'an experimental design based on a theory'. Others define a model in a looser way, emphasizing the notion of establishing a framework for action. Greenberger, Crenson and Crissey (1976), for example, give the following definition:

> 'the model is a repository in which elements of knowledge too numerous to be accommodated simultaneously and assimilated by the unaided human mind are placed in relation to one another within an integrated framework ... The model ... is an instrument for the management of multiple relationships among complex phenomena'.

In this context then, an even broader definition can be proffered. In fact in planning, it is more meaningful to talk about the modelling process, rather than the concept of a model *per se*. Thus modelling is the process of relating knowledge to action or abstracting knowledge through action, whether it be construed as linking theory to practice, science to design. In short then, in planning, scientific, design, theoretical and practical models all exist but each of these must imply the others as the present discussion suggests.

One final point is worthy of note. The perspective developed here can be easily shown to cast light upon the role of models in planning. The uneasy blend of positive and normative models, for example, in the land-use context, has been a source of great confusion. For example, gravitational models of land-use location and interaction very definitely occupy the theory practice domains, and have been designed primarily with understanding in mind. In contrast, normative land-use models such as those based on operations research methods such as linear programming, fall within the science–design continuum. The fact that it is so easy to distinguish between such models shows up one of the real dilemmas of systems analysis in planning: that from whatever viewpoint models are motivated, in planning they will be viewed from all possible angles. The positive–normative relationship which underpins this discussion shows that as systems analysis has developed in planning, it has rarely been conceived in any integrated way. In fact, problems have been defined with only one viewpoint in mind, and thus when models have come to be applied, it has not been possible to embrace other viewpoints, thus leading to failure of the effort. These are the major hurdles to be overcome and the perspective introduced here provides a basis on which to interpret past and present developments as well as future prospects.

6. ANALYSIS AND MODELLING AS STYLES OF LEARNING

It might appear that the historical development of systems analysis in planning through its curious blend of policy scientism, would admit of little progress through its cycles. A good argument could in fact be made to show that social conflicts over what is possible and desirable in the social domain which are not resolved and which perpetuate, become sterile. Action followed by reaction can certainly imply a blind recurrence of behaviour, but in fact in the application of systems analysis, there has been considerable reflection on the

experience from a variety of viewpoints. And this in itself has
meant that much has been learnt. Indeed, a cogent interpretation of
the last two decades in this area might imply that the predominant
style of learning has been through the activity of systems analysis
and modelling: that the quickest way to learn about the limits to
knowledge and action is by attempting to handle ill-defined situations
with well-defined theory.

Learning that has occurred has been diverse but most of it has
been enlightening. The problem of scale which dominated the earliest
attempts at systems analysis was quickly appreciated and this has led
to much less ambitious, more cautious strategies for analysis. In
this field now, there is much more concern for anticipating and balancing out the conflicting requirements of analysis. For example,
researchers have acquired the ability to discriminate not only with
respect to different modes of analysis in different situations, but
also with respect to whether or not to use systems analysis in the
first place. Such expertise only comes through experience and is a
prime indicator that the field has matured through learning. There is
also a stronger sense of the importance of theory too, which implies
that any relevant approach to problem solving must balance theory and
practice in such a way that the knowledge used is obviously useful.

In organizational terms, less has been learnt but this is largely
because there is so little understanding of how the institutions of
modern society function. Indeed in this field like many others, the
agencies involved often seem incapable of absorbing the simplest and
most obvious of ideas. Such organizations seem only intent, only
capable of a concern for survival. Some of the technological physical
factors influencing analysis are also changing dramatically. What
once posed fundamental constraints on what was possible have now
almost disappeared. For example, the present revolution in computing
means that the future availability of computer resources will rarely
ever be the issue it was. Of course, there are still limits but these
limits now provide a scope for applying models which is several orders
of magnitude larger than that available for the inception of these
ideas some two decades or so ago.

Perhaps the most important progress however has been in injecting
a sense of perspective into the field. The argument presented here is
only one of many related concepts being at present explored throughout
the area of the planning-policy sciences. The distinctions between
developing systems analysis in scientific or design contexts, or in
theory or practice, and the consequent mix, often eluded the earliest
advocates of these ideas. The euphoria of those times seemed to wash
over all considerations such as these, but in hindsight, the development of some perspective on how such analysis should be pursued, was
inevitable. This confusion is most clearly seen in the critiques of
systems analysis mentioned earlier. Many have attempted to develop
their critique from partial or single vantage points, or perhaps from
several but without attempting to integrate them. For example, it is
possible to evaluate a model with respect to what is generally
regarded as 'good science' in a passive sense. And the same model
can be regarded from the viewpoint of what constitutes good policy
analysis and proposals; rarely would the criteria for both be the
same, however. In fact, a view from either perspective is likely to
be rather narrow, for such models are normally developed with both in
mind, and are therefore likely to fail from one or the other. What is

acceptable or not in designing an appropriate model in planning is not
something that is easy and unambiguous to evaluate, for the model-
building process itself is constructed on a multitude of value judgements and trade-offs reflecting personal knowledge.

The quest to evaluate models in planning must thus be seen in
other terms, for example, in terms of what has been learnt about the
limits to analysis and in terms of the ability to discriminate, to
know when to use analysis and when to leave well alone, and develop
other approaches. The dilemmas over criteria resulting from the
tension between science and design, theory and practice are unlikely
to ever be resolved. As Brewer (1979) remarks in discussing the
amount of expenditure and effort devoted to such work so far:

> 'Relative to the *potential* value of the work, expenditures
> have probably been too low; relative to the *current* value of
> the work, expenditures have been too high'.

And this situation is likely to prevail for it reflects the nature of
the field and the notion that in understanding and in changing the
social system, it is always possible to do better.

Partial critiques, however, have certainly established a momentum
which has changed the nature of theory in this field. The origins of
urban systems analysis lay in the construction of fairly pragmatic
methods to give immediate aid in urban policy making, and this has
always been something of a sore point with the intellectual establishment. Thus, there has been a continuing attempt to ground such models
in more secure theory, and at present, considerable effort is being
devoted to such research. The developments are best seen in more
well-defined areas such as transport modelling where assumptions and
requirements for good theory have been somewhat easier to pin down.
The traditional aggregative style of modelling in the area, although
quite 'successful',over a long period, has had little to say about
travel behaviour and the values and motivations of travellers. Both
from an empirical standpoint concerning a description of such behaviour, and from the requisite policies to be derived, a change in
emphasis to a more disaggregate, micro-behavioural base was required.
Indeed, the response has been forthcoming and is destined to shake
the field of transport modelling to its core (Manheim 1979). And
such change has been clearly accomplished through the requirements
for knowledge and action relevant to this field.

Elsewhere there have been strong attempts to provide better theory
in the quest for better theory *per se,* and in terms of policy relevance. In land-use modelling, this quest has been less successful due
to the greater uncertainty involved. As yet, research and applications have not moved on from the aggregative paradigm established in
the 1960s, although there are signs that a change is imminent. Developments in micro-economic theory of cities, the so-called 'new urban
economics', are providing strong momentum for change. Developments
in micro-behavioural transport modelling too are likely to have their
effects on land-use modelling, and in a sense, these are required to
break out of the relatively low ebb in which such work at present
finds itself.

Probably the most dramatic changes however emerge from the ideas
already developed in this paper; that is from the wider context. In
the narrowest sense, a concern with the technicalities of analysis
itself has led to substantial insights into the positive-normative
conundrum. This riddle has been the source of considerable confusion

over the use of models in planning but of late, the confusion has been resolved partially through a concern for technical derivation of model types and a meshing of economic rationality with conventional description. It is well-known in modelling that for every consistent set of equations, it is possible to find several plausible procedures to derive or generate the set and at least one of these procedures will involve the optimization of some objective function. That is, for every model, there is a function which if optimized will yield the model, and in this field there has been a growing concern for discovering the types of function which underpin conventional models.

In other words, in mathematics, differences between positive and normative models can simply be in terms of different generating systems. Technical interest in these areas has been transferred to the methodological arena, in that the development of theoretical models in practice using positive method can be clearly linked to the use of those models in normative terms as science in design. The two problem-solving processes implied by these relationships thus correspond to technical derivation and estimation systems. These ideas are cogently explained by Harris (1979) not only as links between positive and normative models, but as links between aggregate and the more disaggregate micro-behavioural focus. The same can be done for transport models (Williams 1980) and some experience is now being gained in developing these ideas in practice (Manheim 1980).

There are comments emerging now on more wider issues. For example, the whole notion of treating phenomena in systems terms is being attacked in formal and consistent ways (see Berlinski 1976) and this is leading to new insights. Most fundamental of all, however, is the search for new paradigms in which to interpret systems analysis. Sayer (1979) argues that if planning is about problem solving, then systems analysis is part of the problem. Thus any attempt to exonerate, or accept the effort and continue it in its present form is also part of the problem. These notions involve questions of ideology, humanism and morality, and broaden the debate considerably. Yet in one sense, the perspective developed here although hardly radical, does provide a foothold on such ideas through the central concept that systems analysis in planning involves the mediation between knowledge and action.

7. FADS, FASHIONS AND BANDWAGONS

The fact that the cycle of action and reaction seems to aid learning in that the limits of what is feasible and desirable are quickly ascertained, does not imply that such cycles are never undermined by undesirable effects. Indeed, the cyclical form of acquiring this type of knowledge is not necessarily desirable in itself, for there are more stable ways of making progress and increasing knowledge. Cycles, in fact, are often plagued, and accentuated by the role of fashion. The active or optimistic phase followed by the reactive or pessimistic phase often corresponds to the use and fall of a fashion, and it is accompanied by the well-known bandwagon effects. In the early stages, the fact that a new set of ideas holds out any hope at all for solving a problem, attracts its supporters; persons who had not conceived or synthesized the possibilities, until made explicit, regard such developments as 'manna from heaven'. This is the stage when a great euphoria exists, but as the problem is researched, and

techniques applied, the ideas are found wanting in an important way.
The problems appear wicked, squishy, intractable, ill-defined, whatever and the prospect of current analysis leading to the promised land
distinctly pales. Many of the adherents grow disillusioned, some find
new causes, some persist in arguing the case but by this time, an
overall reaction has set in. Those who do remain may well reflect on
this state of affairs and subtly change the ground rules, and if
successful provide the momentum for a new cycle in a slightly different guise.

This phenomenon is hardly new for it is recognizable in many
areas. Downs (1972) refers to it as the 'issue-attention cycle' and
he illustrates it in connection with contemporary social events such
as interest in ecology, race problems and the energy crisis. He
characterizes the cycle in five phases: the pre-problem stage when a
highly undesirable social condition exists but has not yet captured
the imagination of the public; alarmed discovery and euphoric emotion;
the realization of the cost of solving the problem; the gradual
decline in public interest; and the post-problem stage - 'a twilight
realm of lesser attention and spasmodic recurrence of interest'.

Many social problems have this nature but some are closer to the
recurrent cycle implied in the development of more abstract knowledge,
such as the use of systems analysis in planning. For example, public
concern over the plight of the British economy is of this form. But
most substantive planning issues seem to be of the kind Downs refers
to. It is in this more abstract realm that continuing cycles seem to
occur and it is possible to speculate that the same kind of issue-
attention but a recurrent one, exists in the debate over education
policy, technique and teaching, economic modelling and forecasting,
and possibly the general area of military strategy and defence policy
(Brewer and Shubik 1979).

In a slightly different context, such cycles often imply the rediscovery of some concept or theory, long ago worked out and used by
some other group not connected with the present issue. This type of
behaviour amounts to a rediscovery of the wheel, and to a limited
extent, this has occurred through the development of urban systems
analysis. Certainly, the realization that to get any semblance of
success with these types of ideas involves casting the ideas in a
wider framework, is the prerogative of wisdom anyway. Even in the
short history of this field, there are countless examples of the
discovery by particular groups of experts that their expertize might
be relevant to solving problems in domains other than those from which
these ideas were originally culled. And this has been particularly
true of those branches of engineering and mathematics which inform
systems analysis.

But the most obvious role of fashion in the development of urban
systems analysis relates to technique. Although not primarily motivated by technicians in search of a problem, for urban systems analysis
was originally inspired through the dictates of practice, once it was
realized that a certain expertise was required, a flood of 'talent'
appeared (Hoos 1972). The field began to explode as many trained in
quantitative knowledge began to apply the ideas and extend the field
itself. Indeed, once the bandwagons were joined these have had
profound effects upon the style of work produced, especially in more
theoretical terms.

This is clearly seen in certain model-building techniques where

the field often takes on the character of branches of applied mathematics, rather than urban studies. For example, in land-use
modelling, such techniques as entropy-maximizing, optimization methods
more generally, estimation and fitting procedures, methods of aggregation and so on have all been developed to a level where progress is
the prerogative of the mathematician. From the outside too, urban
systems analysis is affected by similar fashions being pursued in the
mathematical sciences more generally. Good examples are Thom's
catastrophe theory and Forrester's systems dynamics models, and such
techniques bring with them an army of experts willing to try their
hand at yet another application. In fact, it has been said that parts
of economic theory and management science now to all intents and
purposes resemble,through their published work in journals and texts,
applied mathematics. Game theory, for example, an important element
in the theory of decisions, is one of those areas now classified as
such in most university libraries.

The same is true of other forms of knowledge in the social
sciences. There is a strong bandwagon effect involving the current
interest in social science in ideology and radical critique. In
itself, this may be no bad thing but its worst side relates to the
naïvety and intolerance with respect to other viewpoints which often
accompanies it. In this case, naïvety is expressed as a lack of
awareness for the wider role of analysis in problem solving and
planning emphasized here, but the same goes for more pragmatic viewpoints emerging from practice. In practice, these effects are often
wider and more blatant. Throughout the 1960s, the cycle was affected
and accentuated by the demands of agency after agency for systems
analytic technique. Furthermore as the demand grew, the chances to
make a fast buck, an individual or corporate name, or some advantage
over related agencies, increased, and urban systems analysis had more
than its fair share of charlatans and tricksters (Brewer 1973).

There is a dual, of course, to add to this, and this reflects the
fashion of not wanting systems analysis, a fashion which grew on the
down-turn of the cycle. Both in theory and in practice, can this
negative effect be observed, until the wheel of fashion turns full-
circle and the cycle picks up again. But through all of this there
has been a kind of progress, and even despite the influence of
fashion, there has been learning. Some believe that a threshold of
knowledge will eventually be reached in which these cycles weaken,
progress will appear steadier, and the 'science' of planning will seem
'normal'. This however is perhaps a dream for it assumes a certain
stability which does not match present uncertainty over what constitutes usable knowledge. It may well be that such a course of
development reflects the nature of these types of problem; if so, the
first stage is in understanding the problem through its social
context, not only through the adequacy of technique, and once this is
broached, the ground can be prepared for researching the most appropriate ways to handle such problems. This I believe to be the stage
at which urban systems analysis is now at.

8.   CONCLUSIONS: FUTURE DIRECTIONS

To repeat the central thesis of this paper, existing critiques of
urban systems analysis have been quite partial in that they have
sought to interpret the experience from particular vantage points -

from a scientific standpoint, from a more pragmatic policy-orientated
standpoint and so on. In these terms, the experience appears problematic and prospects for the future do not seem good. But it has been
argued here that a much broader critique is required, one which blends
a variety of viewpoints. And to this end, a perspective has been
suggested which is based on an inquiry into the nature of problem
solving and planning. Seen in these terms, the experience is more
salutary. Much has been learned about the limits to the possible in
using knowledge in the social domain, and it is this ability to learn
and to discriminate which suggests that the experience is much more
healthy than is often assumed.

Future directions in continuing this kind of debate immediately
suggest themselves. To support the perspective, alternative viewpoints from a more practical standpoint should be considered, for the
ideas presented here relate to reflections on a theory of planning.
More case studies of the type conducted by Hoos (1972) and Brewer
(1973) are necessary and in particular, a survey of attitudes to
technical analysis in a policy context, is essential. Invariably,
first impressions about the nature of this experience are misinformed
as Pack (1978) has so poignantly illustrated. But in all of this, the
ideas suggested and the perspective formed provide an approach to
develop the critique further. And in this spirit, the thesis here
only indicates direction. As Warren McCulloch, the pioneer of the
concept of the neuron was so fond of pointing out, when it was later
realized that his early research was inadequate (McCorduck 1979):
'Don't bite my finger, look where I'm pointing!'

REFERENCES

Ackoff, R.L. (1974) *Redesigning the Future: A Systems Approach to Societal Problems*. New York: John Wiley.
Batty, M. (1979) Paradoxes of Science in Public Policy: The baffling case of land use models. *Sistemi Urbani*, 1, pp. 89-122.
Batty, M. (1980) The limits to prediction in science and design science. *Design Studies*, 1, pp. 153-59.
Beer, S. (1974) *Designing Freedom*. London: John Wiley.
Berlinksi, D. (1976) *On Systems Analysis: An Essay concerning the Limitations of some Mathematical Methods in the Social, Political and Biological Sciences*. Cambridge, Mass: MIT Press.
Brewer, G.D. (1973) *Politicians, Bureaucrats and the Consultant: A Critique of Urban Problem Solving*. New York: Basic Books.
Brewer, G.D. (1979) Operational social systems modelling: pitfalls and prospectives. *Policy Sciences*, 10, pp. 157-69.
Brewer, G.D. and Shubik, M. (1979) *The War Game: A Critique of Military Problem Solving*. Cambridge, Mass: Harvard University Press.
Cole, S. (1974) Limitation of large scale models in forecasting. *The Planner*, 60, pp. 646-49.
Downs, A. (1972) Up and down with ecology: the issue-attention cycle. *The Public Interest*, 28, pp. 38-50.
Dyckman, J.W. (1963) The scientific world of the city planners. *American Behavioral Science*, 6, pp. 46-50.
Friedmann, J.R.P. (1973) *Retracking America: A Theory of Transactive Planning*. New York: Anchor Books/Doubleday.

Greenberger, M., Crenson, M.A. and Crissey, B.L. (1976) *Models in the Policy Process: Public Decision Making in the Computer Era*. New York: Russell Sage Foundation.

Harris, B. (1966) The uses of theory in the simulation of urban phenomena. *Journal of the American Institute of Planners, 32*, pp. 258-273.

Harris, B. (1979) Computer aided urban planning: the state of the art, in *Proceedings, International Conference on the Application of Computers in Architecture, Building Design and Urban Planning*. London: Online Conferences , pp. 335-352.

Hoos, I.R. (1972) *Systems Analysis in Public Policy: A Critique*. Berkeley, California: University of California Press.

Kain, J.F. (1978) The use of computer simulation models for policy analysis. *Urban Analysis, 5*, pp. 175-89.

Lee, D.B. (1973) Requiem for large scale models. *Journal of the American Institute of Planners, 39*, pp. 163-78.

Lowry, I.S. (1967) Comment on Britton Harris. *Papers of the Regional Science Association, 19*, pp. 197-98.

Manheim, M.L. (1979) *Fundamentals of Transportation Systems Analysis, Volume 1. Basic Concepts*. Cambridge, Mass: MIT Press.

Manheim, M.L. (1980) What do we want from travel-demand analysis? This volume.

McCorduck, P. (1979) *Machines Who Think: A Personal Inquiry into the History and Prospects of Artificial Intelligence*. San Francisco: W.H. Freeman.

Pack, J.R. (1978) *Urban Models: Diffusion and Policy Applications*, Monograph Series, No. 7. Regional Science Research Institute, Philadelphia.

Pack, H.R., and Pack, J.R. (1977) The resurrection of the urban development model. *Policy Analysis, 3*, pp. 407-27.

Reitman, W.R. (1965) *Cognition and Thought*. New York: John Wiley.

Rittel, H.W.J. and Webber, M.M. (1973) Dilemmas in a general theory of planning. *Policy Sciences, 4*, pp. 155-69.

Sayer, R.A. (1979) Understanding models versus understanding cities. *Environment and Planning A, 11*, pp. 853-62.

Schumacher, E.F. (1973) *Small is Beautiful*. London: Blond and Briggs.

Simon, H.A. (1977) *Models of Discovery and Other Topics in the Method of Science*. Dordrecht-Holland: D. Reidel Publishing Company.

Steinbruner, J.D. (1974) *The Cybernetic Theory of Decision*. Princeton, New Jersey: Princeton University Press.

Strauch, R.E. (1975) "Squishy" problems and quantitative methods. *Policy Sciences, 6*, pp. 175-84.

Webber, M.M. (1978) A difference paradigm for planning, in Burchell, R.W. and Sternlieb, G. (eds.) *Planning Theory in the 1980s*. Center for Urban Policy Research, Rutgers University, New Jersey, pp. 151-62.

Williams, H.C.W.L. (1980) Travel demand forecasting - an overview of theoretical developments. This volume.

Conclusions

DAVID BANISTER and PETER HALL

This final paper, based on the concluding discussions of the seminar group, goes through two stages or cycles to try to define important research questions and priorities. First it seeks to isolate the broad main issues with which research should be concerned. Secondly, from this is goes on to define more closely a number of key research topics.

1. THE MAJOR ISSUES

(i) *Policy, decision-making and political issues*

The first main area concerns the way transport policies are evolved and implemented. Policy is not made in a vacuum. Transport policy is represented by the accumulation over time of a series of decisions, not every one of which will appear to be entirely consistent with its predecessors; there are constant shifts in the environment against which decisions have to be taken. Although the main lines of policy are governed by political philosophy, in practice decisions seem to be made in response to specific and often short-term pressures. We want to know what constitutes the environment which reacts on the decision-makers and policy-formulators, whether they are politicians or career civil servants at central or local government level. We also want to discover how the policy-makers perceive the external environment and how they adapt to it.

One important issue here is the question of how far research findings do contribute to policy formulation and to what extent they are either ignored or even quoted selectively to justify a course of action whose outcome is in doubt. There are numerous issues – such as the effect of alcohol on road accidents or the wearing of seat belts – where the evidence is clear and unambiguous, but where policy either does not get changed, or is changed on paper without these policies being effectively implemented. It would be useful here to undertake a series of case studies against a general background of common theory.

Another interesting type of study would concern local variations

in policy formulation within a common administrative and financial
framework. Transport Policies and Programmes in Britain are an
obvious example: evidently, local authorities have used the degree of
freedom they have been offered to pursue very different policies,
sometimes broadly along party political lines, but sometimes across
them. For instance, differences in policy, combined with local variation in geographical and economic circumstances, may result in public
transport users being subsidised at an annual rate per passenger mile
that is three times as high in one local authority area as in another.
It would be helpful not only to look at the process that led to such
differences, but also to try to evaluate the different outputs in
terms of costs and benefits to different sections of the client population. And it would be interesting to try to relate this back to the
process of policy formulation - to ask, for instance, how far rising
car ownership tends to inhibit local authorities in pursuing a policy
of strong support for public transport (Research Priority (v), below).

Related to this, it might be helpful to study how different
national governments react to similar (indeed nearly identical)
problems in different ways. During the last ten to fifteen years, for
instance, all Western European governments have had to respond to the
fact of rapidly rising car ownership with its attendant problems of
congestion, road building versus traffic restraint (especially in
urban areas) and the weakening viability of public transport systems.
It is superficially clear that though many of the resultant policies
have similarities from one country to another, there are also great
differences - on the amount and character of road building, the fiscal
treatment of car owning and driving, and the support for public transport. A state-of-the-art review, supplementing work already published
under OECD and TRRL auspices, would be of great value here; it should
desirably go beyond a catalogue of the differences, to explain some of
the possible reasons for them. Related to this, it would be useful to
explore the growing importance of international regulation, especially
through the means of the EEC, in such areas as energy and freight
transport.

Policy issues inevitably shade into political ones - as our
European neighbours rightly recognize by employing the same word for
both. The dividing line might be the distinction, already broached
in the last paragraph, between the *description* of policies and policy
differences, and the attempt to *explain* them in terms of the shifting
balance of forces that produces them. To borrow the terms in Peter
Levin's paper, we need to look both at the processes of policy formulation and implementation, and also at the resulting pattern of
outputs. For these outputs are the test of the system, and the
pressures that operate to produce the policies are mostly for or
against specific outputs - even if the imagined output may be rather
different from the one that in fact emerges.

We need therefore to attempt a conceptual schema of the operation
of policy-making institutions in terms of different groups of actors -
the community in its various guises, the political groups both formal
and informal, and the various professional, technical and administrative bureaucracies (Research Priority (v), below). We then need to
employ this in a series of case studies to illuminate the objectives
of the different groups, how they sought to achieve them, and how
these interactions finally produce a stream of policy. Particularly
important and difficult here will be to trace the interaction of

policies on such large measures as support for the car industry on the
pattern of transport at local level. But, here as elsewhere, it will
be often necessary to go beyond the boundaries of transport policy in
the strict sense, to cover closely related areas such as land use,
urban planning, the national health service and housing policy
(Research Priority (ii), below). The main insights in all this will
surely be those of the political scientist, but other social sciences
– particularly social psychology – must play an important role.

     One important aspect of such studies will obviously be an evalua-
tive one. Policies made through a complex process of political
conflict and adjustment, as is so often the case in Britain today,
will inevitably be different from those made in an earlier age when
the vogue for participation was less well developed. One pessimistic
view is that complex participatory decision-making will tend to
produce a kind of total inertia of the system, in which change takes
place very slowly and only on condition that it offends no single
interest group – with the result that radical shifts in output, that
would actually harm one or another group, become impossible. It
would be interesting to study this hypothesis through a number of case
studies (Research Priority (i), below).

(ii) *Social issues*
Once again, the boundary between this and the previous bundle of
issues is a broad and fluid one. Here we are primarily concerned with
the question of impacts of policies on different groups of people and
on areas – with a particular concern for second round, third round
and even more remote effects. Among the numerous research topics
discussed under this heading, the following seem to be most important.

     The first relates to an understanding of the requirements of the
consumer, primarily in terms of information. Research is required to
answer such issues as how the consumer acquires information, how he
assimilates it or becomes overloaded, and what use he makes of the
information. A policy decision – such as installing a telephone in
all households – may seem to be a benefit, but what are the social
implications? Will it be used? Will it act as a substitute for
personal contact? Will it lead to greater isolation? (Research
Priority (iv), below).

     Related to this is the question of knowledge and rationality in
choice. It is unclear for instance whether those without a car
available are aware of the alternatives open to them, or whether they
can appreciate the actual benefits and costs of different modes, or
how they act on the information if they are aware (Research Priority
(iii), below).

     A second research area is an increased understanding of commun-
ities through historical perspectives which would identify how the
present structural and social relationships have developed. This
investigation would include the changes which have occurred or are
likely to occur in resource allocation, as well as the effects of
changes in service and transport provision. Of importance here is the
relationship between the availability of a particular service and the
rate of take-up in terms of use; this point relates to the accessibility issue (Research Priority (ii), below) where one possibility
would be to test various alternative policies such as some form of
transport network planning with a service hierarchy and a system of
collecting routes. This would help to define different life-style
groups and perhaps give some indication of their accessibility needs

(Research Priority (i), below).

This leads into the third priority issue, namely the establishment of a measure of 'needs' and deprivation. The indicators used by local authorities in the first round of the County Public Passenger Transport Plans are mainly aspatial and based on minimum levels of service. Theoretical and practical research is required to determine a social group based measure, perhaps within a particular spatial context with the community having a role to play. The measure should include all sectors, not just transport, and likewise the allocation of resources should consider the total impact of a decision including the distributional effects (Research Priority (i), below).

A fourth and related area for study would be the whole question of subsidies for particular kinds of transport, both of a general nature (capital and/or revenue support for public transport) and of a particular kind (school transport, especially in rural areas; social service transport both in the statutory and voluntary sectors). But a descriptive study alone is likely to ignore the important question of how different individuals and groups perceive their needs and wants and how they pursue them: policies may be designed in good faith to secure aid for one group of the population, but then work to the benefit of another group altogether. Particularly relevant here is the question of the different perceptions and knowledge of relatively well-educated middle-class groups as opposed to socially-deprived ones. All this merely underlines once again the importance of studies that relate the process of policy formulation, seen as a response to pressures of all kinds, to the analysis of the outcomes of the policy. These issues are taken up again under Research Priority (i), below.

Fifthly, it has been suggested that transport research has fallen conceptually behind other kinds of urban planning and related work. There, there has been a marked shift in the late 1970s from a stress on individual responses, towards a Marxist-type analysis of the roles of groups and institutions. In housing research, for instance, the key questions now being asked are: who provides the finance? How do the developers play their role? How in particular do the public and private sectors decide on where to invest? And what are the resulting patterns of gains and losses for different groups? By and large, such questions are not yet being asked in transport research – yet they could probably provide answers at least as interesting as those in the housing field. Such research would require a broad historical perspective to understand how the present structural and social relationships have developed.

Other areas may require a different approach, based on psychological concepts and in particular the idea of personal risk. Thus any research into the social effects of road accidents would have to reckon with the well-known paradoxes: that safety standards for different modes of transport (rail, air, road) are very different in every country; that apparently society at large is willing to live with a high degree of risk from road accidents, knowing that these could be reduced by particular measures (lower speed limits; tougher drinking and driving laws); but that nevertheless different countries seem to settle for very different standards of risk (compare the Scandinavian and British attitudes to drinking and driving, or the very different accident rates that are apparently regarded as acceptable in different EEC countries). There are complex notions here of an 'acceptable' level of risk, which could profitably be explored.

Related to this are notions of equity involved in depriving people of the right to drive either because of judicial conviction, or because of insurance requirements; the social consequences of this may be very different in different social and geographical environments, ranging from minor inconvenience to personal catastrophe.

To return to the main theme that has recurred in this section: the need is to develop research that traces the interactions between the making of policy decisions, on the one hand, and the pattern of policy output, on the other. Policies will inevitably have specific and very different outcomes for different groups of the population – though these will depend in turn on the very different perceptions of those groups as to the choices before them and their knowledge of alternative possibilities. To trace these interactions, through various case studies, should be a central and recurring theme of the research programme now proposed.

2. RESEARCH PRIORITIES

Against this general background, five major research priorities emerge, and these together with a number of other topics which – though of lesser priority – appear to require substantial research.
    The five priority areas are:
(i)   equity and evaluation;
(ii) transport and land-use interactions;
(iii) theory, methodology, techniques and data requirements;
(iv) energy and its implications for transport;
(v)   institutional forces and their impact on transport policies.

The other topics include regulation, taxation and subsidy, and environmental questions. Although these issues are not explicitly covered in this book, many of the major points have been subsumed elsewhere within the other five headings.

(i) *Equity and evaluation*
Most of the research priorities identified here should be explicitly related to the broad issues mentioned in the previous section, in particular the political processes involved in decision making. Research should first address itself to the definition of equity both in a political context and how the concept is perceived by the public, whether in fact it is of primary concern. Secondly, the means to measure the incidence of equity have to be developed together with the mechanisms for its interpretation. There should be an awareness of the types of statements which can be made on equity and how these relate to the types of impacts as perceived by the decision-maker and the general public.

One possible approach would be to establish an understanding of communities through historical perspectives, as already outlined in section 1; related to this issue is the identification of life-style groups. If these groups could be characterized, either at the individual or household level, then responses to changes in service provision can be assessed through indicators such as levels of access to opportunities. Here, the short-term and long-term adaptations to changes such as a bus service withdrawal, or the opening of a new shop can be assessed through theoretical perspectives or monitoring. Supplementary issues such as whether the availability of transport modes actually increases or decreases inequality can be examined, as

can the effectiveness of present transport provision for special
groups.

The problems facing the public transport operator are particularly
pertinent to the equity question. It is not clear whether the application of accessibility standards actually reduces inequity, or
whether resources could be more effectively used in alternative ways,
such as a direct subsidy to the user in the form of concessionary
fares. The effect of subsidization on transport provision may not be
in the long-term interests of either the operator or the public, and
this question relates to the objectives of policy. The concern of the
present British government is to reduce the public cost of transport
services, but this conflicts with the concern for the individual to
minimize his own private costs; this dilemma is particularly evident
with respect to bus service deregulation and payment for school
transport. A wide perspective should be taken of the effects of allocating resources to maintaining transport services, particularly in
rural areas. Although patronage may be maintained, the subsidy allows
people to travel further and this may result in secondary effects such
as the closure of local facilities. All these issues merit further
research, but it is difficult to come to any firm conclusions on their
relative importance due to the limited research which has been carried
out on the equity question.

Once the nature of the equity issues and the methods of measurement of relevant perceptions of benefit and disbenefit have been
established, the concern then becomes one of evaluating the alternatives. The public and private transport markets have been identified,
together with the effectiveness of present provision for the various
social groups. Assessment should not only be solely based on
aggregate efficiency criteria (such as revenue/cost ratios), but
should also consider the development of alternative frameworks that
would evaluate the patterns of costs and benefits to different groups
or individuals. Secondly, there should be compatibility in evaluation
between different modes of transport, in particular road and rail, and
also between motorized and non-motorized forms of transport. Thirdly,
some research could be initiated on evaluating the Leitch Comprehensive Assessment Framework in the light of the evidence of the last
two years, together with a comparative analysis of this methodology
with other multi-criteria analysis techniques (Research Priority (iii),
below).

The requirements of equity and evaluation measurement techniques
are to estimate the likely effects of decisions without necessarily
including an explicit set of decision rules. A clear indication
should be given on the types of statements which can be made from the
distributions, in terms of who receives what and how much. Secondly,
some indication has to be given of the relative importance of the
impacts, how they affect existing activities and what factors particular individuals or groups perceive to be important.

(ii) *Transport and land use*
The analysis of transport should be placed in a wide context, as
transport is a means by which activities can be reached. Consequently,
with the treatment of transport as a derived demand, movement must be
considered in relation to the distribution of activities. Here, the
concept of accessibility is of vital importance since it allows the
relationship to be established between transport and the location of

the individual within the spatial-temporal framework of activities. However, any measure of accessibility must be behaviourally valid (i.e. it must reflect individuals' perceptions of travel impedance). In general, the most notable omission from the research has been the relationship between different levels of accessibility and the take-up of opportunities at journey destinations. This point relates back to the necessity for behavioural measures which would incorporate perceptions of access.

The effects of large-scale transport investments (for example BART) are likely to lead to a limited increase in accessibility, but of greater significance may be the land-use implications associated with this change in accessibility. These secondary impacts may result in changes in the distribution of employment and residential locations and the consequent changes in travel patterns. A key research area is therefore the establishment of the importance of transport in the location decision, both at the regional and the city-wide scale. Present evidence suggests that transport may not be a key variable in the location decision, and adaptations such as the development of long distance commuting may be more important. However, this statement ought to be qualified, as transport may have a more important role in certain situations. For example, analysis of firms' attitudes and motives has indicated that transport might be a key factor in determining whether they should relocate or not, and secondly, the importance of the transport element in the decision may depend on the complexity of the existing transport infrastructure, whether it is ubiquitous or sparse. These relationships could be analysed from data collected at one point in time, but time-series data would be of primary importance in answering the dynamic aspects of these questions. The effect of a location decision by a household could also be considered for its individual members. Although the journey to work for some household members may be reduced, travel for other members to activities may also be increased. Again, the wide context for transport is apparent with both the household interactions and the land-use implications being considered.

A further issue related to changes over time is the effects of decentralization and migration on the journey length distributions for the journey to work, and in particular the increases in walk distances. Changes may also have occurred in the travel time budgets of individuals, and further work could be carried out on the stability of travel times between areas and over time, together with their distributions. Data collected at two points in time is becoming available, and so an assessment of these changes is now possible. However, there is considerable uncertainty, whether it is possible to generalize from evidence in one area to other similar areas, or whether structural changes are location specific.

The other side of the relationship between transport and land use is the effect that the latter may have on the former. A study of the implications of a settlement policy of concentration or dispersal on the demand for transport could usefully be initiated. Here, particular attention could be placed on the increasing dependence upon vehicular transport and the effects this has had on land uses. This analysis could be assessed within the context of energy policy and the energy demands for different settlement patterns, including the effects that increased costs of movement have on settlement patterns. There may be considerable value here in historical perspectives, which trace the longer-term effects of changes such as those in public transport patronage and land-use policy. If cause and effect can be unravelled, then useful insights could be gained into the impact of planning policies on the growth of 'suburbia' and the changing role for public transport.

Although the transport and land-use research priorities are essentially spatial in nature, time management should also be included. In particular, analysis should cover the use of time as a resource and the adaptations which people make if certain constraints are relaxed. Here, the substitution and stimulation effects of the 'old' and 'new' technology on activities and life-styles would be important. Further research on the behavioural aspects and impacts, in contrast to the technological emphasis, could be initiated, and this may include some monitoring. The questions for social scientists would include the alternative uses to which the time saved could be put and the longer-term changes in location and employment patterns.

(iii) *Theory and methodologies*

At present, the conceptual framework for treating transport as a derived demand (Research Priority (ii), above) is lacking. This organizational framework should include both transport and non-transport effects as well as the longer-term secular changes in society. Two possible directions have been suggested, both of which are proving fruitful areas for research. The first is to develop the activities framework derived from time-geography, and the second would be a sociological understanding of the way in which social position generates a framework of choice and constraint. Research on these issues is currently under way; but when it is complete, it may well be that new initiatives should be taken to develop it further.

Once the conceptual framework has been established, then the role of different methodologies in answering specific policy options can be assessed. Much research in the social sciences has been exerted on the development of transport models, both aggregate and disaggregate. Further research which could usefully be carried out on these conventional models relates to the importance of constraints and uncertainty, where the robustness of the model forms and assumptions used could be tested. If the models are to be extensively used, then their applicability should be demonstrable, and more important, the language should be accessible to decision-makers (i.e. the use of jargon should be minimized and the presentation of the results should be comprehensible). Secondly, the limitations of the models should be made explicit, together with the realization that their structures are not impartial. Thirdly, models tend to be essentially reactive and their output tends to specify the well-known, even reinforcing the present system. Finally, there has been a movement away from the concentration on improvements in supply towards the manipulation of demand to match a given supply (e.g. the pricing and marketing policies of British Railways). In each of these examples, there is a case for a change in the emphasis of research to accommodate the changes in the demands of policy-makers.

There is also a strong argument for a reassessment of the present positivist approach to analysis. This critique would consider the theoretical underpinnings of the present methodologies based in welfare economics rather than the new urban economics, the genuine

concern over the range of policy options tested, and the weakness of
the link between theory and practice, in particular whether radical
rather than incremental changes in policy can be accommodated.

In addition to this necessity for a wide-ranging critique, certain
alternative complementary approaches to transport modelling have been
suggested. Attitudinal methods could be used as a precursor to the
model-building process for the purpose of identifying relevant behavioural attributes for use as independent (or other) variables. Their
secondary role is one of advising on the relative weights to be
accorded to different attributes in evaluation, especially where more
direct evidence of trade-off is lacking. Some concern was however
expressed on whether attitudinal methods really were an advance,
particularly as the measurement problems were not clearly understood
by decision-makers. Secondly, the use of activity-based approaches
permits the effects of changes to be assessed within the household
framework so that the interaction between household members can be
made explicit. There are problems, as with other micro-analytical
techniques, of aggregation, and the allocation of costs to alternative
policies which are being tested has also proved difficult. Simulation
methods would enable a formal modelling analysis to be imposed on more
qualitative techniques (such as the activity-based approaches). The
relationships between transport and land use can also be simulated
within a temporal-spatial framework and the output from the policies
tested would include the implications for both the transport system
and land use as it permits the explicit inclusion of sensitivity
analysis. Finally, other exploratory analysis methods should be
developed to examine activity linkages and sequences (including multi-
purpose and multidestination trips), latent demand, learning and
adaptation. Further studies could include the extent to which travel
patterns reflect personal preferences and the determination of priorities at the individual level.

Several other modelling issues deserve further analysis. In
particular, there is the question of the psychology of choice and the
formation of habits; the choice situation is not an event, but can
usefully be conceptualized as a process of adaptation to changing
constraints. There is however a transitional choice phase when
certain important changes take place and existing habits are re-
assessed; e.g. when a family moves house or a car is purchased. An
important consideration here is the acknowledgement not just of error,
but of systematic bias in most currently available models. These
issues are of current importance as major road building has been cut
back, and 'positive' traffic restraint in urban areas has again been
raised. The second major field is the contribution of attitudinal
surveys to reveal the perceived attributes which are relevant to
choice. Work should be carried out on the consistency in perceptions
and expectations over time, as the measurement and analysis of attitudes has proved difficult, and their representative nature has been
questioned. Perhaps more important is the link between preferences
and actual behaviour; the key point here is whether a stable relationship can be established between behavioural intent and actual
behaviour - the extent to which individuals will actually do what they
say that they would do if a particular change were implemented.

Evaluation techniques, which have also been considered as social
outcomes of policy, must be assessed in terms of such effects as
income and redistributional impacts. The conventional methods of

evaluation based on welfare economics, do not have an explicit concern
with the distributional consequences. However, there should be
methods available which, in addition to assessing the effects of major
changes in resource availability, can also evaluate the distribution
of resources within the transport sector, and which groups benefit or
lose from particular decisions. Costs and benefits should be interpreted in the economic, environmental, social and political context.
Perhaps some form of participatory evaluation could be introduced
where all the principal impacts were summarized together with their
consequences. Then all interested parties, including those affected,
could be consulted before a decision is made. The conclusions from
the seminar group on the role of evaluation in methodology are tentative, and further research on evaluation techniques is a priority
(Research Priority (i), above).

The difficulties of using models should be of importance, both to
researchers and decision-makers. The various available methods should
be considered complementary, with some better suited to particular
applications than others. The recent developments in disaggregate
models have introduced new levels of complexity, and some concern has
been expressed as to what additional advantages in a policy context
they offer over the more traditional aggregate techniques. Secondly,
the output from models is relatively assured with precise methods
being applied to imprecise situations. The complexity of travel
behaviour should be made explicit and uncertainty incorporated at
every stage possible in the modelling process.

Data - Data availability has always been a limitation for transport researchers, but the seminar group has made certain suggestions
concerning the collection and use of data. There are two basic types
of data, namely primary information which is collected for a specific
purpose, and secondary data which, although collected for one purpose,
is also used by researchers for additional analysis. There are
several problems with using existing data sources as they may not
collect information on particular aspects of interest (for example,
short walk trips), and there is often a time lag between the
collection of the data and its availability to researchers; obviously
there are problems such as confidentiality, but more cooperation is
required, at the planning stage of the study, between academic
researchers and others on the collection and use to be made of the
data. More important is the consistency of definitions used, both
between studies and over time, and it is suggested that a standard
set should be produced, perhaps not by academic researchers.

Many transport surveys, although not large samples in themselves,
are large by social survey criteria. It was suggested that market
segmentation could be used as an input to data collection so that the
sample could be structured and the sample size reduced, thus saving
resources. The general move away from large-scale comprehensive data
sets to small problem-specific data sets is to be welcomed, although
it may increase the problems of compatibility and consistency between
studies. Further research could usefully be initiated on the relationship between qualitative and quantitative data, together with
explicit discussion on the problems of implementation, including bias
in questions and interpretation.

The main concern of researchers has been with the development of
techniques rather than questionnaire and interview design. Alternative methods of data collection should be tested; these would include

telephone-based interview techniques and the use of observation rather
than survey methods which involve recall on the part of the respondent. A high priority is the increased use of longitudinal and
monitoring studies where data are collected on a continuing basis
(For example in the Tyne and Wear Metro Impact Study), as the use
which can be made of the information far exceeds a single cross
sectional data collection exercise or even data collected at two
points in time. The dynamic relationships of cause and effect over
time can be established.

Another high priority is the collection of activity information
rather than trip information, since there is, for example, a greater
social value in the data and evidence to suggest greater accuracy in
recall as no time period is unaccounted for. However, there is also
a trade-off between the time and cost involved in the collection of
activity information and the use which is actually made of the additional data. One note of caution here is that activity-based studies
could lead to the collection of data on the same colossal scale as the
Land Use-Transport Studies did in the 1960s; this possibility must
be avoided and relates to the essential link between data collection
and the purpose of that data collection. Overall though, activity-
based data collection should be encouraged.

(iv) *Energy*
Energy demand forecasting through economic models was not
considered a specific priority in the transport sphere, but the search
for alternative methods of forecasting should be continued. One
suggestion is the development of fairly detailed physical and technical models which start from the final uses to which the energy is
put and then to work backwards to the primary energy demand.
Alternatively, the social impacts of 'surprise' scenarios on different
energy futures could provide the basis for more speculative research.

With the government's policy objective of energy conservation and
the control of consumption, there are several important research areas
for social scientists. The increase in petrol prices may not lead to
an increase in the demand for public transport from car users, as
adaptations would probably include not making the trip and consolidation of trips before using the alternative. The exact nature of
these adaptations merit further research, and could be tied into
broader studies of the effects of petrol prices on the structure of
the car market, the purchasing of new vehicles and the use of those
vehicles. The second longer-term area of research would be to examine
the impact of battery-powered vehicles, outside the areas of special
application where they are already being introduced on a private
scale. The level of market penetration, the cost and range, the
distribution of replacement or recharging points and other infrastructure considerations could all benefit from social as well as
operational research.

Studies of car usage, both within the household and in car sharing
schemes, are important within the context of energy savings. Some
analysis of trends in such indicators as occupancy rates by destination could be taken as a starting point, and this could be linked in
with the effects of changes in occupancy on peak-hour congestion and
public transport patronage. Another important trend is the increasing
use of taxis (particularly in London) and the growth in the demand for
shared taxi and private car-hire schemes. These trends, together with
the reduction in the dominance of the work trip, the increase in

leisure activities (including a significant growth in the tourist trade), the grouping of work hours and 'activity spreading', and the growing importance of multipurpose movements, are all research topics worthy of analysis and monitoring.

The impact of other innovations (for example telecommunications, microprocessors) may also have important substitution effects which result in energy saving or the energy being put to alternative uses. However, it is often difficult to discern whether telecommunications actually stimulate or substitute for travel, as they often work in the same direction. Carefully designed case studies could help to unravel these effects. Alternatively, an analysis of how households allocate their resource budgets between transport and other energy uses, particularly in response to high energy costs and increased tax on transport fuels, would provide a possible starting point.

(v) *Institutions and their impact*
Here the first focus must be positive rather than normative: it must try to illuminate our understanding of how institutions operate and how decisions are taken within them. It can and must consider normative questions – such as equity and meeting perceived needs – but only as they are identified and presented within the decision-making machinery.

Studies of decision making within institutions would minimally involve the following elements:

1. a careful definition of the structure of the institutions – not merely in formal terms, though this will be important, but also in terms of the actual (latent) structure of decision-making;
2. an analysis of the interrelation between institutions and of individuals within them;
3. study in particular of the formation of interest groups at every level of decision making and policy formulation;
4. studies of the formulation of attitudes and the definition and recognition of areas of concern, including the role of key individuals, interest groups, opinion formers, and especially the mass media. Particular attention needs to be given here to the diffusion of information and opinions from specialists to the wider general public.

It is recognized that these research questions might not be easy to operationalize – though the few studies in the genre offer promise for the future. But it is felt that an understanding of how and why decisions were actually made is a first essential step towards their possible improvement in the future.

One particular area for research concerned the politics of implementation. It is clearly often easier for governmental institutions to develop broad policies, than actually to deliver them where they matter, on the ground in actual local communities. Rapid shifts of policy in British cities, from highway building to traffic restraint to mass transit to a kind of policy vacuum, provide an obvious example. It may be particularly fruitful here to look closely at conflicts in policy implementation. The highway inquiry procedure provides one set of suitable case studies because of its large-scale breakdown in the mid-1970s in such celebrated cases as Winchester and the Archway Road. The politics of such inquiries, often more complicated than was represented in the media at the time, would provide

classic studies of pressure groups and their relationship to the
central administrative and bureaucratic procedure.

But in any case, such conflicts illustrate very difficult disagreements of principle between very broad policy considerations, often
at national level (such as the development of a national strategic
highway system, or the improvement of links between industrial
districts and ports), and considerations of amenity or environment or
way of life in very local communities. This underlines the argument
made above in the first part of this section: that it is important in
evaluation to balance overall allocative efficiency criteria against
the distributional effects for different groups and areas.

Other issues

Some other issues were discussed by the group, but at the end won less
support as priority topics for research. One of these, perhaps surprisingly, was the *regulation* of transport by measures other than
financial or fiscal ones. This could involve a very wide range of
topics ranging from international regulation such as the EEC tacho-
graph requirement, through issues of licencing of freight transport,
down to restraint measures on urban traffic. It is not that these
topics seemed unimportant in themselves; rather that the social
scientist's approach to them would more properly take the form of an
inquiry under other heads, such as for instance policy formulation,
where indeed a number of regulatory topics have been quoted (Major
Issue (i), above).

Another issue, *taxation and subsidy*, seems to have failed to reach
the first order of priority simply because so many of the important
issues have been covered under the alternative formulation of equity
and evaluation (Research Priority (i), above). Under this head, for
instance, it would be appropriate to look at the distributional criteria used in developing a concessionary fares policy on public
transport for defined groups of people. As with regulation, the
tendency of the group was to prefer to go behind the obvious topic
heads, to the deeper issues that lay behind them at the centre of
public policy making.

The same might perhaps be said about the third omission:
questions of the *environment*. In the last decade, such questions have
sometimes seemed to dominate the transport policy debate. But again,
the question must be to identify the most appropriate social scientific cutting edge. For the social scientist it is difficult to assume
that environmental questions have some absolute primacy. Rather, he
will be concerned with two sets of questions: first, how in fact have
environmental considerations entered into decision making? and
secondly, are there other and improved means of doing so? Such
questions have already been posed more than once in these conclusions
- in discussing decision making and policy issues under Major Issues,
above, and in discussing social questions earlier in this section on
Research Priorities. It seems more appropriate to let them remain
there, while recognizing that to incorporate environmental questions
into evaluation for policy may present special difficulties of
marrying natural and social scientific analysis.

3. EDUCATION AND DISSEMINATION OF RESEARCH

A repeated theme of the discussion was the need for better

communication between researchers and practitioners. Though
refreshing exceptions did exist, building on individual initiatives or
a policy decision by a particular organization - such as the Transport
and Road Research Laboratory, or the Universities Transport Study
Group - still there were surprising gaps. Academics did not readily
communicate with non-academic researchers. Though academic researchers
in the United Kingdom maintained good links with colleagues in the
United States, their contacts with other countries - particularly ones
where the first language of communication was not English - were more
tenuous. Further, academic researchers did not link very closely to
practitioners. And lastly, professional officers and politicians were
felt to have somewhat weak contacts.

This problem of communication reinforced the necessity to identify
special kinds of research which would be suitable to place within
different kinds of research organization - but it also suggested that
a critical question was to improve the rate of information dissemination and the actual take-up of research ideas. There seems to be a
problem of translating the findings from social science research into
a form suitable for implementation.

In fact it appears that many planners and researchers are not
aware of developments that have taken place within transport
research. Too much published material is available; the intended
readers suffer a problem of overload. So journal articles tend not to
be widely read, except by specialists in the particular - often
narrow - subject area. One suggestion to overcome this problem would
be a series of abstracted articles (as with *Geo Abstracts* or *Sage
Urban Abstracts*) or general review articles (as with the new transport
journal, *Transport Reviews*). An experiment, currently being undertaken at the time of writing, consists of specially written State of
the Art Reviews, which may include transport subjects. An alternative
- not necessarily exclusive - would be to hold regular seminar
meetings to discuss progress in particular subject areas, but that
might present difficulties of travel and size of attendance.

A final point concerns the general skill level of professionals
and their incentive to learn. The local authorities, who have the
task of the detailed implementation of policy, often do not have the
data, the expertize or the resources to test new techniques such as
disaggregate models, even if they are aware of them. Education is
really at the root of this problem: professional requirements may
reinforce the formalization and continued employment of older techniques, though the professional institutes themselves would doubtless
maintain that their attitude is a flexible one. In any event, often
it is the educational institutions themselves that are at fault -
which may suggest the need for short refresher courses for both
teachers and professionals.

4. CONCLUDING SUMMARY

In summary, then we conclude with a fairly clear list of priorities
for future transport research, as they have occurred in this paper:
no ranking is implied.

1. The definition of equity by groups of the public and by participants in the political process; the relationship (or lack of
relationship) between different perceptions of equity.

2. The analysis of the equity impacts of policies on different groups - defined particularly in terms of life-style. Public transport policies are particularly susceptible to this kind of analysis.

3. The evaluation of alternative policies in terms of both efficiency and equity criteria, taking particular account of evaluation as between modes - a field so far largely ignored - and perhaps including a participating element.

4. The development of accessibility measurements and the relationship of these to the actual take-up of opportunities, having regard to the use of time as a resource.

5. Closely related, the study of impact of transport improvements on location decisions by individuals, groups and enterprises.

6. The analysis of impact of different activity and land use patterns on the total pattern of transport use, including especially the implications for energy consumption.

7. The development of a theory of transport as a derived demand, with the aid either of a time-space or sociological framework based on the choices and the constraints for different social groups.

8. Critical analysis of the present generation of conventional transport models, both to expose possible weaknesses and to improve their usefulness for the policy-maker.

9. In parallel, the development of new approaches to transport modelling, through either attitudinal or activity-based approaches, and attempting to take into account the interactions between transport and land use. The psychology of choice, and the relationship of attitudes and behaviour, would need extended attention.

10. The encouragement of new sources of data with consistent definitions and perhaps small sample data sets, plus new collection methods and the development of longitudinal surveys, coupled with collection of activity information on a continuous time basis.

11. The effect of energy costs and shortages on travel and activity patterns with special stress on car usage.

12. The possible effects - whether or substitution or stimulation - of telecommunications on transport.

13. The study of how institutions operate in terms of their make-up, the relationships of the individuals in them, the formation of interest groups and the formation of attitudes and areas of concern.

14. The analysis of the politics of policy implementation - including the study of major policy shifts and reversals.

15. The systematic analysis of the resolution of conflicts in transport policy, with special reference to the public inquiry process.

As was stated in the introduction, the purpose has been to present a review of the current state-of-the-art in transport. In particular the contribution of social scientists has been emphasised and this concluding paper itemises some critical inter-disciplinary research topics to which researchers, concerned with transport and public policy making, should be addressing themselves in the 1980s.

Subject index

Author index